TimeOut
Athens

timeout.com/athens

Published by Time Out Guides Ltd, a wholly owned subsidiary of Time Out Group Ltd.
Time Out and the Time Out logo are trademarks of Time Out Group Ltd.

© **Time Out Group Ltd 2005**
Previous edition 2004.

10 9 8 7 6 5 4 3 2 1

This edition first published in Great Britain in 2005 by Ebury Publishing
Ebury Publishing is a division of The Random House Group Ltd,
20 Vauxhall Bridge Road, London SW1V 2SA

Random House Australia Pty Limited 20 Alfred Street, Milsons Point, Sydney, New South Wales 2061, Australia
Random House New Zealand Limited 18 Poland Road, Glenfield, Auckland 10, New Zealand
Random House South Africa (Pty) Limited Endulini, 5A Jubilee Road, Parktown 2193, South Africa

Random House UK Limited Reg. No. 954009

Distributed in the USA by Publishers Group West
1700 Fourth Street, Berkeley, California 94710

Distributed in Canada by Penguin Canada Ltd
10 Alcorn Avenue, Toronto, Ontario, Canada M4V 3B2

For further distribution details, see www.timeout.com

ISBN 1-904978-43-6

A CIP catalogue record for this book is available from the British Library

Colour reprographics by Icon, Crowne House, 56-58 Southwark Street, London SE1 1UN

Printed and bound in Germany by Appl

Papers used by Ebury Publishing are natural, recyclable products made from wood grown in sustainable forests

Time Out Guides Limited
Universal House
251 Tottenham Court Road
London W1T 7AB
Tel + 44 (0)20 7813 3000
Fax + 44 (0)20 7813 6001
Email guides@timeout.com
www.timeout.com

Editorial

Editor Ros Sales
Deputy Editor Dominic Earle
Athens Editor Denny Kallivoka
Copy Editors Edoardo Albert, Debbie Ellis
Listings Checkers Georgina Doutsi, Irene Kladi
Proofreader Tamsin Shelton
Indexer Anna Norman

Editorial/Managing Director Peter Fiennes
Series Editor Ruth Jarvis
Deputy Series Editor Lesley McCave
Business Manager Gareth Garner
Guides Co-ordinator Holly Pick
Accountant Kemi Olufuwa

Design

Art Director Scott Moore
Art Editor Tracey Ridgewell
Senior Designer Oliver Knight
Designer Josephine Spencer
Freelance Designer Tessa Kar
Digital Imaging Dan Conway
Ad Make-up Pete Ward

Picture Desk

Picture Editor Jael Marschner
Deputy Picture Editor Tracey Kerrigan
Picture Researcher Helen McFarland

Advertising

Sales Director Mark Phillips
International Sales Manager Ross Canadé
International Sales Executive Simon Davies
Advertising Sales (Athens) Pivotal Media
Advertising Assistant Lucy Butler

Marketing

Marketing Director Mandy Martinez
Marketing & Publicity Manager, US Rosella Albanese

Production

Production Director Mark Lamond

Time Out Group

Chairman Tony Elliott
Managing Director Mike Hardwick
Group Financial Director Richard Waterlow
Group Commercial Director Lesley Gill
Group General Manager Nichola Coulthard
Group Circulation Director Jim Heinemann
Group Art Director John Oakey
Online Managing Director David Pepper
Group Production Director Steve Proctor
Group IT Director Simon Chappell

Contributors

Introduction Ros Sales. **History** Nick Wyke. **Athens Today** Rachel Howard. **Architecture** Martin Olofsson (*Movers & shapers* Rachel Howard). **Greek Myth & Legend** Amanda Castleman. **No More Moussaka** Rachel Howard. **Where to Stay** Joyce-Ann Gatsoulis. **Sightseeing** Cordelia Madden (*A day in Athens, Lycabettus Hill* Alexia Loundras; *The making of a monument* Ros Sales; *Plaka: the old city* Coral Davenport; *You are here* Joyce-Ann Gatsoulis; *The Central Market, Square deal, Pireos Street redux, Keramikos on the cusp* Rachel Howard; *A stroll around the National Gardens* Androniki Kitsantonis). **Restaurants** Rachel Howard (*Taverna tips* Brian Church). **Cafés** Konstantinos Sarkas (*Café culture* Rachel Howard). **Shopping** Cordelia Madden (*Top city spas* Rachel Howard). **Festivals & Events** Paris Ayiomamitis. **Children** Konstantinos Sarkas. **Film** Konstantinos Sarkas. **Galleries** Stathis Panagoulis, Giorgos Vamvakidis. **Gay & Lesbian** Leo Kalovyrnas. **Music** Martin Olofsson (*City sounds* Maria Paravantes). **Nightlife** Konstantinos Sarkas, with contributions from Alexia Loundras and Othonas Orfanos (*A night in Athens* Alexia Loundras). **Sport & Fitness** John Hadoulis, Will Vassilopoulos (*Fixing the game* John Hadoulis). **Theatre & Dance** Nikos Pitsiladis (*Movers & shapers* Rachel Howard). **Getting Started** Alexia Loundras, Ruth Jarvis. **Attica & the Mainland** Alexia Loundras (*Byron in Greece* Gulya Isyanova). **Northern Peloponnese** Alexia Loundras, Jonathan Cox (*Local treats* Alexia Loundras; *Corinth Canal* Jonathan Cox). **Island Escapes** Alexia Loundras, Androniki Kitsantonis. **Directory** Debbie Ellis (*Greek for cheats* Brian Church).

Maps JS Graphics (john@jsgraphics.co.uk).

Photography Maxime Gyselinck, except: pages 10, 15, 22 Bettman/ Corbis; page 20 Ullstein/ AKG; pages 21, 240, 246, 258 Alamy; page 25 Getty Images; pages 27, 212, 237, 256, 262 Rex Features; page 30 ATHOC/ C. Voulgari; page 43 AKG; page 45 Art Archives; page 47 Bridgeman Art Library; page 66 Athens Hilton Archive; pages 104, 123, 124, 204 Jonathan Perugia; page 189 EPA; page 197 Kobal; page 209 Alexis Maxairos; page 228 AFP/Getty Images; page 234 Empics; page 238 Jonathan Cox; pages 261, 248, 249, 251, 251, 254 Greek National Tourism Organisation.
The following images were provided by the featured establishments/ artists: pages 31, 33, 41, 51, 59, 60, 63, 69, 71, 72, 129, 152, 206, 209, 226, 231, 232.

The Editor would like to thank Andy Hadjicostis, Konstantinos Sarkas, Costas Kapareliotis and everyone at *Time Out Athens*.

Contents

Introduction

So Athens pulled it off. Under the doubting gaze of the world's press, the preparations for the 2004 Olympics were finished in time – just. And the Games were a triumph.

Olympic preparation meant more than just stadiums. The city had a facelift: pavements and roads now have fewer holes; squares have been made green and pleasant; façades were restored; there's snazzy new transport. And the jewel in the city's crown – the omnipresent Acropolis – is now surrounded by a cumbersomely named but effective 'Unification of Archaelogical Sites walkway'. This links the various relics of antiquity in the city centre, creating an 'Archaeological Park' and bringing peace, pedestrianisation and pavement cafés to an area previously dogged by traffic chaos and bad air quality.

The legacy of the Games isn't all rosy, of course. Taxpayers are faced with paying off the 11 billion bill, a process that could take 15 to 20 years. Not all the promised permanent jobs materialised. And, with huge maintenance costs, the fight is on to prevent Olympic venues becoming drains on the public purse.

Venues aside, though, Athens has begun to capitalise on its assets. The Parthenon, peering down on the city from the Acropolis, catches your eye when you emerge from metro stations; it's there on the horizon at the end of concrete-blocked streets. It is one of the most recognised (and most copied) structures in the world, described by French poet Lamartine as 'the world's most perfect poem in stone'. Beneath the Acropolis is the Ancient Agora, where democracy was born in the fifth century BC and where Socrates taught young Athenians to question everything.

These and other monuments now have an environment worthy of them. The Archaeological Park has reduced pollution levels, which will help prevent further erosion. And, in the new Athens, the Acropolis is actually accessible for wheelchair users.

But this city is no ancient world theme park. It lives and works in a busy patchwork of styles and periods: around the Ancient Agora; in tiny old neighbourhoods like the villagey Anafiotika at the foot of the Acropolis; in the neo-classical buildings that staked Greece's claim to modernity and nation-statehood in the early years of independence; in icon-filled Orthodox churches, and in the generic-Mediterranean concrete buildings that are homes and offices for most Athenians.

Whatever the problems, there is an undeniable energy about Athens today. Boutique hotels weren't on the Athens map before the Games; now they're a fixture. Old industrial areas are being regenerated. Disused factories have been transformed into galleries, venues and restaurants, where a young ethos holds sway. But an evening that starts at a shiny new club can easily wind up over a bowl of tripe soup in the Central Market at 3am, or dancing on the tables in a *rembetiko* club. Variety is the spice of Athenian life; this is still a city with some grit.

The challenge for Athens today is to keep the verve, build on the improvements – and make sure it doesn't lose its very own addictive essence in the process.

ABOUT THE TIME OUT CITY GUIDES

The *Time Out Athens Guide* is the another addition to the city guide series produced by the people behind London, Chicago and New York's successful listings magazines. We also have an office in Athens, where a weekly Greek-language *Time Out* magazine is published. Staff there have contributed to this guide to ensure that it is crammed with local expertise.

THE LOWDOWN ON THE LISTINGS

Above all, we've tried to make this book as useful as possible. Transport information, opening times, admission prices, websites and credit card details are all included in our listings. And, as far as possible, we've given details of facilities, services and events, all checked and correct at the time we went to press. However, since owners and managers can change their arrangements at any time, we always advise readers to telephone and check opening times and other particulars. While every effort has been made to ensure the accuracy of the information contained in this guide, the publishers cannot accept responsibility for any errors it may contain.

PRICES AND PAYMENT

We have noted whether venues such as shops, hotels and restaurants accept credit cards or not but have only listed the major cards – American Express (**AmEx**), Diners Club (**DC**),

MasterCard (**MC**) and Visa (**V**). Many businesses will also accept other cards, including Cirrus, Maestro, JCB, Discover and Carte Blanche, along with euro travellers' cheques issued by a major financial institution (such as American Express).

The prices we've supplied should be treated as guidelines, not gospel. Fluctuating exchange rates and inflation can cause charges, in shops and restaurants particularly, to change rapidly. If prices vary wildly from those we've quoted, ask whether there's a good reason. If not, go elsewhere. Then please write and let us know. We aim to give the best and most up-to-date advice, so we always want to know if you've been badly treated or overcharged.

THE LIE OF THE LAND

Athens is a city of distinct neighbourhoods, and we have used these to structure our sightseeing chapters. The same area classifications are used to divide other chapters, such as restaurants; for a map showing the divisions, *see p294*. Every location included in the book has a map reference. These refer to the street maps on pages 296 to 301.

TELEPHONE NUMBERS

The country code for Greece is 30. All Athens numbers start with 210, which needs to be dialled both from outside and inside the city. Where no alternative exists, we have given

(and stipulated) a mobile telephone number. These start with a '6'. For more details of phone codes and charges, *see p278*.

ESSENTIAL INFORMATION

For all the practical information you might need for visiting the city – including visa and customs information, disabled access, emergency telephone numbers, a list of useful websites and the lowdown on the local transport network – turn to the **Directory** chapter at the back of this guide. It starts on page 266.

TRANSLITERATIONS

There is no standard system for the transliteration of Greek characters. We have chosen a method that reflects pronunciation as closely as possible. However, we have frequently broken our own rules where there seemed good reason to do so: for proper names with a well-established spelling; or when people or businesses had their own preferred version, for example. We have chosen, however, not to duplicate the spellings given on street signs, since these are inconsistent and unrecognisable in speech. It's better to follow a map.

We have sourced maps with a similar, but not identical, transliteration system to our own.

LET US KNOW WHAT YOU THINK

We hope you enjoy the *Time Out Athens Guide*, and we'd like to know what you think of it. We welcome tips for places that you consider we should include in future editions and take notice of your criticism of our choices. There's a reader's reply card at the back of this book – or you can email us on athensguide@timeout.com.

There is an online version of this book, along with guides to over 45 other international cities, at **www.timeout.com**.

In Context

History

War and peace, autocracy and democracy.

As with all great cities of the ancient world, any early history of Athens is an exercise in separating myth from (limited) reliable sources.

Graves and wells of neolithic settlers dating back three millennia before Christ have been found on the slopes of the Acropolis. Around 1500 BC the hill became known as Cecropia, after King Cecrops, the successor to King Actaeus, who had given Athens its primary name: Acte (from which the name of the region, Attica, also derives). Cecrops had been attracted by the hill's two copious springs.

But the city's founding myth rose out of a heroic showdown between the male god of the sea, Poseidon, and the female goddess of wisdom, Athena. Both were laying claim to Attica. According to legend, when Poseidon struck the rock of the Acropolis with his trident, a horse leaped out of rushing water. Athena replied by striking a nearby rock with her spear, and an olive tree appeared. The gods of Olympus declared Athena victor and she became protectress of the town, bequeathing

the city both its name and, with the olive tree, an important symbol of peace and prosperity.

By 1400 BC the Acropolis had been fortified as a Mycenaean citadel. The Mycenaeans lived in independent communities clustered around palaces ruled by kings and dominated by a centralised religion and bureaucracy. Their kingdoms were a breeding ground for myths, and yielded the sources on the sack of Troy (which took place some time between 1230 BC and 1180 BC) and the destruction of Thebes that would inspire Homer when writing *The Iliad* four centuries later.

Under Dorian assault and amid internal strife, most of the Mycenaean culture in Greece collapsed in 1200 BC. Somehow, though, the invasion bypassed Athens. This immunity later boosted claims of classical Athenians that they were autochthonous, that is, the true native inhabitants sprung from the soil of their land.

DARK DAYS
Athens couldn't avoid, however, the shadow that veiled Greece during the period 1050 BC to 750 BC, known as the Greek Dark Age.

The bitter infighting of the Mycenaeans had caused widespread poverty; the population plummeted and many people migrated to the Aegean Islands and the coast of Asia Minor.

Few, if any, written records survive from this period and our knowledge is limited to scant archaeological evidence. However, tombs from the age have revealed a proto-geometric style of pottery. This would later develop into the story-telling figurative urns, the archetypes of today's copies sold to tourists in Plaka. Other finds of ivory, gold and, particularly, iron indicate some notable advances in metallurgy, which helped Athens to emerge from its Dark Age.

BIRTH OF A CITY STATE

The collapse of Mycenaean civilisation left a political vacuum in Greece. Around 800 BC Athens began incorporating the outlying villages into its city-state (*polis*) and within 50 years ruled the whole of Attica. By this time other Greek cities had also organised themselves into independent city-states, the most powerful being Chalcis, Corinth and Eretria. The main goal of the city-state was to avoid strong central political power and to share authority among its citizens. Power, however, was still largely concentrated in the hands of the wealthy and privileged. Centuries later, the Greek philosopher Aristotle (384 BC-322 BC) insisted that it was the forces of nature that had created the city-state, and that anyone who existed outside the community of a city-state must be either a beast or a god.

A cultural and economic revival accompanied the emergence of the city-states across Greece and inspired new styles of warfare, art and politics. Greek colonies were established as far away as the Black Sea, present-day Syria, North Africa and the Western Mediterranean.

Athens enjoyed a period of peace and remained the leading artistic centre in Greece until about 730 BC, when it was superseded by Corinth, both culturally and politically. The introduction of coinage and the spread of alphabetical writing came to Athens second-hand via Corinth. It would take until the late Archaic Age (700 BC-500 BC) for Athens to garner any real political clout.

FROM TYRANNY TO DEMOCRACY

The Archaic Period is so called because of a plodding pace of change in comparison to the hyper-progressive Classical Age that succeeded it. It was, nevertheless, a seminal period that produced startling innovations in architecture and art, not to mention the poetry of Homer.

In Athens the city office merged into an annually appointed executive of nine archontes (chief magistrates). After serving his term, an archon became a life member of the council (called the Areopagus, because it met on the hill of Ares). An aristocratic group known as the Eupatridai ('sons of good fathers') had an exclusive right to these posts. The governing class was responsible for war, religion and law. Its hierarchy depended on wealth, gained either from commerce or agriculture.

Across Greece the replacement of monarchy by an aristocracy of nobles had left the common people with few rights. The resulting social tensions prompted a move towards tyranny, where despotically inclined individuals temporarily seized power in the city-states.

In 640 BC, bristling with victory in an event at the Olympic Games, an Athenian nobleman named Cylon attempted to overthrow the aristocracy and seize power in Athens. The coup failed. Undeterred and still upset with the political system, Cylon led an abortive attempt at tyranny in 632 BC. His army of mercenaries briefly occupied the Acropolis. When Cylon fled, his followers sought sanctuary at the sacred altar of Athena, from where they were lured down by promises of reprieve by the archon Megacles and then massacred by Athenian troops. Megacles and his family were banished in perpetuity for sanctioning the murders.

'Solon reorganised the state by breaking the exclusive power of the aristocracy.'

Continued unrest and the constant threat to the aristocracy's supremacy led to the archon Draco's strictly defined law code enacted in 621 BC. It was a harsh code (hence 'Draconian') that sidestepped pressing issues and dealt with menial crimes, such as the pilfering of cabbage, by capital punishment.

Relief came in the guise of Solon, a poet who became archon in 594 BC. His revised code alleviated the system of land tenure and debt for the peasants and implemented trial by jury. He reorganised the state by breaking the exclusive power of the aristocracy and established four classes of Athenian society based on agricultural wealth. A new council was set up, the Boule of 400 Representatives, a sort of popular assembly that sat alongside the Areopagus. Solon encouraged the development of lucrative olive and wine production in Attica, reformed the law courts and coinage, and invited foreign businessmen to the city.

Ideologically Solon paved the way to Athenian democracy, but in practice many of his reforms failed. As controversy heightened over the rule of the archontes, the opportunistic military leader Pisistratos seized power as a tyrant by occupying the Acropolis in 560 BC. Although he was expelled twice (the first time he had been reinstated as a result of a ludicrous plot whereby a woman rode into the city dressed up as Athena and proclaimed Pisistratos's virtues as leader), Athens flourished under his rule.

Arguably the most benign of Athens' tyrants, Pisistratos assembled a hefty navy and extended the city's boundaries on land. He improved the water supply and commissioned the Temple of Olympian Zeus and the rebuilding of the Old Temple of Athena on the Acropolis. A keen culture vulture, he sponsored historians, poets, sculptors and orators and revitalised the Festival of the Great Dionysia, which rivalled those at Olympia and Delphi.

Pisistratos died in 527 BC. He was succeeded by his son Hippias, who, though a patron to poets, became increasingly tyrannical after surviving an assassination attempt in 514 BC in which his brother Hipparchos was killed.

By 510 BC, following a consultation with the Delphic Oracle, Megacles's son Cleisthenes had rallied the support of the Spartans, the premier power of the time, and managed to drive Hippias out of Athens. The exiled tyrant tried to settle scores 20 years later with the help of a Persian army headed by Darius, only to be famously trounced at the Battle of Marathon.

The art of sculpture

Athens led the ancient world not only in philosophy, politics and drama but also in the fine arts, especially excelling in sculpture. During Athens' flourishing Golden Age of the fifth century BC, sculpture metamorphosed in form and function from tombstones produced by labourers to the first pieces of what we might call art.

Greek representations of men begin with the kouros figure – the stiff, unrealistic bods with one foot forward dating from the seventh century BC; there are several in Athens' National Archaeological Museum (see p106). Over the centuries these figures softened, filled out with muscle, took on natural expressions and became the fluid, convincing figure of Athenian art exemplified in the *Critian Boy*, the early sculpture found on the Acropolis (now in the Acropolis Museum, see p82).

Over the years, standing statues had adopted the *contrapposto* pose, leaning the weight on one foot, setting up a dynamic between the hips, shoulders, buttocks and neck, as if the figure were on the brink of movement.

Once sculptors had mastered the technology of creating natural-looking flesh and muscle, they began to make more expressive and complex works. The *Discus-Thrower*, made by the Athenian sculptor Myron in the fifth century BC, is a work that appears natural and evokes all the movement of a sporting man. This world-famous statue adorned Greek coins during the Athens 2004 Olympics. It is testament to Myron's skill that although the statue looks completely fluid and lifelike, the positioning of the limbs would be impossible in a real-life discus-thrower – Athenian sculpture had invented artistic sleight-of-hand centuries before rules of perspective were conceived.

With this innovative art form came the first celebrity sculptor: Phedias (circa 493 to 430 BC), to whom every great piece of Athenian sculpture has been credited at one time or another. It was a saying of the ancients that 'the hand of Phedias alone of men could make the image of the gods'. His work had a Homeric quality to it in terms of its lack of affectation and sublime harmony.

Phedias, working in the same vein as Myron, made flesh the preoccupations of the Athenian people. Their love of the gods, war and games are literally embodied in bronze and marble; the human form is used to express ideas. As the concepts became more refined, so the sculpture became more sophisticated, culminating in Phedias' statue of Zeus in Olympia, which was considered one of the seven wonders of the ancient world.

Although much original Athenian sculpture was cast in bronze and melted down in later years, everyone from the Romans to the Victorians was so overwhelmed with the beauty of what remained that they made marble copies. As a result copies of Greek sculpture can be seen in museums throughout Europe.

Greece does still hold examples of its own sculptural treasures, including the brilliant Slipper Slapper group (now in Delos in the Cyclades) depicting Aphrodite fending off the advances of Pan with her shoe. But perhaps the most dramatic statue of all, Phedias' mighty, 40-foot chryselephantine (coated in ivory and gold) statue of Athena that stood in the Parthenon was destroyed during one of the invasions of the city.

Cleisthenes took over Athens, allied himself with the ordinary people (*demos*) and brought Solon's reforms back. He created ten new tribes based on place of residence to avoid the old political ties of kinship that had existed. Each tribe was composed of *demoi* (village units) with their own political apparatus. The Assembly (an attempt to make the different factions and regions of Athens into one people) now became the focus of political decision-making.

Cleisthenes also introduced the political safety valve of ostracism, whereby citizens could agree to remove a perceived troublemaker for ten years. This was democracy of sorts. All adult male citizens could speak and vote for, or against, motions put before the Assembly, but women, slaves and those not born of Athenian parents were excluded from the political process.

BELLIGERENT ATHENS

Athens had to get a series of Persian wars out the way before it could fully blossom as the cosmopolitan centre of its 'empire'. In 490 BC Darius followed up his threats for 'earth and water' from Athens by amassing an army at least 30,000 strong on the plains of Marathon. Famously a messenger ran the roughly 42 kilometres (26 miles) from the battle site to Athens to announce the news, and his efforts are immortalised in modern marathon races.

Darius expected an early surrender, but instead the vastly outnumbered Athenian hoplites made an impromptu charge and with their superior armour, astonishingly, drove the Persians away. The historian Herodotus, by no means a military expert, estimates the Persian dead at Marathon as 6,400 and the Athenians as only 192. A theory has recently evolved that the horsemen carved on the frieze around the wall of the Parthenon, part of the Elgin Marbles, might represent the 192 soldiers killed at Marathon.

In the war's sequel, ten years later, a fearsome army returned under the command of Darius's son, Xerxes I. By the time the invaders reached Athens, the vastly outnumbered citizens had been evacuated and the Persians burned an empty city. Traces of the 'non-event' have been recognised in bronze arrowheads found by archaeologists, their points twisted by striking against the rock of the Acropolis.

Athens was best placed to fight with its navy, built up from the proceeds of the discovery of a rich vein of silver a few years before. At the Battle of Salamis the Athenian general Themistocles ingeniously defeated the Persian navy by luring its ships into a narrow channel, where the heavier Greek vessels proceeded to ram and sink them. The string of victories sent the Greeks' confidence sky-high.

But for Athens and Sparta the spoils of war were short-lived, for they would soon be at each other's throats. Both sides began collecting allies – Athens sided with the city-states in northern Greece, the Aegean Islands and the west coast of Asia Minor, while Sparta formed the Peloponnesian League with its neighbours, Olympia and Corinth. Athens' Delian League, so called because its treasury was originally located on the sacred island of Delos, moved to Athens in 454 BC. Gradually its members became more dependent on their head city and the Athenian Empire was formed.

Pericles (495 BC-429 BC), a politician from a distinguished local family, is the protagonist of Athens' Golden Age. He used tributes coaxed from members of the Delian League and materials brought back from expeditions to territories in Phoenicia and the Black Sea region to transform the city.

Eventually Pericles overstretched the empire by advising war on too many fronts at once, while at the same time stirring up resistance among allies by making harsh demands on them for protection against the Persians. In 446 BC Athens and Sparta agreed to a 30-year peace treaty. But the mutual mistrust continued.

GOLDEN AGE

With the unflappable Pericles at the helm, peace – coupled with unprecedented power and income – heralded Athens' heyday as the intellectual and cultural centre of Greece and beyond. In just a handful of decades, from approximately 470 BC to 430 BC, many of the city's iconic buildings were built. The Acropolis, left ravaged by the Persians, took shape again. The fusion of Ionic and Doric order columns in the Parthenon and the sheer beauty of the Erechtheum proclaimed the city's imperial pre-eminence.

The rooftop pediments of other majestic buildings, including the Temple of Hephaestus (or Theseion), the Propylaia and the Temple of Poseidon on the hillside at Sounion (where Byron was to graffiti his name on a column), strove towards azure skies. Such buildings, some of which still stand today, would prove to be the blueprint for the architecture of elegance and power down through the ages.

The progressive climate of the period allowed the arts full creative freedom. Drama entered its own golden age with the innovative political satire of Aristophanes and the classical tragedies of Aeschylus, Sophocles and Euripides; Pindar penned lyric poetry, while Socrates, and later Plato and Aristotle, laid the basis of Western philosophy. The glories of the Golden Age were recorded by the historians Herodotus and Thucydides. The latter employed an advanced scientific approach that, for the first time, attempted to clear the historic landscape of dim myths and divine actions.

Sculptors abandoned the rigid formal styles of the Archaic Period for more naturalistic poses eased by the development of more malleable bronze casting techniques. Phidias's sculptures from the Parthenon are good examples of this powerful, new, liberating aesthetic. During the fifth century even the much-prized Attic red-figure pottery reached its artistic zenith, with detailed everyday scenes and mythological stories fired on black vases and wine vessels.

'A succession of generals turned their backs on Sparta's offers for peace and took increasing risks.'

At the vanguard of this progress was Pericles. He never ranked higher than a general, but his sound intelligence and charisma as an orator allowed him to dominate the political scene and oversee the city's extraordinary boom. Thucydides believed that Pericles wielded a calming influence over the worst excesses of government. In an oft-quoted funerary speech, Pericles depicted an idealised state of democratic Athens: 'The city has succeeded in cultivating refinement without extravagance and knowledge without softness.'

Although Pericles also had praise for an individual's freedom, his ardent imperial streak still supported the subjugation of former allies. In terms of political and legal rights, Athenian citizenship was deemed superior to that of other cities within the empire. Out of a population of 200,000 at its peak, only 50,000 males were full citizens. In the mid century, at Pericles's request, citizenship was restricted to those born of both Athenian parents; this protectionism arguably backfired as it never allowed the conquered upper classes to become part of the Athens project.

Pericles's achievements were multifarious. He also proposed the building of the Long Walls around Athens' southern perimeter (linking the city to the port at Piraeus), commissioned the Parthenon, introduced the *theorica*, a state allowance to encourage poorer citizens to attend the theatre, and was a friend and sponsor to many of the leading philosophers and artists of the day, in particular Anaxagoras, Sophocles and Phidias. But with Pericles's demise and the onset of war, the Golden Age lost its sheen.

BACK TO THE FRONT

The Peloponnesian War ran from 431 BC to 404 BC and was triggered when Athens placed Corfu, a colony of Corinth, under its power.

Thanks to Thucydides, detailed accounts of the war still exist. He attributed the 'real' cause of the conflict to Sparta's fear of Athens' expanding imperialism. On paper, Athens had the superior navy; Sparta, the sharper infantry. Pericles's strategy, therefore, was to make sudden navy raids and then retreat behind Athens' defensive walls when Spartan soldiers attacked. The plan might have worked had an epidemic in 430 BC not killed thousands of Athenians packed inside the city, including Pericles himself.

Athens held on for ten more years despite the devastation of its countryside and the loss of income from its silver mines and olive groves. After victories for both sides, including the prestigious capture of 120 Spartan soldiers by the Athenians, the fragile Peace of Nicias, named after the chief Athenian negotiator, was agreed in 421 BC.

But a succession of generals turned their backs on Sparta's offers of peace and took increasing risks. In 413 BC an overstretched invasion force led by Alcibiades, an ambitious student of Socrates, suffered a catastrophic defeat at Syracuse in Sicily. The damage was massive. Thucydides calculated that more than 40,000 Athenian troops and as many as 200 ships were lost in Sicily.

Before leaving for war, Alcibiades had allegedly taken part in a spree that desecrated the Herms, sculpted heads of the god Hermes that protected doorways throughout the city. Because he was thought to have once parodied the Eleusian mysteries, the drug-fuelled initiation ceremonies for the cult of Demeter and Persephone, Alcibiades became a chief suspect and was recalled from Sicily for trial. Rather than face the Assembly, he fled to Sparta and was condemned to death in absentia.

After upsetting the Spartans by seducing the wife of one of their kings, Alcibiades sought refuge in Persia. He was itching to return to Athens, though, and, with the promise of Persian support, made contact with some Athenian oligarchs who were looking to take advantage of the ferment in the city. In 411 BC a moderate oligarchy failed and democracy was restored. Alcibiades switched sides to the democrats and led a four-year campaign regaining Athenian control in the Aegean. He rode back into Athens a hero and that year led the religious procession to Eleusis. Pursued by multiple enemies, Alcibiades was eventually blamed by the fair-weather Athenians for a naval defeat at Notium and he retreated to the safety of a castle.

Plato in discussion with a group of students.

The situation deteriorated in Athens when, in 406 BC, a 5,000-strong crew drowned and the people accused the generals of not having done enough to rescue the sailors. The generals were tried en masse at the Assembly, but Socrates, who happened to be chairman, refused to conduct the case as it contravened an Athenian citizen's right to an individual hearing. Such was the rancour among the people that they condemned the generals anyway. Six, including the son of Pericles, were summarily executed. As Aristotle later noted, ancient democracy was ever susceptible to mob rule.

By 404 BC the population of Athens had grown, but food lines were still cut off. The city had no choice but to surrender and its walls were supposedly dismantled to the sound of flute music while the freedom of Greece was proclaimed.

The war ended Athenian hegemony and shut down the Delian League. Sparta installed a brutal puppet regime in Athens called the Thirty Tyrants. This lasted just a year before Athenian rebels restored democracy.

MACEDONIA RISING

Although the fourth century BC began with the unjust death of Socrates, the baton in the quest for absolute truth was passed on to Plato and Aristotle, who became regular fixtures debating in the agora (market place). The Monument of Lysicrates was built and the polished speeches of Demosthenes, delivered at the people's Assembly, became another highlight of city life in this period. Fourth-century BC Greece was marked by complex power struggles between new alliances, yet more wars and a shift from city-states towards monarchy.

During the first third of the century Sparta and Thebes became embroiled in a feud that ultimately weakened both sides. Athens, fearful of the growing power of her north-western neighbour Thebes, switched allegiance and formed a coalition with Sparta. In 378 BC Athens revived her maritime ambitions and formed the Second Athenian Confederacy, composed of the cities and islands of the Aegean and Ionian seas. However, it lacked the backbone of the Delian League, having neither the resources nor the determination to impose its will, and soon overreached itself.

Ready to capitalise on the power vacuum among the squabbling Greek states was new player Macedonia. Its rise as a superpower was inspired by its king, Philip II, and his son Alexander the Great.

Athens, which had allies on the north-western border, had always been happy to see Macedonia weak. A step ahead of his fellow Athenians, Demosthenes realised that Philip's expansionist policies represented a real threat. In a series of well-varnished speeches known as the Philippics, he warned the Athenians how their indifference contrasted with Philip's energy and decisiveness. Speaking about a rumour that wanted Philip dead, Demosthenes said: 'Is Philippos dead? What does it matter to you? For if this Philippos dies, you will soon raise up a second Philippos by your apathy.' His powerful oratory, though, went unheeded.

The Macedonians made their move in 338 BC in a battle at Chaironeia, in central Greece. Fighting side by side in a phalanx formation and armed with 4.3-metre (14-foot) spears, Philip's light-footed army became a lethal porcupine that could skewer enemies before they got too close.

Post-victory, Philip sent Alexander to Athens on a diplomatic mission to placate the Greeks by returning the ashes of the Athenian dead who had fallen in the battle. He made no punitive demands and asked only that Athens should ally itself with Macedonia. Such had been Alexander's brutal razing to the ground of Thebes when it rebelled in 336 BC, that Athens had the good sense to accept Macedonian rule.

Alexander didn't linger in Athens. Instead he marched east to create the Persian Empire by conquering most of the known world from present-day Turkey as far as Afghanistan, while still only in his 20s. Apparently he loved Homer so much that he slept with a copy of *The Iliad* under his pillow. On news that his brilliant life had been cut short by an illness in 323 BC, the people of Athens reputedly danced in the streets.

In the squabbles among generals that followed Alexander's death, Athens tried to seize back its independence, but was effortlessly defeated. Surrender meant the end of its proud tradition of naval power and the abolition of democracy. As if to symbolise the city's demise, Alexander's successor, Demetrios Falireas, installed a harem in the Parthenon. In 322 BC Athens' most eloquent advocate Demosthenes, who had been chased into exile by the Macedonians, chose suicide by poison rather than be captured.

FROM CITY-STATE TO EMPIRE

In 307 BC Demetrios 'the Besieger' (so called because of his assault on the island of Rhodes) freed Athens and re-established democracy. This marked the beginning of the Hellenistic Age, which is characterised by a shift in perception from an insular city-state mentality to a view of the individual as part of an expansive empire. Adherents of Diogenes, the Cynics in particular, but also the Epicureans, and the Stoics, considered the achievement of self-sufficiency a means of protecting man from a random world at large. These new philosophical patterns were reflected in the arts. Portraits expressed not only the public role of the sitter, but also his or her inner thoughts and feelings. Sculpture was less serene than in the classical period, and began to embody the sensual and a sense of life's drama. Much impressive construction took place throughout the wider empire, but in Athens, notably, the Tower of the Winds and the Stoa of Attalos were built, the latter's neo-classical style echoing the glories of the past.

In 267 BC Athens and Sparta, with the support of the Egyptian king Ptolemy II, attempted one last time to undermine Macedonian hegemony. Demetrios's son Antigonos, however, proved too strong and when he counter-attacked not even the Spartans could save the day. Athens endured

Odeon of Herodes Atticus. *See p18.*

Sex and the (ancient) city

The ancients, it is often said, were just like us. In the case of sex, this means that they did it for fun as well as for procreation, and in a variety of weird and wonderful combinations. Carnality crept into every facet of ancient Athenian life. And like most aspects of life in that society, sex was dominated by men. The adult male's predilection for young boys that has scandalised scholars was, in fact, part of a delicate game of power and submission.

At the pinnacle of Athenian society was the mature male citizen – he could do all sorts of thrilling things such as fight Persians, vote in the *agora* and have homosexual and heterosexual sex. A grown man would pursue a younger one, wooing him with poetry, money and the occasional gift of a dead hare if the youth was particularly toothsome. Any boy still beardless was fair game, especially slaves and foreigners. The act of penetration was an assertion of status – cultural and political status. The citizen-penetrator could also earn a living, something denied the young, foreign or enslaved.

This is not to say that the learned Athenians allowed their sexual proclivities to get in the way of philosophy. Rich families employed a *paedogogus* (chaperone and tutor) to ensure school-age boys were well versed in Socrates and not subjected to the shame of sexual predators.

For Athens to have become the boom city state that it was, though, there had to be other people without beards besides young boys: women. Greek society had two kinds of women – wives and other women. The Greeks had a word for women who weren't anyone's wife – *hetairai*, the other women. These women weren't allowed to vote but they were allowed to make a modest income from attending drinking parties or *symposia*. They were sexually available in much the same way that young boys were, and by allowing people to have sex with them, often in exchange for money, were placing themselves in a lower position in society than a virginal daughter or a wife. But the *hetairai* weren't merely exploited bimbos – many could recite long chunks of Homer.

Finally, once the adult male Athenian citizen had finished asserting his social and political status with boys and female prostitutes, he would sometimes get round to having sex with his wife. Even in the marital bedroom, though, sex could be a power game. In Aristophanes' play *Lysistrata*, the male citizens' sexual rights are subverted when their far less powerful wives withhold sex to encourage a speedy peace treaty. Nonplussed by this unexpected change in power relations, the men find themselves befuddled and floundering. Denied their Zeus-given right to fight Persians and penetrate at will, they capitulate in no time.

---

a Macedonian garrison until 229 BC but, although the city lost any further political claims to lead Greece, it remained an intellectual and cultural centre.

ROMAN OCCUPATION

In the second century BC, Rome, the region's growing superpower, began to wrestle power from Macedonia in Greece. But it was not until 86 BC that the Roman general Sulla occupied Athens. One of his first acts, as a punishment for Athens having supported Mithridates's rebellion in Asia Minor, was to knock down its walls and siphon off art treasures to decorate Rome.

Under the Pax Romana (the imperial peace inaugurated by Augustus in AD 31), Athens benefited from Roman patronage as the intellectual capital of the Graeco-Roman world. In 66-67 Nero toured Greece and won everything he turned his hand to, from athletic to musical challenges – only a brave opponent

would defeat a psychopathic emperor. In peacetime, tourists and the sons of Roman nobility, such as Cicero and Horace, flocked to the city to see its ancient sites and to study at its renowned university. As a token of the esteem with which Rome held all things Greek, emperors began to honour leading Greeks by electing them for the Roman senate and inaugurated a panhellenic festival.

Around this time modifications were made to the Acropolis with the construction of an elegant circular temple dedicated to Rome and Augustus, eastwards of the Parthenon. And the Emperor Claudius built a grandiose stairway leading to the Propylaia, which provided a formal and symmetrical approach to the sacred hill.

But of all the Roman Emperors, it was the passionate philhellene Hadrian (117-38), who made the biggest impact on the city and its heritage. Not only did he introduce the Greeks to Roman laws and give them the rights of Roman citizenship, but he also repaired earlier fire damage to the Parthenon and built the Library to the east of the Ancient Agora. In addition, he solved the crucial problem of the city's water supply by building a great reservoir on the slopes of Lycabettus Hill, which collected water brought there by channels from Mount Parnes. His impressive architectural contribution included the continuation and completion in 131-2 of the Peisistratid Temple of Olympian Zeus and the erection of a huge gateway leading to the *peribolos* (precinct) of the temple, the Arch of Hadrian. The inscription over the monumental entrance reads: 'This is the Athens of Theseus, the old city' on one side, and on the other, 'This is the city of Hadrian, not of Theseus.' The words can still be discerned through the soot today.

Equally evident today is the Odeon of Herodes Atticus (Herodion), a Roman imperial theatre built into a natural slope of the Acropolis in the middle of the second century by the eponymous 'millionaire' and tutor to Marcus Aurelius. The auditorium could seat 50,000, and to this day hosts productions of the great Greek dramas.

During the reign of Valerian (253-60) the walls of Athens were rebuilt. But not well enough to repel the Germanic Heruli tribe, who stormed the city in 267 and left it in rubble. The remaining Athenians moved to a small area to the north of the Acropolis, where they fortified new walls built of marble salvaged from the ruined buildings.

THE COMING OF CHRISTIANITY

According to the Roman writer Petronius, in the early first century AD one could find more gods than citizens in Athens. The well-travelled chronicler Pausanias agreed that the gods interested the Athenians more than anything else. In 52 AD St Paul had preached the gospels on the Areopagus. As the apostle shared his news with the Epicurean and Stoic philosophers on walks through the temples he was shocked to discover a city full of idols. Nonetheless, he was impressed by its beauty. The Athenians relished hearing about a religion whose God 'does not inhabit temples'. It appealed to them on a moral and intellectual plane, but they mocked the concept of resurrection. A handful, however, did convert to Christianity, long before Constantine made it Greece's official faith in the early fourth century (323), when the Roman emperor moved his capital from Rome to the Greek city of Byzantium, renaming it Constantinople.

During the fourth and fifth centuries, Athens experienced a brief regeneration, with its neo-Platonic philosophical schools attracting important students (such as Julian the Apostate, Basil and Gregory) from all over the known world, only to fall into oblivion after Emperor Justinian closed them down in 529. By then, Athens, tormented by waves of Slavic barbarians, plague and earthquakes, had long since faded under the shadow of Constantinople.

BYZANTINE COMPLEXITIES

From about the sixth to the 13th centuries Athens entered another dark age. The former cradle of civilisation became a provincial satellite of the Byzantine empire and a minor centre of religious learning and devotion. Today, all that remains from this period are the foundations of some of the ancient temples that had been converted for early Christian worship and a handful of churches from the 11th and 12th centuries built on the Byzantine cross-in-square plan.

From the 13th century, a host of outsiders took advantage of Athens' run-down state. First came the French. After the creation of the Latin Empire of Constantinople in 1204, the city passed to Othon de la Roche, a French nobleman who became *megaskyr*, or great lord of Athens and Thebes. He was succeeded by his nephew, Guy I. Athens prospered under Frankish rule; the magnificence of the Athenian court was recorded in mid century by a Catalan chronicler.

'They paid a tax to the Turks, but both Jesuit and Capuchin monasteries continued to thrive'

Then, in 1311 the duchy was captured by a band of Catalan explorers who a year later offered the ducal title to King Frederick II of Sicily, a member of the house of Aragón. The Aragón clan carried the title, but Athens was, in fact, governed by the Catalan Grand Company, an unreliable mercenary force that also acquired the neighbouring duchy of Neopatras in 1318.

As the French feudal culture faded, Athens sank into insignificance and poverty, particularly after 1377, when the succession was contested in civil war. Peter IV of Aragón assumed sovereignty in 1381, but ruled from Barcelona. On his initiative, the duchy was settled by Albanians.

Athens again shone briefly after its conquest in 1388 by Nerio Acciaioli, lord of Corinth and member of a family that was 'plebeian in Florence, potent in Naples and sovereign in Greece', according to the historian Edward Gibbon. Nerio helped to establish many of his compatriots as merchants in Athens. One of them, Cyriac of Ancona, kept illustrated diaries of his time in Greece; his scribbles offer a rare insight into lost monuments.

The next 50-odd years witnessed a tug-of-war for the city between the Republic of Venice and the Ottoman Turks. The Venetians had held Athens from 1394 to 1402, but in 1456 the fall of the Acropolis to the Turks marked the beginning of nearly four centuries of Ottoman rule.

Athens once again declined. The few remaining Greeks lived a semi-rural existence. They paid a tax to the Turks, but both Jesuit and Capuchin monasteries continued to thrive. The Erechtheum was used as a harem and the Parthenon, which had already been converted into a Christian church with a campanile, was refashioned into a Turkish mosque, complete with minaret. A French naval officer visiting in 1537 wrote: 'Athens, once worthily called the flower of the world, has now, under heavy servitude, sunk to being the poorest and most miserable of cities.'

When Venetian troops besieged the Acropolis in 1687, the Parthenon, which had been used by the Turks as a gunpowder store, was heavily bombarded, resulting in an explosion that caused a great amount of damage – until that incident the sacred hill had been virtually intact. The Parthenon took a further hit in 1801, when the British ambassador to Constantinople Lord Elgin detached much of the frieze around the temple and shipped it to London.

Gibbon described the city's decline, with Athenians 'walking with supine indifference among the glorious ruins of antiquity'. Foreign visitors, however, seemed more enthusiastic. The 1762 publication of *Antiquities of Athens* by the Society of Dilettanti prompted many travellers to visit the city as a sort of adjunct to the Grand Tour, and proved highly influential on Western neo-classical architecture.

Byzantine Plaka.

GERMAN AND BRITISH ATHENS

In the late 18th century the Greek nationalist movement gained momentum with the founding of a number of secret societies financed by exiled merchants. They were spurred on by philhellenic western European intellectuals such as Goethe and Byron, who did a first-rate PR job for the Greek cause. During the War of Independence, Athens changed hands several times between the Turks and Greek liberators, with the Acropolis, as ever, the seat of power.

By 1827, when the Turks recaptured the hill (which they were to hold for the next six years), Athens had been all but evacuated. Even in 1833, when plans for the new nation had been drawn up by the 'Great Powers' of western Europe, Athens only held about 4,000 people housed below the north slope of the Acropolis.

The first modern Olympics

The Olympic tradition of physical perfection stretches back to 776 BC. From then until 393 AD the ancient Games embodied patriotic pride for the Greek states, with the marathon commemorating the mighty run of the warrior Pheidippides announcing the victory of the Greeks over the Persians in the Battle of Marathon.

In 1896, after a growing movement among the strengthening Greek nation for a revival of the Games, the Olympics returned to Greece. A French enthusiast of organised sports, Pierre de Coubertin, had been inspired by the effort of an Englishman who had organised a village Olympics in Shropshire. Coubertin set up the Congress for the Revival of the Olympic Games in Paris in 1894, his efforts aided by a bequest from patriotic Greek Evangelis Zappas. Athens beat off competition from London and Paris to host the event, and had 18 months to clean the streets, sort out the road surfaces, build a shooting hall and construct a velodrome.

The Athenians also restored the ancient Kallimarmaron (Beautiful Marble) stadium, which had stood in Athens since 329 BC; it housed 60,000 spectators.

Three hundred athletes from 13 countries competed, with Greece triumphing overall with ten gold medals. This was certainly deserved in terms of the size of its delegation, which consisted of 230 athletes. They competed in nine events: swimming, cycling, fencing, gymnastics, shooting,

Modern Athens began to take shape from 1834, when it took over from Nafplion as the capital of a newly independent Greece. If Ioannis Kapodistrias, the mastermind of the War of Independence, had not been assassinated in 1831, chances are that the capital would have remained in the Peloponnese. As it was, the reasoning of the mediating powers was almost completely symbolic. They imposed a hereditary monarchy on Greece and at the tender age of 17 the Bavarian Otto I became the first king of the Hellenes (1832-62).

Installed in the only two-storey house in the city, the teenage monarch set about rebuilding much of Athens along neo-classical lines using German and French architects. The idea was to re-create the glories of the ancient city: broad streets were laid out in

lawn tennis, wrestling, weightlifting and track and field – including the legendary marathon. Several events from the ancient past lingered in the modern Games, including discus and wrestling.

One of the non-Greek heroes of the Games was the American athlete Robert Garrett Jr. After romping home in the shot put and picking up a second and third place respectively in the long and high jump, he visited the stadium one evening and found a discarded discus.

Having thrown it about for a while he decided to enter the competition and won gold, defeating the best Greek athletes. But Greek pride was more than salvaged by an astonishing marathon victory on the last day by local shepherd Spiridion Louis.

New traditions were invented for the modern Olympics in line with the Games' theme of international harmony. The Olympic Creed, for example, was set in stone, incorporating the ultimate fair-play phrase: 'The essential thing is not to have conquered but to have fought well.' The torch was symbolically lit for the first time, and now the continuity with the games of the ancients is emphasised with the fire originating from Olympia every four years. The 300 athletes battling it out in 1896 began a great tradition upheld and amplified by every one of the 11,099 sportsmen and women who processed through the same city in 2004.

grid patterns, incorporating showpiece squares such as Syntagma, and lined with grand public buildings like the Royal Palace, the University, the Academy (built in marble from Mount Pentelicon) and the Observatory.

In keeping with the spirit of the new nation, German archaeologists, most notably Heinrich Schliemann, began stripping away the Frankish and Turkish embellishments on the Acropolis and Parthenon and at other key sites in the city. Clearly impressed by these treasures on a visit to the Acropolis in 1848, the English author Edward Lear wrote: 'Poor old scrubby Rome sinks into nothing by the side of such beautiful magnificence.'

By most accounts 19th-century Athens was a mild-mannered city of elegant tree-lined avenues. Its dwellings, built for the nascent

Changing places

When three million visitors descended on Athens for the 2004 Olympics, the city had plenty of time to prepare for their arrival. But an extraordinary influx of 400,000 refugees in 1923 left it shell-shocked for years afterwards.

Following a series of border struggles with Turkey after World War I, the Greek army was eventually forced to seek a truce. The Turkish army, however, began a bloody offensive against the one million Greeks still living in the area that was then known as Asia Minor. The Turks torched all the Greek sections of the city of Smyrna, where hundreds of thousands of Greek Christians had taken refuge. Up to 300,000 were reported killed, and the Allies refused to send aid, having earlier condemned the

Greek decision to reinstate its monarchy. Tension and fear between Greek Christians and Turkish Muslims ran high in both Greece and Turkey.

In 1923 the Treaty of Lausanne was signed, incorporating the plan of a Norwegian diplomat called Fridtjof Nansen to combat the problem of cultural tensions. There was to be a giant exchange of populations, based on religious identity. The Orthodox Christians, largely ethnic Greeks from parts of Turkey such as Anatolia, were to return to Greece, while Muslims living in Greece would move back to Turkey. As a result, 380,000 Turkish Muslims had to emigrate from Greece, while 1.1 million Greek Orthodox Christians moved back over the Turkish border. The resulting chaos

professional classes, were similar in style to those of Victorian London. Most of these Ottonian-style houses have long since been replaced by concrete, though some of the best surviving examples are on Vassilissis Sofias.

In 1843, the explosive combination of Otto's autocratic rule and croneyism, the continued interference of foreign powers and declining economic conditions led to a bloodless revolution

was such that the League of Nations established a Commission for Refugees, with Nansen as its first secretary.

One million-plus people poured into Greece, destitute and desperate. In Athens, refugees camped out on the beaches, in the ancient palace, in the opera house and in the Parthenon. Winter brought an outbreak of pneumonia, and many refugees brought smallpox and typhus with them. Tent cities were set up around Athens and the harbour of Piraeus, which quickly grew into long-term shanty towns. The population of Piraeus more than doubled, as new settlements with poignant neo-Turkish names sprang up: Nea Kokkinia and Nea Smyrni.

A combination of post-war poverty and the 'catastrophe' of the influx impacted on politics. As coup followed counter-coup, the immigrants were slowly absorbed into an unstable Athenian society, but the country was unable to support its new population. Overcrowding, unemployment and famine became the norm, until the instigation of martial rule in 1936 restored some order to the capital. Cultural shifts occurred as the Byzantine side of these new Greeks emerged. In the refugee areas of the city, clubs modelled on the 'cafés aman' of Asia Minor began to appear, and the folk music of the two cultures began to meld.

Despite the desperate conditions, tensions between old and new Athenians were minimal. There was less diversity after the population exchange than there was before: the immigrants were all Orthodox Christians, the majority of Muslims had left and Greece became a country that was unified and even insular. Influence from Asia Minor gradually faded, and Turkish is now spoken by very few Greeks.

taking place in Athens. The people joined forces with political and military leaders to insist on the restoration of the constitution.

In the 1850s the population still numbered only 20,000 and economic progress was slow. There were no railway routes into the city, roads were poor and the export of currants provided the only source of national income. It was out of a climate of despondency that the governing creed of the century, the 'Great Idea' (Megali Idhea), developed. The thesis advocated a new Greek Empire by the gradual enlargement of Greece's territory at the expense of the declining Ottoman Empire. But for the rest of the century, it was to create tension between liberal and conservative forces. One expression of rebellion against tradition was an enthusiasm for use in literature of the demotic language (popular language) over *catharevousa* (a simplified form of ancient Greek), a debate that led to riots in Athens in 1901.

Between 1854 and 1857 the occupation of Piraeus harbour by the French and British armies increased the discontent among Athenians and eventually led to the expulsion of King Otto in 1862. This had been facilitated by a new generation of graduates from Athens University, which had been re-opened in 1837. However, much to the chagrin of the Greek intellectuals (and due to British influence in the Ionian Islands), George I was enthroned in 1863. He ruled until 1913 and proved a more capable leader than Otto (even if during the first 17 years of his reign there were nine elections and 31 governments). In 1870 George's rule was further marred by the kidnapping and murder of a group of wealthy British tourists on an excursion to Marathon; the crime became known as the Dilessi murders, and was one of more than 100 cases of the time.

Arguably Athens deserved its fin-de-siècle tag as the 'Paris of the eastern Mediterranean'. The opening of the Corinth Canal, begun in AD 62 and completed in 1893, made Piraeus one of the world's great ports. The merchant navy expanded and a shipping industry boom sparked a growth in manufacturing and banking.

Athens had a chance to show off its achievements to the world in 1896, when it hosted the first modern Olympic Games. The Panathenaic Stadium, which seated 70,000 people, was constructed on the site of the original fourth-century BC arena by an expatriate Greek tycoon. But such progress was precarious. A year later, when a dispute broke out over the control of Crete, the Turks were poised within a few days' march of Athens. Once more the city was saved from the Turkish army by the allied powers.

Famine in Athens

In April 1941 the Greek prime minister Alexandros Koryzis shot himself in despair at the Germans' imminent occupation. A week later the Greek flag was lowered on the Acropolis and the Nazi swastika raised in its place. Across Europe, newsreels showed field marshal von Brauchitsch on the sacred hill that Hitler had dubbed the symbol of 'human culture'. So began a three-year period that Churchill called the 'long night of barbarism'.

Almost immediately Athenians started panic-buying and stripped the city's stores bare, partly in response to German scare-mongering that the departing British army had poisoned the water supply with typhoid bacilli. The ill-prepared German army had neglected to bring their own food supplies and arrived in Athens half-starving. Officers looted the city's warehouses and seized supplies. A combination of a debilitated Greek state infrastructure, ruthless plundering by the occupying force and a below-average harvest soon caused acute food shortages.

As a result, the country experienced rampant inflation, which created a black market in which olive oil became the chief commodity and the price of a loaf of bread reached two million drachmas.

As the Germans bickered with the Italians about who should feed Greece, official rations dwindled and soup kitchens, set up by charities, fed people just two or three times a week. Many resorted to eating weeds gathered from the outlying areas of the city. Desperate, people of all ages, particularly those from the slums created by an influx of refugees in 1923, took to the streets to beg.

Children waited patiently for soldiers to discard olive stones, fighting among themselves to suck the stone dry, while brave hawkers cried: 'Buy raisins. A handful will save you from Charon!' To make matters worse, snow fell in Athens that winter and the sub-zero temperatures fuelled disease. Physically and mentally exhausted individuals collapsed crying '*pinoue, pinoue*' ('I'm hungry') as they lay dying. The next morning their swollen bodies were slung in the back of a municipal truck bound for the cemetery.

Reports by German occupation officials that more food was needed in Athens were ignored by the Nazi high command in Berlin. In a memo to Reich leaders of the occupied territories, Goering wrote: 'I could not care less when you say that people under your administration are dying of hunger. Let them perish so long as no German dies.'

For the first time since mortality records began in the Athens/Piraeus zone, the death rate exceeded the birth rate. At the time the BBC's reported over 500,000 deaths during the winter of 1941-2, but more accurate studies put the figure at about 40,000 for the year ending October 1942. By this time grain supplies were arriving from the International Red Cross and the end was in sight.

POPULATION BOOM

The man who had led the uprising to liberate Crete in 1905, Eleftherios Venizelos, was summoned to Athens following a coup d'état by an Athens garrison in 1909. Appointed Prime Minister in 1910, he was an advocate of liberal democracy, who doubled Greek territory during the Balkan Wars (1912-13) and sided with the Allies in World War I.

In March 1913, King George was assassinated by a madman and his son Constantine became king. Constantine, who was married to the sister of the German Kaiser, didn't want to get involved in the war and this caused much tension with Venizelos. For the first three years of the war Greece kept neutral and the city was occupied by British and French troops.

Greece's catastrophic post-war invasion of Smyrna resulted in the 1923 Treaty of Lausanne, which implemented a controlled form of ethnic cleansing and signalled the end of the Great Idea. In an exchange of religious minorities, 400,000 Turks left Greece, and almost one and a half million Christian refugees, mainly Greeks, arrived from Asia Minor. More than half of them came to Athens, where they founded shanty towns on the fringes of the city. The web of suburbs along the metro line to Piraeus bears testimony to the refugees' origins: Nea Smyrni, Nea Ionia, Nea Filadelfia.

At the same time as the slums were expanding, during the political bickering of the inter-war years, the American School began excavations in the Athenian Agora in 1931, culminating in the complete restoration of the Stoa of Attalos.

FASCIST THREAT, COMMUNIST REVOLT

Although a republic was established between 1924 and 1935, its existence was threatened by repeated military coups. When Venizelos was

exiled in 1935, King George II was restored
to the throne by a rigged plebiscite. As prime
minister he installed General Ioannis Metaxas,
who ruled as a fascist-style dictator – his secret
police dealt ruthlessly with leftist opponents and
parts of Thucydides were banned from schools.
Metaxas is best known for his curt reply of
'*ohi*' (no) to Mussolini's request to allow Italian
soldiers to cross Greece. Apparently his actual
response was '*C'est la guerre*', but the proud
Greeks prefer to remember the more emphatic
riposte. The day of the rebuttal, 28 October
1940, is now celebrated as a national holiday.

In April 1941, Hitler's armies advanced
suddenly into Greece. Athen's inhabitants
suffered extreme hardships during the
three-year German occupation in World
War II, especially during the winter of 1941-2,
when hundreds died daily from starvation
(*see p24* **Famine in Athens**).

During the war the Hotel Grande Bretagne
in Syntagma Square housed successively
Greek, British and German headquarters.
Churchill, who was in Athens to show his
support for the Greek government against the
communists, escaped a bomb placed in the
hotel's basement in December 1944 by staying
aboard HMS *Ajax* in Piraeus harbour.

In December 1944 an open communist
revolution broke out in the Thisio area after
a demonstration had been fired on by police

in Syntagma Square. Traces of action from
the Battle of Athens that ensued can still
be seen on some buildings in the city. For
a brief time the government held only the
Parliament building, neighbouring embassies
and a part of Syntagma Square, while the
palace garden was used as a common grave.
British troops eventually restored order and,
at a conference called by Winston Churchill
on Christmas Day, an armistice was arranged;
under its terms Archbishop Damaskinos
became regent.

The country's civil troubles of 1944-9
between pro- and anti-communist factions
seriously retarded the city's recovery.
Athens was virtually severed from the
rest of Greece by roadblocks. Tragically,
more Greeks were killed in the civil war
than during World War II. In response to
the distress and disorder, over a million
Greeks set sail for a more peaceful and
prosperous existence in Canada, Australia
and America. Many of those who stayed
behind headed for Athens, where American
aid was funding an industrialisation
programme, in search of work.

After its wars Greece was isolated as
the only non-communist state in the Balkans.
Communism was declared illegal and
the government introduced its infamous
Certificate of Political Reliability (that gave

Tanks on the streets: the Junta strikes back in November 1973. *See p26*.

proof that the holder was not a Red), which remained valid until 1962, and without which Greeks couldn't vote or easily find a job.

In the 1950s and '60s the metropolis began to take on the sprawling shape that characterises it today. Land clearance for suburban building caused run-off and flooding, requiring the modernisation of the sewer system; at Piraeus in 1959 a burst sewer revealed four superb classical bronzes. The Mornos River was dammed and a pipeline over 160 kilometres (100 miles) long was built to Athens, supplementing the inadequate water supply.

Ideological conflict and political instability led to the seizure of power by a military Junta in 1967. Andreas Papandreou, who would later become prime minister, called it 'the first successful CIA military putsch on the European continent'. During this time persecution and censorship ruled. Greece's favourite actress Melina Mercouri was disenfranchised while out of the country, rembetika clubs were shut down and productions of the classical tragedies forbidden. Sadly during the dictatorship of the Colonels (1967-74) many of the Turkish houses of Plaka and other neo-classical buildings were destroyed.

'The Junta was finally felled in July 1974, after it had precipitated the Turkish invasion of Cyprus.'

On 17 November 1973, student demonstrations against the Junta at Athens Polytechnic were brutally ended when tanks moved in, killing dozens. The occasion provided the name for Greece's lethal November 17 urban guerrilla terrorist group, which has killed 23 targets, including British Brigadier Stephen Saunders, shot dead at point-blank range in Athens' traffic in June 2000. In 2002 Greek police had a breakthrough in rounding up its alleged members following a botched bombing in Piraeus; they were finally put on trial in 2003.

MODERN ATHENS

The Junta was finally felled in July 1974, after it had precipitated the Turkish invasion of northern Cyprus following a disastrous plan to assassinate President Makarios. Konstantine Karamanlis, a leading politician in voluntary exile, returned to streets full of jubilant crowds. As the new prime minister, Karamanlis noted: 'We invented democracy. We were into it before it was cool.' A ban on communist parties was lifted and later that year in a referendum the

Greeks voted by two thirds for the abolition of the monarchy. When King Constantine finally returned to Greece in 1993 for a holiday, the government kept his yacht under constant surveillance by missile boats and planes. Not surprisingly, the tanned London-based king insisted he had no desire to overthrow the Greek constitution.

The new republic now looked to western Europe for orientation with the goal of joining the European Economic Community. On 1 January 1981, thanks to the manoeuverings of Karamanlis, Greece became the tenth member of the EEC. Later that year Andreas Papandreou's Panhellenic Socialist Movement (PASOK) party formed Greece's first socialist government, appealing to the electorate with the simple slogan 'Allaghi' (change). Melina Mercouri was appointed Minister of Culture and wasted no time launching a campaign to return the Elgin Marbles to Greece. In 1985 Athens became Europe's first Capital of Culture.

Papandreou had his comeuppance when his amorous exploits with an air hostess were splashed across the newspapers and the party became tangled up in a financial scandal involving the Bank of Crete. But in January 1992 he was acquitted.

The 1990s were characterised by austere cuts by the government to attain some sort of economic stability and reactive strikes. Power passed from the New Democracy party (ND) back to Papandreou's PASOK. With a 52-strong cabinet on hand, Papandreou virtually ran the country from his private villa in Athens' exclusive Kifisia district, a suburb that had first become fashionable when Herodes Atticus built his villa there in the first century AD.

Since World War II Athens has drawn more than three million people from the countryside and now contains more than 40 per cent of the country's population. In such a megalopolis, the Greek saying that Athens is merely 'the largest village in Greece' is now seriously challenged.

A series of governments had neglected the city's expansion problems and by the early '90s Athens was saddled with a deserved reputation as one of the most traffic-polluted cities in Europe. In 1994, as a response to the worsening *nefos* (smog) that was affecting ancient buildings and monuments, traffic restrictions were introduced in central Athens.

The failed bid for the 1996 Olympic Games inspired some improvements to the city – primarily a shiny new metro system and a gleaming modern international airport. But it was the awarding of the 2004 Games a year later that galvanised planners into action.

Plans were temporarily disturbed when a strong earthquake shook the city on 7

The glittering opening ceremony set the scene for Olympic triumph in 2004.

September 1999. It was the most powerful to hit the region in almost 200 years, killing 120 people and leaving 70,000 homeless. The quake measured 5.9 on the Richter scale and left minor cracks in one of the Parthenon's columns. It also damaged the pottery collection in the National Archaeological Museum.

Following the death of Papandreou in 1996, the Blairite Costas Simitis steered Greece to the European Monetary Union in January 2001 when the euro replaced the drachma, much to the relief of countless tourists. A year later, the city elected its first female mayor, Dora Bakoyianni, who narrowly escaped an assassination attempt not long after her election.

Greece held the presidency of the European Union without incident for the first half of 2003. In March 2004 Costas Karamanlis followed in his uncle's footsteps by leading the conservative New Democracy Party to electoral victory in Greece, narrowly defeating another big family name in Greek politics, the incumbent leader of the Socialist party, George Papandreous.

The 48-year-old nephew of Constantine Karamanlis, the former prime minister and founder of the party who died in 1998, Costas Karamanlis is credited with transforming several of the party's dated conservative ideas into more attractive and contemporary proposals and is pro-Europe.

Later in the year, after a running war with the media as to whether the facilities for the Games would be ready in time, the Olympic torch was lit in Athens at a spectacular opening ceremony on 13 August 2004. The Games had returned to their spiritual home.

Despite worries about potential terrorist attacks, a huge security and volunteer operation ensured that the 28th Olympiad ran smoothly – the Greeks even scooped six gold medals in front of the home crowds. On the closing night of the Games, for the second time in the space of two months, celebratory fireworks lit the night sky of Athens – the first had followed Greece's surprising crowning as European football champions in July at Euro 2004 in Portugal.

'The Olympics came home and we've shown the world the great things Greeks can do,' said Gianna Angelopoulos, president of the Games organising committee, who claimed that not just Zeus but all the gods had been smiling on Athens during the Games.

There are mixed feelings among Athenians about the legacy of the Games. The city's transport infrastructure is radically improved with 120 kilometres (75 miles) of new roads, nearly eight kilometres (five miles) of new metro lines, a 24-kilometre (15-mile) tram network, an ultra-modern traffic management centre and arguably the best airport in the world. This in turn has helped to tackle the notorious smog that shrouded the city in the post-war years. But critics point out that long-term commitments may not be met: sustainable development targets were not achieved and not all of the 65,000 promised permanent jobs have materialised.

Key events

3200 BC Bronze Age in Cyclades and Crete.
Around 3000 BC Neolithic settlements on the Acropolis hill.
1450 BC Mycenas in Knossos.
Around 1400 BC The Acropolis is fortified.
1230 BC-1180 BC Destruction of Troy.
1200 BC Collapse of Mycenean culture.
800 BC Athens expands by incorporating its surrounding villages into its city-state.
776 BC The first Olympic Games take place.
750 BC-700 BC Homer writes *The Iliad* and *The Odyssey*.
750 BC-500 BC The Archaic Age.
594 BC Solon becomes archon of Athens.
496 BC Birth of dramatist Sophocles.
490 BC The Athenians defeat the Persians (led by Darius) at the Battle of Marathon.
480 BC The Persians burn Athens.
470 BC-430 BC Pericles's programme of civic improvement focuses on the Acropolis.
454 BC The Delian League moves to Athens, signalling the start of the Athenian Empire.
431 BC-404 BC Peloponnesian War between Athens and Sparta.
427 BC Birth of philosopher Plato.
399 BC Socrates is sentenced to death.
387 BC Plato sets up his Academy.
338 BC After winning the battle of Chaironeia, the Persians led by Philip II gain control over Athens.
336 BC Philip II's son Alexander (the Great) inherits control of Athens.
323 BC Death of Alexander the Great.
322 BC Death of Aristotle and Demosthenes.
330 BC-215 BC Euclid and Archimedes develop their mathematical theorems.
267 BC Athens fails to rise against Macedonia.
148 BC Romans conquer Macedonia.
86 BC Roman general Sulla occupies Athens.
AD 31 The Pax Romana is inaugurated by Emperor Augustus.
52 St Paul preaches the gospels to Athenians.
66-67 Emperor Nero tours Greece.
124-31 The Roman emperor Hadrian begins architectural reconstruction in Athens.
232 Constantine moves the capital of the Roman Empire to Constantinople.
380 Emperor Thedosius declares Christianity the official religion of the Empire.
529 Emperor Justinian closes down the philosophical schools in Athens.
600-1300 Athens goes into decline. Its temples are converted to Christian churches.

1054 The Christian church is divided into Roman and Greek orthodoxies.
1300-1456 A series of invaders (Franks, Catalans, Venetians, Turks) occupy Athens.
1456 The Turks occupy the Acropolis. They rule Athens for the next four centuries.
1687 In an attempt to recapture Athens, the Venetians bombard the Parthenon.
1801 Lord Elgin removes part of the frieze around the Parthenon and ships it to London.
1821 Start of the Greek War of Independence.
1828 Creation of the first free Greek state. Its president is Ioannis Kapodistrias.
1831 Kapodistrias is assassinated.
1832 The Great Powers of western Europe impose Bavarian King Otto as ruler.
1834 Athens becomes the capital of Greece.
1893 Opening of the Corinth Canal.
1896 The first modern-day Olympic Games take place in Athens.
1910 Eleftherios Venizelos is appointed Prime Minister.
1912-13 The Balkan Wars double the territory belonging to Greece.
1913 King George is assassinated.
1917 Greece sides with the Allies in World War I.
1923 Treaty of Lausanne authorises a population exchange in Asia Minor. Greece gains in excess of one million refugees.
1935 Venizelos is exiled; power is given to general Ioannis Metaxas.
1941-42 German occupation.
1944 An assassination attempt against Winston Churchill fails. The communist revolution starts.
1944-49 Civil war tears Greece apart. A mass exodus begins.
1967 The Junta seizes power.
1973 Student demonstrations against the ruling colonels end in a blood bath.
1974 The Junta collapses.
1981 Greece's first socialist government is elected into power. The country joins the European Community.
1985 Athens is Europe's first Capital of Culture.
1994 Traffic restrictions are introduced in Athens in an attempt to reduce pollution.
1997 Athens is awarded the 2004 Olympics.
1999 An fatal earthquake hits Athens.
2001 The drachma is replaced by the euro.
2004 The Olympics come to Athens after a 108-year hiatus.

Athens Today

Capitalising or coping: what's the state of the city in the wake of Olympic triumph?

Even as the chorus of shrill Greek pop faded and the last fireworks spluttered above the roof of the packed stadium, a palpable cloud of anti-climax settled over the crowd. It was the closing ceremony of the 2004 Olympics, and after seven years of hype, headaches and sheer panic, the party was over. In the weeks that followed, conversations in cafés and headlines in local papers were monopolised by nostalgia for the greatest bash in the city's 3,500-year history. Understandably, Athenians gloated over obsequious apologies in the international press begging forgiveness for the barrage of negative media coverage before the Games and pronouncing the Athens Olympics the most successful ever. Greece had pulled it off.

Innately ebullient, Athenians quickly shrugged off post-Olympic depression – but not post-Olympic recession. The cost of hosting the Games far exceeded initial estimates: the €11 billion price tag is over twice the original budget. And that figure doesn't include costly infrastructure improvements to the capital,

including new highways, flyovers and ring roads, metro lines, a suburban railway and a (strangely sluggish) tram system linking the city centre with the coast. The security budget alone topped €1 billion, an extravagant outlay for one of the safest cities in Europe. In the event, the only Olympic security breaches consisted of a man in a blue tutu belly-flopping into the diving pool and a kilt-clad Irishman gatecrashing the marathon.

Financial analysts reckon taxpayers will be picking up the Olympic tab for the next 15 or 20 years. Even so, most Athenians (though not necessarily most Greeks, many of whom resent the colossal investment in the capital at the expense of regional development) felt that the two-week extravaganza was worth it. Not only did it boost Athens' image abroad as a modern European capital capable of hosting a major-league event; more important for the everyday life of residents, an unprecedented number of public works were fast-tracked in time for the Games, which would otherwise have taken

The showpiece **Olympic Complex**.
See p32.

decades to materialise. The cultural life of the capital was also upgraded. From new museums and designer hotels to a makeover of the central squares, impressive lighting of all the major monuments and an intensive tree-planting campaign, a city notoriously short of parks and heavy on concrete has shed some of its shabbiness. Financial incentives to spruce up building façades have been greeted with enthusiasm. Over 1,600 façades have already been restored and painted. The City Council aims to restore 5,000 homes by 2006, or 20 per cent of Athenian apartment buildings.

RESTORING GLORY

The most impressive improvement to the city centre is the Archaeological Park, the creation of the Unification of Archaeological Sites of Athens project. It links sites surrounding the Acropolis – from fifth-century BC temples to Byzantine chapels, interspersed with outdoor cafés and modern art installations – by a 16-kilometre (ten-mile) pedestrian walkway. Where tour buses were once double-parked in front of the Parthenon, traffic-clogged roads have been replaced with idyllic footpaths strewn with ancient artefacts. 'It's like walking into another century,' says Dora Galani, director of the project. 'But we've also taken great care to connect the ancient and modern, so it's very much a living monument in a living city.'

Pedestrianisation has reduced pollution levels, which will protect the Parthenon from further erosion. There are plans to pave over more roads around the striking new Acropolis Museum, set to open in the next couple of years, with or without the contested Parthenon Marbles, pilfered by Lord Elgin and now in the British Museum. But the museum itself, in the pipeline for over a decade, has been as agonisingly elusive as the marbles. Designed

by Swiss architect Bernard Tschumi, the streamlined glass structure has provoked battles with purists protesting its unashamedly 21st-century design and its location in an archaeologically 'sensitive' area. In a city that looks like a historical layer cake, with relics under every paving stone and a serious shortage of exciting contemporary architecture, neither argument has much credence.

> **'With maintenance costs of €85 million a year, the Olympic venues could easily become white elephants.'**

Launched in 2000, some €10 billion has been invested in the Unification project. The same amount is needed to complete the remaining works, but public funds are in short supply after the Olympics. A ten per cent overall drop in tourism in 2004, fuelled by security fears, feeble marketing, and inflated prices did not help. Since the advent of the euro in 2000, price hikes have not only deterred foreign visitors but have taken their toll on residents, whose salaries are frozen at drachma levels. But with 24-hour traffic jams and tavernas, bars and bouzouki joints booming every night of the week, Athenians are clearly determined to have a good time regardless.

AFTER THE PARTY'S OVER

The Finance Ministry is not having such a great time lately. Greece's budget deficit, which hit 5.5 per cent in 2004, has prompted stern warnings from the European Union. (Euro-zone members must keep deficits below three per cent of gross domestic product.) This was compounded by embarrassing revelations about 'creative book-keeping' by the former

PASOK government to meet the economic criteria for joining the euro, exposed by the conservative New Democracy government soon after it won the March 2004 elections. One of the main reasons the incumbent socialists – in power almost continuously since 1981 – were soundly defeated was the conservative party's promise to stamp out rampant corruption.

An additional drain on the public purse is the dozens of empty Olympic venues, looming like spectres of a glorious past. In the scramble to complete delayed construction work, little forethought was given to their post-Olympic exploitation. With maintenance costs of some €80 million a year, these potential assets could easily become white elephants – as other Olympic host cities have discovered. The stadiums' fate has been the subject of endless speculation – and is likely to be the subject of fierce negotiation once legislation concerning long-term leases to private investors is passed. The government says no venues will be

Movers & shapers Fotis Georgeles

Founder and editor of the *Athens Voice*.

When journalist and editor Fotis Georgeles decided to launch a free, weekly newspaper – independent from the handful of conglomerates that controls the Greek press – most people thought he was nuts. The Athenian public has proved them wrong. In its first year, the *Athens Voice* (in Greek, despite the English name) quickly developed a cult following, with a print run rocketing from 30,000 to 80,000 copies a week, which all disappear within hours of distribution.

'I wanted to create an independent media outlet that would provide an alternative space for original critical thought, and reflect all the citizens of Athens,' Georgeles explains. 'Our city is changing so fast, it needed a voice of its own – one that reflects our real environment and the people who live in it.' For Georgeles, an open-minded philosophy is the essence of a free press. 'Unlike commercial publications, we aren't limited to a narrow target group or trying to promote a certain lifestyle. I'm interested in media activism based on the notion of the internet, where information is free and advertisers rather than consumers of culture pay for content.'

This refreshingly unpartisan approach has produced a publication that captures the Athenian zeitgeist. Drawing on a pool of personal friends – from novelists to TV presenters – Georgeles has attracted some of the best writers in Athens, whose witty columns and acerbic political analysis are worlds apart from the vested interests whose voice dominates most mainstream Greek media. Georgeles's pull-no-punches editorials and regular features – like a problem page called 'Talk Dirty to Me' – are the talk of the town. And if you don't speak Greek, don't despair: there are brief English-language listings and reviews for foreign residents too.

Although the title is an obvious tribute to New York's *Village Voice*, Georgeles researched metropolitan papers from Moscow to Dubai to create a template that expresses the idiosyncrasies of Athens. Quality design also sets the paper apart; each cover is designed by a guest artist or illustrator from Greece and abroad. A record 6,000 people showed up for the opening of an exhibition of *Athens Voice* covers – proof that Athenians have taken their local paper to heart.

Pick up a copy of the Athens Voice *from metro stations and selected bookshops and cafés every Thursday morning.*

dismantled or sold, and has promised their use will be decided only after consultations with local communities. These hunks of prime real estate, mostly in underdeveloped suburbs or coveted seafront locations, could be a huge source of public revenue, as well as improving services to the community.

To date, however, only a handful of venues has been earmarked for public use. The Olympic Village will be converted into affordable housing for public sector workers. The main Olympic Complex, showpiece of Spanish architect Santiago Calatrava, will be open to the public, with football matches held in the 75,000-seat stadium. The International Broadcasting Centre will become a Museum of Greek Olympic Games, while the press centre is now the new headquarters of the Ministry of Public Works.

Various proposals are being considered for other venues, from water parks to shopping malls. The government has promised the dishevelled district of Ano Liossia an Academy of Arts and Digital Museum. The weightlifting centre in Nikaia and Galatsi Indoor Hall will be leisure centres. The equestrian centre at Markopoulos will boast an 18-hole golf course and a new hotel complex. Hopefully, security forces training at the shooting centre nearby will not miss their mark.

ON THE WATERFRONT

Waterfront facilities are most in demand. The regeneration of the coastal zone from Faliron to Agios Kosmas marina could result in the long-awaited revival of the so-called Athenian Riviera. Rumour has it that the beach volleyball stadium will become an outdoor concert hall, the tae kwondo stadium a 5,000-seat conference centre, and shops, cafés and restaurants will line the seaside esplanade at Faliron. An aquarium, ice rink and theme park have also been mooted for the area. The previous government's plans to turn the Helliniko complex, site of the old airport, into parkland are unlikely to materialise. But the Ministry of Culture promises there will be no more bouzouki joints along this seaside strip currently famous for its cheesy nightclubs.

What actually happens to any of these stadiums is still more or less anyone's guess. But the government cannot afford to procrastinate. 'We must prove as a nation that one need not put a knife to our throats to get the job done, but that – of our own accord – we are changing and overcoming bad habits and practices of the past,' Athens Mayor Dora Bakoyianni said recently.

One of a new breed of formidable female politicians, Bakoyianni won her seat in October 2002 by an unprecedented majority of 61 per cent. Like Prime Minister Kostas Karamanlis and opposition leader George Papandreou, Bakoyianni comes from a heavyweight political dynasty. Her father, Constantine Mitsotakis, is president of the New Democracy Party. In the brazenly nepotistic style not uncommon here, he made his daughter chief of staff when he was elected prime minister in 1990. But public sympathy for Bakoyianni was strong. A year earlier, her journalist husband had been assassinated by the November 17 terrorist organisation, which carried out 23 killings between 1975 and 2003, when 15 of the cell's ringleaders were finally caught and convicted.

'The Orthodox establishment has been rocked by lurid tales of sodomy, drug deals and embezzlement.'

Bakoyianni, who escaped an assassination attempt herself in 2002, is clearly a survivor. In the last two years, she secured €23 million from the EU for city improvements (compared to a measly €1.2 million in 2002). Bakoyianni's post-Olympic programme includes renovating run-down neighbourhoods like Metaxourgio and Kolonos and appropriating empty urban sprawl to create more parks. She has launched a massive clean-up campaign, whose slogan – 'Are you a team player?' – has helped instil a sense of social conscience. No mean feat in a town where mind-boggling bureaucracy and unco-operative civil servants make daily life unnecessarily difficult. The oversized and underwhelming Greek civil service is ripe for reform, a politically loaded issue the cautious new government has yet to tackle.

ORTHODOX TROUBLES

Traditionally popular with the religious right, New Democracy has also failed to take a stand on the shocking scandals that have rocked the Orthodox Church, following a series of revelations in February 2005. Lurid tales of sodomy, drug deals and embezzlement by bishops with Swiss bank accounts and obscenely large villas continue to capture the headlines. The allegations have been so outrageous that even the notoriously big-mouthed Archbishop Christodoulos (nicknamed Ava Gardner by the Athenian gay set for his gaudy get-ups) has been relatively reticent in response, refusing either to challenge the offenders publicly or to admit the Church is in trouble.

But with revelations gathering apocalyptic proportions, decisive action to address the extraordinary power and untouchable status of the Orthodox Church seems inevitable.

Opposition leaders have called for a constitutional amendment to separate state and Church, a proposal that has broad popular support. But so far the government has shied away from the issue, claiming the Church should be left to resolve its own problems. So far, though, the Orthodox hierachy seems to be following the adage 'to err is human, to forgive divine': none of the big church cheeses have stepped down or agreed to reform the ecclesiastical system. And at the time of writing the justice system had not become involved. Several judges have been implicated in the scandals, accused not only of taking kickbacks for letting priests and their pals off criminal charges, but demanding Russian call girls too.

The extent of the corruption has rattled even the cynical Greeks, whose sense of identity is bound up with their faith. Ninety-three per cent of Greeks are Orthodox Christians. Black-robed priests carry out ritual blessings at every public function, from launching warships to swearing in the president. Clergy salaries will cost Greek taxpayers a whopping €160 million this year. Yet the Church does not have to pay taxes or publish its accounts. With swathes of real estate nationwide, the Church is by far the wealthiest organisation in the country.

This power translates into stifling control over social policy. Orthodox lobbyists have blocked plans to build the city's first mosque, long overdue in the wake of an influx of Muslim migrants. A decade ago, Greece was one of the least ethnically diverse countries in Europe. Today, the migrant population in Athens alone accounts for roughly one fifth of the population. Though a nation of migrants themselves, Greeks have generally been suspicious towards the sudden surge of newcomers, mainly from the Balkans, Eastern Europe, the Middle East and Pakistan. Knee-jerk anti-Americanism is also alive and kicking, even among the intellectual elite. In an effort to ease integration problems as the metropolis becomes more multicultural, the City Council has established a Migrant Service Centre. But it will take time for Athens to become a truly cosmopolitan city.

The year 2004 may have been a milestone for Greece. But as Europe's oldest city struggles to assimilate its ancient past with its modern identity, the Greek capital still feels like a work in progress.

The **Parthenon**. *See p35.*

Architecture

From classical to concrete.

Roughly speaking, Athens comprises 500 square metres (5,380 square feet) of ancient marble and many, many square kilometres of 1950s concrete. Unlike Rome, which has developed more or less harmoniously since its golden age, incorporating and preserving successive waves of new architectural styles, Athens reached its aesthetic peak early on and, once the Romans departed, in AD 395, trudged on to the present with relatively little to show for it.

The reasons are historic: Athens effectively became a backwater. But it's tempting to hypothesise that so feted were the Acropolis constructions, so technically miraculous and rich in their aesthetics, ambition and materials, that later Athenian builders felt unable to compete. Certainly, rather than creating a fitting environment, they have fashioned one that flatters in relief. The Parthenon's hilltop location guarantees its omnipresence: it is visible from around street corners or between apartment blocks, dominating the city's landscape. The temple is impressively beautiful by any terms, but the contrast with the concrete

animal filling up the whole Athenian basin and climbing up the surrounding mountains makes it truly extraordinary.

The brutally uncontrolled way the urban fabric has spread out around the planned city centre has created a non-monumental city with few connecting open spaces, majestic boulevards or parks. Despite the first impression of chaotic ugliness, though, Athens is richer in small-scale meeting places than most cities, which goes some way towards explaining why it is sometimes called 'the largest village in Greece'. Look beyond its concrete façades, alive with balcony greenery; the David-and-Goliath meeting between a microscopic 11th-century Byzantine church and a 21st-century hotel; or the glimmering city that you see beneath you from Lycabettus at night; and you will find a city that hasn't had the luxury to be picturesque. Soon you might realise that the ugliness is not that bad. You might even find it beautiful.

ANCIENT ATHENS

There is evidence of settlements on the Acropolis as far back as Neolithic times, around 5000 BC, and of the cult of Athena in

Mycenaean times (around 1500 BC). But the real architectural fame for the Athenian hill started in 510 BC. It was in the first century BC that the last Peisistratid tyrant was overthrown and the Delphic Oracle ordered that the Acropolis should be the province of the gods, prohibiting human occupancy of the sacred buildings forever. Today, the achievements of the ancient architects stand as testament to one of the greatest legacies of classical Greece – 2,500 years later they're still the most influential constructions in Western civilisation.

The centrepiece of the Acropolis is the **Parthenon** (see p79), which French poet Lamartine called 'the world's most perfect poem in stone'. Standing on the location of earlier temples, it is dedicated to Athena's incarnation as virgin goddess (Parthenos). Its predecessor was the first Doric temple built entirely from marble – Athenian marble, to be precise, from the quarries of Mount Pentelicon. It was meant to be a monument to the Athenian victory over tyranny and to represent the triumph of democracy. However, the temple was destroyed when the Persians sacked Athens in 480 BC.

Thirty-three years later, in 447 BC, Pericles gathered the best architects available, Iktinos and Kallikrates, under the supervision of the sculptor Phidias, and briefed them to draw up a plan for a reconstruction of the Acropolis buildings worthy of the city's newly found cultural and political position. More or less all substantial remains visible today date from this extraordinarily short time, the golden age of Athens. The current Parthenon was completed in nine years, an astonishing achievement.

Though the Parthenon appears to be an ode to simplicity, it is the most technically perfect Doric temple ever built. The architects used their knowledge of mathematics to calculate the best way to create an impression of complete symmetry, even from a distance. The width and placement of columns, distances between them, volumes and angles – every measurement is a ratio derived from the golden mean system of proportion. Subtle modifications were applied to all straight surfaces: the columns, for example, bulge slightly around the middle and lean somewhat inwards; the corner columns are slightly larger in diameter than the other exterior columns, since they are seen towards the open sky; the stylobate has an upwards curvature towards its centre of six centimetres (2.3 inches) on the east and west ends, and of 11 centimetres (4.3 inches) on the sides. These adjustments counteract the illusion that straight lines, when seen from a distance, appear to bend. The effect of these behind the scenes calculations is a building that seems effortlessly natural and harmonious.

The temple stands on the conventional three steps, below which the foundation platform originally created for its predecessor remains visible. The cella consisted of two rooms end to end. Inside the colonnades, towards the end, stood Phidias' monumental gold-and-ivory statue of Athena Parthenos, representing the fully armed goddess with spear, helmet and aegis (shield), accompanied by a snake, and holding a statue of victory in her extended right arm. The ceiling was made of wood, with painted and gilded decoration. Light was let in, as was the norm in Greek temples, only through the doorway when the great doors were opened.

The Parthenon also showcased a hitherto unseen richness in both quality and quantity of sculptures. The Parthenon had countless more metopes than other temples, all brilliantly sculpted. Unusually for a Doric temple, which would normally only have friezes on the end façades or in the interior (if at all), the Ionic frieze continues around the full perimeter.

The other buildings in the Acropolis are equally important in their influence on later architecture; one famous example is the Brandenburg Gate in Berlin, inspired by the **Propylaeum**. This was the masterpiece of the

Temple glossary

Architrave The main beam which rests across columns.

Caryatid A column in the shape of a sculptured female figure, for example at the Erechtheum.

Cella In Greek *naos*, a plain room in the centre of the temple, not used in worship. It was the seat of the god and left empty except for an image.

Entasis The swelling in the middle of a column.

Hexastyle The most common temple style, with six columns on the short ends. The Parthenon is an octastyle temple (eight columns).

Metopes Blank or sculptured panels above the columns.

Pediment The triangular upper part at the front of the temple, above the base of the roof.

Peristyle The colonnades that surround the larger temples – which makes the Parthenon a peristyle octastyle temple.

Stylobate The base on which the columns and the walls of the cella are placed.

architect Mnesicles. As a gateway it was intended to give a feeling of passing from the mundane world to the sacred; it also blocks the Parthenon from view, so that it appears all at once in its full glory. However, with work disrupted by the Peloponnesian Wars, the Propylaeum remains uncompleted.

The **Erechtheum** is the most exceptional Ionic building on the Acropolis, built 421-406 BC. While the Parthenon exudes elegant simplicity, the grace of the Erechtheum, composed of two adjoining temples, is its unique complexity. An exception to all the rules, it looks like a different building from each of its four sides. The last of the great works of Pericles to be completed, the Erechtheum was regarded with great respect and its site considered particularly sacred. It included, among other relics, the tomb of Cecrops, the legendary founder of Athens; the rock that preserved the mark of Poseidon's trident; and the spring that arose from it. The south porch, known as the Caryatid porch, is the most famous of the four porches, elevated by the alluring Caryae maidens from which it possibly takes it name (the ones you see today are concrete; the originals are kept in the Acropolis Museum). Just to the west of the temple is the spot where Athena's sacred olive tree once stood.

The small, jewel-like **Temple of Athena Nike**, goddess of victory, is the earliest Ionic building on the Acropolis (424 BC), while on the slope of the Acropolis stands the cradle of ancient drama, the sixth-century BC **Theatre of Dionysus**, rebuilt in the fourth century by Lycurgus and believed to have seated 17,000 spectators. This is where giants such as Aristophanes, Aeschylus, Sophocles and Euripides first presented their plays, and where the Festival of the Great Dionysia, a renowned drama competition, would take place. In 334 BC one of the winners, Lysicrates, built a monument to commemorate the victory. The **Lysicrates Monument** in Plaka is the only preserved choregic monument, and has been imitated by many neo-classical architects.

In the western outskirts of the Ancient Agora, the **Temple of Hephaestus**, also known as Theseion, is almost contemporary with the Parthenon. It may lack the Parthenon's extraordinary grace, but it is the best-preserved Greek temple. Externally, that is; the Byzantine Greeks converted it into a church, constructed an apse at the east end and gave the temple its present concrete vault. As in the Parthenon, over the porch the Doric frieze is replaced by a continuous Ionic frieze. The building is almost wholly made of Pentelic marble, bar the lowest of the three steps, which is limestone.

Kaisariani Monastery. *See p38.*

The **Stoa of Attalos**, built in the second century BC by King Attalos of Pergamon as a centre of retail trade, is a two-storey colonnade. Completely renovated in the 1950s (but not as far as the original colours), the building currently serves as the Museum of the Agora. The white marble temples that are so admired now are mere skeletons of what they used to look like. Originally, they were heavily decorated, with gold and bright colours. The image of minimal classicism that they inspire today would not have impressed the architects of the ancient times.

Temples were only one, if important, part of the large sacred precincts with complexes of buildings, lined by sculptures and linked by processional roads, revealing imaginative and organic city planning. The situation outside these precincts was a totally different matter. Private houses from the era were mostly very simple and have left few remnants. The street plans were haphazard in archaic and ancient Greece, with narrow streets, except from the main Panathenaic Way.

ROMAN ATHENS

The Romans captured and sacked Athens in 86 BC, razing the fortification walls and destroying a substantial part of its classical and Hellenistic monuments and artworks. Upon coming to power in 27 BC the Emperor Augustus embarked on a systematic reconstruction programme, showing respect and admiration for the local cultural heritage. In Rome public buildings and monuments were built imitating Athenian models, while in Athens new ideas of

planning and architecture were introduced. The **Roman Forum** (*see p89*) of Caesar and Augustus, with the impressive **Gate of Athena Archegetis** on its west side, was an open space intended as a market area. Just by the Roman Forum, the **Tower of the Winds** (*see p89*), also known as the Clock of Andronikos of Kyrrhos, was probably built in the mid first century BC. The tower was an early version of a meteorological station, for the nearby market merchants to know the time and wind conditions to calculate the approximate arrival time of their deliveries by sea.

The Odeon of Agrippa (*see p91*), in the **Ancient Agora**, was originally intended as a concert hall and shows clear evidence of the interaction of Eastern and Western architectural ideas and techniques. It was burned down by the barbarians and later converted to a gymnasium. Now only three colossal statues remain to be seen.

During his reign, Hadrian implemented a large-scale building programme, and the city expanded to include the present-day Zappeion, National Gardens and Syntagma. The grandest of all Hadrian's projects was the **Temple of Olympian Zeus** (AD 132, *see p102*), the foundation of which had been laid more than 600 years earlier. The Corinthian temple is the largest ancient temple on the Greek mainland.

In a move of confident self-aggrandisement, Hadrian placed a statue of himself next to the one of Zeus, in the sacred cella. **Hadrian's Library** (*see p92*) was another of his grand works – its surviving walls, with their monumental Corinthian columns, stand just next to today's Monastiraki metro station. **Hadrian's Arch** (*see p102*) was erected by the Athenians on the border between the old city and the new to honour the imperial benefactor; the arch is now the starting point of Dionysiou Areopagitou, the newly pedestrianised street that connects the archaeological sites.

The **Odeon of Herodes Atticus** (*see p83*) was built by the wealthy public benefactor as a memorial to his deceased wife. It is a fairly typical Roman theatre, with a semicircular auditorium hewn out of the rocky southern face of the Acropolis hill. The 4,500-seat theatre, with its 30-metre- (98-foot-) high arched façade, had a cedar roof when it was completed in 161. It is now the main venue of the annual Athens Festival.

BYZANTINE

In the fourth century paganism was quashed by Emperor Theodosius, and Athens' temples, including the Parthenon, were converted into Christian churches. Justinian I's decision to close down the schools of philosophy (AD 529) was the final nail in Athens' coffin – the city started to decline. The so-called Dark Ages would last until around the ninth century, when the Byzantine Empire hailed a period of reconstruction and reorganisation that was to last until the 13th century.

Several small cruciform churches from this period still remain, scattered around the city, squeezed in by apartment blocks, gigantic office buildings and hotels. The interiors are usually heavily decorated with mosaics portraying religious figures and the emperor, and marble sculptural ornamentation.

The 12th-century **Panaghia Gorgoepikoos** (*see p87*), next door to the Athens Cathedral and sometimes also called the Little Cathedral, is built with material from ruins of older buildings. This is particularly evident in the upper part of the church's external walls, where fragments of classical marble friezes combine with contemporary reliefs to create a collage of Greek history. The **Church of the Saints Theodore** (on Evripidou) and **Panaghia Kapnikarea** (on Ermou) are two other examples of famous cross-churches dating from the 11th century. The **Kaisariani Monastery** (*see p116*), which was well outside the city when it was built, is now a short walk up on the mountainside from buzzy Kaisariani.

THE TURKS

After two centuries of Frank, Catalan, Florentine and briefly Venetian rule, Athens witnessed the arrival of the Turkish Sultan Mehmet II in 1456. The city would stay under Turkish rule until 1821. However, remarkably little remains from this long period. Athens was never much more than a garrison town and not much money was put into it. And much of what was built was, understandably, destroyed after Greece was liberated. The area of Plaka is built on the Turkish plan, but little is left to see. The oldest Ottoman mosque in Athens is the **Fethiye Tzami**, built in 1458 on the Roman Forum, now used as an archaeological warehouse. Across the street from the Tower of Winds stands one of the few Turkish remains, a gateway and a single dome from a *madrasa*, an Islamic school. The Museum of Traditional Greek Ceramics (*see p92*), just opposite Monastiraki metro station, is situated in the 18th-century **Mosque of Tzidarakis**, without the minaret.

CLEANING UP THE CLASSICAL

After Greece won its independence, many buildings that had been erected during occupation were unceremoniously demolished. This was partly out of rage against the former tyrants, but also, in the case of many Byzantine and Frankish buildings, because they had been built as extensions to classical monuments.

In the classical revival all these monuments were stripped of the extra details added over the centuries, the Acropolis being the most striking example. It is easy to imagine the sacred rock having looked the way it does now for the last two millennia. But the Acropolis has hosted the fortress of every power since Pericles, and has been altered accordingly. The

Parthenon served as a Byzantine and Catholic church and as a medieval fortress under the Franks. Under Ottoman rule, it became a mosque, with minaret and all, and a gunpowder arsenal. This led to the worst damage to date, when the Venetians blew it up. Not so long ago, in one of the darkest times in Athens' history, the Nazi flag flew from the Acropolis. Only at the last minute was the plan by German architect Schinkel to place the royal palace of the new Greek state on the Acropolis scrapped.

The urge to clear the Acropolis of all alterations may have restored a pristine classical appearance, but it also led to the erosion of a vast cultural heritage, interrupting the flow of the city's historical continuity, not to mention the damage caused to the original buildings by the stripping craze.

NEO-CLASSICAL

When Athens was appointed royal seat and capital city of a newly independent Greece in 1834, there was already a detailed city plan by architects Stamatios Kleanthis and Eduard Schaubert, both students of Germany's main man in classical architecture, Friedrich von Schinkel. But after a series of dramatic alterations, the plan was suspended in favour of Leo von Klenze's programme. In his urge to promote a picturesque, human-scale city, Von Klenze narrowed the width of the streets, abandoned the grand boulevards and minimised squares. A great plan, if Athens was never to grow bigger. But it did grow bigger, and Von Klenze can be held partly responsible for undermining the natural growth of the city, and for many of the problems Athens faces today.

Meanwhile, other influential foreign architects poured into the city. They laid the ground for the Athenian school of classicism, maybe the most refined of all neo-classical styles. Their monumental buildings showed the way and set the building style of the city, creating a whole city centre of neo-classical buildings. The majority of these buildings have long since been replaced by modern apartment blocks. Some of the finest, though, such as the **neo-classical trilogy** (*see p95*) on Panepistimiou (comprising the **National Library**, the **University of Athens** and **Athens Academy**), the **Presidential Mansion** and the **Catholic Cathedral**, still stand as monuments of the first decades of modern Athens.

POST-WAR

The first wave of the mass expansion of Athens took place between the wars as a result of the forced return of Greeks from Asia Minor. Some of the capital's finest architecture derives from

Future perfect?

The Greek authorities were playing it pretty safe when they chose Spanish architect Santiago Calatrava to be the inspiration behind the look of the 2004 Olympics. With a CV of prestigious projects behind him (the Barcelona Olympics and Lisbon's main train station to name two), and an impressive, monumental and easily recognisable style, he was a sure thing. This was the man, the authorities were convinced, who could create a single, strong image for the Games.

And he did. The main Olympic Complex covers 100,000 square metres and is undeniably impressive. Calatrava was invited to provide aesthetic unification, linking existing venues with new constructions, and his identity is stamped all over the site. Everything in the complex is white and many smaller constructions and buildings are covered in a broken ceramic-tile cladding, a homage to Gaudi's mosaics and a reference to Athens' ancient heritage.

The two main architectural features of the complex are the Velodrome, with its amazing glass-and-steel translucent roof, and the main Olympic Stadium with its even more famous roof. This roof represents an incredible engineering achievement. Since it couldn't be attached to the existing building, it was built in sections that were slid into place.

The complex also features the Agora Walkway, a monumental promenade covered by high arches that cast a cooling, much-needed fishbone shadow over the ground. The 260-metre- (853-foot-) long and 20-metre- (65-foot-) high Wall of Nations is a screen made of hundreds of vertical strips that pivot on a central tube, creating a wave movement (while also hiding the old sports hall behind it).

Calatrava's work didn't end there. He was also asked to design a pedestrian bridge in Katehaki, crossing Mesogion Avenue from Katehaki metro station. The bridge is full-blown Calatrava: said to be inspired by ancient Athenian vessels, it is constructed in white steel. On one side is a curved 50-metre- (164-foot-) high pillar, which looks a bit like an elephant's tusk, from which thick steel cables hang down, sustaining the bridge's 94-metre (308-foot) span. The design is certainly original, some might say naff, but the bridge offers one great architectural moment – the structure gives the illusion of ramming into the apartment blocks on one side.

Athens Hilton. *See p41.*

this time. The 1920s and '30s apartment blocks, for example, incorporated a Greek identity, which was inspired by Cycladic architecture (plain, white stone walls) and modernist ideas. Architects like Dimitris Pikionis and Aris Konstantinidis were trying to define the Greek identity through modern architecture.

To solve the housing problems in Athens caused by the massive wave of migration from the countryside in the early 1950s, government-commissioned entrepreneurs developed a system of part exchange, *antiparochi*, where land for building was acquired from its owner in exchange for an agreed number of apartments in the finished building. The construction companies didn't have to pay for land, the landowners didn't have to pay for their apartments, and everyone was happy.

Concrete was the obvious choice of material, being cheap, easily available and easily handled by unskilled labourers. The system encouraged the standardisation of apartment blocks, the so-called *polykatoikia*, and soon extended to office spaces and other commercial buildings. The role of the architects was taken over by engineers, owing to the contractors' obvious desire to achieve maximum profit. The result was a rapid growth of new, practical housing, but with poor quality of design and construction. At the same time, the brutally uncontrolled, often illegal and rapid way the city grew itself created a unique form of city (non) planning.

Although the artistic quality of pre-war architecture was far ahead of that of the post-war *polykatoikia*, the concept was more or less the same, one not far from the modernistic utopia of Le Corbusier: a standard box-like construction that could fit all possible activities. One of the results of this, and what makes Athens unique, is that it is, in a visual sense, an egalitarian city, with affluent areas sharing the same architecture and structure with poorer areas. Athens exemplifies the functional model of modernism, in taking density to the extreme, not allowing the luxury of space, striving for the simplest, non-decorative, non-monumental architecture possible. The architecture does not create or enhance in itself the character of an area; this falls to the people. As designated public spaces are rare, the streets had to become the public spaces, which has created an extremely lively street life.

MONUMENTS OF MODERNISM

Another result of the *antiparochi* is the almost total lack of monumentalism, except for the buildings on Leof Vas Sofias, whose construction was controlled by the government. One perfect example of monumentalism and a benchmark in the modern architectural history of Athens is the **US Embassy** (No.91, 1959-61), designed by Bauhaus architect Walter Gropius. Unfortunately, nowadays, building works, tight security and police buses have eliminated the spacious surrounds and the free spirit of the initial design.

Also on a monumental scale is the **Athens Conservatory** (Rigillis & Leof Vas Konstantinou, 17-19 Vas Georgiou II). Finished

in 1976, it was designed by Ioannis Despotopoulos, who studied under Walter Gropius in Weimar. The Conservatory was the only building to be completed in a planned Cultural Centre for Athens. Despite various shortcomings in the construction and implementation of design, it is still a fine example of the radical Bauhaus spirit. The **Athens Hilton** (*see p66* **For glamour, just say Hilton**) caused a huge controversy at the

Movers & shapers Maria Kokkinou & Andreas Kourkoulas

Architects of the Pireos Street Annexe of the Benaki Museum.

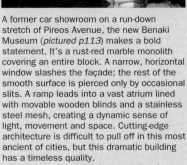

A former car showroom on a run-down stretch of Pireos Avenue, the new Benaki Museum (*pictured p113*) makes a bold statement. It's a rust-red marble monolith covering an entire block. A narrow, horizontal window slashes the façade; the rest of the smooth surface is pierced only by occasional slits. A ramp leads into a vast atrium lined with movable wooden blinds and a stainless steel mesh, creating a dynamic sense of light, movement and space. Cutting-edge architecture is difficult to pull off in this most ancient of cities, but this dramatic building has a timeless quality.

The architects of this instant cultural landmark, Maria Kokkinou and Andreas Kourkoulas, have a refreshingly low-key approach: 'Architecture is increasingly like film production. You need a huge team of creative and cooperative people to get it right.' They credit the Benaki directors for their willingness to create such a daring monument to contemporary culture in a city

notorious as an architectural wilderness after the fifth century BC.

'Architecture is a very social profession: it's not just a question of having talented architects; there must be a balance between market forces and social needs,' explains Kourkoulas. They blame a lack of state support for the absence of a modern architectural movement in Greece. Kokkinou believes the Olympics were a missed opportunity to upgrade the city aesthetically. 'Apart from the Calatrava stadium and the archaeological walkway, there is no Olympic architectural legacy to speak of.'

Kourkoulas cites the recent initiative by PASOK, the Greek socialist party, to stage a competition for young architects to design its regional offices as a step in the right direction. 'Now it's vital the winning designs actually get made,' he adds. Two major public projects in the works – the new Modern Art Museum in the former Fix beer factory and the Bernard Tschumi-designed Acropolis Museum – have been stalled by endless bureaucratic bickering. 'Absurdly, a lot of people are appalled by the idea that a foreigner should design the museum for the symbol of our national heritage. In my view, the more top international architects we can attract to Athens the better.'

For all its eyesores, they love their city. 'Athens is a wonderfully vibrant city blessed with an amazing topography,' says Kokkinou.

Kourkoulas laughs. 'Athens is like someone with a great body wearing a totally unflattering outfit!' Luckily, this glamorous couple will continue to instil their great sense of style into the capital.

time of its construction (1958-63). Accused of being both foreign and offensive, it is now considered one of the finest examples of post-war modernism.

Although the prerequisites for creative activity were sometimes lacking, Athens never lacked gifted urban planners and architects, and there are many interesting talents around today – Dimitris and Suzanna Antonakakis, Zoe Samorkas, Pantelis Nicolacopoulos, Christos Papoulias, for example – who should stand to benefit from Athens' new international perspective and sense of self-esteem.

THE OLYMPICS AND BEYOND

That Athens was ready for the Olympics in time was almost miraculous. A miracle at a very high price: a huge amount of public money was spent while construction quality slacked due to extreme time pressure and, in a majority of cases, there was no planning for the post-Olympic use of the arenas. Less than a year after the Games, many construction works were experiencing problems with electricity and drainage, adding repair bills to the already gigantic cost. The most important of the non-athletic constructions, the **Calatrava pedestrian bridge** in Katehaki (see p39 **Future perfect?**), was closed for repair in March 2004, a little more than half a year after its completion in record time.

Whatever the costs and problems, there is no doubt that the city of Athens went through a major transformation brought about by, or at least triggered by, the Olympics. The biggest of these is the new transport network. The two new metro lines, opened in 2001 after almost 30 years of work, have improved public transport dramatically. They were completed in time for the Games, with new extensions, most importantly the metro line to **Eleftherios Venizelos International Airport**, which itself underwent improvements. Both the metro and the airport could be characterised as architecturally sterile, although the exhibits of the archaeological findings in some of the metro stations, such as Syntagma, give them a distinct character. A tram line to the southern coastal suburbs has met with limited public approval: it's great, but only if you have lots of time to spare.

Of the much talked-about regeneration of the waterfront, there is little evidence so far. On the other hand, parts of the city have been given a dramatic facelift: the refurbishment of Syntagma has given the place a boost, and Omonia at least looks a bit livelier with greenery stuck into the concrete.

If the Olympics didn't contribute any architecture of interest except the Calatrava works, many private initiatives are more

interesting. Boutique hotels weren't part of the Greek vocabulary before the Games. That has changed now. Some of the most interesting examples are the **Semiramis** and **Twentyone**, both situated in the lush suburb of Kefalari. The Semiramis is a colourful lollipop designed by New York-based super designer Karim Rashid, and Twentyone, a stiff creation in the colour scale grey to black, designed by Deca Architecture. The hot young architects from this company have also created the submarine-inspired **Periscope Hotel** in Kolonaki, which features a street-level lounge bar with a panoramic city view, thanks to a periscope that guests can control from the bar. For more on Athens' design hotels, see p72 **Stylish sleeps**.

REGENERATION

The area with most architectural activity in the post-Olympics era is unconnected with the Olympic effort. The grim Pireos Street, one of the city's least glamorous thoroughfares, stretching from Omonia Square to Piraeus, is – against all odds – becoming everyone's top choice for a Sunday walk. The big, dirty, heavily trafficked street, with pavements too narrow for even the stray dogs, formerly lined with abandoned industrial buildings, is finally becoming an important axis in the city's cultural life.

The pioneer was the **School of Fine Arts**, followed by **Foundation of the Hellenic World**, which is now expanding and will open an interactive venue with a spectacular dome, expected to become a new architectural landmark, on Pireos. **Technopolis**, the City of Athens arts centre, opened in 1999 on the district's Gazi site (the old gasworks). It was expanded with two new exhibition spaces in 2004. The new wing of the **Benaki Museum**, designed by architects Kokkinou and Kourkolas, is inspired (see p41 **Movers & shapers**). The large-scale multiplex **Pantheon**, which will house nightclubs, cinemas, restaurants and a hotel among other attractions, is currently under construction. The sculptural façade was designed by one of the country's finest sculptors, Kostas Varotsos. For more on the attractions of Pireos Street, see p112 **Pireos Street redux**.

The government has now latched on to the regeneration and seems keen to promote it: the Ministry of Public Works has announced a renovation of the street, introducing incentives for conservation and new building regulations. It is also trying to secure plots of land for public use, with the aim of creating green strips along its length. Will it actually happen? Watch this space…

Theseus slays the Minotaur. *See p45.*

Greek Myth & Legend

Jason's fleece, Pandora's box, Achilles' heel.

The Hellenic deities weren't exactly wonderful role models. They lied, cheated, squabbled and toyed ruthlessly with humans. Zeus, king of the gods, assumed various shapes – white bull, swan, golden cloudburst – to seduce unwilling women. His enraged wife Hera persecuted his mistresses, even chasing one pregnant rival with a giant python and transforming another into a pet cow. The list of dirty divine deeds is longer – and messier – than a Greek gyro.

The gods' main spin doctors were Homer, whose epic poems *The Iliad* and *The Odyssey* kick-started Western literature in the eighth century BC, and Hesiod, who wrote *The Theogony* in the seventh century BC. Ancient critics sometimes found fault with these saucy tales. 'Homer and Hesiod have attributed to the gods everything that is a shame and disgrace among men, stealing and committing adultery and deceiving one another,' the philosopher Xenophanes later complained. Yet most Greeks didn't mind the bad behaviour,

considering it just as instructive as a good example – and a far better yarn. Even firmly into the days of monotheism myths have been the backbone of education and entertainment. Scholars have memorised ripping tales, then recited them at dinner parties. Politicians have tweaked the stories for propaganda. Artists have depicted scenes on pottery, while poets and playwrights have plumbed this rich vein of melodrama.

The Ancient Greeks believed that deities took a very active role in human affairs and destinies. They wooed them with lavish temples, prayers, rites, offerings and games, like the Olympics. The sacrifice of animals – usually bulls, sheep or goats – was especially popular. Priests would slit the creatures' throats, sprinkle the altars with fresh blood, burn the choice bits for the gods and foretell the future from the entrails.

People could worship any and all of the deities. Cities had patron gods, such as Athena in Athens, as did the trades. New divinities were borrowed freely from other cultures and then woven into local mythology. Oracles, like Delphi, transmitted the gods' cryptic advice and prophecies.

Cults were a major force in Greek society. The most famous took place just outside Athens, in Eleusis, the site of a sanctuary to the fertility goddess Demeter. The celebratory rituals known as Eleusian mysteries were shrouded in secrecy, but rumours of drunkenness and orgies continue to this day.

These pagan rites gave way to Christianity in 324 AD, but Greek myth lives on. The Romans, then the Renaissance, revived these tales, which have since become a cornerstone of Western civilisation.

THE GODS

One creation myth claims the deities and living creatures sprang from the stream Oceanus encircling the world. In the most common version, Mother Earth emerged from the chaos and bore her son, Uranus (sky), while she slept. He showered her with fertile rain and she gave birth to flowers, trees, beasts, birds, the hundred-handed giants, the early gods (Titans) and the one-eyed Cyclops.

> **'In a fit of insecurity, worried that a son might surpass him, Zeus swallowed his pregnant first wife.'**

Family strife led the Titans to attack Uranus. The youngest of the Titans, Cronus, cut off his father's genitals with a flint sickle and became sovereign. He married his sister Rhea, but insisted upon devouring their children, as prophecy declared that a son would dethrone him. He swallowed five babies, then Rhea wised up. She gave birth to Zeus in secret, then hid him with nymph nursemaids on Crete.

Zeus grew to manhood and poisoned his father's honeyed drink, causing Cronus to vomit up the elder siblings – Hades, Poseidon, Hera, Hestia and Demeter (*see p46* **A-Z of Greek gods**). With their help, Zeus vanquished the Titans and became king of the gods and heaven. A dozen major deities dwelled high on Mount Olympus, while Hades brooded in the underworld and Poseidon ruled the ocean. Earth remained a neutral zone.

Supporting the 12 Olympians was a cast of thousands. The three Fates spun, measured and snipped the threads of mortal lives, the Furies punished evil-doers, while nine Muses inspired poets, artists and musicians. Trees contained beautiful female spirits (dryads), as did streams (naiads) and fields (nymphs).

Lusty, goat-legged satyrs frolicked with wild women (maenads) in holy groves. Centaurs, skilled in sorcery and healing, raped and revelled. Other gods included Pan (shepherds), Asclepius (healing), Eros (love), Hypnos (sleep), Helios (sun), Selene (moon) and Nemesis (punishment).

THE GODDESS

The capital's name honours its patron Athena, goddess of wisdom. This bold and brilliant divinity governed all knowledge – from weaving to astronomy and battle strategy. She represented victory and noble defence, unlike Ares, the bloodthirsty god of war. Athena was also the goddess of wit, morality and clear air, and the protector of small children. The flute, yoke, trumpet and plough number among her inventions.

Her birth was extraordinary, even by Greek mythology's standards. In a fit of insecurity, worried that a son might surpass him, Zeus swallowed his pregnant first wife. Soon after a horrible migraine gripped the king of the gods. The pain grew so severe that he begged for his skull to be chopped open with an axe. Out sprang Athena, fully grown, armed and shouting.

Despite the splitting headache, Athena was her father's favourite. Zeus refused her nothing, even allowing her use of his mightiest weapon, the thunderbolt. She remained a virgin, lofty and pure, but still managed to have a son. The smith god Hephaestus tried to ravage her. She fought him off, but some of his semen brushed her thigh and fell to earth, growing into Erichthonius, an early king of Athens.

Athena won the city in a contest against her uncle, the sea god Poseidon. He struck the cliff of the Acropolis with his trident and a salt-water spring gushed from the rock. Athena produced an olive tree. The gods voted her contribution more useful to humans – as it brought food, oil and shelter – and awarded her Athens.

The ancients celebrated her each year at the Panathenea festival. A grand procession wound up the Acropolis, dominated by Phidias's majestic statues of the goddess (one was so massive that sailors in the Saronic Gulf could see her lance and helmet). Her great temple, the mighty Parthenon (meaning 'virgin' in Ancient Greek) still stands today.

THE HEROES

Brave, handsome heroes obsessed with fame and glory star in many tales. More often than not, their ambition wreaked havoc.

Achilles is a prime example. Though he was a magnificent warrior, his 'destructive wrath brought countless sorrows' to his people

The Minotaur devoured young Athenian boys and girls.

during the Trojan War, as Homer recounted in *The Iliad*. His arrogance finally outraged the gods: mid battle, they directed an arrow to Achilles's only vulnerable spot – his heel. Hercules started poorly – with the murder of his wife and children in a bout of madness – but the strongman redeemed himself through the Twelve Labours.

Oedipus unwittingly murdered his father and married his mother. The great musician Orpheus played so sweetly, the gods allowed him to bring his bride back from death – on

one condition: he couldn't look at her until they reached the surface. Riddled with doubt, he glanced back and lost her again. The heartbroken hero soon perished, torn apart by wild animals.

Jason, leader of the Argonauts, captured the coveted Golden Fleece, aided by the sorceress Medea. After ten years of happy marriage, he chucked her out. The vengeful woman murdered their children and his new wife, then fled in a chariot drawn by winged dragons. Medea reappeared briefly as Queen of Athens,

A-Z of Greek gods

Aphrodite
Goddess of: Love.
Strengths: Born naked from the sea foam; also has a magic love-inducing girdle.
Flaws: Addicted to adultery.
Roman name: Venus.
Symbols: Rose, apple, swan, Cupid (her son).

Apollo
God of: Light.
Strengths: Bestowed enlightenment, governed music, medicine, oracles and crops.
Flaws: Cheated in a musical contest, then flayed his rival Marsyas alive.
Roman name: Apollo.
Symbols: Lyre, bow, tripod, laurel wreath.

Ares
God of: War.
Strengths: This natural born killer fathered Eros (Cupid) and Harmonia (Harmony).
Flaws: Lost twice to Athena.
Roman name: Mars.
Symbols: Spear, torch, armour.

Artemis
Goddess of: The hunt.
Strengths: Despite her bloodthirstiness, she protected pregnant women and small children.
Flaws: This eternal virgin turned a peeping tom, Actaeon, into a stag and hunted him.
Roman name: Diana.
Symbols: Bow and quiver, new moon and hind.

Demeter
Goddess of: The earth and fertility.
Strengths: Taught people about agriculture, civic order and wedlock.
Flaws: Starved humans when Hades stole her daughter, then created winter.
Roman name: Ceres.
Symbols: Corn, basket, poppy, serpent.

Dionysus
God of: Wine.
Strengths: Roamed the globe with drunken nymphs, satyrs and wild women.
Flaws: The portable party often spun out of control. Limbs were torn. Lives were lost.
Roman name: Bacchus (aka Liber).
Symbols: Ivy crown, wand, fawn, panther.

Hades
God of: The underworld and the dead.
Strengths: In milder moods, he bestowed wealth or an invisibility helmet.
Flaws: Kidnapped his bride Persephone, whose enraged mother invented winter.
Roman name: Pluto.
Symbols: Three-headed dog Cerberus, pickaxe, cypress tree.

Hephaestus
God of: Fire and metalworking.
Strengths: His fabulous jewellery earned him Aphrodite, the love goddess, as his wife.
Flaws: She cheated on him constantly.
Roman name: Vulcan.
Symbols: Hammer, tongs, a lame leg.

Hera
Queen of heaven, and goddess of marriage.
Strengths: Routinely renewed her virginity bathing in a special spring.
Flaws: This jealous wife chased one rival with a python, kept another as a pet cow.
Roman name: Juno.
Symbols: Peacock, cuckoo, pomegranate.

Hermes
God of: Thieves, traders and messengers.
Strengths: Invented the lyre mere days after his birth (with gut from Apollo's stolen cows).
Flaws: Guided souls to the underworld.
Roman name: Mercury.
Symbols: Herald's staff, winged golden sandals, winged helmet.

Hestia
Goddess of: The hearth and civic harmony.
Strengths: Kept the home fires burning and avoided sexual intrigue on Olympus.
Flaws: Too dull to have one, really.
Roman name: Vesta.
Symbols: Sceptre, hearth.

Poseidon
God of: The ocean and flowing waters.
Strengths: Invented horses (or so he boasted).
Flaws: Caused storms and earthquakes.
Roman name: Neptune.
Symbols: Trident, chariot drawn by foam horses, dolphin.

Zeus
King of the gods, ruler of the sky.
Strengths: Saved his siblings by poisoning their cannibal father, the Titan Cronus.
Flaws: Raped his mother (who advised him not to marry his sister, Hera).
Roman name: Jupiter.
Symbols: Lightning bolt, clouds, eagle, oak.

stepmother to the hero Theseus. She attempted to poison him and was banished. Theseus went on to face the Cretan Minotaur, the half-man, half-bull, imprisoned in the Labyrinth, who devoured young Athenian boys and girls. He killed the monster with the help of Princess Ariadne, then callously abandoned her on the way home. His comeuppance was swift: nearing Athens, Theseus forgot to hoist the white sail, a sign of victory for his worried father Aegeus. The grieving king leaped to his death.

Theseus was strong, but refined, smart and diplomatic, all qualities the ancient Athenians prized. He united the Attica region and laid the foundations of democracy. Perseus, on the other hand, was more of an action hero. He decapitated Medusa, the snake-haired gorgon, whose gaze turned flesh to stone.

Odysseus was celebrated as the cleverest Greek. The wily king fought in the Trojan War to reclaim Helen, the most beautiful woman in the world. His return trip took years, rather than weeks. Homer's *Odyssey* traces this epic journey, plagued by shipwreck, witches, sirens and giant man-eating Cyclops. Finally Odysseus reached his homeland, the island of Ithaca, to discover his faithful wife Penelope besieged by greedy, pushy suitors. He slew them with a great bow and reclaimed his kingdom – an unusually happy ending for ancient mythology.

THE HUMANS

The first generation were the 'golden race', who lived without care. They never grew old, lived off the fat of the land, and died contented. Next came the silver race, eaters of bread. They were so quarrelsome and ignorant that Zeus destroyed them. The insolent bronze race ate flesh and delighted in war. A more noble age, known as the race of heroes, followed. Sired by gods on mortal mothers, the warriors at Troy and the Argonauts were part of this age. The fifth and final race, known as the race of iron, is beset by unworthy descendants: cruel, unjust, lustful and treacherous. Hesiod wrote: 'I wish I were not of this race, that I had died before, or had not yet been born.'

Prometheus stole fire from the heavens and gave it to humans. Enraged, Zeus created the first woman: intelligent, lovely Pandora. The gods gave her a box, containing 10,000 curses. Curious, she opened it and released evil into the world. Pandora quickly slammed the lid, but hope alone remained inside.

The Greeks had a myth for every occasion, from the cradle to the grave. The countless stories tapped into universal themes – jealousy, infatuation, ambition and loyalty, to name a few. Perhaps this resonance explains their continued popularity, nearly 2,800 years after Homer first captured them in song.

Achilles – brought to heel by the gods.
See p44.

No More Moussaka

New verve, new twists: it's Greek food, but not as we know it.

For many travellers, Greek food conjures up an image not dissimilar to British cartoonist Glen Baxter's drawing of a dapper Englishman leaping out of a top-floor window above the caption 'Young Howard could not face another moussaka.' Another Baxter gem features a taverna menu that includes such delicacies as 'peas in sump oil'. Tourist traps in Greek package resorts and dodgy diners and kebab shops abroad are largely to blame for negative stereotypes about Greek cuisine. But Greek food is experiencing something of a global epiphany, thanks to restaurants like Milos in New York, Kokkari in San Francisco and London's the Real Greek, all of which showcase the finest, freshest ingredients prepared with perfect simplicity.

THE CULINARY ART OF REINVENTION

In Athens too – indeed, all over Greece – innovative chefs are reinventing local cuisine to great acclaim. Two chefs are widely credited as the pioneers of 'nouvelle Grecque' cuisine: seafood specialist Lefeteris Lazarou, whose **Varoulko** (*see p144*) is one of only three Michelin-starred restaurants in the capital – the others are **Spondi** (*see p148*) and **Vardis** (*see p154*) – and Chrysanthos Karamolegos, who introduced Greek dishes with a twist at Vitrina in the early 1990s, setting the trend for dozens of eateries to open in the Psyrri neighbourhood and dozens of chefs to copy his subversive spin on Hellenic food. Karamolegos has since moved on from passé Psyrri – though he is still making culinary waves at both branches of his new venture, **Apla Aristera-Dexia** (*see p154*). The site of Vitrina is now home to **Hytra** (*see p144*), where Yannis Baxevannis concocts haute Hellenic dishes like fish soup served with chicory foam and a sea urchin, or sweet and sour calamari, spinach and beetroot salad.

An Italian raised on Corfu, Ettore Botrini combines Italian influences with Ionian elements to stunning effect at **Etrusco** (*see p129*): his signature dish for summer 2005 is grouper in an almond and orange crust afloat in a lobster and mandarin bisque. The other local chef Athenians are drooling over is Christoforos Peskias, who daringly deconstructs Greek classics with dishes like stuffed tomatoes sliced horizontally and renamed tomato sushi, or *imam bayildi* – slow-roasted aubergine, here served with a dollop of feta ice-cream. The decor at Peskias's place, **48 The Restaurant** (*see p136*), is equally dramatic. The whole enterprise is as fashion-conscious as the conceptual art in the gallery next door.

'A vogue for home-style cooking at more affordable prices is gaining ground.'

These trendy temples to cutting-edge cuisine continue to pack in the punters, despite often exorbitant prices. Once conservative in their eating habits, Athenians are suddenly rushing to the sushi bars, trattorias and tapas bars cropping up across town. Locals are even venturing to the Indian canteens and Egyptian falafel stalls that service the growing immigrant communities around Omonia Square (*see p145* **Community centres**).

ROOTS REVIVAL

At the same time, a vogue for home-style cooking at more affordable prices is gaining ground. Once again, Karamolegos is ahead of the game, paring down his experimental fusion food in favour of a return to his culinary roots. 'Traditional dishes instantly bring back memories for Greeks,' he says. 'They provide them with a reference point so they can compare familiar flavours with new combinations, like my *youverlakia* [cabbage leaves traditionally stuffed with mincemeat] filled with seafood.'

'Modern tavernas' are all the rage. These cheerful, contemporary spaces are usually not much pricier than a dirt-cheap traditional taverna, and offer honest nosh like mama used to make but in snazzier surroundings – the joint that kick-started this craze even called itself **Mamacas** (*see p147*), meaning 'Mummy's'.

With its greaseproof paper, barrels of retsina and bum-numbing chairs, the classic taverna will never go out of style. It's no great surprise – anywhere you can gorge on mountains of grilled lamb chops for €10 is bound to be popular. The menu is not all grilled meat either – the vegetarian backpacker's staple diet of *xoriatiki* (Greek salad) and chips has been consigned to history, thanks to a revival of the traditional *mageirio*. Here, customers are invited to peer into pots of stewed vegetables and bean soups (handy for foreigners, who can point to what they fancy).

Vegetarians have also benefited recently from restaurants that celebrate seasonal, regional ingredients. The elegant **Gefseis me Onomasia Proelefsis** (*see p154*), literally 'Flavours of Designated Origin', boasts dozens of exceptional Greek cheeses, rare wild greens and three kinds of olive oil for dunking your home-baked bread into. At the Athens outpost of **Milos** (*see p151*), a colourful canvas of raw ingredients, from scarlet tomatoes to silver sea bream, is laid out like a work of art in front of the open kitchen.

LOVING THE LOCAL

This new appreciation for local produce has spawned several delicatessens that stock natural foods sourced from artisans, co-operatives, bakers and shepherds from all over the country. At **Bakaliko Ola Ta Kala** (*see p151*), eclectic treats like Cretan olive pâté, smoked trout from Ioannina and Santorini's famous fava beans can be taken home neatly packaged or sampled at the chic little café on the premises. 'The village store, or *bakaliko*, traditionally had a few tables where the grocer's wife would rustle up some dishes using whatever happened to be in stock. We've taken that concept one step further,' explains co-owner Vassiliki Kokkota. She and her partners discovered several delicacies they had never heard of in their foraging trips across the country, like *oxymeli*, a vinegar made of sweet red wine, raisins, honey and figs. Their business helps enterprising women in small villages and remote islands sustain their craft and culinary heritage.

Despite the flurry of fashionable new restaurants, the food industry is struggling with the economic slump that has hit Greece. 'Recessions breed bright ideas,' shrugs Karamolegos breezily, who believes the revival of authentic Greek cuisine was partly fuelled by pragmatism: using local rather than imported ingredients cuts costs.

▶ For restaurants, *see pp128-156*.

A LITTLE BIT OF EVERYTHING

The quest for competitive prices has also launched a craze for Mediterranean finger food – a new take on the traditional meze. *Mezedopolia* – the local equivalent of tapas bars – are ideally suited to the kind of casual, communal eating that Greeks love best. Dainty dishes of sun-dried octopus, smoky aubergine purée and crisp filo pastries oozing spinach and feta are passed around or picked at, traditionally accompanied by ouzo or *tsipouro*, but just as good with a glass of rough barrel wine. Grazing on meze also accommodates the bad Greek habit of eating late – and arriving even later. (Don't make the mistake of showing up to a dinner date on time. You'll be blotto by the time your companions show up.)

'Greek cuisine has advanced at lightning speed, but the local clientele is limited because Greeks aren't taught to take food seriously, like the Italians and Spanish,' says Botrini. 'But a new generation of Greek gourmets is emerging.' The majority of Greeks may not know much about gastronomy yet, but they devote plenty of time to good living.

AND TO GO WITH YOUR FOOD...

Given that the ancient Greeks invented oenology, it may seem surprising that local wines have only recently been 'discovered' abroad. *Oenos* (Greek for wine, though the demotic *krasi* is more commonly used) was first produced in Greece more than 4,000 years ago. While the ancients diluted their wine with sea water, modern Greeks generally prefer hard liquor – whether ouzo and its offshoots *tsipouro*

and *raki*, or imported spirits. Four centuries of occupation by the teetotal Turks did not help Greek viniculture to flourish. Today, vineyards are scattered among the country's mountain slopes, plains and islands, cooled from the scorching sun by high altitudes and sea breezes. With almost 100 vintners to choose from, locals are developing a taste for increasingly sophisticated home-grown vintages. The curse of retsina is no more.

The Greek wine renaissance began in the mid 1980s, when a new generation of vintners rediscovered the complexities of over 300 indigenous grape varieties. The most distinctive Greek whites are the citrus-and-smoke **Assyrtiko** from Santorini, and the floral, quaffable **Moschofilero** from the Peloponnese. The top reds are the rich, dark **Xinomavro** from Macedonia, and the velvety, full-bodied **Agiorgitiko** from Nemea. Local grapes are often blended with imported merlots, syrahs and sauvignons, with surprisingly refreshing results. (Try Vivlia Hora's award-winning Ovilos 2003, a melange of semillon with Assyrtiko.) The Greek heat also makes for great dessert wines, notably muscats from Samos and Limnos, and Santorini's vin santo. On this bone-dry volcanic island, vines are grown in baskets close to the ground to protect them from the fierce westerly winds.

Greek wines are still relatively elusive and expensive abroad, since most estates are small, hand-tended enterprises that do not produce exportable quantities. Feuding among winemakers – the Lazarides brothers have rival wineries near Drama, while the Boutari brothers battle it out in Macedonia – is also partly to blame for feeble marketing.

A new awareness of wine, local or otherwise, means that a growing number of Athens restaurants now have sommeliers. At 48 The Restaurant, Yannis Kaimenakis presides over an extraordinary cellar with 600-plus labels, a glowing red room that is a showpiece in its own right. Most restaurants offer a select if not extensive Greek wine list at reasonable prices. At tavernas, you will probably be stuck with their *xyma* (literally 'loose') wine, served in half-kilo or kilo tin jugs. Sometimes this is perfectly palatable. Sometimes it is perfectly awful. But like retsina, the pungent wine made from pine resin, you may find it is an acquired taste. Just don't get too closely acquainted or you will find yourself with a killer hangover.

There are many vineyards surrounding Athens where you can sample Attica's finest harvest straight from the source. The prettiest are **Ktima Haralaftis** in Stamata (210 621 9374), **Semeli** in Stamata (210 621 6811) and **Ktima Efharis** in Megara (210 924 6930).

The best Greek wines

As recommended by Panos Zoumboulis, owner of wine shop **Cava Vinifera** (317 Kifisias Avenue, 210 807 7709).

Agiorgitiko
Ktima Papaioannou or Reserve Haralaftis (2000).

Assyrtiko
Thalassitis by Gaia or Sigalas Vareli (2004).

Moschofilero
Mantinia Tselepou or Moschofilero Skouras (2004).

Xinomavro
Ramnista by Kyr Yianni or Grande Reserve Naoussa by Boutari (2000).

Where to Stay

Where to Stay 52

Features

Where to Stay

What a difference a few months makes.

While the world held its breath waiting for Athens' roads, transport system, facilities and sports venues to be finished in a six-month pre-Olympic mad dash, a less visible but no less legendary effort to renovate most of the city's hotels was also under way. Almost all of the renovations were completed just days or weeks before the thousands of dignitaries, spectators and international Olympic committees breezed through the door. In addition to already existing hotels that were renovated, a dozen brand new places opened up at about the same time.

The result is a boon for travellers. Standards in every price category have improved dramatically, prices have stabilised (and around the four-star category have dropped significantly), and features that used to be expected only in upper price categories have trickled down to budget hotels. A few years ago a dataport was something to get excited about in any Athens hotel, while now even some budget hotels offer wireless or high-speed internet access. Boutique hotels were formerly non-existent, and now a handful of excellent examples of the genre are on offer, many of them around Omonia Square, an area that is emerging as a popular one for hotel development. But most exciting of all is the overnight mushrooming of design hotels, with Athens now an international trendsetter. See *p71* **Stylish sleeps**.

Service in Athens hotels tends to be a bit more personal and less formal than in other European capitals, but sometimes a bit lazier. Rooftop terraces, gardens, pools, cafés and lounges and great views are particular pleasures of many an Athenian hotel, while traffic noise and sad façades are often their major flaws.

The domestic rating system for hotels in Greece, which rates hotels on a 'Deluxe A B C D' scale, is not a very meaningful guide to quality, and runs alongside the more familiar international 'star' rating system. Budget hotels are fairly plentiful, but hotels offering shared facilities and Western European-style pensions are rare. Private apartment rentals are also rare.

Generally speaking, Athens hotel rates are now in line with most European countries – although far cheaper than London – but are more negotiable. Probably because of competition and the rise of internet bookings,

pricing at Athens hotels is now a lot more transparent. Prices listed in this guide are the rates at which rooms were being sold during the summer high season.

Athenian hoteliers know all too well that the average traveller spends just one night in Athens, and can be coaxed into granting discounts for longer stays. Most hotels have a high season running from Easter through October, and offer discounts of around 25-35 per cent in low season. Discounts at budget hotels are smaller. Since upscale visitors tend to avoid central Athens in the summer and business travel slows, travellers can expect significant reductions during July and August at expensive and deluxe hotels downtown. Competition for international clients is so strong that foreign travel agents often offer lower hotel rates than those available within Greece.

Nearly all the hotels we list have **air-conditioning** in the rooms. On the rare occasions where not all rooms are air-conditioned we mention it in the listings.

Acropolis & around

Deluxe

AVA Hotel Apartments & Suites
Lysikratous 9-11, Plaka, 10558 (210 325 9000/fax 210 325 9001/www.avahotel.gr). Metro Acropolis. **Rates** €175 regular apartments; €240 executive apartments; €310 suites. **Credit** AmEx, MC, V. **Map** p301 F6.
These large rooms and suites in the thick of Plaka are ideal for travellers staying more than a few days, executives who may need to use rooms as part-time offices, and families who need a bit more breathing space. The apartments are furnished rather like executive lounges, with desks and in-room DSL internet lines, but well-stocked kitchenettes make feeling at home a little easier. Front-facing rooms have views of the Acropolis and Hadrian's Arch. *Internet: DSL. Kitchenette. No-smoking floor. TV.*

Expensive

Athenian Callirhoe
Kallirois 32 & Petmeza, Makrygianni, 11743 (210 921 5353/fax 210 921 5342/www.tac.gr). Metro Syngrou-Fix. **Rates** €140 single; €140 double; €190 executive room; €260 junior suite. **Credit** AmEx, DC, MC, V. **Map** p301 E7.

When it opened in 2002, the Callirhoe – then a novelty – was hailed as one of the most stylish hotels in Athens, promptly leading to the opening of copycats all over town. The decor is characterised by sleek, sharp-edged metal and glass, while rooms feature fluffy duvets, leather sofas and, in the upper brackets, hot tubs. The newish Etrusco restaurant (*see p129*) is as exquisite as a hotel restaurant can be and chef Ektor Botrini's creative Italian dishes are simply wonderful.
Bar. Business centre. Gym. Internet: ISDN. No-smoking rooms/floor. Restaurant. Room service. Safe. TV: games/pay TV.

Divani Palace Acropolis
Parthenonos 19-25, Makrygianni, 11742 (210 928 0100/fax 210 921 4993/www.divaniacropolis.gr). Metro Acropolis. **Rates** €170 single; €180 double; €300 suite. **Credit** AmEx, DC, MC, V. **Map** p301 E7.
The closest luxury hotel to Plaka and the Acropolis, the Divani Palace Acropolis is popular with wealthy Greeks and ideally located for popping out to catch an evening performance at the nearby Herodeion. There's lots of pink, gilt, mirrors and potted palms in the lobby, while the rooms were spruced up for the Olympics. Two nice features are the roof garden, offering drinks and a great Greek buffet, and the preserved, glassed-in portion of the Themistoclean Wall in the foundations.
Bar. Business services. Concierge. Internet: ISDN. No-smoking rooms. Restaurants (2). Swimming pool (outdoor). Room service (6.30am-11pm). Safe. TV: pay movies.

Electra Palace
Nikodimou 18-20, Plaka, 10557 (210 337 0000/ fax 210 324 1875/www.electrahotels.gr). Metro Monastiraki. **Rates** €160 single; €180 double; €231 triple. **Credit** AmEx, DC, MC, V. **Map** p297/p301 F5.
With a gorgeous neo-classical façade, the Electra Palace is one of the most attractive buildings in the heart of Plaka, which otherwise lacks a smart, full-service hotel. With golden, creamy marble with inlaid designs, antiques with plenty of gold leaf, lots of classic ceiling mouldings, gilded mirrors and dark-wood panelling, and an ethereally lit small indoor pool/hot tub and spa, the Electra Palace experience feels much like the Grande Bretagne on a bit of a budget. A ten-metre-long (33ft) rooftop pool is another attraction, as is the formal, attentive service. The only drawback is some loud motorbike noise from the otherwise quiet residential street that can be audible inside – request a back-facing or garden-facing room.
Bar. Business centre. Concierge. Gym. Internet: dataport. No-smoking rooms/floors. Parking (€12/day). Restaurant. Spa. Swimming pool (1 indoor, 1 outdoor). Room service. TV: pay TV.

Herodion Hotel
Rovertou Galli 4, Makrygianni, 11742 (210 923 6832/fax 210 921 1650/www.herodion.gr). Metro Akropoli. **Rates** €142-€171 single;

Divani Apollon Palace & Spa. *See p68.*

€169-€203 double; €210-€249 triple; €204-€245 junior suite. **Credit** DC, MC, V. **Map** p301 E7.
Under the same excellent management as the Philippos (*see below*), the Herodion shares its chief advantage: a location ideal for drooling at the Acropolis and excellent care and service for a hotel of this size. But where the Herodion differs from its sibling is in the decor, which is much more subdued and traditional, gracefully integrating modern and classical elements. Pink furniture with neo-classical touches dresses up the rooms, which have sumptuous adjoining marble bathrooms. The hotel amenities are good, with a green, atrium-like café, a cosy, elegant bar-lounge, and a modest roof garden with a view of the Acropolis that is as up close and personal as you can get. The location is just a few steps from the ancient Odeon of Herodes Atticus (*see p83*), site of many cultural performances for the summer Athens Festival.
Bar. Business centre. Concierge. Disabled-adapted rooms. Internet: ISDN. Restaurants (2). Room service (8am-1.30am). Safe. Swimming pool. TV.

Philippos Hotel
Mitsaion 3, Makrygianni, 11742 (210 922 3611/ fax 210 922 3615/www.philipposhotel.com). Metro Akropoli. **Rates** €120 single; €156 double; €195 triple. **Credit** DC, MC, V. **Map** p301 E7.
The Philippos is a good choice for those in search of a solid and reliable four-star hotel. While virtually every downtown Athens hotelier claims to be 'under the shadow of the Acropolis', the Philippos really is. Its sleek ground-floor lobby, reception,

Art Gallery Hotel.

lounge and coffee bar have a pleasant postmodern decor, mixing radically different design signatures with seamless elegance. The small rooms are much less extravagantly appointed than the common areas. The service is superb. This hotel attracts a mix of business and leisure travellers who are keen to avoid the 'copy-paste' mould of the giant international hotel chains and are seeking a hotel with some personality.
Bar. Internet: dataport/ISDN. Safe. TV.

Moderate

Acropolis Select Hotel

Falirou 37-39, Makrygianni, 11742 (210 921 1610/ fax 210 921 6938/www.acropoliselect.gr). Metro Syngrou-Fix. **Rates** €110 single; €120 double. **Credit** AmEx, DC, MC, V. **Map** p301 E8.
An uninspired façade hides a renovated, elegant interior. Located just a short walk from the Acropolis, the hotel's lobby, restaurant and bar are stylishly decorated throughout with Italian furniture and original artworks that subtly accent the decor. By contrast, the rooms are furnished in handsome country style, with patterned bedspreads and curtains, and cramped bathrooms. Knowledgeable and professional staff have earned the hotel a fine reputation over the years.
Bar. Business centre. Internet: ISDN. No-smoking rooms/floors/lobby. Parking (free, limited). Restaurant. Room service (7am-9.30pm). Safe. TV: pay movies.

Adrian Hotel

Adrianou 74, Plaka, 10556 (210 322 1553/ fax 210 523 4786/www.douros-hotels.com). Metro Monastiraki. **Rates** €105-€120 single; €130-€145 double; €150 triple. **Credit** MC, V. **Map** p297/p301 E5.
The Adrian is located on Adrianou Street, awash with tourists and souvenir shops selling cheap worry beads and miniature replicas of ancient statues. This places it in the thick of the pedestrian action, and Adrian guests can watch all the neighbourhood animation from their balconies but still close the door on it with double-glazed windows or avoid it altogether with a back-facing room. The Adrian is appropriately priced in the mid-range category, with smart, recently fitted rooms in a pleasant olive motif, Acropolis views from some rooms (for an extra fee), high-speed internet access in rooms, friendly and professional management, a comfortable lounge area, and a beautiful shaded roof garden with an Acropolis view where guests eat breakfast and lounge in the evening.
Café-bar. Internet: shared terminal. Safe. TV.

Art Gallery Hotel

Erechthiou 5, Koukaki, 11742 (210 923 8376/ fax 210 923 3025/www.artgalleryhotel.gr). Metro Syngrou-Fix. **Rates** €75 single; €105 double; €120 triple. Breakfast €7. **No credit cards. Map** p301 E7.
This small, family-run hotel is in a quiet residential area just outside the centre and within reasonable walking distance of the Acropolis. A mishmash of old family furniture and lovingly framed paintings

from a locally celebrated impressionist artist who used the house as a studio decorate the interior. Rooms – which were renovated in 2004 with new bathrooms, air-conditioning, TVs, minibars and a lick of paint – have polished wooden floors and are flooded with light. The earnest service and a good top-floor bar-lounge with views of Filopappou Hill and the Acropolis complete the picture.
Bar. TV.

Hera Hotel

Falirou 9, Makrygianni, 11742 (210 923 6682/ 210 923 5618/fax 210 923 8269/www.herahotel.gr). Metro Akropoli. **Rates** €90-€120 single; €100-€135 double; €180 junior suite. **Credit** AmEx, DC, MC, V. **Map** p301 E7.

On a recent visit to the new Hera Hotel, Frank Sinatra was playing in the lobby while Norah Jones could be heard in the rooftop café. That juxtaposition sums up the feeling of the Hera – classic, but at the same time refreshing and novel. The location is ideal – just a few minutes' walk to the Acropolis and next to all imaginable forms of transport. Other pleasures of the Hera include ultra-courteous if formal service; smart and very comfortable rooms in classic beige and olive tones; a stunning circular indoor courtyard with a soaring 1920s-style iron- and glass-covered sun canopy where breakfast is served; and perhaps the most tasteful and elegant Acropolis-view rooftop café-restaurant in Athens. It's exceptionally good value for money.
Business centre. Café-bar-restaurants (2). Disabled-adapted rooms. Internet: shared terminal. No-smoking rooms. Parking (free, limited). Safe. TV: pay movies.

Magna Grecia

Mitropoleos 54, Plaka, 10563 (210 324 0314/fax 210 324 0317/www.magnagreciahotel.com). Metro Monastiraki or Syntagma. **Rates** €125 single; €140 double; €160 triple. **Credit** AmEx, DC, MC, V. **Map** p297/p301 F5.

Housed in a fine 19th-century neo-classical building in a great location – right on Mitropoleos Square – this small, new 12-room hotel's building renovation gorgeously shows off its fine architectural features – sky-high ceilings, French doors, elaborate original mouldings and hardwood floors. The 'boutique hotel' style is somewhat strained by the odd mix of the neo-classical architectural elements, boxy minimalism of much of the furniture and the wall murals' island kitsch, but while it doesn't quite all come together, it's a novel effort. Rooms are individually decorated and vary quite a bit in terms of style, but all front-facing rooms have gorgeous, open Acropolis views, as does the pleasant rooftop bar.
Business centre. Café-bar. Internet: DSL. Room service. Safe. TV: DVD/CD/MP3.

Parthenon Hotel

Makri 6, Makrygianni, 11743 (210 640 0720/ fax 210 640 0750/www.airotel-hotels.com). Metro Akropoli. **Rates** €105 single; €117 double; €141 suite. **Credit** AmEx, DC, MC, V. **Map** p301 F7.

The Parthenon is the kind of adequate but forgettable, mid-size, somewhat dated three-star hotel that tour operators tend to favour. But aside from its lack of personality, the Parthenon's location is just off the new archaeological walkway, close to the Acropolis, transport is great, and the whiter-than-white hallways and large, turquoise-hued, carpeted rooms are cheery enough. A giant, so-retro-it's-almost-fashionable-again lobby makes for a comfortable meeting point before or after sightseeing.
Bar. Business centre. Internet: WiFi in lobby. No-smoking rooms. Restaurant. Safe. TV.

Hotel Plaka

Kapnikareas 7 & Mitropoleos, Plaka, 10556 (210 322 2096/fax 210 322 2412/www.plakahotel.gr). Metro Monastiraki. **Rates** €115 single; €145 double; €165 triple. **Credit** AmEx, MC, V. **Map** p297/p301 E5.

Once an oasis of style in the Plaka area, the Hotel Plaka now competes with several other reasonably priced sleek hotels downtown. But the hotel still packs in a lot of style and comfort per euro. The decor is minimalist and sleek but by no means cold. The recently renovated rooms are all comfortably and smartly furnished, quiet and spacious. A peaceful roof garden, which guests have at their disposal all day long, offers great views of the Acropolis – as do some of the rooms. Unfortunately, the hotel is as well liked by tour operators as it is by guidebook writers, and is frequently booked up by groups.
Bar (summer). Internet: telephone line. Roof garden (summer). Room service (7am-7pm, beverages only). Safe. TV: pay movies.

Budget

Acropolis House

Kodrou 6 & Voulis, Plaka, 10558 (210 322 2344/ fax 210 324 4143). Metro Syntagma. **Rates** €80 double; €104 triple. **Credit** MC, V. **Map** p295/p299 F5.

After 40 years in business, the verdict is still out on the Acropolis House – people seem to either love it or hate it, as one traveller's faded elegance is another's old-fashioned shabbiness. The best and worst of the hotel is its long history: it's housed in one of Plaka's oldest buildings – a government-designated protected landmark – and retains all its original hand-painted frescoes, gilt-framed wall hangings, gloriously high ceilings and original fittings in the reception area. But the hotel has not been maintained well – the overall impression is dank, musty and somewhat shabby. Rooms are outmoded but practical, and management can be described in much the same way.
Internet access: telephone line. No-smoking rooms. TV.

Hotel Adonis

Kodrou 3, Plaka, 10558 (210 324 9737/fax 210 323 1602). Metro Syntagma. **Rates** €53 single; €80 double; €108 triple. **No credit cards**. **Map** p301 F6.

Just next to the Acropolis House hotel – an excellent location – the Adonis has low room rates for a respectable hotel. The no-nonsense, experienced management serves breakfast on the rooftop, where decor is still cheap 1960s bar/taverna, but the adjacent balcony with just a few tables has one of the best Acropolis views to be had at any budget. Rooms are quite sparsely decorated but are functionally and inoffensively furnished with modern furniture. Tiny en suite bathrooms are balanced by large balconies in many rooms.

Bar. Roof garden. TV.

Athens Backpackers

Makri 12, Makrygianni, 11742 (210 922 4044/ www.backpackers.gr). Metro Akropoli. **Rates** €22 dorm bed with en suite bathroom. **Credit** MC, V. **Map** p301 F7.

'Athens is awesome!' is the earnest slogan of this new hostel, and the friendly Greek-Australian staff do their best to help you believe it. Athens Backpackers is like a fun university dorm right next to the Acropolis. The hostel has a convivial atmosphere, with DIY barbecues on site and affordable sightseeing and club/bar outings. A three-computer internet corner is available, and a casual rooftop, Acropolis-view bar is a great place to start the evening with sunset cocktails. Overall, a hostel to remember.

Bars (2). Internet: pay terminals. Lock-box (some rooms). No-smoking floors. Snack bar. TV room: home cinema.

Hotel Dioskouros

Pitakou 6, Plaka, 10558 (210 324 8165/fax 210 321 9991/www.consolas.gr). Metro Akropoli or Syntagma. **Rates** €35-€40 single; €50-€60 double; €60-€80 triple; €80 quad. **Credit** AmEx, MC, V. **Map** p301 F6.

Time Out Athens won't even list the few real hostels in downtown Athens, as they are miserably located and awfully managed. But, much like the Student & Traveller's Inn (*see p59*), the Dioskouros retains the spirit of a hostel while offering better standards. Guests won't get en suite bathrooms, spacious rooms or fancy furniture, but they will get a small, intimate hostel full of international independent travellers, a clean bed, air-conditioning in all rooms, friendly staff, a dorm-bed option, a peaceful and partially covered garden set among lemon trees to socialise in, and a quiet and convenient location on the edge of Plaka.

Bar. Cooking facilities (Oct-May). Internet point. Parking (free). TV area.

Marble-House Pension

Anastasiou Zinni 35, Koukaki, 11741 (210 923 4058/fax 210 324 3551/www.marblehouse.gr). Metro Syngrou-Fix. **Rates** (breakfast not included) private bath €48 double, €55 triple; shared bath €42 double, €49 triple. **Credit** AmEx, DC, MC, V. **Map** p301 D8.

The small Marble-House Pension is in an unexceptional but quiet cul-de-sac in the Koukaki neighbourhood. But for an off-centre location, it really

---

The best Hotels

For views of the Acropolis
Hotel Adonis, Hera Hotel, Magna Grecia, Hotel Plaka (for all, *see p57*).

For high-end budget design
The Fresh Hotel (*p60*); **Life Gallery** (*p70*); **Semiramis** (*p70*).

For mid-range budget design
Alassia (*p65*); **Athens Art Hotel** (*p65*); **Eridanus** (*p65*); **Polis Grand** (*p65*).

For sea views
Astir Palace Resort (*p68*); **Divani Apollon Palace & Spa** (*p68*); **Poseidon Hotel** (*p69*).

For eating
Etrusco, Athenian Callirhoe (*p52*); **St'Astra, Athens Park Hotel** (*p65*); **Varoulko, Eridanus** (*p65*); **Avenue 103, Life Gallery,** (*p70*); **Vardis, Pentelikon** (*p70*).

For concept
Hotel 21 (*p70*); **Periscope** (*p62*); **Semiramis** (*p70*).

For budget value
Amaryllis Hotel (*p67*); **Athens Backpackers** (*above*); **Fivos** (*p61*); **Tempi** (*p62*).

For art
Athens Art Hotel (*p65*); **Eridanus** (*p65*); **Semiramis** (*p70*).

For history
Hotel Grande Bretagne (*p59*); **Athens Hilton** (*p62*); **King George II** (*p59*); **Pentelikon** (*p70*).

For nightlife on the doorstep
Hotel Arion (*p63*); **Exarcheion** (*p63*); **Xenos Lycabettus** (*p62*).

---

couldn't be more convenient: just a three-minute walk from a metro station, the pension is one metro stop or a brisk walk from the foot of the Acropolis, and two stops from Syntagma Square. And for this minor inconvenience travellers are rewarded with almost unbelievably low prices and a very hospitable atmosphere attracting a crowd of young and young-at-heart budget travellers. The simple bedrooms, with wooden furniture, are thoroughly unobjectionable, and the outside courtyard is serene and tranquil.

Air-conditioning in some rooms only. Kitchenette (in two studios). Safe. TV area.

Student & Traveller's Inn

Kydathinaion 16, Plaka, 10558 (210 324 4808/
fax 210 321 0065/www.studenttravellersinn.com).
Metro Syntagma. **Rates** private bath €55 single,
€65 double, €78 triple; shared bath €50 single,
€55 double, €72 triple. **No credit cards.**
Map p301 F6.

The owner of this long-time low-cost traveller's
favourite only recently started printing brochures,
with one simple explanation: 'The location sells
itself.' Indeed, the location is superb – on the outskirts of the more tasteful part of Plaka, within walking distance of Syntagma Square and metro station,
on a pleasant pedestrianised street. The inn has the
clientele and casual, international camaraderie of a
hostel, with four- and eight-bed dorm rooms with
shared facilities. But it also has the convenient
option of single, double and triple rooms (some
with en suite facilities). Rooms are basic but cheery
enough, and en suite bathrooms have all been renovated. Internet access and a green courtyard for
socialising are more pluses.
Internet: shared terminals. Outdoor snack bar
(vending machines). TV area.

Historic Centre

Deluxe

Hotel Grande Bretagne

Syntagma Square, 10563 (210 333 0000/fax
210 322 8034/www.grandebretagne.gr). Metro
Syntagma. **Rates** (without breakfast) €225-€255
single; €277-€285 double; €330-€345 junior suite.
Breakfast €28. **Credit** AmEx, DC, MC, V.
Map p297/p301 F5.

A manager at a competing five-star hotel has admit-
ted that there's no question about it: the Grande
Bretagne stands head and shoulders above every
luxury establishment in town. Already a landmark
steeped in history, the GB's latest claim to fame is
its reopening after a two-year, head-to-toe renovation, which spared no expense in recapturing its
turn-of-the-19th-century opulence. Antique furnishings, hand-carved architectural details, tapestried
headboards, gold Bavarian cutlery and the like have
all been painstakingly restored to their original
glory. Extra touches like the 24-hour personal butler service add the final decadent finesse. Standard
rooms, however, are not that spacious. If all this
seems rather out of your price range, stop by for tea
(served in hand-painted, gold-trimmed teacups) just
to drink in the history.
Bars (2). Business centre. Concierge. Disabled-
adapted rooms. Gym. Hi-fi (in suites). Internet:
DSL. No-smoking rooms/floors. Restaurants (2).
Room service. Swimming pools (1 indoor,
1 outdoor). Safe. Spa. TV: pay movies.

King George II

Vas Georgiou A2, Syntagma, 10564 (210 322
2210/210 728 0350/fax 210 325 0564/210
728 0351/www.grecotel.gr). Metro Syntagma.

King George II.

Fresh Hotel.

Rates (without breakfast) €220-€260 double; €310-€360 junior suite; €400-€450 suite. Breakfast €25-€32. **Credit** AmEx, DC, MC, V. **Map** p297/p301 F5.

Once one of Athens' most historic hotels, the King George II was closed for 14 years, under renovation for three, and finally opened in great anticipation to reclaim its status as one of Athens' most lavish hotels just before the Olympics. With just over 100 rooms, the hotel is a personalised, upscale deluxe residence with boutique hotel qualities. The effort here is clearly designed to take one back to the previous century, and it succeeds. A marble 'carpet' is the backdrop of the glamorous cream and gold-toned lobby, where armchairs surround circular marble tables and silk brocade curtains drape elegantly around the stately windows overlooking Syntagma Square. There are high-quality antiques throughout, even in the basement gym/health club. Rooms are each uniquely and differently designed, with hand-painted details, hand-made furniture, period desks, custom silk and satin upholstery, and soundproofing; many also have adjustable lighting calibrated to natural light. The elegant rooftop terrace has wonderful views stretching to the Acropolis and beyond.
Bar. Business centre. Concierge. Disabled-adapted rooms. Gym. Hi-fi. Internet: DSL. No-smoking rooms/floor. Restaurant. Spa. Room service (24hrs). Spa. Swimming pool (indoor). TV: DVD (selected rooms only)/games/pay movies.

Expensive

Fresh Hotel

Sofokleous 26 & Klisthenous 2, 10552 (210 524 8511/fax 210 524 8517/www.thefreshhotel.gr). Metro Omonia. **Rates** €130 single; €155-€170 double; €210 triple; €330 suite. **Credit** AmEx, DC, MC, V. **Map** p297 E4.

Like the Semiramis (*see p70*), the Fresh Hotel is not necessarily the kind of place you'd like to live in all the time, but a 'design experience' to revel in for a few days. Also like the Semiramis, electric hues are the design punctuation here, but this time in the context of a straight-lined, minimalist modernism that incorporates wood and 'natural' features like rock gardens. Rooms are small but space is used efficiently: armchairs open into extra single beds and electric blinds can be controlled from the bed. The poolside deck and lounge bar is the height of style.
Bar-restaurant. Business centre. Internet: WiFi. Mini-spa. Parking (€12/day). Restaurant. Room service (7am-2am). Safe. Swimming pool (outdoor). TV: plasma/pay TV.

Moderate

Attalos

Athinas 29, Monastiraki 10554 (210 321 2801, 210 321 2803/fax 210 324 3124/www.attalos.gr). Metro Monastiraki. **Rates** €72 single; €96 double; €120 triple; €147 quad. **Credit** AmEx, MC, V. **Map** p297 E4.

A textbook three-star hotel, the mid-size Attalos has a relaxed, unstuffy atmosphere and is set right next to Monastiraki Square and the metro. The building façade is a standard-issue Athenian concrete box, but rooms, updated in 2003, are classically decorated in warm teak and golden hues. An unfussy, casual Acropolis-view roof garden is adorned with greenery. Service is friendly and informal, and the clientele is wildly diverse, from young, independent travellers to older tour groups.
Café-bar. Internet: ISDN. Room service. Safe. TV.

Cecil Hotel

Athinas 39, Monastiraki, 10554 (210 321 7079/fax 210 321 8005/www.cecil.gr). Metro Monastiraki. **Rates** €65 single; €95 double; €110 triple; €145 suite. **Credit** AmEx, MC, V. **Map** p297 E4.
Both the Cecil Hotel and the street it inhabits are now looking a lot less ragged since undergoing a pre-Olympic spruce-up. Perhaps the most important renovation has been the soundproofing of most of the Cecil's rooms, since noise pollution was previously the hotel's only major flaw. When it comes to the things budget travellers really crave – clean, crisp, pleasant rooms and common areas; a convenient location for sightseeing; crucial amenities like air-conditioning, en-suite bathrooms, televisions, telephones; and a resident cat that gives the place a little personality – the Cecil really delivers.
Air-conditioning. Café-bar. TV.

Hermes Hotel

Apollonos 19, Syntagma, 10557 (210 323 5514/ 210 322 2412/www.hermes-athens.com). Metro Syntagma. **Rates** €115 single; €145 double; €165 triple. **Credit** AmEx, MC, V. **Map** p297/p301 F5.
The Hermes' recent facelift is most welcome in an area which desperately needs more quality affordable hotels. The location is ultra-convenient – just two blocks from Syntagma Square and next to Plaka on an ordinary but not unattractive street. A slightly cold reception leads to a softly lit, relaxing lounge-café/reading room in the back of the lobby. A simple rooftop terrace available to guests has excellent Acropolis views, and the street is fairly quiet. Rooms are simple but efficient if slightly cramped, while bathrooms are luxurious for this price category. A good choice for those travelling with small children.
Café-bar. No-smoking rooms. Safe. TV.

Jason Inn

Agion Asomaton 12, Psyrri, 10553 (210 520 2491/ fax 210 523-4786/www.douros-hotels.com). Metro Thissio. **Rates** €90 single; €110 double; €135 triple. **Credit** MC, V. **Map** p297 D4.
The hotel structure is unimpressive and the street it stands on nondescript, but the Jason Inn borders Thisio, one of historic Athens' less celebrated and more interesting destinations. With good access to excellent restaurants, nightlife, all the ancient sites and the old central market, the area offers a more 'authentic' experience and lower prices than Plaka, just a short walk away. With standard-issue but pleasant rooms, an inviting rooftop garden

restaurant and staff who thoroughly understand the needs of mid-range budget travellers, the Jason Inn is good value for money.
Bar. Restaurant. Room service (7am-midnight). TV.

Omonia Grand Hotel

Pireos 2, Omonia, 10552 (210 523 5230/fax 210 523 1361/www.grecotel.gr). Metro Omonia. **Rates** €130 single; €140 double; €350 junior suite. **Credit** AmEx, DC, MC, V. **Map** p297 E3.
The Grand is Omonia Square's only deluxe hotel, and sits on a corner of the busy square. It calls itself a 'hip hotel', and clearly caters to a youngish, moneyed traveller who wants something stylish, ultra-contemporary and luxurious. Indeed the hotel manages to carry off a modern, artful quirkiness alongside classic refinement. Front rooms, especially the corner ones, feature large glass windows with views over Omonia Square.
Bar. Business centre. Hi-fi. Internet: DSL. No-smoking rooms. Restaurant. Room service. TV: DVD pay movies.

Budget

Hotel Carolina

Kolokotroni 55, Monastiraki, 10560 (210 324 3551/ fax 210 324 3551/www.hotelcarolina.gr). Metro Monastiraki. **Rates** €60-€80 single; €70-€85 double; €90-€120 triple; €90-€150 quad. **Credit** MC, V. **Map** p297 E4.
The recent renovation hasn't turned this frog into a prince but it has been transformed into a slightly more exclusive affair – with somewhat more exclusive prices. The pre-war building lends the hotel a bit of character and history lacking in so many Athens hotels. Brightly coloured matching sets of Greek island-style marine blue furniture make the smallish rooms more efficient and add a touch of warmth to the rather sterile feel of the hotel's spick-and-span, tile-floored rooms.
Bar. Internet: telephone line. TV. Safe.

Fivos

Athinas 23, Monastiraki, 10554 (210 322 6657/fax 210 321 9991/www.consolas.gr). Metro Monastiraki. **Rates** €40-€45 single; €55-€60 double; €60-€70 triple. **Credit** AmEx, DC, MC, V. **Map** p297 E4.
Under the same management as the Dioskouros (*see p57*), the Fivos shares its strengths: dirt-cheap, clean rooms with few amenities and few pretensions. The location could hardly get more practical, within spitting distance of the Monastiraki metro station and very close to all the major central sites. The street on which the Fivos stands, formerly gritty and noisy, has improved considerably since its recent facelift, which increased the pavement area and decreased car traffic. In 2004 the hotel added brand-new bathrooms and air-conditioning to every room, a new breakfast area, and wireless internet on the first and second floors, making it even better value.
Bar. Internet: shared terminal. WiFi (1st & 2nd floors).

Tempi Hotel

Eolou 29, Monastiraki, 10551 (210 321 3175/fax 210 325 4179/www.travelling.gr/tempihotel). Metro Monastiraki. **Rates** without bath €38 single; with bath €50-€58 double, €70 triple. **Credit** AmEx, DC, MC, V. **Map** p297 E4.

For the traveller who has graduated from hostels but doesn't have a gold credit card, the Tempi is the perfect upgrade: the hotel has no curfews or dorm beds to contend with, but does offer some cost-saving features like a simple but well-stocked kitchen available for guest use and the option of shared bathrooms. Rooms were refurbished just before the Olympics, and now have double-glazed windows to cut all noise pollution, air-conditioning, and satellite TV. The neighbourhood is convenient and safe, and its location on a pedestrian street is a relief from busy Athens. The rooms may be nominal, but so are the price tags attached to them. *Cooking facilities. TV.*

Kolonaki & around

Deluxe

Athens Hilton

Vas Sofias 46, Ilissia, 11528 (210 728 1000/fax 210 728 1241/www.athens.hilton.com). Metro Evangelismos. **Rates** €249-€339 single or double; €274 triple; €870 junior suite; €35 extra for Acropolis view. **Credit** AmEx, DC, MC, V. **Map** p299 J5.

In Athens, the Hilton isn't just another standard multinational hotel; it's an institution. Its building design was a minor architectural milestone; scores of famous visitors have spent the night there; it was for years the only hotel offering five-star accommodation and service in the city; and the quality of its pricey eateries and lounges is the subject of hot debate. The hotel is a city landmark, and Athenians have come to call the entire neighbourhood 'Heeltone'. The results of the hotel's frenzied, thorough renovation a couple of years ago, including a new swimming pool and spa (*see p180* **Top city spas**), are lavish, with prices to match. *See also p66* **For glamour, just say Hilton.**

Bars (2). Business centre. Concierge. Disabled-adapted rooms. Gym. Internet: ISDN/web TV. No-smoking rooms/floors. Parking (€27/day). Restaurants (3). Room service. Safe. Spa. Swimming pools (1 indoor, 1 outdoor). TV: pay movies/DVD (suites).

St George Lycabettus

Kleomenous 2, Kolonaki, 10675 (210 729 0711/ fax 210 729 0439/www.sglycabettus.gr). Metro Evangelismos. **Rates** without breakfast €139-€206 double; €315-€370 suite. **Credit** AmEx, DC, MC, V. **Map** p299 H4.

Nestled at the foot of pine-clad Lycabettus Hill, this intimate luxury hotel is just steps away from Athens' top designer shops and museum row, though keep in mind that verdant surrounds in the centre do mean a steep hike or taxi ride up the hill.

Your efforts are rewarded by designer bedrooms in styles ranging from jewel-toned art nouveau to sleek black and white minimalism, and spectacular Acropolis panoramas from the rooftop pool bar and the Grand Balcon restaurant. Downstairs, the 1970s-themed lounge Frame is one of the trendiest nightspots in town.

Bars (2). Business centre. Concierge. Disabled-adapted rooms. Gym. Hi-fi. Internet: ISDN. No-smoking rooms. Parking (€14/day). Restaurant. Room service (6.30am-midnight). Spa. Swimming pool (outdoor). TV: pay movies/LCD TVs (suites).

Expensive

Airotel Stratos Vassilikos

Michalakopoulou 114, Ambelokipi, 11527 (210 770 6611/fax 210 770 8137/www.airotel.gr). Metro Megaro Moussikis. **Rates** €155 single or double; €185 junior suite. **Credit** AmEx, DC, MC, V.

The newish Airotel Stratos Vassilikos is an interesting mix of styles, from the Italian Renaissance-inspired façade – one of the most attractive of any downtown Athens hotel – to the bright florals of its restaurant, the classic style of the guest rooms and the modern futurism of the business centre. The location, on one of Athens' busiest thoroughfares, is less than desirable, but fairly convenient for heading downtown or out to the suburbs.

Business centre. Café-bar. Gym. Internet: DSL. Mini-spa. No-smoking rooms. Restaurant. Room service (7am-midnight). Safe. TV: games/pay TV.

Periscope

Haritos 22, Kolonaki, 10675 (210 623 6320). Metro Evangelismos. **Rates** €160 double. **Credit** AmEx, DC, MC, V. **Map** p299 H4.

The Periscope is a concept hotel where the theme is, bizarrely, surveillance. Staying here is a little like living in an art installation. Bedroom ceilings are entirely covered with photographs of urban Athens landscapes shot from a helicopter, while the lobby bar broadcasts live images on huge flat-screen monitors from the hotel's rooftop periscope, which is controlled by loungers in the lobby bar. Rooms are all black and white, and feature large beds with fine, fluffy linens. Bathrooms have industrial styling and are very sparse. The neighbourhood, a quiet street in Kolonaki, is arty with lots of high-end boutiques for browsing.

Business centre. Café-bar. Gym. No-smoking rooms. Internet: WiFi. Outdoor hot-tub/jacuzzi. Room service (7am-2am). Safe. TV: LCD/DVD/CD/MP3.

Xenos Lycabettus

Valaoritou 6, Kolonaki, 10671 (210 360 0600/ fax 210 360 5600/www.xenoslycabettus.gr). Metro Syntagma. **Rates** €143 single; €173 double; €385 junior suite; €517 suite. **Credit** AmEx, DC, MC, V. **Map** p299 G4.

This newcomer is a sleek, stylish boutique-style hotel. With just 25 rooms, the emphasis is on personal service. The location – on a pedestrianised

street filled with cafés and upscale restaurants in a particularly fashionable yet extremely central part of Kolonaki – is perfect for the fashion-conscious, and the hotel has its own popular café and restaurant. Rooms feature large, marble-swathed bathrooms, but they have a neutral, boxy modern style that's not quite as elegant as the area.
Bar. Disabled-adapted rooms. Internet: ISDN. Restaurant. Room service (7am-9.30pm). Safe. TV: pay movies.

Moderate

Andromeda Hotel

Timoleontos Vassou 22, Ambelokipi, 11521 (210 641 5000/fax 210 646 6361/www.andromeda athens.gr). Metro Ambelokipi or Megaro Moussikis. **Rates** €100-€120 single; €125-€150 double; €145-€160 triple/junior suite. **Credit** AmEx, DC, MC, V.
Offering a more placid atmosphere than its competitors, the boutique-style Andromeda has found its niche catering to discerning business travellers who are averse to the faux-riche decor and impersonal feel of many large hotels in this category, but still expect to be catered for in tasteful surroundings. Service is outstanding and the spacious bedrooms, some of which have been recently renovated, are all plushly decorated. Try to get one with a garden view. The hotel also has some new and very comfortable suites/apartments across the street to accommodate longer stays or families.
Bar. Concierge. Hi-fi (apartments). Internet: ISDN. Kitchenette (apartments). Restaurant. Room service (7.30am-11pm). Safe. TV: pay movies.

Budget

Hotel Dryades/Hotel Orion

Emmanuil Benaki 105, Exarchia, 11473 (210 382 7362/fax 210 380 5193). Metro Omonia. **Rates** with bath €35 single, €45 double, €60 triple; without bath €25 single, €35 double. **Credit** AmEx, MC, V. **Map** p297 F3.
These quiet hotels are in a cul-de-sac on Strefi Hill in the studenty Exarchia district. Both have newly renovated kitchens available for guest use, which makes them good options for independent travellers on tight budgets, although the local tavernas also provide cheap dining options. Rooms in the Orion have shared bathrooms, while all rooms in the Dryades have en suite facilities. Both hotels have undergone partial renovation, and the Orion in particular has been considerably upgraded with a more attractive lobby and rooftop, and all rooms now have newer furniture, air-conditioning and television. Even though these are small establishments, the service can feel a little impersonal. The very low room prices and the cool location draw a young, international crowd.
Cooking facilities. Internet: shared terminal. TV.

Xenos Lycabettus. *See p62.*

Exarcheion

Themistokleous 55, Exarchia, 10683 (210 380 0731/fax 210 380 3296). Metro Omonia. **Rates** €35 single; €45 double; €50 triple. **Credit** MC, V. **Map** 297 F2.
Like the Dryades (*see above*), the Exarcheion offers cheap rooms in the middle of the student district and rather lacklustre service. But unlike the Dryades, the Exarcheion is smack in the middle of the area's café-bar scene, which is exciting or miserable depending on your point of view and how you define relaxation. If getting rest is a priority, then make sure you ask for a top-floor room. The bedrooms are quite generously sized and clean, but simple. The rooftop bar is attractive for soaking up the scene of the buzzing neighbourhood below. If you're looking for proximity to a busy nightlife scene, the Exarcheion is a very good option.
Bar. Internet terminal: ISDN. Room service (7am-midnight). TV.

North of the Acropolis

Expensive

Hotel Arion

Agiou Dimitriou 18, Psyrri, 10554 (210 324 0415/fax 210 322 2412/www.arionhotel.gr). Metro Monastiraki. **Rates** €115 single; €145 double; €165 triple. **Credit** AmEx, DC, MC, V. **Map** p297 E4.

The Arion's draw is its unique position as the only hotel in the heart of Psyrri, one of Athens' more authentic – and tourist-friendly – nightlife areas. The hotel's effort at sleek minimalism in its lobby, bar and breakfast area is a little too stark, but the bedrooms have attractive glass-encased bathrooms and small sitting areas. A pleasant rooftop bar has views of the Acropolis, as do many of the rooms. *Bars (2). Room service. Safe. TV.*

Athens Park Hotel

Leof Alexandras 10, Pedion Areos, 10682 (210 889 4500/fax 210 823 8420/www.athensparkhotel.gr). **Metro** *Victoria.* **Rates** *without breakfast €138 single; €138 double; €200 suite. Breakfast €18.* **Credit** AmEx, DC, MC, V.

Situated on one of the city's central avenues, this recently renovated hotel is a three-minute walk from the Archaeological Museum and the Patision Street shopping area. In contrast to the somewhat dated aesthetic of the lobby and restaurant areas, the attractive, spacious rooms (with a view of the Pedion Areos park across the street) are elegantly furnished and decorated in shades of royal blue. A rooftop swimming pool is good for cooling off on hot summer days, as is a drink from the Astra Café. Also on the rooftop, at the trendy St'Astra lounge-bar and restaurant you can dine with a panoramic view of Athens, including Lycabettus and the Acropolis. *Bars (2). Business centre. Disabled-adapted rooms. Gym. Internet: dataport. No-smoking rooms. Parking (free). Restaurants (2). Room service. Safe. Swimming pool (outdoor). TV: pay movies.*

Residence Georgio

Patision & Halkokondyli 14, Omonia 10677 (210 332 0100/fax 210 332 0200/www.residence georgio.com). **Metro** *Omonia.* **Rates** *€130 single; €145 double; €230-€245 suite.* **Credit** AmEx, DC, MC, V. **Map** p297 E2.

Excellent new five-star hotel attracting an upscale Greek and Cypriot clientele. The lobby has several living room-like 'pockets' that facilitate private conversation. Double rooms have all the luxury amenities: enough space to spread out, high-quality linens and pillows, attractive pearwood decor, jacuzzis in all bathrooms, and great details like closet lights, boutique-brand cosmetics, and complementary wine and fruit on arrival. Great service is the standard here, the hotel is big on facilities, with a health club/spa and rooftop pool. *Bars (2). Business centre. Café. Disabled-adapted rooms. Gym. Internet: WiFi/ISDN. No-smoking floors. Restaurant. Room service. Safe. Swimming pool (outdoor). TV: games/pay TV/plasma (suites).*

Moderate

Alassia

Socratous 50, Omonia, 10431 (210 527 4000/ fax 210 527 4029/www.thealassia.com.gr). **Metro** *Omonia.* **Rates** *€90 single; €120 double; €140 triple.* **Credit** AmEx, DC, MC, V. **Map** p297 E3.

From the orange-lit glass catwalk entrance, waist-high aluminium urns and tall, Cubist-style armchairs in the café-bar in the lobby to the tiny halogen lights set into the creamy marble floors and the cool, subdued, soundproofed rooms, the Alassia is a feast for the aesthete. Unfortunately, the excitement ends at the door of the hotel, as it is situated in a busy, bland commercial neighbourhood. *Business centre. Café-bar. No-smoking rooms. Internet: DSL. Room service. Safe. TV.*

Athens Art Hotel

Marni 27, Omonia, 10432 (210 524 0501/fax 210 524 3384/www.arthotelathens.gr). **Metro** *Omonia.* **Rates** *€60 single; €85 double; €95 triple; €120 suite.* **Credit** AmEx, MC, V. **Map** p297 E2.

The Athens Art Hotel only opened in August 2004, but it has quickly built up a reputation for excellent value and has been booked solid nearly ever since. The rooms are each individually designed, but all feature pinewood floors, giant headboards, individual climate control, ISDN lines, laptop-size safes, double-glazed windows, original paintings, and inspired, high-design lighting and fixtures. Personal service here isn't just an empty promise – every guest gets personal recommendations on sightseeing, dining, culture and nightlife from the staff, who keep up on Athens' cultural and entertainment scene. *Bar-café. Business centre. Internet: ISDN. Restaurant. Room service. Safe.*

Eridanus

Pireos 78, Keramikos, 10435 (210 520 5360/fax 210 520 0550/www.eridanus.gr). **Metro** *Thissio.* **Rates** *€100-€120 double (€160 with Acropolis view); €180 junior suite.* **Credit** AmEx, DC, MC, V. **Map** p296 C4.

The outrageously good-value Eridanus bills itself as a 'luxury art hotel', and the entire place has the feel of an active, bustling gallery. The hotel is on an ugly, busy thoroughfare. However it is situated in an up-and-coming neighbourhood, excellent for quick walking access to nightlife in Psyrri and Thisio. The extremely well-appointed rooms come with designer furnishings, gorgeous deep-green Indian marble bathrooms and original paintings, plus web TV, huge beds and voicemail – all somewhat unusual in Athens. The very personal service and management are excellent. The hotel adjoins Varoulko (*see p144*), one of Athens' most celebrated gourmet restaurants. Some rooms have Acropolis/Filoppapou views. *Bar-bistro. Business centre. Gym. Internet: web TV. No-smoking rooms. Parking (free). Room service. Safe. TV: pay movies.*

Polis Grand

Patision 19 & Veranzerou 10, Omonia, 10432 (210 524 3156/fax 210 523 3688/www.polisgrandhotel.gr). **Metro** *Omonia.* **Rates** *€75 single; €85 double; €140 executive.* **Credit** AmEx, DC, MC, V. **Map** p297 E2.

Along with the Athens Art Hotel (*see above*), the Polis Grand is the best value for money of all the new crop of design-inspired hotels. From top to bottom, the hotel's elements are all in sync: the casual

For glamour, just say Hilton

For most people, the Hilton brand conjures up images of good, solid, run-of-the-mill hotels with a slightly uniform feel. But in Greece, the name resonates with history and glamour. When the Athens Hilton was built in the early 1960s, the arrival of a big, brand-name international chain in the capital seemed to solidify Greece's emerging reputation as a premier European holiday destination. It was also, as the hotel points out, Athens' 'unofficial hotel school', setting the standards for hotels that opened in later years.

The opening was not only important culturally and economically, but artistically too. The Hilton's structure, a semicircular building adorned with wall reliefs derived from ancient mythology, was designed by Greek artist Iannis Moralis. Some contemporary traditionalists considered it ugly and 'foreign', while modernisers saw it as a symbol of the city's progress. Today it's recognised as a minor architectural milestone for Athens – and a fine example of post-war modernism.

Controversial it may have been, but the Hilton's importance to the landscape of Athens was so great that the entire neighbourhood came to be called after the hotel. To this day, Greeks hardly refer to Ilissia – the official name of the area the hotel occupies – but rather to 'Heeltone', the Greek-ified pronounciation of 'Hilton'. A bus stop nearby is also called simply 'Hilton'.

For years, the hotel was the glam set's favourite hangout, the scene of receptions, galas, performances and wildly decadent parties. And the mix of foreign dignitaries and local celebrities was such an alluring cocktail that today a mention of the Hilton still impresses older Athenians.

While the heyday of the Hilton is gone, it still plays a part in the Athens social scene, with its street visibility, high-profile restaurants and hit list of foreign celebrities: Anthony Quinn, Marlon Brando, Jean-Paul Belmondo, Ingmar Bergman, Pierre Cardin, Aristotle Onassis, John Le Carré, Telly Savalas, Jil Sander, Raquel Welch, Rudolf Nureyev, Monaco's Prince Rainier and Prince Albert, and Mark Spitz have all stayed at the Athens Hilton.

Party like it's 1969: the Hilton in its heyday.

elegance of the candlelit, open-air, Acropolis-view roof garden; the sun-drenched lounge café-restaurant offering fresh, light meals; attractive, warm rooms (some with Acropolis and Lycabettus views). A subtle but distinct backdrop of art, which is scattered in mini-installations throughout the hotel, is complemented with high-design features on everything from vases and ashtrays to light fixtures.
Bars (3). Business centre. Internet: WiFi in rooms/lobby. Restaurant. Room service. Safe. TV.

Budget

Alma
5 Dorou, Omonia, 10432 (210 524 0858/fax 210 520 0210/www.almahotel.net). Metro Omonia. **Rates** €35 single; €45 double; €60 triple; €65 quad. **No credit cards. Map** p297 E3.
Simple rooms with country-style pinewood furniture, yellow bedspreads and bold-patterned curtains give a little cheer to this dirt-cheap hotel. A similar motif is repeated in the breakfast room, and the hotel also has its own bar and a minuscule lobby/reception. The location, on a pedestrian street just next to Omonia Square, is convenient.
Bar. Internet: shared terminal. TV.

Amaryllis Hotel
Veranzerou 45, Omonia, 10432 (210 523 8738/fax 210 522 5954/www.greekhotel.com/athens/amaryllis). Metro Omonia. **Rates** €49 single; €61 double; €75 triple. **Credit** AmEx, MC, V. **Map** p297 E2.
One of the best deals in Omonia, the recently renovated Amaryllis has preserved its low rates and now offers even better value for money. In the midst of a busy commercial area, the hotel is located on a comparatively quiet street but is still close to the main square. Ideal for travellers who are on a budget but desire more extensive facilities than the typical fare in this price range, the Amaryllis greets guests with an airy marble-swathed lobby and reception as well as a café-lounge with plush seats. Rooms are cheery, bright and generally more agreeable than other budget hotels, though service can be sour. Eighth-floor rooms include Acropolis views.
Bar. TV.

Hotel Omega
Aristogonos 15, Psyrri, 11743 (210 321 2421/fax 210 325 1116/www.omega-hotel.com). Metro Monastiraki or Omonia. **Rates** €60 single; €70 double; €80 triple. **Credit** MC, V. **Map** p297 E4.
A budget hotel right on Athens' central open-air fruit and vegetable market, which makes for a colourful location. The hotel rooms feel like large 1970s-era dormitories (they operate partly as dormitories for exchange students), with apathetic service to match. The rooms are slightly overpriced, but most have Acropolis views and they're hard to come by at a budget hotel. The roof garden has simple chairs and tables to enjoy the Acropolis views. A good choice for long-stay budget travellers in Athens.
Bar. TV.

Western Athens

Moderate

Oscar Hotel
Philadelphias 25 & Samou, 10439 (210 883 4215/www.oscar.gr). Metro Larissa station. **Rates** €90 single; €105 double; €120 triple. **Credit** AmEx, DC, MC, V. **Map** p297 D1.
Don't be put off by the ugly monolith exterior and unexciting neighbourhood of the Oscar; it's across the street from a major Athens transport hub, with a metro station, train station and suburban railway to whisk guests to the foot of the Acropolis in ten minutes, to the airport in 30 minutes, or outside Athens altogether. 'A luxury you can afford' is how the Oscar describes itself, and while we can't quite muster the enthusiasm to call the Oscar luxurious, its airy, cool, marble-and-brass lobby with stained-glass ceilings, and beautiful pool/rooftop bar with good city views are indeed impressive for a hotel in this price range. The somewhat uninspired rooms and neighbourhood are considerably less awesome.
Bar. Business centre. Internet: DSL. Parking (about €10/day). Restaurant. Swimming pool (outdoor). Room service (8am-1am). TV.

Budget

Hostel Aphrodite
Einardou 12 & Mical Voda 65, 10440 (210 881 0589/fax 210 881 6574/www.hostelaphrodite.com). Metro Victoria or Larissa station. **Rates** €14 dorm bed; €16 quad bed; €40 double. Breakfast €3-€5. **No credit cards. Map** p297 E1.
Though hostels in Greece are rare, they usually offer the best of the genre – cheap beds and a young, convivial atmosphere – without maddening detractions like lockouts, overstuffed rooms and bare-minimum service. Hostel Aphrodite, near Vathis Square, is no exception. Beds are about as cheap as they come, extra services like travel and laundry are readily available, doubles and quads (some with private bath) are also available, and the multinational, young staff create a kind of world-party atmosphere. The location is close to both rail and metro stations, but the gritty neighbourhood should be seriously taken into consideration.
Bar. Internet: shared terminals. No-smoking rooms/floors. TV room.

King Jason Hotel
Kolonou 26, Metaxourgio, 10437 (210 523 4721/www.douros-hotels.com). Metro Metaxourghio. **Rates** €57 single; €72 double; €90 triple. **Credit** MC, V. **Map** p297 D3.
A recent renovation has lifted the profile and customer comfort at this hotel. Rooms are now a warm pinewood style, punctuated with bright colours. The attention to detail and progressive features like dataports and free internet access in all rooms – plus conveniences like room safes and hairdryers –

support the King Jason's excellent reputation. The lounge, breakfast area and bar are all sleek and cool. Staff are friendly and seem to have a sincere interest in helping guests. The hotel's only shortcoming is its decidedly unglamorous neighbourhood.

Bar. Internet: DSL. Parking (free). Restaurant. Room service (8am-midnight). Safe. TV.

Syngrou & Southern Suburbs

Deluxe

Astir Palace Resort

Apollonos 40, Vouliagmeni, 16671 (210 890 2000/ fax 210 896 2582/www.astir.gr). Bus 114 from Glyfada Square. **Rates** *Arion* €350-€430 single; €380-€460 double; *Nafsika* €310-€380 single, €340-€410 double; *Afroditi* €270-€330 single, €300-€360 double. **Credit** AmEx, DC, MC, V.

This tranquil resort, reachable only via a security-guarded access road, sprawls over a private pine-clad peninsula 25km (16 miles) from Athens. The complex is actually made up of three hotels, which offer magnificent sea views, private beaches and dozens of activities ranging from windsurfing, tennis and jet-skiing to private Pilates lessons. Its isolation makes the Astir a popular site for top-level international conferences; keep your eyes open for hob-nobbing dignitaries, such as recent visitors Tony Blair and Jacques Chirac.

Bars (2). Business centre. Concierge. Disabled-adapted rooms. Gym. Internet: DSL/web TV. No-smoking rooms. Parking (free). Restaurants (2). Room service. Safe. Swimming pool (outdoor). TV: plasma/pay TV.

Athenaeum InterContinental

Syngrou 89-93, Neos Kosmos, 11745 (210 920 6000/fax 210 920 6500/www.intercontinental.com). Metro Syngrou-Fix (1km away). **Rates** €170 single/ double; €305 junior suite. **Credit** AmEx, DC, MC, V.

Athens' largest hotel specialises in efficient luxury. Spacious rooms are furnished in cool white marble and blue and green fabrics, with touches such as sunny sitting areas, double-headed showers and two or more phones per room. Executive suite floors have private check-in, an Acropolis-view lounge with an all-day buffet, and private meeting rooms on top of the vast conference facilities. But all businesslike restraint melts away in the shamelessly decadent Presidential Suite, which has hosted prominent guests including Bill Clinton and the Rolling Stones. Café Zoe, the hotel's all-day restaurant, is a must.

Bar. Business centre. Concierge. Disabled-adapted rooms. Gym. Internet: WiFi. No-smoking rooms. Parking (€14/day). Restaurants (2). Room service. Safe. Swimming pool (outdoor). TV: pay TV.

Divani Apollon Palace & Spa

Agiou Nikolaou 10 & Iliou, Vouliagmeni, 16671 (210 891 1100/fax 210 965 8010/www.divanis.gr). Bus A2 from Akadimias Street, then 116, 117 from Glyfada. **Rates** €200 single; €320 executive single; €220 double; €340 executive double; €1,600 suite. **Credit** AmEx, DC, MC, V.

Although it's part of a local hotel chain, the Divani Apollon Palace & Spa offers the business or leisure traveller a true Athens beachside haven. The service is exceptionally good, as are the hotel amenities: a gorgeous location on Kavouri beach, verdant gardens, two large outdoor swimming pools with towering palm trees, a jacuzzi, a children's playground and tennis courts. The spacious rooms all have sea views. A romantic dinner can be had in the hotel's restaurant, Mythos tis Thalassas, with seafront tables and great seafood. Another major plus point is the new, extensive spa.

Bar. Business centre. Concierge. Gym. Internet: DSL/web TV. Parking (free). No-smoking rooms/ floor. Restaurants (3). Room service. Safe. Spa. Swimming pools (1 outdoor in hotel, 1 indoor in spa). TV: pay TV/DVD (executive rooms).

Margi

Litous 11, Vouliagmeni, 16671 (210 896 2061/fax 210 896 0229/www.themargi.gr). Bus E22 from Akadimias Street, then 114, 116 from Glyfada. **Rates** €220 single; €250 double; €600 executive suite. **Credit** AmEx, DC, MC, V.

The Margi seems inspired by a Moorish castle, with its stone walls, distressed leather chairs, antique trunks, randomly placed candles and herbs in silver pots, and gauzy linens draped over outdoor arches. It's all deliciously atmospheric, though rooms still offer plenty of mod cons, including internet facilities and, in upper price brackets, hot tubs. And castle-dwellers never experienced such lavish American buffet breakfasts or elegant lounge bars offering sushi with their cocktails.

Bars (2). Internet: DSL. No-smoking rooms. Parking (free). Restaurant. Room service (24hrs). Safe. Swimming pool (outdoor). TV: pay TV/DVD (executive rooms).

Expensive

Metropolitan Hotel

Syngrou 385, Faliro, 17564 (210 947 1000/fax 210 947 1010/www.chandris.gr). Bus A2, B2 from Akadimias Street. **Rates** €145 single or double; €190 junior suite; €233 corner suite. **Credit** AmEx, DC, MC, V.

Yet another hotel upgraded in preparation for the 2004 Olympics, the 360-room Metropolitan is now one of the most luxurious places to stay and houses a fitness centre, outdoor swimming pool and beauty salon. Standard double rooms come in pleasant earth tones and seem slightly small only because they are crowded with comforts. By contrast, the executive rooms and suites are positively palatial. The hotel has also addressed its major drawback – accessibility to the city centre – with a free shuttle bus to Syntagma Square (the journey takes about 15 minutes). The hotel is a good choice for those heading to Piraeus, as it has a relatively good link via

Live like a suburban lord at the deliciously Moorish **Margi**. *See p68.*

Syngrou Avenue, or those with a car, since the hotel has its own garage. Like many hotels of this size, though, it may not suit guests looking for a highly personalised service.
Bar. Business centre. Disabled-adapted room. Gym. Hi-fi (executive & suites). Internet: DSL. No-smoking rooms/floor. Parking (free). Restaurant. Room service. Safe. Swimming pool (outdoor). TV: games/pay movies.

Poseidon Hotel
Posidonos 72, Paleo Faliro, 17562 (210 987 2000/ fax 210 982 9217/www.poseidonhotel.com.gr). Tram from Syntagma. **Rates** €135 single; €156 double; €190 triple; €250 junior suite. €30 extra for sea-view rooms. **Credit** AmEx, DC, MC, V.
With a brand new tramline connecting Paleo Faliro to central Athens, spending a holiday or conducting business in this coastal suburb is an attractive option since it now has easy access to the centre and is also relatively close to Piraeus port and marinas. The Poseidon Hotel, located right on the Athens coastline, has its own private beach (separated by a busy thoroughfare) and pleasant café-taverna right on the sand. Alternatively, guests can opt for its excellent rooftop restaurant, which has great views of the Saronic Gulf. There's also a swimming pool for those who don't want to venture into the sea, and good cafés and nightlife near the hotel during the summer. An internet point and smallish conference halls also make the Poseidon a good-value option for business meetings.
Bars (2). Business centre. Internet: DSL shared terminal/ISDN in rooms. No-smoking rooms. Restaurants (2). Swimming pool (outdoor). TV.

Moderate

Best Western Coral
Posidonos 35, Paleo Faliro, 17561 (210 981 6441/ fax 210 983 1207/www.coralhotel.gr). Tram from Syntagma. **Rates** €110 single; €130 double; €150 triple. **Credit** AmEx, DC, MC, V.
Located in Paleo Faliro, a popular summer suburb about 20 minutes from downtown Athens, the Coral has good facilities for a casual seaside conference or a semi-urban beach vacation. The hotel is located on the main coastal highway, across the street from a beach, a new seaside boardwalk and a number of beach tavernas, cafés and bars. Rooms, many of which have ocean views, are subdued and efficient. There are two marinas nearby, offering a convenient way to visit the nearby Saronikos islands.
Bar. Business centre. Disabled-adapted rooms. Gym. Internet access: WiFi. No-smoking rooms. Parking (free). Restaurant. Room service. Safe. Swimming pool (outdoor). TV: pay movies.

Emmantina Hotel/ Palmyra Beach Hotel
Emmantina: Posidonos 33, Glyfada, 11675 (210 898 0683/www.emmantina.com). Palmyra: Posidonos 70, Glyfada, 16675 (210 898 1183/ www.palmyra.gr). **Rates** *Palmyra* €75 single; €90 double; €115 triple; €250 suite. *Emmantina* €88 single; €95 double; €114 triple. **Credit** AmEx, DC, MC, V.
Two hotels offering value for money in the seaside suburb of Glyfada, about 25 minutes away from downtown Athens. Under the same management,

Sightseeing

they have comparable rooms and prices. The Palmyra is on the coastal side of Poseidonos Avenue and the larger Emmantina across the road, slightly closer to the golf course. The name Palmyra is something of a misnomer, but there is a large public beach just 50m away from the hotel. Both hotels are a five-to ten-minute walk from the main square of Glyfada, southern Athens' shopping and dining centre, one kilometre from the popular golf course and within close proximity of the south coast summer nightlife. Pools at each hotel are another major attraction, as is the free airport transfer.

Emmantina: *Bars (2). Business centre. Internet: WiFi throughout hotel/DSL in rooms. No-smoking rooms. Parking (free). Restaurant. Room service (6.30am-2am). Swimming pool (outdoor). TV.*
Palmyra: *Bar. Business centre. No-smoking rooms. Parking (free). Restaurant. Room service (7am-11pm). Swimming pool (outdoor). TV.*

Northern Suburbs

Deluxe

Life Gallery
Thiseos 103, Ekali, 14565 (210 626 0400/fax 210 622 9353/www.blue.gr). **Rates** €250 single; €350 studio; €500 suite. **Credit** AmEx, DC, MC, V.
Life Gallery is one of the new hotels aiming to attract business travellers who don't want their trip to be just about business. The hotel promises no less than 'a symphony of balance and a source of energy', reflecting the elements of life' and aims to 'embrace personal and business life, body and soul satisfaction, providing the ultimate experience to the modern business traveller'. As for body and soul, it offers a state-of-the-art spa with a fitness centre, and yoga, meditation and treatment rooms, in addition to a sauna, Turkish bath and 'raindrop therapy'. Sleek rooms have a Japanese style to them, and bathrooms – some with two sinks – are distinct in their Zen-like design. Jean-Louis Capsalas' creations in the Avenue 103 restaurant are a gastronomic pleasure.
Bar. Gym. Internet: DSL. No-smoking rooms. Parking (free). Restaurant. Room service (24hrs). Spa. Swimming pools (2 outdoor). Safe. TV: plasma.

Pentelikon
Deligianni 66, Kifisia, 14562 (210 623 0650/ fax 210 801 0314/www.hotelpentelikon.gr). Metro Kifisia. **Rates** €235 single; €250 double; €513-€1,900 suite. **Credit** AmEx, DC, MC, V.
The height of grand old luxury, the Pentelikon, built in 1929 and roused again with a 1980s renovation carefully preserving its belle époque style, seems less like a hotel than a country club or private estate. It is located in a residential neighbourhood in Kifisia just a short walk away from Kefalari Square's fine eateries, and Vardis (*see p154*), its gourmet restaurant, is Michelin-starred. Grand staircases, ballrooms, carefully kept expansive gardens and silk curtains all preserve an age long gone. Many of Greece's famous politicians, artists and celebrities

stayed here during the hotel's 1930s heyday, and today a new generation of stars is regularly spotted here. The Pentelikon's sumptuous bedrooms are all individually decorated for those who crave a unique experience.
Bar. Business centre. Concierge. Parking (free). Restaurant. Room service (6.30am-2am). Safe. Swimming pool (outdoor). TV.

Semiramis
Harilaou Trikoupi 48, Kifisia, 14562 (210 628 4400/fax 210 628 4499/www.semiramisathens. com). Metro Kifissia. **Rates** €180-€265 single; €230-€265 double; €260-€300 bungalow. **Credit** AmEx, DC, MC, V.
The newly renovated Semiramis boasts that it's 'Athens' only design-inspired hotel', and while that's probably too bold a claim, the strength of the design ethic is readily apparent in every last detail of Karim Rashid's new creation. The place feels positively futuristic, in contrast with most other hotels in Kifisia that hark back to the days of old. The hotel, aimed at art (not to mention hotel) enthusiasts, is positively daring, with a pink, green, orange and yellow colour scheme and a façade made of glossy white ceramic tiles. T-1 internet connections on flat-screen monitors, remote-controlled curtains, cordless phones and digital locks in rooms just add to the futuristic feel of the Semiramis. *See also p72* **Stylish sleeps.**
Bars (2). Business centre. Concierge. Gym. Hi-fi. Internet: T-1/web TV. No-smoking rooms/floors. Parking. Room service (24hrs). Safe. Swimming pool (outdoor). TV: LCD/plasma/pay TV.

Expensive

Hotel 21
Kolokotrini 21 & Mykonou, Kifisia, 14562 (210 623 3521/fax 210 623 3821/www.twentyone.gr). Metro Kifissia. **Rates** €160 single/double; €200 loft suite. **Credit** AmEx, DC, MC, V.
The brand new Hotel 21 is a unique addition to the growing number of hotels around Kifisia's Kefalari Square. Double rooms are very spacious, featuring giant beds with luxuriously fine linens, and large glass-encased bathrooms that have an innovative, dual-entrance design to allow two people to use en suite facilities at the same time. Split-level loft suites feature star-gazing sunroofs with electric blinds. Paintings in rooms each tell a part of a story, the whole of which is displayed in the reception. This is something of a 'scene' hotel, with a huge, fashionable outdoor café in front of the hotel with tables sunk into the ground, and an all-black café-bar inside. Front-facing rooms are ideal for people-watching, while back-facing rooms are more private. Freebies like wireless internet access, good-quality toiletries, DVD/CD/MP3 players, slippers and bathrobes are nice extra touches.
Bar-restaurants (2). Business centre. Internet: ISDN. No-smoking rooms. Parking (free). Room service (24hrs). Safe. TV: LCD/DVD/CD/MP3.

Stylish sleeps

In a city dominated by cement-box architecture, Athenians have come to expect little of modern building design. So when three hoteliers promised to uncover radical new looks for the Olympics, locals would have been forgiven for not believing the hype.

But just a few days before the Games, three hotels – the Semiramis, the Fresh Hotel and Life Gallery – all opened, with architectural and interior designs that were not merely up to date, but positively of the moment.

'Hotels today make you feel like you're living in the previous century,' says British-Egyptian designer Karim Rashid, who created the new **Semiramis** (see p70). 'That's the last thing I wanted to do.'

Against a modern white backdrop, the Semiramis features shocks of hot magenta, electric lime, glowing orange, radiant yellow and other energised hues. These rampant colours are contrasted by smooth, organic curves. There's hardly a straight line to be seen in the hotel.

There's nothing Rashid's hand hasn't touched. From the amoeba-shaped pool and the symbols on the rooms instead of numbers, to the hallways that each glow a different colour and the LCD displays outside guest rooms with various messages, there's a purity of design execution that starts with the architectural features and trickles all the way down to the light switches. Even the universally young, stylish staff seem to have been hand-picked to frame the concept.

Electric hues are also the design punctuation at the **Fresh Hotel** (see p60), this time used in the context of straight-lined minimalist modern design. 'Many people say they like a certain hotel because it reminds them of home,' says Fresh's sales and marketing director Panos Theodoridis. 'But I think people will like the Fresh Hotel because it doesn't remind them of home.'

The Fresh Hotel's most visible triumph is its extraordinary reworking of a decidedly unspectacular exterior façade, like thousands in central Athens, into something that's retro, futuristic and totally individual. Inside, a highly functional design prevails: small, efficient rooms with armchairs that open into extra single beds; electric blinds controlled from the bedside that give guests a view of the indoor rock gardens; and coloured glass dividers that bring atmosphere to the bathrooms.

The seriously sleek **Semiramis**.

Glass is a big player in the design at the **Life Gallery** (see p70). The hotel's all-glass façade invites people to view the action inside; and the elevated, glass-encased swimming pool is akin to a human goldfish bowl. Rooms have a Japanese-style design harmony and, like the Semiramis, art is everywhere: pop art in the dining areas, photo panels in the rooms, designer plants set like living works of art, rock installations – there are artistic moments throughout the hotel.

Whether or not these bright new hotels are going to stand the test of time remains to be seen. Let's hope they survive to serve as tangible reminders of a thrilling period, when all eyes were on Athens and the city really did live up to its own hype.

Sightseeing

Piraeus

Travellers on their way to or from the islands by ferry who want to stay in Piraeus overnight have limited options, with deluxe accommodation non-existent. The **Savoy** (Iroon Polytechniou 93, 210 428 4580, www. savoyhotel.gr, €110 double) is probably the best hotel in the port area. Other fairly reliable, smart digs within walking distance of the port include the **Park Hotel** (Kolokotroni 103, 210 452 4611, www.bestwestern.com, €90 double), and the less expensive **Triton** (Tsamadou 8, 210 417 3457, http://users.otenet.gr/htriton, €60 double without breakfast). Travellers on tighter budgets can try the simple but efficient **Glaros Hotel** (Harilaou Trikoupi 4, 210 451 5421, www.glaros-hotel.gr, €58 double) or the **Anita Argo Hotel** (Notara 23-25, 210 412 1795, www.hotelargoanita.com, €70 without breakfast per double), also just a few steps from the main port.

Moderate

Mistral Hotel

Alexandrou Papanastasiou 105, Piraeus, 18533 (210 411 7094/fax 210 412 2096/ www.mistral.gr). Metro Piraeus, then trolleybus 20. **Rates** €110 single; €140 double; €168 triple. **Credit** AmEx, MC, V.

Towering above one of Attica's most polluted and congested areas, the Kastella neighbourhood – with a port lined with fish tavernas and other restaurants – the Mistral is actually in a very fashionable residential area. Rooms are standard mid-range fare, with subdued blue motifs. A pleasant location for an overnight stay on the way to the islands, and a short distance but a world away from the noisy, polluted main port of Piraeus.

Bars (2). Internet: dataport. Parking (free). Restaurant. Room service. Swimming pool (outdoor). TV: pay movies.

Attica region

Deluxe

Sofitel Athens Airport

Eleftherios Venizelos International Airport, Spata (210 354 4000/fax 210 354 4444/www.sofitel.com). Metro/suburban railway to Venizelos Airport. **Rates** €186-€213 single; €250-€270 double; €280-€300 suite. **Credit** AmEx, DC, MC, V.

Since its opening alongside Athens' new international airport, the Sofitel has been collecting lots of compliments. It's one of the more pleasant airport hotels in Europe; the main draw is its ideal location within walking distance of the airport itself. There are plenty of conference spaces in addition to its pleasant rooms.

Bars (2). Business centre. Concierge. Gym. No-smoking floors. Internet: DSL. Parking. Restaurants (2). Room service. Spa. Swimming pool (indoor). TV: DVD (suites)/pay movies.

Camping

Athens Camping

Athinon 198-200, Peristeri, 12126 (210 581 4114/ fax 210 582 0353). Bus 075 from Agios Antonios metro. **Rates** €6/person, €3 under-10s. Campers €7, caravans €5, cars €3, small tents €4, large tents €5, electricity €4. **Credit** MC, V.

This campsite is in the middle of nowhere, although technically it is still in Athens. The site has just undergone a badly needed renovation and has upgraded almost all of its facilities. It includes a proper restaurant, a mini-market for necessities and self-service laundry facilities on the grounds. It is within walking distance of a neighbourhood with plenty of dining options and provisions. A nearby bus transports campers to Omonia Square in 20 to 40 minutes. The place is often full, so early reservations are recommended.

Bar. Parking (prices above). Restaurant. TV room.

Life Gallery.
See p70.

Sightseeing

Features

Introduction

Welcome to 5,000 years of history.

THE ACROPOLIS AND AROUND

Conveniently, most of Athens' significant
ancient landmarks are close to each other,
connected by a pleasant pedestrian promenade
dotted with shady cafés. Dominating from on
high, the **Acropolis** lies at the centre. The
Odeon of Herodes Atticus and **Theatre
of Dionysus** are on its southern slopes and
the vast, verdant **Agora** is to the north-west.

Spread around the eastern edge of the
Acropolis is the picturesque, though heavily
touristed district of **Plaka**. Its pedestrianised
winding streets are full of ancient ruins,
medieval churches, neo-classical museums and
vine-covered tavernas. Behind the Agora lies the
modern-day market area of **Monastiraki**, while
to the west is once-decrepit, now revitalised
Thisio, full of lively coffee shops and bars.

South of the Acropolis is the green expanse of
Filopappou Hill, the highest point in southern
Athens and a cool retreat from the bustling

centre. Below Filopappou is **Makrygianni**, a
quiet, residential district that is set to become
home to the massive, multimillion-euro
Acropolis Museum.

THE HISTORIC CENTRE

The modern city – the one constructed in the
19th century as a worthy capital of a newly
independent Greece – evolved to the east of
the Acropolis. Many greats of neo-classical
architecture contributed, among them Ernst
Ziller, Friedrich von Gartner and the Hansen
brothers. Some of their handsome structures
remain (most notably the University trio on
Panepistimiou and the Royal Palace on
Syntagma Square, now the Parliament building),
but many were destroyed between the 1920s
and 1970s, making for today's somewhat
uncomfortable juxtaposition of magnificent
colonnaded mansions and grimy modern blocks.

Within the area known as the **Historic
Triangle**, bounded by Mitropoleos (Plaka's
northern border), Athinas and Akadimias (the
two latter joining at the unlovely Omonia traffic
circle, *see below* **North of the Acropolis**) is
the commercial heart of the city, containing
both the colourfully chaotic Central Market and
the Stock Exchange. Situated at the head of the
main shopping street, Ermou, Platia Syntagma
is probably the city's busiest square. South and
east of Syntagma lies the wonderfully tranquil
oasis of the **National Gardens**.

KOLONAKI AND AROUND

Posh, pricey and some would say pretentious,
Kolonaki is home to eye-poppingly expensive
real estate, countless designer boutiques and
some of the city's priciest cafés and clubs. To
the north-west is the grungy, characterful,
student quarter of **Exarchia**, while to the east
is heavily populated **Ambelokipi**. All three
neighbourhoods creep up the foothills of
Lycabettus Hill, once a barren wilderness but
now home not only to acres of shrubs and pines
but also a tiny sugar-cube chapel, an acclaimed
restaurant and a popular open-air concert area.

NORTH OF THE ACROPOLIS

North of Monastiraki is the formerly run-down
neighbourhood of **Psyrri**. For centuries, this
was a dark, seedy place, populated mostly by
craftsmen's workshops and hash dens. But in
the late 1990s it began to sprout edgy art

galleries, restaurants, bars with live music and strictly face-controlled clubs, and now it's one of the hottest nightlife neighbourhoods in town. West of Psyrri are the neighbourhoods of **Keramikos** and **Gazi**, where new galleries and cafés are springing forth among soulful 19th-century ruins. North of Psyrri is **Platia Omonia**, a major roundabout and traffic hub for several of Athens' main boulevards. In the 19th century Omonia was a genteel *platia*; today, it's still a central point through which most visitors will pass, but it's degenerated into a dodgy, traffic-clogged meeting point for drug addicts, prostitutes and down-and-outs. Most of the area around Omonia also fits that description, and is best avoided after dark. But the appearance of a few hip new art spaces and restaurants in nearby **Metaxourgio**, directly to the west of Omonia, hint that it may one day follow the gentrification path of Gazi and Psyrri.

ATHENS SUBURBS
Extending south along the Attica coast are affluent suburbs such as **Glyfada** and **Vouliagmeni**, home to some half-decent beaches, glamorous seaside nightclubs, marinas full of extravagant craft, and a number of 2004 Olympic venues.

North of central Athens, the vital artery of Leof Kifisias flows up through **Marousi**, past the Santiago Calatrava-designed main Olympic complex, to the green and stately suburb of **Kifisia**. This elegant district was where rich Athenians once built their holiday retreats, and it remains, to some extent – despite becoming incorporated into Athens' urban sprawl – an area of old money. **Paleo Faliro** to the south was equally a place of costly summer retreats, but its handsome old villas have mostly been torn down to make way for towering blocks that compete for views over the Saronic Gulf.

PIRAEUS
Athens' sister city and main port has grown so large that it's now pretty much joined up with the capital, but still retains its own character, filled with tavernas and old *rembetika* dives.

SIGHTSEEING TIPS
Sightseeing in Athens, especially in summer, can be heavenly or hellish – which of the two depends chiefly on timing. Central Athens at noon in the white-hot sun of midsummer should be avoided at all costs. Do most of your active sightseeing in the morning and evening. Some archaeological sites stay open later than official closing times on summer evenings, while a few museums are initiating seasonal late-night hours – up to midnight – one day a week. And there's always a corner café or even the cinema to retreat to for a blast of revivifying air-con.

Spend early mornings wandering around and visiting museums. At noon, escape to the shady tavernas of Plaka for a leisurely outdoor lunch, followed by a visit to one of Athens' few properly air-conditioned museums. The Cycladic and Benaki Museums stay well chilled, and the National Archaeological Museum has just installed a comprehensive new air-conditioning system.

Guided tours
Private companies and travel agents can tailor walks to specific themes or interests, while guides provided by the Union of Official Guides can lead you around the archaeological sites.

Bus tours give a good overview of the best sites, so you can pick where you'd like to go back and spend more time. The standard package bus tour of Athens lasts around four hours and includes a guided tour of the Acropolis and National Archaeological Museum; it also drives by most other major sites and finishes up with lunch in a Plaka taverna. Reservations can be made through most hotels or any travel agency. The tours run daily, year-round, and cost between €45 and €50. Reserve at least one day in advance. CHAT Tours and Key Tours have good guides.

CHAT Tours
Xenofontos 9, Syntagma (210 322 2886). Metro Syntagma. **Open** 9am-7.30pm Mon-Sat. **Credit** AmEx, DC, MC, V. **Map** p297/p301 F5.
Tours depart from just in front of the Hotel Amalia (Leof Vas Amalias 10).

Hop In Sightseeing
Zani 29, Piraeus (210 428 5500/www.hopin.com). **Open** 7am-9pm daily. **Credit** MC, V.
Tours depart every morning from the Panathenaic Stadium (*see p116*) and take in most of the major sights of Athens, allowing passengers to get on and off for stops of up to an hour. The ticket is good for 24 hours, so you can come back the next day. It's best to book both in advance. Hop In offers a courtesy pick-up service from or near your hotel.

Key Tours
Kallirois 4, Southern Suburbs (210 923 3166/www. keytours.gr). Metro Akropoli. **Open** 7am-8pm daily. **Credit** AmEx, MC, V. **Map** p301 F7.
Tours depart from the head office, located on a major thoroughfare south of the Temple of Olympian Zeus.

Other tours

Amphitrion Holidays
Syngrou 7, Koukaki (210 924 9701/www. amphitrion.gr). Metro Akropoli. **Open** 9am-5pm Mon-Fri. **Credit** AmEx, DC, MC, V. **Map** p301 E9.

Sightseeing

A day in Athens

There is so much to see in Athens it's impossible to do it all in a day. But with a little determination, a pair of comfortable shoes and an early start, you can at least get a flavour of what the city has to offer.

Kick off the day at the **Tomb of the Unknown Soldier** in Syntagma Square (*see p98*). Every hour on the hour the tall, striking miniskirt-clad Evzones (ceremonial guards) perform their elaborate march up to the tomb (on Sundays at 10.45am they complete their manoeuvres to the strains of a military band). With the guards changed and back at attention, cross the newly renovated marble square and enter the old city via the ultra-modern shopping thoroughfare of Ermou at the far end of Syntagma. Wander down the wide street until you reach the beautiful 11th-century church of **Kapnikarea** (*see p95*), juxtaposed with Ermou's gleaming shopfronts.

Cutting through to the left of the square takes you into the winding streets of Plaka. Head past the **Roman Forum** (Eolou & Pelopida, *see p89*) and immerse yourself in the bric-a-brac of these narrow streets, then take Pritaniou and Stratonos into the heart of the dreamy island-style district of Anafiotika on your way up to the **Acropolis** (*see p79*).

After exploring the monuments of this most famous rock, amble down newly pedestrianised Apostolou Pavlou, where you can enjoy a laid-back lunch. **Filistron** (Apostolou Pavlou 23, *see p159*) and **Stavlos** (Iraklidon 10) are recommended spots for a break.

Work off lunch with a stroll back down Dionysiou Areopagitou to **Hadrian's Arch** (*see p102*) and the **Temple of Olympian Zeus** (*see p102*). Having taken in the glorious fallen columns, follow Leof Vas Olgas to the impressive **Panathenaic Stadium** (*see p116*), home to the first modern Olympics and one of the venues for the 2004 Games. Cut into the shaded calm of the **National Gardens** (*see p102*), taking in Zappeion on your way. Alternatively, walk up Irodou Attikou past the Presidential Palace.

Having emerged on Leof Vas Sofias, head for the excellent **Benaki Museum** (*see p103*), crammed with precious artefacts – from art and jewellery to ceramics and everyday objects – spanning thousands of years of Greek civilisation. On Thursday opening hours are extended until midnight and entrance is free.

With your appetite for antiquities nicely sated, head up Koumbari to Platia Kolonaki and immerse yourself in café society for a well-deserved frappé and a spot of people-watching. And that, for most, will mark the end of a full and fruitful day of sightseeing.

The extremely energetic, on the other hand, can window-shop their way up to the corner of Aristipou and Ploutarchou high above Kolonaki to take the funicular up to the day's final destination – the glorious promontory of **Lycabettus Hill** (*see p104*). A sunset drink here lets you marvel at Athens' sights from a breathtaking new perspective.

Offers four-hour tours of the city by minibus or taxi, and individually tailored walking tours of Plaka and the Acropolis with or without a guide.

Athenian Days
210 864 0415/6977 660798/www.athenian-days.co.uk.
Personal guided tours for groups of up to six. Start off with a one-hour talk on a subject chosen by the group (Greek religion, everyday life in ancient Athens) over cold drinks or a snack lunch, then a professional guide will take you round related sites. Pre-booking on the internet is recommended.

Union of Official Guides
Apollonos 9A, Syntagma (210 322 9705). Metro Syntagma. **Open** 9am-3.30pm Mon-Fri. **Map** p301 F5. Provides licensed guides for individual or group tours, starting at about €120 for a four-hour tour of the Acropolis and its museum.

The Acropolis & Around

The birthplace of Athens.

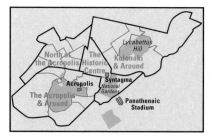

It's impossible to imagine Athens without the **Acropolis**. The rectangular limestone hill that juts out from the very heart of the city served as both a defensive citadel and sacred site in antiquity. It was here, according to both myth and history, that the city was born.

Ringed by the mountains of Hymettus, Penteli and Parnes, and bordered to the south-west by the sea, the high, flat-topped rock was a natural site for defence, administration and religious worship, and as such has been inhabited since the earliest days of human settlement. The hill and the area around it, as the oldest continuously populated parts of Athens, are layered with the seemingly endless remains of all the civilisations that have existed here. The most impressive of these are from the fifth-century BC classical period, also known as the Golden Age of Athens, during which the Athenian leader Pericles initiated the building of the complex of temples and structures that now graces the top of the Acropolis. Around its southern base are classical structures including the **Theatre of Dionysus** and **Lysicrates Monument**, while lying in its south-western skirts of pines and scattered antiquities is the impressive **Odeon of Herodes Atticus**, added in the second century AD by the wealthy Roman of that name. To the north of the Acropolis is another Roman addition: the **Forum**, or central marketplace, ordered neatly around the unique eight-sided **Tower of the Winds**, which dates back to 50 BC.

The Byzantine era filled the area with dozens of tiny, frescoed churches. During the Ottoman occupation, Turkish rulers built mosques (like the one that remains in the Roman Forum) on the ancient sites. Relics of Ottoman daily life also appear in the form of structures like Athens' only remaining Turkish bathhouse.

UNIFICATION OF ARCHAEOLOGICAL SITES WALKWAY

The best way to explore this most historic part of Athens is via the stone-paved **Unification of Archaeological Sites walkway**. If there's one Olympic-era venture that has changed the face of central Athens sightseeing, it is this project. Universally hailed as a success, the project has brought peace and pedestrianisation to an area previously dogged by traffic chaos and bad air quality – the very same area that is home to the city's most important monuments. The project links the city's main sites in an 'archaeological park' by means of a ten-mile walkway.

Beginning opposite Hadrian's Arch (*see p102*) at the wide, neo-classical villa-lined street of Dionysiou Areopagitou, the walkway runs seamlessly into Apostolou Pavlou, with its lively cafés and views over the Ancient Agora, before rounding a bend, crossing the train tracks and turning into the lower part of Ermou to reach Keramikos (*see p113*).

Until a few years ago, these streets were part of the main goods thoroughfare across Athens. Constantly congested with traffic and choked with exhaust fumes, they were hardly a good advertisement for the care Athens was taking of its antiquities. But with the Olympic bid in mind, along with the concomitant effort to secure the return of the Parthenon Marbles, the Ministry of Culture turned its attention to improving the monuments and their environs – transforming sightseeing in central Athens into an altogether more relaxing experience.

It may be a pedestrian route but don't assume you won't encounter vehicles: the walkway is popularly seen as a convenient, traffic-free shortcut by many a cunning moped rider and delivery van driver, and is actually the sole means of vehicular access to their homes for some residents of Plaka and Thisio.

In the four years since Dionysiou Areopagitou and Apostolou Pavlou were pedestrianised, the buildings have slowly shaken off decades of grime and been restored to their former glory as magnificent neo-classical mansions (many now remodelled into contemporary cafés and restaurants). The Ermou part of the walkway, on the other hand, which previously belonged to the industrial area that encircles Gazi (the former gas works),

Sightseeing

Church of St Dimitrios Loumbardiaris.

Classical composition – the awe-inspiring **Acropolis**.

remains, at the time of writing, dotted with half-derelict warehouses and factories, a deserted nightclub or two, and the central bus depot.

THE NEIGHBOURHOODS

Branch off from the pedestrian promenade to discover the fascinating neighbourhoods that have grown up around the Acropolis and its surrounding sites. To the north and east of the walkway lies the charming, if heavily touristed (at least in summer) area of **Plaka**, packed with ancient ruins, neo-classical houses, winding cobblestoned streets and tavernas festooned with bougainvillea.

To the south of the Acropolis is shady **Filopappou Hill**, the highest point in southern Athens and the best place for outstanding views of the Acropolis. Surrounding Filopappou are the residential districts of **Makrygianni** and **Koukaki** to the east and working-class **Petralona** to the west. A mix of cement-block flats and restored neo-classical villas, these areas are interesting for a stroll. They may lack the instant appeal and abundant sightseeing of Plaka, but they are also free from touting taverna-owners and throngs of backpackers.

In the area just north of the Acropolis beats the true heart of classical Athens: the sprawling Agora – the marketplace where citizens haggled over the price of olive oil, where bureaucrats hammered out the tricky points of the first democracy and where the likes of Socrates paced among the stalls asking mind-bending questions. The marble ruins of the **Ancient Agora**

constitute the biggest, greenest and, some say, most fascinating archaeological site in Athens. On its northern boundary is **Monastiraki**, the most colourful and attractive of the surrounding areas. Since Ottoman times, this small, vibrant quarter has taken over the Agora's mantle of the marketplace, playing host to Athens' most famous flea market (*see p172* **Sunday morning in Monastiraki**), filled with antiques and junk dealers, clothing and craft stalls.

At the western boundary of the Agora is **Thisio**, an area that underwent a major revival with the arrival of the Unification of Archaeological Sites walkway. Today, you'll find dozens of cafés packed on main Apostolou Pavlou and its narrow, once-residential satellite streets. Venturing off the walkway, you'll find still more cafés, bars and tavernas, as well as a mixture of tumble-down neo-classical houses, new blocks, edgy galleries, a renovated 19th-century hat factory and the old royal stables, as well as countless chaotically parked cars and mopeds belonging to café customers.

Acropolis & Filopappou Hill

Maps p300 & p301

Acropolis

Dionysiou Areopagitiou (210 321 0219/www.culture. gr). Metro Akropoli. **Open** *Apr-Dec* 8am-sunset daily. *Jan-Mar* 8.30am-2.30pm daily (museum opens 11am Mon). **Admission** (including entry into

Temple of Dionysus, Ancient Agora, Roman Agora, Keramikos & Temple of Olympian Zeus) €12; €6 concessions; free under-18s. Free to all Sun Nov-Mar. **No credit cards. Map** p301 D6/E6.

Looming in quiet splendour over modern Athens, the Acropolis (or 'high city') is omnipresent: often glimpsed between apartment blocks or at the end of central streets, it can be dimly discerned through a blanket of yellow-tinged summer smog, or clearly highlighted against the night sky, illuminated by hundreds of spotlights. But nothing prepares the viewer for the breathtaking magnificence of this monument when seen up close. The awe it inspires comes from more than sheer beauty: the Acropolis temples represent the greatest achievement of classical Greece, combining mathematical proportion with a glorious aesthetic to create an effect both human and sublime.

The Acropolis was a seat of royalty and a focus of religion as far back as Neolithic times. After the 11th century BC, however, everything grew up around Athena (*see p43*). Most of myths surrounding the Acropolis are associated with the goddess of wisdom: it was on this rock that she battled Poseidon for control of Attica's greatest city. The god of the sea struck the rock with his trident and out gushed a spring, his offering to the people. Athena offered the less flashy but more useful gift

of the olive tree (providing food, oil and shelter), and the citizens awarded her patronage of the city that still bears her name.

The earliest Acropolis temples to Athena date from 650 BC, but it was during the late fifth century BC, known as the Golden Age of Athens, that the Athenian general Pericles launched an ambitious programme of works by Greece's greatest artists and architects, resulting in the timeless monuments we see today. Though the temples' influence may be eternal, their physical state is not. The Acropolis has weathered invasions by the Spartans, Persians, Ottomans and Nazis but its downfall may come from a more modern foe: the infamous Athenian smog is slowly eroding the marble. A team of international experts has been working for nearly 20 years to restore and protect the monuments, meaning that not only are all the structures propped up to some extent with scaffolding, but that the entire Acropolis rock is littered with Portakabins, cranes and teams of workmen – yet somehow it manages to maintain its majesty.

The Acropolis is entered through the **Propylaeum**. The work of the architect Mnesicles, this colossal gate obscures the view of the Parthenon and so stands alone on the horizon in all its grandeur, creating a theatrical passage from the profane to the

The making of a monument

For the thrillseekers and fans of antiquity of late 18th-century and early 19th-century Europe, who braved danger and disease to catch a glimpse of 'real' Greek architecture, the first sighting of the Parthenon could be almost transcendental. For them the structure was the embodiment of the classical ideal: art, they believed, had reached a state of perfection in classical Greece during the fifth century BC, and the Parthenon was its most sublime example. To see it was like finding the holy grail.

Though they may have swooned, the ruin that greeted these travellers was very different from the ancient Parthenon. The structure had had different lives under various rulers, functioning as a church, a mosque and a gunpowder store. And the Acropolis site contained a Turkish village, a minaret, a Renaissance palace and a structure known as the Frankish tower. At times it had accommodated a harem and a garrison.

Earlier visitors had taken these multiple uses for granted. Able to admire the architecture, and the culture that had created it, they nevertheless remained supremely confident that the proper use for a building

of this stature was as a place of worship for their own religion, first Christianity (the Parthenon became a church in the sixth century AD), then Islam. The concept of preserving historical structures as monuments was an idea whose time had not yet come.

After the Ottoman takeover in 1458, the conversion of the Acropolis to a garrison and wars in Europe put the Parthenon off-limits for western visitors for some time. In September 1687 the garrison's gunpowder stores exploded, putting the Parthenon out of practical use. By the 18th century western visitors were drifting back and the tenor of their accounts is twofold. They drooled over the 'exquisite symmetry', while expressing dismay at the Parthenon's ruined state. Blame was laid firmly at the feet of Turks and locals who took stones for building and otherwise contributed to its disintegration.

Of course, ignorant locals and 'barbarous' Turks were not alone in denuding the Parthenon. The reaction of many 19th-century western visitors to the structure was to want a piece of it. Lord Elgin is most famous for his wholesale removal of the Parthenon marbles, but smaller parts of the Parthenon appeared

sacred. The Propylaeum's north wing, known as the Pinakothiki (art gallery), was decorated with frescoes of scenes from Homer and filled with recliners where visitors could rest. Construction on the Propylaeum began in 437 BC, but was suspended five years later with the onset of the Peloponnesian Wars and never completed.

On your right, as you stand before the immense Propylaeum, is the **Temple of Athena Nike**. Built in 424 BC, this tiny temple to the goddess of victory was demolished in 1686 by the Turks to make way for gun emplacements, then painstakingly reconstructed in the 1830s. Since 2000 it has been undergoing major restoration to correct inaccuracies and inadequacies of both the 1835-45 reconstruction and a subsequent 1935-40 repair job. It was initially hoped that the temple could be completed by summer 2004; it now appears that a further two years or so are required to finish the mission. The originals of its small but exquisite friezes showing battle scenes with Greeks, Persians and gods are displayed in the on-site Acropolis Museum.

The main focus of the Acropolis is, of course, the **Parthenon**. The temple honours the incarnation of Athena as virgin goddess (Parthenos). Designed by the great sculptor Phidias, he also supervised its construction between 447 BC and 438 BC. It seems incredible that such a magnificent work could be completed in only nine years; the early second-century biographer and historian Plutarch commented, 'It is this, above all, that makes Pericles' works an object of such wonder to us – the fact that they were created in so short a span and yet for all time.' Despite its apparent simplicity, the Parthenon is the result of countless advanced calculations. Every measurement used in the construction of the temple is based on the golden mean: a ratio-based geometrical system of proportion that still preoccupies mathematicians today. And, to counteract the optical illusion that straight lines viewed from afar seem to bend, its columns bulge slightly and lean a few degrees inward (if their lines were extended, they would eventually meet). The result of such intricate mathematical wizardry is to create a perfect structure, balanced in every way, that gives the impression of somehow being alive.

The Parthenon's decorations were no less marvellous than its structure. The metopes (part of the friezes) were sculpted with scenes of gods and celebrated mortals, their dynamism and detail surpassing everything the Greeks had created up until then. The pediment sculptures were the most magnificent: the east pediment showed the birth of Athena, springing fully formed from the head of Zeus, while

in collections around Europe during the century. The nationalism inherent in the 19th-century drive to collect and collate was clear even in the writings of those criticising Elgin. 'While we indignantly reprove and deeply regret the irreperable damage that has been done to the Athenian monuments, we must not overlook that advantage which the fine arts in our country will derive from the introduction of such estimable specimens of Greek art,' wrote Edward Dodwell, an eyewitness to the removal of the marbles.

A far more emotional response came from one of Elgin's most vehement contemporary critics, romantic and lover of Greece Lord Byron: 'Cold is the heart, fair Greece/That looks on thee/Nor feels as lovers o'er the dust they lov'd./Dull is the eye that will not weep to see/They walls defac'd, they mouldering shrines remov'd/By British hands...'

The Greek War of Independence (1821-2) and subsequent Turkish seige (1826-7) turned the Acropolis into a war zone once again. The conflict drew a new kind of traveller – philhellenes from western Europe, romantic amateur fighters in love with the classical ideal, keen to save the 'cradle of democracy' from the Turks. Some of them ended up holed up on the Acropolis under seige. Graffiti scratched on the columns is still visible. 'M Blondel, Philhellene, 1826' reads one piece.

Peace secured, a Bavarian prince was imported to take up the job of monarch of the newly independent nation state. Otto came from a country where philhellenism was a popular trend. He wasted no time in exploiting ancient Greece's number one symbol – the Parthenon – to bolster his own shaky claim to legitimacy: the days of barbarism were over and he would lead the new state in a return to the glories of the classical era. He pressed the point at a ceremony of glorious kitschness, in which he rode up to the Acropolis, was greeted by white-clad Athenian maidens, and sat on a throne in the Parthenon.

A plan to build his palace on the Acropolis was eventually abandoned. Instead, this symbolic site was to be preserved in pristine classical condition. All evidence of post-ancient use was dismantled, and there were sporadic attempts to reconstruct the original structures, leaving the site more or less as modern visitors see it. An 'ancient monument' was born.

the west pediment depicted Athena and Poseidon's battle for the city. Though many of these sculptures survive, you won't see them in Greece. About two-thirds were removed from the Parthenon during the early 19th century – a frenzied period of antiquity acquisitions – by a team of agents for the seventh Earl of Elgin, Thomas Bruce, who was then British Ambassador to Constantinople. These pieces, which include the greater part of the frieze from within the Parthenon, 15 metopes and various sculptures from the triangular pediments, were bought by the British Museum, where they remain to this day on display in the Duveen Gallery, the subject of controversy.

Elgin was not the first to take treasures from the Acropolis, nor did the rock escape other forms of vandalism. A reportedly breathtaking 12-metre (40-foot) gold-and-ivory statue of Athena, by Phidias, disappeared after just a few centuries. The Byzantine emperors consecrated the Parthenon as a Christian church and the Ottomans later used it as a mosque. Under the Ottomans it also served as a gunpowder magazine; when the Venetians shelled the building in 1687 the powder ignited and blew the roof off. In the 15th century the Florentine rulers built a Frankish tower on the Acropolis, which is still visible in early to mid 19th-century etchings and watercolours of the rock. This structure was removed in 1875 by the archaeologist Heinrich Schliemann, an act considered vandalism by some, although purists were pleased to see it go. Nineteenth-century representations also show the low dwellings that once stood on the Acropolis, built by the Turkish settlers with stones 'borrowed' from the nearby temples.

The simplicity of the Parthenon is contrasted with the fascinating complexity of the **Erechtheum** opposite. It was completed in 406 BC, on the spot

Acropotips

● Hold on to your ticket. It will give you free entry to all the other sites on the Unification of Archaeological Sites walkway for up to a week. The sites are: Acropolis site and museum, Ancient Agora (*see p91*), Theatre of Dionysos (*see p83*), Keramikos (*see p113*), Temple of Olympian Zeus (*see p102*) and Roman Forum (*see p89*).
● When you have your ticket checked, ask for a copy of the free guide to the site (in English). It's packed with info, but ticket-checkers usually don't bother to hand it out.
● Bring your own (large) bottle of water – the on-site vendors tend to charge higher prices.
● Go first thing in the morning to avoid the heat and the crowds, or in the early evening to watch the sunset from the temples. After 5pm the colours are fabulous.

where Athena and Poseidon are said to have battled for Athens. The structure unites two separate temples: the east porch once sheltered an olive-wood statue of Athena (now the goddess must make do with just a young olive sapling, growing in her honour on the western side of the temple), while the west porch was devoted to Poseidon. The most famous feature is the south porch, held up by six columns in the shape of voluptuous, drapery-clad maidens. These are known as the Caryatids, possibly after the women of Caryae, who were famed for their beauty and served as Athenian slaves. This latter fact may have been what inspired the Ottoman commanders to convert the temple to a harem during their occupation. Like the Parthenon, the Erechtheum survived its different uses unscathed.

The Caryatids on the Erechtheum today are copies: one of the originals is in the British Museum, the other five are in the **Acropolis Museum**, tucked away and camouflaged in a sunken corner of the Acropolis. Although it's small, rather run-down and populated by a large number of gossiping public employees, its holdings make it one of the most important museums in the world. Its star pieces are undoubtedly the temple friezes from the Athena Nike and the one-third of the Parthenon series left by Lord Elgin, but don't miss the pediment exhibits – some of which still show some traces of their original, vivid colours – and the impressive collection of korai maidens.

Since summer 2004 the Acropolis has been open to wheelchair-users, who previously were kept out by the steep slopes, numerous steps and uneven, slippery ground. Entrance is free of charge to those in wheelchairs, as well as to one able-bodied companion per chair. Keeping the main entrance to the Acropolis (under the Propylaeum) on your right, head through a large gate marked with a wheelchair sign and bear left on a dust path through a wooded, shady glade in the shadow of the Acropolis until you come across what Paralympic visitors rather unkindly described as a 'tin can on a stick'. It may look precarious, but it will take you straight up the northern face of the rock, depositing you just in front of the Erechtheum. An even path leads up to the Parthenon; from then on it's rather rocky going until you reach the museum, which is accessed by a small lift. Keep in mind that on very windy or rainy days, the wheelchair lift is out of action.

Disabled visitors have to leave the site the same way they came in, but others are recommended to exit by way of the **Theatre of Dionysus** (*see p83*). Wander down through the sweet-scented pines, with the Parthenon towering above, admire the auditorium, then stroll out – passing the 19th-century chapel of St George on your left – on to the lower end of Dionysiou Areopagitou, opposite Acropolis metro station and the site of the new Acropolis Museum.

This controversial multi-million-euro project is way behind schedule. The original, ambitious hope was that it would be completed (and housing the Parthenon Marbles) in time for the Olympics in summer 2004. The scheme was stymied by legal challenges, change of government and firm refusals from the British Museum to hand over the marbles for temporary exhibition. No new completion date has been announced. An exhibition showcasing plans for this mammoth development is at the neighbouring Weiler Building (Dionyssiou Aeropagitou and Makrygianni, 210 924 1043) until 31 May 2005, and is likely to be extended through summer 2005. Pop in to see the scale model and watch the virtual tour (entrance is free), but also to peer at the ongoing construction of the museum next door: at the time of writing it was just a massive crater stretching for an entire block, encircled by the half-demolished remains of Makrygianni residents' homes.

Areopagus

Outside the entrance to the Acropolis. Metro Akropoli. **Map** p301 D6.

Named after Ares, the god of war, this high, slippery limestone rock began life in officialdom as ancient Athens' highest court. According to myth, Orestes fled here after murdering his mother, Clytemnestra. Though the Furies had planned to kill him, Athena insisted on a jury trial (Orestes was acquitted), marking a transition from blood feuds to rule of law. Athens' judicial council convened on the same spot from the eighth to the fifth centuries BC. In AD 51, when St Paul visited Athens, he delivered his famous 'Men of Athens' sermon here, converting Dionysus (a namesake, not the debauched god himself), who would later become the first bishop of Athens. The speech, immortalised in the Bible (Acts 17:22-34), is carved on a bronze plaque at the bottom of the rock, which is often visited by pilgrims.

Odeon of Herodes Atticus

Dionysiou Areopagitou, near intersection with Propylaion (210 323 2771/www.culture.gr). Metro Akropoli. **Open** only during performances. **Tickets** vary with performance. **Map** p301 D6.

If the Theatre of Dionysus was the most important venue in classical Athens, this has been its equivalent since Roman times. Built in AD 174 by the wealthy Herodes Atticus (friend to Emperor Hadrian and a benefactor of the city) in memory of his wife, it has marvellous acoustics and a beautiful backdrop with tiers of Roman arches. More commonly called Herod Atticus or, in Greek, Irodio, the theatre is now the venue of the annual Athens Festival (*see p189*), hosting moonlit performances nightly every summer. Artists such as Luciano Pavarotti and the Bolshoi Ballet have performed here, and the theatre is a regular host to interpretations and adaptations of the ancient Greek tragedies and comedies. Though the Odeon is only open for performances, you can appreciate its architecture and setting from the outside and look down on it from the Acropolis.

Theatre of Dionysus

Dionysiou Areopagitou (210 322 4625/www. culture.gr). Metro Akropoli. **Open** *May-Oct* 8.30am-7pm daily. *Nov-Apr* 8am-sunset daily.

Porch of the Caryatids. *See p82.*

Admission €2; €1 concessions; free to holders of €12 Acropolis ticket. **No credit cards**. **Map** p301 E6.

This spot saw the birth of drama as we know it: it was the site of the sixth-century BC Festival of the Great Dionysia, honouring the god with performances that led to the renowned fifth-century BC drama competitions. The tragedies of Sophocles and Euripides, as well as the comedies of Aristophanes, were first performed here. In its original state, the theatre seated 15,000. The best seats were reserved for the priests of Dionysus: you can still see the head priest's throne in the centre, carved with satyrs and adorned with lions' paws.

Filopappou Hill

Dionysiou Areopagitou & Apostolou Pavlou (www. culture.gr). Metro Akropoli or Thissio. **Map** p300 C7/ p301 D7.

One of the best places in Athens from which to view the Acropolis, this verdant 173-acre landscaped park contains a wealth of archaeological finds and is

Plaka: the old city

Sightseeing

This walk wanders through a mix of colourful central streets, into tranquil, flower-filled corners that still seem astonishingly removed from the passage of time and it won't take you more than an hour and a half. Sights range from 2,500-year-old ruins to incense-filled churches to modern-day museums. A word on the latter: this walk will take you past five of them, each a small, focused entity offering a slice of modern (ie the past 500 years) Greek culture. While only the most fervent history buffs need feel obliged to see all five, keep in mind that the excellent displays therein are often overlooked by tourists blinded to all but fallen pillars and muscular *kouroi*, to their own detriment. Remember that most museums close at around 2pm.

Start the walk at the Russian Orthodox **Church of the Holy Trinity**. It was built as a small chapel in the 11th century then, 800 years later, sold to the Russian government, which expanded it to its current size. Inside, Russian embroideries are on display and, if you're lucky, you may hear the renowned female chanters practising. Cross the street and turn right on to Kydathinaion. This is a quintessential Athenian moment: the turn takes you suddenly from a modern, traffic-filled artery on to a stone-paved walkway lined with neo-classical mansions, leading straight to the heart of the old city. Head down Kydathinaion, and on your right you'll see the Byzantine **Church of the Transfiguration of the Saviour** (Kydathinaion 10, 210 322 4633), set in a shaded garden, around which neighbourhood men gather to play backgammon. Originally built in the 11th century, the church has been rebuilt and added to many times; most of the current exterior dates from the 19th and 20th centuries. Opposite the church is the excellent **Museum of Greek Folk Art** (*see p89*), the biggest and most comprehensive of the museums on this walk. Continue down Kydathinaion to pleasant, leafy Platia Filomousou. At some point everyone visiting Athens passes through this shady *platia* lined with cafés, both old-world and modern-day.

At the bottom of the square, turn left on to Farmaki, which will take you to the **Church of St Catherine** (*see p88*), then turn right on to Lysikratous, which leads to the **Lysicrates Monument** (*see p89*). In the 17th century the monument was incorporated into a Capuchin monastery where Lord Byron stayed while writing the first canto of *Childe Harold*. The names of the branching streets reflect the celebrity guest: Vyronos (the Hellenised version of Byron) goes off to the south, while to the north Selley (Shelley) recalls Byron's Romantic buddy.

Have a gander round the souvenir shops on Adrianou and then continue on Thespidos, walking by the traditional taverna **Giouvetsakia** (*see p131*), with a history of over 50 years in Plaka. Walking straight along Thespidos will take you up to the base of the Acropolis. Turn right, following the rock to the whitewashed island-style **Church of St George of the Rock**. The church marks the entrance to Anafiotika (*see p87*), a picturesque hidden neighbourhood literally clinging to the side of the Acropolis. The steps carved into the rock at the left of the church will take you straight into Anafiotika's heart. Emerging, you'll likely find yourself on Pritaniou, near Mnisikleous, or Theorias, near Klepsydras. Head downhill on either Mnisikleous or Klepsydras, near the **Roman Forum** (*see p89*).

If you take Klepsydras, make a short detour at your second right on to Thrasyvoulou, which will lead you to the **Church of the Holy Sepulchre** (*see p88*). Go back to Mnisikleous, continuing down the stairs. Turn left on to Kyrristou, which will lead you to the square of the Forum.

If you came via Klepsydras, you can head to the east side of the square and turn right on Kyrristou, to check out the recently restored **Turkish Baths** (see p90).

Now take a wander around the **Roman Forum** and the **Tower of the Winds** (see p89). On leaving, turn right on to Diogenous; on your left is the **Museum of Greek Musical Instruments** (see p89), where you can listen to recordings of regional folk music. You could continue down Diogenous for lunch under the enormous plane tree at **O Platanos**

(Diogenous 4, 210 322 0666) before heading back to the Roman Forum on Diogenous. Turn right at Eolou, then take the first left on Adrianou. On the right, you can look into the ruins of the once-luxurious **Hadrian's Library** (see p92). Follow the library to Areos, where you'll turn right, passing multinational street vendors on your way to Monastiraki.

In an intriguing visual surprise the ancient library's next-door neighbour is a mosque, which you can go into to see the **Museum of Traditional Greek Ceramics** (see p92). From here you can hop on the metro (at Monastiraki station) to head anywhere in town.

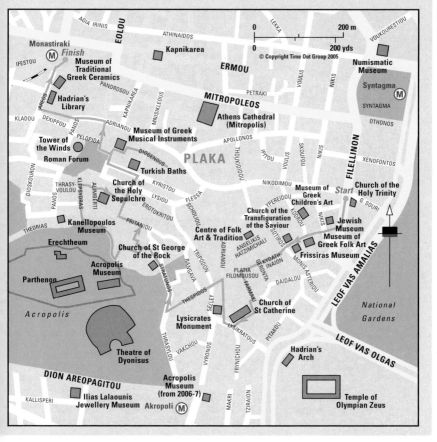

home to a wide range of indigenous flora. In antiquity, it was known as the Hill of the Muses, and poets thronged its slopes for inspiration; in wartime generals garrisoned themselves atop it because of its sweeping views out to sea; now it attracts a daily crowd of local dog-walkers and joggers, as well as weekend brigades of smooching couples, grandparents babysitting the kids, groups of picnickers, and tourists. Beautiful all year round, with its pines and cypresses and its winding walks, Filopappou really comes into its own in spring, when the bulbs blossom and the grassy slopes are covered with poppies and daffodils. After Clean Monday (the first day of Lent), though, when it is traditional for families to drive up Filopappou and fly kites, the flowers are gone – plucked to wither and die in apartments throughout the city.

Before you get started on Filopappou itself, check out the Culture Ministry's Acropolis Museum Shop in the coach park at the bottom of the hill. It's worth a quick once-round if you're looking for some fairly predictable souvenirs such as postcards, clay replicas of pots and statuettes, and reproduction jewellery, as well as more imaginative items like puzzles of the Parthenon friezes and silk scarves with ancient patterns.

There was a furore when the ministry started constructing this shop in 2002: it was part of a grand plan that included fencing off the entire hill as an archaeological site and constructing an open-air exhibition area in the old quarry. Most of the fencing was pulled down by angry residents who believed an admission charge to the hill would be the next step; the exhibition space never progressed further than a pitifully ugly slick of concrete daubed with graffiti and pierced by a number of metal posts, but the shop and its adjacent grass-roofed toilet block actually turned out less of a problem than the locals had feared.

At the foot of Filopappou is the pretty, mosaic-tiled church of **St Dimitrios Loumbardiaris**, built in 1460 (*see below*). Behind the church is the tourist pavilion (210 923 1665), a blissfully quiet, scenic little café offering sweeping views to the Acropolis. Opposite the church you will see a small cave said to be Socrates' prison, where the philosopher was held after being sentenced to death for corrupting the youth of Athens. One of these corrupted youths, Plato, wrote a version of his mentor's deathbed words in this prison in his *Phaedo*, a seminal work of Western philosophy.

Take a while to wander along the wonderfully peaceful, unevenly paved paths that wind around the hillside, shaded by trees and shrubs and provided with stone benches on which to rest and admire the panoramas across to Piraeus and the Saronic Gulf beyond: all this is the work of the little-known architect Dimitris Pikionis who, in the 1950s, landscaped the Acropolis and Filopappou area, linking the sites with characteristic pathways that use irregularly shaped stones and hundreds of indigenous shrubs and flowers.

At the peak of the hill is the AD 116 **Tomb of Filopappus**, a Roman senator who loved Athens so much he was made an honorary citizen. This is the spot to take that postcard-perfect shot of the Acropolis – and to look all the way out over the city to the sea. On the way down the hill is Athens' **National Observatory**, Greece's oldest functioning research centre, housed in a beautiful neo-classical mansion. Further down the hill is a grassy, idyllic spot with some piles of stones and a few foundations. This is all that's left of the **Pnyx**, which could be considered the exact birthplace of democracy: when Athens converted from the rule of one governor to rule by the people, in 594 BC, the Athenians built a 5,000-seat amphitheatre here, which was where the first voting by, of and for the people, for their own leadership, took place. Now, between April and October, the Pnyx is the scene of nightly sound and light shows, complete with coloured spotlights and a melodramatic voiceover recounting the glorious history of Greece.

On the west side of the hill, cut into the green slopes, is the **Dora Stratou Dance Theatre** (*see p235*), which hosts performances of Greek folk dancing.

Church of St Dimitrios Loumbardiaris

Filopappou Hill, off Dionysiou Areopagitou. Metro Akropoli. **Open** during services. **Admission** free. **Map** p301 D6.

This church's scenic location and handsome interior mean it is highly popular for weddings and christenings – in summer the horn-blaring cavalcades on their way to and from the church don't cease all evening. The peculiar name, 'St Dimitris the Bombardier', is said to have been given because, in 1656, an Ottoman commander planned to attack the church with cannon fire on the feast day of St Dimitrios, but the saint intervened, striking the garrison with a bolt of lightning to foil the attack.

Plaka

Maps p297 & p301

Starting at the base of the rock of the Acropolis, Plaka is the city's most tourist-heavy area – a maze of narrow, cobblestoned medieval streets that twist through ancient sites, packed *platias* and lovely Byzantine courtyards. It's hard to imagine that not so long ago it was a hive of brothels and seedy nightclubs. In the 1980s the Ministry of Culture, then under the redoubtable rule of *Never on Sunday* actress and Parthenon Marbles campaigner Melina Mercouri, set in motion a tide of change by buying up all the uninhabited neo-classical buildings (and some inhabited ones) to renovate them and turn them into ministry offices and museums (like the **Frissiras Museum** and the **Museum of Greek Children's Art**, for both, *see p89*). Meanwhile, those seeking late-night licences

Odeon of Herodes Atticus – great acoustics, even better view. *See p83*.

for after-hours joints found their applications refused. Gradually, the residents crept back, mansions were restored and dozens of more salubrious (if often overpriced) tavernas, restaurants and cafés opened up.

Plaka's tourist shop-packed main street, Adrianou, has perhaps managed to maintain something of the tackiness of yesteryear. Named after the Emperor Hadrian, the street winds up to the library he built in AD 132.

The most beautiful section of Plaka is the tiny village of **Anafiotika** (*see below*), a cluster of houses at the very base of the Acropolis.

Anafiotika

Bounded by Stratonos, Pritaniou & Alimberti streets. Metro Akropoli. **Map** p301 E6.
This tiny district hidden under the Acropolis crag is one of the most quirky and charming spots in all of Athens. Just a stone's throw from the bustling modern centre of the city, in the very heart of Attica, the wanderer comes across a perfectly reconstructed version of a Cycladic town, erected in the 19th century by stonemasons brought from the island of Anafi to build the king's palace in the new Greek capital. They missed home so much that they recreated a pocket of it, complete with sugar-cube houses, blazing banks of bougainvillea and winding stone passages. It's easy to get lost in this maze of alleyways, and wind up in someone's minuscule front room, all scattered flokati rugs, icons and yawning cats. Go quietly here: although some of it may look run-down it's still very much occupied, in many cases by descendants of the original Anafiotes.

Athens Cathedral

Platia Mitropoleos (210 322 1308). Metro Monastiraki. **Open** *Oct-May* 6.30am-7pm daily. *June-Sept* 6.30am-8pm daily. **Admission** free. **Map** p301 E5/F5.
The large, lavishly appointed Athens Cathedral, known as Mitropolis, is one of Athens' best-known landmarks. It is the seat of the Greek Orthodox archbishop (one of the nation's most influential – and controversial – figures) and is regularly packed when thousands of Greek grandmothers turn out to kiss touring holy relics, or when Athens' high society floods in for weddings, baptisms or funerals. One of the best times of the year to appreciate the cathedral is during the elaborate Easter celebrations: most of central Athens gathers here, shoehorned inside or spilling out on to the marble forecourt, to light candles and say '*Christos anesti*' ('Christ is risen'), '*Alithos anesti*' ('Truly he is risen') to each other at midnight on Easter Saturday. Though the icons and ecclesiastical objects are impressive, the building's architecture is fairly standard. Of far greater artistic importance is the tiny Panagia Gorgoepikoos (also known as Mikri Mitropolis, or Little Cathedral) next door. It was built in the 12th century, on the ruins of an ancient temple devoted to the goddess of childbirth, Eileithyia. What makes it unique are its building materials: the walls are made entirely of Roman and Byzantine marble relics, sculpted with reliefs depicting the ancient calendar of feasts.

Centre of Folk Art & Tradition

Angelikis Hadzimichalis 6 (210 324 3972). Metro Akropoli. **Open** 9am-1pm, 5-9pm Tue-Fri; 9am-1pm Sat, Sun. **Admission** free. **Map** p301 F6.

You are here

Don't know where you've been, where you are or where you're going? In Athens, these are not only philosophical considerations, but practical ones too. If you're lost, you'd be advised to do what Athenians do: ask directions rather than try to figure it out with the aid of a map.

Good maps are as hard to come by in Athens as beefsteaks are in Delhi. Athenian taxi drivers – who don't know Athens streets any better than the average resident – rarely have maps in their cabs. If they do have one, it is inevitably falling apart (from age, not overuse). If you suggest using it, expect to be outright refused, eyed derisively, and perhaps asked if you are Swiss.

Part of Greeks' apparent aversion to maps is really just unfamiliarity. Modern maps of the city are still based on a quarter-century-old template commissioned by the Greek army (and updated since). Before that, a comprehensive map of Athens didn't exist – which might go a long way to explaining why most Greeks over 50 are not in the habit of using them.

The powers that be have taken some dramatic stabs at remedying the dire map situation, but most have failed. An attempt at producing a comprehensive public transport map three years ago looked as if it might be a success. But once posted at city centre bus shelters the maps were rendered useless by condensation – and remain so today. A few bus stops in the suburbs have weatherproofed, well-framed maps of the immediate neighbourhood, but inexplicably don't indicate any bus routes at all. A publishing consortium promised state-of-the-art aerial satellite-image maps by the 2004 Olympics, but the company went bust before the project even began. The transport maps published for the Olympics looked downright cartoonish.

Finding a good map is only half the battle. You still have to deal with the fact that the street signs in Athens are often missing, and the numbers on the buildings are absent even more often.

It can be argued that the Greek uneasiness with maps is a reflection of a more general dislike of overexactitude. This characteristic has its benefits: you won't need one- or two-cent coins in this country, as all prices are rounded to the nearest ten cents and cashiers will always forgive a customer who can't scrounge up the last few cents for any purchase over two euros. You won't find taverna glasses with parsimonious measurement lines as in booze-measuring-obsessed Britain. Until a few years ago, the national telephone company refused to provide itemised telephone bills. You'll have to search long and hard for a public clock and, metro aside, you'll be hard-pressed to find one that tells the right time. So now, not only do you not know where you are, but you also don't know what time it is. Welcome to Athens.

The rooms in the mansion of folklorist Angeliki Hadzimichali have been set up to depict the traditional Greek way of life, with housewares, ceramics and kitchen utensils from the 19th century. Museum exhibits include embroideries and family portraits.

Church of the Holy Sepulchre

Thrasyvoulou (210 325 0322). Metro Syntagma/Monastiraki. **Open** by appointment. **Admission** free. **Map** p297 E5/p301 E5.

According to legend, this lovely church was built in the eighth century by Byzantine empress Irene, an Athenian orphan. During the Turkish occupation, the church's well was a hiding place for dissidents. The pretty, shady courtyard is filled with ancient bits of marble, and is a tranquil place to sit and rest.

Church of the Holy Trinity

Filellinon 21 (210 323 1090). Metro Syntagma. **Open** Sun mornings & during choir rehearsals. **Admission** free. **Map** p297 F5.

Built in the 11th century, this church had some of its outer walls pulled down by the brutal Turk Ali Haseki in 1780, to help build fortifying walls around Athens. In later years, the chapel (also known as Agios Nikodimos) was sold to the Russian Orthodox Church, and in 1852 Tsar Alexander II had it restored with a new terracotta frieze and bell tower. Today, it is still the stronghold of Russian Orthodoxy in Greece, and contains displays of ornate Russian embroidery. The church is famed for its chanters: stop by during the Sunday services to listen to them.

Church of St Catherine

Herephontos 14 & Lysikratous (210 322 8974). Metro Akropoli. **Open** *May-Oct* 8am-noon, 5-7pm daily. *Nov-Apr* 8am-noon, 4-6pm daily. **Admission** free. **Map** p301 F6.

This 11th-century church is built over the ruins of what some say is an ancient temple, while others believe it to be a sixth-century paleochristian church;

some of the columns still stand in the courtyard. Although the main body of the church, beautifully decorated with well-restored frescoes, is Byzantine, the two outer chapels were added in the first half of the 20th century. The church choir is reputed to be one of the best in the city.

Frissiras Museum

Monis Asteropi 3 & 7 (210 323 4678/www.frissiras museum.com). Metro Syntagma/Akropoli. **Open** 11am-7pm Wed, Thur; 11am-5pm Fri-Sun. **Guided tours** 12.30pm Sat, Sun. **Admission** €6; €3 concessions. **No credit cards. Map** p301 F6.

A stylish recent addition to Athens' cluster of small museums and galleries, this collection of contemporary European paintings is fresh and varied. Past exhibitions have included works by Francis Bacon and Lucian Freud, among many other illustrious names. The rotating display is housed in two beautifully restored neo-classical houses. In the four years since it opened, the Frissiras has already earned a reputation for spotting top new Greek and international talent.

Jewish Museum

Nikis 39 (210 322 5582/www.jewishmuseum.gr). Metro Syntagma. **Open** 9am-2.30pm Mon-Fri; 10am-2pm Sun. **Admission** €5; €3 concessions. **No credit cards. Map** p301 F6.

Archaeological digs have unearthed a synagogue in the Ancient Agora, evidence of the existence of a Jewish community in Athens as far back as the fifth century BC. Some 87 per cent of the Jewish population of Greece was killed during the Holocaust, one of the highest percentages in Europe. This well-run museum has excellent displays documenting the history of the country's Jewish community, including engravings, historical and religious artefacts, intricate carvings and works of art, and written records dating back 2,300 years.

Kanellopoulos Museum

Panos 12 & Theorias (210 321 2313/www. culture.gr). Metro Monastiraki. **Open** phone to check. **Admission** ring to check. **Map** p301 E6.

Closed for restoration and extension since December 2004, this museum is expected to reopen in July 2005. It has a fine collection of Greek art from the third century BC right up to the 19th century; some of the most important exhibits include icons from the 14th to 17th centuries, a selection of Byzantine jewellery, vases and jugs dating to the eighth century BC and a second-century marble head of Alexander the Great.

Lysicrates Monument

Platia Lysikratou (www.culture.gr). Metro Akropoli. **Map** p301 F6.

Each year, winners of the Dionysian drama festival (who included Aristophanes, Sophocles and Euripides) were awarded a decorative tripod – the ancient equivalent of an Oscar. In 335 BC Lysicrates, the producer of the winning play, built this marble public display for his prize – ostentatious, perhaps, but unbeatable PR. Six Corinthian columns are arranged around a circular base, carved with Dionysian emblems. In the 17th century the monument was incorporated into a Capuchin monastery, the foundations of which could be seen until recently in a pleasantly overgrown green space around the monument. However, in summer 2003 the whole area was paved over with gravel, an aesthetically unfortunate move that caused the area to be dubbed a 'giant litterbox'.

Museum of Greek Children's Art

Kodrou 9 (210 331 2621/www.childrensart museum.gr). Metro Syntagma. **Open** 10am-2pm Tue-Sat; 11am-2pm Sun. Closed Aug. **Admission** €2; free under-18s. **No credit cards. Map** p301 F6.

Remember the scene in *Six Degrees of Separation* when the art dealer played by Donald Sutherland walks into a classroom hung with children's paintings and is struck by how the five-year-olds paint like Matisse? That's how it feels when you enter this sunny exhibition space, one of only two museums of its kind in the world. Children's pictures are displayed with the same dignity given to the work of great artists: the result is vivid, colourful, thought-provoking and surprising. The museum offers daily workshops and programmes for children.

Museum of Greek Folk Art

Kydathinaion 17 (210 322 9031/www.culture.gr). Metro Syntagma. **Open** 10am-2pm Tue-Sun. **Admission** €2. **No credit cards. Map** p301 F6.

The dimly lit, government-run building won't win any prizes, but inside are five floors packed with rich, beautiful folk art, including filigree jewellery, fine embroideries worked with gold and silver, Greek shadow puppets and highly skilled carvings in stone and wood. Don't miss the room of wall paintings by naif painter Theophilos Hadzimichali, transported intact from his home on the island of Lesbos. Limited information in English.

Museum of Greek Musical Instruments

Diogenous 1-3 (210 325 0198/www.culture.gr). Metro Monastiraki. **Open** 10am-2pm Tue, Thur-Sun; noon-6pm Wed. **Admission** free. **Map** p301 F6.

There's a lot more to Greek music than the bouzouki that plucked out the theme to *Zorba the Greek*. The displays in this unassuming but fascinating little museum trace how Asian, Middle Eastern and European influences filtered through the Hellenic sensibility to create instruments such as Byzantine lutes, the sitar-like *santouri* and the *gaida* (a Balkan take on the bagpipes). The instruments themselves are beautiful, intricately carved with precious metals, ivory and tortoiseshell; the displays are accompanied by headphones playing recordings.

Roman Forum & Tower of the Winds

Eolou & Pelopida (210 324 5220/www.culture.gr). Metro Monastiraki. **Open** 8am-7.30pm daily. **Admission** €2; €1 concessions; free to holders of €12 Acropolis ticket. **No credit cards. Map** p297/p301 E5.

Sightseeing

One of Athens' most interestingly layered sites. Its earliest and most striking feature is the marvellous eight-sided Tower of the Winds, built in 50 BC by Syrian astronomer Andronikos Kyrrhestas. The combination sundial, weathervane and water clock was unlike any other building in the ancient world.

A century later, the Romans shifted Athens' central marketplace from the sprawling Ancient Agora (*see p91*), creating a smaller, more orderly one around the tower. The Ottomans made their mark by building a mosque on the same site. In the 20th century archaeologists used the Forum as a repository for unclassifiable smaller finds from all over Attica, which explains the presence of the odd Byzantine grave marker or garlanded sarcophagus.

Turkish Baths

Kyrristou 8 (210 324 4340). Metro Monastiraki. **Open** 9am-2.30pm Mon, Wed, Thur-Sun. **Admission** free. **Map** p297/p301 E5.

Under Ottoman rule, every Athenian neighbourhood had one of these public baths, used not only for steams and scrubs, but also as essential meeting places. After Greece won independence, all Turkish baths (or hammams) in the city were destroyed except this one, which has been recently renovated and reopened to the public. You can't actually bathe, but you can walk around the rooms and picture the languor of a lost era. Imagine being massaged on the marble slabs, dappled with pinpricks of light from the pattern cut in the high domes, with scantily clad attendants fetching tea and scented oils.

Koukaki & Makrygianni

Maps p300 & p301

The area directly to the south of the Acropolis, Makrygianni, has changed irrevocably in the last five years. The pedestrianisation of the area's main boulevard, Dionysiou Areopagitou, has unquestionably been a success, but it has pushed a lot of traffic on to the surrounding residential streets, forming a daily gridlock of tourist coaches blocked by the parked cars of strollers on the pedestrian way. Just off Dionysiou Areopagitou, the **Ilias Lalaounis Jewellery Museum** (*see below*) is a showcase for this jeweller's craft.

On a far grander – national – scale, the construction of the new Acropolis Museum (*see p82*) drastically changed the face of the neighbourhood in 2003-4 as Makrygianni home-owners were forced out and their houses demolished to create space for the gigantic site.

Makrygianni is named after the Greek War of Independence hero General Yiannis Makrygiannis (the name translates as 'John Long-John'), of whom a large bronze statue stands at the corner of Dionysiou Areopagitou and Vyronos. Vandals regularly snap off the imposing general's sword, and his macho military image is often compromised further by a bouquet of freshly picked flowers gathered and put into his hands by locals.

South of residential Makrygianni is the lively district of Koukaki. Cheaper, more working class than its neighbour, Koukaki is full of cars, souvlaki joints and mom-and-pop shops trying desperately to compete against the inexorable surge of international chains that have already killed off a number of the area's hardware shops, grocers and corner stores.

Ilias Lalaounis Jewellery Museum

Karyaditon & Kallisperi 12, Makrygianni (210 922 1044/www.addgr.com/jewel/lalaouni). Metro Akropoli. **Open** 9am-4pm Mon, Thur-Sat; 9am-9pm Wed; 11am-4pm Sun. **Admission** €3; €2.30 concessions. Free to all 3-9pm Wed, 9-11am Sat. **No credit cards** (AmEx, MC, V accepted in gift shop). **Map** p301 E7.

Located on a leafy residential street running parallel to Dionysiou Areopagitou, this museum displays the works of Ilias Lalaounis, the world-famous, Greek-born jewellery designer who has haughty boutiques in New York, Paris and London. Admire decades of Lalaounis's work, ranging from reproductions of antiquities to minimalist, modern, molecule-inspired pieces, then visit the shop for some precious souvenirs.

Monastiraki

Maps p297 & p301

Monastiraki Square lies at the heart of Athens' modern marketplace. It is given over to commerce, with overloaded carts of bananas and pineapples, peddlers hawking mobile phones of dubious origin, stalls of cheap and cheerful knick-knacks and trays of nuts and seeds. From this central hub, the spokes leading out in every direction are filled with a varied assortment of shops, each street with its own characteristic selection. Heading down towards Thisio is Ifestou: a loud, brash alley of cut-price jeans, slogan T-shirts and knock-off trainers, interspersed with traditional holes in the wall selling backgammon sets and copper coffee containers. Branching off from Ifestou are the antique streets – sleepy, sunny passages of tarnished silver, curling posters and old furniture. This area comes alive every Sunday with the renowned **flea market** (*see p92*), a bazaar that has flourished since Ottoman times, centring on Platia Avyssinias and Ifestou.

Leading up from Monastiraki Square towards Athens Cathedral, Pandrossou is a bustling, claustrophobic lane with shops stocked mainly with items designed to tempt tourists – Grecian sandals, worry beads, replica vases, jewellery and even a Panathinaikos Football Club souvenir shop. Meanwhile, to the north of the square are Athinas and Ermou, two of Athens' busiest commercial thoroughfares. Athinas used to be the shoe street, but now it sells a diverse mix of gardening equipment, copper tins and trays, T-shirts, fabrics and, as the street creeps closer to the Central Meat Market and Omonia Square, olives, spices, nuts and crates of frightened rabbits and chickens waiting to be slaughtered, as well as glass containers of puppies and kittens to tempt impulse buyers. The Syntagma end of Ermou is all classy shoe shops and high-street clothing stores; by the time it reaches Monastiraki it features mostly fast-food eateries. On towards Thisio it used to be full of small supplies stores for the nearby workshops, but it is gradually being upgraded since the pedestrianisation of its lowest end, and now boasts a trendy hairdresser, designer coffee shop and a costly restaurant.

As always in Athens, though, just beyond the new lies the ancient, and Monastiraki Square provides one of the best vantage points to the layers of history that shaped the city. The square itself takes its name ('little monastery') from the tiny tenth-century church that stands in the square, alongside the shiny new metro station. The church was destroyed and then rebuilt in 1678 as part of a large convent whose buildings, over the following 200 years, spread all around the surrounding areas, up to what is now the Central Meat Market. Most of the buildings were destroyed during the late 19th century during archaeological excavations and railway construction. The little church is all that remains. Just behind the church is an 18th-century mosque, one of the most distinctive reminders of the Ottoman occupation (today the mosque is the **Museum of Traditional Greek Ceramics**, *see p92*). Nearby **Hadrian's Library** is a monument to the city's Roman past. The classical temples of the Acropolis, rising above, give perspective to it all. And only a stone's throw from the square lie the ruins of Athens' **Ancient Agora**, one of the most important sites in the classical world.

Ancient Agora

Entrances on Adrianou & on the descent from the Acropolis (210 321 0185/www.culture.gr). Metro Monastiraki/Thissio. **Open** *May-Oct* 8am-7pm daily. *Nov-Apr* 8am-5pm daily. Museum closes 30mins before site. **Admission** €4; €2 concessions; free to holders of €12 Acropolis ticket. **No credit cards**. **Map** p301 D5.

If you find the sprawling site confusing to navigate, that's partly because the market, founded in the sixth century BC, was the city centre for 1,200 years, witnessing the construction and destruction of overlapping stoas (colonnades fronting the market), temples and government buildings. But it's mainly because the market was far more than a place to shop: it was the centre of all public life, including arts, politics, commerce and religion. A typical Athenian, for whom participation in public life was as essential as breathing, would spend all day here, listening to the likes of Socrates, Demosthenes or St Paul holding forth among the oil and spice stalls, checking in at the circular *tholos*, where a council of

Church of St Marina. *See p92*.

50 administrators was available 24 hours a day, and lighting a candle at the shrine to Hephaestus, which overlooked the whole scene. The latter is still the best-preserved classical-era temple in Greece – get up close and look at the friezes, which depict the adventures of Theseus and Heracles. The restored Stoa of Attalos, which functioned rather like an ancient shopping mall, today houses the excellent Agora Museum, focusing on artefacts connected to the incipient democracy.

Hadrian's Library

Dexippou & Areos, (www.culture.gr). Metro Monastiraki. **Map** p301 E5.

The Roman Emperor Hadrian built this luxurious library in AD 132. Most of the space was a marble courtyard with gardens and a pool, but there were also lecture rooms, music rooms, a theatre and a small place for storing scrolls. Though the site is closed to the public, you can easily see the remaining Corinthian columns from the street.

Monastiraki Flea Market

Monastiraki (no phone). Metro Monastiraki. **Open** 8.30am-3pm Sun. **Map** p297 D5.

Platia Avyssinias comes to life on Sunday mornings when Athens' best flea market fills the space and spills out on to the streets around it. Here's where you'll find everything you didn't know you needed: pink cut-glass Turkish liquor sets, 100-year-old telephones, antique carved-wood desks, gold-framed maps of the Balkans and a whole set of Russian nesting dolls. Bring your haggling skills. For a guided walk around the area, *see p172* **Sunday morning in Monastiraki.**

Museum of Traditional Greek Ceramics

Areos 1 (210 324 2066/www.culture.gr). Metro Monastiraki. **Open** *Sept-June* 9am-2.30pm Mon, Wed-Sun. *July, Aug* hours vary. **Admission** €2. **No credit cards. Map** p301 E5.

Built in 1789 by the city's Turkish governor, this is the only Ottoman-era mosque in Athens still open to the public. After Greek independence, Athenians stripped the mosque of its minaret and turned it into a military barracks and then a jail. In 1918 it was turned into a government-run museum of ceramic art, against the wishes of many Greeks who would have preferred to see all remnants of the hated occupiers destroyed. The collection here is small and limited mostly to pieces from the second half of the 20th century – though many are beautiful, the main appeal of the museum is just being inside Athens' only mosque, in the heart of what was once the old Turkish bazaar.

Thisio

Maps p296 & p300

Until recently, Thisio was just a rather grubby, low-rent neighbourhood – albeit with fantastic views of the Acropolis – at the far western end of Ermou. But with the advent of the pretty, paved walkway linking up the area with the rest of ancient Athens' major sites, it has been transformed. Old buildings have been renovated into cultural spaces (such as the **Melina Mercouri Cultural Centre**) and Thisio has been inundated with cutting-edge galleries, buzzing cafés, restaurants and bars. The places to see and be seen are mainly around the newly landscaped metro station, where all the bright young things hang out waiting for their dates, on bustling Iraklidon (named after Heracles, Theseus' companion), and quiet, tree-lined Eptachalkou, home to a number of galleries, homely ouzeries and a couple of small churches.

The area is also home to one of the city's most popular churches, **St Marina**, on the edge of Filopappou Hill.

Thisio takes its name from the best-preserved classical-era temple in Greece. Although the shrine, in the Ancient Agora, was built to the blacksmith god Hephaestus and is formally known as the **Hephaestum** (*see p36*), among its most notable features are the reliefs of Athenian hero and king Theseus carved on its metopes. It informally became known as the Theseion (Temple of Theseus), subsequently lending its name to the surrounding neighbourhood.

Church of St Marina

North-east edge of Filopappou Hill (210 346 3783). Metro Thissio. **Open** *Apr-Sept* 7.30am-noon, 5-7.30pm daily. *Oct-Mar* 7.30am-noon, 5-6.30pm daily. **Admission** free. **Map** p301 D7.

This cheerful church honours the protectress of pregnant mothers and infants. St Marina's many domes are higher and narrower than those of most Orthodox churches, giving it a sprightly, buoyant feel, definitely enhanced by the red-and-white peppermint striped façade. This is one of the most popular churches in Athens, hosting a week-long festival to the saint every July.

Melina Mercouri Cultural Centre

Iraklidon 66 & Thessalonikis (210 345 2150). Metro Thissio. **Open** 9am-1pm, 5-9pm Tue-Sat; 9am-1pm Sun. **Admission** free. **Map** p300 D7.

This former hat factory has undergone an industrial-to-arts-space transformation, keeping the original stone walls and airy spaces in a clever conversion that has rendered it a fresh, modern venue for temporary art exhibitions. There is one permanent display: a nostalgic re-creation of a 19th-century Athenian street, complete with meticulously put-together shop windows of authentic paraphernalia like cigarette cards, food tins, elaborate hats and tin toys; a pharmacy where the chemist weighs out drugs on antique scales; and, of course, a *kafenio* with wrought-iron chairs, little cups on marble tables and overflowing ashtrays.

The Historic Centre

The commercial and political heart of modern-day Athens.

Neo-Classical University Complex.
See p95.

The Historic Triangle

Maps p297 & p299

The heart of modern Athens – the area between
a triangle of boulevards formed by Akadimias,
Mitropoleos and Athinas – is a complicated
juxtaposition of glorious neo-classical
buildings, hastily thrown-up post-war blocks,
tiny Byzantine churches and the occasional
ancient ruin. Just 170-odd years ago, though,
when Greece had wrested its independence from
the Ottoman Empire and was looking for a
capital, that area was hardly built on and the
whole city was little more than a country town,
devastated by years of war and occupation.

Up until Ottoman times the commercial and
cultural centre of the city was based in the
area around the Acropolis and Ancient Agora.
Visitors in the early 1800s described Athens as
a city in ruins, a desolate, deserted place whose

houses were roofless and whose once-proud
churches were now reduced to piles of rubble.
Dust paths connected the houses that lay
scattered on the lower slopes of the Acropolis
and its surrounding plain, and the population
barely surpassed 6,000.

But its resonance with Greece's ancient
glories – embodied by the magnificent
Acropolis rising from the ruins – made it

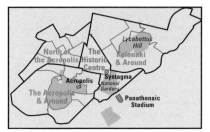

the choice for the independent country's new capital, and Greece's first statesmen set about constructing a 19th-century neo-classical city worthy of the country's glorious past. A new king, Otto, was imported from Bavaria to introduce a monarchy to the fledgling state. Numerous ideas for his residence were submitted – including, incredibly, a blueprint for transforming the Parthenon and its surrounding buildings into a palatial complex – until eventually a plan for a building on Syntagma Square was settled upon. The handsome yet somewhat austere Royal Palace was constructed in 1836, now redesignated as Greece's **Parliament Building** (*see p98*).

The authorities invited Stamatios Kleanthis and Edouard Schaubert, a Greek and a German, to submit a plan for a brand new city. Working on the assumption that once Athens became capital the population would mushroom, Kleanthis and Schaubert designed a city for 40,000 inhabitants – a modern European capital of wide boulevards, courtyards, botanical gardens, a public library, ministries and a cathedral – on the plain to the north of the Acropolis, an area that offered the benefits of open space, clean air, easy access and the possibilities for drainage and sewage. Their grid plan showed a marked rejection of the higgledy piggledy Ottoman style of building. Kleanthis and Schaubert were determined to preserve Athens' ancient heritage while getting rid of non-classical (Turkish and Byzantine) elements. Their plans were eventually modified by the architect Leo von Klenze, who favoured a more human-scale city. For more on the birth of neo-classical Athens, *see p38*.

The city shot up almost overnight, with stonemasons brought in from the Cycladic islands and noted foreign architects arriving to make their individual mark. The German Friedrich von Gartner was responsible for building the Royal Palace and planning the gardens behind; Hans Christian and Theophilus Hansen, two Danish brothers, between them built some of the city's most outstanding public buildings, including the complex of the **Academy of Arts**, **National Library** and **National University** on **Panepistimiou** (for all, *see p95*), the Mint on Klafthmonos Square (demolished in 1939) and the **Grande Bretagne Hotel** on Syntagma Square (*see p58*). But Ernst Ziller, a pupil of Theophilus Hansen, had perhaps the greatest impact on the face of the new city. The German, who in 1868 settled permanently in Athens, built neo-classical masterpieces such as the **National Theatre** (*see p233*), the building that is now the **Presidential Palace** (*see p101*), a number of central hotels, the **Stathatos Mansion** on

Vassilisis Sophias (now part of the Goulandris Museum of Cycladic Art, *see p105*), and was responsible for restoring the ancient Panathenaic Stadium for the 1896 Olympics.

With such a glittering roster of talents involved in its creation, it is hardly surprising that Athens was once considered home to some of the finest neo-classical architecture in Europe. City planners had a chance to work on an almost blank canvas, with the classical jewel of the Acropolis in the background as inspiration for handsome, colonnaded public buildings and intricately sculpted mansions. Sadly, their architectural pearl would not survive intact.

By the 1920s, with the sudden influx of more than a million refugees from Asia Minor, the city had expanded and exploded – some 12,000 hastily built homes were put up in 1922, and in the post-World War II years, as more and more Greeks flocked to the city from outlying regions, spacious, gardened neo-classical villas were brutally hacked down to make room for faceless modern blocks. And the destruction continues. While antiquities are revered, anything built in the last two centuries is still regarded as fair game by rapacious property developers. A pre-Olympics facelift by the Athens municipality restored the façades of some 1,000 old buildings in the city centre and along the so-called Olympic routes, but most pre-war houses are still seen as nothing more than real estate waiting to be developed.

The best place to start your neo-classical Athens experience is on **Platia Klafthmonos**, a famous gathering point for politicians who would come here to commiserate on electoral defeats. The **City of Athens Museum** here has a fascinating scale model of the city in 1842, showing the handsome, orderly city in its early days as the Greek capital. A walk down Stadiou will bring you to Greece's first modern Parliament building, today the **National Historical Museum** (*see p95*). Then head up to Panepistimiou, home to the **Neo-Classical University Complex** (*see p95*) and what is now the **Numismatic Museum** (*see p98*). The latter was originally Heinrich Schliemann's house, designed by Ziller. On nearby Akadimias, the **Cultural Centre of Athens** houses a fascinating and comprehensive collection of theatrical mementos.

The 19th century also saw the commercial needs of the city addressed. In 1870 the **Central Market** (*see p96*) was built on Athinas and since then has remained the capital's most vital and vibrant marketplace. Throughout the 19th and 20th centuries the historic triangle filled with shops and restaurants, old-time *rembetakika*, modern banks, shops and traffic of every kind.

But this area is no bastion of crisp modernity by any stretch of the imagination. As with all of Athens, there are still many, many layers: dotted throughout the centre are some of the city's oldest, smallest and most fascinating Byzantine churches, including the **Church of the Saints Theodore** (*see below*) and **Kapnikarea** (*see below*). Almost all are still in use. Ancient Athens makes an appearance too, whether in the remains of the Themistoclean Wall (sometimes surprisingly well preserved, like the section in the foundations of the National Bank of Greece, on Eolou), or in the little sixth-century **Church of St John of the Column** (*see below*), which is actually built around an ancient Corinthian pillar.

Church of the Saints Theodore

Aristidou & Evripidou (no phone/www.culture.gr). Metro Panepistimio. **Open** generally mid morning-mid evening daily. **Admission** free. **Map** p297 E4.
This tiny 11th-century church is one of Athens' oldest remaining Byzantine monuments. Many of the frescoes have been damaged by smoke and age, but towards the front and right there's a nice fresco of saints Jacob, Thomas and Simon, with beautiful floral detailing beneath.

Church of St John of the Column

Evripidou 72 (no phone). Metro Omonia. **Open** generally mid morning-early evening daily. **Admission** free. **Map** p297 E4.
Locally known as Agios Ioannis Kolonastis, this quirky little church is located at the intersection of Omonia's migrant community, Evripidou's spice market and Psyrri's gritty old workshops and edgy new nightlife. This tiny chapel, dating from about the sixth century, was built around an ancient Corinthian column which protrudes incongruously from the roof.

City of Athens Museum

Paparigopoulou 5-7, Platia Klafthmonos (210 324 6164). Metro Panepistimio. **Open** 10.30am-6pm Mon, Tue, Thur-Sun; noon-8pm Wed. **Admission** €5; €3 concessions. **No credit cards. Map** p297 F4.
Otto, Greece's first king – a teenager brought over from Bavaria – lived here while waiting for construction of his first palace (now the Parliament Building) to finish. Most of the museum consists of re-creations of the rooms as they were when the king and his bride Amalia lived in them, including a throne room. There's a lot of pink and gilt rococo – perhaps to remind them of home. Don't miss the collection of paintings of Athens from the early 19th century, when it was little more than a village, and the absorbing model of the town as it was in 1842.

Cultural Centre of Athens

Akadimias 50 (210 362 1601/210 362 9430/ www.culture.gr). Metro Panepistimio. **Open** *Theatre Museum* Sept-June 9am-2pm Mon-Fri. July, Aug 9am-1pm Mon-Fri. **Admission** free. **Map** p297 F3.

The pretty Cultural Centre is fronted by several statues of Greek notables, but everyone only looks at one sculpture: the woman whose robe seems to magically evaporate around her gravity-defying breasts is the famous Greek actress Kiveli, second wife of the former prime minister, George Papandreou. Inside the centre, there's a Theatre Museum with exhibits on the ancient Greek stage and lots of memorabilia from the likes of Melina Mercouri and Maria Callas, and a gallery that shows new works by Greek artists. At the back, you can join Athens' students and intellectuals at its popular café.

Kapnikarea

Kapnikarea & Ermou (210 322 4462). Metro Monastiraki or Syntagma. **Open** 8am-1pm Mon, Wed, Sat; 8am-1pm, 4.30-7.30pm Tue, Thur, Fri; 8-11am Sun. **Admission** free. **Map** p297 E5.
The beautiful 11th-century church of Kapnikarea appears suddenly and felicitously, smack in the middle of the bustling shopping strip of Ermou. The church, dedicated to the Blessed Virgin Mary, was built over the ruins of an ancient temple dedicated to a goddess, possibly Athena or Demeter. It is laid out in the typical Byzantine cross-in-square plan, with three apses on the east side and a narthex on the west. Inside, it is decorated with a mix of medieval mosaics and paintings by renowned 20th-century Greek artist Photis Contoglou.

National Historical Museum

Stadiou 13, Platia Kolokotroni (210 323 7617/ www.culture.gr). Metro Panepistimio or Syntagma. **Open** 9am-2pm Tue-Sun. **Admission** €3; €1.50 concessions; free under-18s. Free to all Sun. **No credit cards. Map** p297 F4.
The heroes of Greece's War of Independence were essentially bandits who lived in a network of mountain hideouts during their rebellion. That doesn't seem to have precluded a taste for luxury, however: their paraphernalia, displayed here, includes lavishly engraved weapons and embroidered outfits galore. There are also paintings and engravings of key battles, personal items of war hero Lord Byron, and the embalmed heart of war hero and Greek president Konstantine Kanaris. The building itself was Greece's first Parliament, whose chamber is still preserved intact. The plumed bronze statue out front is Theodoros Kolokotronis, a lowly mountain bandit who became the war's greatest general. Even today, you may see floral wreaths left at the statue's base.

Neo-Classical University Complex

Panepistimiou, between Ippokratous & Sina (University 210 361 4301/Academy 210 360 0209/ Library 210 338 2541/www.culture.gr). Metro Panepistimio. **Open** *Library* Sept-June 9am-8pm Mon-Thur; 9am-2pm Fri, Sat. Closed Aug. *Academy & University* closed to the public. **Admission** free. **Map** p297 F4.
Though the formal name of this street is Eleftherios Venizelos, it's known to everyone – and even written on maps – as Panepistimiou ('University') thanks to these buildings, which are among the most

The Central Market

Every Athenian neighbourhood has its weekly *laiki agora* or street market, where locals jostle for the freshest fruit, vegetables, herbs and oversized underpants. The boisterous *laiki* is a blaze of colour that changes with the seasons – from the Day-Glo tang of clementines in December to oozing purple figs in August. Each market is also a reflection of its locale.

In the chi-chi district of Kolonaki, well-heeled ladies elbow each other over the rocket and coriander at the Friday market on Xenokratous Street, while in bohemian Exarchia's Kallidromiou Street, students haggle over African statuettes and bunches of chrysanthemums.

A permanent version of the *laiki* is the Central Market on Athinas Street, where pungent whiffs of pork sausage, salt cod, caged canary and pickled garlic hit you in quick succession. Spruced up for the 2004 Athens Olympics, the fruit and vegetable market on Varvakeio Square now has paved walkways and a café. Dipping into a barrel of olives or snaffling a handful of pistachios is perfectly acceptable, although unlike other markets, traders here won't let you choose your own produce. Consequently, though prices are dirt cheap, you might find your purchases are less than perfect when you get them home.

The covered fish and meat markets, which date back to 1870, are not for the squeamish. In the fish market, sunlight filters through the glass ceiling and glitters off fish scales of every hue, while shiny octopus and purple squid wallow on mounds of crushed ice. In the blood-splattered meat market, butchers bark out prices as they make mincemeat of hunks of flesh with giant cleavers. Open 24 hours, the meat market is at its liveliest after 3am, when clubbers stagger into the trio of all-night restaurants that specialise in tripe soup (*patsas*), allegedly a miracle cure for hangovers. Taverna Papandreou (210 321 4970) is the best of the three. Another late-night haunt is the Stoa Athanaton (210 321 4362), a *rembetiko* club where dancing on tables is de rigueur.

Central Market

Athinas Street, between Evripidou & Sophocleous. Open 7am-3pm Mon-Sat.

The lush **National Gardens**. *See p102.*

Its marble entry is based on the columns of the Acropolis temple Erechtheum, and its classical-style friezes are modelled after those on the Parthenon: one depicts the birth of Athena; another the battle between the gods and the giants. In front, the building is flanked by seated statues of Plato and Aristotle, while on either side rise high columns topped by statues of Apollo and Athena. On the far left is the **National Library**. It was built in 1902, and was also designed by Theophilus Hansen. Its entrance has Doric columns and is modelled after the Temple of Hephaestus in the Ancient Agora.

Though these three buildings were founded as the country's premier educational institutions, their stairs and huge courtyards are oddly empty – today's Athenian university students are rarely allowed within spitting distance of them. Most teaching takes place in gritty buildings around Patision, while the University is reserved for administrative offices and the Academy only opens for special events. The library is open to the public, but only students, public servants and others with special passes can enter the stacks. Even though you won't see students entering and leaving the buildings, you're unlikely to miss them altogether – along with anarchists and religious groups, they often hold demonstrations here.

Numismatic Museum

Panepistimiou 12 (210 364 3774/www.culture.gr).
Metro Panepistimio. **Open** 8.30am-3pm Tue-Sun.
Admission €3; €2 concessions. **No credit cards**.
Map p297 F5.
It's worth taking a look at this small museum, even if you're not interested in coins, just to walk around the mansion of Heinrich Schliemann, the famed German archaeologist who fulfilled his lifetime obsession when he discovered the rich Mycenaean kingdoms believed to be those described in *The Iliad*. The mansion is decorated with wonderful Pompeii-style frescoes and mosaics, carved marbles and moulded ceilings. It's a gorgeous showcase for the display of ancient gold, silver and bronze coins, many engraved with gods and mythical symbols. Displays include, among others, ancient Athenian coins bearing exquisite reliefs of Athena on one side and the owl, symbol of wisdom, on the other.

Parliament Building & Tomb of the Unknown Soldier

Syntagma (no phone/www.culture.gr). Metro
Syntagma. **Open** *Parliament Library* 9am-1.30pm
Mon-Fri. **Admission** free. **Map** p299 G5.
Once the domain of royalty, later a shelter for starving refugees, and today the seat of government, Greece's Parliament Building has many stories to tell. It was built in 1842 to house Otto, Greece's first king. Over the next 70 years, the palace swung between opulence and neglect as various kings were exiled and returned. In 1922, after thousands of Greeks were forced to flee Asia Minor during the Greek-Turkish population exchange, the building acted as a shelter to the newly homeless. All this left

impressive structures in modern Athens. These models of neo-classical design were all built in the years after Greece gained independence, and exemplify what the new state hoped that it would become: a blend of its classical heritage and modern, Western-style statesmanship.

The central building housed Athens' first **National University**. It was designed by the Danish architect Hans Christian Hansen and built in 1842. The Ionian entryway columns are replicas of the columns of the Propylaeum, the entrance to the Acropolis. Inside the portico, there are colourful frescoes depicting Greece's first king, Otto, sitting on his throne surrounded by ancient Greek gods and heroes.

To the right of the University is the ornate, marble **Academy of Arts**, designed by Theophilus Hansen (brother of Hans Christian) and built in 1859.

Square deal

'*Pame platia*' ('let's go to the square') –
a catchphrase coined by comedian Lakis
Lazopoulos – captures the Athenian habit
of hanging out in the neighbourhood square,
checking out the other people hanging out
there. It didn't matter that the squares were
often grimy and traffic-clogged – they were
the place to be. The pre-Olympic clean-up
changed all that. After enduring months of
dusty hoardings and pounding bulldozers,
Athenians can now strut their stuff at several
spanking new squares. Most of the new looks
around town are a result of international
architecture competitions, but not all the
renovations have been equally successful.
The makeover of the two main squares,
Syntagma (*see p74*) and **Omonia** (*see p75*),
are equally loved and loathed. Syntagma, a
grand expanse of white marble stretching
below Parliament, has benefited from a pair
of waterfalls and two elegant cafés with
outdoor tables. Brilliantly lit, the square
looks even better after dark. Though
Omonia has been criticised for its drab grey
surface and scant greenery, compared to
the junkie junction – singularly lacking
in redeeming features – it was
before, the simple, sloped
landscape architecture is a great
improvement. Ten olive trees,
symbols of ancient Athens, have
been planted, and the mishmash
of neo-classical shopfronts and
concrete 1960s façades has
been scrubbed up. A chaotic
traffic junction, Omonia will never
be somewhere to linger for long,
but it does have great views of
the Acropolis.

Once home to former Prime
Minister Koumoundouros – and
more recently to hundreds of
Kurdish refugees sleeping rough
– **Koumoundourou** Square is
unrecognisable since acquiring
108 new trees and over 1,800
plants. Linking the neighbourhoods
of Psyrri and Keramikos,
Koumoundourou is now a meeting
point for art lovers visiting the
National Gallery (*see p115*),
skateboarders hurtling down
its ramps and Orthodox
worshippers dropping into Agioi

Anargyri church. Alfresco concerts were
staged in the lovely little amphitheatre
during the Olympics.

Of the smaller oases scattered about town,
tiny **Mousaion** in Plaka, with its miniature
amphitheatre overlooking the remains of
Kitsouk Tzami ('Little Mosque'); raised
Varvakios in the Central Market, with its café
looking down on lively market traders; and
Asomaton, at the heart of the archaeological
park, are all worth a pit stop.

Less pretty – though much busier – are
Kolonaki (*see p103*), with its kitsch fountains
and excess of concrete, and **Exarchia** (*see
p105*), which looks worse than it did before
months of excavation (luckily the bars lining
the square liven up the dreary surroundings).
Monastiraki (*see p90*), potentially one of the
capital's most stunning squares, with the
Pandanassa monastery and mosque (now
the Museum of Greek Ceramics, *see p92*),
has been relegated to a parking lot for
motorbikes. The award-winning architects are
so appalled by the shabby implementation of
their original design that they are threatening
to sue the government.

Sightseeing

A stroll around the National Gardens

This three-hour route, taking you through lush greenery and past some handsome historical sites, makes for a pleasant and romantic afternoon walk.

It is impossible to rush a stroll through the **National Gardens** (*see p102*). Enter the grounds next to the Parliament Building on Leof Vas Amalias and lose yourself in a refreshing setting of towering palm trees, pines and cypresses, scattered with little bridges over brooks and shaded corners. At your exit, on the east side, a café named Kafenio, with an ivy-covered terrace, serves rather rough and ready fare but is a nice shady place to have a rest and a cool drink. Emerging from the park on to the immaculate Irodou Attikou – one of the most heavily policed streets in Athens thanks to its high-ranking residents – is an abrupt reality check.

Directly opposite the exit, on the right, are the **Maximou Mansion**, the prime minister's official residence, and the **Presidential Palace** – both neo-classical structures. The latter – home to Greece's kings until Constantine left in 1967, now used mainly for entertaining visiting dignitaries – is guarded by Evzones who march solemnly towards each other at regular intervals.

At the end of Irodou Attikou, turn right on to Leof Vas Konstantinou, then continue on to Leof Vas Olgas and around 200 metres (220 yards) on you will see the elegant **Zappeion Exhibition Hall** on your right. Next door, the **Aigli Bistro Café** is a haunt of politicians and their entourages, but also pulls in its fair share of families fresh in from the weekend promenade around Zappeion.

Strolling away from Zappeion, across busy Ardittou and left up Leof Vas Konstantinou, will bring you to the marble Panathenaic Stadium (also known as Kallimarmaro, *see p116*). A 19th-century reconstruction of the ancient Olympic Stadium, it was the site of the first modern-day Olympics in 1896 as well as the 2004 Olympics archery competitions and the finish of the marathon races. It is next to the pine-covered **Ardittou Hill**, allegedly haunted by the ghosts of those murdered during the Nazi occupation of Athens, who were hastily buried here. Following Ardittou uphill will take you to the neighbourhood of **Mets**, one of the few central Athenian districts to have preserved some of its traditional flavour.

A turn on to Nikiforou Theotokou will give you a taste of the neighbourhood – rows of pre-1940s houses with tiled roofs and flower-covered balconies on ascending levels of an uphill slope, connected by little staircases. Alternatively, turn on to Markou Mousourou, and head towards **Pangrati** – another picturesque residential district. A short stroll along Markou Mousourou and a left turn takes you on to Archimidou – the *mezedopolio* Xanthippe (Archimidou 14, 210 756 0514) is great for lunch or dinner.

Going back down along Markou Mousourou you will come to Trivonianou on your left, which leads you to the striking Bauhaus-style entrance of Athens' **First National Cemetery** (*see p115*). This graveyard is a veritable museum, housing the works of Ianoulis Halepas, the famous belle époque sculptor from the Aegean island of Tinos, whose masterpiece *I Koimomeni* (*Sleeping Girl*) is around 300 metres (330 yards) in on the right.

Leaving the cemetery, head down Anapafseos (directly opposite the cemetery gates) until you emerge on to a busy junction where you will see the **Temple of Olympian Zeus** (*see p102*) – the largest temple ever constructed in Greece, which now retains only some of its columns. On the same site, but in a somewhat better state of preservation, is **Hadrian's Arch** (*see p102*). Athenians built

---

it in a sorry state and, after the return of a national parliamentary government in 1926, the building was gutted, renovated and reopened as a single-chamber council for the parliament. Today, it is the scene of parliamentary debates, broadcast on state television through a live camera. Most of the building is closed to the public, although its elegant library is open to researchers and often holds public exhibitions.

In the square below the building is the Tomb of the Unknown Soldier, erected in 1929, a monument to Greece's fallen. Carved on the tomb is a dying soldier, based on a fifth-century BC sculpture from Aegina, and an excerpt from Pericles' 430 BC funeral oration, given in honour of the Athenians who died in the Peloponnesian Wars. The tomb is guarded by the kilt- and stocking-clad Evzones, with a ceremonial changing of the guard every hour.

Platia Klafthmonos
Metro Panepistimio. Map p297 F4.
This square once played an important role in modern Greek politics. The name translates as the 'Square of Wailing', and it's where politicians who

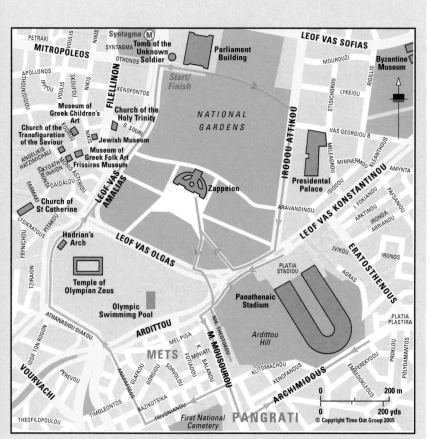

the arch in AD 131 in honour of the Roman Emperor Hadrian. Continuing up Leof Vas Amalias will bring you back almost full circle, to the edge of Zappeion. Stop at the classic **Oasis** café on the corner of Amalias and the main Zappeion promenade for a welcome sit-down in the shade and something cold to drink.

had lost office traditionally went to console each other after the elections. The sculpture in the centre is called *National Reconciliation*.

Around the National Gardens

Map p299

Once part of the Royal Palace and located south-west of the Historic Triangle, the **National Gardens** (*see p102*) are a godsend: thick, beautiful and shady, and dead in the centre of downtown Athens. Unsurprisingly, the real estate around them is among the city's most desirable. This is easy enough to see if you take a stroll down Irodou Attikou, where you'll pass the lovely **Presidential Palace** (*see above* **A stroll around the National Gardens**), designed by Ernst Ziller (the Bavarian architect who created many of modern Athens' most important buildings), and, on the corner of Leof Vas Georgiou, the stately **Maximou**. This building is the official residence of the prime minister and is thus frequently surrounded by television reporters hoping to get exclusive soundbites from visiting ministers. They quickly have to get out of the way when the high-kicking Evzone ceremonial guards march up the street – this whole scene, set against the verdant backdrop of the park, makes for a great modern Athenian moment.

Byzantine Museum

Leof Vas Sofias 22 (210 721 1027/www.culture.gr). Metro Evangelismos. **Open** 8.30am-3pm Tue-Sun. **Admission** €4; €2 over-65s; free students. **Map** p299 H5.
The Byzantine Museum has a world-renowned collection of icons, mosaics, sculptures and religious art. Renovation is more than doubling its permanent exhibition space, and never-before-seen parts of the collection – such as rare illuminated manuscripts – will be displayed for the first time. In addition, archaeologists have discovered the site of Aristotle's Lyceum on the grounds; this ongoing dig will also be open to the public. The current renovations will run through to 2006, during which time the museum will be open only intermittently – it's best to call ahead.

Hadrian's Arch

Leof Vas Amalias & Dionysiou Areopagitou (no phone/www.culture.gr). Metro Akropoli. **Open** 24hrs daily. **Admission** free. **Map** p301 F6.
To thank the Roman Emperor Hadrian for finally completing the Temple of Olympian Zeus (*see below*), Athenians built this arch in his honour in AD 131. Hadrian also saw to it that the arch clarified his own sovereignty. He had its west side inscribed: 'This is Athens, the ancient city of Theseus'. The east side was inscribed: 'This is the city of Hadrian and not of Theseus'. Sculptures of Theseus and Hadrian probably stood atop the arch. Nearby is some more honorific masonry: the statue of Byron at the corner of Amalias and Olga.

National Gardens

Leof Vas Amalias 1 (210 721 5019). Metro Syntagma. **Open** 7am-sunset daily. **Admission** free. **Map** p299 G5/G6.
The lush National Gardens were originally planted in 1839 as a private sanctuary adjoining the Royal Palace (now the Parliament). Amalia, Greece's first queen, had over 15,000 domestic and exotic plants brought in from Genoa, nearby Sounio and Evia. Many of these trees still remain. The garden was opened to the public in 1923, and is now a welcome deep-green – sometimes even jungly – oasis in the parched city centre. Winding paths lead past statues, fountains and trellised promenades with such mock-natural abandon that it's actually possible to get lost. There is also a botanical museum, children's library, duck ponds, a depressed collection of caged wildlife, a playground, a piece of Roman mosaic, a shaded café and a colony of felines fed and sterilised by the local charity Friends of the Cat.

National War Museum

Leof Vas Sofias & Rizari 2 (210 725 2974/ www.culture.gr). Metro Evangelismos. **Open** 9am-2pm Tue-Sun. **Admission** free. **Map** p299 H5.
Admittedly, three sprawling floors on the history of Greek warfare, from Alexander the Great's battle plans through to the sticky stew of the Balkan conflicts, might not be everyone's cup of tea. But a certain stripe of visitor will be in heaven. Meanwhile, anyone should enjoy a brief foray into the Saroglos Collection, which includes suits of armour, *Three Musketeers*-style foils and engraved Turkish scimitars. Outside there are real tanks and warplanes, which visitors can climb up into for a closer look. Avoid weekday mornings in term-time – busloads of hyperactive kids are deposited to run riot among the planes. Interpretive panels are in Greek only.

Temple of Olympian Zeus

Leof Vas Olgas & Leof Vas Amalias (210 922 6330/ www.culture.gr). Metro Syntagma. **Open** 8.30am-3pm daily. **Admission** €2; €1 concessions. Free to holders of €12 Acropolis ticket. **No credit cards.** **Map** p301 F6.
In a city infamous for bureaucracy and construction delays, this colossal temple still holds the record for the longest tie-up – nearly 700 years. The tyrant Pisistratos commissioned the largest temple in Greece in 515 BC, ostensibly to honour Zeus, but mainly to keep his subjects occupied. After he was overthrown, the citizens of the new democracy refused to complete what they saw as a monument to tyranny. And so the Temple of Olympian Zeus languished for centuries, until the Roman Emperor Hadrian recognised the opportunity it presented. He had the temple finished in seven years, fitted out with a gigantic gold-and-ivory sculpture of the god, and, for good measure, added a similar one of himself. Today, only 16 of the original 104 columns remain, but their majesty still overwhelms.

Zappeion

Leof Vas Amalias (210 323 7830). Metro Syntagma. **Open** *Garden* 24hrs daily. *Exhibition Hall* during exhibitions. **Admission** free. **Map** p299 G6.
On the south side of the lush and overgrown National Gardens are the orderly Zappeion Gardens, centred on the stately Zappeion Exhibition Hall, built in 1888 by Theophilus Hansen, the Danish neoclassical architect who also designed parts of the University complex on Panepistimiou. As was typical of his designs, Hansen combined an entrance reminiscent of an ancient temple with a main body that referenced contemporary Mediterranean buildings, to pleasing effect. The building hosts conferences and exhibitions, the latter open to the public; it was also the first headquarters of the Olympic organising committee. The area in front of the building frequently hosts outdoor concerts and events, while the pretty complex of buildings just to the east of the Exhibition Hall includes the restaurant and café Aigli, a restored outdoor cinema and a summer-only nightclub in the middle of the park.

Kolonaki & Around

The home of Greek chic.

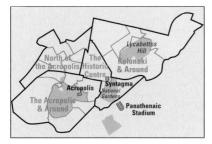

Thrusting up above Kolonaki, Ambelokipi and Exarchia in a taller, steeper and greener echo of the Acropolis, Lycabettus Hill has origins shrouded in myth – it is said to have had a violent start to life as a rock thrown by the goddess Athena. Certainly, in ancient times, the hill was considered an uninhabitable wilderness far from the centre of Athens. By the early 20th century, however, it had become a popular place to graze sheep, and a mere 100 years later, the lower slopes of Lycabettus Hill have been completely transformed.

Since the 1950s Kolonaki, which snakes around and creeps up the southern slopes of Lycabettus, has indisputably been the chicest address in Athens and today it's home to the city's top designer shops, trendiest restaurants, most see-and-be-seen cafés and face-must-fit nightclubs, as well as block after block of pretty neo-classical mansions-cum-apartment-buildings housing all manner of high-society party-goers, from diplomats to pop stars. This is the place to people-watch and spend money – though it is possible to enjoy Kolonaki without doing too much of the latter, just by strolling under its flowering trees, browsing its art galleries and window shopping.

On the north-eastern side of Kolonaki and Lycabettus is **Ambelokipi**, today a densely packed and busy district. Its name, translated as 'little grapevines', also betrays its rural origins – it was once full of vineyards supplying Athenians with wine. Although Ambelokipi has no tourist sights or museums, it is a good area to keep your radar on – it's packed with good tavernas, restaurants, cinemas and, increasingly, small, friendly nightclubs that lack both the cachet and ludicrous prices of their Kolonaki brethren.

Kolonaki

Map p299

Kolonaki's hub – where business deals are completed, the morning's papers perused, the scandal of the day discussed and tomorrow's media stars discovered – is **Platia Kolonaki**. This small, concrete- and waterfall-filled square hums with activity generated by the cafés, art galleries and designer shops that line its edges. Radiating off the square are some of Athens' best streets for shopping and going out: start on Tsakalof, Anagnostopoulou or Patriarchou Ioakim for boutiques, and Milioni or Skoufa for a surfeit of cool places to imbibe caffeine or cocktails. *See also p174* **How to do Kolonaki**. In the midst of the designer stores, the **Greek Costume Museum** (*see p104*) is devoted to what Greeks of yesteryear were wearing.

Heading uphill (and we really mean uphill) towards Lycabettus, you'll reach another hub, this one rather quieter. **Platia Dexamenis** is home to the chic St George Lycabettus hotel (*see p62*) and its trendy café, Frame, plus one of Athens' nicest outdoor cinemas, the Dexameni (*see p195*). Heading west, you can see some of Athens' most exclusive real estate. If you're here on a Friday morning, walk down **Xenokratous**, which hosts one of Athens' liveliest fruit and vegetable markets. You'll see housekeepers, Filipina maids and even pearl-wearing, poodle-clutching old ladies bargaining at the stalls below the mansions – a nice reminder that even in this most genteel of neighbourhoods, the old-fashioned village *laiki* (market) still thrives. To the east of Platia Dexamenis, on the edge of Lycabettus Hill, is the **Gennadius Library** (*see p105*), the world's largest private collection on matters Greek.

To the south, Kolonaki is bordered by the boulevard of Leof Vas Sofias, home to Athens' Museum Row: on the north side it's got the **Goulandris Museum of Cycladic Art** (*see p105*) and the **Benaki Museum** (*see below*), while on the south are the **Byzantine** (*see p102*) and **National War** museums (*see p102*).

Benaki Museum

Koumbari 1 & Leof Vas Sofias (210 367 1000/ www.benaki.gr). Metro Evangelismos or Syntagma. **Open** 9am-5pm Mon, Wed, Fri, Sat; 9am-midnight Thur; 9am-3pm Sun. **Admission** €6. Free to all Thur. **No credit cards. Map** p299 G5.

Lycabettus Hill

Sightseeing

Athens is a city of breathtaking sights but one of the finest is 277 metres (908 feet) above its bustling streets. From the top of Lycabettus Hill, you can see right across the dusty, sprawling city to the port of Piraeus and the Saronic Gulf on a clear day.

According to mythology, this jagged rock separating Kolonaki from neighbouring Ambelokipi owes its location to a missile hurled by the goddess Athena, in a tempestuous fury, at the daughters of the mythological King Cecrops, who was half-man, half-snake. She missed her target and the hill fell where it now remains. Another legend has it that Athena was trying to bulk up the Acropolis and carrying a huge piece of rock from nearby Mount Pentelicon when she heard some bad news and dropped the rock in dismay. Once a wilderness far from human habitation, the hill is no longer home to the wolves (lykoi), from which it is said to have got its name, but it remains a pine-studded outcrop, with woodland paths snaking their way to the summit.

Today, the Lycabettus summit is home to the chapel of Agios Georgios (St George), which dates back to the 1780s. This Greek islandesque gem is a working church; the highlight of its year is Good Friday midnight mass, when Athenians flock to witness the city's candlelight processions from this incredible vantage point (*see p191* **Christos anesti!**). The hill also provides a dramatic location for an open-air amphitheatre, the Lycabettus Theatre, which has played host to international music talent ranging from Philip Glass, Calexico and PJ Harvey to Dido. In summer 2005 both Duran Duran and Franz Ferdinand are playing this unique venue. Having no ticket doesn't preclude fans from enjoying the music: skinflint punters perch on the treacherous clifftops that surround the venue to watch for free. Classical theatre is also staged here during the Athens Festival (*see p189*).

Most visitors, though, just come to eat, drink and – above all – to take in the panorama. A little below the chapel, the elegant restaurant Orizondes (*see p152* **Food with a view**) is popular and has an unbeatable view. There is also a low-key café-restaurant, Prasini Tenta, conveniently placed halfway up the steep steps to the peak; a sunset drink here is delightful. All this is accessible by road or paths through the pines, but it's a steep walk; many prefer to take the funicular to the top and then amble down along the winding, shady trails.

Getting there

Funicular from Aristippou & Ploutarchou (210 722 7065). Metro Evangelismos. **Open** *Funicular* 8am-3pm daily (every 30mins). *Chapel of St George* Sun. **Admission** *Funicular* ¤ 4.50. *Chapel* free. **Map** p299 H4.

If you're walking up, take either the circular road, Sarantapichou (the easiest route), or the steep Ploutarchou and then the still steeper woodland paths.

This museum is housed in the gorgeously restored mansion of the wealthy 19th-century Benakis dynasty. It's also a pre-eminent collection: the works of Greek art, spanning the eras from antiquity to the 20th century, are top notch. Don't miss the sumptuous gold Hellenistic jewellery, the Byzantine shrines or the intricate re-creations of Ottoman-era sitting rooms. The gift shop is a destination in itself, offering exquisitely reproduced ceramics and jewellery.

Gennadius Library

Souidias 61 (210 721 0536/www.ascsa.edu.gr/ gennadius/genn.htm). Metro Evangelismos. **Open** 9am-5pm Mon-Wed, Fri; 9am-8pm Thur; 9am-2pm Sat. **Admission** free. **Map** p299 J4.

Turn-of-the-19th-century Greek diplomat John Gennadius scoured bookshops across Europe for rare and valuable publications on his country; the 27,000 gold-bound multilingual volumes he amassed represent the largest private collection on anything

Greek. You can peruse whatever you desire within the luxurious reading room, and also check out displays including Lord Byron memorabilia, the papers of Nobel laureate George Seferis and the first edition printed in Greek of Homer's works.

Goulandris Museum of Cycladic Art

Neofytou Douka 4 & Irodotou (210 722 8321/ www.cycladic.gr). Metro Evangelismos. **Open** 10am-4pm Mon, Wed-Fri; 10am-3pm Sat. **Admission** €5; €2.50 Sat. **No credit cards. Map** p299 H5.

The world's largest collection of Cycladic art is one of Athens' must-sees. While Greek sculpture reached its pinnacle with the Parthenon Marbles, the first seeds in that tradition had been sown some 2,000 years earlier, in the Cycladic Islands of the Aegean. There, between 3,200 BC and 2,200 BC, a unique matriarchal culture flourished. Though contemporary with the Egyptians and Mesopotamians, it produced a totally different kind of art featuring elegant, angular, marble female figures with emphasised breasts and genitalia. The influence of the prehistoric figures can be seen in the work of Modigliani and Picasso, and they continue to inspire artists to this day. In addition to the fascinating Cycladic pieces, the museum also owns a small but first-rate collection of ceramic items from the classical period, as well as the adjoining Stathatos Mansion, a Bavarian-style neo-classical building designed by Ernst Ziller. There, among sparkling chandeliers, velvet drapes and antique furniture, the museum holds highly acclaimed temporary exhibits.

Greek Costume Museum

Dimokritou 7 (210 362 9513). Metro Syntagma. **Open** 9am-2pm Mon-Fri. Closed Aug. **Admission** free. **Map** p299 G4.

This boutique-sized museum devoted to the history of clothing and fashion is located in the midst of Kolonaki's designer clothes stores. The 25,000 dresses and accessories include centuries-old folk costumes from every region of Greece, and copies of Minoan, Byzantine and classical Greek fashions.

Exarchia & Pedion Areos

Maps p297, p299

Bohemian Exarchia will never be known as a beautiful neighbourhood, but it holds a place in the heart of nearly every modern Greek, as evinced in the number of times it is referenced in Greek folk songs and novels from the 1970s onwards. It is home to the most important event in recent history: it was here, in 1973, that the students of the **Athens Polytechnic** (*see p106*) rose up in protest against Greece's hated military dictatorship. Many of those students went on to become Greece's most prominent left-wing politicians; meanwhile, the neighbourhood has remained a gathering spot for students and intellectuals, its many cafés and tavernas alive with political debate.

Café-table politics in bohemian **Exarchia.**

While the front of the polytechnic is often filled with students and demonstrators passing out leaflets against the latest Western imperialist offence, its neighbour is often fronted by huge, shiny tour buses disgorging hundreds of people, all there to see one of the essential sights of Greece: the **National Archaeological Museum** (*see p106*), home to the mythical treasures of Mycenae, the sculptures of classical masters and much more.

On the east side of the polytechnic, Stournari leads up to the heart of the neighbourhood, **Platia Exarchia**, the place for all your intellectual café-sitting needs. Its cafés and bars are always filled with students and old-time lefties, but you're just as likely to see middle-aged businessmen or taxi drivers having a drink – many Greeks like to come here when they feel the pull of their political consciousness. Don't be alarmed if you're approached by down-and-out figures asking for some change or a cigarette: they're harmless and won't protest if you say no. If you have a car, though, you may wish to park it further out of Exarchia – broken windshields and even Molotov cocktails chucked at vehicles (as well as banks and other symbols of greedy capitalism) are not uncommon here.

Of architectural interest in the square is the Bauhaus-style building that houses the Floral café: it looks a bit faded and tatty today, but this was Athens' first apartment block, built in 1932-3. Away from the square is a mix of crepit neo-classical houses, blocks daubed with passionate and scores of second-hand book record shops, hippie clothing stores, independent cinemas that show nothing but art flicks, simple tavernas serving up hearty, home-made food to accompany philosophical banter and some of the best places in town to hear *rembetika*, the gritty Greek blues.

One of the best streets to see life in action in Exarchia is **Kallidromiou**, where you'll find a cluster of small cafés much favoured by locals and intellectuals. Saturday mornings see this narrow thoroughfare transformed into one of Athens' largest outdoor markets as the vendors take over with their stalls of (mostly) fresh fruit and vegetables as well as flowers, herbs and fish. The pedestrianised part of **Valtetsiou** is also pleasant to wander on, especially in the evening when you can take your pick of lively street cafés and bars housed in renovated old mansions, an open-air cinema and Athens' only organic restaurant, Giantes.

If you follow Kallidromiou east, it eventually runs into **Neapoli**, a pretty but quiet residential district that acts as a buffer between the lefty grit of Exarchia on one side and the posh consumerism of Kolonaki on the other. It is mostly populated by genteel but shabby writers and academics, who tend to frequent its many tavernas and *rembetatika*.

To the north of Exarchia and Neapoli is **Pedion Areos**, Athens' largest park. Sounds good, but some caveats should be noted: because of its location in a slightly down-at-heel area, the park sees a fair few homeless people and a decreasing number of maintenance workers looking after the place. That said, it is still spacious and green, decidedly welcome qualities anywhere in town.

Athens Polytechnic

Patision & Stournari. Metro Victoria. **Map** p297 F2.
The date that resonates most deeply in the heart of many Greeks is 17 November 1973. On that day, thousands of students at the Athens Polytechnic rose up in protest against Greece's military junta. The colonels countered with guns and tanks, killing at least 20 students. Though the day was one of the darkest in modern Greek history, it was also the turning point that led to the overthrow of the dictatorship the following year. Today, the bravery of the students is commemorated with a moving monument to the slain in the polytechnic's courtyard, which thousands of Greeks turn out to cover with flowers every year on the anniversary of their death.

Epigraphical Museum

Tositsa 1 (210 821 7637/www.culture.gr).
Metro Victoria. **Open** 8.30am-3pm Tue-Sun.
Admission free. **Map** p297 F2.

Located on the ground floor of the National Archaeological Museum (*see below*), with a separate entrance from the pedestrian street that runs between the museum and the polytechnic, this collection of inscriptions includes a 480 BC decree by the Assembly of Athens to flee the city before the Persian invasion; a sacred law concerning temple-worship on the Acropolis; and a stele with the Draconian laws on homicide.

National Archaeological Museum

Patision 44 (210 821 7717/www.culture.gr).
Metro Victoria. **Open** *Apr-Oct* noon-7pm Mon;
8am-7pm Tue-Sun. *Nov-Mar* 8.30am-3pm Tue-Sun.
Admission €6; €3 concessions. At the time of going to press, opening times and admission prices for summer had yet to be finalised. **No credit cards.**
Map p297 F1/F2.

It hosts one of the most important collections in the world, so it's no surprise that you can't really do justice to this museum in one visit. If you can, plan at least two trips so you can properly take in and appreciate its astounding array of treasures. If you really don't have time to visit twice, it may be a good idea to hire one of the English-speaking guides to fill you in on the key pieces. Bear in mind that such a tour could take up to two hours.

The museum was closed from the beginning of 2002 until late 2004 for extensive remodelling – new lighting and air-conditioning were installed, damage from the 1999 earthquake was rectified and the exhibits were rearranged. At the time of writing, the upper floor – with its galleries of artefacts from the kingdom of Thira (Santorini), including the exquisite Thira frescoes showing scenes of prehistoric daily life, as well as the museum's rich collection of painted vases and pottery from the 11th to sixth centuries BC – was still closed. It is expected to reopen by summer 2005. You may wish to ring ahead to find out which, if any, galleries are still being renovated.

The best way to tackle the museum is chronologically: in other words, start on the ground floor in Gallery 5, a long, thin room at the left of the central hall (Gallery 4). Here you will find Neolithic artefacts dating from 6800 to 3300 BC, the time of the first documented settlements on the Acropolis. Exhibits include pottery and household objects, clay models of people and animals, tools and a small collection of fabulous gold ornaments confiscated from plunderers in 1997 and 1999. The gallery also hosts some early and mid Bronze Age vessels – vases, bowls – found on the Acropolis and dating from 3200 BC.

Then head out across the central hall to the Early Cycladic room (Gallery 6), to survey the remarkably modern-looking naïve statues of women, mostly naked, standing with their arms folded below their chests. The most impressive of all the figurines in this room is the girl on the right of the door, at 1.52m (5ft) the largest known example, preserved complete from around 3200 BC. Also fascinating are the 'frying pan vessels' (thought perhaps to have been used as mirrors), intricately decorated with spirals, circles, triangles, stars and even Cycladic ships.

The astounding **National Archaeological Museum** – 7,000 years of BC history. *See p106.*

Next, go into the central gallery (4), home to some of the museum's most celebrated finds, the Mycenaean antiquities. The Mycenaeans, renowned for their prowess as warriors, flourished between 1600 and 1100 BC, and fought the Trojans with the aid of Athena in *The Iliad*. Homer described their citadel, overseen by King Agamemnon, as 'well-built Mycenae, rich in gold'. This was thought to be myth until German archaeologist Heinrich Schliemann unearthed their settlement in 1876. Prepare to be astonished by the stunning hoard he found, including

a gold death mask, that was originally believed to be Agamemnon's but later dated to the 16th century BC, long before the king would have lived. Also found were a perfectly preserved 16th-century BC gold diadem and the 15th-century BC golden Vaphio cups, embossed with scenes of capturing wild bulls and similar to cups described by Homer.

When you've had your fill of ornate gold jewellery and prancing bulls, make for the sculpture galleries in the outer circle of the museum's maze. Galleries 7-13 are full of *kouroi* from the seventh to the fifth

Athens Polytechnic – the scene of a brutal student massacre in 1973. *See p106.*

centuries BC. These statues of youths and maidens were the first monumental works in Greek art. The earliest are stiff and stylised, but by following the forms through the centuries, you can see artists learning to depict the body more naturalistically. It is also interesting to plot the changing influences, from Egyptian (as seen in the larger-than-life Sounion *kouros* from 600 BC) to Roman.

Galleries 14-28 have some of the most marvellous achievements of sculpture in classical Greece. Most of the classical sculptures were made in bronze, which was later melted down and used for tools and weapons, but among those that survive is a famous 460 BC sculpture of a god, believed to be either Poseidon or Zeus, poised to throw (depending on who it is) a trident or thunderbolt. There are also several later marble copies of the bronze originals, such as the one of an athlete binding his hair, a 100 BC copy of a bronze by the renowned sculptor Polycleitos, originally made in the fifth century BC.

These galleries also include many moving funerary sculptures: many were so large and luxurious, as families competed to spend more and more money to create showier monuments, that they were actually banned in 317 BC. The scenes in these beautiful marble carvings typically show the deceased on the right and the survivors on the left, as well as an object characteristic of the dead. Suddenly, just when you may be becoming a little overwhelmed by marble, you come across what is perhaps the most celebrated exhibit in the whole museum: the Artemision horse and jockey. Created in bronze around 140 BC and retrieved in pieces from a shipwreck off Cape Artemis on Evia, this racehorse and

his child jockey have been sculpted in such lifelike detail that it seems that if you reached out to touch the animal's strained, veined, flaring-nostrilled nose, it would be warm and damp with sweat. Whether the boy actually belongs with this horse has been the subject of much discussion – scientific arguments aside, from a purely visual point of view he seems to be on a far smaller scale than the horse.

The final sculpture galleries (29-33) show Hellenistic statuary dating from the second century BC to the first century AD. Having started your tour of Greek sculpture with the stiff, solid archaic monuments, here you can see how far the artists have come. These sculptures are full of vigorous movement and sensuality, especially the 100 BC group of Aphrodite, Pan and Eros and the statue of a wounded Gaul.

Should you wish for some earthly sustenance after this heavenly visual feast, the museum has a basic café operated by the fast-food chain Grigoris (you can, at least, look out over a charming courtyard filled with classical statues). There is also a gift shop selling postcards, guidebooks, replicas of statues and jewellery, and various other mementos.

Pedion Areos

Leof Alexandras & Patision. Metro Victoria. **Open** 24hrs daily. **Admission** free. **Map** p297 F1.
Athens' largest park is a shady, welcome refuge from the smog and congestion, but not really a place to stroll if you are after scenic landscape. It has more of a working-class feel, with old folks on benches, kids playing football, stray dogs, and vagrants sleeping under trees. The park's proximity to the student district of Exarchia means it's frequently the site of political rallies, book fairs and free concerts.

North of the Acropolis

Cutting-edge culture and post-industrial chic.

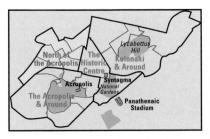

Described by the historian Thucydides in 430 BC as 'the most beautiful quarter outside the city walls', ancient **Keramikos** was a tranquil, cypress tree-filled area in the valley of the Eridanus river. It was divided roughly in half by the fifth-century BC Themistoclean Wall: the inner zone was where potters produced the famous ceramics for which the region was named, while the outer edge was the site of the state cemetery, the burial ground for the dead of the Persian wars and notable Athenian males.

With the wall's two key portals – the Dipylon, leading to Plato's Academy, and the Sacred Gate, leading to Eleusis – right in the middle of Keramikos, it hardly comes as a surprise to learn that the district was also home to a number of insalubrious edge-of-the-city activities: prostitutes held al-fresco assignations with soldiers; moneylenders, wine-sellers and other shady dealers gathered here to do business.

For centuries Keramikos and the neighbourhoods around it kept their ancient reputation intact, becoming home to a chaotic flea market, humble workshops and hashish dens. But in recent years, bright, cool new restaurants, trendy cafés, hip artists' studios and clubs have been emerging.

To the south-east of Keramikos is **Psyrri**, which for years was a dark, scruffy quarter of workshops and craftsmen's studios. Today, some of these still run as they always have, but popping up among them are innovative galleries, hipper-than-thou restaurants and nightspots, and hole-in-the-wall music joints, making this one of the hottest places to go out in central Athens.

South of Keramikos, at the very end of Ermou, is **Rouf**, a truly revitalised former urban wasteland. On the northern fringe of this area is a former foundry, now transformed into the huge, multi-use Technopolis arts complex (*see p113*) that, by proxy, has filled the surrounding streets with happening galleries, theatres and clubs galore.

Radiating out from Rouf and Keramikos are miles of decayed and decaying urban wilderness. To the south of Rouf are lonely abandoned factories, a few of which are gaining new life as dance clubs. To the north is Metaxourgio, a grey, congested cement block-flat region where migrants pack into low-income housing. While this wouldn't seem the most promising spot for arts and nightlife, some venues have started to crop up, with planners taking advantage of low rent, proximity to the centre and the patina of authentic grunge wherever they can find it.

Psyrri

Map p297

Wander Psyrri in the daytime, and you'll see glimpses of an Athens of yesteryear: elderly, black-clad women shuffle along, hunched over bags of shopping from grocery shops that exude the scent of mothballs; old men in suits sit outside crumbling, fine neo-classical houses overrun with stray cats; hawkers carry poles festooned with fluttering lottery tickets; street vendors sell feather dusters or fresh fruit, and roasted chestnuts from barrows. Tiny corner stores tend to specialise heavily – one sells just plastic flowers, another carnival costumes, and a third walking sticks and little leather animal harnesses. As the streets approach the main thoroughfare of Evripidou, things start to get more and more multicultural: Sikhs gather to exchange news at pavement curry houses; Chinese traders sell bargain clothing from hastily set-up shops festooned with red lanterns.

By night Psyrri is entertainment central, with everything from traditional Greek *bouzoukia* to posh fashion-police-patrolled clubs and tiny, jazzy, smoky bars. Much of the action centres on the three squares of Iroon, Agion Anargyron and Agion Asomaton (home to the **Benaki Museum of Islamic Art**, *see p110*), where cheery tavernas, hipster-filled outdoor cafés and sleek DJ bars cluster around old churches. It's well worth getting lost in

Psyrri's winding streets at night – there's always some new find cropping up on a once-forgotten corner.

Benaki Museum of Islamic Art

Agion Asomaton & Dipylou (210 325 1311/210 325 1314/www.benaki.gr). Metro Monastiraki. **Open** 9am-3pm Tue, Fri-Sun; 9am-9pm Wed. **Admission** €5; €2.50 concessions. Free Wed. **No credit cards** (except in the gift shop). **Map** p297 D4.

In two gloriously restored neo-classical mansions on the edge of Psyrri, just a stone's throw from Keramikos, is this world-renowned collection of Islamic art. Antonis Benakis (also founder of the outstanding Benaki Museum, *see p104*) spent much of his life in Egypt, where he painstakingly amassed the 8,000-piece collection, now displayed over four floors. Exhibits hail from regions of the old Islamic world as diverse as Spain and India, and date from the early days of Islam up until the 19th century. Items include an impressive collection of ceramics – ranging from 11th-century Fatimid pieces from Egypt to a colourful 16th-century Ottoman bowl from Iznik in modern Turkey, decorated with the then mega-fashionable tulip. From the early Islamic period a stand-out piece is a pair of carved doors from eighth-century Mesopotamia. Fabrics, jewellery and ornaments, battle equipment and tombstones also feature. Don't miss the exquisitely detailed tenth-century gold belt from Samarra, modern Iraq; gold 12th-century earrings from Spain with Arabic inscriptions; a 14th-century universal astrolabe, the only known surviving piece of medieval astronomical equipment of its kind; and a series of 19th-century Iranian daggers in gem-encrusted or painted ceramic cases that manage to make even such deadly instruments look beautiful. Also from Persia is a small gold turban decoration intricately decorated with flowers and the face of a young maiden (Persian art had no qualms about representing the human form). Fabrics are impressive too, from simple woollen cloth with animal forms and kufic inscriptions from Fayoum in Egypt (tenth century) to a sumptuous red velvet saddle-cloth, embroidered with gold and silver thread, dating from the 16th century, from Bursa. The museum also displays the entire marble-inlaid reception room of a 17th-century Egyptian official's mansion – complete with a fountain surrounded by sunken seats, stained-glass windows and gold-woven silk wall hangings – transported piece by piece from Cairo.

The café on the top floor has magnificent views not only over Keramikos, but also of the Acropolis, Filopappou and its observatory, the hills surrounding Athens and the sparkling Saronic Gulf.

Rouf & Tavros

Map p296

Rouf's defining landmark is **Technopolis**, the foundry-turned-arts-centre at the crossing of Ermou and Pireos. A century ago, black exhaust from its smokestacks coated the surrounding area, giving it the name **Gazi** ('gaslands'). Today, the structure remains, with all the harsh beauty of its industrial architecture, but now the chimneys are illuminated with coloured lights that draw arty types to the complex's concerts and galleries. The revival of the once-sooty surrounding streets has been complete: Persefonis, Technopolis's southern border street, is home to some of Athens' sleekest restaurants, and the smaller roads radiating off it are full of theatres, arts spaces and cool bars. Pireos Street, the long avenue leading towards Omonia Square, has enjoyed a new lease of life (*see p112* **Pireos Street redux**).

Among its highlights are the new annexe of the **Benaki Museum** (*see below*) and the **Foundation of the Hellenic World** (*see p113*), housed in a converted factory. Arts space **Athinais** (*see below*), also a converted industrial space, is on the outskirts of Rouf, in the neighbourhood of Votanikos.

South of Rouf are the vast old factories of **Tavros**. Though these are not very easy to get to, their sheer size seems to have inspired several transformations into nightclubs and party spaces.

Athinais

Kastorias 34-36, Rouf (210 348 0000/www.athinais. com.gr). Metro Metaxourgio or Thissio, then 20min walk. **Open** 9am-10pm daily. **Admission** free. **Map** p296 B3.

Athinais exemplifies the best of the industrial-to-arts space conversions that are transforming Athens' downtown landscape: the former silk factory on the outskirts of Rouf is now a sophisticated arts complex housing Greece's only Museum of Ancient Cypriot Art, containing treasures dating from the ninth century BC, gallery spaces, a concert hall, a theatre and a cinema that screens classic or art films. It also has two excellent restaurants – the lush Red and the more affordable brasserie Votanikos – and the sleek Boiler Bar. Unfortunately, the complex, which is still swathed in its original 1920s stonework, has had no knock-on effect on its run-down, out-of-the-way surroundings.

Benaki Museum, Pireos Street Annexe

Pireos 138 & Andronikou (210 345 3111/www. benaki.gr). **Open** 9am-5pm Wed, Thur; 10am-10pm Fri-Sun. **Admission** depends on exhibition/performance. **No credit cards.**

The Benaki Museum's younger sibling was built to accommodate temporary exhibitions, but it also acts as an arts space for other cultural events from film screenings and theatre performances to poetry evenings and concerts. During summer 2004 it hosted the acclaimed Ptychoseis display, exploring the role of drapes, folds and pleats in dress from ancient

Benaki Museum of Islamic Art.
See p110.

Pireos Street redux

Stretching from Omonia Square to the port of Piraeus, Pireos Street has long been a drab no-man's land, all abandoned factories and car mechanics. But since the late 1990s, this post-industrial area has been morphing into a cultural melting pot. Bouzouki clubs, galleries and theatres rub shoulders with strip joints, and once-decrepit neo-classical houses are being converted into hotels and restaurants.

The **School of Fine Arts** (*see p198*) – all shabby chic and artful dodgers – made the first move, taking over the old Hellenic Textiles factory in Tavros. Next door, the glossy **Foundation of the Hellenic World** (*see p113*) makes a stark contrast, with its interactive exhibitions and virtual tours of ancient Greece – great for children.

In a converted railway warehouse, the stunning cement façade of the **Pantheon** – it's studded with crystals – was designed by local sculptor Kostas Varotsos. Opening in 2005, the 24-hour multiplex will house a hotel, spa, theatre, cinema, restaurants, galleries, bars, and roof garden. Its **Athinon Arena** music hall (*see p216*) is already open, with Yorgos Dalaras and Antonis Remos headlining.

Contemporary art aficionados look sharp in the sleek café of the new **Benaki Museum** (*see p110*), an architectural landmark with mesh blinds opening on to a dramatic atrium and an excellent shop showcasing Greek design. The free 'trash art', comics and jazz festivals at **Technopolis** (*see p113*), the municipal arts centre in the former gasworks, are highlights of the capital's cultural calendar. After dark, Technopolis's glowing red chimney lures revellers to bars in the surrounding backstreets of Gazi. At **Bios** (*see p210* **Bios world**), an innovative arts centre furnished with modern antiques, expect an eclectic line-up, from electro-punk gigs to underground cinema to multimedia installations.

The hipsters who hang out at Bios relish the grunge factor. But with entrepreneurs paving the way, the Ministry of Public Works has promised to posh up Pireos Street, planting trees in empty plots, removing billboards and upgrading listed buildings. These promises have already attracted some glamorous openings. Lefteris Lazarou's Michelin-starred restaurant **Varoulko** (*see p144*) has moved from Piraeus into the new **Eridanus Hotel** (*see p65*), one of the most comfortable and reasonably priced downtown hotels.

Car showroom to cultural landmark: **Benaki Museum, Pireos Street Annexe.** *See p110.*

Greece to the present day, with exhibits including pieces by Mariano Fortuny, John Galliano and Issey Miyake. For more on the building's architects, *see p41* **Movers & shapers**.

Foundation of the Hellenic World

Pireos 254, Tavros (210 483 5300/www.fhw.gr). Metro Kalithea. **Open** *Mid Sept-mid June* 9am-2pm Mon, Tue; 9am-9pm Wed-Fri; 10am-3pm Sun. *Mid June-mid Sept* 9am-4pm Mon, Tue, Thur; 9am-7pm Wed; 11am-3pm Sun. **Admission** free.
This vast, multi-purpose space is a fantastic use of a converted factory; it's now a cultural centre that is devoted to multimedia and virtual reality exhibits on ancient Greece. These take you through sound-and-light tours of ancient Miletus, the Temple of Olympian Zeus and the ancient Olympics. There is also abundant theatre and gallery space, which is often used for educational programmes.

Technopolis

Pireos 100, Gazi (210 346 0981/www.culture.gr). Metro Thissio, then 10min walk. **Open** 9am-9pm Mon-Fri during exhibitions. **Admission** free.
Map p296 B5.
When the City of Athens bought this abandoned foundry and converted it into a huge, multi-purpose arts and performance space, it led to the transformation of the dingy surrounding neighbourhood, Gazi, into Athens' edgiest nightlife district, and kick-started a much-needed urban renewal trend: suddenly, Athenians cottoned on to the hipness of opening galleries and fusion restaurants in old lofts and factories all over town. The Technopolis buildings preserve their original industrial lines, and make an excellent home for everything from exhibitions of cartoon art to avant-garde theatre to rave concerts. The one permanent exhibit is the Maria Callas Museum, a small collection of the diva's personal items, including a handful of photos, mementos and costumes. If you visit the museum during the day, you'll need to find someone in the central office to let you in. Check local listings for exhibits and evening events.

Keramikos

Map p296

Until recently, Athens' tranquil classical cemetery was bounded on two sides by hectic, pollution-churning thoroughfares – visitors to Keramikos had to venture at their peril down the narrow pavement of roaring Pireos Street before, thankfully, slipping in the gate and entering the quiet, verdant oasis.

Since the Olympics, the Unification of Archaeological Sites walkway has made the approach to Keramikos substantially more pleasant, and the neighbourhood is slowly but surely sprouting shoots of change (*see p114* **Keramikos on the cusp**). Wander down from the Acropolis on the cobbled promenade, passing cafés full of lively young people, cross the train tracks at Thissio metro station then, keeping the beacon of Technopolis ahead, follow the railings around the edge of the Keramikos site until you reach the entrance, which is usually guarded by a couple of friendly stray dogs.

Keramikos

Ermou 148 (210 346 3552/www.culture.gr). Metro Thissio. **Open** *Oct-Mar* 8.30am-3pm daily; *Apr-Sept* 8am-8pm daily. **Admission** €2; free to holders of €12 Acropolis ticket. **No credit cards. Map** p296 C4.

Peaceful, green Keramikos, with its daisies, grassy hillocks, butterflies and tortoises, has been many things during its long life – shrine, city gates, hangout of prostitutes and soldiers, artists' quarter and the oldest and largest cemetery in Attica. What these uses have in common was that they were all suited to a site on the edge of the (ancient) city. The site's name derives from the prevalence of potters' workshops on the grassy banks of the River Eridanus, which cut through the site, and marked the northwest boundary of ancient Athens. In 478 BC that boundary was built in stone with the construction of the Themistoclean Wall around the entire city. The wall's foundations still mark the outer edges of Keramikos. Despite being built in haste, in fear of a sudden enemy attack, the walls were studded with grand gates. At the south-west edge of the site are the remains of the Dipylon Gate, the main entrance to Athens and the largest gate in ancient Greece. The roads from Thebes, Corinth and the Peloponnese led to this gate, and many ceremonial events were staged here at important arrivals and departures.

To the south-east of the site is the Sacred Gate, reserved for priestesses to pass through on the Sacred Way (Iera Odos) to Eleusis, to perform ancient Greece's most important religious rites, the mysteries of the goddess of agriculture, Demeter, and her daughter Persephone. Along the sides of the sacred road grew Athens' main cemetery, resting place for war heroes and wealthy statesmen – it was definitely prestigious to be buried here, as evinced by the many elaborate tombstones. The earliest tombs are probably the seventh-century BC tumuli – high, round burial mounds built to honour great warriors. But 200 years later, the classical Athenians decided they wanted a lot more than just mounds of dirt, hence the showy monuments. The most distinctive of these is the fifth-century BC marble bull on the tomb of Dionysios of Kollytos, a man praised for his goodness, who died unmarried, mourned by his mother and sisters. The tomb of Dexileos, who died in 394 BC, shows a sculpture of the young man astride a rearing horse, while the lovely fifth-century BC stele of Hegeso shows the dead woman, seated on the right, taking a trinket from a box held by her maid.

As on the Acropolis, many of the sculptures that are exposed to the elements are actually copies, with the originals displayed in the small but fascinating on-site Oberlander Museum. The museum also contains other fabulous cultural remains like pottery shards depicting erotic scenes, used in a brothel once on the site, and bits of marble carved with curses, which people would slip into the graves of their enemies.

Keramikos on the cusp

Catch it while you can. Keramikos is teetering towards cool.

One of the last central Athens neighbourhoods to escape gentrification, Keramikos is on the cusp of coolness. The area is named after one of the city's loveliest and least visited sites, the ancient cemetery and pottery of Keramikos (*see above*), brilliantly exposed by the recent pedestrianisation of lower Ermou Street. With its rambling neo-classical buildings and patchwork of paved streets, the area is attracting artists and galleries priced out of nearby Psyrri. The **Gazon Rouge** gallery (*see pxxx*) recently relocated here, following in the footsteps of the **Attis Theatre** (Leonidou 7, 210 522 6260), run by one of Greece's most innovative directors, Theodoros Terzopoulos, and **417** (Mylerou 22 & Keramikou, 210 523 0417, www.417.gr), a stylish arts space that hosts everything from wine tastings to yoga workshops and contemporary dance.

But even in Keramikos things are on the move, and property prices have doubled in the last two years. Trendification could gradually force out the junk shops, junkies, immigrants and brothels (hookers don't cruise here, but look out for the tell-tale lit bulbs outside the cute cottages lining Iasonos Street). The city council is cleaning up, installing street lights and restoring heritage buildings, especially around Dourouti Square, overlooking the old Silk Factory. A modern art museum and digital library will open here in 2006. In the meantime you can watch kids playing football in the square over a cold beer at **Archangelos** café (Giatrakou 12, 210 522 8840) and then move next door for a romantic dinner at mellow Mediterranean restaurant **Astivi** (Giatrakou 10, 210 522 2696).

Future plans for Keramikos include the pedestrianisation of Iera Odos, the ancient route of the Eleusinian Mysteries, and a small park at the intersection between Iera Odos and Keramikos. An ambitious proposal to create a Cultural Park connecting Keramikos and Gazi is on hold for now.

Athens Suburbs

Head for the hills (and beaches) beyond the urban jungle.

Greek chic in **Kifisia**. *See p117.*

Surrounded by roaring traffic on Omonia or Syntagma squares, or surveying a seemingly endless sprawl of grey concrete blocks, it may be hard to imagine ever finding peace and quiet, greenery or fresh air in this chaotic capital. But cupped within the Athenian basin are, in fact, myriad ways to escape the urban grind. With the herb-scented, flower-filled rambles of Mount Hymettos, the soothing, medicinal waters of Lake Vouliagmeni, the people-watching possibilities of Kifisia's posh tree-lined streets and the seaside promenade that overlooks the glittering Saronic Gulf, the city's outskirts offer a whole new insight into Athenian life and leisure.

Eastern Suburbs

Maps p299 & p301

Useful transport: Metro Evangelismos, Syngrou-Fix.
To the east of central Athens, just beyond Zappeion Gardens and the Temple of Olympian Zeus, the ground starts to rise into the foothills

of **Mount Hymettos**. The elevated eastern suburbs run along most of the 16-kilometre (ten-mile) length of the mountain. Most of these are fairly ordinary residential neighbourhoods, with **Pangrati**, the one closest to central Athens, the most interesting to visitors. Further up the mountain, you can take a break from smoggy central Athens with a walk on trails scented with wild herbs.

Pangrati

Pangrati's most dominant feature is the huge, marble **Panathenaic Stadium** (*see p116*), site of the first modern Olympics in 1896. To the south of the stadium is the steep but lovely street of Markou Mousourou, shaded by flowering trees and filled with the scent of jasmine and bougainvillea from the balconies of the surrounding neo-classical buildings. Markou Mousourou borders **Mets**, one of Athens' prettiest residential neighbourhoods. Heading up Markou Mousourou and then turning right on Trivonianou, you'll reach the entrance of the tranquil, shady and fascinating **First National Cemetery** (*see below*).

First National Cemetery

Anapafseos & Trivonianou (210 922 1621). Metro Akropoli or Syngrou-Fix, then 10min walk. **Open** 7am-sunset daily. **Admission** free.
The wide, overgrown rows of century-old marble mausoleums in Athens' largest cemetery are good for a contemplative, off-the-beaten-path stroll. All of modern Athens' most famous are buried in lavish tombs here, including actress, culture minister and national heroine Melina Mercouri, War of Independence hero Theodoros Kolokotronis and the Nobel laureate George Seferis. The cemetery is planted with cypress trees, whose tall, pointed shape is believed to help guide souls up to heaven.

National Gallery

Leof Vas Konstantinou 50 (210 723 5857/ www.nationalgallery.gr/www.culture.gr). Metro Evangelismos. **Open** 9am-3pm, 6-9pm Mon, Wed; 9am-3pm Thur-Sat; 10am-2pm Sun. **Admission** €6.50. **No credit cards**. **Map** p299 J5.
The highlight of Greece's finest art gallery is a collection of El Greco's masterpieces. The museum is also a regular stop on the circuit of premier international exhibitions, and has showcased Cézanne and Picasso, among others.

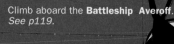

Climb aboard the **Battleship Averoff**.
See p119.

Panathenaic Stadium

*Leof Vas Konstantinou (210 752 2986/www.
culture.gr). Metro Evangelismos.* **Open** 8am-sunset
daily. **Admission** free. **Map** p299 G7/H7.
This enormous marble stadium, which boasts a seating capacity of around 50,000, was originally built
in 330 BC to host the first Panathenaic Games. It
later fell into ruins, and much of its marble was used
for the construction of other buildings. In the 19th
century it was rebuilt to host the first modern
Olympics (1896). The reconstruction used marble
from nearby Mount Penteli, famed for its beauty –
hence the stadium's nickname, Kallimarmaro, meaning 'beautiful marble'. The marble was meticulously
cleaned and restored for the 2004 Olympics, during
which the stadium hosted the archery competition
and marathon finish. The shady path around the top
of the stadium is popular with local joggers, especially on cooler summer evenings.

Mount Hymettos

A magnificent natural backdrop to the creeping
suburbs of eastern Athens, Mount Hymettos is
the nearest and arguably the most pleasant
place to escape Athens' urban jungle. Its gentle
slopes are traced with paths that wind through
pine forests, dells of bulbs and acres of
scrubland dotted with indigenous herbs and
wandering tortoises. But even if you never set
foot on it, you can enjoy one of Hymettos's most
famed qualities: at sunset, a spectacular display
of rosy hues illuminates the mountain, starting
off a soft pink and deepening to a vivid purple
as the evening wears on. This phenomenon has
been admired since antiquity, with the fifth-
century BC poet Pindar describing the hill as
'iostephanos' or violet-crowned.

The ancient Greeks believed the mountain
was the original source of honey. It's not hard to
see why. Honey from the mountain's abundant
wild herbs – fragrant thyme, sage and lavender
scent the air and make any walk up here a treat
– is still considered among the finest in Greece.

The best way to experience Mount
Hymettos is to visit the beautiful **Kaisariani
Monastery** (*see below*), set in a pine and
cypress copse on Ethnikis Antistaseos, the
road to the top of the mountain.

Kaisariani Monastery

*Ethnikis Antistaseos, Kaisariani (210 723 6619).
Bus 223 or 224, then 20min walk.* **Open** *Apr-Oct*
noon-7pm Mon; 8am-7pm Tue-Sun. *Nov-Mar* 8.30am-
3pm Tue-Sun. **Admission** €2; €1 concessions. Free
to all Sun Oct-Mar. **No credit cards.**
It's a mere 20-minute drive from Athens following
the mountain road known as Ethnikis Antistaseos,
but this Byzantine monastery on pine-clad Mount
Hymettos feels a world away from the city. The
monks still hold services in the two chapels, one

built in the 11th century, the other 500 years later. Have a wander around the fresco-filled sanctuaries and feel free to taste the spring water gushing from the ram's-head fountain (it's said to boost fertility). Then, setting off through the picturesque 11th-century olive grove, follow one of the many mountain trails to get unrivalled views over the Attica basin and to breathe in the fresh, thyme-scented air.

Northern Suburbs

Useful transport: Metro Irini, Kifissia, Maroussi.
Heading north out of Athens, the boulevards of Leof Kifisias and Mesogeion run through increasingly expensive, spacious and leafy suburbs. Not that one could tell while driving on either road, though – they are filled with a huge, ugly build-up of randomly set shopping malls, business centres, supermarkets, neon signs and advertising hoardings. But behind this façade are neighbourhoods like **Paleo Psychiko**, with graceful neo-classical buildings, old flowering trees and diplomats' residences, and **Neo Psychiko**, home to ground-breaking gallery DESTE (*see p198*).

Athens' northern suburbs are framed by mountains on all sides – Tourkovounia to the west, Penteli to the north, Hymettos to the east. That means the wealthy residents who get to live on their foothills have space, clean air, greenery and a different climate from the denizens of central Athens – in winter, these districts may see up to 30 centimetres (12 inches) of snow, while downtown sees nary a flake. (The mountains are also the reason that the city's infamous pollution ends up getting trapped in the lowland city basin.)

The two main suburbs of interest to tourists are **Kifisia**, 16 kilometres (ten miles) from central Athens, and **Marousi**, 12 kilometres (7.5 miles) from the city. The former is an attractive, wealthy and tree-lined district full of parks, cafés, posh shops, outstanding restaurants and two museums. It is a wonderful refuge from Athens in midsummer. Marousi is home to the Santiago Calatrava-designed **Athens Olympic Sports Complex**, the 2004 Olympics' main venue (*see also p39* **Future perfect?**).

Kifisia

Kifisia started life as a cool, green and gracious summer resort for Athens' wealthiest citizens, who built airy neo-classical holiday homes along its neat, tree-lined streets. The urban sprawl of Athens didn't fully reach Kifisia until the 1970s, and though it's now a fully fledged suburb, it still retains the main qualities (shady, pretty and pricey) that made it so appealing to its earlier inhabitants.

By far the easiest way to get to Kifisia is on the Line 1 metro, which terminates here. Walking out of the metro, you'll head up Adrianou, which flanks a pretty park filled with cafés. Continuing up the street, you'll pass Leof Kifisias to enter the commercial centre of the area. This is focused around Kassaveti, Kolokotroni, Kyprou and Georganta streets, all lined with some of Athens' best restaurants and nightclubs, most expensive designer shops and chicest people-watching cafés.

Gaia Centre

Othonos 100 (210 801 5870). Metro Kifissia.
Open 9am-2.30pm Mon-Thur, Sat; 10am-2.30pm Sun. **Admission** €5; €3 concessions. *Gaia Centre & Goulandris Museum of Natural History* €7; €4 concessions. **No credit cards.**
The Gaia Centre is part environmental research lab, part edutainment. The Centre, affiliated with the Museum of Natural History (*see below*) down the street, has three floors of well-made displays on ecosystems and the environment, including plenty of interactive video, computer and tactile displays. There's an exhibit on solar power, where you can cover and reveal the sun with varying degrees of cloud to see how fast it will run an engine; a touch-screen game where you can try to make your organic crop succeed on its own or by using pesticides; and a laser-light rotating-globe show every hour. The exhibits, designed in association with London's Natural History Museum, are well made and a big hit with children. Unfortunately, almost all the information is in Greek.

Goulandris Museum of Natural History

Levidou 13 (210 801 5870/www.culture.gr). Metro Kifissia. **Open** 9am-2.30pm Mon-Thur, Sat; 10am-2.30pm Sun. **Admission** €5; €3 concessions. *Gaia Centre & Goulandris Museum of Natural History* €7; €4 concessions. **No credit cards.**
The extensive, excellently researched exhibit on Greece's rich natural wildlife makes the Museum of Natural History a fitting stop in leafy Kifisia. The displays include insects, mammals, birds, reptiles, shells, rocks, minerals and fossils. The botanical collections have over 200,000 species of Greek plants, 145 of which have been discovered and recorded only recently, thanks to the museum's research.

Marousi

Up until the end of the 20th century, Marousi was little more than a sprawling suburb, whose main attributes were a good hospital and a football stadium. The 2004 Olympics transformed the area, with the development of the **Athens Olympic Sports Complex**, along with some of the other biggest projects of the Games, including a gigantic broadcasting and press centre. Construction continues post-Olympics, with vast new shopping centres, office blocks and other structures springing up in the gashes where until only a few years ago stood small, village-type houses with hens in their gardens. Proximity to the Sports Complex has also highlighted the neighbouring **Museum of 20th-Century Design**.

Athens Olympic Sports Complex

Leof Kifisias 37 & Spiros Louis (210 683 4060). Metro Irini.

The main, multi-stadium complex for the 2004 Olympics has long been Athens' biggest venue for sports and major concerts; but the stadium itself was shabby and its surrounds little more than a concrete wasteland. But for the Games the stadium was given a pricey facelift by renowned Spanish architect Santiago Calatrava, whose modern works for the Barcelona Games have become veritable landmarks. Calatrava's contributions to the Olympic Complex include soaring, graceful glass-and-steel arches over the main stadium, a new velodrome and, most ambitious of all, the transformation of the surrounding area into a landscaped park filled with sculpture and lined with undulating glass-covered walkways. *See also p139* **Future perfect?**.

Museum of 20th-Century Design

Patmou 4-12, Technal Plaza (210 685 0611/ www.designplaza.gr). Metro Irini. **Open** 10am-6pm Mon-Wed; 10am-8pm Thur, Fri; 10am-3pm Sat. **Admission** free.

This may once have been the most random museum in Athens: a stylish collection of furniture, lamps and interior design pieces by some of the top 20th century architects (Salvador Dali, Le Corbusier, Frank Lloyd Wright, Mies van der Rohe and Antoni Gaudi) located next to a football stadium in a far-flung suburb of the city. But now that the stadium is a landmark Olympic monument by Santiago Calatrava, whose name is starting to rank in importance with some of those displayed in the museum, it's all beginning to make some weird kind of sense. If you're at the stadium and inspired to see some more good design, it's a worthwhile place to visit.

Syngrou & Southern Suburbs

Map p300

Useful transport: Metro Syngrou-Fix; bus A2, E2.
Syngrou Avenue runs from central Athens, south to its coastal suburbs and beaches. Like the major arteries to the north, Syngrou is one of the ugliest roads around, home to a haphazard smattering of big-box buildings, abandoned or run-down blocks of flats (many built to house Greek refugees when they fled from Asia Minor in 1923), business centres and perpetual construction work. It is also, due to a combination of fast-flowing traffic and unpleasant underground pedestrian passes that many avoid, site of many a fatal traffic accident.

But Syngrou does have its attractions. A lot of those big-box structures house Athens' largest nightclubs and *bouzoukia*. Their names, ownership and decor change almost every year, keeping them fresh, trendy and always exclusive, so international clubbing types should definitely put a night out here on their agendas. As with much in Athens, there's a quirky appeal to making your way through an arbitrarily gritty area, then suddenly finding yourself in one of the most wildly posh nightclubs in the Mediterranean; perhaps even more in driving by and seeing all the beautiful people lined up on the road's edge.

The northern part of Syngrou is also a hot-spot for Athens' sex industry, lined with strip clubs and, late at night, prostitutes and transvestites. Nothing wildly posh here: this is a particularly sleazy red-light district, staffed almost entirely by Eastern European women forced into the sex trade by their illegal status.

Once the road hits the coast, things get much better. From Syngrou, the busy Leof Posidonos, named after the god of the sea, runs along the coast through the wealthy seaside suburbs of Faliro, Glyfada, Voula and Vouliagmeni. The locals have taken to calling this area the 'Athenian Riviera', and there's something to be said for that: it's lined with clean, well-maintained public and pay-per-visit beaches (*see p123* **Beaches**), all invariably full of the requisite topless, thong-clad bathing beauties.

Between the beaches are enormous, luxurious seaside nightclubs, which entertain Athens' party people in summer, when the Syngrou clubs close down. Like their downtown equivalents, these spots are huge, seasonal, pricey and trendy, but they have the added advantage of wide, open-air beachfront locations. Some are open all day, drawing Athens' chicest and showiest to lounge and have coffee in their stunning settings. Many have decks that go right up to the water, pools, gauzy draperies and model-perfect waiting staff. Some are also restaurants, importing brand-name chefs to serve up astronomically expensive and beautifully presented fusion food. All heat up after midnight, when long lines of designer-clad wannabes wait for admission from the fashion police at the doors.

Before the Olympics, major changes were made to this coastal area – most obviously through the construction of beach volleyball and tae kwondo arenas at **Paleo Faliro** (the Trocadero Marina here is home to the **Battleship Averoff**, *see p119*), replacement of the rather seedy hippodrome at the end of Syngrou with a concrete park, the conversion of Agios Kosmas to host Olympic sailing events, and the transformation of the old airport at

Hellinikon into a vast complex of Games venues. Since the Olympics and Paralympics came to an end in September 2004, many of these multi-million-euro projects have fallen into disrepair and anything that was not completed in time for the Games (for example, the 'environmental' park and promenade that was to link the Peace and Friendship Stadium at **Neo Faliro** with the two Paleo Faliro venues) has been left, strewn with debris, in mid construction.

Another change brought about by the Olympics was the opening of a tram line from central Athens to Vouliagmeni and Neo Faliro, meant to shorten and ease the trip from the city to the seaside and Olympic venues. The tram was also supposed to be of permanent benefit to residents of the southern suburbs, but a painfully long journey time, extended by traffic lights, too many stops and, often, vehicles obstructing the lines, has resulted in widespread rejection of this form of transport. Trams were first introduced to Athens in 1882, but were abolished in 1959. The public was so opposed to this decision that the public works minister at the time, Constantine Karamanlis, went to the tram depot under cover of night to personally oversee the removal of the first rails so the trams could not set off in the morning. As the new tram was a project of the previous, socialist government, one wonders whether the current conservative prime minister (Costas Karamanlis, ironically none other than the nephew of the original tram abolisher) may also take steps to put an end to the system. Public outrage seems unlikely this time around.

Battleship Averoff

Trocadero Marina, Paleo Faliro (210 983 6539/ www.bsaverof.com). Metro Piraeus, then bus 909 to Oulen bus stop. **Open** *Oct-May* 9am-1pm Tue, Thur; 9am-1pm, 3-5pm Mon, Wed, Fri; 11am-3pm Sat, Sun. *June-Sept* 9am-1pm Tue, Thur; 9am-1pm, 5-7pm Mon, Wed, Fri; 11am-3pm Sat, Sun. **Admission** €1. **No credit cards**.

Between 1910 and 1920 the *Averoff* was the fastest ship in the Greek fleet, and famously played a decisive role in the Balkan Wars, turning the tide between Greece and Turkey and forcing the return of Greece's major islands. The ship served in both World Wars, before being decommissioned in 1958. Since 1985 it has been moored at the Trocadero Marina, restored to its original state and operating as museum. You can explore everything from the bridge to the captain's quarters to the engine room, but bear in mind that there are still a couple of navy officers living on board, so don't be surprised to find personal knick-knacks and a few signs saying 'keep out'. On-board exhibits tell the stories of the ship's wartime exploits. Berthed next to the *Averoff* is the reconstructed trireme that was used to bring the Olympic flame into Piraeus after the torch relay of the islands in summer 2004. This vessel, a hand-made replica of a 2,500-year-old Greek warship, is powered by 170 oarsmen. She has toured the Greek islands and even been as far as London.

Lake Vouliagmeni

Leof Posidonos, Vouliagmeni (210 896 2239). Bus A2 or E2 to Platia Glyfada, then bus 114. **Open** *Summer* 7am-8pm daily. *Winter* 8am-5pm daily. **Admission** €6. **No credit cards**.

This lake is beautifully set inside a huge jutting rock on the inland side of the coast road. Its blue-green mineral-infused waters come partly from the nearby sea and partly from a deep, but still unknown, freshwater source. What is known is that the water stays at an approximate 24°C (75°F) year round, making this a popular spot for winter bathing. The waters are said to be curative for conditions such as rheumatism, which explains the preponderance of genteel, elderly, bathing-capped crowds. They also appreciate the free parking, attractive landscaping and old-fashioned café on one bank. Behind the café there is a small spa facility, where visitors can have hydrotherapy massages in the lake waters.

National Museum of Contemporary Art

Amvrosiou Frantzi 14 & Kallirois, Syngrou (210 924 2111). Metro Syngrou-Fix.

A fine example of modern industrial architecture, the old FIX Beer brewery on Syngrou had been empty for so long that much of it had fallen into ruin. Works for the nearby metro station further decimated it. But the good news is that the brewery is finally being restored and renovated, in order to be converted into Athens' first comprehensive museum of modern art. The museum – which will display works by artists such as Ilya Kabakov, Gary Hill, Nan Goldin, George Hadjimichalis, Pavlos and Allan Sekula – is scheduled to open by late summer 2007. Features of the plan include a rooftop restaurant and sculpture garden, a 'rock curtain' at the museum's entrance and water walls within as a tribute to the Ilissos river, which used to flow along neighbouring Kallirois Avenue until it was asphalted over in the 1950s. The museum is currently in temporary accommodation at the Athens Concert Hall (Vas Sofias & Kokkali 1, 210 924 2111, www.emst.gr).

Evgenidio Planetarium

Syngrou 387, Paleo Faliro (entrance from Pentelis 11) (210 946 9600/www.eugenfound.edu.gr). Bus 040 from Syntagma Square, 161 from Akadimias. **Open** 5.30-8.30pm Wed-Fri; 10.30am-8.30pm Sat, Sun. **Admission** *Feature film presentation* €8; €5 concessions. *Digital presentation* €6; €4 concessions. **No credit cards**.

Athens' planetarium shows documentary films as well as stars and planets on its overhead domed screen. Commentaries for the films and exhibitions are in Greek, but earphones with English-language commentaries are often available. Call ahead to check screening times and programmes.

Sightseeing

Piraeus

Set sail for Athens' nautical neighbour.

Useful transport: Piraeus metro. For
Mikrolimano, Piraeus metro then trolleybus 20.
With its strategic position at the crossroads of
the continents of Europe, Africa and Asia –
not to mention the proximity of several dozen
popular island destinations – Piraeus is not
only the busiest port in the Mediterranean but
also the third busiest in the world. Around 12
million passengers pass through this Greek
harbour city annually, and over 30,000 ships
dock here every year.

Thousands of years ago Piraeus was an
island. Even after the thin channel that
separated it from the rest of Greece dried up
and it rejoined the mainland, it took nearly
another 1,000 years before the great Athenian
general Themistocles, in the fifth century BC,
recognised Piraeus's potential as Attica's best-
situated natural harbour. Until then, Athenians
had moored in the bay of Faliro, today a wealthy
seaside suburb (*see p118*).

Themistocles had his new port built up to
accommodate Athens' many ships, but his
greatest accomplishment was the construction
of the **Long Walls** in 478 BC. These

fortifications, which surrounded the entire port
and ran all the way back to the city of Athens,
are still the most impressive remains in Piraeus
today – walking through the modern city,
you're likely to come upon fenced-off areas
containing foundations of the walls and the
settlements around them. In the mid fifth
century AD, under Pericles, the city of Piraeus
was laid out in blocks by Ippodamos of Miletus
– it grew and thrived under the city plan, which
is still the same one used today (you can
appreciate its ruler-straight lines best from the
air, but they can also be seen furrowing through
the city from the nearby island of Aegina).

In medieval times, the port became known as
'Porto Leone', after the colossal stone lion that
guarded its entrance. The lion was removed in
1688 and taken to Venice, where it remains.

By the 19th century Piraeus was a busy,
fast-growing city. In 1923 it grew even more:
the Greek-Turkish population exchange
brought thousands of refugees from Asia Minor
to Greece; many of them settled here. The port
became known as a colourful but seedy place,
full of hashish dens and dives where the Greeks

Piraeus Flea Market. *See p121.*

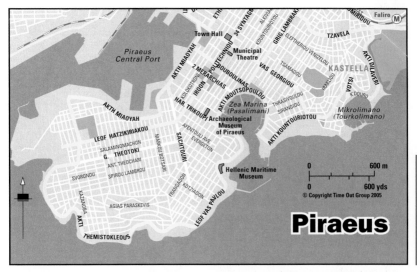

Sightseeing

Piraeus

from Turkey sang gritty *rembetika*. This image persisted into the mid century, immortalised in the movie *Never on Sunday*, where the whisky-voiced blonde film star Melina Mercouri (who later became minister of culture) plays a lively prostitute with a heart of gold who loves to swim in the harbour.

Today, Piraeus has grown in size to the point where it's hard to say whether it's a sibling to Athens, or just part of the city itself. But there's no question that it retains its own character. Most visitors arrive by train in the middle of the chaotic central harbour, surrounded by enormous ships, dozens of shipping company offices, street hawkers and people departing and arriving from all over the Med. Behind the station, around Alipedou and Skylitsi, is the **Piraeus Flea Market**. The market proper is held on Sundays from 7am to 3pm; a number of antique-cum-kitsch-cum-junk shops are also open during the week. A walk through this proletarian district will eventually lead you to Piraeus's must-see **Archaeological Museum**, housing the bronze sculptures of Athena and Artemis that graced the port in Themistocles' day.

South of the museum are Piraeus's two smaller and more scenic harbours, **Zea Marina** and **Mikrolimano**. The larger of the two is **Zea Marina**, also known as Pasalimani; this is the harbour for yachts plying the Saronic Gulf islands (and a good place to go millionaire-spotting). It's lined with buzzing cafés and bars, and is also home to the **Hellenic Maritime Museum**. Pretty Mikrolimano (also known as

Tourkolimano), filled with fishing boats and seafood restaurants overlooking the sea, is the main destination for tourists, and with good reason. Behind Mikrolimano rises the pretty neighbourhood of **Kastella**, Piraeus's most fashionable district. Lined with attractive, narrow streets and pastel-painted neo-classical mansions, it has the most lovely view of the entire harbour.

Archaeological Museum of Piraeus

Harilaou Trikoupi 31, Pasalimani (210 452 1598/ www.culture.gr). Metro Piraeus. **Open** 8.30am-3pm Tue-Sun. **Admission** €3. **No credit cards.**

That this little sister of the National Archaeological Museum (*see p106*) sees less than half the visitors of its downtown sibling is perhaps understandable, but it's a shame nonetheless, for it is home to some of the most magnificent works of classical Greek art in existence. The greatest pieces by the Greek classical sculptors were generally made in bronze, but few survive, as most were melted down for weapons or tools in the intervening centuries. Some, however, were lost in the waters of Piraeus, where they stayed, perfectly preserved, for centuries, until they were found during an underwater excavation in 1959. Such is the fate that befell the marvellous bronze statues of Athena, Apollo and Artemis, the undisputed stars of this museum.

It's worth stopping by just to see Room 3, with the centrepiece of a brilliantly sculpted and perfectly intact bronze of Athena, believed to date either from the fourth century BC or from a first-century BC sculptor imitating the earlier classical style. Either way, it is a masterpiece, with a noble, helmeted head and a sash made of writhing snakes, and bearing the

Zea Marina – home to the Maritime Museum (and a few gin palaces). *See p121.*

head of Medusa. In the same room is a well-sculpted bronze of Apollo, believed to date from around the sixth century BC, two lovely bronzes of Artemis and a perfectly intact fourth-century BC bronze tragic mask, with a wild, snaky beard, sunken cheeks and dramatically dismayed eyebrows.

Room 4 has another don't-miss: a large fourth-century BC shrine to the mother of the gods, with the goddess seated on a throne with a lion next to her. Room 7 has what may have been the largest funerary monument in ancient Greece. Built by a merchant from Istria for his son, the piece is the size of a small temple, with larger-than-life sculptures of the merchant, his son and their servant surrounded

by friezes of Greek heroes. It was the lavish ostentation of pieces like this that led to the banning of funerary monuments in Athens in 317 BC.

Hellenic Maritime Museum

Zea Marina (210 451 6264/www.culture.gr). Metro Piraeus. **Open** 9am-2pm Tue-Sat. **Admission** €3; €1.50 concessions. **No credit cards**.

From Odysseus to Aristotle Onassis, the nautical world has always been fundamental to Greece's psyche. The 2,500 exhibits at this museum begin with models of prehistoric ships, and include sophisticated ancient navigating equipment, paintings, maps, flags, guns and models galore.

Beaches

Sweeping stretches of sand and tiny, rocky coves are within easy reach along the coastline south of Athens.

Sightseeing

The Greek islands are famous for their pristine waters, but few visitors to Athens are aware that the capital's coastline also consistently scores highly on the EU's 'Blue Flag' list of clean beaches. This may come as a surprise to those who have seen the unwholesome flotsam and jetsam lapping around the bay of Piraeus, who are aware of the 'sewage island' of Psytallia just off the coast of Piraeus, and who have read that if Melina Mercouri did her *Never on Sunday* stunt of leaping into the harbour waters today she would probably not have survived as long as she did. But around the corner from Piraeus, lining the coastal road that runs from Alimos to Vouliagmeni and further, are a number of clean and attractive beaches – and the nearest is only about half an hour from the city centre. So after a hot climb up the Acropolis, you can grab your swimsuit, hop on the tram or bus, and set off for the seaside.

Beaches in the Athens area can be roughly divided into publicly maintained free beaches and semi-public, privately managed, paying beaches. Heavy privatisation in the past few years means that very few of Athens' beaches are public and free, but they do exist and are reasonably maintained, if predictably crowded.

If you want more than just sea and sand from your ideal beach, then look to Athens' privately managed beaches. They are perfect for high-maintenance types and more closely resemble stylish clubs than merely convenient spots in the sand. And while they can be pricey, they do offer a number of services and conveniences. For the admission price you normally get an umbrella and chair, changing cabins, WCs and a cold rinse-off shower. Often there are also small children's playgrounds, a bit of greenery, a snack bar or kiosk/mini-market, a first-aid station and areas for racket-ball or beach volley. Lifeguards are employed at all privately managed beaches but should never be relied on, as they are often absent from their posts.

Athens' beaches are at their most crowded on summer weekends, between 11am and 2pm. The umbrella and chair you've paid for may not be available right away – a fact that you may or may not be informed of unless you ask. The roads too are busy at peak times and the buses full; a taxi is a sensible option.

Beaches usually close at sunset regardless of their stated 'official' hours. Sadly, midnight dips aren't an option except on public beaches; privately managed beaches are closed (and usually fenced off) at night. Crime of any sort is still unlikely, but common-sense precautions

The best Beaches

For peace and quiet
Agios Kosmas, *see p124.*

For sports and facilities
Asteria, *see p125.*

For style by the sea
Varkiza Beach, *see p126.*

For a beach-side temple
Astir Beach, *see p126.*

For long stretches of sand
Attica Vouliagmeni Beach, *see p126.*

Where the smart set like to sunbathe – popular but pricey **Astir Beach**. *See p126.*

like keeping an eye on your belongings apply. Your biggest problem is likely to be getting socked by a tennis ball from 'rackets' games, which are ubiquitous on all beaches.

Animals are not allowed on any private or public beaches in Greece. It's easy to get away with taking your dog for a seaside stroll during winter or a swim at a deserted island beach, but you are likely to get into trouble trying to bring him with you to any of the popular places listed below during the height of summer.

The best...

The following beaches are listed in geographical order, travelling from north (Faliro) to south (near Varkiza). For more beach options, *see p241* **Roadside beaches**.

Edem Beach ❶ ↖

Leof Posidonos coastal road, Paleo Faliro (in the Flisvos/Edem districts of Paleo Faliro). Tram from Syntagma ('Edem' stop)/bus A1, B1, B2, E1, E2, 101, 217, X96. **Open** *24hrs daily.* **Admission** *free.*
Athens' most urban beach may not be its best but it is certainly the most convenient. Set in the seaside suburb of Faliro, Edem is skirted by an attractive promenade running between the coast and Leof Posidonos. The long beach, which is mostly sandy but with a few pebbles to contend with, is flanked at one end by a couple of tavernas, while the other end stretches towards the rather seedy Flisvos area (the redeeming feature of which is a very pleasant

open-air cinema). Since the beach is publicly managed, it is free of charge and largely a self-service experience. However, the Hotel Poseidon (which is actually located over the road but operates the Poseidon taverna and beach bar on the sand) offers private beach facilities (with sunbeds, drinks service, changing room, shower and lifeguard), while the nearby Edem taverna serves up reasonably priced meals. If driving, be aware that parking is notoriously difficult in the Paleo Faliro area. You're much better off taking the tram from Syntagma – it stops right at the entrance to the beach.

Agios Kosmas ❷

Off Leof Posidonos coastal road, Elliniko (next to the Ethniki Athlitiko Kentro [National Athletic Centre], turn off at the sign marked 'Agios Kosmas beach'). Tram from Syntagma ('2nd Ayios Kosmas' stop)/ bus A1, A2, B1, E1, 140. **Open** *mid May-mid Sept 9am-9pm daily.* **Admission** *Mon-Fri €5; €2 concessions. Weekends €8; €5 concessions.*
Slightly off the beaten track, tucked in between a number of strictly fenced-off sporting complexes, Agios Kosmas is well worth the extra effort needed to find it. One of Athens' smallest, most tasteful and peaceful beaches, in some ways it feels more like a sleepy island resort than an Athens 'scene' beach. The water is clean and boosted by an extra filter/barrier in place for environmental pollution, while security guards are in place to throw out the human sort of pollution (guests behaving badly). Regulars as well as large groups can expect some discounts on request. Generally, facilities, as well as the beach itself, are well maintained. Toilets are especially

modern and clean; the outdoor showers less so. A small green garden is available for a little shade, and private parties on occasion; there is also a snack bar. Next door, the vast expanses of concrete are where crews launched their vessels from and viewers sat during the 2004 Olympic sailing events.

Asteria ③

Entrance on Leof Vas Georgiou B, between Platia Katraki Vasos and Platia Kritis, Glyfada. Tram from Syntagma (get out at Glyfada on Metaxas and walk down to the sea, or at 'Palia dimarchio' stop and walk along the coast)/bus A1, A2, E2, 114, 116, 149, X96. **Open** *Beach* mid May-mid Sept 8am-9.30pm daily (last entry 8pm). Lifeguards on duty until 8pm. *Pool area* mid May-mid Sept 10am-7pm, 9pm-3am daily. **Admission** *Mon-Fri* €7; €3.50 concessions. *Weekends* €10; €5 concessions. **Parking** Cars €5; motorbikes €2.

With door staff who act like bouncers, landscaped gardens and a nightclub, Asteria feels like an exclusive beach club. And although it isn't a private membership club, it is the priciest Athens beach and encompasses a giant complex and huge beach on a bay in the seaside suburb of Glyfada, with easy access from Athens city centre. With immaculate WCs, extensive dressing rooms, huge gardens, a playground, a volleyball court, a pool complex, a few shops, watersports (water volleyball, inner tubes and blow-up teeter-totters) and several cafés, the Asteria is particularly popular with scenesters and upscale families. Which is not to say the beach has a really refined or restrained quality about it – it's as rowdy as any other beach and at high season can become a virtual sea of people. A unique feature is the elegant pool area, surrounded by cabanas, which transforms into a cocktail bar/café/lounge/disco/restaurant at night.

Voula A & Voula B ④ ⑤

Leof Alkyonidon, Voula. Voula A: opposite the Asklipeo Voula Hospital complex; Voula B: close to the Voula Dimarhio (town hall). Bus A1, A2, E1, E2, E22, 114, 116, 149 (Voula A); bus A1, A2, E1 (Voula B). **Open** early May-mid Sept 7am-9pm daily. **Admission** (each beach) €4; €1.50 concessions.

Under the same management and just a couple of kilometres apart on the same thoroughfare, these two private beaches are nearly identical. Both are on the cheaper side, and tend to be less crowded than some of the other beaches. Both have generous grounds with gardens, generic snack bar and shops, plus sports facilities such as beach volleyball. Voula A is directly next door to a large, pleasant beachside bistro-café, Palmie (meals around €20), while Voula B has tennis courts and has just finished building seven cute one-room bungalows that can be rented out on a short-term basis during the summer. Surrounded by palm trees and looking out over the glittering sea, these little guesthouses are idyllic at sunset and sunrise when the beach is closed, but not so peaceful during the heat of the day.

Kavouri-Vouliagmeni ⑥

Parallel to Iliou, near Agios Nikolaos church, in the Kavouri district of Vouliagmeni. Bus E1, E2, 114, 116, 138, 149. **Open** 24hrs daily. **Admission** free.

The incredibly popular Kavouri-Vouliagmeni is a long stretch of sand near the Divani hotel (*see p68*). This public beach is packed throughout the summer; if you can't find a patch of sand, join the others and play 'rackets' by the sea. Though this is a strictly self-service resort, there is a string of fish tavernas (all rather upscale) alongside the beach, and some

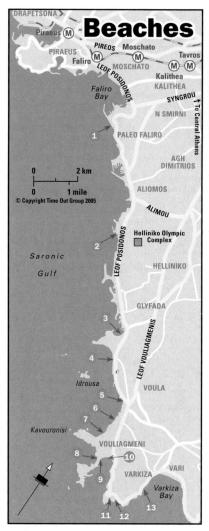

pleasant places for strolls amid them. The main problem here is space, so if there isn't enough, head to nearby Megalo Kavouri (*see below*).

Megalo Kavouri ⑦

Off Leof Kavouriou, in Kavouri district of Vouliagmeni. Bus 114 (get off at Strofi Kavouriou, a leafy square). **Open** 24hrs daily. **Admission** free.
Although set in the middle of one of the most expensive real-estate areas in Athens, Megalo Kavouri has a casual, downmarket feel. The large beach includes an up-close view of an ancient temple ruin on a tiny island opposite. Shallow waters mean it's a good place for swimmers who are less than proficient, which is probably why swarms of families flock to it. Besides several nondescript, inexpensive cafés, no basic beach services are available (not even changing cabins or outdoor showers), but a shady, tree-dotted area just next to the beach makes for a great do-it-yourself picnic site. Parking is readily available.

Astir Beach ⑧
(also known as Asteras)

Entrance via Platia Aiglis, on Apollonos, Vouliagmeni Bay. Bus 114, 116 from Platia Glyfada. **Open** 8am-8pm daily. **Admission** *Mon-Fri* €10; €5 concessions. *Weekends* €15; €8 concessions.
Open all year round, this popular though pricey private beach attracts keen racket-players, winter swimmers and sunseekers. Set in a sheltered bay – with an ancient temple devoted to Apollo and the gourmet fish restaurant Ithaki on one flank, the Astir Palace resort on the other – the beach offers an extensive range of watersports, beach volley and racket-ball areas, a bar and shop. Parking in July and August is extremely difficult. Easy access for the disabled is a positive distinguishing feature.

Attica Vouliagmeni Beach ⑨

Opposite Platia Aiglis & next to Apollonos, Vouliagmeni Bay. Bus 114 from Glyfada. **Open** 24hrs daily. **Admission** free.
Opposite the private Astir Beach (*see above*), this is the free part of Athens' largest beach. It may not boast an ancient temple, sports facilities or even sunbeds and umbrellas, but it does have a gorgeous view. The narrow stretch of sand definitely attracts a younger, alternative crowd, so if that doesn't sound like your thing, continue on to the privately managed section (*see below*), which, although virtually the same beach, has a separate entrance.

Attica Vouliagmeni Beach ⑩

On Vouliagmeni Bay. Entrance at the point where Leof Athinas becomes Leof Posidonos, next to the Dimarhio (town hall) at Platia 24 Iouliou, Vouliagmeni Bay. Bus 114, 116. **Open** *mid May-mid Sept* 8am-9.30pm (last entry 8pm) daily. **Admission** €5. Animals not allowed.
Excellent value, and stylish to boot, the recently privatised Attica Vouliagmeni Beach (formerly known as Vouliagmeni A Beach) is perhaps the best compromise between the high-frills Astir (*see above*) and the free-for-all Attica Vouliagmeni (*see above*). This

well-organised beach is set on an enormous stretch of sand on Vouliagmeni Bay, perhaps Athens' most beautiful coastline. A low-ish admission fee offers visitors an elegant chaise longue and umbrella, snack bars, two small children's playgrounds, volleyball, tennis and basketball courts, and the usual amenities like changing rooms, WCs and open showers. Tennis courts can be booked in advance.

...and the rest

While not exactly proper beaches, **Agnanti** and **Lambros** (named after the eateries they are adjacent to), two mini-beaches opposite Lake Vouliagmeni, deserve a mention. These makeshift beaches with a stylish café and taverna flanking them tend to be very windy, so they are great for extra-hot days. However, they practically disappear in high tides. Both boast shallow waters, making them good alternatives for those with little confidence in their own – or their children's – swimming abilities. The beaches have no closing hours, and can be reached via bus 114 or 116 from Glyfada.

Limanakia A & Limanakia B ⑪ ⑫

Between Vouliagmeni & Varkiza. Bus 116, 149, E2. **Open** 24hrs daily. **Admission** free.
'Little Lakes A' and 'Little Lakes B' are misnomers, as neither is a lake, rather a series of small, rocky coves. Resting on an otherwise nondescript stretch of Athens coastline, they are easy to miss, but well worth a stop if only to gape at the stunning bays, which are beautifully lit up at night. Descend one of the small dirt paths leading steeply downhill towards the rocks. Limanakia B (just a short walk from A) leads down directly towards a quiet, rather private area of the rocks. A section of this beach is a well-known gay nudist haven (*see p205*). The steep rocky path at Limanakia A descends towards a café built into the rocks, which offers access to the water below. There's a bona fide scene at the rocks and the café-bar is bursting with teenagers and twenty-somethings, and is host to all-day parties throughout the summer.

Varkiza Beach ⑬

Varkiza Bay. Bus 116, 125, 171. **Open** *mid May-Sept* 8am-8pm daily. **Admission** €12; €3 concessions.
You can't miss the vast, multicoloured beach bar-restaurant that marks the entrance to the recently renovated private part of this sprawling bay. Drop in for a cold coffee and to admire the orange Perspex walls and geometric white sofas straight from the pages of a design magazine, then join the beautiful people sunning themselves on the beach. Lifeguards, watersports, drinks service – you name it, they've got it at this hip and happening beach, which belongs to the Grecotel chain. If you're more of a rough and ready type, head next door to the public part of the beach, where on windy days you can watch kitesurfers whisking perilously from one edge of the bay to the other.

Eat, Drink, Shop

Restaurants

Traditional tavernas and cutting-edge cuisine.

Eat, Drink, Shop

Eating out – and eating outside – is an integral part of Greek culture; it's hard to over-estimate the pleasure of a meal in a leafy garden or overlooking moonlit waves on a summer evening. If you want to dine with the locals, make your reservation for late evening – Greeks hardly ever go out for dinner before 10pm.

Recent years have seen changes and improvements to the Athenian restaurant scene. People in the city are venturing away from trusted taverna fare. The overall boom in the restaurant industry has brought a multitude of new trends with it. Traditional Greek food is undergoing a process of reinvention, while classic foreign cuisines like French and Italian, as well as more exotic, multi-ethnic alternatives, Asian, Moroccan and fusion, are finding their way on to restaurant tables. The global craze for sushi has taken Greece by storm of late, with new restaurants springing up all the time. More and more chefs are now going abroad to train and then returning to Greece to put their newly found creative expertise to good use in the city's kitchens. Three Athens restaurants, **Spondi** (*see p148*), **Vardis** (*see p154*) and **Varoulko** (*see p144*), have been awarded a Michelin star for their high standards.

In spite of an influx of modern trends, there's no real fear that the old-style taverna will go out of favour with the majority of the population. What has happened, though, is that these past couple of years have seen the birth of 'modern' tavernas aimed at the city's younger crowd, where traditional Greek food is served in a much fresher environment and with more attention to detail.

Making a table reservation is an absolute necessity in club-restaurants and in most quality eateries in general. Your tip should be around 10-15 per cent on top of the bill (check whether service is included). Be warned that the combination of good food and a great eating environment doesn't come cheap in Athens – although the comparatively high restaurant prices in these places don't seem to deter people in the slightest. Seafood, in particular, is surprisingly expensive, and if it seems like it isn't, it's probably frozen.

GREEK EATS

Eating at traditional tavernas and *mezedopolia* is a must-do; unquestionably one of the best experiences to be had in Greece. Both serve the hearty, deeply flavourful dishes based on the precepts that have governed Greek cooking for centuries: fresh, seasonal ingredients, lots of extra virgin olive oil, local cheeses and a few fragrant herbs and spices. These are assembled sometimes with a wonderful simplicity that shows off the best of dishes, like *horta* (wild greens) with lemon, or sometimes with the inspired creativity that is a hallmark of much peasant food, and comes from taking the only ingredients available and combining them in the most interesting, flavourful way possible. An example of the latter is the winter classic, *stifado*, where rabbit is stewed with dark Mavrodaphne wine and hundreds of tiny onions.

Tavernas are friendly, cheap and informal, and usually have tables covered in butcher paper that is changed for each customer, cosy interiors lined with wine barrels (from which you may sometimes be asked to draw your own wine), outdoor gardens draped in bougainvillea, and cats winding their way around your chairs. Many tavernas have no written menus, and, even when they do, you'll often find that there's plenty of discrepancy between what's on the menu and what's in the kitchen. Usually, the waiter will just reel off what's cooking today, and you'll pick from his list. In many cases, customers are welcome – even expected – to go into the kitchen and just point to what looks most appealing. So don't be afraid to ask to do this. Though it may be intimidating, the taverna staff will consider it par for the course, and you can order exactly what you want, even without understanding a word of Greek.

There are three main types of dishes available. You'll start with a selection of *salates* (salads) and *orektika* (appetisers), a category that includes the dozens of aromatic dips like tzatziki, and small plates of cooked vegetables,

Price guide

€ up to €20
€€ €21-€35
€€€ €36-€50
€€€€ €50 and over
For a meal for one including starter, main course and dessert.

Etrusco – dinstinctive and sophisticated Greco-Italian fusion.

like *kolokithokeftedes* (fried courgette-and-potato balls) or *mavromatakia* (marinated black-eyed peas). Main courses include simply grilled or roasted meat and fish, but vegetarians (or just those who don't want slabs of meat at every meal) should be sure to inquire about *mageirefta* (cooked stews, vegetable dishes, and casseroles, such as *briam* and moussaka). All this is accompanied with carafes of *hima* (local barrel wine), and often with the serenades of strolling musicians. For advice on choosing a good taverna, *see p135* **Taverna tips**.

If you're in the mood to sample dozens of dishes in one sitting – and to drink a lot – head to a **mezedopolion**. These serve *mezedes*, lots of small dishes, rather than large main courses, meant as much as an accompaniment to wine, ouzo and gossip. In some *mezedopolia*, ordering couldn't be easier. The waiter will come out with a large tray of all the dishes available, and you'll choose from those. In others, you might pick from a menu or in the kitchen.

Though the focus is ostensibly on nibbles to accompany your meal, most *mezedopolia* serve dishes just as well made and delicious as you'll find at a taverna. If it turns out this is your favourite way of eating – and it certainly has the advantage of allowing you to try everything – you can also turn your taverna experience into a meze feast. Simply order one of all the salads and appetisers.

Mezedopolia are also known as *ouzerie*, as ouzo, the aniseed-flavoured spirit distilled from the remains of grapes from the wine press, is the traditional accompaniment. You'll also come across other members of the ouzo family: *raki* (the basic drink with or without the aniseed flavouring), *tsipouro* (with aniseed but weaker than ouzo) or *tsikoudia* (Cretan *raki* without aniseed). All are served with water and ice.

Acropolis & around

Creative

Etrusco
Athenian Callirhoe Hotel, Kallirois 32 & Petmeza, Makrygianni (210 921 5353). Metro Syngrou-Fix. **Open** 8.30pm-12.30am Tue-Sat. **Average** €€€. **Credit** AmEx, DC, MC, V. **Map** p301 E7.
Having made his name as the finest chef on Corfu, Ettore Botrini has brought his distinctive Greco-Italian fusion to Athens. He has also bagged one of the capital's loveliest roof gardens, with close-up Acropolis views. Botrini cures his own fish and meat. The results – such as beef carpaccio with green tea jelly and caviar chocolate – are sublime. Other sophisticated combinations include grouper in an orange and almond crust floating in a citrus crab sauce. Desserts – created by Botrini's equally charismatic wife Monica – are dramatic: try semifreddo Amaretti with vanilla and pumpkin sauce. In winter, the restaurant moves to a less atmospheric dining room on the ground floor of the Athenian Callirhoe Hotel but Botrini supervises the kitchen in person, whereas in summer he decamps to Corfu. *See also p152* **Food with a view**.

Greek contemporary

To Kouti
Adrianou 23, Monastiraki (210 321 3229). Metro Monastiraki. **Open** 1pm-1am daily. **Average** €€. **Credit** AmEx, MC, V. **Map** p297/p301 D5.
All the restaurants along Adrianou Street have breathtaking views of the Acropolis and Ancient Agora, but most serve faux-Greek fodder. This boho

> ► For more on Greek food, *see pp48-50* **No More Moussaka**.

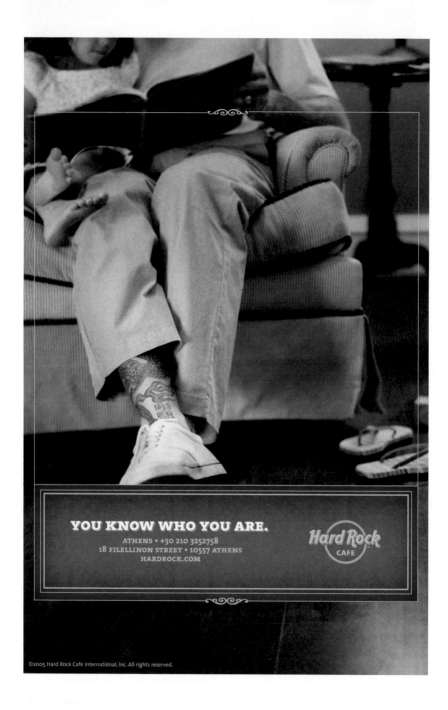

YOU KNOW WHO YOU ARE.

ATHENS • +30 210 3252758
18 FILELLINON STREET • 10557 ATHENS
HARDROCK.COM

haunt painted in pretty pastels stands out from the crowd. From the menus hand-written in picture books to the rose petal ice-cream, this offbeat spot is unabashedly romantic. With the trains chugging past and the moon rising above the Acropolis, it is even more magical after dark. Quirkily named dishes are a bit hit-and-miss, but there are lots of great vegetarian options like mushroom pie, fluffy leek soufflé and pasta with gorgonzola sauce.

Greek traditional

Café Abyssinia

Kinetou 7, Platia Avyssinias, Monastiraki (210 321 7047). Metro Monastiraki. **Open** 11am-midnight Tue-Sat; 11am-7pm Sun. Closed mid June-mid Aug. **Average** €€. **Credit** MC, V. **Map** p297/p301 D5.

Among the dusty china and antique furniture strewn about Abyssinia Square, the heart of the Monastiraki flea market, Café Abyssinia has the bohemian feel of a 1950s cabaret, complete with a feisty chanteuse. Tiny tables are squeezed among the market stalls, crowded with locals tucking into sardines wrapped in vine leaves, baked feta and fat chips dunked in creamy taramasalata. Starters are generally better than main courses, though the giant beefburger with red pepper relish is a crowd-pleaser. You won't want to share the delicious chocolate pot dusted with crystallised orange. For a quieter tête-à-tête, book a window seat on the mezzanine, with dreamy views of cats prowling the tin roofs crowned by the Parthenon.

Giouvetsakia

Adrianou 144 & Thespidos, Plaka (210 322 7033). Metro Akropoli. **Open** 10am-2am daily. **Average** €. **Credit** MC, V. **Map** p297 D5.

There is still a handful of authentic eateries in souvenir- and souvlaki-infested Plaka. This traditional taverna, run by the same family since 1950, is postcard pretty with its red-checked tablecloths and ivy-covered walls. At the bustling junction of Kydathinaion and Adrianou, it is the perfect spot for people-watching while you guzzle fried aubergines dipped in tzatziki, Greek salad and tasty stuffed tomatoes. Giouvetsakia is named after the house specialty, *giouvetsi* – a tender hunk of lamb baked in an earthenware pot with orzo (small pieces of pasta shaped like rice) and tomato sauce. Courteous staff will bring you complimentary fruit dusted with cinnamon for dessert.

To Steki tou Ilia

Thessalonikis 7, Thisio (210 342 2407). Metro Thissio. **Open** *mid June-mid Sept* 8pm-1am daily. *Mid Sept-mid June* 8pm-1am Tue-Sat; 1.30-5pm Sun. Closed 2wks in Aug. **Average** €. **No credit cards.** **Map** p296 B5.

Situated on a peaceful pedestrian street only a block away from the bustling cafés of Thisio, this homespun grill-house is a mecca for thrifty carnivores who keep coming back for the pièce de resistance: huge platters of *paidakia*, char-grilled 'lamp chops', served with grilled bread drizzled in olive oil and oregano. The dish is best enjoyed with a simple salad of wild greens, garlicky aubergine purée, and a hunk of feta.

Eat, Drink, Shop

The best Restaurants

For seafood

Thalatta's (*see p147*) location – in gritty Gazi – may seem incongruous, but the seafood is superb. **Milos** (*see p151*) uses the minimum of fuss and the freshest of ingredients. Simplicity is key at **Trata** (**O Stelios**, *see p151*) too, where fish is grilled to perfection. Athenians rush to the waterside to **Diasimos** (*see p156*) as soon as the sun comes out.

For old-school taverna food

Lefka (*see p139*) is a throwback to a bygone era. Old-fashioned **Philippou** (*see p139*) is great value for Kolonaki. There's top-notch taverna food at rock-bottom prices at **Nikitas** (*see p145*).

For contemporary Greek food

Humble taverna staples are treated with creative flair at **Apla Aristera-Dexia** (*see p154*). **Hytra** (*see p144*) is a pioneer of Greek haute cuisine. **Yiandes** (*see p145*) serves revved-up Greek dishes at palatable prices.

For ouzo

Ouzadiko (*see p136*) and **Ivi** (*see p137*) have dozens of varieties – and gorgeous Greek dishes to go with it.

For vegetarian food

Quirky **To Kouti** (*see p129*) has plenty to tempt vegetarians, as do traditional and modern tavernas of all stripes.

For top cuisine

There's a distinctive Greco-Italian twist to the food at rooftop **Etrusco** (*see p129*), and a superb wine collection to go with innovative Greek dishes at **48 The Restaurant** (*see p136*). Delicate and daring combinations rule at **Spondi** (*see p148*), while **Vardis** (*see p154*) has classic quality. **Varoulko** (*see p144*) majors in extraordinary seafood dishes.

Historic Centre

Creative

Tudor Hall

*King George II Hotel, Vassileos Georgiou A3,
Syntagma Square (210 322 2210). Metro Syntagma.*
Open 12.30-4.30pm, 7pm-midnight Mon-Sat.
Average €€€€. **Credit** AmEx, DC, MC, V.
Map p297/p301 F5.

Despite its pompous name, this grand restaurant on
the top floor of the King George II hotel has nothing
remotely medieval about it. Greek columns, fake
chandeliers, and gold brocade drapes provide the
backdrop for middle-aged couples speaking in
hushed tones. Professional waiters in bow ties and
white jackets cruise the room (they should ditch the
name tags – a giveaway that this is part of a hotel
chain). In contrast with the decor, the excellent
French cuisine is exquisitely unpretentious – pumpkin consommé with soft cheese, prosciutto chips and
baby mushrooms; saffron risotto decorated with
parmesan and gold leaf, complemented by crisp
fillets of sole; and divine tagine-steamed bream with
black truffles. Petits fours of Rice Krispies dipped in
cooking chocolate strike the only false note.

Greek traditional

Athinaikon

*Themistokleous 2, Omonia (210 383 8485).
Metro Omonia.* **Open** 11.30am-12.30am Mon-Sat.
Average €. **No credit cards. Map** p297 F3.

A stone's throw from hectic Omonia Square,
Athinaikon offers authentic meze in marvellously
old-fashioned surroundings. The dark wood interior,
with its marble-topped tables and black and white
chequerboard floor, bustles day and night with
office workers, solitary old codgers, and stray
tourists. Waiters handle the constant turnover with
brisk good humour, while cooks in white hats churn
out dishes from a four-page menu featuring excellent prawn fritters and grilled sardines.

Diporto

*Theatrou & Sokratous, Central Market (No phone).
Metro Omonia.* **Open** noon-6pm Mon-Sat. **Average**
€. **No credit cards. Map** p297 E4.

Duck down into this grungy basement lined with
wine barrels, where blood-spattered butchers and
suit-clad brokers have been savouring Barba Mitsos'
pot-luck lunches and potent wine for as long as anyone can remember. If it's crowded (and it usually is)
he will sit you at any table with empty seats, so be
prepared to mingle with the market traders as you
scoff chickpea soup, fried whitebait, and the freshest
Greek salad, all sourced from the market upstairs.

Doris

*Praxitelous 30, Platia Klathmonos (210 3232671).
Metro Omonia.* **Open** 7.30am-6pm Mon-Sat.
Average €. **No credit cards. Map** p297 F4.

Doris has been dishing up delicious Greek grub in
this cheerful pink space, serviced by polite staff in
white coats, since 1900. It's one of the few places
where you can get a traditional Greek breakfast of
rice pudding and *loukoumades* (baby doughnuts
dunked in honey, walnuts and cinnamon). The lunch
menu, with dishes of the day chalked up on the blackboard, is incredibly cheap and as close as it gets to
home cooking. Try the spinach salad with pine nuts
and manouri cheese, slow-roast aubergines, baked
broad beans, and stuffed tomatoes.

To Paradosiako

*Voulis 44A, Syntagma (210 3214121). Metro
Syntagma.* **Open** 10am-2am Mon-Sat; 10am-9pm Sun.
Average €. **No credit cards. Map** p297/p301 F5

It would be easy to walk right past this hole-in-the-
wall on the fringes of Plaka, with just a handful of
tables squeezed on the pavement beside the parked
cars. But it would be a shame to miss this great-
value lunch spot smack in the centre of town but a
world apart from the tacky tourist traps that litter
the neighbourhood. Pull up a chair and tuck into
delicious traditional dishes, like leek and carrot pilaf,
baked chickpeas and whole grilled calamari.

Mediterranean

Aigli Bistro Café

Zappeion Gardens (210 336 9363). Metro Syntagma.
Open 1-4.30pm, 8.30pm-12.30am daily. **Average**
€€€€. **Credit** AmEx, DC, MC, V. **Map** p299 G6.

This Athenian landmark trades on its enchanting
setting in Zappeion Gardens. The elegant terrace is
ideal for a light lunch, while the formal dining room,
with picture windows overlooking the park, is
atmospheric after dark. The lunch menu focuses on
bistro-style standards, while the French-Med dinner
menu is more refined (with prices to match). After
catching a movie at the outdoor cinema next door,
treat yourself to sea bream with asparagus and
coriander, followed by cheesecake with date compote
and kumquat coulis.

Fresh Air

*Fresh Hotel, Sofokleous 26 (210 524 8511). Metro
Omonia.* **Open** May-Oct 8.30pm-1am daily. Closed
Nov-Apr. **Average** €€€. **Credit** AmEx, DC, MC, V.
Map p297 E4.

Sashay through the pink reception area and ride the
lift to the top floor of the Fresh Hotel. You emerge
in an urban oasis concealed among the TV aerials,
tower blocks and twinkling city lights. Artists and
stylists swap gossip at the moodily lit bar or nibble
fusion finger food on the designer sofas. Modern
Mediterranean mains are sourced from the nearby
Central Market.

GB Roof Garden

*Hotel Grande Bretagne, Syntagma Square (210 333
0766). Metro Syntagma.* **Open** May-Oct 7.30pm-
1.30am daily. Closed Nov-Apr. **Average** €€€€.
Credit AmEx, DC, MC, V. **Map** p297/p301 F5.

Step back in time at bohemian **Café Abyssinia**. *See p131.*

Eat, Drink, Shop

The swanky rooftop restaurant of the Hotel Grande Bretagne has unbeatable bird's eye views of the National Gardens, the Parthenon and Parliament – a quintessentially Athenian vista with the Greek flag fluttering in the breeze. Posing on plush sofas and elegantly laid tables under the pergola, Athenian socialites graze on standard five-star hotel fare, such as tartare of yellow-fin tuna, pan-fried tiger prawns and rocket salad. The Wagyu steaks imported from Japan are worth the hefty price tag. For a cheaper taste of the high life, go for a champagne cocktail at the small bar. It's essential to book in advance.

Oriental

Noodle Bar

Apollonos 11 (210 331 8585). Metro Syntagma. **Open** 11am-midnight Mon-Sat; 5pm-midnight Sun. **Average** €. **No credit cards**. **Map** p297/p301 F5.

Cheap and cheerful, the Noodle Bar is ideal for a slap-up lunch when the thought of another Greek salad is stomach-churning. The cosy red-and-blue dining room with its open-plan kitchen can get steamy, but there is a handful of tables on the pavement, popular with office workers on their lunch

The house of mister Pil-Poul
(restaurant- bar)

View à la carte

the house of mister

Apostolou Pavlou & Poulopoulou, Thissio, tel.: 210 34 23 665

break. Apart from every noodle dish imaginable, from pad thai to chicken chow mein, there is a wide range of Asian soups, satays and spring rolls. **Other locations**: Irodou Attikou 4, Halandri (210 680 0064-5); Polytechniou 52-54 & Haras, Iraklio (210 281 5500).

Kolonaki & around

Bar-restaurants

Balthazar
Vournazou & Tsocha 27, Ambelokipi (210 644 1215). Metro Ambelokipi. **Open** *May-Oct* 9pm-2am daily. *Nov-Apr* 9pm-1.30am Tue-Sat. **Average** €€€€. **Credit** AmEx, MC, V.
Balthazar has been the place to see and be seen since it opened 20 years ago in one of the grandest 19th-century mansions in Athens. Its greatest asset is the walled garden canopied by palm trees and swaying Chinese lanterns, where advertising executives schmooze over cocktails at the long outdoor bar. The restaurant suffers from an excess of style over substance, but reliable dishes include pumpkin purée with sour cream and sweet chilli, ravioli with spinach and truffle oil, and knock-out espresso ice-cream with hot chocolate and orange fondant.

Mommy
Delfon 4, Kolonaki (210 361 9682). Metro Panepistimio. **Open** noon-2am daily. **Average** €€. **Credit** AmEx, DC, MC, V. **Map** p300 C8.
This groovy bar-restaurant on a pedestrian street packed with cafés is a hit with the fashion and media crowd. All mismatched armchairs, printed lamp-shades and arty photos, it can get noisy indoors as the night goes on. But the wooden deck scattered with wicker armchairs and floral cushions is magical on hot summer nights. Pretty young things nibble mini turkey burgers wrapped in bacon and chicken satay, while their beefy beaux dig into squid ink tagliatelle and banoffi pie.

Ratka
Haritos 32, Kolonaki (210 729 0746). Metro Evangelismos. **Open** *Oct-May* 9am-2am Mon-Fri; 1-5pm Sat. Closed Jun-Sept. **Average** €€€ **Credit** AmEx, DC, MC, V. **Map** p299 H4.
Ratka doesn't need to advertise. A cross between a bistro and a bar, nothing has changed at this chic Kolonaki bolthole since it opened 30 years ago. It is still as fashionable as ever, especially among fortysomething movers and shakers from ministers to movie directors. The multi-ethnic menu ranges from spaghetti al pesto to steak, snails and surprisingly good sushi.

Taverna tips

There are hundreds of tips for finding a good Greek taverna, but only one vital piece of advice upon which your life, or at least your stomach, depends: go where the Greeks go.

Walk past a taverna where you don't understand a word being spoken by the people eating outside and you've found your place. Local Greeks invariably choose the best tavernas – by taste, value for money and atmosphere. Don't worry, entering a taverna full of Greeks is nothing like going into a tightly knit English pub.

Ninety-nine percent of the battle for a good meal is won before entering the taverna. Once in, many tourists will be too polite to leave, however bad their meal. And there's little room for surprise. Tavernas tend to be uniformly bad, uniformly reasonable or uniformly excellent. Avoid places where someone outside is trying to drag you inside. Nearly always it's standard tourist fare – and possibly worse. Good tavernas let their cooking do the talking. Recommendations from hotels are sometimes not to be trusted as staff may have a particular place to plug. If you're here for a few days, one option is to go for a small snack and see how you get

on in a taverna before committing yourself to the full monty. The strong-willed can take up the invitation of many tavernas, good and bad, to look at food in their kitchens, and then leave without ordering.

Ignore set meals. They're not good value and, in some places, the food has already been served up on dozens of plates, waiting for people like you. Several outfits cater to the plate-breaking, bouzouki-dancing Greek stereotype. Have a good time by all means, but keep an eye on the bill.

To avoid being ripped off in tavernas you must have a menu to see the prices. Fresh fish can be extremely expensive, likewise bottles of wine. The taverna's own wine (ask for '*hee-ma*'), served out of a barrel, is cheaper and usually perfectly acceptable. But when it's bad, it is bad.

Should you have a reasonable complaint, speak quietly with the waiter or, if not yet satisfied, with the owner. Greeks don't like being confronted in front of others. If you're getting nowhere, seek the help of fellow Greek diners. They will very likely back you up. There's nothing like a good argument to end a nice meal.

48 The Restaurant

Eat, Drink, Shop

Creative

48 The Restaurant

Armatolon & Klefton 48, Ambelokipi (210 641 1082). Metro Ambelokipi. **Open** 9pm-1am Mon-Sat. **Average** €€€. **Credit** AmEx, DC, MC, V.

All brushed concrete, green glass and light sculptures that change colours, 48 was last year's hottest meal ticket. Chef Christoforos Peskias, who trained at El Bulli, twists classic Greek dishes into surprising new variations: intense mackerel tartare, battered cod with beetroot chips and a trio of garlic sauces, or rare charolais fillet of beef in caper sauce served with a cone of hand-cut chips. The clued-up sommelier oversees an outstanding wine list, showcased in the scarlet cellar downstairs. Desserts are deadly. Limit yourself to refreshing tangerine sorbet and honeyed halva ice-cream, or succumb to the Chocolate Theme – a chocoholic's downfall.

Ethnic

Altamira

Tsakalof 36A, Kolonaki (210 361 4695). Metro Syntagma. **Open** 1pm-1.30am Mon-Sat. Closed July, Aug. **Average** €€. **Credit** MC, V. **Map** p299 G4.

The multi-ethnic menu in this cosy, colonial-themed restaurant works surprisingly well. From Indian tandoori chicken to Mexican quesadillas with guacamole to crispy Peking duck, you can scoff your way around the world at a single sitting. The knowledgeable staff and hefty portions make Altamira a firm favourite among foreign residents.

Other locations: Perikleous 28, Marousi (210 612 8841).

French

L'Aubrevoir

Xenokratous 51, Kolonaki (210 722 9106). Metro Evangelismos. **Open** 12.30-4.30pm, 8.30pm-12.30am daily. **Average** €€€. **Credit** AmEx, DC, MC, V. **Map** p299 H4.

One of the few French restaurants in Athens, L'Aubrevoir serves up classic Gallic fare like steak tartare, foie gras, and crêpes suzette. The shady garden in the sleepy end of Kolonaki is perfect for Sunday lunch, provided you're prepared to fork out at least €60 each.

Cellier

Panepistimiou 10 (in the arcade), Syntagama (210 3638525). Metro Syntagma. **Open** *Sept-May* 10am-2am daily. *June-Aug* 10am-6pm Mon-Sat. **Average** €€€. **Credit** AmEx, DC, MC, V. **Map** p297 F4.

This stylish bistro could be in Paris. Waiters in waistcoats attend to bon viveurs surrounded by vintage French posters, giant mirrors and chandeliers. The exceptional wine list contains about 250 Greek and international labels, many available by the glass, plus special offers on top-quality bin-ends that change every couple of months. The food is equally excellent, from traditional dishes of the day to caviar, oysters, and superior salads.

Greek contemporary

Ouzadiko

Karneadou 25-29, Kolonaki (210 729 5484). Metro Evangelismos. **Open** 12.30-5.30pm, 8pm-midnight Tue-Sat. **Average** €€. **Credit** AmEx, DC, MC, V.

Despite its unpromising location in a deserted shopping mall, Ouzadiko is packed every night. Once inside, the atmosphere is cosy and the conversation lively, but it's the outstanding food that keeps the connoisseurs coming back time and again. Choose from dozens of varieties of ouzo accompanied by dozens of delicious Greek dishes with a twist – spinach and cumin patties, taramasalata made with smoked trout, cheesy chickpea fritters, and stewed octopus with black-eyed peas.

Where the locals eat

Unless they are entertaining visitors from out of town, you'll rarely see Athenians eating out at Plaka's quaint tavernas or the pricey seafood restaurants lining picturesque Mikrolimano port. Those in the know head to residential Petralona for home-cooked Greek food and venture away from the seafront for fresh fish at affordable prices. Petralona's Troon Street is home to several unpretentious tavernas, like the excellent value **Oikonomou** and **Skoufias**. Nearby, **Monopolio Athinon** is popular for imaginative regional delicacies from all over Greece and **Therapeftirio** for some of the cheapest, freshest fish in town.

The backstreets of Piraeus boast two cult establishments for seafood at rock-bottom prices: **Margaro**, a slap-up joint that serves nothing but flash-fried fish, battered shrimps and Greek salad; and **Kollias**, a family-run restaurant tucked among the apartment blocks of Tambouria. Sunday lunch at the fish restaurants lining Kesariani Square is an institution. **Trata** is far and away the favourite on this strip. *See also p156* **Piraeus**.

The Psyrri district has more *mezedopolia* per square metre than anywhere in Athens. Many of these meze bars are more about the live music and see-and-be-seen vibe than the menu. **Naxos**, with its tender grilled octopus, and **Ivi**, with over 20 varieties of ouzo and raki, are two notable exceptions.

Since the 1960s Athenians have been making pilgrimages to the northern suburb of Drosia, where over a dozen restaurants do a brisk business in *peinirli*. These dough-boats oozing cheese, ham, sausage and tomato arrived in Greece with refugees from Asia Minor in the 1920s. The most famous *peinirli* place is **Tehlikides**, whose owner shared his secrets with chef Christoforos Peskias. Peskias made the humble *peinirli* fashionable again at 48 The Restaurant (*see p136*), using ingredients like truffles and sea urchins.

Taverna Oikonomou

Troon 41, Petralona (210 346 7555).
Metro Petralona. **Open** 8.30pm-1.30am Mon-Sat. Closed few days in Aug. **Average** €.
No credit cards.

Skoufias

Troon 63, Petralona (210 341 2210).
Metro Petralona. **Open** 8pm-1am Mon-Sat.
No credit cards.

Monopolio Athinon

Ippothontidon 10, Petralona (210 345 9172).
Metro Petralona. **Open** 8.30pm-1.30am Tue-Sun. Closed end May-end Sept. **Average** €€.
Credit AmEx, MC, V.

Therapeftirio

Kallisthenous & Kydantidon 41, Petralona (210 341 2538). *Metro Petralona.* **Open** noon-1.30am Mon-Sat; noon-7pm Sun. Closed 1wk in Aug. **Average** €€. **No credit cards**.

Margaro

Hatzikyriakou 126, Piraeus (210 451 4226).
Metro Piraeus. **Open** noon-midnight Mon-Sat; noon-5.30pm Sun. Closed Aug. **Average** €€.
No credit cards.

Kollias

Stratigou Plastira 3, Piraeus (210 462 9620).
Metro Piraeus. **Open** 8pm-1am Mon-Sat; noon-5pm Sun. **Average** €€. **Credit** AmEx, DC, MC, V.

Trata

Platia Anageniseos 7-9, Kesariani (210 729 1533). **Open** noon-1am daily. Closed 2wks in Aug. **Average** €€. **Credit** MC, V.

Naxos

Platia Chrystokopidou 1, Psyrri (210 321 8222). *Metro Thissio.* **Open** 7am-2am daily.
Average €. **No credit cards**. **Map** p297 D4.

Ivi

Navarhou Apostolou & Ivis 10, Psyrri (210 323 2554). *Metro Monastiraki or Thissio.*
Open 1pm-1.30am Tue-Sun. **Average** €.
No credit cards. **Map** p297 D4.

Peinirli Tehlikides

Argonafton 4, Drosia (210 622 9002).
Metro Kifissia. **Open** 7.30pm-midnight Mon-Fri; noon-midnight Sat, Sun. **Average** €.
Credit AmEx, DC, MC, V.

Eat, Drink, Shop

MOSCHOFILERO BOUTARI

All about white!

Moschofilero Boutari. From selected vineyards of Mantinia at an altitude of 650 meters. From the homonymous, famous, indigenous white grape. Aromatic, fresh, full-bodied and well balanced, it represents modern Greek wine-making, signed by the country's best known winery: Boutari. Rewarded for excellence in Greece and abroad. Moschofilero Boutari. All about white.

BOUTARI

QUALITY OF LIFE

www.boutari.gr

Greek traditional

Dexameni

Dexameni Square, Kolonaki (210 723 2834). Metro Evangelismos then 15min walk. **Open** *May-Oct* 8am-2am daily. Closed Nov-Apr. **Average** €. **No credit cards**.

An Athenian landmark, Dexameni reopened in summer 2004 under new management. Although regulars are nostalgic for the rickety chairs and quick-witted waiters, this outdoor oasis in a small park is still blissful. Passers-by parade down the sloping walkway lined with tables, watched by leisurely diners knocking back jugs of house wine and simple snacks like bite-sized filo pastries, courgette croquettes, and rocket and tomato salad.

Kafeneio

Loukianou 26 & Patriarchou Ioakim, Kolonaki (210 722 9056). Metro Evangelismos. **Open** noon-midnight Mon-Sat. Closed Aug. **Average** €€. **Credit** DC, MC, V. **Map** p299 H5.

Distinguished gents, ladies who lunch and yuppie couples all love this Kolonaki classic, where waiters in black jackets and starched white shirts have been dishing up superior Greek staples for years. The consistent quality and immaculate service make Kafeneio extremely foreigner-friendly. Try the house salad of cucumber, avocado and spring onions; creamed leeks with bacon; stuffed squash; and roast suckling pig. The dark wooden interior is reassuringly old-fashioned. In summer, lunch can last for hours at one of the pavement tables.

Lefka

Mavromichali 121, Exarchia (210 361 4038). Metro Omonia, then 5min walk. **Open** 8pm-1am Mon-Sat. Closed few days in Aug. **Average** €. **No credit cards. Map** p297 F3.

A throwback to a bygone era, this dirt-cheap taverna is one of the most atmospheric eateries in town. Though the no-frills interior with its wooden tables and rickety chairs squeezed below wine barrels has bags of character, Lefka comes into its own in summer when the walled courtyard fills up with laid-back locals. Take your pick from steaming pots of beef stew, lemon chicken and baked broad beans on display in the kitchen. Or order char-grilled chops and meatballs, served with fabulous chips. You'll be hard pressed to spend more than €10 a head.

Philippou

Xenokratous 19, Kolonaki (210 721 6390). Metro Evangelismos. **Open** 1-5pm, 8pm-midnight Mon-Fri; 1-5pm Sat. Closed 10 days in Aug. **Average** €€. **Credit** V. **Map** p299 H4.

This old-school taverna (founded back in 1923) is one of the best-value spots in an area where fancy design tends to prevail over fine food. A good lunch spot, this low-key local specialises in *mageirefta*, traditional casseroles like *arakas* (pea, potato and dill stew), *hirino lemonato* (pork with lemon) and *briam* (slow-roast vegetables). Though the dining room is

St' Astra. See p143.

rather dowdy, you can admire the doodles by famous Greek artists who have dined here over the years. On summer nights, the tables creep up the steps outside and spill on to the pavement opposite – a mellow place to while away an evening with a jug of red house wine.

Italian

Il Postino

Grivaion 3, Kolonaki (210 364 1414). Metro Panepistimio. **Open** 1pm-1.30am Mon-Thur; 1pm-2am Fri, Sat. **Average** €. **Credit** MC, V.

Antonio has run a string of successful Italian restaurants in Athens. His latest venture is a cosy osteria where you can savour home-style Italian cooking at surprisingly affordable prices almost any time of day or night. Neapolitan love songs welcome you into a narrow space lined with photos of Italian movie stars and old postcards. Choose the *vitello tonnato* (veal with tuna) and marinated anchovies from the tray of starters. Follow that up with fresh tagliatelle with porcini mushrooms and rabbit and rosemary stew.

Japanese

Kiku

Dimokritou 12, Kolonaki (210 364 7033). Metro Syntagma. **Open** 7.30pm-1am Mon-Sat. **Average** €€€€. **Credit** AmEx, DC, MC, V. **Map** p299 G4.

The best Japanese restaurant in Athens, Kiku introduced Athenians to sashimi and tempura long before the current sushi fad kicked in. Although the minimalist interior is discreetly screened from the street by white blinds, this is where moneyed Athenians come to flash their cash and show off their skills with chopsticks. But genuine lovers of Japanese cuisine also come to enjoy authentic and unusual dishes like *tori tsukune, yakisoba* and exquisite udon noodles.

Mediterranean

Bakaliko De Toute Façon

Skoufou 48, Kolonaki (210 361 5700). Metro Syntagma. **Open** 11am-1am Mon-Sat. **Average** €€. **Credit** AmEx, MC, V. **Map** p301 F5.

Hellenic chic meets French gastronomy courtesy of Gallo-Greek owner Eric Artigault, whose impeccable sense of style pervades this deli-café. Pick up organic olives and olive paté in the grocery, then head up to the loft to brunch with local bon viveurs on smoked swordfish, leek and courgette tart or spinach and bacon salad with goat's cheese. Ask about the dishes of the day, which change with the seasons. It is also worth checking into Bakaliko De Toute Façon to sample the excellent pastries, which taste great with sour cherry cordial from the island of Chios.

Middle Eastern

Alexandria

Metsovou 13 & Rethymnou 7, Exarchia (210 821 0004). Metro Victoria. **Open** 8.30pm-12.30am Mon-Sat. Closed Aug. **Average** €€. **Credit** MC, V. **Map** 297 F1.

Located behind the Archaeological Museum, this is an excellent Egyptian restaurant, surprisingly not on the tourist trail. The cosy interior, with its mellow light and antique floor tiles, is separated into two spaces – opt for a table on the left, lined with aromatic herbs and spices. Authentic Middle Eastern treats include *fatoush* salad (diced tomato and cucumber with pitta croutons and mint), *koubepia* (lamb rissoles with pine nuts and raisins)

and Om Ali, a creamy pudding studded with dates, nuts and sultanas. The pretty courtyard is equally seductive. Booking is essential at weekends.

Oriental

My Sushi Express

Ploutarchou 7 & Karneadou 30, Kolonaki (210 729 9300). Metro Evangelismos. **Open** noon-midnight Mon- Sat. Closed 3wks in Aug. **Average** €€. **Credit** AmEx, MC, V. **Map** p299 H5.

For quick, fresh sushi, this new addition offers better value for money than the spate of mediocre sushi bars that have recently hit Athens. The vibe at My Sushi Express is casual and the service friendly. Slip into a booth or perch at the wooden counter and watch the dexterous chefs slice and roll your *maki* and salmon *nigiri*. Both the miso soup and *edamame* are good too.

Other locations: Agiou Konstantinou 40, Aithrio Shopping Centre, Marousi (210 610 0300).

Freud Oriental

Xenokratous 21, Kolonaki (210 729 9595). Metro Evangelismos. **Open** 8pm-1am Mon-Sat. Closed Aug. **Average** €€€. **Credit** MC, V. **Map** p299 H4.

As you enter this posh Japanese restaurant you are greeted by sushi masters sharpening their knives behind an oval cut-out counter. The minimalist interior – all low, cream sofas and exposed stone – contrasts strongly with the glitzy clientele. Start with some melt-in-the-mouth tuna *tataki* and special *temaki* (hand-rolled shrimp, avocado and asparagus), followed by *kurodai* tempura teriyaki – exquisitely light sea bream tempura on a bed of crispy noodles. Choose carefully from the impressive but expensive sake selection – a small carafe can set you back as much as €80. For a clandestine rendezvous, bag one of the handful of tables in the tiny, candlelit garden at the back.

Spanish

Mi Sueno

Akadimias 30 & Lykavitou, Kolonaki (210 361 6271). Metro Syntagma. **Open** noon-2am Mon-Sat; 7pm-2am Sun. Closed Aug. **Average** €€. **Credit** AmEx, DC, MC, V. **Map** p299 G4.

This new tapas bar is divided into a small, white dining room, a central bar and a rather cramped counter where you can watch the action in the open kitchen. Pop in at lunchtime for a couple of tapas and a glass of Manzanilla, or settle in for the evening with a bottle of Rioja and work your way through saucily named dishes like Atracción Fatal (Galician octopus stew), Propsición Indecente (green salad with tinned palm hearts and asparagus in sherry vinegar) and Viagra (chocolate soufflé). The *pata negra*, chickpeas with spinach, and roast suckling pig are the best dishes. The Latin soundtrack can get loud later on in the evening.

Street eats

For most Athenians, breakfast is a cappuccino and *koulouri* (sesame-studded bread ring) wolfed on the hoof. Street vendors sell *koulouria* and sugary 'donats' (a steal at €0.50), but for the freshest snacks head straight to their source: the all-night **Koulouria Bakery** in Psyrri, full of red-eyed ravers.

Athens is littered with *fastfoudadika* – fast-food joints *à la grecque*. These holes-in-the-wall serve *tost* (toasted sandwiches), *piroski* (a stodgy sausage roll) and all kinds of *pittes* (pies). At **Ariston**, the humble *tyropitta* (feta pie) has been elevated to an art form. There's always a huddle of customers outside this pie shop, which has been churning out flaky pastries since 1910. Try the *spanakopitta* (spinach), *prassopitta* (leek) or *kolokythopitta* (courgette). The tomato-filled *tyropitta* from **Takis** bakery a few blocks below the Acropolis has an equally devoted following.

Souvlaki is every Greek's illicit treat – hot pitta bread full of grilled meat, raw onion, tomato, tzatziki and chips. There are several variations of this post-pub staple: the standard souvlaki is stuffed with hunks of skewered meat; *gyro* (pronounced 'yee-roh') with shavings of pork or lamb; and kebab with minced beef mixed with onions, garlic and spices. Follow the smell of sizzling fat to Monastiraki Square, where three souvlaki joints sweat it out at the junction with

Mitropoleos Street. Legend has it these meat-meisters made more money than anyone else during the Olympics. The grub is as tasty – and service as gruff – at **Savvas** and **Baraiktaris**, but **Thanasis** is the favourite.

Koulouria Bakery
Karaiskaki 23, Psyrri (210 321 5962). **Open** 24hrs daily. **Map** p297 D4.

Ariston
Voulis 10, Syntagma (210 322 7626). **Open** 7.30am-5pm Mon, Wed; 7.30am-9pm Tue, Thur, Fri; 7.30am-4pm Sat. **Map** p297/p301 F5.

O Takis
Misaraliotou 14, Acropolis (210 923 0052). **Open** 6am-9pm Mon-Fri. **Map** p301 E7.

Savvas
Mitropoleos 86, Monastiraki (210 324 5048). **Open** 10am-2am daily. **Map** p297/p301 E5.

Baraiktaris
2 Platia Monastiraki, Monastiraki (210 321 3036). **Open** 10am-2am daily. **Map** p297/p301 E5.

O Thanasis
Mitropoleos 67-69, Monastiraki (210 324 4705). **Open** 8am-3am daily. **Map** p297/p301 E5.

Eat, Drink, Shop

North of the Acropolis

See also **Ivi** and **Naxos**, *p137* **Where the locals eat.**

Bar-restaurants

Soul

Evripidou 65, Psyrri (210 331 0907). Metro Monastiraki. **Open** 9.30pm-1.30am Mon-Sat. **Average** €€. **Credit** DC, MC, V. **Map** p297 E4.
A Mojito in Soul's back garden – with palm trees and red walls – feels like a trip to the tropics. The fairly priced dinner menu is limited but tasty. Opt for Mediterranean rather than Asian dishes like mixed leaves with manouri cheese, chicken stuffed with goat's cheese and sun-dried tomatoes, and pasta with smoked salmon. In the stylish dining area indoors the music can muffle conversation as the bar gets busy. Later, head upstairs to the small, smoky Stereo club to work off your dinner on the dancefloor.

Creative

Red

Athinais Complex, Kastorias 34-36, Votanikos (210 348 0000). Bus A25, A26. **Open** 8.30pm-12.30am Tue-Sat. Closed mid May-mid Sept. **Average** €€€. **Credit** AmEx, DC, MC. **Map** p296 B3.
All undulating red velvet sofas, gold nude busts, exposed stone walls and silver candelabras, Red feels like a cross between a monastery and a bordello. Maybe it's the opulent decor or the smooth service that encourages customers to speak in hushed tones. Or perhaps they're concentrating on chef Michalis Dounetas' refined cuisine, which is heavy on lobster, foie gras and guinea fowl. The *dégustation* menus are good value (four dishes for €35 or five for €45), and you can match a different wine with each course from the extensive Greek wine list. Stand-out dishes are delicate fillet of grouper in a rich caramelised onion sauce, lobster and asparagus risotto with truffles, and venison in bitter chocolate sauce. The Valrhona chocolate soufflé served with Madagascar vanilla ice-cream oozes pleasure, though the 'stuffed egg surprise' on the side – suspiciously like a home-made Cadbury's Creme Egg – is superfluous to proceedings.

St' Astra

Park Hotel, Leof Alexandras 10, Pedion Areos (210 889 4500). Metro Victoria. **Open** 8pm-2am Mon-Sat. **Average** €€€. **Credit** AmEx, DC, MC, V. **Map** p297 F1.
Chef Hervé Pronzato (who was previously at Michelin-starred Spondi) now oversees the menu at this glamorous glass box of a restaurant on the top floor of the Park Hotel. A bamboo bar, cowhide rugs and Murano chandeliers provide a suitably snazzy backdrop for innovative dishes like parfait of foie gras with fig and Mavrodaphne coulis; *kataifi*

Hytra. *See p144.*

Fairy lights and fantastic seafood at **Thalatta**. *See p147.*

stuffed with goat's cheese, prosciutto and sun-dried tomatoes; and duck with onion marmalade and a ginger and redcurrant sauce, served with a spring roll. The small portions and big prices are not quite so appetising.

Varoulko

Pireos 80, Keramikos (210 522 8400). Metro Omonia. **Open** 8.30pm-1am Mon-Sat. **Average** €€€€. **Credit** AmEx, DC, MC, V. **Map** p296 C4.

Greece's most famous chef, Lefteris Lazarou, made his name for his extraordinary way with seafood, from pesto calamari to legendary poached monkfish. Lazarou recently relocated from Piraeus to purpose-built premises beside the Eridanos Hotel on Pireos Street. Though the lofty, multi-level space with its glass floors and see-through kitchen lacks atmosphere, the food is better than ever, with the addition of equally innovative meat dishes. Goat and chocolate risotto, and wedding pilaf with marrow sound awful but taste amazing. For dessert, try the subtle pineapple, orange and passionfruit soup. Lazarou likes to surprise his customers with an endless parade of dishes, though you can order à la carte if you like (safer on the wallet). Whatever you do, be sure to book well in advance.

Greek contemporary

There is also a branch of **Apla Aristera-Dexia** in Gazi, *see p154.*

Hytra

Navarchou Apostoli 7, Psyrri (210 331 6767). Metro Thissio. **Open** Oct-May 8.30pm-1am Mon-Sat. **Average** €€€. **Credit** AmEx, DC, MC, V. **Map** p297 D4.

The uncluttered space – white linen tablecloths, red banquettes and stark prints of cooking utensils – suggests this is a place for people who take food seriously. Chef Yiannis Baxevanis also takes his role as a pioneer of Hellenic haute cuisine seriously. The menu showcases the finest Greek ingredients, with attention-grabbing dishes like octopus marinated in aniseed, seaweed and soy sauce; and red snapper served in a broth of spinach and black-eyed peas.

Baxevannis has also reinvented the Greek dining tradition: his tasting menu is actually a superior selection of about 15 *mezedes* (great value at around €45). Sweets are beautifully presented; try the *tiganites* (doughnuts) with chocolate and orange or the caramelised dried fruit souvlaki served with a tart yoghurt-and-coffee mousse.

Iridanos
Plateon 15, Keramikos (210 346 2983). Metro Omonia, then 5min walk. **Open** 9pm-1.30am Mon-Sat. **Average** €€. **No credit cards. Map** p296 C4.
Closed for almost a decade, Iridanos was a legendary bar-restaurant back in the late 1980s. The same management is back in brand new premises – a restored neo-classical house in the up-and-coming neighbourhood of Keramikos with an ace up its sleeve: a huge courtyard. The new look is bright and modern, with blow-up portraits of movie stars on the table-tops, so you can find Clark Gable grinning at you as the waiter whisks away your plate. The Mediterranean menu is perfectly respectable, if unexceptional. Green salad with avocado and roquefort goes well with penne in rich courgette, broccoli and gorgonzola sauce.

Yiandes
Valtetsiou 44, Exarchia (210 330 1369). Metro Omonia, then 10min walk. **Open** 1pm-1am daily. **Average** €€. **Credit** MC, V. **Map** p299 G3.
Yiandes has a seasonally adjusted menu of revved-up Greek dishes at palatable prices. Owned by the head of Greece's organic farmers' association,

organic ingredients are used to create unusual regional dishes such as chicken with honey, raisins and coriander; and quince stuffed with lamb and rice. The terracotta and azure courtyard draped in ivy is blissfully tranquil, while the barn-like interior with its yellow chairs and mellow jazz warms up a winter evening.

Greek traditional

Chryssa
Dimofondos 81, Ano Petralona (210 341 2515). Metro Ano Petralona. **Open** 9pm-1am Mon-Sat. **Average** €€€. **Credit** MC, V.
This sedately stylish restaurant in a lovely old house is perfect for a quiet dinner date. Mellow music, soft lighting and creamy colours create a seductive mood. The attentive proprietor, Chryssa Protopapa, who personally serves guests, instantly puts you at ease. She brings warm rolls with white tarama and red pepper purée while you browse the short but creative menu. Stand-out dishes include duck in cranberry sauce, chicken with lime and mustard, and superb crème brûlée.

Nikitas
Agion Anargyron 19, Psyrri (210 325 2591) Metro Monastiraki. **Open** 10am-7pm daily. **Average** €. **No credit cards. Map** p297 D4.
Just about the last old-time taverna in Psyrri, this unpretentious little joint is now hemmed in by bars and gimmicky music-and-meze joints. But Nikitas

Community centres

The influx of migrants from Eastern Europe, the Middle East, the Indian sub-continent and Africa that began in the early 1990s initially caused some consternation among locals, although the Athens Municipality has taken some positive steps to integrate and cater for foreigners. Most of the city's migrant communities are centred in neighbourhoods around Omonia Square, and they offer some of the tastiest snacks in town.

In Athens' Little India – the spice-scented triangle between Menandrou, Evripidou and Sofokleous streets, you can pick up a bargain bowl of pilau rice, curried mutton and chapatis at the **Green Garden** (Geraniou 10, Omonia, 210 523 7010) or **Bengal Garden** (Korinis 12, Platia Koumoundourou, 210 325 3060). Then indulge in a wedge of halva from **Milan Sweets** (Keramikou 6, 210 523 7675), a Pakistani pâtisserie that supplements its sweets with an

extraordinary line in custom-decorated cakes (think plastic flamingos and ballerinas).

The Middle East has a fair selection of Athenian outposts. Don't miss the Armenian-Lebanese bakery **Masis** (Menandrou 24, Omonia, 210 520 2659) for delicious spinach and tahini pitta triangles, and chickpea and potato samosas. For a taste of Egypt, head to **Cleopatra** (Kratinou 11-13, Omonia, 210 522 7975) for fresh harissa and dates, and **Raja Jee** (Sofokleous 47, Omonia, 210 324 5272) for delicious, dirt-cheap falafel.

Mostly from Nigeria and Ethiopia, the African community is centred in the Kypseli district in the northern suburbs. You can eat Ethiopian at **Axum** – if you can stomach the fermented injeran pancakes (Drosopoulou 183, Kypseli, 210 201 1774).

There are no great Chinese restaurants in Athens, but **Imperial Town** (Geraniou 44, Omonia, 210 524 6485) has some unusual dishes from Shanghai.

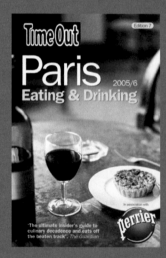

has preserved its friendly character and still turns out top-notch taverna food at rock-bottom prices throughout the day and late into the night. Order the souvlaki, fava (split-pea purée), *horta* (stewed greens), and that increasing rarity, hand-cut chips, plus extraordinary baked quince for pudding.

Mamacas

Persefonis 41, Gazi (210 346 4984). Metro Thissio. **Open** 1.30pm-1.30am daily. **Average** €€. **Credit** AmEx, MC, V. **Map** p296 B4.
A modern spin on the old-time taverna, Mamacas pioneered the Gazi neighbourhood revival back in 1998. With whitewashed walls and pared-down chic, Mamacas may have become a little too trendy for its own good, but it still serves wholesome Greek grub like mama used to make. Models and pop stars tuck into meatballs in tomato sauce; calamari and spinach stew; and Cretan rusks topped with sheep's cheese, capers and tomatoes. Waiters in tight white T-shirts and starched aprons are equally mouth-watering.

Oineas

Aisopou 9, Psyrri (210 321 5614). Metro Monastiraki. **Open** 6pm-2am Mon-Fri; noon-2am Sat, Sun. **Average** €€. **Credit** DC, MC, V. **Map** p297 D4.
With pistachio walls covered in vintage ads, antique tins and colourful bottles, Oineas combines cheerful style with fresh flavours. The lively crowd of locals and tourists share out-of-the-ordinary appetisers like fried feta in a light honey and black sesame batter, spinach salad with warm goat's cheese in a walnut crust, and grilled portabello mushrooms with lashings of garlic. Friendly waiters add to the easygoing vibe, though things can get frantic at weekends.

Tellis

Evripidou 86, Psyrri (210 324 2775). Metro Monastiraki. **Open** 9am-1am Mon-Sat. **Average** €. **No credit cards. Map** p297 E4.
There is only one thing to order at this cult meaterie: giant-sized portions of pork chops and chips. Who cares about the neon lights, greaseproof paper tablecloths and uncomfortable chairs, when you can stuff yourself with prime meat for peanuts? Go the whole hog and have a huge cabbage salad and baked feta with tomato and chilli peppers on the side. Punters range from artists to lawyers to bouzouki singers.

Mediterranean

Prosopa

Konstantinoupoleos 84, Gazi (210 341 3433). Metro Metaxourghio, then bus B13. **Open** 8.30pm-2.30am daily. **Average** €€. **No credit cards. Map** p296 B4.
Although a favourite with hot young actors and artists, Prosopa is cosy and unpretentious thanks to the low-key ambience created by the charming staff. The inspired owners were the first to set up shop beside the train tracks in the tail end of Gazi, sparking a flurry of openings in what is now dubbed Athens' 'gay village'. But Prosopa still has the edge both in terms of atmosphere and food. Delicious

modern Mediterranean dishes include beetroot and goat's cheese salad, creamy penne with artichoke hearts and courgettes, and chicken with mint and yoghurt sauce. Don't over-order: the gracious waiters will bring you a trio of complimentary desserts too good to resist – cheesecake, chocolate brownie and banana cream pie.

Seafood

Thalatta

Vitonos 5, Gazi (210 346 4204). Bus O49 or trolleybus 21 from Omonia. **Open** *early May-mid Nov* 8pm-1am Mon-Sat. *Mid Nov-early May* 8pm-1am Mon-Sat; 1-5pm Sun. **Average** €€€. **Credit** AmEx, DC, MC, V. **Map** p296/p300 B5.
This fancy fish restaurant on an unlikely backstreet behind Pireos Street is for people who are serious about seafood. The nautically themed interior borders on kitsch, but the courtyard strung with fairy lights is peaceful and pretty. The expansive owner, Yiannis Safos, makes a point of visiting every table to explain dishes or make recommendations. Besides an impressive selection of shellfish, octopus with fava and sun-dried tomatoes, and salmon in champagne sauce are outstanding.

Therapeftirio

Kallisthenous & Kydantidon 41, Ano Petralona (210 341 2538). Metro Petralona. **Open** noon-1.30am Mon-Sat; noon-7pm Sun. Closed 1wk in Aug. **Average** €€. **No credit cards. Map** p300 B6.
The residential neighbourhood of Petralona is full of unpretentious restaurants serving super homestyle nosh. As well as plenty of seasonal vegetables and meat casseroles, Therapeftirio is well known among local gourmets for very fresh fish at friendly prices. Home-made taramasalata, *garides saganaki* (prawns sautéed with tomato and cheese), and pan-fried red mullet go down a treat with a steaming bowl of *spanakorizo* (rice with spinach and tomato) and an ice-cold beer. With food this good and service with a smile, it is easy to overlook the drab interior, especially if you can nab a table on the pavement under the orange trees.

Thai

Bar Guru Bar

Platia Theatrou 10, Psyrri (210 324 6530). Metro Monastiraki. **Open** 9.30pm-1.30am daily. Closed late July-late Aug. **Average** €€. **Credit** AmEx, MC, V. **Map** p297 E4.
Still hotter than a green curry after seven years, this Thai bar-restaurant never goes out of style. A postmodern pagoda presides over actors and architects swapping gossip over real Thai food. The hot tom yam goong soup (shrimps, lemongrass, chillis and coriander), goong tod (fried baby shrimps with sweet and sour peanut sauce) and gean gai rama (Burmese chicken curry with caramelised onions and coconut milk) are especially delicious. The

Eat, Drink, Shop

The menu

Avgolemono: a sauce made out of lemon, egg yolks and chicken stock. Also used for a soup made with rice, chicken stock, lemon and egg yolks.

Baklava: a pan-Middle Eastern sweet made from sheets of filo pastry layered with nuts.

Barbouni: red mullet, usually selected by the customer, grilled and served with olive oil.

Bekri meze: cooked pork marinated in wine, usually topped with melted cheese.

Briam: a vegetarian casserole of aubergines, courgettes, tomatoes, potatoes, bay and spices, similar to ratatouille.

Dolmades: young vine leaves stuffed with rice, spices and (usually) minced meat.

Fasolia plaki or pilaki: white beans in a tomato, oregano, bay, parsley and garlic sauce.

Fava: a dip made of puréed yellow split peas, usually topped with chopped red onions.

Garides: large prawns, fried or grilled.

Gemista: tomatoes or peppers stuffed with a combination of rice, mince, herbs, pine nuts and raisins.

Gigantes or gigandes: white beans baked in tomato sauce; pronounced 'yigandes'.

Halloumi or hallumi: a cheese traditionally made from sheep's or goat's milk, but increasingly from cow's milk. Best served fried or grilled. Primarily a Cypriot speciality.

Horiatiki: 'Peasant' salad of tomato, onion, cucumber, feta and sometimes green pepper, dressed with ladolemono (oil and lemon).

Horta: salad of wild greens.

Htipiti: tangy purée of matured cheeses, flavoured with red peppers.

Kalamari, kalamarakia or calamares: small squid, usually sliced into rings, battered and fried.

Kataifi or katayfi: syrup-soaked 'shredded-wheat' dessert rolls.

Keftedes or keftedakia: herbacious meatballs made with minced pork or lamb (rarely beef), egg, breadcrumbs and possibly grated potato.

Kleftiko: slow-roasted lamb on the bone (often shoulder), flavoured with oregano and other herbs.

Kokkinisto: chunks of meat – usually lamb or beef – baked with tomatoes and herbs in an earthenware pot, which seals in the juices and flavours.

Loukanika or lukanika: spicy coarse-ground sausages, usually made with pork and heavily herbed.

Loukoumades: tiny, spongy doughnuts dipped in honey.

Loukoumi: Turkish delight, made with syrup, rosewater and pectin, often studded with nuts.

Mageirefta: cooked vegetable dishes such as casseroles and stews. (This is a useful word to know in restaurants with no menus, where the waiter might say, 'We have such-and-such for salads, such-and-such for meats and such-and-such for mageirefta.' Also a

dimly lit mezzanine is like an upmarket opium den, perfect for a secret rendezvous. The later you go to Guru the better. After midnight, the bar is swamped with beautiful people fighting for the fantastic frozen Margaritas and Thai Martinis. The top-floor jazz club, where local bands jam with an impressive line-up of international guests, is less of a crush.

Eastern Suburbs

Creative

Spondi

Pyrronos 5, Pangrati (210 752 0658). Trolleybus 2, 4 or 11 from Syntagma. **Open** 8pm-midnight daily. Closed 1wk in Aug. **Average** €€€€. **Credit** AmEx, DC, MC, V.

Year after year, Michelin-starred Spondi is cited as Athens' best restaurant. This year, it also made it on to the Relais & Châteaux hot list. The revamped

interior is more colourful, but the stone courtyard shaded with bougainvillea creates a surprisingly low-key backdrop to the elaborate creations of executive chef Jerôme Serrés. His signature dishes include sea bass in rose petal sauce; hare and truffle mille-feuille; and sweetbreads with truffles, chestnuts and salsify. Don't miss the daring desserts, created in collaboration with Parisian pâtisserie Bristol, like banana-pineapple purée in a basil-saffron sauce. The excellent wine list is a revelation.

Greek traditional

Vlassis

Pasteur 8, Ambelokipi (210 646 3060). Metro Ambelokipi. **Open** 1-5pm, 9pm-1am Mon-Sat; 1-5pm Sun. **Average** €. **No credit cards.**

This old-school taverna down a dead-end street is hard to find but worth the effort. Every table in the three-storey house is packed after 9.30pm. Vlassis

Papoutsaki: aubergine 'shoes', slices stuffed with mince, topped with sauce, usually béchamel or similar.
Pastourma(s): dense, dark-tinted garlic sausage, traditionally made from beef.
Saganaki: fried cheese, usually *kefalotyri*; also means anything (mussels, spinach) made in a cheese-based red sauce.
Skordalia: garlic and breadcrumb or potato-based dip, used as a side dish.
Soutzoukakia: baked meat rissoles, often topped with a tomato-based sauce.
Souvla: large cuts of lamb or pork slow-roasted on a rotary spit.
Souvlaki: chunks of meat quick-grilled on a skewer (known to London takeaways as kebab or shish kebab).
Spanakopitta: small turnovers, traditionally triangular, stuffed with spinach, dill and feta.
Spetsofai: a stew of sausages and peppers cooked with wine and bay leaf.
Stifado: a rich meat stew (often rabbit) with onions, red wine, tomatoes, cinnamon and bay.
Tarama, properly taramasalata: fish roe pâté, originally made of grey mullet roe (*avgotaraho* or *botargo*), but now more often cod roe, plus olive oil, lemon juice and breadcrumbs.
Tyropitta: like spanakopitta, but usually without spinach and with more feta.
Tzatziki: a dip of shredded cucumber, yoghurt, garlic, lemon juice and mint.

useful word for vegetarians or people who don't want to eat hunks of grilled meat or fish at every meal.)
Marides: picarel – small fish best coated in flour and flash-fried.
Melitzanosalata: purée of grilled aubergines.
Meze (plural mezedes): a selection of appetisers and main dishes that can be either hot or cold.
Moussaka(s): a baked dish of minced meat, aubergine and potato slices and herbs, topped with béchamel sauce.
Oktapothdi: octopus, usually grilled fresh and served with lemon and olive oil.

Eat, Drink, Shop

is not bothered with culinary trends; the recipe for its success remains unchanged – honest Greek grub in relaxed surroundings. Brisk waiters bring a tray piled high with mezedes to your table, which makes ordering a doddle for non-Greek speakers. Just point to the aubergines with yoghurt, leek and feta pie, and stuffed cabbage leaves. For main courses, you can't go wrong with the pork with quince and whole grilled calamari. Simple puddings are limited to yoghurt and honey or baked fruit.

Italian

Pecora Nera
Sevastoupoleos 158, Ambelokipi (210 691 4183). Metro Panormou. **Open** noon-2am Mon-Sat. **Average** €€. **Credit** AmEx, MC, V.
Owned by an actor, there's a touch of theatre to this split-level trattoria. Good-natured young waiters, funky music and first-rate cocktails create a lively

setting for casual dining. The big communal table by the bar is fun for birthday parties, the cute conservatory lined with sofas is ideal for dinner à deux, but the mezzanine can be noisy. Excellent appetisers include crunchy bruschetta with gorgonzola and pears. The pork with polenta and bona fide spaghetti carbonara are equally accomplished.

Mediterranean

Mets
Markou Moussourou 14, Mets (210 922 9454). Bus 209 from Syntagma. **Open** noon-2am daily. **Average** €€. **Credit** MC, V.
Thankfully, this timeless jazz bar-bistro in one of Athens' most elegantly bohemian neighbourhoods reopened last year after a hiatus of several years. The classic decor – a long, L-shaped wood and marble bar, green pool hall lights and terracotta floor tiles – has barely changed over the years, but the

Pecora Nera.
See p149.

simple but sophisticated menu is better than ever. Go for gravadlax, fresh pasta with mushrooms and truffle oil, and mango sorbet. There's an interesting selection of wines by the glass, plus a range of malt whiskies to help you prop up the bar afterwards. Tables by the glass front look out on to a pretty street; there's a more intimate little loft at the rear. Mets is likely to be closed for much of summer 2005 for renovations.

Seafood

Milos

Athens Hilton, Vas Sofias 46, Ilissia (210 724 4400). Metro Evangelismos. **Open** noon-4.30pm, 7.30pm-midnight daily. **Average** €€€€. **Credit** AmEx, DC, MC, V.

Costas Spiliades single-handedly rebranded Greek cuisine at his restaurants in Montreal and New York. Now he has brought the Milos phenomenon home, albeit to a somewhat sterile space in the Athens Hilton. Spiliades sources the freshest ingredients from fishermen and farmers around the country. These raw materials – piled high in a dazzling array of colours around the sizzling open kitchen – are handled with the minimum of fuss, letting the flavours of Greece speak for themselves. Flash-fried slivers of aubergine and courgette with yoghurt sauce are as light as tempura, and hand-picked *horta* from Crete is barely wilted and dressed in nothing but purest olive oil and a squirt of lemon. One bite of Spiliades' whole bream baked in sea salt and you're transported to a star-spangled beach. Traditional Greek pastries like *galaktoboureko* (custard cream oozing between sheets of syrup-soaked filo) are equally well handled.

Trata (O Stelios)

Platia Anagenniseos 7-9, Kaisariani (210 729 1533). Bus 224, 214 from Akadimias. **Open** noon-1am daily. **Average** €€. **Credit** MC, V.

Simple grilled fish is the trademark at Trata, by far the best of the seafood restaurants lining this lively square where Greek families flock for Sunday lunch. Intensely flavoured fish soup and battered prawns are delicious. Consistently fresh seafood is complemented by fast, polite service, essential for a restaurant that is always jammed to the gills.

Southern Suburbs

Greek contemporary

Bakaliko Ola Ta Kala

Gianitsopoulou 1 & Kiprou, Platia Eleftherias, Glyfada (210 898 1501). Bus A3, B3 from Akadimias. **Open** *Café* 9am-1am Tue-Sat; 9am-6pm Sun. *Deli* 9am-9pm Mon-Fri; 9am-6pm Sat. **Average** €€. **Credit** MC, V.

This chic little deli-café stocks traditional specialities sourced from artisans and co-operatives all over Greece. Sample great home-made treats like smoked

Eat, Drink, Shop

Food with a view

Summer in Athens is all about escaping to the seaside. For those stranded downtown, the alternative is rooftop dining. At many restaurants where the biggest draw is the view, prices can be sky-high and tables are by reservation only. The following places don't rest on the laurels of their location.

On the summit of Lycabettus Hill, the 360-degree view from **Orizondes Lykavitou** stretches as far as the sea. Accessible only by cable car or a sweaty slog up pine-forested footpaths, this glitzy restaurant is the showpiece of TV celebrity chef Yannis Geldis. Further down the hill, **Grand Balcon** atop the St George Lycabettus Hotel boasts equally panoramic views from its silver leather seats. Resident DJs occasionally spice up the funky terrace decked with Swarowski chandeliers and see-through plexiglass chairs. The liveried waiters at the **House of Mr Pil Poul** reckon this is the most popular spot in town to pop the question. The marble roof garden of this fancy restaurant is certainly hard to beat for romance, with its jaw-dropping vistas of the moonlit Acropolis. The posh nosh, like steak with truffles and grouper in champagne sauce, is rather disappointing. **Etrusco** (*see p129*) combines heavenly food with sublime views, while the chic **GB Roof Garden** (*see p132*) is booked days in advance.

cheese from Metsovo, Santorini's famous fava beans and swordfish carpaccio courtesy of Etrusco (*see p129*). Delicious dishes of the day, such as cuttlefish and spinach stew or lentil soup with yoghurt, are written up on the blackboard. For dessert, don't miss the *masourakia* from Chios, crispy filo rolls oozing nuts and honey, delicious with a Greek coffee served with a slice of Turkish delight. Prettily packaged goodies from the grocery make great gifts.

Greek traditional

Louizidis

Ermou & Iasonos 2, Platia Vouliagmenis, Vouliagmeni (210 896 0591). Metro Dafni, then bus 171. **Open** noon-midnight daily. **Average** €. **Credit** AmEx, DC, MC, V.

Kyria Athina wears the trousers at this family-owned taverna. She runs a tight ship, turning out classics like moussaka, *pastitsio* and octopus macaroni. Baked dishes and stews often run out later in the day, but you can always make do with barbecued meat. The flower-filled veranda is a blissful oasis in this posh coastal suburb.

Italian

Vincenzo

Gianitsopoulou 1, Glyfada (210 894 1310). Bus A3, B3 from Akadimias. **Open** 1pm-1.30am daily. **Average** €. **Credit** MC, V.

This cosy pizza place caters to jazz aficionados with regular gigs. The pizzas are the next best thing to the genuine Italian article. As in Italy, a perfectly

You don't have to pay astronomical prices to dine under the stars. Right on the walkway ringing the Acropolis, the pretty roof terrace of **Filistron** is a serene spot to quaff palatable house wine as you share *bekri meze* (pork stew), grilled potatoes with smoked cheese, and char-grilled haloumi. On a less frequented side street nearby, **Greek House Attikos** is where performers at the Herodes Atticus outdoor theatre come to unwind over tasty salmon crêpes and schnitzel after the show. (You can watch the performance for free from the front tables.) Above the atmospheric antique market of Monastiraki, **Brachera** is a mellow bar-restaurant popular with locals for its close-up Acropolis views, great cocktails and decent Mediterranean dishes.

For after-dinner drinks, head to the top-floor chill-out zone of **Home**, the hottest new addition to Gazi's club scene, which hosts some of the world's top DJs downstairs. The cocktails may be overpriced and finger food average, but the view from the Hilton's 13th-floor **Galaxy** bar is unbeatable. The sunken bar allows you to gaze out at the sweeping cityscape, which is even more spectacular from the terrace as cars speed by far below.

Orizondes Lykavittou

Lycabettus Hill, Kolonaki (210 722 7065). Metro Evangelismos. **Open** noon-1.30am daily. **Average** €€€. **Credit** AmEx, DC, MC, V. **Map** p299 J3.

Grand Balcon

St George Lycabettus Hotel, Kleomenous 2, Kolonaki (210 729 0712). Metro

Evangelismos. **Open** 7pm-2.30am Tue-Sat. **Average** €€€. **Credit** AmEx, DC, MC, V. **Map** p299 H4.

The House of Mr Pil Poul

Apostolou Pavlou & Poulopoulou, Thisio (210 342 3665). Metro Thissio. **Open** 8pm-1.30am Tue-Sun. **Average** €€€€. **Credit** AmEx, DC, MC, V. **Map** p297/p301 D5.

Filistron Apostolou

Apostolou Pavlou 23, Thisio (210 346 7554). Metro Thissio. **Open** noon-2am Tue-Sun. **Average** €. **Credit** DC, MC, V. **Map** p297/p301 D5.

Greek House Attikos

Garivaldi 7, Acropolis (210 921 5256). Metro Thissio/Akropoli. **Open** 7pm-1am daily. **Average** €. **Credit** DC, MC, V. **Map** p301 D7.

Brachera

Platia Avyssinias 3, Monastiraki (210 321 7202). Metro Thissio. **Open** *May-Oct* 8pm-2am daily. *Nov-Apr* 8pm-1am Tue-Sun. **Average** €€. **Credit** AmEx, DC, MC, V. **Map** p297/p301 D5.

Home

Voutadon 34, Gazi (210 346 0347). Metro Thissio. **Open** 9pm-3am daily; last orders 1.30am. **Average** €€€. **Credit** DC, MC, V. **Map** p296 C4.

Galaxy

Hilton, Leof Vas Sofias 46, Kolonaki (210 728 1402). Metro Evangelismos. **Open** 6pm-3am Mon-Thur; 6pm-4am Fri, Sat. **Average** € (finger food). **Credit** DC, MC, V. **Map** p299 J5.

thin crust is topped with a couple of simple ingredients – prosciutto and rocket, or crushed cherry tomatoes and mozzarella. Blow the diet with a decadent profiterole and a shot of frangolino mulberry liqueur. The back garden brimming with basil plants is quieter than the buzzing terrace at the front.

Mediterranean

Aioli

Artemidos 9, Platia Esperidon, Glyfada (210 894 0181). Bus B3 from Akadimias. **Open** 7pm-1am Mon-Fri; 1pm-1am Sat. Closed Aug. **Average** €€. **Credit** AmEx, MC, V.

A favourite date venue, this romantic little restaurant feels like a corner of Provence. The cute, candlelit space is decorated in pastels, with flower-print

wallpaper and rose-patterned plates. Start with delicious walnut bread and a bowl of smooth aïoli. Then make eyes over goat's cheese soufflé, canola filled with parmesan and rocket, fillet steak with orzo, and baked apple in mastic sauce.

Café Tabac

Margi Hotel, Litous 11, Vouliagmeni (210 967 0924). Bus A2 from Akadimias; where bus terminates take local bus 114 or 116 to Apollonos bus stop. **Open** 11am-1am daily. **Average** €€€€. **Credit** AmEx, DC, MC, V.

Despite the animal prints and ambient music, the colonial dining room at the Margi Hotel feels rather formal, but the candlelit terrace is quietly exclusive. The lunch menu, which focuses on bistro standards like rocket and parmesan salad, char-grilled vegetables, and grilled salmon, is unadventurous but

Eat, Drink, Shop

perfectly good. The expensive dinner menu features more exciting options like marrow and peanut butter ravioli or a perfectly poached grouper in an earthy sauce of shiitake mushrooms, fennel and ruby port. You can also sample the sushi menu as you show off your tan on loungers by the pool.

Northern Suburbs

Creative

Semiramis
Hotel Semiramis, Harilaou Trikoupi 48, Kifissia (210 628 4500). Metro Kifissia. **Open** noon-1am daily. **Average** €€€. **Credit** AmEx, DC, MC, V.
Cheekily kitsch or awfully pretentious? Whatever. Since opening last summer, this retro-futuristic bar-restaurant designed by Karim Rashid is always packed. Squidgy pink sofas and amoeba-shaped tables interconnect to accommodate unexpected dinner guests. Fresh-faced waiters in pastel flares and silver sneakers are eager to please. The chef, Yiannis Loukakos, has not been swayed by the flashy surroundings: the food, a blend of fresh Asian and Mediterranean flavours, is straightforward but accomplished. Pair tuna steak in a pepper crust with a dollop of *caponata* with a sweet and sour lobster and mango salad. Finish with dense fig tart.

Vardis
Hotel Pentelikon, Deligianni 66, Kifissia (210 623 0650). Bus 550 from Kallimarmaro, A7 from Platia Kaningos. **Open** 8.30pm-1am Mon-Sat. Closed Aug. **Average** €€€. **Credit** AmEx, DC, MC, V.
This Michelin-starred restaurant in the old-fashioned Pendelikon Hotel is the epitome of gastronomic grandeur. In a classic dining room lined with Venetian mirrors, attentive waiters dance around tables set with Riedel crystal, starched linen and porcelain tableware. Chef Betrand Valegeas has created some outstanding dishes like Solea Solea (sole meunière with gnocchi), *côte de veau* with morilles risotto, and cauliflower couscous with grilled red mullet. The frothy soufflé with Grand Marnier and fruits of the forest is a sublime finale.

Greek contemporary

Apla Aristera-Dexia
Harilaou Trikoupi 135 & Ekalis 39, Erythrea (210 620 3102). Metro Kifissia, then bus 561. **Open** 8pm-12.30am Tue-Thur; 8.30pm-1.30am Fri, Sat; 8.30pm-midnight Sun. **Average** €€. **Credit** MC, V.
The understated interior – stripped wooden tables simply laid out in a light space walled with shattered glass – belies the extraordinary Greek food cooked up by Chrysanthos Karamolegos. He turns humble taverna staples into a gourmet affair – think battered baby calamari with harissa sauce; tempura of sardines with fig vinaigrette and lemon paste; and lamb fillet marinated in honey, lemon and mint. The Greek salad with pitta croûtons and feta vinaigrette

is anything but traditional. Karamolegos also makes a mean risotto, not to mention killer puddings. Service is polished but relaxed. Surprisingly, prices are not much higher than an upscale taverna.
Other locations: Tzaferi 11, Gazi (210 342 2380).

Gefseis me Onomasia Proelefsis
Leof Kifisias 317, Kifisia (210 800 1402). Metro Kifissia or bus 550 from Kallimarmaro, A7, B7 from Platia Kaningos. **Open** June-mid Sept 8.30pm-1am Mon-Sat. Mid Sept-May noon-5.30pm, 8pm-12.30am Mon-Thur, Sat; 8pm-12.30am Fri; 12.30-5pm Sun. Closed 1wk in Aug. **Average** €€€€. **Credit** AmEx, MC, V.
Vintner Panos Zoumboulis (who owns the wonderful Vinifera wine shop next door) has converted the glorious, rambling villa where he and his ten brothers grew up into a gourmet Greek restaurant, where ingredients are sourced from small producers and artisans nationwide. From Dinos, the impeccable maître d', to the cheerful chef Nena Ismirnoglou, who takes time to explain new dishes, there is no doubt the people who run this place are passionate about what they do. And it comes across in the cooking. Peasant dishes like fava (split-pea purée) are tarted up with caramelised beetroot chips. Marinated anchovies with shavings of apple, purslane and celery have the subtlety of sushi. Goat baked between layers of aubergine and tomato in a yoghurt crust is a wonderfully earthy main dish. The intense chocolate tart with delicate praline crust is ingenious.

Greek traditional

Ta Kioupia
Dexamenis & Olimpionikon 2, Politia (210 620 0005). Metro Kifissia, then bus 561. **Open** 6pm-1am Mon-Sat; 1pm-5am Sun. **Average** €€€. **Credit** AmEx, DC, MC, V.
Be prepared to overeat: there is no menu here, but an army of waiters brings a seemingly endless array of dishes, each announced like a guest at a ball. Even the choice of breads is overwhelming. You may not manage to munch through all 38 different dishes, but be sure to try mushroom patties, parsley salad, and rooster marinated in coffee. Many meat dishes are slow-roasted in wood ovens or clay pots (*kioupia*) overnight. Visiting celebrities from Margaret Thatcher to Marco van Basten have come all the way to suburban Politia to eat here. The entrance opens on to a terrace with sweeping cityscapes.

Oriental

Square Sushi
Deligianni 56, Kefalari (210 808 1512/210 808 1881). Bus 550 from Kallimarmaro. **Open** June-Sept 7.30pm-12.30am daily. Oct-May 1pm-midnight daily. **Average** €€. **Credit** AmEx, DC, MC, V.
Square Sushi's strongest point is the interesting variety of maki – lobster with mayonnaise, cucumber, mint and plum paste – and the caterpillar roll

The real Greek: Costas Spiliades sources the freshest ingredients for **Milos**. *See p151.*

with eel, avocado, caviar and omelette. The sleek setting, all black lacquer and mauve, is casual enough for a mellow date but elegant enough for a formal dinner.
Other locations: Dinokratous 65, Kolonaki (210 725 5219).

Spanish

Mayor
Harilaou Trikoupi 92, Kefalari (210 808 0460). Bus 550 from Kallimarmaro. **Open** 8pm-1am Tue-Sat; 1-5pm Sun. **Average** €€€. **Credit** AmEx, DC, MC, V.

Everything is imported from Spain at this smart, Gaudi-inspired restaurant, from the superb ham to the talented Basque chef, Assier Hernandez, who cut his teeth at Conran's Cantina del Ponte. Young, friendly staff, with a genuine interest in Spanish cuisine, will recommend the best sherry to accompany starters of baby eel with burnt garlic, sautéed shrimps, and rich Pamplona sausage with onion rings. Portions are generous, so don't order too many tapas. Move on to hearty suckling pig served with potato cake and asparagus, great with a robust Rioja. The luscious *crema catalana* is a smooth foil to cognac with orange and spices. Finish with fantastic handmade chocolates and a shot of espresso.

Square Sushi. *See p154.*

Turkish

Tike

Kritis 27 & Harilaou Trikoupi, Kifisia (210 808 4418). Metro Kifissia, then bus 525. **Open** 1-4.30pm, 8pm-midnight Tue-Thur; 1-5pm, 8pm-12.30am Fri, Sat; 8pm-12.30am Sun. **Average** €€. **Credit** AmEx, MC, V.

This outpost of the award-winning Istanbul restaurant chain has won over the locals who can't get enough of the brilliant kebabs. The glass-walled space sits pretty in a garden with a mosaic fountain. There's only a hint of the Orient to the buzzing red-and-black interior, with its round tables and bejewelled lampshades. The two dining areas are divided by an impressive grill and wood oven that turns out fantastic *tavuk adana* (tender chicken kebab served with paper-thin bread) and *fındık lahmacun* (spicy minced meat on a crisp pitta base). Try not to wolf the puffy pitta breads with garlic butter before the starters of velvety *mütebbel* (char-grilled aubergine with yoghurt) and tomato and onion salad dressed with pomegranate juice arrive. Finish with *helva* – a warm, crumbly semolina pudding studded with pine nuts that conceals a heart of vanilla ice-cream.

Piraeus

See also p137 **Where the locals eat.**

Seafood

Diasimos

Akti Themistokleous 306-308 (210 451 4887). Metro Piraeus, then bus 904. **Open** 10am-1am daily. **Average** €€. **Credit** AmEx, MC, V.

With the first hint of summer, locals flock to the waterfront for a taste of the sea. You can spot Diasimos among the many (mostly tacky) fish restaurants along the coastal strip of Freatida by the sign outside ordering you to STOP! The entrance is strung with octopus hanging out to dry and crates of cockles, shrimps and fish. This is the place for the quintessentially Greek supper: a whole grilled fish simply dressed in olive oil and lemon. The spaghetti with shrimps is also delicious, and the service is fast and friendly.

Kollias

Stratigou Plastira 3 (210 462 9620). Metro Piraeus or bus O40 from Akadimias, then bus 843. **Open** noon-4pm, 7.30pm-1am Mon-Sat; noon-6pm Sun. **Average** €€. **Credit** AmEx, DC, MC, V.

Although way off the beaten track in an unpromising apartment block in the backwaters of Piraeus, Kollias is a landmark among local gourmets. Fish fetishist Tassos Kollias will take you on a tour of his kitchen so you can choose your supper from ice boxes bulging with clams, oysters and all manner of obscure sea creatures from every corner of the country. As soon as you sit down on the flower-filled terrace decked with nautical paraphernalia, you're presented with a shot of heavenly fish soup. Follow that with squid cooked in its ink, sea urchin salad and the catch of the day.

Plous Podilatou

Akti Koumoundourou 42, Mikrolimano (210 413 7910). Metro Piraeus, then bus 915. **Open** 9am-4pm, 7pm-1am daily. **Average** €€€. **Credit** AmEx, MC, V.

Of all the seafood restaurants squeezed along post-card-perfect Mikrolimano – otherwise known as the Athenian Riviera – Plous Podilatou boasts the most elegant decor and inventive menu. As a full moon rises above the tinkling masts and star-spangled sea, indulge in Greek salad served in pitta bread, grilled aubergine with smoked octopus and chilli, and lemon sole with shrimps and capers.

Cafés

Nes, frappé or freddo: the Athens day revolves around coffee.

Relax in style at the **Athinaion Politeia**.

Coffee rituals punctuate the Athenian day, and at times it can seem as if the entire city is fuelled by caffeine. What kind of coffee you enjoy and where you enjoy it depends a lot on age, class and gender considerations. To unravel the complexities of who drinks what, where, *see p160* **Café culture**.

Good weather means coffee can often be enjoyed outdoors: in the summer months you'll be hard pushed to find a free table outside at one of the popular cafés in Thisio, Kolonaki or Plaka. From old men slurping noisily at their tiny cups of Greek coffee to pretty young things toying with the straws in their tall glasses of frappé (Greece's very own Nescafé and condensed milk concoction), everyone derives great pleasure from the coffee ritual. Café owners also take a lot of pride in their product, paying attention to both flavour (be

sure to specify if you want a weak brew) and presentation (a little cookie often comes tucked between the spoon and the saucer). Even instant coffee, or *'nes'* as it's known, comes with an appealingly frothy head.

Acropolis & around

Amaltheia
Tripodon 16, Plaka (210 322 4635). Metro Akropoli.
Open 10am-1am Mon-Thur, Sun; 10am-2am Fri, Sat.
No credit cards. Map p301 E6.
This small, traditional pastry café specialises in dairy-based sweets, and while few in variety, they are certainly good. Amaltheia is well known for its yoghurt, which comes topped with honey and walnuts, chocolate sauce or diced fruit. It is also a classic stop for savoury crêpes.

aPLAKAfe
Adrianou 1, Monastiriki (210 325 5552). Metro Thissio. **Open** 10am-2am daily. **Credit** MC, V.
Map p297/p301 D5.
In one of the most beautiful spots in town, aPLAKAfe offers a great view of the Acropolis and a fantastic vantage point for people-watching on the junction of the Apostolou Pavlou and Adrianou pedestrian walkways. Be sure to try a plate of the delicious *loukoumades*, traditional deep-fried dough-nuts topped with warm honey and a scoop of ice-cream; or a syrupy slice of *ekmek politico me pagoto*. The selection of special coffees includes double espresso with cream in a caramel and truffle-frosted glass and 'coffee time' espresso, with vodka and Cointreau, topped with orange peel.

Athinaion Politeia
Akamantos 1 & Apostolou Pavlou, Thisio (210 341 3795). Metro Thissio or Akropoli.
Open 8am-2am daily. **Credit** AmEx, DC, MC, V.
Map p296 C5/p294 D5.
An old mansion has been transformed into a café with a great view of the crowds on Apostolou Pavlou and the Acropolis. There's a great range of coffees on offer here, from basic Greek coffee to the likes of espresso corretto, a wonderfully explosive mix of espresso coffee and sambuca. The terpsichori crêpe with chocolate and fresh fruit is an indulgent and very popular snack.

Dioskouri
Dioskouron 13, Plaka (210 321 9607). Metro Monastiraki. **Open** *May-Sept* 8.30am-midnight daily. *Oct-Apr* 8.30am-2am daily. **No credit cards. Map** p301 E5.

Aiolis.
See p159.

While the frappé isn't anything to write home about, the tables here have a magnificent view of the Agora, with Gazi and Keramikos fading into the urban Athenian background. Dioskouri is best avoided at summer lunchtimes, though, as there's very little shelter from the sun.

En Athinais
Iraklidon 12, Thisio (210 345 3018). Metro Thissio. **Open** *May-Sept* 9am-3am daily. *Oct-Apr* 9am-2am daily. **Credit** V. **Map** p296/p300 C5.
Housed in a restored neo-classical building, En Athinais has a splendid view of the Acropolis through its large windows. Outside, the tables on the pedestrianised street are a great place to people-watch with a good cup of coffee or a light meal.

Filistron
Apostolou Pavlou 23, Thisio (210 342 2897/210 346 7554). Metro Thissio. **Open** *June-Sept* 6pm-2am daily. *Oct-May* noon-1.30am daily. **Credit** DC, MC, V. **Map** p297/p301 D5.
Filistron (which means 'manic passion' in ancient Greek) is a pleasant hangout for light meals, snacks and good coffee. Its best asset is its terrace, which is lush with climbers and flowers and has a lovely view across the city. For indulgence, try a delicious alternative frappé: it comes with a ball of vanilla ice-cream instead of milk. Tables are hard to find at lunchtime or during the evening.

Gallery Café
Adrianou 33, Monastiraki (210 324 9080). Metro Monastiraki. **Open** 10am-2am Mon-Sat; 9am-2am Sun. **No credit cards**. **Map** p297/p301 D5.
Next door to the Stoa of Attalos (*see p92*), the Gallery Café is highly recommended for its relaxed loungey atmosphere, good espresso and indulgent brownies served with chocolate sauce and a generous scoop of vanilla ice-cream on the side. After 4pm, the bar starts serving cocktails (with or without alcohol) and cranks up the volume in preparation for the evening. A good place to take a break while sightseeing.

Ionos
Geronta 7, Platia Filomousou, Plaka (210 322 3139). Metro Akropoli. **Open** 8am-4am daily. **No credit cards**. **Map** p301 F6.
Ionos is one of the best places to get a frappé in Plaka. Alternatively, try the ice-cold 'special' chocolate milkshake. There are also backgammon boards for those who fancy a game.

Melina Café
Lysiou 22, Plaka (210 324 6501). Metro Akropoli. **Open** *May-Sept* 10am-3am daily. *Oct-Apr* 10am-2am daily. **Credit** AmEx, MC, V. **Map** p297/p301 E5.
Located on a picturesque cobblestone street, this café (it's named after the legendary actress-turned-activist Melina Mercouri) is a great place to enjoy a cappuccino along with a slice of apple pie and vanilla ice-cream.

Tristrato
Geronta & Dedalou 34, Plaka (210 324 4472). Metro Akropoli. **Open** 9am-1am daily. **No credit cards**. **Map** p301 F6.
A blast of cool air hits you as soon as you push open Tristrato's wooden door. Try one of the home-made baklavas, cream pies (*galaktoboureko*) or cheesecakes with cherries (€4.50). The menu is rich with herbal teas, such as fresh mountain tea, as well as a broad selection of coffees.

Historic Centre

Aigli Bistro Café
National Gardens, Syntagma (210 336 9363). Metro Syntagma. **Open** 9am-4am daily. **Credit** AmEx, DC, MC, V. **Map** p299 G6.
An all-time classic spot for a classic Greek coffee, located in a picture-perfect setting – among the flowering trees and fountains, beside the Zappeion Exhibition Hall in the National Gardens. The Aigli Bistro Café is an ideal shady refuge from the sizzling summer heat.

The best Cafés

For classic frappés
Ionos (*see above*) and **Athinaion Politeia** (*see p157*) froth it up nicely.

For location, location, location
aPLAKAfe (*see p157*) and **Athinaion Politeia** (*see p157*) have amazing views of the Acropolis; **Dioskouri** (*see p157*) has the Agora in its sights; **Aigli Bistro Café** (*see above*) is set among the flowering trees and fountains of the National Gardens.

For fashion and style
Kolonaki's coolest hang out at **Tribeca** (*see p162*); **Skoufaki** (*see p162*) is the height of fashion; the design-conscious love **Eau de vie** (*see p162*).

For the sweet and lovely
Amaltheia (*see p157*) is known for its for yoghurt, complete with gorgeous toppings; for an alternative frappé, made with vanilla ice-cream, try **Filistron** (*see above*); **aPLAKAfe** (*see p157*) does delicious *loukoumades* – doughnuts with warm honey and ice-cream; **Dodoni** (*see p162*) is the last word in ice-cream.

For a classic cup of Greek coffee
Aigli Bistro Café (*see above*) makes coffee the traditional way.

Aiolis

Eolou 23 & Agias Irinis (210 331 2839). Metro Monastiraki. **Open** 10am-2am daily. **No credit cards.** **Map** p297/p301 E5.

Though jam-packed and busy during the day, the pedestrianised shopping strip of Eolou can become quite deserted at night. But the small tables of the Aiolis café are hardly ever empty. This former local caff, housed in an attractive neo-classical building, was given a facelift several years ago and its classic decor now attracts thirtysomethings who call in for an espresso, a chocolate soufflé or a perhaps a refreshing Mojito.

Ethnikon

Platia Syntagma (210 331 0576). Metro Syntagma. **Open** 6am-3am daily. **No credit cards.** **Map** p297/ p301 F5.

Thanks to its Olympic facelift, Syntagma, the city's most central square, now boasts two new cafés in its paved tree-shaded heart, providing great spots for rest and recuperation right in the middle of downtown Athens. At Ethnikon, be sure to try Greek coffee served the traditional way, in a *briki* with a bronze base, and accompanied by a complementary sugary *biskotoloukoumo* sweet. Other popular sweets include a sumptuous chocolate cake with layers of melted chocolate and a strawberry garnish, as well as the various *glyka tou koutaliou*, or spoon sweets.

Flocafé

Stadiou 5, Syntagma (210 324 3028). Metro Syntagma. **Open** 7am-midnight Mon-Fri; 8am-midnight Sat; 10am-midnight Sun. **No credit cards.** **Map** p297 F4.

This home-grown café chain is standing up to the competition from Starbucks, which has branches popping up around the city. It offers a huge number of coffee options, and also serves up great snacks. Like most Greek cafés, the music and the conversation can get loud, especially in the evening. **Other locations:** throughout the city.

Café culture

No matter that a cup of coffee costs a small fortune since the advent of the euro, there's still a café on every corner of Athens – and they're always packed. The kind of coffee you order – and where – speaks volumes about your social standing, not to mention your age and gender. Coffee can be roughly divided into three categories: *ellinikos* (Greek), *frappé* (chilled Nescafé) and *freddo* (iced cappuccino). Whatever your poison, it can be ordered *sketo*, *metrio* or *glyko* – plain, medium or sweet.

The sludgy *ellinikos* is an acquired taste, favoured by the grizzled patrons of *kafenia*, nicotine-stained coffeehouses where many an elderly gent idles away an afternoon as the slam of backgammon and click-clack of worry beads beat slow time. The number of *kafenia* in downtown Athens is dwindling, but some self-consciously old-school enterprises now serve Greek coffee brewed the traditional way in a tiny copper beaker heated over hot ash (or *sti hovoli*). It is usually served with a wedge of Turkish delight or a cinnamon biscuit and always with a glass of cold water. **Aigli Bistro Café** (*see p159*) is the perfect place to savour a Greek coffee with a dash of panache.

Ouzo may be the Greek cliché, but frappé is the national drink – a frothed-up blend of Nescafé, sugar, cold water and condensed milk slurped by twentysomethings who frequent a modern café (*kafeteria*) like

Athinaion Politeia (*see p157*), on the scenic pedestrian walkway circling the Acropolis. Since it's cool and refreshing, it goes down a treat in the hot Greek summer, when it becomes ubiquitous.

These days, the hipster's coffee of choice is a freddo, to be sipped slowly while people-watching at fancy coffee shops like **Da Capo** (*see p161*). This Kolonaki Square landmark also serves the best espresso in Athens. The buzz on a Saturday afternoon is deafening as patrons barefacedly eye up the bottle blondes parading up and down pedestrianised Tsakalof Street.

Although Starbucks has infiltrated Athens, we are happy to report that it hasn't taken over the city's café culture. Every neighbourhood square has a couple of rival cafés with their own faithful regulars (there was a time when patrons of *kafenia* were strictly divided according to their political affiliation, though this is no longer so). Athenians plan their day around their (multiple and leisurely) coffee breaks. Even midweek at noon, you'll have a hard time finding a free table at one of the crammed cafés along Skoufa Street in Kolonaki, Adrianou Street in Plaka or Iraklidon Street in Thisio. And Athenians don't just come to cafés for a caffeine fix; they swap gossip, seal deals and break hearts. So when a local suggests *'Pame gia kafe?'* ('Shall we go for a coffee?'), be prepared for anything.

Pulsar

*Romvis 24A, Syntagma (210 331 3150). Metro
Syntagma.* **Open** 8am-3am daily. **Credit** DC, MC, V.
Map p297/p301 F5.
Turn into tiny Romvis Street and you'll come across
this delightful three-storey townhouse, now a modern café with an all-day loungey vibe, where you'll
feel equally comfortable having an afternoon coffee
or an evening meal.

Niki's Café

*Nikis 3, Syntagma (210 323 4971). Metro
Syntagma.* **Open** 7am-2am daily. **No credit
cards.** **Map** p297/p301 F5.
Ideal for a coffee stop when you're out shopping or
strolling along nearby Ermou Street, this crowded
but cosy little hole-in-the-wall café-bar also offers
light meals and snacks.

Yellow Café

*Karagiorgi Servias 9 & Voulis (210 331 9029).
Metro Syntagma.* **Open** 8.30am-8.30pm Mon,
Wed; 8.30am-10pm Tue, Thur, Fri; 8.30am-7pm Sat.
No credit cards. **Map** p297/p301 F5.
After a morning of sightseeing, pop into the jolly
Yellow Café for a sandwich on home-made bread,
followed by a chocolate brownie accompanied by a
classic strong espresso.

Kolonaki & around

Cafeina

*Kiafas 6 & Zoodochou Pigis, Exarchia (210
384 1282). Metro Panepistimio.* **Open** 10.30am-
3am Mon-Fri; noon-3am Sat; 2pm-3am Sun.
No credit cards. **Map** p297 F3.
You'll be hard pressed to find a much smaller café
than Cafeina, a cosy yet avant-garde hangout in
bohemian Exarchia. Its plush, comfortable sofa is
ideal for long conversations with a group of friends,
the coffee is good, the hot chocolate's even better
and the speakers normally pump out a wicked selection of freestyle and deep house beats.

Cake

*Irodotou 13 & Kapsali, Kolonaki (210 721 2253).
Metro Evangelismos.* **Open** 9am-10pm Mon-Fri;
11am-6pm Sat. **No credit cards.** **Map** p299 H5.
Kolonaki has a wealth of cafés to choose from but
this particularly tiny one, serving beverages and all
kinds of fragrant cakes, stands out from the rest. Pop
in and try to grab one of the three stools for a slice
of the heavenly chocolate fudge cake or the
American-style cheesecake.

Da Capo

*Tsakalof 1, Platia Kolonaki, Kolonaki (210 360
2497).* **Open** 7am-2am daily. **No credit cards.**
Map p299 G4.
Renowned for its cappuccino freddo, Da Capo is
also known for its elite clientele (not to mention its
rather limited seating). There is a selection of sweets
and cakes to accompany the fabulous coffee. It's
expensive, but stylish.

Wunderbar. *See p162.*

Eau de vie

Skoufa 47-49, Kolonaki (210 363 8980). Metro Syntagma or Panepistimio. **Open** 9am-3am Mon-Fri; 9am-4am Sat. **No credit cards.** **Map** p299 G4.

This new arrival in Kolonaki, next to the classic Skoufaki (*see below*), might not be expansive in size but it certainly makes up for it in terms of its impressive decor. Fuchsia pink quilted walls, royal purple sofas and ornate avant-garde decorative items on the walls create an atmosphere that is part Almodovar and part *Twin Peaks*. Choose from a variety of coffees, grappas and champagne to the strains of modern electronica.

Minim's

Skoufa 48, Kolonaki (210 363 0045). Metro Panepistimio. **Open** 8am-3am Mon-Fri; 9am-3am Sat, Sun. **Credit** AmEx, DC, MC, V. **Map** p299 G4.

The latest addition to the café scene in and around trendy Kolonaki is this youthful café where you can enjoy a coffee, drink or meal at any time of the day. The millefeuille comes highly recommended.

Prytaneion

Milioni 7, Kolonaki (210 364 3353). Metro Syntagma. **Open** 9am-2am daily. **Credit** AmEx, DC, MC, V. **Map** p299 G4.

Located in one of the most cosmopolitan pedestrianised streets in Athens, Prytaneion is a great all-day place for watching the crowds go by. Take a break from shopping in upmarket Kolonaki to cool off at one of the outside tables and enjoy upbeat music along with a great casual atmosphere.

Rosebud

Skoufa 40 & Omirou 60, Kolonaki (210 339 2370). Metro Panepistimio. **Open** 9am-2am daily. **No credit cards.** **Map** p299 G4.

This café-bar is a regular meeting point for arty types and cinephiles. The decor is mainly a cute combination of wood and velvet, and the speakers put out a pleasant mixture of jazz and soul.

Skoufaki

Skoufa 47-49, Kolonaki (210 364 5888). Metro Panepistimio. **Open** 10am-3am Mon-Thur; 10am-4am Fri-Sun. Closed Aug. **No credit cards.** **Map** p299 G4.

A fashionable café-bar where young crowds flock to get their evening going with a shot of caffeine or perhaps something stronger, drunk to the strains of a variety of sounds ranging from electronica to jazz and R&B.

Ta Tria Gourounakia

Skoufa 73, Kolonaki (210 360 4400). Metro Panepistimio. **Open** 8am-3am Mon-Fri; 10am-3am Sat; noon-3am Sun. **Credit** MC, V. **Map** p299 G4.

This colourful, multi-faceted café-restaurant-club is named after the three little pigs in children's literature. The upbeat pop music puts a spring in your step and it gets louder as the day wears on. The small couches are invariably occupied by students cramming over a cappuccino freddo. Favourite desserts are chocolate soufflé with ice-cream and millefeuille with white chocolate. The very friendly service is another plus.

Tribeca

Skoufa 46 & Omirou, Kolonaki (210 362 3541). Metro Panepistimio. **Open** 9am-4am daily. **No credit cards.** **Map** p299 G4.

This café might be the size of a dolls' house but it still manages to attract the coolest crowd in Kolonaki, who let their hair down to the accompaniment of a wide variety of tunes, ranging from 1980s new wave to R&B.

Wunderbar

Themistokleous 80, Exarchia (210 381 8577). Metro Omonia. **Open** 9am-4am daily. **No credit cards.** **Map** p297 F3.

Earthy colours reign at Wunderbar, and colourful sofas seat a young, stylish crowd. Stop by for a good cappuccino in the daytime; in the evening a clubby atmosphere pervades.

Yachting Deluxe

Sina 6, Kolonaki (210 364 5575). Metro Panepistimio. **Open** 8am-3am Mon-Fri; 9am-3am Sat; 1pm-3am Sun. **Credit** DC, MC, V. **Map** p297 F4.

A comfortable café-restaurant with kitschy nautical decor. A good choice for a coffee stop or a spot of lunch after visiting the nearby Academy and the National Library (*see p98*).

North of the Acropolis

Ta Serbetia tou Psyrri

Eschylou 3, Psyrri (210 324 5862). Metro Monastiraki. **Open** 10am-3am daily. **No credit cards.** **Map** p297 E4.

This café is dedicated to good home-made cakes. There's a folk-arty feel to the hand-decorated furniture and yet more artistry in the kitchen. Here delicacies are prepared such as the *galaktoboureko* cream pie and preserves (raspberry, cherry, grape, bergamot, quince), served either with yoghurt or the traditional northern Greek sweet *kazan dipi*.

Eastern suburbs

Dodoni Ice Cream

Ymittou 95, Pangrati (210 751 4445). Metro Evangelismos, then 15min walk. **Open** 8am-2am daily. **No credit cards.**

Greece's premier ice-cream parlour chain is highly recommended for sweet-toothed coffee drinkers. At any of the branches across the capital you can combine a cappuccino or freddo with one of the many heavenly ice-cream flavours on offer, including gourmet almond caramel choco, mango sorbet and gourmet tiramisu.

Other locations: throughout the city.

Shops & Services

Sandals, mastic, jewellery, ceramics: Athens is full of affordable gems.

In urgent need of a sunhat, shades or a bikini? Looking for presents for friends back home – things they'd really like? In search of some local delicacies to make up an impromptu picnic? Can't take another step in those blistering flip-flops? Whatever you need in the way of retail therapy, Athens can provide it. And the good news is that most of its main shopping areas are within easy walking distance of each other.

Different areas have their own specialities and price brackets, as shops here tend to congregate like with like. The central street **Ermou**, although home to some of the most expensive real estate in Europe, tends to attract affordable high-street clothing and footwear brands. Posses of teenagers gather along this pedestrian way to snap up the newest trends, while families flock here to buy basics.

In the warren of roads between Ermou and Kolokotroni are excellent haberdashery and bargain clothing shops (**Agiou Markou**, which starts life as Evangelistrias where it intersects Ermou, is well known for cut-price outfits and accessories; it also has some of Athens' rare outsize shops), while down towards **Athinas** the focus switches to hardware and food, culminating in the vast meat and fish markets and their satellite stalls selling cheeses, cold meats, olives, herbs and spices and preserved vegetables. Further into **Psyrri**, the immigrant influence manifests itself in the numerous shops selling Indian, Pakistani and Chinese foods and clothing.

Touristy **Plaka** and **Monastiraki** are full of shops selling souvenirs, from leather bags and designer knock-off sunglasses to flokati rugs and traditional backgammon boards via antique furnishings and the ubiquitous priapic satyrs, while the moneyed district of **Kolonaki**, to the east of the city centre, is home to designer clothes shops (*see p174* **How to do Kolonaki**).

Venture out of the city centre and you'll find similarly upmarket fashion boutiques in the stately northern district of **Kifisia** (once the site of holiday homes for rich Athenians before central Athens spread out its concrete tentacles and incorporated it into the urban sprawl), while on the south coast, **Glyfada** has a mix of street brands and classy designer labels lining its wide central promenade.

Greek shops have rather complicated hours, but in general they open from morning to mid-afternoon on Monday, Wednesday and Saturday and morning until dusk on Tuesday, Thursday and Friday. The siesta has been all but done away with these days – while some of the smaller, family-run shops may close for a short break during the afternoon of late-opening days (Tuesday, Thursday, Friday), the majority of stores stay open all day. Shops in tourist areas are allowed to open all day every day, including Sunday. At the time of writing, the government was discussing longer shopping hours, which would see even small, family-run shops open till 9pm daily, but the shopkeepers' and employees' unions are fighting the changes.

Art & antiques

Martinos
Pindarou 24, Kolonaki (210 360 9449/www. martinosart.gr). Metro Syntagma. **Open** 10am-3pm Mon, Wed, Sat; 10am-2pm, 5-8pm Tue, Thur, Fri. **Credit** AmEx, MC, V. **Map** p299 G4.
The Kolonaki branch of Martinos has high-quality antique pieces from around the world, including eighth-century Chinese ceramics, African tribal masks and traditional Greek pottery. The shop in Monastiraki specialises in Byzantine pieces and antiquities, but beware of buying one to take home – it is illegal to take antiquities out of Greece without a special licence from the Archaeological Service. **Other locations**: Pandrosou 50, Monastiraki (210 321 2414).

Zoumboulakis
Kriezotou 7, Historic Centre (210 363 4454). Metro Syntagma. **Open** 10am-3pm Mon, Wed, Sat; 10am-8pm Tue, Thur, Fri. **Credit** AmEx, DC, MC, V. **Map** p299 G4/G5.
The celebrated gallery hosts exhibitions of paintings and sculptures by the crème de la crème of contemporary Greek artists, while at the nearby shop you can buy numbered, signed silk screens or prints and objets d'art (both local and imported).

Books

Eleftheroudakis
Panepistimiou 17, Historic Centre (210 325 8440/ www.books.gr). Metro Panepistimio. **Open** May-Sept 9am-9pm Mon-Fri; 9am-6pm Sat. Oct-Apr 9am-8pm Mon-Fri; 9am-6pm Sat. **Credit** AmEx, DC, MC, V. **Map** p297 F4.

TAKING A BREAK IN THE USA?

PACK A TIME OUT CITY GUIDE

Looking for the latest bestseller to entertain you on that lengthy ferry ride to the islands, a copy of *The Iliad* to brush up on your classics, a biography of Maria Callas or a coffee-table tome with glossy photos of the Acropolis? This eight-floor megastore is the place to go. The choice includes novels and classics (in English and Greek), cookery and travel, guidebooks, maps and children's books. For a break from browsing, pop up to the Food Company café. **Other locations**: Nikis 20, Syntagma (210 322 9388); Lazaraki 27, Glyfada (210 894 3892); Kifisias 268, Kifisia (210 623 6677).

Reymondos International Bookstore
Voukourestiou 18, Kolonaki (210 364 8189). Metro Syntagma. **Open** 8am-6pm Mon, Wed; 8am-8pm Tue, Thur, Fri; 8am-3pm Sat. **Credit** AmEx, DC, MC, V. **Map** p299 E4.
This shop is well known for having the most comprehensive collection of foreign-language magazines in Athens, plus newspapers from most European countries, fiction, travel and coffee-table books.

Children

Alouette
Pindarou 26-28, Kolonaki (210 362 8049). Metro Syntagma. **Open** 9am-3.30pm Mon, Wed; 9am-9pm Tue, Thur, Fri; 9am-4pm Sat. **Credit** AmEx, DC, MC, V. **Map** p299 G4.
This spacious, well-laid-out store offers a range of reasonably priced Greek-made clothing alongside more pricey pieces by Lacoste, Gant and Miniman.

Jack in the Box
Haritos 13, Kolonaki (210 725 8735). Metro Evangelismos. **Open** 10am-3pm Mon, Wed, Sat; 10am-2.30pm, 5-8.30pm Tue, Thur, Fri. **Credit** AmEx, DC, MC, V. **Map** p299 H4.
Traditional wooden toys and puzzles, cuddly soft toys, board games, musical boxes, wind-up tin cars and all manner of other carefully chosen, nostalgic toys from the past line the shelves (and floor) of this treasure trove of a shop.

Lapin House
Anagnostopoulou 2, Kolonaki (210 724 6227). Metro Evangelismos. **Open** 9am-3pm Mon, Wed; 9am-8.30pm Tue, Thur, Fri; 9am-4pm Sat. **Credit** AmEx, DC, MC, V. **Map** p299 G4.
The place for proud parents to fuel a future designer addiction in their young, with children's clothes and shoes from DKNY, Prada, Dolce & Gabbana and Ralph Lauren, among other brands.

The Little Baby Shop
Spefsippou 10, Kolonaki (210 724 5640). Metro Evangelismos. **Open** 11am-3pm Mon, Wed, Sat; 11am-2pm, 5-8pm Tue, Thur, Fri. **Credit** AmEx, MC, V. **Map** p299 H4.
Decorated like an old-fashioned English nursery, complete with Beatrix Potter pictures and pastel-painted walls, this charming shop is stocked with

humorous slogan Babygros, pretty floral frocks, personalised pillows and hand-knitted bootees and hats, mostly imported from the UK.

Mothercare
Voukourestiou 23, Kolonaki (210 360 1295). Metro Syntagma. **Open** *May-Sept* 9am-4pm Mon, Wed; 9am-9pm Tue, Thur, Fri; 9am-5pm Sat. *Oct-Apr* 9am-4pm Mon, Wed; 9am-8pm Tue, Thur, Fri; 9am-5pm Sat. **Credit** AmEx, DC, MC, V. **Map** p297/p301 E5.
Mothers will be glad to know that the Athens branch of the international baby and mother chain stocks a wide variety of maternity clothing (including underwear), clothes and shoes for babies and older children, pushchairs, prams, cots, blankets and everything else an infant might need.

Mouyer
Kanari 8, Kolonaki (210 361 7714). Metro Syntagma. **Open** *May-Sept* 9am-3.30pm Mon, Wed, Sat; 9am-9pm Tue, Thur, Fri. *Oct-Apr* 9am-3.30pm Mon, Wed, Sat; 9am-2.30pm, 5-8pm Tue, Thur, Fri. **Credit** AmEx, DC, MC, V. **Map** p299 G5.
Quality, well-fitted, durable footwear for children from four months old and up. As well as Mouyer's own label, you'll also find kids' brands from Italy and France. Adults with smallish to medium-sized feet can shop here if they happen to have a penchant for childish styles (particularly Mary Janes) – sizes go up to a European 40.

Neverland
Solonos 18, Kolonaki (210 360 0996). Metro Syntagma. **Open** 9am-3pm Mon, Wed; 9am-3pm, 5-8.30pm Tue; 9am-8.30pm Thur, Fri; 9am-3.30pm Sat. **Credit** DC, MC, V. **Map** p297 F3.
This delightful shop is a veritable Aladdin's cave of goodies for youngsters (and for parents with an eye for quality collectibles), with its realistic furry animals, micro-scooters and board games, lifelike dolls and elaborately detailed sets of furniture and crockery for old-fashioned doll's houses. The kids may just never want to leave.

Wrap
Haritos 36, Kolonaki (210 729 3659). Metro Evangelismos. **Open** 10am-3pm Mon, Wed, Sat; 10am-2.30pm, 5-8.30pm Tue, Thur, Fri. **Credit** DC, MC, V. **Map** p299 H4.
The perfect place to find a christening or birthday present. It sells cheery, colourful hand-painted pictures, teddies, fleece blankets and handmade decorations, and also creates beautiful, unique baptismal bonbonières (sugared almonds in little containers) for stylish Kolonaki mums.

Department stores

Attica
Panepistimiou 9, Historic Centre (211 180 2500). Metro Syntagma. **Open** 9am-6pm Mon, Wed; 9am-9pm Tue, Thur, Fri; 9am-5pm Sat. **Credit** AmEx, DC, MC, V. **Map** p297 F4.

Don't go home without…
Athens' ten best souvenirs.

Shoes
Follow in the footsteps of Sarah Jessica Parker, John Lennon and Jackie O and purchase a pair of handmade ancient Greek-style thongs from the celebrated 'Poet Sandalmaker' (*see p184* **Pantelis Melissinos**), or go upmarket with some elegant 1950s-inspired creations from the showroom of dapper stylist-turned-designer **Vassilis Zoulias** (*see p178*).

Olive oil
We all know how good it tastes, and now the scientists are proving how good it is for us too. In the area near the Central Market you can find kegs of pure, raw, green virgin oil whose vivid flavour is a far cry from some of the pallid, insipid bottles that lurk on supermarket shelves abroad. A word of warning: store the oil in a dark container as exposure to light spoils the taste.

Pistachio nuts
These plump, purple-green nuts from the sun-kissed slopes of nearby Aegina island can be bought in or out of their shell, salted or unsalted, warm or cold. It's just a shame you can't take the entire sack home.

Ceramics
The colourful, detailed pottery of Rhodes and Skyros is world famous. Even if you don't have a chance to visit these islands during your stay, the pretty, practical plates, bowls and jugs can be found in the **Centre of Hellenic Tradition** shop (*see p183*) and various other specialised ceramics outlets around Athens.

Natural cosmetics
In London, New York and Paris, Korres cosmetics can be found in chic boutiques and high-end department stores, but in Athens they are right there on the shelves of your nearest chemist. Made to homeopathic formulae, these effective and affordable lotions and potions cure all ills, from dandruff to acne and sunburn.

Worry beads
Banish your cares the Eastern way with a string of glowing amber or rare black coral beads. Variations on these age-old accessories have been used by generations of Greek men to while away the hours spent sitting and sipping at the *kafenio*; now they are just as likely to be used by impatient drivers in an Athens traffic jam. *See p183* **Kombologadiko**.

Herbs and spices
Forget fussy little jars of musty dust: visit the spice shops of Psyrri's Evripidou Street and bring home bags of fresh, pungent oregano, sage and thyme just gathered from the hillside, threads of extravagant saffron from northern Greece, nutmeg, cinnamon sticks and cardamom pods.

A huge, newly opened department store right in the heart of commercial Athens. Some 300 shops-in-shops, spread over eight floors, sell around 800 different labels of clothing, accessories, cosmetics and homewares. International brands represented include Missoni, Loewe, Sonia Rykiel, Accessorize, Armani, Burberry, Diesel, Adidas and Napapijri. Parents in search of trendy togs for their tots can find a great selection, sports fanatics can browse happily for hours in the athletics section, and girls with a footwear fetish will enjoy the collection on the lower ground floor.

Fokas
Stadiou 41, Historic Centre (210 325 7740/ 210 325 7750). Metro Panepistimio. **Open** 9am-5pm Mon, Wed, Sat; 9am-8pm (9am-9pm Apr-Oct) Tue, Thur, Fri. **Credit** AmEx, DC, MC, V. **Map** p297 F4.

In the basement you can find sports- and casualwear from the usual suspects (Nike, Puma, Reebok, Fila, and so on). The ground floor is home to fashion-conscious clothing and accessories, while the upper levels have an admirable selection of lingerie, swimwear and everyday clothing for ladies, gents and kids.

Notos Galleries
Eolou 99 & Lykourgou 2-6, Historic Centre (210 324 5811). Metro Omonia. **Open** *May-Sept* 9am-6pm Mon, Wed; 9am-9pm Tue, Thur, Fri; 9am-5pm Sat. *Oct-Apr* 9am-6pm Mon, Wed; 9am-8pm Tue, Thur, Fri; 9am-5pm Sat. **Credit** AmEx, DC, MC, V. **Map** p297 E3.

Seven floors of clothing, perfumes and cosmetics, bags, children's fashions and more. The international labels represented are fairly generic – Benetton, Lacoste, Bostonians – although there are one or two more upmarket brands like Trussardi Jeans. The top

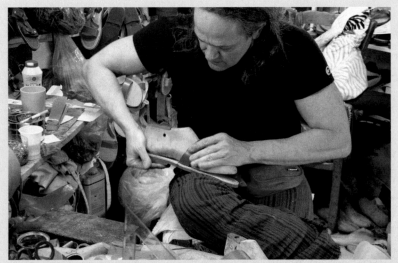

'Poet sandalmaker' **Stavros Melissinos** – purveyor of sandals to the stars. *See p184.*

Jewellery

Since antiquity, the Greeks have been creating magnificent pendants, chokers, earrings and bangles, and the country is still celebrated for its gold- and silversmiths. Choose between breathtaking reproductions of museum pieces, genuine antiques and innovative designs by talented young creators.

Mastic

Cultivated only in the south of Chios island, the sticky resin of the mastic tree allegedly cures a veritable A-Z of ills. Try the traditional shards of mastic chewing gum (which become surprisingly adhesive) and, if you get a taste for it, branch out into resin-flavoured biscuits, chocolates and liquor (*see p184* **Mastiha Shop**).

Ouzo

There's simply nothing better for bringing back nostalgic memories of days in the sun than a cool, cloudy tumbler of ouzo (accompanied by a dish of pistachios). The best ouzos come from Lesvos: try the acclaimed Ploumari brand, which comes in cute mini-versions with corks.

floor, called 'Loft', is dedicated to trendy items for young people, with names such as Custo Barcelona, Nolita and Michiko Koshino. Around the corner on Platia Kotzia, Notos Home (210 374 3000) will fulfil all your home furnishing needs.

Dry-cleaning & laundry

5 a Sec

Xenokratous 40, Kolonaki (210 721 5914). Metro Evangelismos. **Open** 8am-8pm Mon-Fri; 9am-4pm Sat. **No credit cards. Map** p299 H4.
Cheap, quick dry-cleaning and laundry services, but don't expect individual attention – this is a business chain and staff just want to get the job done. Jumpers cost around €2.50, trousers about €3.50 and leather jackets and coats from €35.
Other locations: throughout the city.

National Dry Cleaners & Laundry

Apollonos 17, Historic Centre (210 323 2226). Metro Syntagma. **Open** 8am-4pm Mon, Wed; 8am-8pm Tue, Thur, Fri. **No credit cards. Map** p297/p301 F5.
This friendly, family-run dry-cleaners is especially good at cleaning suede and leather items. It also dyes leather, a point worth bearing in mind if you spill a glass of red wine down your pale leather jacket.

Electronics

Computer purchase & repairs

Germanos

Kanari 26, Kolonaki (210 361 5798/freephone 8001 140000). Metro Evangelismos or Syntagma. **Open** 9am-4pm Mon, Wed; 9am-8pm Tue, Thur, Fri; 9am-3pm Sat. **Credit** AmEx, DC, MC, V. **Map** p299 G5.

The Germanos chain mainly sells and connects mobile phones, but it also has a range of internet services and can arrange PC repairs.
Other locations: throughout the city.

Photography

Camera Gallery
Anthimou Gazi 15, Syntagma (210 324 2310). Metro Syntagma. **Open** 10am-6pm Mon, Wed; 10am-8pm Tue, Thur, Fri; 10am-3pm Sat. **Credit** MC, V. **Map** p297 F4.
A little store where you'll find a large selection of collectable cameras dating from 1890 up to 1980, as well as all the necessary accessories. The store caters mainly for collectors and professionals but amateurs are more than welcome to come in and discover simpler models.

Kodak Express
Xenofontos 14 & Nikis, Syntagma (210 322 9135). Metro Syntagma. **Open** 8am-8.30pm Mon-Fri; 8.30am-4pm Sat. **Credit** AmEx, DC, MC, V. **Map** p301 F5.
This Kodak Express franchise is handily located just near Syntagma Square, offering film exposure (both regular and digital) within 30 minutes, retouching and enlargements, as well as a portrait photography service.
Other locations: throughout the city.

Fashion

Boutiques

Antonios Markos
Skoufa 21, Kolonaki (210 362 3036). Metro Syntagma. **Open** 10am-4pm Mon, Wed, Sat; 10am-9pm Tue, Thur, Fri. **Credit** AmEx, DC, MC, V. **Map** p299 G4.
As well as the eponymous Greek design duo's elegantly deconstructed garments for men and women, this minimalist gallery/shop stocks diverse pieces from a range of labels including Rokha, Anna Heylen, Bernard Willhelm, Xavier Delcour, Age and Dice Kayek. Also hats by Jacques le Corre, Irina Volkonskii bijoux and the complete range of Paul Frank clothes and accessories, for which Antonios Markos has the Greek distribution rights.

Bettina
Pindarou 40 & Anagnostopoulou 29, Kolonaki (210 339 2094). Metro Syntagma. **Open** 10am-3.30pm Mon, Wed, Sat; 10am-8.30pm Tue, Thur, Fri. **Credit** AmEx, DC, MC, V. **Map** p299 G4.
This simple, white, minimalist gallery is home to the collections of Greece's home-grown fashion talents Sophia Kokosalaki and Angelos Frentzos, as well as such revered international labels as Comme des Garçons, Junya Watanabe, Cerruti 1881 and Martine Sitbon. Find the prices a bit steep? Check out the stock shop full of last season's pieces (*see p171*).

Carouzos
Kanari 12, Kolonaki (210 362 7123). Metro Syntagma. **Open** *May-Sept* 10am-3.30pm Mon, Wed; 10am-8.30pm Tue, Thur, Fri; 10am-4.30pm Sat. *Oct-Apr* 10am-3.30pm Mon, Wed; 10am-8pm Tue, Thur, Fri; 10am-5pm Sat. **Credit** AmEx, DC, MC, V. **Map** p299 H4.
This leading fashion retail chain offers prestigious women's and men's clothing brands and accessories by Prada, Fendi, Donna Karan, Celine, Valentino, Emanuel Ungaro, Ermengildo Zegna, Salvatore Ferragamo, Corneliani, Jil Sander and Brioni.
Other locations: Patriarchou Ioakim 14, Kolonaki (210 724 5873); Metaxa 23, Glyfada (210 898 3597); Kassaveti 19, Kifisia (210 808 3991).

Ice Cube
Tsakalof 28, Kolonaki (210 362 5669). Metro Syntagma. **Open** 10am-3.30pm Mon; 10am-8.30pm Tue, Thur, Fri; 10am-4pm Wed, Sat. **Credit** AmEx, DC, MC, V. **Map** p299 G4.
Undisputedly the trendiest lifestyle boutique in Athens, this designer emporium boasts many of the hottest labels in London fashion today (Lara Bohinc, J Maskrey, Liza Bruce, Frost French, Gharani Strok and Temperley, to name a few) as well as a sprinkling of young Greek talent, Italian shoes and bags, glassware from Murano and scented French candles.
Other locations: Ioannou Metaxa 40A, Glyfada (210 898 2803).

Occhi
Sarri 35, Historic Centre (210 321 3298). Metro Monastiraki or Thissio. **Open** noon-5pm Mon; noon-9pm Tue-Fri; noon-6pm Sat. **Credit** AmEx, MC, V. **Map** p297 D4.
A concept clothes and accessories store in the centre of Athens with designs by young, up-and-coming designers from all around Europe. Discover handmade clothes with an art space aesthetic that are all based on the idea that art can be worn and used (all designs convey a unique, playful and multifunctional character). Designs are mainly for women who like to stand out in a crowd but there are also a few interesting men's items too. Take as much time as you like to discover unique accessories in the store's various drawers.

Rere Papa
Skoufa 62, Kolonaki (210 364 4300). Metro Panepistimio. **Open** *May-Sept* 10.30am-3pm Mon, Wed; 10.30am-8.30pm Tue, Thur, Fri; 10.30am-6pm Sat. *Oct-Apr* 10.30am-3pm Mon, Wed; 10.30am-8pm Tue, Thur, Fri; 10.30am-6pm Sat. **Credit** AmEx, DC, MC, V. **Map** p299 G4.
Rere Papa features an idiosyncratic selection of garments and accessories, highlighted by the beautiful, feminine creations of young Greek design duo Rebecca Papastavrou and Renata Papazoglou (get the shop's name now?). There are also flamboyant clothes by Cypriot designer Erotokritos and some unusual bags made from loom-woven wool and lurex by his compatriot Joanna Louca, plus imported pieces (including Shellys shoes from London).

YEShop

Pindarou 38, Kolonaki (210 361 5278). Metro Syntagma or Evangelismos. **Open** *May-Sept 11am-4pm Mon, Wed, Sat; 11am-9pm Tue, Thur, Fri. Oct-Apr 10am-4pm Mon, Wed, Sat; 10am-3pm, 5-9pm Tue, Thur, Fri.* **Credit** AmEx, MC, V. **Map** p299 G4.

Alongside Greek designer Yiorgos Eleftheriades' avant-garde tailoring for men and women with unconventional tastes, this *Wallpaper**-favoured boutique sells a great selection of top-notch accessories garnered from all corners of Europe and the States: sunglasses by Selima, Kirk Originals and IC! Berlin, hats by Viennese legend Muhlbauer, bags by Eva Blut and Robert Leheros, and one-off handmade pieces by up-and-coming Greek talents. Well worth checking out.

International brands

Benetton *Skoufa 20, Kolonaki (210 361 2451). Metro Syntagma.*
Bershka *Ermou 50, Syntagma (210 331 4440). Metro Syntagma.*
Body Shop *Ermou 13, Syntagma (210 331 1186-7). Metro Syntagma.*
Celine *Alonion 28 & Kyriazi, Kifisia (210 808 0946). Metro Kifisia.*
Diesel *Skoufa 3, Kolonaki (210 362 2748). Metro Syntagma.*
DKNY *Solonos 8, Kolonaki (210 360 3775). Metro Syntagma.*
Emporio Armani *Solonos 4 & Milioni, Kolonaki (210 338 9101). Metro Syntagma.*
Ermenegildo Zegna *Skoufa 18, Kolonaki (210 361 3700). Metro Syntagma.*
Escada *Tsakalof 33, Kolonaki (210 361 3918). Metro Syntagma.*
Furla *Patriarchou Ioakim 8, Kolonaki (210 721 6154). Metro Evangelismos.*
Gant *Kapsali 3, Kolonaki (210 722 2535). Metro Syntagma.*
Giorgio Armani *Koumbari 8, Kolonaki (210 361 3603). Metro Syntagma.*
Gucci *Tsakalof 27, Kolonaki (210 361 0870). Metro Syntagma or Evangelismos.*
Guess *Skoufa 14, Kolonaki (210 360 2511). Metro Syntagma.*
Habitat *Kolokotroni 3-5, Syntagma (210 321 5402). Metro Syntagma.*
Hermes *Athens International Airport, Schengen departures Gate B (210 353 4307). Metro Athens Airport.*
IKEA *Athens Airport Retail Park, Building 501 (210 354 3400). Metro Athens Airport.*
Intimissimi *Voukourestiou 27 & Solonos, Kolonaki (210 364 6996). Metro Syntagma.*
Jacques Dessange hair salon *Patriarchou Ioakim & Marasli 33, Kolonaki (210 721 4395). Metro Evangelismos.*
Karen Millen *Anagnostopoulou 11, Kolonaki (210 362 3172). Metro Syntagma or Evangelismos.*
La Perla *Spefsippou 14, Kolonaki (210 729 9720). Metro Syntagma or Evangelismos.*

Levi's *Pindarou 19, Kolonaki (210 360 2066). Metro Syntagma.*
Loewe *Patriarchou Ioakim 30-32, Kolonaki (210 725 7480). Metro Evangelismos.*
Longchamp *Voukourestiou 6, Syntagma (210 325 8750). Metro Syntagma.*
Louis Vuitton *Voukourestiou 19, Kolonaki (210 361 3938). Metro Syntagma.*
Marina Rinaldi *Skoufa 8, Kolonaki (210 363 8741). Metro Syntagma.*
MaxMara *Akadimias 14, Kolonaki (210 360 2142). Metro Syntagma.*
Naf Naf *Ermou 45, Syntagma (210 321 6712). Metro Syntagma.*
Nautica *Kanari 2, Kolonaki (210 361 7685). Metro Syntagma.*
Nike *Tsakalof 34, Kolonaki (210 363 6188). Metro Syntagma or Evangelismos.*
Paul & Shark *Anagnostopoulou 6, Kolonaki (210 339 2334). Metro Syntagma or Evangelismos.*
Polo Ralph Lauren *Pindarou 22, Kolonaki (210 363 6342). Metro Syntagma.*
Pull&Bear *Panepistimiou 56, Omonia (210 383 3538). Metro Omonia.*
Puma *Kanari 17 & Solonos, Kolonaki (210 361 0516). Metro Syntagma.*
Replay *Ermou 53, Syntagma (210 324 5217). Metro Syntagma.*
Sisley *Skoufa 17 & Iraklitou, Kolonaki (210 361 6200). Metro Syntagma.*
Swatch *Adrianou 107, Plaka (210 323 0280). Metro Monastiraki. Ermou 5, Syntagma (210 331 3833). Metro Syntagma.*
Tod's *Voukourestiou 13, Kolonaki (210 335 6425). Metro Syntagma.*
Toi & Moi *Panepistimiou 54 & Emmanuil Benaki, Omonia (210 384 0229). Metro Omonia.*
Tommy Hilfiger *Milioni 3, Kolonaki (210 338 9420). Metro Syntagma.*
Toni & Guy *Ermou 118, Historic Centre (210 322 2120). Metro Monastiraki or Thissio.*
Wolford *Skoufa 9, Kolonaki (210 363 2353). Metro Syntagma.*

Eat, Drink, Shop

Rere Papa. *See p168.*

Budget

Mango

Ermou 39, Syntagma (210 322 7657). Metro Syntagma. **Open** 9.15am-6pm Mon, Wed; 9.15am-8.30pm Tue, Thur, Fri; 9.15am-5pm Sat. **Credit** AmEx, DC, MC, V. **Map** p297/p301 F5.

Located in the heart of what is perhaps the most well-known shopping street in Athens, this popular Spanish womenswear chain carries affordable versions of catwalk looks, classic suits and basics, and casuals like jeans and sweats.

Other locations: Iroon Polytechniou 49, Piraeus (210 413 0175); Village Park, Thivon 228, Rendi (210 425 0966).

Zara

Stadiou 59, Historic Centre (210 321 8141). Metro Omonia. **Open** *May-Sept* 9am-6pm Mon, Wed; 9am-9pm Tue, Thur, Fri; 9am-5pm Sat. *Oct-Apr* 9am-6pm Mon, Wed; 9am-8pm Tue, Thur, Fri; 9am-5pm Sat. **Credit** AmEx, DC, MC, V. **Map** p297 E3.

Everyone's favourite high-street chain is well represented in Greece, with elegant branches housed in stylishly restored neo-classical buildings popping up across the country. Here you can buy trendy, catwalk-inspired garments and accessories or chic, classic clothing for men, women and children at very reasonable prices. Go early to avoid the crowds.

Other locations: throughout the city.

Street

Energie-Shop

Skoufa 29, Kolonaki (210 360 3264). Metro Panepistimio. **Open** *May-Sept* 9.30am-4pm Mon, Wed, Sat; 9.30am-9pm Tue, Thur, Fri. *Oct-Apr* 9.30am-4pm Mon, Wed, Sat; 9.30am-8.30pm Tue, Thur, Fri. **Credit** DC, MC, V. **Map** p299 G4.

Both branches of this funky clothes shop (in Kolonaki and on Patision) stock a wide selection of items from the hip Miss Sixty and Energie brands. The former is rich in super low-waisted jeans, tourniquet minis and pop-art tops for girls, while menswear label Energie shows loose pants and laid-back styles, as well as the occasional see-through T-shirt for trendy guys who aren't afraid to show off their perfect pecs.

Other locations: Patision 52, Historic Centre (210 882 6054).

Nine Below

Tsakalof 16, Kolonaki (210 362 5668). Metro Syntagma. **Open** 10am-3.30pm Mon, Wed; 10am-9pm Tue, Thur, Fri; 10am-4pm Sat. **Credit** AmEx, MC, V. **Map** p299 G4.

Nine Below features cool urban European and US clothing labels, including Dico Copenhagen, Paul Frank, Soochi, 2Ckep and Punk Royal. Come here for customised vintage army pants, kooky T-shirts, unisex bags and funky flip-flops.

Other locations: Stock shop at Sinopis 3, Ambelokipi (210 777 8475).

Stock shops

Bettina

Voukourestiou 4, Syntagma (210 323 8759). Metro Syntagma. **Open** 10am-3pm Mon, Wed, Sat; 10am-6pm Tue, Thur, Fri. **Credit** AmEx, DC, MC, V. **Map** p297/p301 F5.

Tucked away in an arcade behind Syntagma Square's grand line-up of hotels, this boutique has a selection of previous seasons' pieces from designers such as Comme des Garçons and Balenciaga – as well as a selection from Greek-born stars Sophia Kokosalaki and Angelos Frentzos – at greatly reduced prices.

Carouzos Stock

Agiou Metaxa 41, Glyfada (210 894 6202/210 894 6181). Tram to Glyfada stop. **Open** 10am-3.30pm Mon, Wed; 10am-8.30pm Tue, Thur, Fri; 10am-5pm Sat. **Credit** AmEx, DC, MC, V.

If you have a good eye and you time it right, then you can pick up some really amazing bargains at Carouzos Stock: deals might include Prada tops reduced to 70% of their original price or Yves Saint Laurent suits down to just €100. Other labels on offer range from Celine to Emanuel Ungaro, Jil Sander and Salvatore Ferragamo.

Vintage

American Market (Amerikaniki Agora)

Sofokleous 19, Historic Centre (210 321 7051). Metro Omonia or Monastiraki. **Open** *May-Sept* 9am-2.30pm Mon, Wed, Sat; 9am-2.30pm, 5.30-8.30pm Tue, Thur, Fri. *Oct-Apr* 9am-2.30pm Mon, Wed, Sat; 9am-2.30pm, 5-8pm Tue, Thur, Fri. **No credit cards**. **Map** p297 E4.

Suspended over the central meat market, with potent smells wafting up through the open windows in the height of summer, this second-hand clothing outlet attracts everyone from students on a budget to designers searching for inspiration. If you're prepared to spend hours sifting through the kilos of junk bulk-bought from the States, then you might just get lucky and happen upon a glamorous 1930s gown, a Calvin Klein top or a piece from Donna Karan's last collection.

Borell's

Ypsilantou 5, Kolonaki (210 721 9772). Metro Evangelismos. **Open** 10am-3pm Mon, Wed, Sat; 10am-2pm, 5-7.30pm Tue, Thur, Fri. **Credit** DC, MC, V. **Map** p299 H5.

If you are a costume jewellery aficionado, be sure to visit this antique jewellery emporium on a residential street close to the British and German embassies. It is packed with genuine 1930s, '40s and '50s bijoux items, many signed by such luminaries as Miriam Haskell, Trifari and Kenneth Lane, collected by the shop's owner during her regular trips to antique fairs in Britain.

Sunday morning in Monastiraki

A walk around the flea market.

The Monastiraki flea market, centred on Platia Avyssinias, should not be missed, no matter whether your idea of shopping is strictly designer or more like a couple of dirty postcards and a bottle of ouzo. Located next to Athens' Ancient Agora, where traders from throughout the Mediterranean once peddled their wares, crowded, colourful Monastiraki has become the meeting place for sellers of everything, from antique furniture and rare books to clothes, kitsch and junk from around the world. Sunday, when the rest of the city shuts down completely, is the liveliest market day, when dealers from all over crawl out of the woodwork to hawk their choicest and cheapest offerings. A word to the wise: haggling is expected, indeed, de rigueur, no matter how low the initial price may seem.

When planning a day at the market, remember to start fairly early. Stalls and shops open at about 8.30am and close around 3pm.

Begin the walk at Thissio metro station, going down pedestrianised Adrianou. Take note on your right of the sprawling ruins of the Ancient Agora, where fifth-century BC vendors once told riff-raff like Socrates to shove off and stop scaring away customers. Continue down Adrianou, turning left on to Thisio, lined with twittering birdcages and traders selling fake furs, silver cutlery and Russian dolls on blankets. Have a poke round **Erato** (Thisio 9,

210 331 1991), a favourite bookstore of Athenian literati, full of foreign-language books, prints and leather-bound rare editions. Across the street, **Palaiopoleion O Alexandros** (Thisio 10, 210 321 5926, closed Mon) is a fascinating jumble of oddities such as engraved art nouveau cigarette holders, tiny silver salt-and-pepper sets, erotic Arabic prints and antique medical supplies. The shop is co-owned by a Venetian and is often stocked with handmade Venetian carnival masks and colourful Venetian glass. Continue down Thisio, turning right on Astigos or Ermou, either of which will take you past a handful of intriguing junk shops while leading you to Platia Avyssinias, the heart of the market. In the centre of the square, dealers sell painted trunks, coloured cut-glass Turkish tea sets, frilly knickers, pastel-painted Jesus figurines and other such treasures from makeshift stalls. Those on the hunt for true antiques should explore the shops surrounding the square. Platia Avyssinias 3 can yield some good finds: at street level, **Costas Alexandros** (210 321 1580) has antique desk sets with ink bottles and working quills, battered marble-topped rococo writing tables, 1920s typewriters, Victrolas and old Greek toys. Downstairs, **Motakis** (210 321 9005) is one of the few stores in Athens licensed to carry certified

antique furniture. On the other side of the square, **Kougianos** (Platia Avyssinias 6, 210 321 2473) has old Greek musical instruments, wooden signs from the early 1900s and funky upholstered furniture.

If you need a break, stop at **Café Abyssinia** (Kinetou 7, 210 321 7047), a family-run institution whose Arabic and French takes on Greek classics burst with flavour.

Leaving the square, turn left on to Ifestou. It's full of shops selling cheap clothes and trinkets, but keep your eyes open for the small entryways that lead downstairs into dusty storehouses of junk and treasure. Be sure not to miss Normanou, a sunny alley on the left of Ifestou. Here you'll find shops selling maps, prints, old photos and everything else for your walls. Try **Darousos Theotokis** (Normanou 7, 210 331 1638) for prints of old Greek ads. From here head to Ermou and cross the street into Agia Theklas to visit **Stavros Melissinos** (see p184). The white-haired 'Poet Sandalmaker' has morphed into a tourist-attraction parody of himself, more than happy to pose for pictures and push his books on guide-toting tourists. Be that as it may, this is probably still the best place in Athens to buy handmade leather Jesus sandals – there's a huge selection, which Melissinos (in keeping with his 'poet-as-man-of-the-people' image) custom-fits for each buyer. Back on Ifestou, look for **Vavas** (see p185). Barely even a hole in the wall, this stand has been selling carved *tavli* (backgammon – the national pastime of Greece's café-sitters) sets for ages. At Ifestou 24, duck into the arcade of stores selling old Greek records. At the front of the arcade is **Nasiotis** (Ifestou 24, 210 321 2369), where bibliophiles can get lost in the stacks of rare and first editions, prints, old magazines and Greek movie posters. Ifestou ends at Monastiraki metro station. Just beyond the station, stamp and coin collectors should check out **Kiritisis** (Areos 1, 210 324 0544) – a tiny stall full of coins, stamps and wartime paraphernalia.

Dada

Emmanuil Benaki 82, Exarc[...] Metro Omonia. **Open** 11am[...] 11am-8.30pm Tue, Thur, Fri. **Map** p297 E3.

Dada is bursting with impo[...] ing – dresses, shirts (€25-€3[...] accessories for twenty- to thirtysomethings. No need to worry about hygiene – everything is sterilised and dry-cleaned before going on sale.

Le Streghe son Tornate

Haritos 9, Kolonaki (210 721 2581). Metro Evangelismos. **Open** 10.30am-3.30pm Mon, Wed, Sat; 10.30am-8.30pm Tue, Thur, Fri. **Credit** AmEx, DC, MC, V. **Map** p299 H4.

With its classic Chanel suits, flamboyant designer gowns and leopardskin coats, this colourful boutique stands firmly in the category of 'vintage' rather than 'second-hand'. The prices are high but the selection, chosen by Athens' celebrated thrift expert Riana Kounou, is first class.

Underwear & swimwear

Delta of Venus

Haritos 4, Kolonaki (210 722 6829). Metro Evangelismos. **Open** *May-Sept* 10.30am-3.30pm Mon, Wed, Sat; 10.30am-8.30pm Tue, Thur, Fri. *Oct-Apr* 10.30am-3.30pm Mon, Wed, Sat; 10.30am-8pm Tue, Thur, Fri. **Credit** MC, V. **Map** p299 H4.

A pink-and-black boudoir filled with saucy lingerie (think frilly French knicks, cutaway balconette bras and lacey babydolls), rhinestone-studded whips and masks and a variety of other bedroom toys – well, what do you expect from a shop named after Anaïs Nin's soft-porn classic? Stylists love this place because, apart from the lingerie, it also stocks cutting-edge fashions imported from London.

Filidono

Tsakalof 11, Kolonaki (210 361 6780). Metro Syntagma. **Open** 10am-3.30pm Mon, Wed, Sat; 10am-8.30pm Tue, Thur, Fri. **Credit** AmEx, DC, MC, V. **Map** p299 G4.

This abundantly stocked basement shop is where all the smart Athenian girls come to stock up on bikinis for the long, hot summer. Brands include D&G, DKNY, Moschino, Replay, Calvin Klein and Blu Bay. There is also a range of sexy, vibrant-hued bikinis imported from Brazil that are cheap and cheerful but strictly for the well toned.

Sine Qva Non

Patriarchou Ioakim 25, Kolonaki (210 729 2537). Metro Syntagma. **Open** 9am-4pm Mon, Wed, Sat; 9am-8.30pm Tue, Thur, Fri. **Credit** AmEx, DC, MC, V. **Map** p299 H4.

Irresistible frou-frou lingerie that is far too pretty to be kept under wraps. With labels including La Perla, Wolford and Parah, this shop certainly isn't a cheap option, but it's a great place for a birthday/ Valentine's/Christmas gift.

How to do Kolonaki

If you don't have a designer handbag, a jeep with tinted windows, a drop-dead gorgeous companion or a yen to encounter all of the above, don't come to Kolonaki. Once a prestigious residential district of neo-classical dwellings and neatly turned-out, French-speaking families with au pairs, over the last 30 or 40 years this central district has been transformed into a mecca for shopaholics, bar-hoppers and people-watchers.

Morning and evening, Kolonaki's central square (Plateia Filikis Etairias) is a chattering, cellphone-ringing, purchase-displaying, smoking, cappuccino-drinking, double-parking chaos. Get a feeling for the area with a coffee at **Da Capo** (*see p161*), Kolonaki's best-known café. Here, among the models, TV personalities, businessmen, ladies who lunch and eager wannabes, is where deals are done, political scandals are uncovered, new faces are discovered, old friends are reunited, gossip rags' front pages are written and paparazzi shots are snapped.

When you've absorbed enough tittle-tattle and caffeine to set you up for the morning, cross the road to go and join the women staring longingly at the new designs from Casadei, Luciano Padovan, Prada and Marc Jacobs in the window of shoe emporium **Kalogirou** (*see p177*). Then head down the side of Kolonaki Square past the glittering windows of **Serkos** (*see p177*), purveyor of exceptional, extravagant jewellery and timepieces. Just round the corner, on Kapsali Street, make-up junkies will be pleased to see **Beautyworks** (Kapsali & Neofitou Douka, 210 722 5511), a pricey little boutique

selling Shu Uemura and other upmarket brands. Turn on to Irodotou Street to find **Body 'n' Soul** (*see p181*), which stocks Kiehl's, Aesop's, Nars and plenty more treats. Stock up on some store cupboard luxuries at **Maison du Fromage** (10 Kapsali & Irodotou, 210 724 8101) – try the olive oil from Andros and *avgotaraho*, salty fish-roe paste – then pop into **Cake** (*see p161*) next door for a slice of home-made carrot cake or a mini-cheesecake with hot caramel sauce.

After this introductory splurge, it's time to hit Kolonaki's famed designer clothing stores. Head up Irodotou to **Enny di Monaco** (No.18, 210 721 7215) to drool over the itsy-bitsy bikinis by Tomas Maier and the trendy pieces by designers from Roland Mouret to Luella, then on to **Carouzos** (*see p168*), which stocks illustrious names like Prada, Fendi and Celine. Love the looks but choking on the price tags? Check out Enny di Monaco's stock shop on nearby Alopekis Street – you'll find last season's pieces at up to 70 per cent off.

On residential Loukianou Street, a couple of upcoming Greek designers have set up their showrooms. Lena Katsanidou's **Where to Wear** (Alopekis 17 & Loukianou, 210 722 3923) is a colourful den of beaded jewellery, chunky leather belts and kaftans, dresses and separates; meanwhile, **Elena Syraka** (No.21, 210 722 0113) creates gorgeous but practical totes and handbags, jewellery that combines vintage elements with precious metals, and some stylish sandals.

When you hit Patriarchou Ioakim Street, take a tiny detour to choose one of **Thalassa**'s (Nos.30-32, 210 725 8525)

Vraki

Skoufa 50, Kolonaki (210 362 7420). Metro Panepistimio. **Open** *May-Sept* 10am-3.30pm Mon, Wed, Sat; 10am-9pm Tue, Thur, Fri. *Oct-Apr* 10am-3.30pm Mon, Wed, Sat; 10am-8.30pm Tue, Thur, Fri. **Credit** DC, MC, V. **Map** p299 G4.

A funky outlet selling Thessaloniki-made label Modus Vivendi underwear. Mainly for guys, but there are also cute cotton briefs and vests for girls.

Menswear

De Toute Façon

Voukourestiou 43, Kolonaki (210 361 4017). Metro Syntagma. **Open** 10.30am-3.30pm Mon, Wed; 10.30am-8.30pm Tue, Thur, Fri; 10.30am-4pm Sat. **Credit** DC, MC, V. **Map** p299 G4.

Discerning gentlemen, this way please. This small, unobtrusive shop draws sartorially savvy customers who believe in paying for the best. Incomparably soft John Smedley cashmere tops, Duchamp cufflinks and ties, Cutler and Gros sunglasses, Alessandro Gherardeschi shirts and trousers, and Trickers and Sabelt shoes.

Glou

Ermou 49, Historic Centre (210 331 3101-2). Metro Syntagma. **Open** 9am-7pm Mon, Wed; 9am-8pm Tue, Thur, Fri; 9am-6pm Sat. **Credit** AmEx, DC, MC, V. **Map** p297/p301 E5.

Shirts, suits and casual clothing galore, and all at surprisingly affordable prices. This centrally located store also stocks the entire range of Puma sportswear as well as some Nike and Reebok items. During

pure silk pareos, cross the road to admire the intricate gold insect brooches at **Fanourakis** (No.23, 210 721 1762), then, keeping the verdant slopes of Lycabettus Hill in front of you, head to Haritos Street, with its antique shops, art galleries, fashion boutiques, vintage clothing store and well-stocked pet shop. Turn on to the small parallel street (Xanthou) for a browse in **Elena Votsi**'s (*see p176*) celebrated jewellery workshop.

Anagnostopoulou Street, which Xanthou leads into, is packed with top-notch fashion boutiques. Take your pick from **Sofos** (No.5, 210 361 5922; Diane von Furstenberg, Martine Sitbon), **Prince Oliver** (No.3, 210 364 5401; Matthew Williamson, Etro, Pal Zileri), **Karen Millen** (*see p169*), **Studio Avra** (No.27, 210 364 1990; Hussein Chalayan, Philip Treacy), **Bettina** (*see p168*; Sophia Kokosalaki, Comme des Garçons) and **Baton Premier** (No.10, 210 360 1611), which, along with shoes from Costume National and Gaultier, sells accessories by Greek designer Dukas Hadjidoukas. Turn down Pindarou Street at irresistible French pâtisserie **Amelie** (Pindarou & Anagnostopoulou, 210 361 1573), past **YEShop** (*see p169*), where you can find the creative collections of Yiorgos Eleftheriades, and on to Tsakalof Street. **Sotris** (41 Voukourestiou & Tsakalof, 210 361 0662) should be your first port of call, then make for the bags at **Gucci** (*see p169*) before chilling out at lifestyle emporium **Ice Cube** (*see p168*).

Still up for more? Follow Voukourestiou Street down towards the town centre and you'll pass **Louis Vuitton** (*see p169*), **Tod's**

(*see p169*), **Longchamp** (*see p169*), myriad jewellery shops including **Ilias Lalaounis** (*see p176*), and end up at the **Attica** department store (*see p165*), an eight-level emporium boasting a plethora of luxury labels, shop-in-shops, accessories and cosmetics booths, cafés and a vast gym/health club complex.

the sales periods (February and August), Glou's prices plummet to almost ridiculous depths. A suit for €50, anyone?

Other locations: throughout the city.

Oxford Company

Patriarchou Ioakim 12C & Irodotou, Kolonaki (210 721 1133). Metro Evangelismos. **Open** *May-Sept* 9am-3.30pm Mon, Wed; 9am-4pm Sat; 9am-9pm Tue, Thur, Fri. *Oct-Apr* 9am-3.30pm Mon, Wed; 9am-8.30pm Tue, Thur, Fri; 9am-4pm Sat. **Credit** AmEx, DC, MC, V. **Map** p299 H4.

Take the inspiration of two Greek businessmen, the best of Italian fabrics and workmanship and a sensible pricing policy, and you get an extremely successful shirt-and-tie shop. The Oxford Company chain sells an impressive range of styles, shapes and patterns of shirts (for work and play) to suit every age and taste. Get your initials embroidered under the pocket – it only costs a couple of euros extra and gives that all-important tailor-finished impression. The shop also sells ties, cufflinks and a limited selection of jumpers.

Pagoni, Maison des Cravates

Voukourestiou 21A, Kolonaki (210 362 7649). Metro Syntagma. **Open** *May-Sept* 9am-4pm Mon, Wed, Sat; 9am-9pm Tue, Thur, Fri. *Oct-Apr* 9am-4pm Mon, Wed, Sat; 9am-8.30pm Tue, Thur, Fri. **Credit** AmEx, DC, MC, V. **Map** p299 G4.

Looking for a designer tie? You name it, they've got it at this tiny but comprehensively stocked neckwear emporium. Every label under the sun, from Cacharel, Fendi and Paul Smith right down to Walt Disney, is

Eat, Drink, Shop

sold here. In summer, pick up an attractive (and laughably inexpensive) beach bag from the capsule collection made in India especially for Pagoni.

Fashion accessories

Achilleas

Ermou 34, Historic Centre (210 324 9708).
Metro Syntagma. **Open** 9am-4pm Mon, Wed,
Sat; 9am-9pm Tue, Thur, Fri. **Credit** DC, MC, V.
Map p297/p301 E5.
This highly successful chain is Greece's home-grown equivalent of the UK-based accessory brand Accessorize. It's not the best place if you're looking for lasting quality items, but it is great for cheap and up-to-the-minute bags, belts, sarongs, bijoux and hair baubles.
Other locations: throughout the city.

Folli Follie

Ermou 18, Historic Centre (210 323 0729). Metro
Syntagma. **Open** 9am-3.30pm Mon, Wed, Sat; 9am-8.30pm Tue, Thur, Fri. **Credit** AmEx, DC, MC, V.
Map p297/p301 F5.
There is nowhere better for reasonably priced, good-quality jewellery, watches, bags and scarves than this global accessories chain, which started right here in Athens. The K Collection of one-off necklaces with precious stones and antique elements is particularly impressive.
Other locations: throughout the city.

I&D Colors

Tsakalof 7-9, Kolonaki (210 363 3859). Metro
Syntagma. **Open** 9.30am-4pm Mon, Wed, Sat; 9.30am-8.30pm Tue, Thur, Fri. **Credit** AmEx, DC, MC, V.
Map p299 G4.

Need a quick fix to brighten up an unexciting outfit for the evening? Find it at this bright basement shop on Kolonaki's main pedestrian row, which is a treasure chest of affordable, trendy faux bijoux imported from India. You can also buy silk scarves, sarongs and lengths of embroidered sari fabric in vivid hues.

Jewellery

Elena Votsi

Xanthou 7, Kolonaki (210 360 0936). Metro
Evangelismos. **Open** 10am-3pm Mon, Wed, Sat; 10am-8.30pm Tue, Thur, Fri. **Credit** AmEx, DC, MC, V.
Map p299 H4.
Making international headlines when she was chosen to redesign the Olympic medals, this talented Greek designer worked for Gucci's accessories division before launching her own line to the delight of A-list celebrities and jewellery aficionados. Votsi's impeccably finished creations that marry chunky semi-precious stones with 18-carat gold are the epitome of classic Greek elegance.

Lalaounis

Panepistimiou 6 & Voukourestiou, Historic Centre
(210 361 1371). Metro Syntagma. **Open** 9am-3.30pm Mon, Wed, Sat; 9am-8pm Tue, Thur, Fri.
Credit AmEx, DC, MC, V. **Map** p299 G4/G5.
For decades the shops of Ilias Lalaounis, one of the earliest masters to make a name for Greek jewellery on the international stage, have been attracting discerning customers for the jewellery designer's top-quality, Byzantine-inspired solid gold necklaces, bracelets and earrings. The recent DNA range incorporates more modern elements in an unusual series of molecular jewellery.

Li La Lo

Voukourestiou 2 & Stadiou, Syntagma (210 331 9864). Metro Syntagma. **Open** 9am-5pm Mon, Wed, Sat; 9am-9pm Tue, Thur, Fri. **Credit** AmEx, DC, MC, V. **Map** p297/p301 F5.

Li La Lo offers fashionable pieces in various combinations of silver, gold or white gold with precious and semi-precious stones. The selection of silver gifts for christening presents is especially good. **Other locations**: Patriarchou Ioakim 3, Kolonaki (210 725 5264); Grigoriou Lambraki 16 & Ioannou Metaxa, Glyfada (210 898 2554); Iroon Polytechniou 48, Piraeus (210 411 3983).

Patrick Fabre Gallery

Anagnostopoulou 22, Kolonaki (210 361 0490). Metro Syntagma. **Open** 10.30am-3.30pm Mon, Wed; 10.30am-8.30pm Tue, Thur, Fri; 10.30am-4pm Sat. **Credit** AmEx, MC, V. **Map** p299 G4.

Located in the heart of Athens – close to Kolonaki Square – the Patrick Fabre Gallery offers a chance to buy, or just admire, some unusual merchandise: ethnic jewellery sourced from Asia and Africa and a rare collection of objects from Ethiopia. The gallery also stocks cotton creations by designer Brigitte Singh from Jaipur in India.

Petaie Petaie

Skoufa 30, Kolonaki (210 362 4315). Metro Syntagma. **Open** 9.30am-3.30pm Mon, Wed; 9.30am-2.30pm, 5-9pm Tue; 9.30am-9pm Thur, Fri; 9.30am-3.30pm Sat. **Credit** AmEx, DC, MC, V. **Map** p299 G4.

This tiny hole-in-the-wall shop sells a select range of works by talented young Greek jewellery designers, including Vangelis Polizo's amber inventions, Erato Boukogianni's coral-and-gold necklaces, Yiannis Tjovenis's collection of silver pieces, and a

range of orna sea-glass ban self, Ioanna K

Serkos Je

Kapsali 1, Plat 7975). Metro 2.30pm Mon, W Thur, Fri. *Oct-* 9.30am-2.30pm Fri. **Credit** Am This swanky g Rolex, Cartier, Muller. The gift selection is also interesting and includes silver ornaments, vases and frames. The service is impeccable.

Trambakopoulos

Stadiou 7, Syntagma (210 331 6661). Metro Syntagma. **Open** 9.30am-3.30pm Mon, Wed, Sat; 9.30am-8.30pm Tue, Thur, Fri. **Credit** AmEx, DC, MC, V. **Map** p297 F4.

Jewellery is this shop's strong point, with many pieces on display created by the shop's owners themselves, but it also stocks a fairly decent selection of investment timepieces by Rolex, Cartier and Vacheron Constantin.

Shoes

Kalogirou

Patriarchou Ioakim 4, Kolonaki (210 335 6401). Metro Evangelismos. **Open** *May-Sept* 9am-3.30pm Mon, Wed; 9am-9pm Tue, Thur, Fri; 9am-5pm Sat. *Oct-Apr* 9am-3.30pm Mon, Wed; 9am-8pm Tue, Thur, Fri; 9am-5pm Sat. **Credit** AmEx, DC, MC, V. **Map** p299 H4.

Mesogeia. *See p179.*

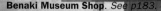

Benaki Museum Shop. *See p183.*

Shopaholics from all over Greece and Cyprus flock to jockey for viewing positions at the windows of this formidable Kolonaki shoe emporium, which sells a pricey selection of own-brand footwear as well as the latest mouthwatering creations from Prada, D&G, Miu Miu, Tod's and Casadei. Well-off professional gentlemen come here to buy their classic Church's brogues here.
Other locations: Panagitsas 5, Kefalari (210 335 6404); Ioannou Metaxa 18 & Grigoriou Labraki, Glyfada (210 335 6407).

Rollini

Tsakalof 11, Kolonaki (210 360 9643). Metro Syntagma. **Open** 9am-5pm Mon, Wed, Sat; 9am-9pm Tue, Thur, Fri. **Credit** AmEx, DC, MC, V. **Map** p299 G4.
A tempting range of shoes for both men and women from Rollini's own label are sold at this shop, as well as a selection of imported footwear by the likes of Pura Lopez and Dolce & Gabbana.
Other locations: Patision 133, Patisia (210 864 3359); Ippokratous 1, Historic Centre (210 261 6030); Platonos 12A-14, Halandri (210 684 6129); Kiriazi 6-8, Kifisia (210 808 8710); Vas Georgiou 21A, Piraeus (210 413 3133).

Spiliopoulos

Ermou 63, Historic Centre (210 322 7590). Metro Monastiraki. **Open** 10am-4pm Mon, Wed, Sat; 10am-8.30pm Tue, Thur, Fri. **Credit** AmEx, DC, MC, V. **Map** p297/p301 E5.
A bargain hunter's delight, this shop stocks seconds and last season's styles made by such sought-after names as Manolo Blahnik, Kate Spade, Narciso Rodriguez, Calvin Klein, Donna Karan and many others at a fraction of their original prices. We should really have kept this one a secret…
Other locations: Adrianou 50, Monastiraki (210 321 0018).

Vassilis Zoulias Old Athens

Kanari 17, Kolonaki (210 361 4762). Metro Syntagma. **Open** 9.30am-3.30pm Mon, Wed; 9.30am-8.30pm Tue, Thur, Fri; 9.30am-4pm Sat. **Credit** AmEx, DC, MC, V. **Map** p299 G5.
Greek *Vogue* stylist Vassilis Zoulias takes inspiration from the elegant films and photographs of the 1950s and '60s for his beautiful collections of handmade pointy stilettos, ballet pumps and cute kitten heels in satin, ostrich or tweed. Matching bags are also available, as well as luxuriously soft leather Gilda gloves.

Food & drink

See also p96 **The central market** *and p153* **Street eats**.

Greek specialities

Elixir

Evripidou 41, Psyrri (210 321 5141). Metro Monastiraki. **Open** 7.30am-3.30pm Mon-Wed, Sat; 7.30am-6pm Thur, Fri. **Credit** AmEx, DC, MC, V. **Map** p297 E4.
Stuck in the middle of a rather insalubrious area of central Athens, close to the meat market, this shop is well worth a visit for its tasteful interior and spectacular array of mountain herbs, spices, teas, local honeys and traditional homeopathic remedies. Great bunches of oregano and chamomile are suspended from the ceiling, baskets of dried rosebuds sit in the entrance, and the walls are lined with deep glass-fronted wood drawers full of all manner of aromatic twigs and powders.

Gnision Esti

Christou Lada 2 & Anthimos Gazi 15, Historic Centre (210 324 4784). Metro Panepistimio. **Open** 10am-2pm, 5.30-7.30pm Mon-Fri; 10am-3pm Sat, Sun. **Credit** AmEx, DC, MC, V.
Barely more spacious than a larder, this shop is deservedly renowned for its traditional savouries and drinks, sourced from small, family-run producers all over the countryside who have perfected the art of making one delicious item: melt-in-the-mouth *koulourakia* (cookies), fiery *tsipouro* spirit, flavoursome honey, creamy scoops of feta cheese or green-hued virgin olive oil.

Loumidis

Eolou 106, Omonia (210 321 6965/210 321 4426). Metro Omonia. **Open** 8am-8pm Mon-Fri; 8am-3.30pm Sat. **No credit cards. Map** p297 E3.
The oldest *kafekopteio* (coffee grinders) in Athens, Loumidis offers a wide selection of caffeinated – and some decaf – beverages to suit all tastes, from bitter, thick Greek coffee to Colombian beans or fruity teas. You can also buy all the necessary accoutrements for preparing and serving coffee here, as well as the accompanying biscuits and chocolates.

Lutece

Koumbari 5, Kolonaki (210 362 7744/210 362 9204). Metro Evangelismos or Syntagma. **Open** 8.30am-8.30pm Mon-Fri; 8.30am-6pm Sat. **Credit** AmEx, MC, V. **Map** p299 G5.
Along the left-hand side of this narrow shop is a refrigerator crammed with hunks of cold meat and salami, French cheeses, pâté, smoked fish and other imported goodies, while the shelves on the right contain elusive gourmet ingredients ranging from dried

Eat, Drink, Shop

shiitake mushrooms to truffle oil and spicy Asian sauces. Head towards the back of the shop for an excellent range of cheeses from all over Greece, as well as items like *gigantes* (white haricot beans in oil and tomato sauce), *fava* (chickpea purée) and *dolmadakia* (little parcels of rice wrapped in vine leaves). Don't forget to pick up a bottle of Greek wine from the small but well-chosen selection to accompany your meal.

Mesogeia

Nikis 52 & Kydathinaion, Plaka (210 322 9146). Metro Syntagma. **Open** *May-Sept* 9am-5pm Mon, Wed, Sat; 9am-8pm Tue, Thur, Fri. *Oct-Apr* 9am-5pm Mon, Wed, Sat; 9am-8pm Tue, Thur, Fri; 10am-3pm Sun. **Credit** MC, V. **Map** p301 F6.

If you happen to be in Plaka, then do your food shopping at this small store packed to the gunnels with traditional (and often organic) goodies. The selection includes crusty *paximadia* (rusks), local olive oil, Greek wines and liqueurs, cheeses and other edible specialities gathered from all over Greece and its islands.

Tsaknis

Panepistimiou 49, Historic Centre (210 322 0716). Metro Panepistimio. **Open** *May-Sept* 9am-4pm Mon-Sat. *Oct-Apr* 9am-7pm Mon-Fri; 9am-4pm Sat. **No credit cards. Map** p297 F4.

Tucked away in the façade of a handsomely restored neo-classical block, this cupboard of a shop has for the past 70 years been selling the finest, freshest sun-dried pistachio nuts from the isle of Aegina. It also has kegs of almonds, walnuts, peanuts and sesame seeds, as well as a selection of dried fruit and bottles of metaxa brandy, whisky and gin to accompany the nuts.

Tyria Outra

Sofokleous 17, Historic Centre (210 322 1135). Metro Omonia. **Open** 6am-8pm Mon-Sat. **No credit cards. Map** p297 E4.

The perfect place to come and stock up on traditional Greek hors d'oeuvres, this unpretentious deli sells a great variety of local cheeses, cold meats, tempting kegs full of fish marinated in oil or grilled red peppers, octopus tentacles in vinegar and stuffed vegetables. Got a sweet tooth? Try Tyria Outra's selection of sweet, chalky *halva*.

Supermarkets

Marinopoulos

Kanari 9, Kolonaki (210 362 4907). Metro Syntagma. **Open** *May-Sept* 8am-9pm Mon-Fri; 8am-6pm Sat. *Oct-Apr* 8am-8pm Mon-Fri; 8am-6pm Sat. **Credit** AmEx, DC, MC, V. **Map** p299 G5.

Marinopoulos is a small, run-of-the-mill city supermarket where you can pick up your basic staples: dairy produce, fruit and vegetables, alcohol and beverages, cosmetics, tinned and frozen goods and pet foods. The delicatessen section is pretty good, as is the limited range of warm, ready-cooked lunch

options. Make sure that you arrive there early if you want to sample the whole free-range chickens and freshly baked, floury loaves – they tend to sell out by noon.

Vasilopoulos Delicatessen

Stadiou 19, Historic Centre (210 322 2405). Metro Panepistimio. **Open** 8am-8pm Mon-Fri; 8am-3.30pm Sat. **Credit** AmEx, DC, MC, V. **Map** p297 F4.

Pricier than other supermarkets, this deli is stocked with unusual finds like Green & Black chocolate, organic and gourmet eats, local specialities such as olive oil and feta cheese, and some generic household staples. Unfortunately, the staff tend to be on the grumpy side.

Wine & spirits

Cellier

Kriezotou 1, Historic Centre (210 361 0040). Metro Syntagma. **Open** 9am-5pm Mon, Wed; 9am-8.30pm Tue, Thur, Fri; 9am-3pm Sat. **Credit** AmEx, DC, MC, V. **Map** p299 G4/G5.

Cellier offers an excellent selection of fine wines – including many from Greek vineyards – champagnes and spirits, as well as a few pots and jars of tempting appetisers to serve alongside the booze. The goody-packed Christmas and New Year hampers are famed throughout Athens. Before you do your shopping here, pop into the Cellier Bistro next door for a spot of wine tasting.

Health & beauty

Beauty parlours & nail bars

Cavalliert

1st Floor, Irodotou 18, Kolonaki (210 721 3546). Metro Evangelismos. **Open** 10am-1pm, 4-8pm Mon-Fri. **Credit** MC, V. **Map** p299 H5.

In their old-fashioned Kolonaki apartment, the Cavallieratos couple and their capable assistants cleanse, squeeze, knead, stroke and press away the troubles and imperfections that plague tired, unhealthy, badly nourished city complexions. Pambitsa unblocks blackheads and purifies pores with her magic fingers. Her husband Takis massages using creams made by hand to the Cavalliert recipe from flowers and plants grown on their organic estate in southern Attica.

E-nail

Anagnostopoulou 9 & Tsakalof 6, Kolonaki (210 364 3558). Metro Syntagma. **Open** 9am-6pm Mon; 9am-7pm Tue, Thur, Fri; 9am-8pm Wed; 9.30am-5.30pm Sat. **Credit** V. **Map** p299 H4.

A small but cute nail store famed for the quality of its artificial nails. It takes just 90 minutes to give your own nails a brand-new appearance or have false ones added. Don't forget that they'll need upkeep – each pair lasts for roughly one month.

Eat, Drink, Shop

Top city spas

Ananea Spa

Life Gallery Hotel, 103 Thiseos Avenue, Ekali (210 626 0456). Bus 550 from Kallimarmaro or A7 from Kanigos Square, then bus 507, 508, 509, 536 from Kifisia. **Open** 10am-7.30pm Mon-Fri; 11am-6pm Sat, Sun. **Credit** AmEx, DC, MC, V.

All marble and blue glass, this small spa in the sleek Life Gallery Hotel is pure Zen. Choose from a range of treatments from Bali, Polynesia and Morocco using Elemis products, then unwind in the candlelit meditation room. **Best treatment**: The energising and deeply relaxing Thai Yoga Massage (€80 for an hour) is a mixture of acupressure, stretching and reflexology.

Cocoon Urban Spa

9 Souliou & Erifylis, Agia Paraskevi (210 656 1975). Metro Ethniki Amyna, then bus A5. **Open** noon-10pm Mon; 10am-10pm Tue-Fri; 10am-6pm Sat. **Credit** AmEx, MC, V.

Owned by two glamorous Greek-American sisters, this minimalist three-storey spa decked out in dark wood and brushed concrete is a haven of soothing sophistication. Besides facials, massages, waxing and various treatments for men, there are drop-in Pilates and yoga classes. **Best treatment**: The Ayurvedic Shirodhara is sure to de-stress you. After a ginger body rub, warm scented oil is gently

GB Spa Grande.

poured over the third eye, followed by a full body massage with healing oils (€120 for 90 minutes).

Divani Athens Spa & Thalasso Centre

10 Agiou Nikolaou & Iliou, Vouliagmeni (210 891 1900). Bus E22 from Akadimias. **Open** 10am-10pm Mon-Fri; 10am-8pm Sat; 11am-7pm Sun. **Credit** AmEx, DC, MC, V.
The only thalassotherapy centre in Athens, this lavish beachside spa has an endless selection of treatments inspired by the sea, such as the bizarrely named but deeply detoxifying algotherapy, thalgobodytherm, plus hydromassage on giant aqua-beds – especially good for getting rid of cellulite.
Best treatment: The Bamboo Massage (€95 for 50 minutes) uses bamboo sticks to detox, stimulate circulation and boost energy.

GB Spa Grande

Hotel Grande Bretagne, Syntagma Square (210 333 0772). Metro Syntagma. **Open** 6am-10pm daily. **Credit** AmEx, DC, MC, V.
With its E'SPA products, herbal steam rooms, marble foot spas and indoor pool lined in blue glass, the Grande Bretagne spa is the ultimate pampering treat smack in the centre of town.
Best treatment: The Nourishing Yoghurt, Honey and Sugar Treatment (€150 for 70 minutes) combines a foot ritual, an all-over scrub with olive oil, sugar and lemon, a yoghurt and honey body wrap and scalp massage.

Glow Irodotou

Irodotou 10, Kolonaki (210 729 4396). **Open** 10am-7pm Mon, Wed; 10am-8pm Tue, Thur, Fri; 10am-5pm Sat. **Credit** MC, V.
This funky little space is perfect for a quick beauty fix between hitting Kolonaki's designer boutiques. The friendly staff specialise in pedicures and manicures, but also offer expert eyebrow shaping, eyelash tinting and make-up.
Best treatment: Sink back into a massage chair for a relaxing Pedicure Spa (€30 for an hour) that will leave your feet feeling sandal soft.

Cosmetics

Beauty Shop

Milioni 2 & Kanari, Kolonaki (210 362 9925). Metro Syntagma. **Open** *May-Sept* 9am-8pm Mon, Wed; 9am-9pm Tue, Thur, Fri; 9am-5pm Sat. *Oct-Apr* 9am-8pm Mon, Wed; 9am-8.30pm Tue, Thur, Fri; 9am-5pm Sat. **Credit** AmEx, DC, MC, V. **Map** p299 G5.
You'll discover all the famous brands of cosmetics (Lancôme, Clinique, Estée Lauder, La Prairie, etc) and fragrances, as well as face and body products to cater for your every need. If you're after a bargain, try Beauty Shop's own brand of products, which you'll find in the self-service department – some of them are outstanding.
Other locations: Patision 12, Omonia (210 382 5759).

Body 'n' Soul

Irodotou 23, Kolonaki (210 722 2424). Metro Evangelismos. **Open** *May-Sept* 10am-3pm Mon, Wed; 10am-9pm Tue, Thur, Fri; 10am-4pm Sat. *Oct-Apr* 10am-3pm Mon, Wed; 10am-8.30pm Tue, Thur, Fri; 10am-4pm Sat. **Credit** AmEx, DC, MC, V. **Map** p299 H5.
A product-packed boutique that is simply paradise for beauty connoisseurs, featuring some of the finest and most exclusive cosmetics from around the world. Make-up from Stephane Marais, T Le Clerc and Nars, soaps and perfume from L'Artisan Parfumier and shaving products by Santa Maria Novella are just a handful of the many enticing items to be found here.
Other locations: Fivis 17, Glyfada (210 894 5737); Omirou 11, Neo Psychiko (210 677 4554).

Sephora

Ermou 24, Syntagma (210 331 3167/210 325 7744). Metro Syntagma. **Open** *May-Sept* 9am-6pm Mon, Wed; 9am-9pm Tue, Thur, Fri; 9am-5pm Sat. *Oct-Apr* 9am-6pm Mon, Wed; 9am-8.30pm Tue, Thur, Fri; 9am-5pm Sat. **Credit** AmEx, DC, MC, V. **Map** p297/p301 F5.
The Athens branch of the famous red-carpeted international beauty supermarket is somewhat smaller than many of its international siblings, but it still manages to pack in a good many must-have brands. Check out Sephora's own line of beauty accessories – affordably priced brushes, tweezers, cosmetics cases and so on.

Hairdressers & barbers

Bitsikas Hairlines

Xanthippou 2, Kolonaki (210 721 3573). Metro Evangelismos. **Open** by appointment. **No credit cards. Map** p299 H4.
Presided over by hair guru Stathis, this contemporary salon features a men's floor that resembles a futuristic airport lounge. There's also a pretty pampering parlour for the ladies. The salon specialises in trendy, funky cuts.

Eat, Drink, Shop

Ilias Zarbalis

Spefsippou 4 & Irodotou, Kolonaki (210 723 2939).
Metro Evangelismos. **Open** 10am-5pm Mon; 8am-
7pm Tue, Thur, Fri; 8am-5pm Wed, Sat. **Credit**
AmEx, MC, V. **Map** p299 H4.

This celebrity salon is where local celebs pop in to
have their roots touched up and their locks cropped
into the latest look. Check out the super-stylish
new branch in Neo Psychiko (Ethnikis Antistaseos
103, 210 675 4901), which more closely resembles an
elegant furniture showroom than a hairdressing
salon, and boasts luxurious massage armchairs at
each styling station.

Opticians

Optika Stavrou

Akadimias 60, Kolonaki (210 364 3012). Metro
Syntagma. **Open** 8.30am-3.30pm Mon, Wed; 8.30am-
8.30pm Tue, Thur, Fri; 9.30am-3.30pm Sat. **Credit**
AmEx, DC, MC, V. **Map** p297 F3.

Whether you've lost a lens or just want a trendy pair
of shades to attract the paparazzi flashes on
Kolonaki Square, this shop will solve your problem.
It has everything from prescription lenses to the
latest designer frames.

Pharmacies

Litos

Stadiou 17, Historic Centre (210 322 2200). Metro
Panepistimio. **Open** May-Sept 8am-2.30pm Mon,
Wed; 8am-2pm, 5.30-8.30pm Tue, Thur, Fri. *Oct-Apr*
8am-2.30pm Mon, Wed; 8am-2pm, 5-8pm Tue, Thur,
Fri. **Credit** AmEx, DC, MC, V. **Map** p297 F4.

One of the oldest pharmacies in central Athens, this
shop has everything you could need, from sunscreen, shampoo and mosquito repellent to vitamin
pills, aspirin and prescription medicines (most of the
latter, interestingly, are available over the counter
in Greek chemists).

Home

Htypa Xylo

Vouliagmenis 376, Kalamaki (210 994 0920/210
994 0216). Bus 108, B3 from Akadimias, 109, 171
from Dafni metro station. **Open** May-Sept 10am-
5.30pm Mon, Wed, Sat; 10.30am-9pm Tue, Thur,
Fri. *Oct-Apr* 10am-5.30pm Mon, Wed, Sat; 10am-
8.30pm Tue, Thur, Fri. **Credit** AmEx, MC, V.

Htypa Xylo (Knock on Wood) is the place to go for
20th-century European furniture (mainly from the
Netherlands, Belgium and Scotland). Here you can
pick up anything from a 1970s wooden magazine
stand to a three-seater Chesterfield sofa. Choose
items to add a vintage air to your pad including fans,
copper candelabras, lamps, settees and dining tables.

Ionia

Patriarchou Ioakim 11, Kolonaki (210 722
4125). Metro Evangelismos. **Open** May-Sept
9am-3.30pm Mon, Wed, Sat; 9am-9pm Tue, Thur,

Fri. *Oct-Apr* 9am-3.30pm Mon, Wed, Sat; 9am-
8.30pm Tue, Thur, Fri. **Credit** AmEx, DC, MC, V.
Map p299 H4.

Ionia sells affordable, locally made china, crockery
and cutlery. Whether you require a full dinner service for a wedding present or just a couple of cheap,
comic mugs for the children, it's well worth a visit
to see what's in stock.

Other locations: throughout the city.

Mofu

Sarri 28, Psyrri (210 331 1922). Metro Thissio.
Open 10am-3pm Mon, Wed; 10am-3pm, 5.30-9pm
Tue, Thur, Fri; 10am-6pm Sat. **Credit** MC, V.
Map p297 D4.

One of the best options around town if you're after
truly special objects for the home. The shop's stock
has been collected by the owners themselves during
their travels around the world, giving Mofu an identity all of its own. The groundbreaking design, the
1960s and '70s atmosphere, as well as the various
pieces of designer furniture that are now a part of
history, won't allow you to walk past here without
wanting to take a good look inside.

Pallet Stores

Evangelistrias 17, Historic Centre (210 323 2344).
Metro Syntagma or Monastiraki. **Open** 9am-6pm
Mon, Wed; 9am-9pm Tue, Thur, Fri; 9am-5pm Sat.
Credit AmEx, DC, MC, V. **Map** p297/p301 E5.

It's almost impossible to shoehorn yourself in here
on a Saturday morning, and even midweek this
cheap and cheerful shop is jam-packed with bargain
hunters in search of odds and ends for the house.
Candles, lamps, kitchen utensils, cups and saucers
– they're all here, if you can fight through the crowds
to reach them.

Other locations: throughout the city.

Music

Metropolis

Panepistimiou 54, Historic Centre (210 380
8549). Metro Omonia. **Open** 9am-9pm Mon-
Fri; 9am-6pm Sat. **Credit** AmEx, DC, MC, V.
Map p297 F3.

Five storeys of music catering to most mainstream
tastes. Prices average €18-€20 for an imported CD,
but there are often good sales racks with relatively
recent releases for €10 or less.

Other locations: throughout the city.

PMW

Panepistimiou 66 & Patision 2, Omonia (210 380
3030). Metro Omonia. **Open** 8.30am-9.30pm Mon-
Fri; 8.30am-7pm Sat. **Credit** AmEx, DC, MC, V.
Map p297 E3.

At this six-floor emporium you can pick up chart
pop CDs – both Greek and international – for
between €5 and €10 less than you would expect to
pay at other mainstream music stores. Apart from
its significantly lower prices, PMW is also worth a
visit for its selection of non-chart music (classical,
jazz, heavy metal) and DVDs.

Shoe repairs

Iliopoulos

Voulis 42, Historic Centre (210 324 5028). Metro Syntagma. **Open** *May-June* 7am-6pm Mon-Fri; 7am-2pm Sat. *July-Apr* 7am-3pm Mon, Wed; 7am-6pm Tue, Thur, Fri; 7am-2pm Sat. **No credit cards.** **Map** p297/p301 F5.

In his tiny workshop, elderly Mr Iliopoulos does an impeccable job re-heeling, re-soling, dyeing or just tidying up your scruffy but beloved shoes and boots.

Takouni Express

Voulis 12 & Karageorgis Servias 16, Historic Centre (210 322 1545). Metro Syntagma. **Open** 9am-4pm Mon, Wed, Sat; 9am-9pm Tue, Thur, Fri. **Credit** DC, MC, V. **Map** p297/p301 F5.

This shoe repair chain offers swift, efficient and reasonably priced service for basic operations such as replacing heels. Takouni Express also sells a range of basic slippers and flip-flops.

Other locations: Skoufa & Pindarou, Kolonaki (210 363 7003); Filonos 35, Piraeus (210 412 2453).

Souvenirs & gifts

Benaki Museum Shop

Koumbari 1 & Leof Vas Sofias, Kolonaki (210 367 1045). Metro Evangelismos or Syntagma. **Open** 9am-5pm Mon, Wed, Fri, Sat; 9am-midnight Thur; 9am-3pm Sun. **Credit** AmEx, DC, MC, V. **Map** p299 G5.

The perfect place to find a tasteful souvenir or gift, this gift shop inside the Benaki Museum (*see p103*) sells replicas of ancient Greek artefacts, icons, jewellery and toys displayed in the museum, as well as books on Hellenic and Byzantine history, modern Greek photography and art, plus postcards, silk scarves and local pottery.

Centre of Hellenic Tradition

Mitropoleos 59, Plaka (210 321 3023). Metro Monastiraki. **Open** *May-Sept* 9am-8pm daily. *Oct-Apr* 9am-6pm daily. **Credit** AmEx, DC, MC, V. **Map** p297/p301 E5.

The arcade leading to the Centre of Hellenic Tradition is filled with wonderful display cases of hand-painted pottery, icons and embroidery, giving a pretty good idea of what the extensive gallery upstairs specialises in. Here you will find traditional handicrafts – ceramics, tapestries, lace, carved wood and sculptures, paintings and rugs – garnered from every corner of Greece.

Kombologadiko

Koumbari 6, Kolonaki (210 362 4267). Metro Evangelismos or Syntagma. **Open** 10am-4pm Mon, Wed, Sat; 10am-9pm Tue, Thur, Fri. **Credit** AmEx, DC, MC, V. **Map** p299 G5.

Where traditional worry beads (*komboloi*) are transformed into works of art. Made from some of the rarest, finest quality materials from around the world, prices for these elegant strings can rise into thousands of euros (for a version in precious red

Kombologadiko.

amber) but start at a mere €10. Choose between intricately worked Yusuri sets of black coral inlaid with turquoise and silver, Faturan Egyptian strings with handmade amber beads, delicate mother-of-pearl rosaries or simple, affordable sets made from cat's eye or crystal.

Kori

Mitropoleos 13 & Voulis, Syntagma (210 323 3534). Metro Syntagma. **Open** *May-Sept* 9am-5pm Mon, Wed, Sat; 9.30am-9pm Tue, Thur, Fri. *Oct-Apr* 9.30am-4.30pm Mon, Wed, Sat; 9.30am-8.30pm Tue, Thur, Fri. **Credit** AmEx, DC, MC, V. **Map** p297/p301 E5.

A treasure trove for the discerning souvenir hunter, this small but well-stocked shop offers not only replicas and reproductions but also plenty of eye-catching contemporary ornaments and jewellery made by talented young Greek artists.

Lamarinoupolis

Athinas 17 & Kakourgiodikeiou 2, Psyrri (210 324 8345). Metro Monastiraki. **Open** *July, Aug* 8.30am-3pm Mon-Fri. *Sept-June* 8.30am-3pm Mon, Wed; 8.30am-7.30pm Tue, Thur, Fri; 8.30am-2.30pm Sat. **No credit cards. Map** p297 E4.

Many of Yiannis Terikoglou's wares are visible from the street outside – tin cooking pots and trays are hung temptingly around the doorway and on the surrounding walls – but duck down the steps into his workshop to see the full selection. Perhaps the best souvenirs are the traditional three-strutted *kafenio* trays (which start at just €8), but there are also practical baking trays and many more essential items for the home.

Mastiha Shop

Panepistimiou 6 & Kriezotou, Historic Centre (210 363 2750). Metro Syntagma. **Open** 9am-9pm Mon-Fri; 9am-5pm Sat. **Credit** MC, V. **Map** p297/p301 F5.

Just about everything you can imagine made from the resin of the southern Chios mastic tree – a gum that is said to be a panacea for all ills from stomach ulcers to cancer. Whether you're after mastic chewing gum, sweets, essential oils, candles, beauty products or just a book about the island of Chios, this is the place to find it. Don't miss the line of natural cosmetics made by Korres (*see p166* **Don't go home without…**) especially for the Mastiha Shop.

Pantelis Melissinos

Agias Theklas 2, Monastiraki (210 321 9247). Metro Monastiraki. **Open** 10am-6pm Mon-Sat; 10am-4pm Sun. **No credit cards. Map** p297/p301 E5.

Plaka and Monastiraki are full of attractive leather shops, but generations of knowledgeable visitors from all over the world instead duck into this rather less flamboyant shop to stock up on Stavros Melissinos' long-lasting, handmade leather sandals. The smiling 'Poet Sandalmaker' (he is the author of several tracts) began making shoes in 1954, has expanded the original few styles to feature around

32 classically inspired designs. He has reputedly sold to the likes of John Lennon, Sophia Loren and Jackie Kennedy Onassis, so you'll be in illustrious company if you buy a pair.

Pelekanos Folk Art

Adrianou 115, Plaka (210 321 9846). Metro Akropoli. **Open** *May-Sept* 9am-2am daily. *Oct-Apr* 10am-10pm daily. **Credit** AmEx, DC, MC, V. **Map** p301 E5.

Come in for a traditional beaten copper carafe for keeping your wine cool (even in the midsummer heat) and you might just be tempted to invest in a couple of the pretty cake tins or other decorative copper items too. Everything at Pelekanos Folk Art is handmade and, although the shop is located bang in the middle of the tourist trail, its prices are not ridiculously exaggerated.

Mastiha Shop. *See p184.*

R Touch

Athinas 17, Historic Centre (210 321 0285/210 324 7402). Metro Monastiraki. **Open** 10am-3pm Mon-Sat. **Credit** MC, V. **Map** p297 E4.

A welcome surprise among the gardening tool stores that line the southern end of Athinas, this tiny shop is crammed with lucky charms and strings of beads. Everything is made by Rodi Constantoglou, whose family has been in the trade since the 1850s. Her creations can also be found in the gift shop of the Benaki Museum, and a wider selection is available around the corner at the showroom on Miaouli Street.

To Fylakto Mou

Solonos 20, Kolonaki (210 364 7610). Metro Syntagma. **Open** 10am-3pm Mon, Wed, Sat; 10am-8pm Tue, Thur, Fri. **Credit** AmEx, DC, MC, V. **Map** p299 G4.

Ward off evil the traditional Greek way by buying one of the lucky talismans on sale here. Matia (blue glass 'eyes'), aromatic phials of frankincense, keyring amulets to keep you safe on the roads, detailed painted icons and silver crosses – all are available at a range of prices to suit any pocket, starting from as low as €4.

Vavas

Ifestou 30, Monastiraki (210 321 9994). Metro Monastiraki. **Open** 9am-9pm daily. **No credit cards. Map** p297/p301 E5.

So small you can barely step inside, this tiny alcove can hardly be described as a shop, but it still manages to stock a fine selection of traditional wooden *tavli* (backgammon) boards. Prices start from around €10. Look out for the unusual hand-painted sets and the mini, pocket editions that are ideal for travellers.

What Londoners take when they go out.

Arts & Entertainment

Festivals & Events

Sporting events, music and theatre festivals and popular religious commemorations punctuate the Athenian year.

Easter – the most important event in the Greek religious calendar. *See p189.*

Nearly half of Greece's population is concentrated in Athens, so it's hardly surprising that most of the nation's annual festivals and arts and sports events happen here. This is the case all year round, but never more so than in the summer months. While in the past many Athenians would escape the maddening summer heat, the capital's varied menu of cultural events is now tempting more people to postpone their holidays to breathe in something more than just pollution.

New Mayor Dora Bakoyianni has continued where her predecessor left off, promoting a wide range of cultural activities and backing efforts to 'humanise' the city. To this end, in 2004, the year of the Oympics, the City of Athens promoted over 650 events, and 2005 built on that Olympic momentum with an ever-widening variety of cultural events.

Exhibitions are held regularly at the city's cultural centres, art galleries and museums, and there are plenty of outdoor events too. The city's New Year celebrations at Syntagma, while not on a par with Scottish Hogmanay, are getting people out into the streets (in 2004 the festivities moved to Kotzias Square opposite Athens town hall on Athinas Street); local municipalities organise summer festivals; newly pedestrianised avenues and long-neglected inner-city areas now serve as the stage for innovative modern art exhibitions, book fairs and music festivals; and the city's splendid outdoor amphitheatres stage concerts, plays and festivals.

For more information on events taking place in Athens during your stay, consult *Kathimerini* (a supplement of the *International Herald Tribune*), *Time Out Athens* or visit www.athensnews.gr (updated weekly). Also worth checking out are www.cultureguide.gr, which lists all cultural events in English, or the City of Athens website (www.cityofathens.gr). Alternatively, you can call the citizens' helpline on 195 (English speakers are available) or tune into the English-language radio station AIR 104.4FM.

Spring

Agia Evdomada (Easter Week)
Various churches around Athens, including Mitropolis. Metro Monastiraki. **Map** p297/p301 E5/F5. **Date** Mar/Apr.
Equivalent in importance to Christmas in Britain, Pascha (Easter) in Athens is a rewarding and colourful experience, drawing deep on Greece's rich Orthodox heritage. S*ee p191* **Christos anesti!**

Labour Day
Date 1 May.
Labour Day is usually celebrated with a mass exodus to the countryside for picnics. For those who stay in town there are marches organised by left-wing groups and workers' unions.

Summer

The Athens Festival
Lycabettus Theatre, Lycabettus Hill, Kolonaki (210 928 2900/www.hellenicfestival.gr). Metro Evangelismos or Megaro Moussikis. **Map** p299 J3. *Odeon of Herodes Atticus, Acropolis. Metro Akropoli.* **Date** May/June-Sept/Oct. **Map** p301 D6.
The Athens Festival is the urban incarnation of the Hellenic Festival. Since its inception in 1945 it has been a major highlight of the Greek capital's summer cultural activities (a time when indoor venues tend to suspend activities). Music concerts ranging from jazz to classical, along with drama and dance productions, take place at the Odeon of Herodes Atticus and the Lycabettus Theatre. One couldn't ask for better settings – the latter boasts the best views of the city from the top of the hill, while the former offers the classical splendour of the Parthenon as a backdrop for performances. At the Herodeion heels are frowned upon (for fear of damage to the marble), even though Athenian socialites tend to ignore the rules. Stilettos are not an issue at the Lycabettus, and a small bus shuttling to the theatre from the foot of the hill means you can give your Manolos a good outing. The likes of Placido Domingo, Jose Carreras and the Philharmonia Orchestra are to appear at the Herodeion in 2005. Massive Attack, Moby, Madredeus and Alvin Ailey are some of the names to have played at the Lycabettus in recent years. For big-name events, book well in advance – tickets tend to sell out pretty quickly. *See also p233* **Classics in situ**.

Acropolis Rally
Various locations throughout the city (www.acropolis rally.gr). **Date** mid June.
Launched 50 years ago, the rally has developed a huge following. The route starts at the foot of the Acropolis and takes drivers through rugged terrain on the Greek mainland for three days before leading them to the finish line at the Panathenaic Stadium. Join the rest of Athens by standing at the side of the road and watching the drivers whizz past.

Glyfada Festival
Exoni Theatre, Hydras 11, Glyfada (210 891 2200). Bus A1. **Date** June-July.
Taking place in the eerie surroundings of an abandoned quarry, this music festival has been hosting contemporary Greek singers such as Nikos Papazoglou, Orpheas Peridis and Dionyssis Savvopoulos since 1992.

Rematia Festival
Rematia Theatre, Halandri, Northern Suburbs (210 680 0001). Metro Halandri. **Date** June-July.
The search for Greece's musical roots has really taken off in recent years and thousands gather at this open-air theatre to watch live shows with a focus on traditional Greek and ethnic music from the Balkans and Asia.

Vyronas Festival
Melina Mercouri Vrahon Theatre, Vyronas, Eastern Suburbs (210 765 5748). Bus 214/tram 11. **Date** 6wks June-Sept.
The municipality of Vyronas has done a pretty good job of attracting well-known Greek and foreign acts to an otherwise drab area. Sixteen years since its inception, the festival (dubbed the People's Festival) offers jazz, rock, ethnic and contemporary Greek music at good prices under the shadow of a huge rocky outcrop.

Rockwave Festival
Various venues around Athens (210 882 0426/ www.didimusic.gr). **Date** 3 days late June, early July.
Since 1996 Rockwave has been taking its ear-splitting show to venues in and around Athens, to the delight of hairy head-bangers and pale Goth rockers. The festival also includes juggling events and parties. In 2005 the venue is the Malakassa junction, 37km (23 miles) north of Athens on the Athens–Lamia highway. Dinosaur rockers Black Sabbath and Velvet Revolver are headlining.

Anti-Racism Festival
May 1st Square, Evelpidon (210 381 3928). **Date** early July.
This three-day event is organised by the Network for Social Support for Refugees and Immigrants. Since its debut in 1996, the festival hasn't looked back. Involving some 40 migrant communities and more than 100 human rights and anti-racism groups, the event includes live music and dance by non-Greek groups (recent festivals have showcased Syrian, Kurdish and Thai acts), exotic refreshment stalls and a chance to mingle with people from Athens' various foreign communities.

International Aegean Sailing Rally
Along the Saronic coast. Hellenic Offshore Racing Club, Akti Dilaveri 3, Mikrolimano, Piraeus (210 412 3357/210 411 3201/www.aegeanrally.gr/ www.horc.gr). **Date** early July.
Sailing fans have been heading down to the coast for one of Greece's biggest sailing events ever since 1964. Organised by the Hellenic Offshore Racing

Arts & Entertainment

Club, the regatta gathers contestants from all over the world. You can watch the aquatic action from any of the seaside suburbs.

Full Moon Day

Acropolis & Roman Forum, Acropolis & Plaka. Metro Akropoli or Monastiraki. **Map** p301 E6/E5. **Date** 9pm-1am 2nd wk in Aug.

Since it began six years ago, Full Moon Day has been a major success, drawing thousands to experience the city's archaeological sites by moonlight. Live outdoor cultural events are also held.

Autumn

Athens International Film Festival

Various venues around Athens (210 606 1363/ www.aiff.gr). **Date** 10 days 2nd wk in Sept.

Not to be confused with the better-known Thessaloniki Film Festival, the AIFF is becoming an important event in its own right. Local buffs get to feast on more than 100 features and short films from over two dozen countries.

International Month of Photography

Hellenic Centre of Photography, Chatzichristou 3, Makrygianni (210 921 0545/www.hcp.gr). Metro Akropoli. **Map** p301 E7. **Date** mid Sept-mid Nov.

Always expanding its subject matter, this two-month event brings together different photographers – from young Greek artists to established international names – in a range of venues across the city.

Athens Book Fair

Information 210 330 3942. **Date** late Sept.

Now in its third decade, this highly popular 16-day fair exhibits books from a wide range of Greek publishers. Dozens of stands and over 300 booksellers set up, while buskers and food stalls complete the picture. In 2004, the fair took place under the Acropolis, as its usual venue, Pedion tou Areos park, received a makeover. It is expected to return to Pedion tou Areos (Leof Alexandras & Patision, metro Victoria) in 2005. The books are in Greek, of course.

Trash Art – Marathon of Creation & Recycling

Technopolis Gallery, Pireos 100, Rouf (210 346 0981). Metro Thissio, then 10min walk. **Map** p296 C4. **Date** Oct.

Founded in 1998, Trash Art (which is exactly what it sounds like) is as popular as ever. Fashion events inspired by recycling are also held in parallel. Some of the city's best DJs set the tone for the funky parties that follow.

Ohi Day

Date 28 Oct.

This national holiday commemorates Greece's resounding rejection '*ohi*' ('no') of an ultimatum from Italy's Benito Mussolini demanding that his troops be allowed to pass through Greece during World War II. School parades take place in the heart of the city (Leof Amalias, in front of the Greek Parliament).

Winter

Athens Marathon

www.athensmarathon.com. **Date** Sun early Nov.

Runners from Greece and abroad follow the original 42km (26-mile) route of Phidippides, the man who ran to Athens from Marathon in 490 BC to report that the invading Persian army had been defeated before dropping dead from exhaustion. The race begins at the modern village of Marathon and ends at the Panathenaic Stadium (site of the first modern Olympic Games in 1896).

17 November

Begins at Athens Polytechnic, Patision & Stournari, & ends at the US Embassy, Leof Vas Sofias. Metro Omonia. **Date** 17 Nov.

Although to outsiders 17 November is inextricably linked to the urban guerrilla group of that name, it's also the day that marks an important event in Greece's recent troubled history. Every year without fail, a march takes place to commemorate the night of 17 November 1973, when the military dictatorship brutally broke up a student protest at the Athens Polytechnic, killing 34 demonstrators. The uprising's tragic end was a factor in the downfall of the Junta the following year. Organised by left-wing groups and workers' unions, the march has broad appeal and cuts through generations. The US Embassy is pelted with eggs and other objects, and graffiti is sprayed on neighbouring buildings – in protest at Washington's widely acknowledged support for the colonels. Depending on the political climate of the time, there is sometimes a stop at the British Embassy. Although more sedate in recent years, in the past the march would routinely deteriorate into street clashes between self-styled anarchists and riot police.

Christmas & New Year

Date 24, 31 Dec & 5 Jan.

Not as important as in Western Europe, but still a major event on the Greek calendar. Children sing carols door to door while charity groups do their rounds. After midnight on New Year's Eve, a cake (*vassilopitta*) containing a coin is sliced. The person who gets the coin is blessed with good fortune for the year to come.

Epiphany

Along the Piraeus coast. **Date** 6 Jan.

The traditional Blessing of the Water that takes place every Epiphany is steeped in Orthodox tradition, with roots stretching perhaps as far back as pagan antiquity. The faithful congregate by the sea to watch the spectacle of young men diving into the chilly waters to retrieve a cross hurled by the presiding priest. The diver who retrieves the crucifix is blessed with good fortune.

Apokries (Carnival season)

Various locations. **Date** last wk Feb/beginning of Lent.

Municipal orchestras and choirs, jugglers, mime artists, singers and float parades take to the streets, and fancy dress parties and lots of booze are the norm. A pervasive 'anything goes' atmosphere grips the city, particularly in Plaka, where groups of young males roam around bashing just about anybody they can find with plastic clubs. Celebrations climax with the traditional party (*koulouma*) on Kathari Deftera (Ash Monday), with kite-flying spectacles and picnics at Filopappou Hill. Ash Monday also marks the beginning of Megali Sarakosti (Lent), leading up to Easter.

Independence Day Parade

Leof Vas Amalias, in front of Parliament. **Map** p299 G5. **Date** 25 Mar.

Military jet fighters whizz by as Athenians turn out in their droves to watch the military and school parades to celebrate the proclamation of the Greek revolution in 1821 against the Ottoman Empire. The feast of the Annunciation is also celebrated on the same day.

Christos anesti!

If you have the good fortune to visit Athens during Agia Evdomada (Orthodox Easter Week), set aside the evening of Good Friday for a wander around town. Easter (Pascha) is the most important event of the Greek religious calendar (on a par with Christmas in Britain and the US) and on this night you'll find Athens a city transformed. In the darkness hymns and chants emanate from churches; bells toll; candlelit church processions pass through the streets, accompanied by chanting and clothed in clouds of incense. In each procession an *epitaphios* (bier) is carried, representing Christ's funeral. The heady mix is especially thick in Plaka, and Good Friday evening is best experienced wandering from church to church here breathing in the atmosphere (along with the incense).

Churches in Plaka particularly worth checking out include **Agia Ekaterini** (Hairephontos Street), **Metamorphosi Sotiros** (Kydathinaion Street) and **Agia Sophia** (Dionysiou Aeropagitou Street). It's also interesting to visit the Russian church of the **Agia Triada** (Holy Trinity) on Filellinon Street at midnight on Saturday. Many Greeks attend to listen to the awe-inspiring Russian Orthodox hymns, and to watch the priests bless baskets of food (including bread and eggs) laid out by the faithful in the churchyard.

The most important Good Friday procession begins at **Mitropolis Cathedral** and winds through the streets of central Athens. Syntagma Square is a good vantage point to see several processions, as many of them cross on Filellinon Street. And the procession that climbs Lycabettus Hill to the chapel of **Agios Georgios** is a dramatic one to follow: the view from the hill is awesome.

On Saturday, at around 11pm, people gather once again in churches, this time holding unlit candles. They are waiting for Christ's symbolic resurrection, *Anastasi*, at midnight. It's a dramatic ceremony: as the hour strikes, the church is plunged into darkness. Then a priest emerges from behind the curtains concealing the altar with a lit candle and proclaims, '*Christos anesti!*' ('Christ is risen'). He passes the flame to the congregation, who light their own candles and greet each other with cries of '*Christos anesti*', or the response '*Alithos anesti*' ('Indeed he is risen'). Firecrackers go off all around the city and church bells peal. Then familes head home to mark the end of Lent with a feast of *mageiritsa* (a soup made of lamb innards), *tsourkeia* (a sweet Easter bread) and, of course, Easter eggs. Only in Greece they're not made of chocolate. Instead, the Greeks crack boiled eggs painted red to symbolise the blood of Christ in a tradition that links pre-Christian rites of spring with Byzantine Christian culture. The egg, an ancient and universal symbol of rebirth, is used here to represent the crucifixion and resurrection.

Celebrations culminate on Easter Sunday (Kiriaki tou Pascha) when lambs are roasted on spits and most Athenians spend the rest of the day eating and drinking. Everywhere is closed, so you may as well join them: this is a good day to have lamb in tavernas around Plaka.

When you're planning your Easter in Athens, bear in mind that the Eastern Orthodox churches use the Julian rather than the Gregorian calendar, so Easter dates don't coincide.

Easter Sunday 2006 23 April.
Easter Sunday 2007 8 April.

Arts & Entertainment

Children

Athens is capital for kids – just steer clear of the midday sun.

The prospect of spending time in Athens with kids in tow may seem daunting at first, bearing in mind the city's dearth of facilities dedicated to the young. But before you decide that Athens and children definitely don't mix, take a moment to consider that this paradoxical society adores children and welcomes them into most public places (bars aside). Your kids may even make some Greek friends without having to battle against the language barrier, as locals learn English at a young age.

Animal encounters

Attica Zoological Park
Yalou, Spata, Attica (210 663 4724). Bus 319 to end of route; change to bus 304, 305; bus stop Zoological Park. **Open** *May-Sept* 9am-8pm daily. *Oct-Apr* 9am-5pm daily. **Admission** €11; €9 under-12s. **Credit** MC, V.
Lions, apes and many different kinds of birds feature in this zoo. A new extension was recently opened with tigers and pygmy hippos; by the time it's finished (scheduled for mid 2005) the extra areas will also house wild dogs, alligators and trained seals.

Cinemas

There are several multiplexes dotted around the city, but children are likely to find a trip to an outdoor cinema more exciting, though screenings are in the evenings only (and in summer only). Most films tend to be shown in their original language, but animated films and other movies aimed at youngsters are often dubbed. Listings in the press should indicate this. For cinemas, *see p194* **Film**.
Young visitors should also be impressed with a visit to the **Evgenidio Foundation's Planetarium** (*see p119*). The state-of-the-art domed projection screen is the size of two and a half basketball courts and displays include short films on topics ranging from space to the natural environment.

Eating & drinking

You'll find that children are allowed in all restaurants, and genuinely welcomed in most. For those that simply won't do without their fast-food fix there are plenty of Pizza Hut and McDonald's outlets as well as Greece's own home-grown hamburger joint, Goody's. Dinner

tends to be a late-evening affair. One of the restaurants listed below has special features for children; the other is close to the Allou! Fun Park (*see p193*) and welcomes younger diners.

Barras
Kanapitseri 4, Rendi, Southern Suburbs (210 562 3559). Tram 21 to Kan Kan stop. **Open** 10am-3am Mon-Thur, Sun; 10am-5am Fri, Sat. **Credit** AmEx, MC, V.
An ideal spot to take the kids before or after a visit to the nearby Allou! Fun Park. Barras offers reasonably priced Mediterranean dishes in vibrantly decorated surroundings.

Pale Pote
Grigoriou Lambraki 75, Glyfada (210 963 2739). Bus B3 from Akadimias. **Open** 9pm-4am Thur-Sat; 1.30-7pm Sun. Closed June-Aug. **Credit** AmEx, MC, V.
This classic Greek restaurant has an indoor play area (Sundays only).

Museums

At the **Foundation of the Hellenic World** (*see p113*) kids can go on a virtual reality tour around ancient Militos, while a trip to the **Museum of Greek Children's Art** (*see p89*) could prove inspiring to budding artists. The **Greek Children's Museum** in Plaka features interactive educational exhibits offering an insight into a variety of subjects including the human eye, the deep and nutrition. Greeks are proud of their traditional shadow-puppet theatre (*karaghiozis*), so a visit to the **Spathario Museum of Shadow Puppets** is also worthwhile. Future pilots can jump into the cockpit of a World War I plane at the **National War Museum** (*see p102*), while the displays at the **Museum of Greek Musical Instruments** (*see p89*) offer a fun introduction to Greek music.

Greek Children's Museum
Kydathinaion 14, Plaka (210 331 2995). Metro Akropoli/Syntagma. **Open** 10am-2pm Tue-Fri; 10am-3pm Sat, Sun. **Admission** free. Programmes €5.
Map p299 F6.

Spathario Museum of Shadow Puppets
Vas Sofias & Ralli D, Platia Kastalias, Marousi (210 612 7245). Metro Marousi. **Open** *May-Sept* 10am-1.30pm Mon-Fri. *Oct-Apr* 10am-1.30pm Mon-Fri; 10.30am-1.30pm Sun. **Admission** free.

Parks

For a pleasant stroll with younger children visit the **National Gardens** (see p102), near Syntagma, where you'll find a duck pond, mini-zoo, playground and narrow winding paths shaded by towering trees. It's also worth heading for the **Municipal Park of Glyfada**, a couple of blocks inland from the marina, where kids can work on their rollerblading, cycling and skateboarding skills.

Municipal Park of Glyfada
Bus A3 or B3. **Open** 9am-9pm daily.

Playgrounds

Indoors

These indoor play areas make a point of catering to English-speaking kids as well as their Greek counterparts, so your youngsters won't have any difficulty communicating. You can let your children run free all you like – they'll be safe and well looked after.

Balloons
Georgiou Papandreou 49, Zografou, Eastern Suburbs (210 777 7861). Bus 22 or 235 to IKA bus stop. **Open** *Sept-June* 10am-1pm Mon, Wed, Fri; 5.30-9.30pm Tue, Thur; 10am-2pm, 5-10pm Sat; 10am-10pm Sun. *July, Aug* 10am-1pm Mon, Wed, Fri; 5.30-9.30pm Tue, Thur; 10am-2pm, 5-10pm Sat; 10am-2pm, 5-10pm Sun. **Admission** €6 (unlimited juice included). **No credit cards**.
A well-organised playground with loads of games and toys for children up to the age of 12. Certain weekday sessions also feature a resident clown. **Other locations**: Kifisias 243, Kifisia (210 808 1883).

Paramithi
Ifigenias 39, Nea Ionia, Northern Suburbs (210 271 1811). Bus A8. **Open** 11am-2pm, 5-10pm Mon-Fri; 10am-10pm Sat, Sun. **Admission** €8; €7 members. **Credit** MC, V.
Decked out like a medieval castle, Paramithi is a great place for kids to play, watch shows and have some serious fun. For children up to 12.

Outdoors

Almost every neighbourhood in Athens has its own small public playground. Those worth a mention are in the National Gardens (see p102) and the Municipal Park of Glyfada.

Sightseeing

Avoid the midday heat by starting early with a visit to the Parliament Building (see p98) in Syntagma, where you can watch the slow-motion goose-stepping *evzones* (guards). Then take a stroll down to Plaka (see p86) for a tour of the capital's oldest neighbourhood on the open 'train' that departs from the corner of Eolou and Adrianou (35 minutes; €5, €3 under-12s). Older kids will get more out of a visit to the Acropolis (see p80) if you employ the services of a guide (book on 210 322 0090/ xenagoi@otenet.gr).

In summer, with temperatures soaring past 35°C (95°F) on some days, it's best to avoid the city centre. Instead, take the metro and head north to leafy Kifisia (see p117), where kids love the 'grand tour' by horse-drawn carriage (Platia Kefalari, €15 for a 15-minute ride).

A visit to one of Attica's many beautiful and sandy beaches is not only fun in its own right but a good way to integrate. For suggestions, see p123 **Beaches**. The water is clean and free of dangerous currents or drops, but note that lifeguards can be unpredictably absent.

Visiting a public pool is a real hassle because you need a certificate from a paediatrician, so it's much easier to use hotel pools and beaches.

Theme parks

Agios Kosmas Go-Kart Centre
Posidonos, Agios Kosmas, Southern Suburbs (210 985 1660). Bus A2 to 2nd Agios Kosmas bus stop. **Open** 9am-3am daily. **Admission** €10/10mins. **No credit cards**.
Kids aged ten and upwards can have a crazy Go-Kart race followed by a cool dip in the sea at the nearby Agios Kosmas beach, opposite the Helliniko Olympic Complex. There are lessons for novices from 9am to 11am.

Allou! Fun Park
Kifisou & Petrou Ralli, Rendi, Southern Suburbs (210 425 6999). Tram 21 to Kan Kan stop. **Open** 5pm-1am Mon-Fri; 10am-2am Sat, Sun. **Admission** free. **Rides** €2-€5. **No credit cards**.
This large entertainment park is the closest you'll get to Disneyland in Greece. Attractions like the Carousel and Bongo should get younger children going while adults will enjoy La Isla, where you can try rafting, and the adrenalin-inducing Shock Tower. There are all sorts of refreshments available on site and, if you're driving, the added benefit of free parking. This past year has also seen the addition of the Kidom extension with attractions especially tailored to toddlers and children up to 13.

Oropos Water Park
Chalkoutsiou, Skala Oropou, Attica (22950 37570/1). Bus to Oropos from Mavromateon Street, bus stop Skala. **Open** 31 May-6 Sept 11am-7pm Mon-Fri; 10.30am-7.30pm Sat, Sun. **Admission** €9; €7 5-11s; free under-4s. **No credit cards**.
This well-organised, safe water park provides a kiddies' pool, waterslides, a restaurant and snack bar.

Film

But, oh, those summer nights...

Athens is a cinema-loving city, with arthouse theatres, neighbourhood cinemas and massive multiplexes in abundance. During the autumn the capital hosts several small, independent festivals, such as the Athens International Film Festival in September (see p190) and the Panorama Film Festival in October, which showcases European films with limited distribution deals.

But for most Athenians, summer cinema is the highlight of the year. While other European cities write off the summer months as a dead season for film, with only the occasional Hollywood blockbuster to liven things up, Athens takes its films outdoors; most 'normal' cinemas close their doors and cinema under the stars becomes a hugely popular evening entertainment. The experience is uniquely atmospheric: there's nothing quite like recapping on some of the best films of the year or watching a Fellini classic with the dark, star-covered sky as your ceiling.

There's always a small bar or kiosk for refreshments; some serve wine by the glass, some provide snacks. The real world only manifests itself in the sometimes very visible signs of the cinema's sponsor – on the chairs you sit on and often on a huge banner above the screen. But if that's the price we have to pay for the survival of these amazing venues, it's a small sacrifice.

LANGUAGE NOT A PROBLEM
Indoors or outdoors, non-Greek speakers need not miss out; films are generally shown in their original language, with subtitles. As everywhere, Hollywood tends to dominate, but European and independent films also get a fair run at the box office.

GREEK CINEMA
Greece might not be internationally renowned for filmmaking or major film festivals, but things have been steadily moving in the right direction in recent years. The Thessaloniki International Film Festival – the biggest in the Balkans – attracts a considerable amount of foreign interest, and the domestic film industry has just started to recover after a long period in the doldrums.

It's still a far cry from the golden age of the 1950s and '60s, when Greece produced over 60 films a year, compared to around 20 today.

During this period Greeks flocked to cinemas to enjoy tear-jerking melodramas and light-hearted comedies featuring local stars revered by an adoring public. Famous names include blonde legend Aliki Vougiouklaki, her dark-haired nemesis Jenny Karezi, Alekos Alexandrakis, Dimitris Papamichael and many more. Domestic film production won international renown through the likes of Michael Cacoyannis, the director of *Alexis Zorbas* (*Zorba the Greek*, 1964), actresses Melina Mercouri and Irene Papas, and composers Mikis Theodorakis (*Zorba the Greek*) and Manos Hadjidakis, who won an Oscar for *Pote tin Kyriaki* (*Never on Sunday*, 1960).

Attikon. *See p196.*

In the early 1970s, as the sun began to set on the heyday of popular Greek cinema, the internationally acclaimed New Greek Cinema, a school similar to the French New Wave, was emerging and beginning to blossom. Directors had to work under the censoring eye of the Junta, but some profoundly personal and poetic films were made during this difficult period, such as Theo Angelopoulos's *Anaparastassi* (*Reconstruction*, 1970) and Alexis Damianos's *Evdokia* (1971).

After the fall of the Junta, the film industry made a brief recovery, but the introduction of video in the 1980s almost wiped it out. It would be a decade before the industry began to bounce back with box-office hits like Olga Malea's *O orgasmos tis ageladas* (*The Cow's Orgasm*, 1996) and Sotiris Goritsas's *Valkanisateur* (*Balkanisateur*, 1997). In 2000 *Safe Sex* topped the country's ticket sales chart, the first Greek film to do so in 30 years. The early years of the new millennium have seen Tasos Boulmetis's *Politiki kouzina* (*A Touch of Spice*, 2003) and Pantelis Vourgari's Martin Scorsese-produced *Nyfes* (*Brides*, 2004) storm the local box office. The most recent success story is promising young director Constantinos Giannaris, who took his film *Omiros* (*Hostage*, 2005) to this year's Berlin Film Festival.

On the international stage, Greek cinema is synonymous with director Theo Angelopoulos, one of Europe's great filmmakers. The 1998 winner of Cannes' Palme d'Or with *Mia aioniotita kai mia mera* (*Eternity and a Day*), Angelopoulos is now celebrating more than 40 years in the industry. His slow, contemplative and intellectual works present rather a different picture from that revealed by most Greek films.

TICKETS AND INFORMATION

Adult ticket prices tend to hover around the €5.50-€8 mark. English-language listings can be found in *Athens News* and *Kathimerini*. Screening times at both indoor and outdoor cinemas are normally around 9pm and 11pm. During the lighter summer months, it is wise to catch the late screening (11pm), since Mother Nature doesn't switch the lights off until about half an hour into the earlier show. Don't forget that all venues apart from multiplexes have intermissions here, so don't leave if you find the ending a bit abrupt – it's just half time. And, this being Greece, you can smoke in the open-air cinemas.

Some Athenian cinemas carry the name of their sponsors. Since these may change with time, we have used the original name of the venue in the guide; be ready for variations in local listings.

Summer cinemas

The cinemas listed below usually operate between May and September. The **Alfaville** (*see p196*) indoor cinema also converts to an open-air venue in summer.

Aigli
Zappeion (in the National Gardens), Historic Centre (210 336 9369/210 336 6970). Metro Syntagma. **Tickets** €7. **No credit cards**. **Map** p299 G6.
A classic outdoor cinema, built in the early 20th century and located within the leafy National Gardens. It shows mainly American blockbusters.

Athinaia
Haritos 50, Kolonaki (210 721 5717). Metro Evangelismos. **Tickets** €7; €5 concessions. **No credit cards**. **Map** p299 H4.
Tell anyone you went to the Athinaia last night, and the first question will be: 'How was the cheese pie?' And then maybe they'll ask what film you saw. Legendary home-made *tiropitas* aside, this is a good modern summer cinema with a half-decent sound system. However, that's almost irrelevant on Friday and Saturday nights, when the loud buzz from the busy bars on Haritos, literally outside the cinema, will make it nearly impossible to hear a single line of dialogue.

Cine Paris
Kydathinaion 22, Plaka (210 324 8057/210 322 2071). Metro Monastiraki. **Tickets** €7; €6.50 concessions. **No credit cards**. **Map** p297 F6.
One of the largest, most picturesque cinemas in the city and the only one in Plaka, Cine Paris is perched on a rooftop, right in the heart of the action. If you sit up high enough you can alternate your gaze between a 21st-century blockbuster and the fifth-century Acropolis.

Ciné Psirri
Sarri 40, Psyrri (210 324 7234/210 321 2476). Metro Thissio. **Tickets** €7; €5 concessions. **No credit cards**. **Map** p297 D4.
In the heart of urban Psyrri, this cinema has a good bar in the back of the yard, its own restaurant and a repertoire of modern (and not-so-modern) classics (think Coen Brothers, Bergman and Hitchcock) mixed with re-runs of last year's blockbusters. Even the decor is Hitchcockian, with the cinema's whisky-making sponsor managing to place its little grouse on just about every free space.

Dexameni
Platia Dexamenis, Kolonaki (210 362 3942/210 360 2363). Metro Evangelismos. **Tickets** €7; €5 concessions. **No credit cards**. **Map** p299 H4.
Situated on a quiet little square in the heart of Kolonaki, this cinema next to an *ouzerie* is surrounded by trees and greenery and has late-night Friday and Saturday screenings of various art/cult films. You might sometimes be surprised by the soundtrack to your favourite film, though – the

Arts & Entertainment

sound system has a hard time competing with the blaring music from the adjacent outdoor Mykonos-style Frame bar. Jennifer Lopez meets *Citizen Kane*, anyone?

Ekran
Zoodochou Pigis & Agathiou, Exarchia (210 646 1895). Metro Panepistimio, then 10min walk. **Tickets** €7; €5 concessions. **No credit cards.**
A good old cinema in Exarchia. Everything is just as it should be: a little kiosk with a little old woman selling pre-printed tickets, and a little old man next to her clipping it for you and selling photocopied programmes for the films.

Riviera
Valtetsiou 46, Exarchia (210 383 7716/210 384 4827). Metro Panepistimio. **Tickets** €7; €5 concessions. **No credit cards.**
Your average desktop speakers are probably more efficient than the Riviera's sound system. And then you have to contend with the insects and leaves falling on you from the big trees, and the lush vegetation covering a good portion of the screen. But don't let that put you off – they show some very good films here and some of Athens' friendliest bars and restaurants are just around the corner for the post-movie post-mortem.

Thisseion
Apostolou Pavlou 7, Thisio (210 347 0980/ 210 342 0864). Metro Thissio. **Tickets** €7; €5 concessions. **No credit cards. Map** p296/p300 C5.
The Unification of Archaeological Sites walkway has benefited many of Athens' ancient sights, and it has helped the Thisseion too. While it used to suffer heavily from the traffic outside, it is now one of the quietest cinemas in town. Add to that the view of the Acropolis and the countless cafés and bars in Thisio, and you have a serious contender for best open-air cinema in Athens.

Arthouse & rep

Alfaville
Mavromichali 168, Exarchia (210 646 0521). Metro Panepistimio, then 15min walk. **Tickets** €6.50; €5 concessions. **No credit cards.**
In Exarchia, Athens' alternative 'hood, the Alfaville rules. This classic, slightly run-down cult cinema in a theatre-dense area is a true art house, offering retrospectives of '60s Japanese film, French New Wave and so on. In summer, the roof opens and the cinema becomes an open-air venue.

Apollon
Stadiou 19, Historic Centre (210 323 6811/210 325 2817/www.cinemax.gr). Metro Panepistimio. **Closed** July-mid Sept. **Tickets** €8; €6 concessions. **No credit cards. Map** p297 F4.
One of the home cinemas of the Athens Film Festival Opening Nights and the Panorama Festival, and one of the most popular downtown cinemas, the Apollon shows mostly European films.

Astron
Leof Kifisias 37, Ambelokipi (210 692 2614/210 692 4823). Metro Ambelokipi. **Closed** July-mid Sept. Tickets €7; €6 matinées; €5.50 concessions. **No credit cards.**
An inviting venue on the cinema high street of Athens, Leof Kifisias. The roomy upper circle and the balcony overlooking the bustling road below make this place special.

Attikon
Stadiou 19, Historic Centre (210 322 8821/210 325 2817/www.cinemax.gr). Metro Panepistimio. **Closed** July-mid Sept. **Tickets** €8; €6 concessions. **No credit cards. Map** p297 F4.
Built as a theatre in 1914 and converted to a cinema four years later, the Attikon boasts handsome plaster arches and an impressive chandelier. Arguably the flagship cinema of Athens, its programme comprises European and American quality features. Along with Apollon and the Danaos, the Attikon is one of the home cinemas of the Athens International Film Festival.

Danaos
Leof Kifisias 109, Ambelokipi (210 692 2655). Metro Panormou. **Closed** July-mid Sept. **Tickets** €7. **No credit cards.**
For Athenians, the name Danaos is synonymous with seriously non-Hollywood, quality films and the Athens International Film Festival in September. The duplex cinema also entices with a nice bar, sophisticated crowds and a range of film books for sale in the foyer.

Mikrokosmos
Leof Syngrou 106, Eastern Suburbs (210 921 5305). Metro Syngrou-Fix. **Tickets** €7; €5.50 concessions. **No credit cards.**
With cutting-edge minimal design, this brand new player on the cinema circuit is more Hoxton or SoHo than Syngrou. The design makes the most of the limited space in the foyer and the likeable owners will always greet you with a smile. Art house and avant-garde are the main staples here.

Multiplexes

One of the main attractions of mutiplexes (sound quality and comfortable seating aside) is their air-conditioning, making them a natural escape from a fetid summer day. Most of the large ones are on the outskirts of the city.

Village Cinemas Pangrati
Ymittou 110 & Chremonidou, Pangrati (210 757 2440/www.village.gr). Trolley 2, 11 from Syntagma. **Tickets** €7.50. **Credit** MC, V (by phone). **Map** p299 H7.
It may only be a five-screener, but the big advantage of this mini-multiplex is its city centre location. It's housed in the modern Millennium shopping centre, which provides all the usual international shopping and eating opportunities.

Diaspora directors

Sure, the Greek film industry might be just about pulling itself out of a 30-year slump, but all the while – and for longer – sons of the diaspora have been hard at work carving a name for themselves in the international film industry. So next time someone asks you what links Alexander Payne, John Cassavetes, Costas Gavras and Elia Kazan, you'll know the answer: they're all Greeks, of course.

Granted, Alexander Payne doesn't even sound Greek (his family changed their name from Papadopoulos), but he is proud of his roots, was a jury member at the Thessaloniki Film Festival in 2004, and is a frequent visitor to the country. His most recent film, *Sideways*, garnered five Oscar nominations and his other Oscar-nominated works include *Election* (1999) and *About Schmidt* (2002).

John Cassavetes, the son of Greek immigrants, started his career as a Hollywood bit player in the 1950s. In 1959 he directed *Shadows*. Shot on a shoestring budget, the film broke new ground: jumpy editing, free-focus camerawork and naturalistic dialogue pushed towards a new genre and opened up a whole new career for Cassavetes. Except for a few Hollywood acting gigs like *Rosemary's Baby* and *The Dirty Dozen*, the next 30 years saw him in the director's chair. Stand-out masterpieces include *Faces* (1968), *A Woman under the Influence* (1974) and *Gloria* (1980).

The 1960s found a young Greek named Costas Gavras studying in Paris and assisting top French directors such as Jean Renoir and Jacques Demy. Labelled a communist by the Greek post-war regime, Gavras saw France as an ideal cradle for his polemic style of filmmaking. His first major success, *Z* (1969), an indictment of the repressive Greek Junta, won him the Oscar for foreign-language film.

Throughout the '70s, Gavras continued chanelling his hatred of political oppression through films such as *The Confession* (1970) and *State of Siege* (1973). His first American film, *Missing* (1982), exploring the disappearance of a young American writer during the Chilean coup of 1973, won Gavras an Oscar for his screenplay. His politically committed work continued with *Hannah K* (1983), a film that caused controversy with its pro-Palestinian stance at a time when the cause was little understood.

The man who was perhaps the most successful filmmaker of Greek origin was also arguably the most controversial. Elia Kazan, born Elias Kazanjoglou, made a huge mark on film history but also incited anger by co-operating with the anti-communist McCarthy witch-hunt in 1950s Hollywood. Kazan first gained notoriety directing Broadway productions such as *A Streetcar Named Desire* and *Death of a Salesman*, before Hollywood came calling: his 1947 film *Gentleman's Agreement* earned him his first directing Oscar. After forming the famed New York Actors Studio with Lee Strassberg in 1948, Kazan went on to direct classics such as *A Streetcar Named Desire* (1951), *On the Waterfront* (1954), *East of Eden* (1955) and *America, America* (1966).

A Streetcar Named Desire.

Galleries

A thriving contemporary art scene supports new spaces and galleries.

Contemporary art in Athens is on the move. Literally, in some cases. The **National Museum of Contemporary Art** is currently in temporary accommodation at the Athens Concert Hall (Vas Sofias & Kokkali 1, 210 924 2111, www.emst.gr), since its new home is still under construction, but this hasn't prevented it from staging a series of successful shows with socio-political themes, mostly focused on video and new media art. The museum has also recently boosted its collection with works by international artists including Bill Viola, Jannis Kounelis and Shirin Neshat.

The central area of Psyrri, traditionally the domain of craftsmen and small-scale industry, has gained itself a reputation as one of Athens' main culture zones and is home to an ever-increasing number of galleries, bars and cafés, and artists' studios. Meanwhile, the former industrial wasteland of Pireos Street is fast gaining ground as an art hub. The stunning **Benaki Museum – Piraeus Street Annexe** (*see p110*) stages occasional exhibitions, including recent shows of work by German ceramicist Gerd Knapper and contemporary painter and sculptor Marina Karella. The huge, multi-purpose **Technopolis** (*see p113*) also includes art exhibitions among its other cultural activities, while the **School of Fine Arts** (Pireos 256, 210 480 1315) is known for shows by new artists as well as retrospectives and exhibitions by top contemporary Greek artists. Another art space worth watching, stuck out in the Rouf neighbourhood, is former silk factory **Athinais** (*see p110*). It currently houses contemporary work from the Pieridis collection.

A number of other private collectors have opened their collections to the public through various foundations and exhibition spaces: the **Emfietzoglou Collection** (Terma Finikon, Anavrita-Marousi, 210 802 7026) of modern and contemporary Greek art; the **Portalakis Collection** (Pesmatzoglou 8, 210 331 8933, www.portalakiscollection.gr) of mainly modern Greek art; the **Frissiras Museum** (Monis Asteriou 3-7, Plaka, 210 323 4678, www.frissirasmuseum.com), which occupies two neo-classical buildings in Plaka and whose permanent collection is focused on figurative paintings of the human form; and the **DESTE Foundation** (Omirou 8, Neo Psychiko, 210 672 9460, www.deste.gr), owned by über-collector Dakis Joannou. The DESTE showcases cutting-edge contemporary international art with regular exhibitions of emerging or established artists. In summer 2004 the crème de la crème of the art world came to Athens to catch 'Monument to Now', a major exhibition organised by the DESTE, with recent acquisitions of the Dakis Joannou collection, which took place in two prominent venues totally refurbished for the show. In summer 2005 the DESTE is holding an exhibition of works by the nominees of the fourth DESTE Prize, a biennial award that this time will be presented to a Greek artist under the age of 40.

Most galleries close for the summer between July and September, and there's usually little to see between scheduled shows during the rest of the year. It's a good idea to phone ahead or pick up a copy of the free brochures *Art & the City* and *Athens Contemporary Art Map* (available at most galleries and online, in English, at www.artandthecity.gr and www.athensartmap.net) to find out what's on.

AD gallery

Pallados 3, Psyrri (210 322 8785). Metro Monastiraki. **Open** noon-9pm Tue-Fri; noon-4pm Sat. **Map** p297 E4.
In operation for more than ten years, AD gallery focuses primarily on modern and conceptual Greek art. Its repertoire has included such international artists as Jan Fabre, plus well-known mid-career artists such as Maria Loizidou and Cris Giannakos.

a.antonopoulou.art

4th Floor, Aristofanous 20, Psyrri (210 321 4994). Metro Monastiraki. **Open** 4-9pm Tue-Fri; noon-4pm Sat. **Map** p297 D4.
The work of renowned architect Aris Zampikos, Angeliki Antonopoulou's gallery is one of the best-designed art spaces in Athens – and also boasts a great view of the Psyrri area. It concentrates on Greek contemporary work: artists who have exhibited here include Alexandros Psychoulis, Sia Kiriakakos and Maria Papadimitriou.

The Apartment

5th Floor, Voulis 21, Syntagma, Historic Centre (210 321 5469/www.theapartment.gr). Metro Syntagma. **Open** noon-8pm Wed, Thur; noon-4pm Fri, Sat; by appointment only Mon, Tue. **Map** p297/301 F5.
Located on the fifth floor of an office building in Syntagma and owned by curator Vassilios Doupas, the Apartment has a mixed exhibition programme

Arts & Entertainment

featuring both Greek and foreign artists such as Larry Sultan, Delia Brown, Caroline May and Kostas Avgoulis. The gallery's mission is to exhibit and promote the work of international emerging artists, and it encourages artists to work on a project basis.

Bernier/Eliades

Eptahalkou 11, Thisio (210 341 3935/www.berniereliades.gr). Metro Thissio. **Open** 10.30am-8pm Tue-Fri; noon-4pm Sat. **Map** p296/300 C5.

One of the oldest and most respected galleries in Athens, the Bernier/Eliades was founded in 1977 by Jean Bernier and Marina Eliades and, over the years, has shown a wealth of big names (such as Tony Cragg, Juan Munoz, Tony Oursler and Thomas Schutte). This gallery has made a significant contribution towards introducing the Greek public to international contemporary art.

The Breeder

Evmorfopoulou 6, Psyrri (210 331 7527/www. thebreedersystem.com). Metro Monastiraki or Thissio. **Open** noon-6pm Wed-Sat. Closed 3 July-31 Aug. **Map** p297 D4.

The Breeder showcases some of the most interesting up-and-coming young contemporary artists: Jim Lambie, Scott Myles, Marc Bijl, Kostis Velonis and Jannis Varelas, for example. A very active international programme involves solo presentations, group shows and gallery swaps, and features artists such as Romanian twins Gert and Uwe Tobias, and Mexican Abraham Cruzvillegas.

Eleni Koroneou Gallery

Mitsaion 5-7, Makrygianni (210 924 4271/www. koroneougallery.gr). Metro Akropoli. **Open** 11am-1pm, 5-8pm Tue-Fri; 11am-2pm Sat. By appointment only July, Aug. **Map** p301 E7.

Opened back in 1988 with a programme centred on painting and photography, recent shows here have included John Bock, Christopher Wool and the renowned Swiss artist Dieter Roth.

Els Hanappe Underground

Melanthiou 2, Psyrri (210 325 0364/http://els.hanappe. com). Metro Monastiraki. **Open** noon-4pm Wed, Sat; noon-8pm Thur, Fri. Closed July, Aug. **Map** p301 E7.

With a penchant for young artists from Glasgow, London and Los Angeles working in diverse styles and media, this gallery's past exhibitions have featured the likes of Adam Chodzko and Katja Strunz. Young Greek artists represented include Vangelis Vlahos. Summer 2004 also saw Naya Fragouli's videos and drawings featured in a solo show.

Gallery 7

Zalokosta 7, Kolonaki (210 361 2050). Metro Syntagma. **Open** 11am-2pm, 6-9pm Tue-Fri; 11am-2pm Sat. Closed July, Aug. **Map** p299 G5.

Established 20 years ago, Gallery 7 has recently begun to place emphasis on a younger generation of emerging artists, many of whom are graduates of the Athens School of Fine Arts. Gallery artists include Daphne Angelidou and Irene Mastouki.

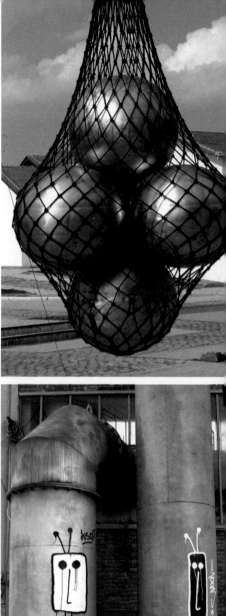

Technopolis. *See p198.*

a.antonopoulou.art. *See p198.*

Gazon Rouge

Victoros Ougo 15, Metaxourgio (210 524 8077/ www.gazonrouge.com). Metro Metaxourgio. **Open** noon-8pm Tue-Fri; noon-4pm Sat. **Map** p297 E4.

One of the modish young galleries that have opened in recent years, Gazon Rouge focuses mostly on the younger generation of Greek artists and on artist-initiated shows – past exhibitions have featured performances by rising art star Georgia Sagri. The gallery is located on the first floor of a newly refurbished neo-classical building; there is a coffee shop and an art bookstore on the ground floor.

Ileana Tounta Contemporary Art Center

Armatolon 48 & Klefton, Lycabettus, Neapoli (210 643 9466/www.art-tounta.gr). Metro Ambelokipi. **Open** *July* 11am-8pm Tue-Fri. *Sept-June* 11am-8pm Tue-Fri; noon-4pm Sat. Closed Aug.

Opened in October 1988, the Ileana Tounta Center includes two exhibition halls, an art shop and the stylish 48 The Restaurant (*see p135*). The gallery holds shows by contemporary Greek and foreign artists such as Joao Onofre and Dimitris Foutris.

Millefiori Art Space

Haritos 29, Kolonaki (210 723 9558). Metro Evangelismos. **Open** *May-Sept* 10.30am-3.30pm Mon, Wed, Sat; 10.30am-8.30pm Tue, Thur, Fri. *Oct-Apr* 10.30am-3pm Mon, Wed, Sat; 10.30am-8pm Tue, Thur, Fri. Closed 2wks in Aug. **Map** p301 H4.

This energetic young gallery hosts interesting group shows, mostly by British artists. Past collaborations have included the likes of Phillip Allen and Christian Ward. Located on the first floor of a charming neo-classical building in the hip street of Haritos, the gallery also has a small shop selling art books and Philip Treacy millinery.

Nees Morfes

Valaoritou 9A, Kolonaki (210 361 6165/www.nees morfesgallery.gr). Metro Syntagma. **Open** 10am-2pm, 6-9pm Tue-Fri; 10am-3pm Sat. Closed July, Aug. **Map** p299 G4.

The oldest contemporary art gallery in Athens, Nees Morfes was established by Julia Dimakopoulou in 1959. The gallery's focus over the years has been painting, particularly abstraction, holding solo presentations of established Greek painters. Recently, it has introduced younger artists as well, such as Nikos Charalambidis.

Rebecca Camhi

Themistokleous 80, Platia Exarchia, Omonia (210 383 7030/www.rebeccacamhi.com). Metro Omonia. **Open** 10am-8pm Tue-Fri. Closed Aug. **Map** p297 F2.

Greek and international artists show here, and the gallery regularly holds parallel events, such as talks by artists and curators. Past collaborations have included Nan Goldin, Rita Ackermann, Nobuyoshi Araki and Mantalina Psoma.

Vamiali's

1 Samou, Platia Karaiskaki, Metaxourgio (210 522 8968/www.vamiali.net). Metro Metaxourgio. **Open** 2-8pm Wed-Fri; 1-5pm Sat. By appointment only July, Aug. **Map** p297 D1/D2.

A new space run by curator Sofia Vamiali and her artist sister Dimitra, who invite Greek and foreign artists to use the gallery's workshop and then hold exhibitions of the works created during their stay. Recent shows include 'Magic', a group show with young artists including Michal Chelbin, Joao Onofre and Efrat Galnoor, curated by Andrea Gilbert.

Xippas

Sofokleous 53D, Historic Centre (210 331 9333/ 210 331 9341/www.xippas.com). Metro Omonia. **Open** noon-8pm Tue-Fri; noon-4pm Sat. Closed Aug. **Map** p297 D1.

Renowned architect Eleni Kostika designed this Athens outpost of the established Greek-owned Paris gallery Xippas. It's one of the largest and best-designed commercial spaces in the Greek capital. Artists exhibited here have included Vic Muniz, Panos Kokkinias, Peter Halley and Takis.

Zoumboulakis

Platia Kolonaki 20, Kolonaki (210 360 8278/www. zoumboulakis.gr). Metro Evangelismos. **Open** 11am-2pm, 6-9pm Tue-Fri; 11am-3pm Sat. **Map** p297 G5. *Kriezotou 7, Kolonaki (210 363 1951/www. zoumboulakis.gr). Metro Syntagma.* **Open** 10am-3pm Mon, Wed, Sat; 10am-8pm Tue, Thur, Fri. **Map** p299 G4.

One of the best-known and most commercially successful gallery names in Athens, the two Zoumboulakis galleries are now operated by Daphne Zoumboulaki. With a focus on representative Greek painting, the galleries collaborate with established artists such as Yiannis Moralis. An art shop operates at the Kriezotou branch, selling silk-screens and editions by famous artists such as Yiannis Tsarouhis.

Gay & Lesbian

As more and more Greeks say goodbye to the closet, Athens' gay scene is finally coming of age.

The Athenian gay scene is an odd but captivating mixture of European-style bars and clubs, and others with a distinctly eastern Mediterranean feel. Gay bars are generally teeming with people, especially at weekends, but like their clientele, few of them are really out. However, a gentle breeze of change is blowing across the city. More and more gay Greeks are slowly but surely stepping out of the closet, providing their braver favourite haunts with the impetus to do likewise.

You won't find any of the huge gay dance clubs you may be used to in Northern Europe or the US, but then again you will get a feel of the Mediterranean way of painting the town red. Be advised that nightlife starts late in Greece; hardly anyone goes out before 11pm or midnight, and clubs are practically empty until 1am.

Despite changes, being male, gay and Greek remains a complicated business for many. It's common for men to be hung up about their sexuality, which can make flirting difficult. Most tend to be friendlier to foreigners than to fellow gay Greeks. The age of consent is 17.

SO, WHERE DO I MEET THE BOYS?
Gay Greeks tend to congregate in three main hotspots in the city: around the crossroads of Iera Odos and Konstantinoupoleos Street (the nascent gay village at Gazi), in the neighbourhood around the beginning of Syngrou near the Temple of Zeus, and in the area south of the Victoria metro station.

AND WHAT ABOUT THE GIRLS?
There are fewer exclusively lesbian bars, but women are welcome at and frequent all but the most hardcore gay bars. Fairytale, So Bar So Food, Troll and Sodade are the venues most favoured by gay women in Athens.

Cafés

Apsendi
Amynta 4, Pangrati (210 724 0087). Metro Evangelismos. **Open** *Summer* noon-2am daily. *Winter* noon-6pm daily. **No credit cards**. Map p299 H6.
Not far from the marble Panathenaic Stadium, this is a cosy café-bar with seating under the shady trees on the square across the road. Attracts all ages.

Blue Train
Konstantinoupoleos 84, Gazi (210 346 0677/www. bluetrain.gr). Bus 049, B18 from Omonia. **Open** 8pm-4am daily. **No credit cards**. Map p296 B4.
A gay café that plays the latest hits and spills out on to the street, with tables right by the railway tracks where you can watch the trains – and the boys – go by. It transforms into a bar as the evening progresses and is perfect for an early drink before you hit the clubs in the area.

Dadee
Sinopis 8, Athens Tower, Northern Suburbs (210 777 7367). Metro Ambelokipi. **Open** 10am-1am Mon-Fri; 3pm-2am Sat, Sun. **No credit cards**.
Decorated *à la* Almodovar, and with a very friendly atmosphere, this café is a delightful spot to enjoy a variety of coffees, a light meal or a cocktail over a board game. There is an Octapus shop inside, selling all kinds of adorable knick-knacks. The only gay place near the Athens Tower.

En Merei
Stournari & Kapnokoptiriou 5, Exarchia (210 822 3105). Metro Omonia. **Open** 1pm-1am Mon-Fri; 4pm-late Sat, Sun. **No credit cards**. Map p297 F2.

The best Spots to…

…watch the boys go by
Aleco's Island (*see p202*); **Blue Train** (*see above*); **Granazi** (*see p203*); **Play my music** (*see p204*).

…watch the girls go by
Fairytale (*see p202*); **So Bar So Food** (*see p204*); **Sodade** (*see p204*); **Troll** (*see p204*).

…wear your heels
Koukles (*see p203*); **Strass** (*see p204*).

…get cruisey
Lamda (*see p203*); **Olympic** (*see p205*); **Star** (*see p205*).

…get in a sweat
Athens Relax (*see p205*); **Flex** (*see p205*).

…have dinner à deux
En Merei (*see above*); **Prosopa** (*see p202*); **Trelli Papia** (*see p202*).

Arts & Entertainment

A gay and lesbian café in a neo-classical house complete with charming courtyard and a Greek island feel. You can start with coffee around 1pm and move on to ouzo and *mezedes* (a rich selection of starters), as well as some home-made main courses, until late at night. It's close to the Archaeological Museum, with seating outside in the quiet pedestrian street.

Enidrío Internet Café
Syngrou 13 & Lembesi, Makrygianni (210 921 2050/www.enydrio.gr). Metro Akropoli. **Open** 8pm-1am Mon-Thur; 24hrs Fri, Sat; 5.30pm-1am Sun. **No credit cards. Map** p301 E7.
This is the perfect spot to check your email or arrange a hot date (at all hours over the weekend), while having a light snack, lunch, dinner, ice-cream or drink. It's very close to Lamda (*see p203*) and Granazi (*see p203*).

Kirki
Apostolou Pavlou 31, Thisio (210 346 6960). Metro Thissio. **Open** 10am-2pm daily. **No credit cards. Map** p301 D5.
An open-air café with a mesmerising view of the Parthenon, great for relaxing after a stroll along the stunning pedestrian walkway below the Acropolis. Less popular with the gay and lesbian crowd than it used to be.

Wunderbar
Themistokleous 80, Exarchia (210 381 8577). Metro Omonia, then 10min walk. **Open** 9am-3am daily. **No credit cards. Map** p297 F2.
The hippest of Athens tribes hang out at this gay-friendly café-bar on Exarchia Square.

Restaurants

Cookou Food
Themistokleous 66, Exarchia (210 383 1955). Metro Omonia, then 10min walk. **Open** 1pm-1am Mon-Sat. **Average** €. **No credit cards. Map** p297 F2.
Modern and imaginatively decorated, Cookou Food is a central, gay-friendly restaurant in the bustling Exarchia area, offering a superb and inexpensive culinary experience. Great for lunch downtown before heading off to the nearby Archaeological Museum.

Petalo
Xanthis 10 & L Karayanni, Northern Suburbs (210 862 2000). Metro Victoria, then 15min walk. **Open** 8.30pm-late Tue-Sat. Closed June-Aug. **Average** €. **No credit cards.**
Athens' first gay-friendly traditional Greek taverna, tucked away in a tiny street off the Fokionos Negri pedestrian zone in Kypseli. There's a wide variety of delicious dishes, great house wine and low prices (around €13 per person). Don't miss the pies with filo pastry and quince and grape preserves.

Prosopa
Konstantinoupoleos 84, Gazi (210 341 3433). Bus 049, B18 from Omonia. **Open** 8pm-2am daily. **Average** €€. **No credit cards. Map** p296 B4.

Cool ambience and reasonably priced, innovative food with a Mediterranean flair are the hallmarks of this gay-friendly restaurant. Perfect for a romantic dinner or a meal with your mates before you hit the area's bars and clubs. There is also seating outdoors right by the railway.

Trelli Papia
Triptolemou 26, Gazi (210 346 8720/www.trelli papia.gr). Bus 049, B18 from Omonia. **Open** 7pm-late Tue-Sat. **Average** €€. **Credit** MC, V. **Map** p296 B4.
A straight-friendly gay restaurant – with exquisite Italian cuisine and alfresco seating too. It's a darling little place to have dinner à deux or a fun time with your mates before heading out clubbing. It's owned by the ever-so-friendly Belgian chef Werner Debuysere, who also does catering for the Belgian and Canadian embassies.

Bars & clubs

Aleco's Island
Sarri 41, Psyrri (no phone). Metro Monastiraki. **Open** 11pm-3am daily. **No credit cards. Map** p297 D4.
The historic Aleco's Island, where scores of young men have taken their first steps out of the closet, recently moved to this new location. Ideal for an early drink as it's one of the few bars to get going before midnight.

Almodobar
Konstantinoupoleos 60, Gazi (mobile 6946 457442/ www.almodobar.gr). Bus 049, B18 from Omonia. **Open** 9.30pm-late daily. **No credit cards.**
Almodobar is a small but impressive gay-friendly place with a mixed crowd who come for the electro music. It often hosts live shows with artists from the Greek electro scene.

Big
Falesias 12 & Iera Odos 67, Gazi (210 347 4781). Bus 049, B18 from Omonia. **Open** 9pm-2am Mon-Thur, Sun; 9pm-late Fri, Sat. **No credit cards. Map** p296 C4.
The first Athenian bar-club to cater to bears, cubs and everyone who loves them. Very friendly atmosphere and cheap drinks.

Fairytale
Koletti 25, Exarchia (210 330 1763/www.fairytale. gr). Metro Omonia, then 10min walk. **Open** 11pm-3am daily. **No credit cards. Map** p297 F3.
Small, low-key bar with mixed music, safe drinks and a friendly feel. A favourite spot for women who love women. It is located in the lively and colourful Exarchia area, within walking distance of En Merei (*see p201*) and Cookou Food (*see above*).

Fou Club
Iera Odos & Keleou 8, Gazi (210 346 6800). Bus 049, B18 from Omonia. **Open** 11pm-5am daily. **No credit cards. Map** p296 B4.

Arts & Entertainment

The only gay club in Athens to proudly fly the rainbow flag. The music selection is mainstream, with Greek and foreign hits, and the clientele is easygoing. Don't miss the hot 'wet' shows every Friday and Saturday at around 2am, as well as several other frequent fun events.

Granazi

Lembesi 20 & Kallirois, Makrygianni (210 924 4185). Metro Akropoli. **Open** 6pm-4am daily. **No credit cards. Map** p301 E7.
Granazi has the distinction of being the oldest gay bar in Athens. Close to the Acropolis, it's very laid-back and friendly, with predominantly Greek music for a generally older crowd and their friends. A must-go during your stay in Athens.

Group Therapy Bar

Lepeniotou 11, Psyrri (210 323 4977). Metro Monastiraki or Thissio. **Open** 7pm-late Mon-Fri; noon-late Sat, Sun. **No credit cards. Map** p297 D4.
Gay- and straight-friendly bar in the heart of Psyrri. It's pretty relaxed early in the evening, but the mood heats up as the night progresses. Great vibes and real group therapy sessions organised by the Psychognosia Centre (call for more details).

Inoteca

Platia Avyssinias, Monastiraki (210 324 6446). Metro Monastiraki. **Open** 2pm-2am Tue-Sun. **No credit cards. Map** p297 D5.
A cool, gay-friendly establishment to while away an evening to the sounds of lounge, freestyle, ambient and trip hop in one of the most theatrical settings in Athens, amid the antique shops of the old flea market (*see p172* **Sunday morning in Monastiraki**). The pace picks up after dark.

Kazarma

1st Floor, Konstantinoupoleos 84, Gazi (210 346 0667). Bus 049, B18 from Omonia. **Open** midnight-5am Wed-Sun. **No credit cards. Map** p296 B4.
Upstairs from Blue Train (*see p201*), this is the club to dance among all the sweet young things swaying to the mix'n'match music. Popular with all ages.

Koukles

Zan Moreas 3, Koukaki (no phone). Metro Syngrou-Fix. **Open** 11pm-5am Wed-Sun. **No credit cards. Map** p301 D8.
Home to the best drag shows in town at weekends; most of Athens' transvestites and their admirers hang out here.

Lamda

Lembesi 15 & Syngrou 9, Makrygianni (210 922 4202/www.lamdaclub.gr). Metro Akropoli. **Open** 11pm-4am daily. **No credit cards. Map** p301 E7.
This Athens classic is not to be missed, particularly at weekends when it gets packed to the rafters. It's on two floors, with a dancefloor upstairs playing the latest hits, and a more cruisey area downstairs that sports a backroom – the only one in town.

Lamda.

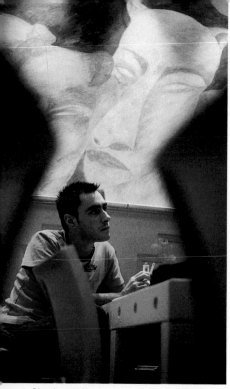

Check out the talent at **Kirki**. *See p202.*

LoveConnection
Triptolemou 35, Gazi (210 345 8118). Bus 049, B18 from Omonia. **Open** 11pm-5am daily. **No credit cards. Map** p296 B4.
Always packed and pumping, LoveConnection covers all tastes, but has a penchant for Greek tunes.

Mayo
Persefonis 33, Gazi (210 342 3066). Bus 049, B18 from Omonia. **Open** 8pm-5am daily. **No credit cards. Map** p296 B4.
Gay- and straight-friendly bar, with minimalist decor, a lovely inner courtyard and just about the greatest rooftop in Athens, with a captivating view of the Acropolis. Don't miss it.

Play my music
Konstantinoupoleos 78, Gazi (210 341 1141). Bus 049, B18 from Omonia. **Open** 11pm-5am daily. **No credit cards. Map** p296 B4.
This fun club plays a mixture of Greek and foreign music and often gets jam-packed with gay men. Its small garden with white benches creates a wonderful ambience.

So Bar So Food
Persefonis 23, Gazi (210 341 7774). Bus 049, B18 from Omonia. **Open** 10pm-4am Tue-Sun. **No credit cards. Map** p296 B4.

Gay-friendly and very popular with hip lesbians, So Bar So Food attracts all ages and plays a mixture of Greek and non-Greek music ranging from chart to house. The fabulous garden is a big plus during the summer months.

Sodade
Triptolemou 10, Gazi (210 346 8657). Bus 049, B18 from Omonia. **Open** 10.30pm-6am daily. **No credit cards. Map** p296 B4.
You're bound to be swept off your feet by the best dance music in town in one of Sodade's two rooms, which are connected by a corridor where girls and boys are only too happy to rub shoulders, and other body parts, with you.

Troll
Alikarnassou 7, Northern Suburbs (210 515 8920/ www.troll.gr). Metro Attiki, then 10min walk. **Open** 11pm-5am daily. **No credit cards.**
The only exclusively lesbian club in town. Opens daily as a bar, but at weekends it turns into a dance club. Greek and foreign mainstream music.

Alternative bars

For those in search of adventure…

Fantastiko
Aristotelous 37, Northern Suburbs (no phone). Metro Victoria. **Open** 10.30pm-3am Mon-Fri, Sun; 10.30pm-5am Sat. **No credit cards. Map** p297 E1.
Small and cosy, with loud music and daring go-go boys from former Eastern bloc countries strutting their stuff on the makeshift stage every Friday and Saturday after 2am.

Sammi's
Filis 34, Northern Suburbs (210 882 2134). Metro Victoria. **Open** 11pm-5am Wed-Sun. **No credit cards. Map** p297 E1.
Multi-ethnic gay boys and their fans party long and hard here, especially on Saturday nights.

Strass
Odissea Androutsou 32, Koukaki (210 922 1622). Metro Syngrou-Fix. **Open** 10.30pm-4am daily. **No credit cards. Map** p300 C8.
Popular with a host of drag queens, transsexuals and their admirers.

Test Me
Pipinou 64, Platia Victoria, Northern Suburbs (210 822 6029). Metro Victoria. **Open** 10.30pm-4am daily. **No credit cards.**
A meeting place for the older crowd and those who seek them, with sweet young things from former Eastern bloc countries and Asia.

The Guys
Lembesi 8, Makrygianni (210 921 4244). Metro Akropoli. **Open** 10pm-3am Mon-Wed, Fri-Sun. **No credit cards. Map** p301 E7.
Quiet and small, preferred by older men and the boys who like them.

Bookshops

Colourful Planet

Antoniadou 6, Platia Victoria, Northern Suburbs (210 882 6600/www.colourfulplanet.com). Metro Victoria. **Open** 9am-8.30pm Mon-Fri; 9am-5pm Sat. **No credit cards.**
The first and only gay bookshop in Greece. You'll find the largest collection of Greek gay literature, fiction and non-fiction, as well as calendars, gay foreign press and knick-knacks. The staff are very friendly and helpful.

Saunas

Athens Relax

Xouthou 8 & Sokratous, Omonia (210 522 2866). Metro Omonia. **Open** 1-8.30pm Mon-Sat. **Entrance** €16. **No credit cards. Map** p297 E2.
All the usual facilities including steam room, rest rooms, sauna, private cabins, lockers, bar, showers and masseurs. You can rent a locker or a cabin. It's rather expensive, and note the very unusual opening hours for a gay sauna.

Flex

Polyklitou 6, Monastiraki (210 321 0539). Metro Monastiraki. **Open** 5pm-2am Thur-Sun. **Entrance** €15. **No credit cards. Map** p297 E4.
New, very central and easily accessible by metro. Spacious lockers, sauna and gym facilities. Very clean, but small.

Ira Baths

Zinonos 4, Omonia (no phone). Metro Omonia. **Open** noon-8pm Mon-Sat. **No credit cards. Map** p297 D3.
This traditional men's baths is looking rather run-down these days and cleanliness leaves an awful lot to be desired. There's no steam room or sauna; just a little old lady in a pinafore handing out towels and bars of soap. Highly surreal.

Porn cinemas

Porn cinemas are a good spot for cruising, regardless of whether the film shown is gay or straight.

Athinaikon

Kratinou 11, Platia Dimarchiou, Omonia (210 524 3876). Metro Omonia or Monastiraki. **Open** 8am-3am daily. **Tickets** €3.50. **No credit cards. Map** p297 E3.
Gay films are screened at the Athinaikon from 10pm to 3am every day.

Olympic

Filonos 88, Piraeus (210 429 4701/www. olympic-cinema.com). Metro Piraeus, then 10min walk. **Open** 8am-3am daily. **Tickets** €3.50. **No credit cards.**
The only porn cinema in Piraeus, with a proportion of gay screenings.

Star

Agiou Konstantinou 10, Omonia (210 522 5801/ www.star-cinema.gr). Metro Omonia. **Open** 8am-3am daily. **Tickets** €3.50. **No credit cards. Map** p297 D3.
Huge cinema with neo-classical decor. Very cruisey, particularly on the first and second balconies. Gay films screened on the first floor.

Media

There are two gay magazines and two gay guides in Greece. *Antivirus* and *10%* are bi-monthly community editions printed in Greek. *Deon* and *The Gay Guide* come out in English in early summer.

Internet

www.10percent.gr

The online edition of *10%* is very impressive, but only available in Greek. However, there is one section in English (www.10percent.gr/issues/ 200408en), with useful information about being gay in Greece, cruising, health and so on.

www.deon.gr

The most useful site for foreign tourists, as it contains a lot of information in English about cruising and gay places across the country.

http://clubs.pathfinder.gr/ lesviakiomadaathinas

The Lesbian Group of Athens site has a lot of useful information, but only in Greek.

Beaches

Pack your towel, suntan lotion, swimming trunks (optional) and mosquito repellent (essential) and take the express bus E22 from Akadimias, getting off at Limanakia (the third stop). You can also catch the tram to Glyfada and then hop on the E22 bus there – ask a driver or another passenger to tell you when it reaches the third stop.

Limanakia is a gay-frequented area comprising three consecutive coves between the southern suburbs of Vouliagmeni and Varkiza. From the two parking lots opposite the one and only roadside canteen (this is your last chance to stock up on snacks and water), follow the trails down the slope to the sea. There is not a single inch of sand or a tree in sight (you jump directly into the clear blue water), but the view more than compensates: bronzed men in various states of undress are sprawled all over the rocks sunbathing. Limanakia gets especially cruisey around sunset, and it's not unusual to see some open-air action around dusk.

Arts & Entertainment

Music

From folky *entekno* to experimental electro.

The Greek National Opera takes to the stage. *See p207.*

Your musical experience of Athens will vary depending on when you visit. Winter is about intimate musical moments: an early morning in a smoky *rembetika* joint in Kipseli; a sweaty basement in a small club in Exarchia; enjoying a recital in Megaron or a night with Puccini at the Greek National Opera. Or, if you really want to blend in with the locals: on the sofa in front of reality TV show *Fame Factory*.

The long summer nights bring bigger, more glamorous outdoor events. International divas are flown in, followed by the large symphonic orchestras. Big rock bands come with trucks of equipment and, post-Olympic finances allowing, there might be free concerts in the squares. Athenian outdoor venues are second to none, the flagships being the Odeon of Herodes Atticus and Lycabettus, the former 2,000 years old while the latter dates from the 1960s. They both offer the most astonishing backdrop to any concert.

TICKETS AND INFORMATION

Tickets can be bought from the relevant venues and from ticket agencies such as Tickethouse. On the net, www.cultureguide.gr lists most events. For smaller venues, check the listings in the weekly English-language press – *Athens News* or *Ekathimerini* (www.ekathimerini.gr).

Ticket Hellas

1st Floor, Aithrio department store, Agiou Konstantinou 40, Marousi (210 618 9300/ www.ticket-hellas.gr). Metro Marousi. **Open** 9.30am-6pm Mon-Fri; 10am-3.30pm Sat. **Credit** MC, V.

Tickethouse

Panepistimiou 42, Historic Centre (210 360 8366/ www.tickethouse.gr). Metro Panepistimio. **Open** 10am-6pm Mon, Wed; 10am-9pm Tue, Thur, Fri; 10.30am-4pm Sat. **No credit cards.** **Map** p297 F4.

Classical & Opera

Few people travel to Athens for a night at the opera; indeed, for a city of this size, the chances to hear classical music are limited. But then, Athens is not like any other European city. Western classical music is a relatively new phenomenon here. In 1828, when the Turks left the country and the first generation of Greek composers like Nikolaos Mantzaros and Manolis Kalomiris started out, Beethoven was already dead and the rest of the world was well into the Romantic era.

Although there are regular performances of classical music in the city the scene is very centralised, with most of the action taking place in the Athens Concert Hall, the **Megaron Mousikis**. Inaugurated in 1991, with major extensions completed in 2004, Megaron is part-funded by the state, but the brainchild of publishing tycoon Christos Lambrakis, a very powerful man in Greek cultural and media life (too powerful, say some). Architecturally, Megaron is anachronistic and bombastic, with vast shiny marble surfaces and an orgy of brass details. But for Athens, it is more than just a music venue. The long-awaited building also embodies the modern cultural aspirations of the city and its desire to be on a par with other EU capitals. Megaron has long been unrivalled as a modern purpose-built arts venue, but the recent move of cultural activities to Pireos Street promises healthy competition (*see p112* **Pireos Street redux**).

The other main venue is the **Ethniki Lyriki Skini**, or Greek National Opera. Surprisingly, the opera has a much more independent and artistically interesting profile than Lambrakis's musical tanker on Vas Sofias. Still, one would expect the country that gave the world Maria Callas to honour the opera company where she started her career. But the Lyriki Skini, founded in 1939, has never had a permanent home and is still in temporary accommodation at the Olympia Theatre on Akadimias. Every new government makes, and then breaks, its pledge to find the company a home. Despite this, the audience is loyal, enthusiastic and growing. This is no doubt due to the inspired stagings, under the leadership of the artistic director Loukas Karytinos.

Another proof of the artistic energy of the GNO is the new Experimental stage, which is directed by composer Theodore Antoniou. It has a capacity of just 200 and is on Pireos Street, thus moving 'classical' music out from the traditional historic centre to the new art district of Athens.

Other venues worthy of a mention are the Odeia (Music Schools), the most important being **Filippos Nakas** (*see p208*), and the foreign institutes, such as the **Goethe Institut** and the **French Institute**, which regularly schedule classical music concerts. The Goethe Institut is quite an institution – in the 1960s Günther Becker, one of the forgotten heroes of Athens' musical life, started to arrange concerts of German and Greek contemporary music there. During the Junta years the institute became a meeting point for composers, musicians and music lovers, playing a vital role as a centre of unofficial art.

In the summer, the action moves outdoors. One of the main programmes is the **Athens Festival** (*see p189*), from May to September, with the major events, including concerts and operas from the main Greek orchestras and big international names, taking place in the **Odeon of Herodes Atticus** (*see p83*) and at the **Lycabettus Theatre** (*see p213*).

Considering the limited venues available, the number of Athens-based classical groups is impressive, with two symphonic ensembles, two major chamber orchestras and the opera orchestra. Apart from the **Camerata Friends of Music**, none can compete with the top ensembles in Europe, but they are still able to surprise under the leadership of an inspired conductor.

Venues

Principal venues

Ethniki Lyriki Skini (Greek National Opera)

Main stage *Olympia Theatre, Akadimias 59-61*. **Second stage** *Acropol Theatre, 9-11 Ippokratous, near Panepistimiou*. **Experimental stage** *Pireos Street, Historic Centre (210 361 2461/www.national opera.gr)*. *Metro Panepistimio*. **Open** *Box office* 9am-9pm daily. **Tickets** €20-€52. **Credit** MC, V. **Map** p297 F3/F4.

The Greek National Opera is a competent company that hasn't had the means to develop fully owing to the limitations of its temporary home: the Olympia Theatre seats only 800. Artistic director Loukas Karytinos runs the activities in the problematic venue while fighting for a new purpose-built opera house. The indoor opera season runs from November to May. In the summer the company plays at the Odeon of Herodes Atticus and occasionally tours other parts of Greece and abroad. The Acropol Theatre stages operettas and children's shows and the new Experimental stage puts on Greek operas commissioned by the GNO, and presents first performances in Greece of 20th-century works (like Bernstein's *Trouble in Tahiti*).

Arts & Entertainment

Megaron Mousikis
(Athens Concert Hall)

*Leof Vas Sofias & Kokkali, Kolonaki (box office
210 728 2333/information 210 728 2000/www.
megaron.gr). Metro Megaro Mousikis.* **Open** *Box
office* 10am-6pm Mon-Fri; 10am-2pm Sat. **Tickets**
€15-€90. **Credit** AmEx, DC, MC, V.

The completion of the extension of Megaron in 2004
makes it undoubtedly one of the major cultural centres of the city, housing conference halls, exhibition
areas, a music library, shops and restaurants.
Megaron hosts mainly operas and symphonic and
chamber music, from Greek and international
names; it is also the home of the Camerata Friends
of Music. The main Hall of the Friends of Music,
renowned for its flawless acoustics, seats around
1,960; the smaller Dimitri Mitropoulos Hall around
450. The new Alexandra Trianti Hall (opened in
2004), intended mainly for opera and other staged
productions, seats 1,750. The season runs from
October to June.

Other venues

Athens French Institute

*Sina 31, Kolonaki (210 339 8600/www.ifa.gr).
Metro Panepistimio.* **Open** 8am-9pm Mon-Fri.
Tickets free. **Map** p299 H3.

Benaki Museum – Pireos Street
Annexe

*Pireos 138 & Andronikou, Gazi (210 345 3111/
www.benaki.gr). Bus O49 from Omonia.* **Open** 9am-
5pm Wed, Thur; 10am-10pm Fri-Sun. **Tickets** prices
vary. **Map** p296/300 A5

Since opening in 2004 the new Benaki Museum
annexe in Pireos Street has become one of the most
interesting cultural sites in Athens. It now showcases classical music, and hosts a chamber music
concert series promoted by the music website
www.classicalmusic.gr.

Goethe Institut

*Omirou 14-16, Historic Centre (210 366 1000/
www.goethe.de/athen). Metro Syntagma.* **Open** *June,
July, Sept* 9am-6pm Mon-Fri. *Oct-May* 9am-9pm
Mon-Fri. Closed Aug. **Tickets** free-€10. **No credit
cards**. **Map** p297 F4.

Hellenic-American Union

*Massalias 22, Kolonaki (210 368 0900/www.hau.gr).
Metro Panepistimio.* **Open** 9am-10pm Mon-Fri; 9am-
3pm Sat. **Tickets** free. **Map** p299 G3.

Odio Filippos Nakas

*Ippokratous 41, Historic Centre (210 363 4000/
www.nakas.gr). Metro Panepistimio.* **Tickets**
prices vary. **Closed** mid July-mid Aug.
Map p297 F3.

Founded in 1969, the Filippos Nakas Conservatory
is one of the most important music institutions in
Athens, or Greece. The conservatory stages recitals
by guest performers as well as concert cycles featuring young musicians.

Athens State Orchestra

*210 725 7601/www.megaron.gr/www.athens
festival.gr.*

'The main symphony orchestra in the history of
Greek music' (as it calls itself) was formed over 100
years ago, though the current name goes back only
to 1942, when the ensemble was assured the state
funding it still enjoys. The current chief conductor,
Vyron Fithedjis, is committed to performing new
(and rediscovering old) Greek music.

Camerata Friends of Music

210 724 0098/www.megaron.gr.

Formed in 1991 as the Megaron house band, in just
over a decade this chamber orchestra has, under the
devoted leadership of Alexandros Myrat, achieved
international renown. Respected Academy of St
Martin-in-the-Fields maestro Sir Neville Marriner
was appointed honorary chairman in 2001, adding
lustre. The other leading figure is Myrat, who has
been with the orchestra from the start.

ERT National Symphony Orchestra

*Symphony office 210 606 6802/Megaron Mousikis
box office 210 728 2333/Athens Festival box office
210 322 1459/928 2900/www.megaron.gr/
www.athensfestival.gr.*

The Radio Orchestra sticks mostly to recording for
radio and TV, so the chances to see it in concert are
few and far between. However, the ensemble does
occasionally perform at Megaron and more often at
the Athens Festival in the summer.

Hellenic Group of
Contemporary Music

*Megaron Mousikis box office 210 728 2333/www.
megaron.gr.* **Open** 10am-6pm Mon-Fri; 10am-2pm Sat.

The leading contemporary music ensemble in
Greece, formed by composer/conductor Theodore
Antoniou, professor of composition at Boston
University and the president of the National Greek
Composers Organisation. Antoniou recently also
became the director of the Experimental stage at the
Greek National Opera. The ensemble has no per-
manent venue, but Megaron is your best chance.

Orchestra of the Colours

*210 362 8589/www.megaron.gr/www.orchestra
ofcolours.gr.* **No performances** Aug.

The much-loved composer/conductor Manos
Hadjidakis formed this ensemble in 1989 with the
intention of performing works not usually included
in conventional repertoires. The maestro succeeded
in this heroic task by investing in extensive
rehearsals and financing his vision with his own
money. Since Hadjidakis's death in 1994, the orchestra has been under a shaky state patronage. The current chief conductor is Miltos Logiadis. The
ensemble regularly performs at Megaron and the
Melina Mercouri Cultural Centre, and organises the
annual Dimitris Mitropoulos competition.

Arts & Entertainment

Byzantine Sacred Music

The fact that Greece 'missed' the first centuries of Western classical music is more than compensated for by its alternative musical history. In ancient Greece music was considered the highest form of art. It is believed to have accompanied everything from religious rites to labour. Recently, there have been many efforts to re-create the music of the classical era, but it's hard to say how close to the source the results are, and how much ancient music has influenced later Greek music. What is certain is that even in 21st-century Greece, music remains omnipresent.

The greatest contribution to the Greek music world was made without doubt by the unique Byzantine chant, a musical system dating back to the first centuries of Christianity and the scholarly music of the vast Byzantine Empire. Created somewhat before Gregorian chant, with its own principles and a sophisticated use of notation, Byzantine chant is still alive and well, although after the fall of the empire in 1453, the Greek Orthodox Church pursued its own course of artistic expression.

Byzantine music has remained essentially vocal. It is monophone and has inherited microtonal intervals, probably from the music of ancient Greece. Without the use of harmony or counterpoint, it has created a world of rich melodies and complex musical forms. Byzantine chant forms a solid base from which, much later, Greek secular music has sprung.

Venues & ensembles

The best place to hear Byzantine chant is Sunday mass. Chants start at 7am and go on until 11am. **Agias Irini** on Eolou is the home of the renowned Greek Byzantine Choir (210 862 4444/www.cs.duke.edu/~mgl/gbc/), performing the classic monophone chants on Saturdays (winter only) and Sundays. At **Agios Dionysos** on Skoufa you can hear the rival (and less common) school of polyphonic chant.

Rock & Pop

If Athens set the world standard, bands like Calexico, Tindersticks and Godspeed You! Black Emperor would be international household names. Greece has never boasted a band with any real international success. Dig really deep and you come up with progressive

Peggy Zina at the **Apollon**. *See p216.*

rockers Aphrodite's Child, big in France in the 1960s, and Leuki Symphonia, who are said to have been on MTV in 1989.

This doesn't mean that there's no scene, though. The grandaddies of Greek rock, Trypes, which formed in 1983 and disbanded a few years ago, were domestically influential and incredibly popular. Indie rockers Closer released some good albums in the 1990s, as did Pyx Lax and Diafana Krina. Raining Pleasure is the most succesful rock band in Greece at the moment, having supported at the Dandy Warhols Athens gig in Lycabettus in 2003, and Pleasure was only the second English-speaking band in Greece ever to be signed to a multinational label. On an underground level, there are local bands, but not enough small clubs for them to play in, or enough fan and small-label support to generate a buzz.

The electropop scene is more vital. In the 1990s pioneers Stereo Nova could have easily competed on the international stage had there been any promotional push. The two members of Stereo Nova, Michel D and Konstantinos B, pursue critically acclaimed solo careers, the latter having released *Transformations* in 2003, a kind of remix CD of the classic songs of Manos Hadjidakis, a beautiful album that is a great introduction to Greek music past and present. There's a handful of small electro labels, like Floor Filler Production, Bios Records, Antifrost and Pop Art Records, promoting surprisingly experimental artists, such as Barcelona-based Ilios (Antifrost), Drog-A-Tek and Poptraume (Bios). The commercial offspring of the genre are Dadaist electro-poppers Mikro, who had a massive hit with 'MikroTronicPlasma' in 2003 and released the album *180 Mires* (180 degrees) in early 2005.

Bios world

Bios is a truly multi-purpose venue for music, electronic and digital arts and more, and a very successful one, drawing crowds with an incredibly ambitious programme of screenings, concerts and lectures.

The space has an unusual provenance – the world of advertising. First, the Bios company decided to dabble in art and music, and set up a record label and an electronic music festival. But the lure of a bar (complete with events, exhibitions and all sorts of cultural activity) proved irresistible, and Bios – the venue – opened in an old, listed industrial building.

Except for installing the long bar and cleaning the floors, not much was done to the space. It was left to speak for itself, with the original old storage shelves as main decoration and not even a sign on the façade. The furniture is a mixture of funky vintages, and is all for

Two annual festivals take place in Athens with an impressive cast of international, experimental electronica artists: the Electrograph Festival (www.electrograph.gr) features more experimental noise and electro-acoustic music, while the Bios Festival (www.biofighter.com) has names like Mouse on Mars, PanSonic and Fennescz. The rockers get their share in the summer festival Rockwave (*see p189*).

Venues

See also p210 **Bios-sphere**.

An Club

Solomou 13-15, Exarchia (210 330 5056). Metro Omonia. **Open** *Oct-May* from 8pm Thur-Mon (can vary with event). Closed June-Sept. **Tickets** prices vary. **No credit cards. Map** p297 E2.
One of Athens' smallest but best-loved rock clubs is set right in the heart of rocker- and anarchist-packed

sale, and the graphic work is brilliant. But Bios is not only about cool aesthetics, or drinking. The art's the thing here. Whether it's video dance, Austrian laptop improvisation, Mexican electronica acts or photo exhibitions the place is rammed. Why is this? Because it's unpretentious and the formalities that often surround the art experience are erased. The venue is adjacent to the bar and you can

go to and fro as you please. And the final lure? Entrance is free or very cheap, in a city where 30 is standard for a gig ticket.

Bios Pireos 84

Pireos 84, Gazi (210 342 5335/www. biofighter.gr). Metro Metaxourgio. **Open** 11am-4am daily. **Admission** free. **No credit cards. Map** p296 C2.

The divine Callas

It wasn't just her voice that made her La Divina – the diva of divas. Her life had all the ingredients of adversity, tragedy and personal relationships played out before the merciless flash of photographers' bulbs that you normally associate with stars from other fields of music. You could call her the Judy Garland of the aria.

Maria Anna Sofia Cecilia Kalogeropoulos was born in New York in 1923 to Greek parents, but returned to Athens in 1937. There she attended the National Conservatoire and made her stage debut in 1939, followed in 1941 with her first prima donna role as *Tosca* for the Greek National Opera.

The dark days of occupation followed, and when Greece was eventually liberated by the British in 1944, Callas worked as an interpreter, before rejoining her father in America in September 1945. While the material conditions were much easier in the United States than in Greece, the country was flooded with expatriate Italian opera singers and Maria made little headway. The offer of *La Gioconda* in Verona was a godsend, and Maria left for Italy. That and subsequent performances of the *bel canto* operas made her a star, singing around the world and famed for the dramatic intensity and performing flair she brought to the stage.

During this period she met and married Italian industrialist Giovanni Meneghini. But his is not the name that is coupled with Callas in the popular imagination. That belongs to Aristotle Onassis, the Greek shipping tycoon she met in 1957 and the man who broke La Divina's heart.

But he can't be blamed for what happened to her voice. During the 1950s the strain on it became increasingly clear, until by 1958 she could no longer properly sing many roles. Critics have maintained that she regularly pushed her voice beyond its natural limits, at the expense of beauty of tone, but perhaps

that is part of the reason for the effect she had on so many listeners. Callas really did sing her heart out.

In 1959 she left her husband for the already married Onassis. Onassis never married her and, nine years later, in one of the most notorious splits in the world of celebrity, he left her for Jacqueline Kennedy.

'First I lost my voice, then I lost my figure and then I lost Onassis,' La Divina once lamented. She made a half-hearted attempt at a stage comeback in 1973, but her voice was gone.

Maria Callas's final years were lived largely in seclusion in Paris, where she died in 1977. But the drama did not end there. Her ashes were stolen from the Père Lachaise cemetery, but later recovered, and finally scattered in the Aegean Sea, where she had so often sailed with Onassis.

Exarchia. This is a great place to catch local acts as they play their first riffs on their way towards stardom, as well as the odd international act that you probably won't have heard of.

Club 22

Leof Vouliagmenis 22, Neos Kosmos, Southern Suburbs (210 924 9814/www.club22.gr). Metro Syngrou-Fix. **Open** from 11.30pm Wed-Sun (can vary with event). **Tickets** €12 including drink Wed-Fri; €15 including drink Sat, Sun.
No credit cards.
A club that also organises gigs, with acts like Thievery Corporation and Pink Martini. In the summer, the venue relocates along the coast, to Glyfada.

Gagarin 205 Live Music Space

Liosion Thymarakia, Vathi, Western Suburbs (210 854 7600/www.gagarin205.gr). Metro Attiki. **Open** Oct-May 9pm-3am Mon, Thur-Sun (can vary with event). Closed June-Sept. **Tickets** €20-€30. **Credit** MC, V.
This converted garage has been turned into a mid-sized, very sympathetic rock venue featuring artists like Beth Orton, Lambchop, Archive and a fair dose of industrial. It also converts to a cinema from time to time, showing music films and cult movies.

Half Note Jazz Club

Trivonianou 17, Kinossargous, Southern Suburbs (210 921 3310/www.halfnote.gr). Metro Syngrou-Fix, then 10min walk. **Open** Oct-May from 10.30pm Thur-Sat; from 8.30pm Sun. Closed June-Sept. **Tickets** €30 (including 1 drink); €20 concessions. **Credit** MC, V. **Map** p301 F8.
The Athens jazz scene circles more or less entirely around this legendary venue next to the First Cemetery. A great club with the right atmosphere, attracting international and Greek names in both jazz and world music.

House of Art

Sachtouri 4 & Sarri, Psyrri (210 321 7678/ www.house-of-art.gr). Metro Monastiraki. **Open** Oct-May varies with event. Closed June-Sept. **Tickets** prices vary. **Credit** MC, V. **Map** p297 D4.
A cabaret-like venue in Psyrri, often featuring international avant-garde names, like Arto Lindsay.

Lycabettus Theatre

On top of Lycabettus Hill, Kolonaki (210 722 7209). Metro Evangelismos or Megaro Mousikis, then 15min walk. **Funicular** every half hour 8am-3am daily from corner of Aristippou & Ploutarchou. **Open** Theatre June-Sept. Box office from 2hrs before performances. **Tickets** prices vary. **Credit** AmEx, MC, V. **Map** p299 J3.
This modern amphitheatre, which hosts major acts, local and international, was created by one of the country's most important architects, Takis Zenetos. In the last few years artists like Radiohead, Massive Attack and Jane Birkin have played here. From up here, the chaotic city becomes a calm carpet of lights far below. Tickets can be pricey, but you can listen for free by climbing up the surrounding rocks

(though agility is required). You don't even need to bring booze: freelance entrepreneurs climb around selling ice-cold drinks.

Melina Mercouri Vrahon Theatre

Vyronas (210 764 8675/210 766 2066). Bus 214/ trolleybus 11. **Open** Theatre June-Sept. Box office from 6pm on performance days. **Tickets** prices vary. **Credit** MC, V. **Map** p301 E5.
This outdoor theatre, impressively located in front of a cliff face, hosts concerts by top Greek musicians, with a liberal sprinkling of international acts – from an African drumming festival to David Byrne.

Mikromousiko Theatro (Small Music Theatre)

Veikou 33, Koukaki (210 924 5644/www.small musictheatre.gr/smt). Metro Akropoli. **Open** Oct-May 9pm-3am daily. Closed June-Sept. **Tickets** €5-€15. **No credit cards. Map** p301 E7.
A tiny venue with grand programming. It started in 2000 with the focus on experimental, free improvised and electronic music. But it also features avant-rock, jazz, folk and chamber music, local rock bands and, once in a while, the odd international act, like Dirty Three and Laura Veirs. Not content with that, it hosts the 2:13 Experimental music club, with monthly live dates, and the yearly three-day 2:13 December Festival with both Greek and international artists.

Palenque

Farantaton 41, Platia Agiou Thoma, Ambelokipi (210 775 2360/www.palenque.gr). Metro Ambelokipi. **Open** Oct-May 9pm-3.30am daily. Closed June-Sept. **No credit cards.**
The temple of Latin music in Athens, with live shows almost every day. Dance lessons are included in the price, so why not brush up your salsa steps before the gig? If you prefer to tango, Sunday is Tangueria night.

Rembetika & Folk

Arguably the only genuine Athenian music, **rembetika** can be described as songs from the urban underworld (or the blues of the Balkans). The roots of the genre can be traced to the 1920s Piraeus hash dens, populated by the immigrants from the big population handover between Greece and Turkey. Drawing inspiration from Turkish café music, or *aman*, rembetika adopted a simple style and instrumentation, and became the voice of the dispossessed and miserable immigrant workers in Piraeus. Originally, the main instruments were the bouzouki and the smaller *baglamas*; the rhythm was tapped with feet, spoons on glasses or anything else to hand. The lyrics, often improvised, focused mainly on prostitutes, drugs and how to humiliate the police. *Rembetika* became popular during the 1930s, turning some of the poor *rembetes* into stars driving Rolls-Royces, before falling into oblivion until a new generation, oppressed by the Junta, rediscovered the old songs and their rebellious lyrics, and turned them into their national songs of freedom.

The legendary names are the members of the Piraeus Quartet: Markos Vamvakaris, Stratos Payoumdzi and Giorgos Batis. But for the fourth member, Anestos 'Artemis' Delias, fortune was short-lived: he died in the streets at the age of 29, after he became addicted to hard drugs. But if *rembetika* had a superstar it was bouzouki wizard Yiannis Tsitsanis, who was connected with the westernisation of *rembetika*.

Today, *rembetika* is synonymous with Greek music and seen as fundamental in much of the contemporary scene. Pure *rembetika* no longer exists, living on only in preserved-in-aspic recordings. But various venues strive to keep the form alive. The quality of the singers varies, but there are still a couple of performers out there with that old *rembetes* feel in their veins. And *rembetika* certainly exists in the hearts of the Greek people. It's truly amazing listening to generations of Greeks at family gatherings, singing along to the old *rembetes* praising hookers and dope.

Rembetika should not be confused with folk music, which in Greece differs widely from region to region and is a major chapter in itself, with influences from ancient Greece, Byzantium and the later occupying powers. A good place to hear the real stuff is at the **Dora Stratou Garden Theatre** (*see p235*), where it comes complete with authentic costumes. Don't be put off, though – this is not a touristic Real Greek Music show, but a serious institution based on extensive ethnographic research under the direction of Professor Alkis Raftis. Another artist to look out for is Domna Samiou, who recorded thousands of folk songs in villages across Greece and is counted as one of the finest folk singers around. She co-operates with young musicians such as *lyra* player Sokratis Sinopoulos. Percussionist Andreas Pappas creates a tasteful blend of folk music and modern sounds with his group Krotala.

Rembetika

Mantala – rembetiko steki
Ydras 14 & Kipselis, Kipseli, Northern Suburbs (210 823 4511). Bus 022 from Kolanaki Square. **Open** *Oct-May* 11pm-4am Fri, Sat. Closed June-Sept. **Admission** free. **No credit cards**.

This is a classic neighbourhood *rembetika* joint in densely populated Kipseli. Try to catch a night with Babis Goles, one of the best singers/bouzouki players around.

Perivoli t'Ouranou
Lisikratous 19 & Leof Vas Amalias, Plaka (210 322 2048). Metro Akropoli. **Open** *Oct-May* 10pm-4am Wed-Sat. Closed June-Sept. **Admission** free. **Credit** AmEx, MC, V. **Map** p301 F6.

Located right by the Acropolis, this tasteful venue has remained in business for over three decades on a fine entertainment-and-food principle. Home to respectable old-school *laiko* and *rembetika* acts, it has maintained a delightful traditional character, suggesting Athenian nightlife as it was in the 1960s.

Stoa Athanaton
Sofokleous 19, Historic Centre (210 321 4362). Metro Omonia. **Open** 3-7.30pm, 10pm-4am Mon-Sat. Closed June-Sept. **Admission** free. **No credit cards**. **Map** p297 E4.

Athens' premiere *rembetatiko*. Old-timers with suits and cigars shower musicians with flowers and, when the mood strikes, dance passionately to songs of heartbreak and destitution. Reservations are essential on Friday and Saturday.

Taximi
Harilaou Trikoupi & Isavron 29, Exarchia (210 363 9919). Metro Omonia, then 15min walk. **Open** *Sept-May* 10pm-2am Thur-Sun. Closed June-Aug. **Admission** free. **No credit cards**.

Most of Greece's greatest *rembetika* musicians have played here at some point, and the atmosphere remains deliciously old-time, illuminated mostly by red candles and burning cigarettes. The smoke-stained walls are adorned with black-and-white pictures of the greats.

Folk

To Baraki tou Vasili
Didotou 3, Kolonaki (210 362 3625). Metro Panepistimio or Syntagma. **Open** *Oct-May* 10.30pm-3am daily (can vary with event). Closed June-Sept. **Tickets** €13 (including 1 drink). **No credit cards**. **Map** p299 G3.

A small, cosy venue in a quiet street, run by a music freak who unfailingly introduces performers to audiences. It stages up-and-coming local acts, both traditional and contemporary and, less frequently, established artists too.

Greek Popular Music

Greek popular music, or **laiko** (literally 'music of the people'), descends from the gritty strains of *rembetika* but morphed, via 1950s lounge singers, plate-smashing nightclubs and an

Arts & Entertainment

affinity for love songs and glitter, into a one of a kind music (and entertainment) experience that blends the centuries-old bouzouki with the showmanship of Western pop. There are different strains of *laiko*, but in the same way that most Western pop can trace its origins to gospel, jazz and blues, so the roots of Greek popular music can be found in the earthy, almost Middle Eastern sounds of *rembetika*. In the 1950s and '60s, as opulent nightclubs made their appearance in Athens, a few musicians who'd once made their names in *rembetatika* began emerging into this larger, showier world. They replaced the dark lyrics of *rembetika* songs with softer themes of love and longing, accompanied by dazzling, showy bouzouki musicianship. Bigger bands, bigger hair, sparkling costumes and floorshows soon followed. This music, and the clubs that play it, are called **bouzoukia**, after the primary instrument involved.

In the 1960s *bouzoukia* became famous for over-the-top revelry, with customers breaking plates during songs, and stories of excess doing the rounds, like the gentleman who paid $100 (a lot of money then) for a pair of scissors to cut his favourite singer's evening gown into a mini-dress. Remnants of this attitude still prevail in today's *bouzoukia* – though breaking plates has been replaced by throwing flowers. This kind of revelry and conspicuous consumption may seem like a Western influence, but it actually comes from the same deep, dark roots as the music's *rembetika* ancestry: a fatalistic Balkan sensibility that destruction and death may well come tomorrow, so it's best to live it up to the dizzying heights tonight.

In modern Athens, *bouzoukia* fall into a couple of different categories. Though all favour fancy stage shows, vast consumption of alcohol, liberal spending and thoroughly decked-out performers and clientele, some play a high quality of more traditional Greek music, with old-school singers like Costas Makedonas, Dimitris Bassis, Eleni Tsaligopoulou, Gerasimos Andreatos and Yiannis Kotsiras.

Another branch of *bouzoukia* is heavily mixed with Western, commercial pop – these performances tend to favour laser-light spectacles and catchy tunes that are often made into videos. The kings and queens of this scene are just as likely to perform in tight leather pants and bustiers as in sparkling evening gowns. The ruling divas here are Anna Vissi, Kaiti Garbi and Despina Vandi.

City sounds

Greek-language hip hop, europop, beat-based electronica, nostalgic instrumental music, art song (*entekno*), vibrant folk music and the often tacky but usually entertaining pop-*laiko*: these are just some of the many sounds you can hear around Athens.

Top of the pop crop is Cypriot-born crooner Mihalis Hadjiyannis, who combines boy next door charm with a velvety voice that won him five music awards in 2005, or Greek-Swede Eurovision sex kitten Elena Paparizou, with her upbeat blend of europop and techno dance. Or all-dancing heart-throb Sakis Rouvas. But for a distinctively Greek sound, there really is no one to beat the chart-topping first lady of pop-*laiko*, the Madonna of Greece, Anna Vissi.

Away from the europop and pop-*laiko* axis, the jazzy house of Mikael Delta, one of the few Greek artists with an international label deal, is great to chill out to. Fusion outfit Mode Plagal – motto 'naming music or making music, naming the feel or feeling the feel, borrowing traditions or making your own' – lets its funky improvisations of traditional Greek *demotika* (folk) do the talking. Composer Stamatis Kraounakis and his boisterous Speira-Speira troupe offer music and much more. Crammed with vocal talent, the group puts on one of the most entertaining shows in town, mixing instrumental works, rock 'n' roll, *laika*, drama, vaudeville, *entekno*, tango and parodies of 1970s and '80s hits.

The crystal-clear, resonant voice of Alkistis Protopsalti aims straight for the heart with songs that are integrally Greek, yet internationally influenced, while world music star Eleftheria Arvanitaki's spine-chilling vocal acrobatics have enchanted fans. Other distinctive voices include Mario Frangoulis, who has one foot in opera and the other in popular music, and serves up some mesmerising sounds, and Savina Yannatou, an artist of exceptional talent. Her vocal mannerisms – raw and primitive one minute, lyrical and sublime the next – strike an openly religious note. Armed with a sensuously gruff voice, a style with its roots in *rembetika* and a gripping stage presence, Haris Alexiou (known lovingly as Haroula) embodies Greek spirit.

The lowest form of *bouzoukia* is called *skiladiko*, literally 'dog clubs'. These are places where the level of tackiness and ostentation is so high, and the quality of music (and level of décolletage) so low that they attract the lowest class of customer – fascinating if you're into cultural anthropology, but not recommended if you are interested in real *bouzoukia* music. If you want to see this scene, it's best to book a table at one of the clubs (for which you'll also pay for an obligatory meal). Expect the cost of ticket, meal and drinks for a couple to run to around €200 – more if you buy flowers to throw at the singer.

But *laiko* isn't confined only to the kitschalicious world of *bouzoukia*. There's also a much less commercial and more sophisticated take on modern Greek music. In the 1960s, when nightclub singers were co-opting *rembetika* and marketing their pop version to the masses, Greece's most celebrated classical composers, Mikis Theodorakis and Manos Hadjidakis, combined traditional Greek music with Western-style symphonies, and accompanied them with lyrics by major poets, including Nobel Prize winners Odysseus Elytis and George Seferis.

These innovative and beautiful pieces are usually performed at Greece's most prestigious venues, as part of high-profile festivals. But what's also important about them is that they laid the groundwork for a new type of *laiko* called **entekno**, meaning 'art music', a sophisticated and more difficult-to-define sound, found in small clubs and record stores, rather than in *bouzoukia*. *Entekno* still sounds very Greek but is definitely open to various influences, generally more folky and international rather than Western and commercial. *Entekno* artists like Socrates Malamas, Orpheas Peridis and Thanassis Papaconstantinou tend to be deep-digging songwriters rather than straight-out entertainers. But, even so, they can provide a heady night on the strength of their material and rapport with fans. Shows are usually limited to short runs at clubs with 400-500 capacities, because the acts aim to 'keep it real'.

Venues

Bouzoukia

Apollon
Syngrou 259, Nea Smyrni, Southern Suburbs (210 942 7580). Metro Moschato, then 10min walk. **Open** *Nov-Easter* 11pm-4am Wed-Sun. Closed Easter-Oct. **Tickets** standing room €15 (including 1 drink); table for 4 €150 (including alcohol). **Credit** AmEx, DC, V.

One of Athens' most popular venues, showcasing top acts like the Greek take on Britney Spears, Peggy Zina, as well as classic divas like Kaiti Garbi. Expect extravagant shows with dozens of costume changes, laser effects and wailing declarations of passion.

Athinon Arena
Pireos 166, Tavros, North of the Acropolis (210 347 1111). Bus 049 from Omonia. **Open** *Nov-Mar* 11pm-4am Thur-Sat. Closed Apr-Oct. **Tickets** standing room €15 (including 1 drink); table for 4 €170 (including alcohol). **Credit** AmEx, DC, V.

This new arena, unprecedented in everything from cost to size to technology, is the Las Vegas of Greek music. It opened in December 2004 with popsters Yorgos Dalaras and Antonis Remos in an excellent double show. The venue can hold 7,000 people and is part of the Pantheon (still under construction), a huge entertainment complex featuring nightclubs, cinemas, restaurants and hotels.

Fever
Syngrou & Lagoumitzi 25, Neos Kosmos, Southern Suburbs (210 921 7333). Metro Neos Kosmos. **Open** *Dec-May* (season may vary) 10.30pm-4am Thur-Sun. Closed June-Nov. **Tickets** standing room €15-€20 (including 1 drink); table for 4 €180 (including alcohol). **Credit** AmEx, DC, V.

A massive space with high-tech stage mechanisms that recently showcased Sakis Rouvas and Elena Paparizou. Be warned: they've both represented Greece in the Eurovision Song Contest, the latter twice, solo and as part of the group Antique.

Rex
Panepistimiou 48, Omonia (210 381 4591). Metro Omonia. **Open** *Dec-mid Apr* 11pm-4am Thur-Sun. Closed mid Apr-Nov. **Tickets** standing room €20 (including 1 drink); table for 4 €190 (including alcohol). **Credit** AmEx, DC, V.

One of the few big clubs in the centre. It recently featured a true diva, Despina Vandi, together with *Fame Factory* products Kalomira and Thanos Petrelis.

Romeo Plus
Kallirois 4, Syngrou (210 923 2648). Metro Syngrou-Fix. **Open** *Nov-Apr* 11pm-4am Wed-Sat. Closed May-Oct. **Tickets** standing room €10-€15 (including 1 drink); table for 4 €130 (including alcohol). **Credit** AmEx, DC, V.

One of the hottest places for pop-*laiko*. In the summer the club moves to the coastal area, at Ellenikou 1, Glyfada (210 894 5345).

Entekno

Zygos
Kydathinaion 22, Plaka (210 324 1610). Metro Syntagma. **Open** *Nov-Apr* 11pm-3am Thur-Sat; 9pm-1am Sun. Closed May-Oct. **Tickets** €15 (including 1 drink); table for 4 €160 (including alcohol). **No credit cards. Map** p301 F6.

This historic venue in the city centre is the hub of Athenian *entekno*.

Nightlife

Forget the sightseeing – it's after midnight that Athens really hots up.

Athenians might spend the whole day working hard but there's no doubt they live for the night. While older people still enjoy the more traditional venues with exclusively Greek fare, the city's young people are far more international about their clubbing habits. Early closing times aren't an issue here: Athenian clubbers set out late (midnight is early) and then just keep going till dawn. Though the clubbing scene here is decidedly more small-scale than in, say, London or Berlin, in terms of quality it's up there among the best of them, with at least one or two international DJs (recent guests include Sven Vath, Sasha and Felix Da Housecat) flying in every weekend during the summer months. Pick up a copy of the weekly *Time Out Athens* (in Greek).

The past three or four years have seen Athens fall for R&B in a big way, but many dance venues and bars still retain their fondness for house and techno with clubbers also gradually turning towards harder, more progressive electro sounds. Bar-wise, all tastes are catered for, from jazz and rock to trip hop.

Most of the big dance clubs close their downtown venues in the summer months to relocate to the cooler northern or coastal southern suburbs, or even ship out to the islands. Just a five-minute walk away from Omonia Square you'll find the **Psyrri** neighbourhood, an inner-city playground packed with numerous bars and small clubs. It attracts young, hip, fun-loving Athenians and clubbers often congregate here before grabbing a cab and zipping down to the beachside venues.

The neighbouring district of **Gazi** shares similar characteristics and is within easy walking distance of the metro station in Thisio (another area with a cluster of small bars with outside tables, nice for a relaxed evening drink). **Exarchia** has something for everyone and is home to the city's best alternative venues. **Kolonaki Square**, coupled with the string of small bars on Haritos Street, can be found roughly 15 minutes away from Omonia Square and draws a more affluent crowd. The northern suburb of **Kifisia** is for visitors who demand good service and are free of budgetary constraints.

Posidonos, the coastal avenue in the southern suburbs, pulls in crowds from all over the city during the summer thanks to the abundance of big clubs situated along the strip: think open-air, swimming pools, chic decor, beautiful people, state-of-the-art sound systems and the funkiest tunes to boot. The only drawbacks to the coastal venues are the high prices and the time it takes to get there, thanks to the traffic mayhem they generate.

In **Piraeus** expect to find a younger clientele at the various café-bars that remain open throughout the day and into the night in the Mikrolimano area. If you have your own transport or don't mind splashing out on a hefty cab fare, you may want to make the trek up to the northern **Attica** region, which has some beautifully situated clubs.

BEWARE BAD BEVERAGES

Just like every other large city Athens has its fair share of seedy joints that charge an arm and a leg for, at best, a mediocre experience. And the gleaming bottles of branded whisky and vodka – or any other spirit for that matter – that are lined up behind the bar may not be all they seem. Some venues cut on costs by diluting their spirits with illegally imported rough – and potent – alcohol. These adulterated spirits are referred to as *bombes* by Athenians and large doses are potentially lethal. Once you've downed a few, your taste buds will hardly notice but your head, and your liver, definitely will. This underhand practice has yet to reach epidemic proportions but it is worth being careful. The best way to tell if drinks are spiked somewhere is to see what everyone else is drinking – if they're all on the bottled beer there's usually a good reason.

THE LISTINGS

In the following listings you'll notice that many of the bars and clubs operate as restaurants as well. The listed opening hours refer to the bar sections. Opening hours in general are flexible. Places may stay open way past the listed closing time if they're busy, or close early if they're not.

The clubs in the Southern Suburbs section, in places like **Glyfada** and **Vouliagmeni**, are open during the summer only. These summer nightclubs often pride themselves on redecorating every season, so themes can change. Also bear in mind that venues come and go; this is especially true of Athens' summer clubs.

Arts & Entertainment

THESE BOOKS ARE MADE FOR WALKING

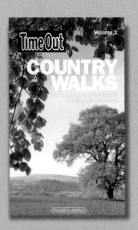

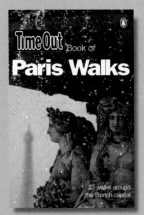

Acropolis & around

Gallery Café
Adrianou 33, Monastiraki (210 324 9080). Metro Monastiraki. **Open** 10am-2am Mon-Sat; 9am-2am Sun. **Admission** free. **No credit cards.** **Map** p297/p301 E5.
This quaint café is on bustling Adrianou Street with the majestic Acropolis in full view. Come nightfall, Gallery turns into an inviting little bar where you can enjoy cool lounge grooves surrounded by stone-and-wood decor. Keep an eye out for various exhibitions and live events.

Inoteka
Platia Avyssinias 3, Monastiraki (210 324 6446/ www.intoteka.com). Metro Monastiraki. **Open** 4pm-5am Mon-Sat; 2pm-5am Sun. **No credit cards.** **Map** p297/301 D5.
Set in the middle of the old Athens flea market, this shadowy, minimalist beacon offers DJ-spun electro-pop, scuzzy leftfield beats and dirty house to a trend-setting crowd. The outdoor tables, set away from the frazzled baselines, offer a good alternative for a traditional quiet drink.

Loop
Platia Agion Asomaton 3, Thisio (210 324 7666). Metro Thissio. **Open** 9.30am-5am daily. **Admission** free. **No credit cards.** **Map** p297 D4.
A great DJ bar for fans of electronica, Loop loves anything from down-tempo and trip hop to nu jazz and deep house. On most nights you'll find a musically well-informed crowd of twentysomethings crowding around its long bright-red bar inside or fighting over the few outside tables and chairs in the newly pedestrianised Agion Asomaton Square.

Stavlos
Iraklidon 10, Thisio (210 346 7206/www.stavlos.gr). Metro Thissio. **Open** 10am-3.30am daily. **Admission** free. **Credit** AmEx, MC, V. **Map** p296 C5.
An all-time classic choice in the heart of Thisio. Laze the afternoon away in the tree-lined courtyard to the soft strains of chilled-out funk, soul and jazz. In the evening the mood gets livelier as trendy crowds of all ages turn up to enjoy the DJs spinning everything from house and electro-pop to retro classics.

Historic Centre

Bar Guru Bar
Platia Theatrou 10 (210 324 6530). Metro Omonia. **Open** 10pm-3.30am daily. Closed 25 July-25 Aug. **Admission** free. **Credit** AmEx, MC, V. **Map** p297 D4.
A lively and endearing bar-club run with a passion that you're sure to find infectious. The mixed crowd includes young, funky twentysomethings about town and older couples who come for the Thai finger-food menu in the restaurant. Weekly live jazz events in the upstairs bar are sure to keep musos happy. Downstairs, the crowds get down to 1970s soul, grizzled house and R&B.

Kolonaki & around

Baila
Haritos 43, Kolonaki (210 723 3019). Metro Evangelismos. **Open** 8.30pm-3am daily. **Admission** free. **Credit** MC, V. **Map** p299 H4.
A great meeting point for socialising in pedestrianised Haritos Street. The decor is sleek, stylish and red all over, and the stream of radio-friendly hits are kept at an amiably conversation-encouraging level.

Balthazar
Vournazou & Tsocha 27, Ambelokipi (210 641 2300). Metro Ambelokipi. **Open** 9pm-4am daily. **Admission** free. **Credit** AmEx, MC, V.
For the past 30 years, Balthazar has been making its presence felt on the Athens nightlife circuit. Housed in a neo-classical mansion, it offers one of the most refreshing venues in the city centre. Local celebrities and out-of-towners flock to the island-esque courtyard bar where there's also a garden restaurant serving Mediterranean cuisine.

Briki
Dorilaiou 6, Platia Mavili, Kolonaki (210 645 2380). Metro Megaro Moussikis. **Open** 8.30am-3.30am Mon-Thur, Sun; 8.30am-5.30am Fri, Sat. **Admission** free. **No credit cards.**
This small but lively watering hole holds a special place in the hearts of all those who have visited it throughout the years. Located in the conveniently central Mavili Square, it's a great place to either start or end your night. The eclectic mix of funk, acid jazz and rock with infectious beats is guaranteed to raise the spirit and the killer air-con system makes sure you stay cool in the hot and sticky summer evenings.

Caffeina
Kiafas 6 & Zoodochou Pigis, Exarchia (210 384 1282). Metro Panepistimio. **Open** 10.30am-3am Mon-Sat; 2pm-3am Sun. **Admission** free. **No credit cards.** **Map** p297 F3.
Come early if you want to grab one of the few comfy sofas at this tiny but cute café-bar in the heart of the city. This is where stylish (and in some cases avant-garde) groups of twentysomethings gather for a good chat and get down to a fair bit of electronica.

En Delphis
Delfon 5, Kolonaki (210 360 8269). Metro Panepistimio. **Open** 8am-3am Mon-Sat; 9am-3am Sun. **Admission** free. **No credit cards.** **Map** p299 G3.
The king of bars on Delfon for a number of years now, En Delphis is a spacious, sophisticated hang-out. The soundtrack is chart pop with a few house beats thrown in for good measure. If you fancy a spot of lounging, head for the upstairs room where you'll find soft orange seats and window benches.

Frame Bohemian Bar
St George Lycabettus, Platia Dexamenis, Kolonaki (210 721 4368). Metro Evangelismos. **Open** 11am-3am daily. **Admission** free. **Credit** AmEx, DC, MC, V. **Map** p299 H4.

Located on the ground floor of the St George Lycabettus hotel (*see p62*), this lounge-restaurant-bar is a popular hangout with VIPs, businessmen and a generally well-heeled clientele, but the colourful yet simple 1970s retro-style decor creates a welcoming atmosphere for everyone. In the summer, the action moves across the street to the garden area of Dexamenis Square, where you can sit back on comfy sofas and enjoy lounge/chill-out music. Both the indoor and outdoor bars have a fun swing-armchair that you can reserve when booking.

Galaxy

Athens Hilton, Leof Vas Sofias 46, Kolonaki (210 728 1000). Metro Evangelismos. **Open** 6pm-3am Mon-Thur, Sun; 6pm-4am Fri, Sat. **Admission** free. **Credit** AmEx, DC, MC, V. **Map** p299 J5.

An impossibly chic classic lounge bar located on the top floor of the Hilton hotel (*see p62*). Galaxy is a great place to enjoy a relaxed drink with a fantastic bird's eye view of the city skyline and the Acropolis. The spectacular vistas come at a price, though, as drinks are on the expensive side. But then again, you get what you pay for.

Mike's Irish Bar

Sinopis 6, Ambelokipi (210 777 6797/www.mikesirishbar.gr). Metro Panormou. **Open** 8pm-4am daily. **Admission** free. **No credit cards.**

Every Monday and Tuesday this fun basement pub gets jam-packed as the microphones come out for anyone wanting to try their luck at karaoke (oddly, somewhat of a novelty in Greece). Homesick pub lovers will feel right at home as they look around to see Irish flags and football shirts on the walls and people playing darts with a pint of Murphy's in hand. The large screens regularly show sports events. On non-karaoke nights live bands playing mainly classic rock and pop entertain punters.

Mommy

Delfon 4, Kolonaki (210 361 9682). Metro Panepistimio. **Open** 11am-3am daily. **Admission** free. **Credit** AmEx, MC, V. **Map** p299 G3.

A hugely popular meeting place for trendy young Athenians, this cool yet boisterous bar-restaurant impresses with its decor. The interior is set out like a house and decorated with kitschy accessories and comfy low sofas. Keep an eye out for mini exhibitions of paintings adorning the walls from time to time. In summer, head for the outdoor area where mainstream dance music kicks off the night and later turns to joyous pumping house.

On the Road

Ardittou 1, Zappeion (210 347 8716/210 345 2502). Metro Syntagma, then 10min walk. **Open** 10.30pm-5am daily. **Admission** free. **No credit cards.** **Map** p299 G7.

This aptly named open-air bar-club certainly gets high marks for being an unusual venue: it's actually situated on a long, narrow piece of land in the middle of busy Ardittou Street. The decor is bright (sky

blue dominates) and the 30-plus regulars while the night away on the dancefloor to the strains of a broad-ranging playlist. Theme nights include golden oldies, R&B and oriental.

Palenque Club

Farandaton 41, Platia Agiou Thoma, Ambelokipi (210 775 2360/www.palenque.gr). Metro Ambelokipi. **Open** 9.30pm-4.30am Mon-Thur; 10pm-6am Fri, Sat; 9pm-4am Sun. **Admission** (including 1 drink) €10. **No credit cards.**

The city's premier Latin club has built up a sturdy reputation over the years and the sexy mambo, salsa and samba sounds emanating from its speakers are guaranteed to get you on the dancefloor. If you feel you need to work on your tango, experienced teachers are on hand most days of the week to offer early evening (9-11pm) dance lessons. Palenque also regularly plays host to various events and live performances by Latin American and European bands.

Tribeca

Skoufa 46, Kolonaki (210 362 3541). Metro Panepistimio. **Open** 10am-3am Mon-Thur, Sun; 10pm-4am Fri, Sat. **Admission** free. **No credit cards.** **Map** p299 G4.

There's a distinctly Manhattan feel to this incredibly hip bar, which is something like a minimalist living room in appearance. Young and energetic go-for-it crowds pile into the small indoor space to jiggle (and on occasion sing) along to a rainbow of alternative pop tunes. Expect White Stripes, Joy Division, Red Hot Chili Peppers and Talking Heads. The pavement tables are quieter, but crackle with the same swish atmosphere.

North of the Acropolis

Astron

Taki 3, Psyrri (mobile 6937 146337). Metro Monastiraki. **Open** 9.30pm-4am daily. **Admission** free. **No credit cards.** **Map** p297 D4.

Perhaps the smallest bar in the middle of Psyrri, Astron is a year-round hotspot that regularly gets filled to bursting point so you're most likely to end up sitting on the pavement outside with your beer. Fortunately, the pumping electronica, deep house and progressive sounds blare out so that everyone can hear, inside or out. The atmosphere's friendly and it's worth braving the crowded interior to gawk at the ironic glowing photos of sunsets in fluffy frames that lighten up the heady atmosphere.

Banana Moon

Iera Odos & Megalou Alexandrou 139, Gazi (210 341 1003/210 341 1513). Bus A17, B17 from Omonia. **Open** 8pm-3.30am Sun-Thur; 8pm-4.30am Fri, Sat. **Admission** free. **Credit** AmEx, MC, V. **Map** p296 B4.

The recently renovated Banana Moon has got summer written all over it: the mainly wooden decor in earthy colours is enhanced by banana trees all around and banana-shaped half-moon lanterns hang from any available space. The music policy embraces old-school dance hits and also throws in a few new ones for good measure.

Bee

Miaouli 6, Psyrri (210 321 2624). Metro Monastiraki. **Open** 1pm-3.30am Mon-Thur, Sun; 1pm-5am Fri, Sat. **Admission** free. **Credit** AmEx, DC, MC, V. **Map** p297 E4.

There's a touch of Almodovar about the avant-garde decor of this happy disco bar that will put you in a good mood for your night out on the town. Its smart, thirtysomething crowd mingles to the strains of lounge, rock, upbeat R&B grooves and, on weekends, a fair bit of house too.

Bios

Pireos 84, Metaxourgio (210 342 5335). Metro Metaxourgio. **Open** noon-2.30am daily. **Admission** free. **No credit cards**. **Map** p296 C2.

This cutting-edge bar in a modern art and events space (a former warehouse) is mostly frequented by the hippest crowd in Athens, artists and generally anyone open to something a little bit different. There are regular exhibitions and short films are even projected on to the no-nonsense concrete walls. You'll hear anything from house, dance and electro to avant-garde noise and trippy chill-out tunes at varying sound levels, depending on the DJ's mood.

Corto Maltese

Karaiskaki 31, Psyrri (no phone). Metro Monastiraki. **Open** noon-5am daily. **Admission** (including 1 drink) €6. **No credit cards**. **Map** p297 D4.

The fact that this bar is named after an obscure but cult comic-book hero that only a small, hip section of Athenians would have even heard of is indicative of the kind of pop culture-savvy clubbers it aims for. The music policy is equally cool: the DJs spin a mix of alternative or indie rock and electro-pop sounds.

En Delphis.
See p219.

Gazaki

Triptolemou 31, Gazi (210 346 0901). Metro Thissio, then 10min walk. **Open** 9pm-3.30am Mon-Thur, Sun; 8pm-5am Fri, Sat. **Admission** free. **No credit cards**. **Map** p296 B4.

The oldest watering hole in Gazi, Gazaki is a regular hangout for the ever-sociable Greek theatre crowd. Still, the friendly atmosphere in this bustling yet relaxed bar welcomes everyone and the outside pavement tables are ideal for a long summer evening drink. The bohemian charm of Gazaki is reflected in its rustic, wooden, dark-blue decor and the sounds here are eclectic to say the least (anything from old-school rock, funk, jazz and soul to 1960s movie tunes).

Mamacas

Persefonis 41, Gazi (210 346 4984). Bus 049/B18 from Omonia to Gazi bus stop. **Open** 9.30pm-4am daily. **Admission** free. **Credit** AmEx, MC, V. **Map** p296 B4.

One of the major meeting points in lively Gazi, this atmospheric all-white island-themed bar attracts a flirty and stylish young crowd with a fondness for

Bee. *See p221.*

mingling and cocktails. After 1am, once the DJ gets into gear with a selection of deep and jazzy house, the roof opens to reveal the Athenian sky – a true summer experience.

Nipiagogio

Elasidon & Kleanthous 8, Gazi (210 345 8534). Metro Thissio, then 10min walk. **Open** 9pm-3.30am Sun-Thur; 9pm-6am Fri, Sat. **Admission** free. **No credit cards. Map** p296 B5.

Set in an old nursery school, Nipiagogio (or 'kindergarten') retains the kind of fun, carefree vibe synonymous with finger painting. Silhouetted kiddie designs line the walls and stained-glass flowers spruce up the place. A small dancefloor at the top end of the room is packed with a friendly bunch of twenty- to thirtysomethings who relive their childhood – well, sort of – to lounge and electronica. A dream-like walled garden, lit with fairy lights and floating, light-air balloons, acts as a second chill-out room; the specially selected soothing tunes are perfect for winding down.

Soul Garden

Evripidou 65, Psyrri (210 331 0907). Metro Monastiraki. **Open** 9.30pm-3.30am Mon-Thur, Sun; 9.30pm-6am Fri, Sat. **Admission** free. **Credit** DC, MC, V. **Map** p297 E4.

One of the most popular bar-restaurants in the Psyrri area, including a club on the top floor that opens only on Fridays and Saturdays. Its summer pulling power (with all ages) lies in its gorgeous garden decked out in a profusion of plants, comfy sofas and big bar that serves a range of refreshing cocktails, including one

of the best Mojitos in town. The music is a breezy blend of carefully selected chart pop, hip hop, R&B, house and electronica.

Tapas Bar

Triptolemou 44, Gazi (210 347 1844). Metro Thissio, then 10min walk. **Open** 8pm-3am Sun-Thur; 9pm-4am Fri, Sat. **Admission** free. **Credit** AmEx, MC, V. **Map** p296 B4.

One of the most interesting stops in Gazi, the small but always upbeat Tapas Bar plays more downtempo jazz and funk on weekdays when crowds turn up for a meal or a quiet drink, and spicy upbeat Latin sounds at the weekend. The drinks selection is excellent, as are the refreshing cocktails.

Southern Suburbs

These venues are the place to go for beachside summer clubbing. They are open from May until the end of September.

Akrotiri Club Restaurant

Leof Vas Georgiou B5, Agios Kosmas (210 985 9147-9). Bus A2 from Akadimias. **Open** 11pm-5am daily. **Admission** (including 1 drink) €10 Mon-Thur, Sun; €15 Fri, Sat. **Credit** AmEx, DC, MC, V.

A massive open-air club with a capacity of around 3,000, Akrotiri attracts a mixed crowd of twenty- to thirtysomethings who come to pose with a drink in hand as they gaze at the amazing sea views through thin white curtains wafting in the summer breeze. Mainstream club sounds (and a few Greek chart tunes) are the playlist staples.

Anabella

*Ethnarchou Makariou 10, Peace & Friendship
Stadium, Faliro (210 483 4190). Metro Faliro.* **Open**
10pm-5am daily. **Admission** (including 1 drink) €10
Mon-Thur, Sun; €15 Fri, Sat. **Credit** MC, V.

You'll have to navigate around the giant stadium to
reach this club – keep going and you'll find it eventually. The concept is that of a retro 1970s or early
'80s disco with a bit of up-to-date glamour thrown
in for good measure. Thirtysomethings wanting to
relive their youth come here for the old-school tunes,
the breathtaking view across the Saronic Gulf and
the summery vibe.

Balux

*Posidonos 58, Glyfada (210 894 1620). Bus A2 from
Akadimias.* **Open** 11pm-5am Wed-Sun. **Admission**
(including 1 drink) €12 Wed, Thur, Sun; €15 Fri, Sat.
Credit AmEx, MC, V.

Arguably one of the most summery of all the bars
and clubs along Athens' coastal strip, the impressive swimming pool and sea view at Balux draw a
very trendy crowd. The hip young clientele of models, athletes, artists and rich kids let their hair down
on the wooden decks (or even the sand) to mainstream and sometimes more progressive sounds.

Bebek

*Posidonos 3, Kalamaki (210 981 3950). Bus A2, 103
from Akadimias/tram Kalamaki.* **Open** 9.30pm-5am
daily. **Admission** (including 1 drink) €10 Mon-Thur,
Sun; €15 Fri, Sat. **Credit** MC, V.

This recently opened club-restaurant (or dinner club,
as it likes to call itself) attracts a thirtysomething
crowd. The interior is full of mirrors and twirling
blue spotlights, while the outside area with wooden
decks and a marina view offers a romantic summer
spot for a meal or drink. The music is mainstream,
which in this case means you'll hear both foreign
and Greek chart-toppers.

Destijl

*Karamanli 14, Voula (210 895 9645). Bus E2, A2
from Akadimias to the bus terminal.* **Open** 11am-
5am daily. **Admission**. **Credit** MC, V.

Style and attitude are vital in places like this, so
remember to dress sharp. Boasting one of the best
sea views of all the seaside venues and a gorgeous
beachside cocktail bar, Destijl has been redecorated
in a style inspired by the Costa Carayes in Mexico.
Plush sofas, huge lamps and metal swallows over
the DJ box complete the picture. The DJs crank out
a steady stream of mainstream and Greek hits.

Envy Mediterraneo

*Platia Agia Kosma, Helliniko (210 985 2994/mobile
6937 033303). Bus A2 from Akadimias/tram 1st
Agia Kosma.* **Open** 11.30pm-5am Mon-Sat; 9pm-4am
Sun. **Admission** (including 1 drink) €10 Mon-Fri;
€15 Sat, Sun. **No credit cards**.

Greek youngsters love this mainstream open-air
club, which is swathed in shades of pink, fuchsia,
white and light green. Book one of the private tables
under the tents on the beach for that extra summertime vibe. Wednesday is Greek Hits Night so steer
clear if that's not your bag. Opt for the Sunday
Sunset Parties instead, which start at 9pm and crank
out anything and everything from 1980s and pop to
R&B and house.

Fuego

*Omirou 69, Nea Smyrni (210 931 9075). Metro
Tavros, then bus 219.* **Open** 10.30pm-3.30am Wed-Fri,
Sun; 11pm-4am Sat. Closed mid June-Sept. **Admission**
(including 1 drink) €10. **No credit cards**.

The lively crowds that frequent this popular dance
club invariably get down to some frantic Latin dancing. With its vibrant Latin American decor and live
music it's sure to spice up your evening. Tuesday is
Brazilian night while on Thursdays Fuego plays
host to traditional Cuban bands. If you're not too
confident about your dance moves, you can take
dance lessons every Wednesday and Sunday.

Galea

*Karamanli 4, Voula (210 894 4990). Bus A2 from
Akadimias.* **Open** 10pm-4am daily. **Admission** free.
Credit AmEx, MC, V.

A mainstream club that attracts a mixed crowd of
VIPs and VIP-wannabes, Galea is a massive yet
inviting space where the beautiful people get down
to house, R&B and Greek pop. The decor has an air
of the aristocratic about it and features impressive,
lit-up marble stands and an attractive veranda.

Island

*Limanakia Vouliagmenis (210 965 3563). Metro
Dafni, then bus 171 or A2 to the bus terminal, then
change to 114 and get off at Limanakia bus stop.*
Open 9.30pm-4am Mon-Fri; 9.30pm-5am Sat, Sun.
Admission free. **Credit** AmEx, MC, V.

It may be a long trek to get to Island's enchanting
location but it's certainly worth it: the amazing sea
view will make you feel like you're on an Aegean
island. The minimal decor blends elements from
various Mediterranean summer destinations including Corsica, Barcelona, Tangiers and St Tropez.
Although pricey, snappily dressed customers at this
trendy venue can dine at the finger-food bar and
dance under the stars in what is a lush spot for a
romantic night out. Island attracts all ages with
tunes ranging from loungey ethnic beats and chill-
out house to disco. It regularly issues its own CD
compilations of summer anthems.

Mao

*Diadoxou Pavlou, Glyfada (210 894 4048). Bus A2,
B3 from Akadimias, Paralia Glyfadas.* **Open** 10pm-
3am Mon-Thur, Sun; 10pm-5am Fri, Sat. **Admission**
(including 1 drink) €10 Mon-Thur, Sun; €15 Fri, Sat.
Credit MC, V.

One of the most popular mainstream clubs in Psyrri
moves to a massive 5,000-capacity venue in the
southern suburbs for the summer. The decor is
inspired by the Far East (with a modern edge) and
the predominantly twentysomething crowd gathers
round a swimming pool surrounded by sofas and
recliners to the strains of mainstream club sounds.

Arts & Entertainment

Molly Malone's
Giannitsopoulou 8, Glyfada (210 894 4247). Bus B3 from Akadimias/tram Platia Esperidon. **Open** noon-4am daily. **Admission** free. **Credit** AmEx, DC, MC, V.

The best pint in Athens, no doubt about it. Anyone homesick for their local back home will be as right as rain after a visit to Molly Malone's. The Irish atmosphere is authentic and friendly, and you'll find a good selection of beers (Murphy's, Kilkenny) as well as a range of Irish malts (Bushmills, Powers). If you're feeling peckish, you can also sample the agreeable pub food, which includes (what else?) fish and chips.

Skipper's
Marina Kalamakiou, Kalamaki (no phone). Bus B2 to Edem bus stop/tram Marina Alimou. **Open** 9am-4am daily. **Admission** free. **No credit cards**.

Though this venue is a bit out of the way – a five-minute walk from the main road – it is pretty impressive: built to resemble the deck of a large ocean liner, Skipper's comes complete with a tall protruding mast with fairy lights running down each side that can be seen from afar. Get there early on Friday and Saturday nights if you want to secure a seat on deck. Majestic flamenco and salsa, plus occasional trip hop beats, attract a more mature pack.

Venue
Next to Riba's, 30th km of the Athens–Sounion coastal road, Varkiza (210 897 1163/210 897 0333). Bus E22 from Akadimias. **Open** 11.30pm-5am Fri, Sat. **Admission** (including 1 drink) €15 . **Credit** MC, V.

Perhaps the ultimate dance club on the seafront due to its strong following of young, hip clubbers and its ability to attract well-known international DJs. It might be a long trek to get here along the winding Athens–Sounion road but the location is beautifully deserted. Don't forget your sunglasses – the music doesn't stop here until well after the sun comes up.

Northern Suburbs

Cosmos
Omirou 8, Neo Psychiko (210 672 9150). Bus 450, 550/trolleybus 13. **Open** 10am-4am Mon-Sat. **Admission** free. **Credit** AmEx, MC, V.

The New York vibe and comfy sofas at this swish bar-restaurant attract well-to-do young professionals and VIP guests who chatter among themselves to mainstream and house sounds. The low lighting highlights the original art by Jeff Koons on the walls. The narrow inside bar opens up to a small but cool open-air courtyard.

Local
Christou Lada & Olympou 21, Kifisia (210 801 8236). Bus 550. **Open** 9pm-1.30am Mon-Sat. **Admission** free. **Credit** AmEx, MC, V.

Perhaps the funkiest and hippest of the bars in the northern suburbs, Local attracts an affluent crowd from the surrounding area. Make a beeline for the small, verdant garden and while the night away with a cool selection of reggae, Latin and soul sounds.

Wabi
Eleftherotrias 25, Politeia (210 801 7673). Metro Kifissia, then bus 524. **Open** 10am-3am daily. **Admission** free. **Credit** DC, MC, V.

The minimal decor of this Zen-inspired bar in the shady northern suburb of Politeia attracts a stylish crowd. Mainstream house and lounge sounds are the order of the day.

Western Suburbs

Enzzo de Cuba
Agias Paraskevis 70, Bournazi (210 578 2610). Metro Aghios Antonios. **Open** 9am-4am Mon-Fri, Sun; 10am-7am Sat. **Admission** free. **Credit** V.

This popular bar-restaurant sways to Latin rhythms every night. Located on the most popular square in Athens' western suburbs, the authentic decor evokes the atmosphere of a Cuban neighbourhood. Take in a live tango and Latin show or lounge on white sofas for a great view of the lively goings-on in Bournazi's main square. The mostly young crowd you'll find here comes from the surrounding suburbs with tequila drinking and flirting in mind.

Piraeus

Lemon
Akti Themistokleous 154, Piraiki (210 428 1164). Metro Piraeus, then bus 904. **Open** 10am-1am Mon-Thur, Sun; 10am-2am Fri, Sat. **Admission** free. **No credit cards**.

An ideal place for chilling out in Piraeus, not least because of the amazing sea view. The pop art decoration at Lemon creates a playful atmosphere and the adventurous electronica beats emanating from the speakers are sure to grab your attention.

Attica

Atlantis Club
Halkoutsiou, Skala Oropou (229 503 1832/229 503 4120). Athina-Skala Oropou or Athina-Dilesi bus from Mavromateon Street. **Open** 11pm-4am daily. **Admission** *Sat only* (including 1 drink) €15. **Credit** AmEx, MC, V.

An ideal choice if you're staying in the northern suburbs. Atlantis is basically two clubs in one. The open-air club-restaurant is decked out in white and attracts a thirty- to fortysomething crowd. The music policy is strictly mainstream with 1980s and '90s hits as well as Greek chart-toppers. The indoor club next door attracts a much younger clientele that congregates around the large circular outdoor bar for pumping house beats that occasionally give way to the odd Greek pop tune on Fridays and Saturdays.

A night in Athens

Gazaki.

Athens – so much to see, so much to do. But it's after the sun sets that things really start hotting up. The hedonistic pursuit of pleasure has always been integral to the Athenian way of life. After midnight you'll find city dwellers flocking around favourite watering holes like gazelles at an oasis. For those seeking to sample the best on offer, a meze-like pick 'n' mix approach is thoroughly recommended.

Kick the night off with a decadent cocktail at the impossibly cool **Galaxy** bar (*see p220*). The spectacular bird's eye view of that monumental heap of stone also known as the Acropolis is worth the price of the (yummy) drinks alone. Then, while you still have cash to burn, tear yourself away from the stunning views and pop up the road to the intimate **Briki** (*see p219*), where the eclectic tunes and mellow atmosphere will set you up nicely for a bit of a boogie.

Suitably warmed up, drop by Kolonaki's über-trendy **Mommy** (*see p220*) for a blast of 1960s-inspired Technicolor kitsch before heading on to the fabulously funky **Bar Guru Bar** (*see p219*). This lively oriental-themed bar-cum-club bubbles over with an infectious feel-good atmosphere guaranteed to get even

the most bashful bums wiggling with abandon. Afterwards, escape to the island-esque garden of the nearby **Soul Garden** (*see p222*) and recharge your batteries in the Club Tropicana surroundings.

No nocturnal Athenian visit is complete without an exploration of Psyrri's labyrinthine streets, so wonder freely through the winding alleys, taking in the heady scents and sounds of the bustling, bar-infested area on your way to Gazi. Once in the neon-edged shadows of the towering former gas works-turned-arts centre, check out **Mamacas** (*see p221*) for a dose of upmarket island-flavoured fun. If you're looking for something a little more relaxed, then join the gregarious crowds at the bohemian **Gazaki** (*see p221*) just around the corner.

With morning now almost upon us, step back in time with a visit to the wonderfully laid-back and very slightly surreal **Nipiagogio** (*see p222*). Exhaust yourself shaking your thang to the tunes of yesteryear before moving out into the dream-like garden of this former kindergarten to wind down and watch the sun come up. Then it's back to your bed, for tomorrow is another big day.

Sport & Fitness

Football still reigns supreme in post-Olympics Athens.

Keep on running: Athens has plenty of hi-tech facilities for amateur athletes.

It has to be said that many modern Greeks do not follow in the footsteps – fitness-wise – of their once-athletic ancestors. Today's typical Hellene tends to jump behind the steering wheel for a trip to the kiosk, and take the lift rather than walk up a single flight of stairs. But this nonchalant attitude to fitness belies a nationwide obsession with sport – albeit one that is practised from the comfort of the sofa.

Spectator sports

Football, basketball, volleyball and water polo compete (in that order) for attention in a country of paltry stadium attendance but generous television coverage. In the wake of Olympic success, athletics, gymnastics and weightlifting have also acquired an important fan base.

Athens alone boasts nine sports dailies, not counting an equivalent number of metro handouts, betting papers and fanzines. The papers' allegiance is evenly distributed among the capital's football powerhouses – AEK, Olympiacos and Panathinaikos – and widely differing accounts of the same Sunday match are not uncommon.

For its amateur athletes, the city has its fair share of pools, sailing marinas and open-air, multi-sports grounds. The city marathon

(www.segas.gr), a 42-kilometre (26-mile) uphill slog from the town bearing that name to central Athens, attracts thousands of runners every November. There is also a wealth of five-a-side courts, particularly popular among office employees looking for a post-work match.

Lastly, the construction of some two dozen new facilities for the Athens 2004 Olympics has significantly boosted the capital's sports potential, although future public access to many of these costly arenas is currently up for debate.

Football

Athens and the port of Piraeus dominate the Greek first division (A' Ethniki Katigoria), a championship that 16 teams contest for a few months before the silverware invariably ends up with AEK Athens, Olympiacos Piraeus or Panathinaikos. The last time one of the Big Three did not win the tournament was in 1988, when Larissa FC, a club from rural central Greece, pulled off an upset tantamount to Greece's Euro 2004 victory in Portugal.

But the Greek league has at least improved in one key respect – in contrast to recent years, when paying to watch a small side face one of the giants was a complete waste of time, the big clubs have ceased to have it easy. In a tournament still racked by rumours of match-fixing and other shady dealings, this is a measure of consolation.

AEK Athens
Grammou 69-71, Marousi (210 612 1371/www.aekfc.gr).
A club originally formed by refugees from Asia Minor who fled to Athens following the 1922 ethnic purge of Greeks in Turkey, AEK traditionally carry the old Byzantine Empire symbol – a double-headed eagle – on their shirts. Currently homeless after the demolition of their derelict ground in Nea Filadelfia, the team have rented out the Olympic Stadium (OAKA sports complex, Spyrou Loui Avenue, nearest metro Irini) until a new ground is built.

Olympiacos Piraeus
Platia Alexandras, Zea Marina, Piraeus (210 414 3000/www.olympiacos.gr).
Historically the club of sailors and dock workers – hence their nickname 'anchovies' – Olympiacos sealed a deal with the state in 2003 to tear down and reconstruct their home pitch, Karaiskaki Stadium, in time for the Athens 2004 Olympics. In return, they secured a 49-year lease on Greece's best football ground (Poseidonos Avenue, nearest metro Faliro).

Panathinaikos
Irodou Attikou 12A, Marousi (210 809 3630/www.pao.gr).
Panathinaikos is traditionally linked to the wealthier elements of Athenian society; nevertheless, until May 2005 they played in one of the capital's most run-down stadiums, the Apostolos Nikolaidis (also known as Leoforos, 'the Avenue'). The Greens have been talking about building their own place for years, but in summer 2005 the team's managers decided to rent out the Olympic Stadium (OAKA Sports Complex, Spyrou Loui Avenue, nearest metro Irini) until this happens.

Panionios
Chrysostomou 1, Nea Smyrni (210 931 1189/www.panionios.gr).
Another team of Asia Minor origin founded in 1890, Panionios are among Greece's oldest sports clubs and a regular purveyor of talent. Sadly, the team's Nea Smyrni stadium missed out on the Olympic bonanza. Built in 1939, the ground feels nearly as venerable as the historic club itself (1 Chrysostomou Street, nearest tram station Megalou Alexandrou).

Basketball

Greece's favourite sport in the late 1980s and '90s, basketball owed its popularity to the Greek national team's unexpected capture of the European championship in 1987. The Greek A1 league briefly ranked as Europe's most competitive in the mid '90s, before a glut of mediocre talent and an excess of TV coverage sent bored fans back to football.

AEK Athens
Gravias 4, Marousi (210 616 1380/www.aekbc.gr).
AEK were the pioneers of Greek basketball glory in Europe, winning the 1968 European Cup in front of 80,000 home fans at the all-marble stadium built for the 1896 Olympics. The club now play at the brand-new Galatsi Indoor Hall (113 Veikou Avenue, Galatsi, buses 608, 444), purpose-built for the gymnastics tournament at the 2004 Olympics.

Olympiacos Piraeus
Platia Alexandras, Zea Marina, Piraeus (210 414 3000/www.Olympiacos.gr).
The sole Greek club ever to have won a 'triple crown' of titles – the European championship, domestic championship and cup in 1997 – Olympiacos enjoyed unparalleled home success during the '90s, with five straight league titles between 1993 and 1997. Their fortunes have since taken a turn for the worse, following the management's decision to focus on the club's football section. The team play at the renovated Peace and Friendship Stadium (Poseidonos Avenue, nearest metro Faliro).

Panathinaikos
Kifissias 38, Maroussi (210 610 7160-1/www.paobc.gr).
With 25 domestic and three European championships under their belt, Panathinaikos are Greece's top basketball club. The first Greek team to win the European championship in 1996, the Greens have since built a reputation for no-nonsense efficiency, snapping up the best players without bothering too much about the cost. The club play at the Indoor Hall of the OAKA Olympic Stadium complex in Maroussi (Spyrou Loui Avenue, nearest metro Irini).

Active sports

Bungee jumping

Zulu Bungy
Corinth Canal, Corinth, 75km south of Athens (210 514 7051/mobile 6946 301462 English, German, French, Italian/6932 702535 Greek, English/www.zulubungy.com). Trains from Larissa station (a shuttle bus from Athens is due to operate in 2005). **Open** *Apr-mid June, mid Sept-end Oct noon-6pm Sat, Sun; mid June-mid Sept noon-7pm Wed-Sun.* **Rates** €50 per jump; plus €12 if you want a VHS/DVD recording your fall.
The Corinth Canal cuts mainland Greece off from the Peloponnese peninsula – jumping from the sheer, steep banks into the depths below is very dramatic.

Gyms

Athens Hilton – Sport Academy
Leof Vas Sofias 46, Kolonaki (210 725 7072). Metro Evangelismos. **Open** *6am-11pm Mon-Fri; 9am-9pm Sat, Sun.* **Day pass** €50. **Credit** AmEx, DC, MC, V. **Map** p299 J5.

The 2004 Olympics has raised the fan base for sports such as gymnastics.

The Hilton Sport Academy opened its doors in 2004. The price tag may seem steep, but included in the price is a fully equipped gym with personal trainers on site, an indoor pool with hydrotherapy available, a sauna and steam room. That isn't bad value for lounging around with the rich and famous.

Joe Weider Gym

Stadiou & Korai 4, Historic Centre (210 324 1441/ www.joeweider.gr). Metro Panepistimio. **Open** 7am-11pm Mon-Fri; 9am-5pm Sat; noon-8pm Sun. **Day pass** €15. **Credit** AmEx, DC, MC, V. **Map** p297 F4.
The Joe Weider Company has gyms and spas throughout Greece. The gyms are clean and airy, with a good range of up-to-date equipment, aerobics classes and a sauna. All welcome day guests.

Universal Studios

Xenofontos 32, Glyfada (210 963 5300). Tram Glyfada. **Open** 8am-1am Mon-Fri; 9am-1am Sat; 10am-1am Sun. **Day pass** €15. **Credit** AmEx, MC, V.
If you are into pumping iron before heading to the beach, this Glyfada gym is the place for you. It offers jacuzzi, sauna, aerobics and yoga classes.

Mini-soccer

Mini-soccer fields have been sprouting up all around Athens recently, attracting mostly men and a few women, who proudly don the kit of their favourite teams and head on to the synthetic pitches in teams of between five and eight. Pitches can be booked at a cost of around €60-€80 per hour. So, should you and your friends fancy a kickabout, call one of the numbers listed below and book yourselves a game. The people in charge should be able to organise some opposition.

Paradise

Metamorfoseos 100, Agios Sotiras, Acharnes, Northern Suburbs (210 246 6466/www.minifootball paradise.gr). Bus A9. **Open** 9am-1am daily. **Rates** €65/75mins. **No credit cards.**
The club also houses a spa, not included in the price.

Protasof Club

Kapodistriou 2 & Marathonomachon, Cheroma, Vari, Southern Suburbs (210 9653 400). Metro Dafni, then bus 171. **Open** 4pm-midnight Mon-Fri; 5-10pm Sat, Sun. **Rates** €60/hr. **No credit cards.**

Running

The old Panathenaic Stadium (*see p116*) is popular with joggers, who either use the track on the surrounding hill or run up and down the marble stadium's steps. The National Gardens are a reasonable central option, though they can often be people- and pushchair-choked. If you prefer a more sociable jogging experience, try going out with the Athens branch of the Hash House Harriers. Entirely non-competitive and requiring no level of fitness, the ad hoc group meets weekly at 7pm on Mondays during summer and 11am on Sundays in winter. An hour's run or walk around town or into the surrounding hills is followed by a taverna meal and drinks – this is as much about socialising as exercising. Visitors are welcome; you can often cadge a lift from a metro station. Contact Brian Kirman on 6946 969154 (mobile), visit the Harriers' website (www.athenshash.com) for the next featured run or look for listings in the *Athens News*.

Scuba diving

For more watersports, *see pp123-126* **Beaches**.

Divers Club – Marathon Bay

Avenue Marathon 417, Marathon (229 406 9196/ 229 409 7477/mobile 6977 223391/www.divers club.gr). Buses from Pedio to Areos. **Open** *May-Oct* 9am-9pm. **Rates** €50-€80 per dive, all equipment included. **Credit** AmEx, MC, V.

Specialising in shipwreck diving, the Divers Club organises excursions in Attica and South Euboic

Fixing the game

When Greece captain Theodore Zagorakis lifted the Euro 2004 trophy to the rafters of Lisbon's Da Luz Stadium in July of that year, fans at home held their collective breath. The Greek team had just done the impossible: romped their way through Portugal to emerge as victors, earning a place in history as the most unfancied side ever to win the European Championship.

The Greeks hailed their triumph as providing a unique opportunity to clean up their own football act. When close to a million Athenians lined the streets for the national squad's return that summer, officials saw a chance to breathe new life into a sport long plagued by fan violence and appalling conditions, both on and off the pitch.

So far, success has been limited. In a league where fans are used to acting with impunity, change comes slowly. A succession of football laws has brought little response from the police, who see arrested hooligans released with suspended sentences a few days later. Clubs have also been accused of using their supporter armies to coerce the government into granting favours. At a February 2004 Panathinaikos match, for example, fans demanding a state-sponsored stadium carried banners reading: 'Either a stadium now or on 7 March [the date of the national election].' Although it's not clear what effect this kind of threat has or the extent of the club's involvement, it's unlikely that the banners would have appeared without club permission. Panathinaikos are not alone in challenging the government. In July 2004 some 5,000 AEK fans marched in central Athens to demand that the government save their team from relegation to the fourth division because of unpaid debts to the state. And in early 2005 Olympiakos fans were talking about a street demo in central Athens after points were docked for

stadium violence. The points were eventually restored. Was there a connection? Who knows? What is clear, though, is that clubs have taken no action to stamp out the protests and claim to be powerless to rein them in.

If Euro 2004 gave a kick-start to improving the game and its environment, hosting the 2004 Olympics arguably did even more to fix the Greek league – literally. Having poured millions of euros into new stadiums, the government now expects clubs to pay for damage. Feeling the pinch in their coffers, many teams are making more effort to keep their fans in order. Better still, a camera network installed for Olympic security purposes is beginning to bear fruit on the violence front, helping the police identify repeat offenders and paving the way for a future hooligan database.

Sadly, the improvements have so far made a difference only in stadiums used during the Olympics. At other grounds, conditions are pretty much the same as they were before the Games, when in the words of one top club official, 'there was hardly a stadium with a decent toilet'.

On the other hand, Greek football wasn't built on posh facilities, gourmet food and smiling toddlers. It's passion for the game that counts, and there is certainly no shortage of that here. To enjoy a trouble-free game, a tip is to avoid the (usually cheaper) seats behind the goals. The middle seats are generally a better bet. Once inside the ground, don't fret if you can't understand the chants. In most cases, they have something to do with sexual acts involving the opponents' immediate family. One key term is *malaka*, which can be loosely translated as 'wanker'. But for the most part, the word you'll want to catch – goal – will be in English anyway, as are 'foul', 'offside' and 'penalty'.

Bay. Courses are available for beginners and experienced divers and the club also has a private beach at Zouberi in Nea Makri, where other sports are available too.

Vythos

Leof Eleftheriou Venizelou 56, Nea Smyrni, Southern Suburbs (210 933 3260/www.vithos.com). Bus 110. **Open** 8am-3pm Mon, Wed, Sat; 8-9pm Tue, Thur, Fri. Closed Sun. **Rates** 2wk courses from €260. **Credit** AmEx, DC, MC, V.

As well as organising classes for beginners, Vythos operates experienced divers' excursions around the coast of Attica. The cost varies for short dives, depending on the equipment needed, while the two- to three-week courses start at €260.

Swimming

Summertime in central Athens can be sweltering, so it's nice to know that there are plenty of pools open to the public where you can cool off. Though hotel pools are rather pricey, you may find them preferable to their municipal counterparts owing to the excessive admission bureaucracy of the latter.

Athens Hilton

Leof Vas Sofias 46, Kolonaki (210 728 1000). Metro Evangelismos. **Open** *May-Sept outdoor pool* 10am-6pm daily. Closed Oct-Apr. *Year-round indoor pool* 10am-6pm daily. **Rates** €20 Mon-Fri; €35 Sat, Sun. **Credit** AmEx, DC, MC, V. **Map** p299 J5.

The Hilton's impressive outdoor swimming pool – the largest in central Athens – was an integral part of the hotel's €96 million refurbishment and re-opened in August 2003 with a swanky party. If you want to lounge around the pool with the in crowd, this is the place to go. And at €20 per day during the week, it isn't bad value for the luxury.

Athens Municipal Swimming Pool

Leandrou & Iphigenias, Kolokynthous, Northern Suburbs (210 515 3726). Metro Sepolia. **Open** 8.30am-6pm Mon-Fri; 9am-2pm Sat, Sun. Closed Aug. **Rates** €24 for 13 swims per mth. Members only. **No credit cards.**

To swim here you'll need a health certificate from a pathologist or a cardiologist, another one from a dermatologist, two passport-sized photos and a photocopy of your passport. So, if you're only in Athens for a short stay, you're better off heading to one of the hotel pools.

Holiday Inn

Michalakoupolou 50, Kolonaki (210 727 8000). Metro Megaro Moussikis. **Open** *May-Oct* 10am-7pm daily. Closed Nov-Apr. **Rates** €25 (towels included). **Credit** AmEx, DC, MC, V.

The Holiday Inn's pool isn't exactly big, but with superb views of Lycabettus Hill, its smart rooftop setting (complete with a bar and restaurant) is a great place to cool down and unwind while Athens life continues apace beneath you.

Tennis

Pete Sampras may be the son of Greek immigrants, but Eleni Daniilidou is the nearest Greek tennis has to its own star. There are plenty of courts in Athens for budding Serenas and Leytons to practise. As well as the tennis courts at the public beaches of Voula A and Attica Vouliagmeni (for both, *see pp123-126*), the following courts are worth a try.

Athens Tennis Club

Leof Vas Olgas 2, Historic Centre (210 921 5630). Metro Syntagma. **Open** *Non-members* 7am-2pm Mon-Fri. **Rates** *Non-members* €15 per person per hr. **No credit cards. Map** p301 F6.

This centrally located upmarket club has ten outdoor courts (six clay, four artificial grass, all floodlit). There are also three squash courts and a gym. Such facilities come at a price.

Ilioupolis Municipal Court

Angelou Evert 1 & Keffalinias, Ilioupoli, Southern Suburbs (210 993 0452). Bus 237. **Open** 3.30-11pm Mon-Fri; 9am-1pm, 5-10pm Sat, Sun. **Rates** free.

These five clay and three hard courts are free to use and therefore very busy.

Ten-pin bowling

Athens Bowling Centre

Patision 177, Patisia, Northern Suburbs (210 865 6930/210 866 5573). Metro Ano Patissia. **Open** 10am-2am daily. **Rates** €4.50 per game Mon-Fri; €5.50 per game Sat, Sun; €2.50-€3.50 per game concessions. **No credit cards.**

Recently renovated eight-lane alley that, while perhaps not Athens' best, is certainly its most central.

Super Bowl

Kanapiteri 10, Rendi, Western Athens (210 561 3447/210 561 3678). Bus B18. **Open** 10am-2am daily. **Rates** €5 per game; €3.50 per game Mon-Thur am; €3 per game concessions. **Credit** AmEx, MC, V.

This 30-lane, well-equipped modern bowling centre is worth the short trip out of town.

Trekking

Trekking Hellas

Filellinon 7, Plaka (210 331 0323/www.trekking.gr). Metro Syntagma. **Open** 9am-5pm Mon-Fri. **Rates** €20-€70. **Credit** AmEx, MC, V. **Map** p297/p301 F5.

Attica's countryside will come as a pleasant surprise to those who thought Greece was nothing but sun, sea and sand. Trekking Hellas's simple yet interesting four-hour trek close to Athens is highly recommended. Starting in the foothills of Mount Parnitha at the Church of St Triada, it takes you through Skipiza spring and ends up at the Bafi lodge. It costs €20 for a group of six to eight people and includes a picnic lunch.

Theatre & Dance

Ancient drama is joined by a lively experimental theatre scene.

First-class theatre at **To Treno sto Rouf** – a converted train carriage. *See p235.*

It seems fitting that the capital of Greece, birthplace of ancient drama, should have a flourishing modern theatre scene. Athens today has around 170 venues – many of them brand new – that host productions ranging from comedies to contemporary tragedies, where exuberant Broadway musicals meet with experimental audio-visual performances, where the likes of Shakespeare, Chekhov and Ibsen co-exist with the ancient dramatists.

When it comes to the venues themselves, the ones located closer to the centre of town (in Syntagma, Panepistimio and Kolonaki) combine luxurious facilities with expensive productions. You shouldn't hesitate, though, to visit the smaller but cosier theatres in areas like Monastiraki, Psyrri and Gazi.

Athens hasn't forgotten its ancient dramatic heritage. The Athens Festival and nationwide Hellenic Festival provide unique opportunities to see ancient drama in ancient surroundings. *See below* and *p233* **Classics in situ**.

SEASONS AND FESTIVALS

The theatre season runs from mid October to the end of April, after which many companies leave town to tour the provinces. In summer, focus shifts to the open-air theatres (Park, Alsos and Athineon) in the triangle made by Leof Alexandras, Patision and Prigiponison, which usually host light comedies or *epitheorises*, a theatrical descendant of Aristophanian comedy with sharp political and social commentary punctuated by musical numbers.

If you are in town during the Athens Festival (*see p189*), you can watch ancient Greek drama staged by guest companies (some from as far away as Japan) in the Odeon of Herodes Atticus (popularly known as the Herodeion) or the Lycabettus Theatre. During the festival, the Herodeion also stages various other shows and concerts. Another venue for classical drama is Epidaurus, an ancient site situated a couple of hours' drive from the city (*see p233* **Classics in situ**).

Costume drama: **Ethniko Theatro** – Athens' National Theatre. *See p233.*

TICKETS AND TIMES

Many mainstream theatres are closed on Mondays and Tuesdays. Performances start late, at around 8.30-9.30pm, and at weekends there are additional matinées. Shows popular with young audiences usually have an after-midnight performance on Fridays or Saturdays. Ticket prices are around €15-€25, with the cheapest offered by the National Theatre and for matinées at all venues. Students pay a little over half price. You can buy your tickets directly from theatre box offices or book in advance by credit card at an agency for an additional 16.5 per cent charge. For most of the shows at the Megaron Mousikis, Olympia Theatre and Herodeion and Lycabettus, you should book as far as a month in advance.

Tickethouse

Panepistimiou 42 (210 360 8366/www.tickethouse.gr). Metro Panepistimio. **Open** 10am-6pm Mon, Wed; 10am-10pm Tue, Thur, Fri; 10.30am-4pm Sat. **No credit cards. Map** p297 F4.
This is a useful central walk-in office, but payment is cash only.

Major venues & theatres

Alma

Agiou Konstantinou & Akominatou 15-17, Omonia (210 522 0100). Metro Omonia. **Open** *Box office* 10am-1pm, 5-10pm Tue-Sun. Theatre closed May-Oct. **Tickets** €22; €10 concessions. **No credit cards. Map** p297 D3.

Right in the heart of the city, this new venue hosts theatre, music and dance events by artists from Greece and abroad. The 280-seat auditorium has some of the most advanced equipment in town. Its debut play was Joanna Murray-Smith's *Honour.*

Amore (Theatro tou Notou)

Prigiponison 10, Pedion Areos (210 646 8009/www. amorenotos.com). Metro Victoria. **Open** *Box office* 10am-10pm daily. Theatre closed July, Aug. **Tickets** €20; €14 concessions. **No credit cards.**
Often focusing on some of Shakespeare's less frequently staged plays (such as *King John*), but also embracing contemporary international theatre – Caryl Churchill's *Far Away* was a great success in 2005 – Amore is one of the most successful venues in the capital. It has broken through the formerly stagnant waters of the Athenian scene and offered shelter to some of the most promising young Greek talent. Its artistic directors have worked extensively throughout Europe.

Coronet

Frynis 11, Pangrati (210 701 2123/www.coronet.gr). Metro Evangelismos, then 20min walk. **Open** *Box office* 9am-9pm daily. Theatre closed May-Sept. **Tickets** prices vary. **Credit** MC, V. **Map** p299 J7.
This former cinema has been transformed into a luxurious theatre hosting a variety of companies. One of these is the Black Theatre of Prague, whose unique dream-like technique, famous among theatre fans around the world, has its roots in the 17th century and was an influence on Stanislavsky. The Czech performers use body language and mimicry so you can feel comfortable that your Greek will not be tested.

Ethniko Theatro (National Theatre)

Agiou Konstantinou 22-24, Omonia (210 522 3242/ www.n-t.gr). Metro Omonia. **Open** *Box office* 10am-1pm, 5-10pm Tue-Sun. Theatre closed June-Oct. **Tickets** €15-€20; €10 concessions. **No credit cards. Map** p297 E3.

Housed in a beautiful neo-classical building, designed by German architect Ernst Ziller, the National Theatre hosts a variety of shows – classic and modern theatre, and musicals. It has staged some innovative work: a recent production on the theatre's New Stage was Lars von Trier's *Dogville*, adapted for the stage by Christian Lolique and directed by Antonis Kalogridis. The theatre has several other locations scattered around Omonia, such as the Experimental Theatre, where productions often get rave reviews.

Club22

Leof Vouliagmenis 22, Eastern Suburbs (210 924 9814/www.club22.gr). Metro Syngrou-Fix. **Open** *Box office* 11.30am-11.30pm Mon-Fri; 1-10pm Sat; hrs vary Sun. Theatre closed May-Oct. **Tickets** prices vary. **No credit cards. Map** p301 F7.

One of the most innovative and alternative clubs in town – famous for its theme nights – Club22 hosts everything from stand-up comedy to cabaret and drag shows. After the show, the dancefloor is pumping until the early hours.

Ilisia Ntenisi

Leof Vas Sofias 54, Kolonaki (210 721 0045). Metro Megaro Mousikis. **Open** *Box office* 10am-1pm, 5-9pm Tue-Sun. Theatre closed May-Oct. **Tickets** €21-€23; €18-€21 concessions. **Credit** V.

Named after the Greek star Mimi Denisi, this is a wonderfully extravagant venue – thick red carpets, velvet seats and a huge stage – that programmes some of the most extravagant and exuberant shows in town. A short walk south of Ilisia Ntenisi, at Papadiamantopoulou 4, is an intimate studio-like venue, Ilisia Volanaki, which usually presents contemporary plays featuring the most promising young Greek actors.

Classics in situ

Seeing ancient drama in its birthplace, preferably in an amphitheatre where it would have been performed in classical times, is a quintessential Greek experience. It's best to make a summer (July-September) trip to the Ancient Theatre of Epidaurus, but there are also frequent performances in Athens during the summer months, at the Odeon of Herodes Atticus (Herodeion) or the Lycabettus Theatre.

The most commonly produced plays are Aristophanes' gender-reversal comedy *Lysistrata* and Sophocles' tragedy *Oedipus Rex*. Other works by these two writers are also common, along with works by Euripides. Theatre-goers will know that classical theatre is far from dull. At times it gives Tarantino a run for his money with its violence and wry social commentary. It is, of course, in Greek, so take a translated text with you or read the plot summary in the programme before the lights go down.

Most shows use modern theatrical conventions and technology, and they are all translated into modern Greek. They do not have an all-male cast, as they used to in the classical period, except for some Aristophanes productions. Accordingly, the actors very rarely wear masks as they used to. Costumes tend to be modern or stylised in keeping with the overall design; rarely, though, you will see the typical ancient Greek costumes (long pleated white dresses). Generally speaking, the productions stick to original conventions, which means that there's no interval: bringing cushions and refreshments is a good idea.

Renowned for its acoustics and beauty, the Ancient Theatre of Epidaurus, which dates back to the fourth century AD, has a capacity of 14,000. Coach and ferry trips there and back are arranged by Hellenic Festival organisers, and at weekends extra buses are added to the usual schedule. The Musical July Festival is held in the nearby Little Theatre of Ancient Epidaurus. Peformances at the Lycabettus Theatre and Herodeion are part of the Athens Festival, the Hellenic Festival's urban incarnation. For more details, *see p189*.

Hellenic Festival Box Office

Panepistimiou 39, Historic Centre (210 928 2900/www.greekfestival.gr). Metro Panepistimio. **Open** 8.30am-4pm Mon-Fri; 9am-2.30pm Sat. **Credit** MC, V. **Map** p297/p301 F5.

Tickets for the Epidaurus Festival are available here, at the Herodeion box office and at Epidaurus's two box offices, which open two hours before the performance. Credit card bookings are accepted on the above number until 4pm on the day of the performance.

Odou Kykladon

Kefallinias & Kikladon 11, Northern Suburbs (210 821 7877). Metro Victoria. **Open** *Box office* 10.30am-1.30pm, 5-8pm Tue-Sun. Theatre closed June-Nov. **Tickets** €20; €14 concessions. **No credit cards**. The artistic director of this venue is Lefteris Vogiatzis, one of the country's most acclaimed directors. The theatre has staged both foreign and Greek,

and modern and classical, drama. Molière's *Les Femmes Savantes* was a great success in 2004.

Theseion

Tournavitou 7, Keramikos (210 325 5444). Metro Thissio. **Open** *Box office* 5-9pm Mon, Wed-Sun. Theatre closed July-Aug. **Tickets** €20; €14 concessions. **No credit cards**. **Map** p297 D4.

Movers & shapers
Dimitris Papaioannou

Director of the opening and closing ceremonies of the Athens 2004 Olympics.

When Dimitris Papaioannou was chosen to direct the opening and closing ceremonies of the Athens Olympics, it was an inspired but unconventional choice. Though feted at home and abroad as one of the most exciting contemporary choreographers around, Papaioannou's iconoclastic style was a world away from the average kitsch Olympic extravaganza.

A former painter (he studied under Yannis Tsarouchis) and comic artist (he scooped first prize at the Marseilles Comics Biennale in 1991), the consistent feature of his varied career has been a desire to experiment. 'Comics were a way for me to tell stories through images,' he explains. 'Then I discovered contemporary dance, which allowed me to tell stories that evolve in real time and space.' Big-money mega-productions, however, were not on his

agenda. 'That territory of big, mainstream shows is not something I ever really intended to pursue.'

In 1986 Papaioannou co-founded the Omada Edafous company with dancer Angeliki Stellatou. With sell-out shows, from *Medea*, staged on water, to *Forever*, featuring a romantic duet between two male dancers in a gorilla suit and tutu, Omada Edafos pioneered the Greek modern dance explosion of the early 1990s. Papaioannou later worked with many leading Greek artists, from actress Irene Papas to pop singer Haris Alexiou, before landing the artistic directorship of the Athens Olympics.

Papaioannou's spectacular shows, watched by five billion viewers worldwide, were hugely influential in the rebranding of Greece. He is modest about his achievements and cagey about his future plans. 'After three and a half years of being isolated and dedicated to a specific goal, right now I need the rest.' But Renaissance man Papaioannou is unlikely to rest on his laurels for long. Next year, he plans to stage a 'live show' featuring Greek and international performers. He may even take to the stage again.

Despite a flurry of offers from abroad, for now Papaioannou cannot imagine leaving the city he has always called home. 'Athens is a monstrous, chaotic city that you can easily fall in love with. It will never be a pretty, civilised city for people to come to with their families. It should be visited for its frantic, wonderful energy, and for its monuments.' He believes the Games created a cleaner, though just as vibrant, city. 'Last year, Athens was the centre of the world's attention, but nobody visited because of paranoia about terrorism. I hope this year more people will come to see the new face of Athens.'

This minimalist venue, very close to the Acropolis, is unique in Athens. It hosts one of the city's most experimental and internationally renowned theatre companies, the Theseum Ensemble. One of its productions, *The National Anthem*, which ran for two years in Athens and abroad, has won various awards in local and foreign theatre festivals. In 2005 the Theseum Ensemble presented *2004*, a symbolic piece reflecting on the effect of the Olympics and other world events such as 9/11 on ordinary life.

To Treno sto Rouf

Leof Konstantinoupoleos & Petrou Ralli, Rouf (210 529 8922/mobile 6937 604988). Metro Thissio, then 15min walk. **Open** *Box office* 10am-2pm, 6-9pm Tue-Sun. **Tickets** €20; €14 concessions. **No credit cards. Map** p296/p300 A5.

A carriage of a train has been transformed into a venue. Shows are followed by a candlelit dinner in an Orient Express atmosphere.

Dance

The first Athens International Dance Festival, held in 2004 and supported by the Cultural Olympiad as part of the celebrations for the Athens Games, was hailed as a great success, offering talented Greek artists the chance to 'share' stages with some of their more internationally known colleagues. This wasn't the city's first dance event: mini-festivals were already taking place regularly in venues such as the post-industrial Roes and the romantic Dora Stratou Garden Theatre.

Classical ballet remains the city's missing link, though, and there is little local ballet activity. Megaron Mousikis and the Olympia Theatre usually host foreign guest companies during the winter.

THE COMPANIES

Groups to look out for include the Dimitris Papaioannou's well-established Omada Edafous; Konstantinou Rigou's alternative Octana; Ermi Malkotsi, Dimitri Sotiriou and Kiki Baka's Sinequanon; Ioanna Portolou's Griffon; and newcomers such as Katerina Papageorgiou's AdLib and Fotis Nikolaou's X-it.

Venues & festivals

Dora Stratou Garden Theatre

Filopappou Hill, Acropolis (central box office 210 921 4650/www.grdance.org). Metro Akropoli, then 15min walk. **Open** *Central box office (Skoliou 8, off Adrianou 122, Plaka)* 8-10.30pm Tue-Fri. Theatre closed Oct-May. **Performances** 9.30pm Tue-Sat, 8.30pm Sun. **Tickets** €15. **Credit** MC, V. **Map** p300 C7.

Founded by Dora Stratou, a cornerstone of the movement to keep traditional Greek dance alive, this venue is known as 'the living museum of Greek dance'. The 900-seat garden theatre is located in the beautiful surroundings of Filopappou Hill. Dances, songs and music are presented in the form they were (or are still) performed in the villages where they originated, thanks to Stratou's meticulous research. Even the costumes are museum pieces, handmade in villages a century ago. Dora Stratou also offers workshops in Greek folk dance and culture, with English-speaking instructors. The daily programme includes dance classes, visits to the theatre's extensive wardrobe of over 2,500 village-made costumes and entrance to the evening's performance.

Kalamata International Dance Festival

Pan Kessari 6, Kalamata (27210 83086/www. kalamatadancefestival.gr). **Tickets** €20; €15 concessions. **Credit** MC, V.

Trisha Brown, Jerome Bell, Jan Fabre and Greek dance group Sinequanon are just some of the artists that have participated in Greece's most important dance event. The festival is held in Kalamata, a city less than three hours away from Athens, usually in July. Audiences appreciate the opportunity to see the best-known Greek dance groups, along with the crème de la crème of the international dance scene.

Leda Shantala 'Shantom'

Tripoleos 35A & Evoias, Halandri (210 671 7529/ www.shantala.gr). Metro Halandri. **Open** *Box office* 10am-8pm Mon-Fri. **Tickets** prices vary. **Credit** MC, V.

Choreographer and dancer Leda Shantala created this small venue after spending years in India studying all there is to know about Indian culture and dance.

Megaron Mousikis

Leof Vas Sofias & Kokali 1, Kolonaki (210 728 2000/www.megaron.gr). Metro Megaro Mousikis. **Open** *Box office* 10am-6pm Mon-Fri; 10am-2pm Sat. *Performance days* 10am-8.30pm Mon-Fri; 10am-2pm, 6-8pm Sat, Sun. Box office closes 2hrs before the start of each performance. Theatre closed July-mid Sept. **Tickets** prices vary. **Credit** AmEx, DC, MC, V.

This theatre often hosts foreign dance companies.

Olympia Theatre

Akadimias 59, Historic Centre (210 361 1516/ 210 361 2461/210 364 3725/www.national opera.gr). Metro Panepistimio. **Open** *Box office* 9.30am-9pm daily. Theatre closed May-Sept. **Tickets** prices vary. **Credit** MC, V. **Map** p297 F3.

The Olympia Theatre, home of the Greek National Opera, Lyriki Skini and Megaron Mousikis (*see above*) are the places to go for classical ballet. These venues host lavish productions by some of the world's foremost companies. Book well in advance.

Roes

Iakhou 16, Rouf (210 347 4312). Metro Thissio, then 15min walk. **Open** *Box office* hours vary. Theatre closed mid June-late Oct. **Tickets** prices vary. **No credit cards. Map** p296 B4.

A modern venue that accommodates some of the city's most established companies.

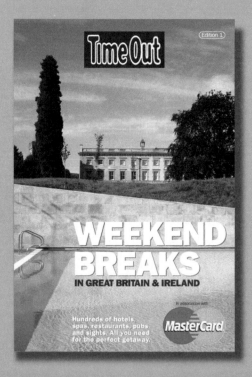

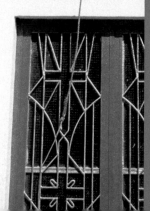

Trips Out of Town

Features

Getting Started

Ancient sites, snow-capped mountains and pristine beaches are all just a short hop from the city.

Athens has much to recommend it – from a glorious historic legacy to a newfound, thriving cosmopolitan edge. But it's also remarkable for its location. With coastal roads running like arteries out of the city, it makes an excellent launch pad for the discovery of a whole host of Hellenic delights. So with the Acropolis and its environs thoroughly explored, step outside Athens' bustling borders and enter a world of forgotten ancient communities and azure coastlines. With idyllic beaches just an 80-kilometre (50-mile) drive down the Attica peninsula, islands a 40-minute hydrofoil trip away, heavy-hitting archaeological sites at Delphi and Olympia, and vibrant cities such as Nafplio and Patra, you can savour the quintessential flavours of Greece just a stone's throw from the city's doorstep.

GETTING AROUND

Buses run from Athens to all the major destinations covered in this chapter, though it can be problematic to travel between them by bus. You can get to parts of the Peloponnese by rail, but there are fewer trains than buses, and there's little or no saving on journey time. Car hire companies are listed on page 269: driving is a far simpler business away from the Athens traffic, and there are English transliterations of most road signs. You'll need a good map, though. Road Editions' Greece map is the best we've found available locally, but it's impractically large: we recommend you buy one in your home country. The AA/AAA's are good. If there are several of you, a taxi becomes a reasonable option for travel to destinations in Attica.

You can also arrange trips through tour operators (*see p75*).

TOURIST INFORMATION

Tourist information is only patchily available. Use the Greek National Tourist Organisation's internet database (*see p279*) ahead of your journey. Many destinations have a Tourist Police office (dial 171 country-wide), where you can ask for advice if you have any difficulties.

BASICS

Hotel rates are given as a range (from the cheapest double room in low season to the most expensive in high season) and should be taken as guidelines only: they are the official 'rack' rates and will rise and fall with the availability of rooms.

Phone numbers are given as dialled locally and from Athens; if you're calling from outside Greece you need to preface them with the country code (+30).

It's easy to do nothing in the lovely old town of **Nafplio**. *See p253*.

Trips Out of Town

Trips Out of Town

© Copyright Time Out Group 2005

Attica & the Mainland

Dive into the crystal-clear waters of the Aegean or dip into Attica's rich archaeological history.

Smog permitting, the views are spectacular from **Mount Parnitha**, Attica's highest peak.

The area outside Athens is often overlooked, seen as somewhere to pass through on the way to somewhere more interesting. This is unfair. While there may be more fabulous beaches, picturesque towns and villages and impressive ancient sites elsewhere in Greece, the Attican peninsula has its own charms – within easy distance of the capital. On its west coast, the scenic road to the temple of **Sounion** takes you over headlands to tiny fingernail coves, sandy beaches and some great fish restaurants; to the east are some lesser-known though evocative ancient sites, such as **Thorikos** and the **Sanctuary of Artemis Brauron**, that seem hauntingly suspended in time. Further up the eastern coast lies the resort of **Porto Rafti** and the port of **Rafina**, which both have their allure. Further away, but still within striking distance, are two major sites: **Marathon**, interesting more for its history than the ruins that remain, and majestic **Delphi**.

Athens Environs

Mount Parnitha National Park

Snow-capped in winter and a tinderbox during the long, hot summer, Mount Parnitha – Attica's highest mountain at 1,413 metres (4,636 feet) – towers over the Athens basin. On a good day (smog permitting), the views of the sprawling city beneath are quite breathtaking. But for Athenians, the pine-strewn rugged mountain is famous mainly for two things: as the epicentre of the devastating earthquake of 1999 and for its hotel/casino, the formerly illustrious **Mont Parnes**. Served by a funicular, the casino boasts all the usual slot machines, as well as 54 gaming tables, including roulette, baccarat and blackjack. And, if you're feeling peckish, it offers a reasonably priced buffet dinner, complete with cracking views, in the glass-walled dining room.

The hotel is currently out of action (undergoing much-needed renovation), but the the casino remains open and retains a sepia-tinted (if a little nicotine-stained) retro feel that harks back to its glamorous 1960s heyday, when even Greek royalty would try their luck at the roulette tables – you half-expect Dean Martin's Rat Pack to come strolling in.

Aside from spinning the wheels of fortune (and gawping at the view), Parnitha offers little other reason to make the trip out of town.

Mont Parnes

Karageorgi 2, Parnes (210 242 1234). **Open** 24hrs daily. **Admission** €6; free 7am-8pm Mon-Thur, Sun. **Credit** DC, MC, V. **Dress code** smart. No under-18s. Passport ID required.

Getting there

By bus

The Mont Parnes casino runs a free bus service with pick-up and drop-off from outside the Athens Hilton hotel (Leof Vas Sofias 46). The bus leaves at 4pm and 6pm and takes over an hour to reach its destination; return trips leave the casino at 10.30pm, 1.45am and 2.45am. Otherwise take bus 714 from Platia Vathis (also known as Platia Anexartisias), near Omonia. Tickets cost €0.45 regular; €0.20 student.

By car

Take National Road 1 (Ethniki Odos) towards Mount Parnitha, which is clearly signposted. From the foot of Parnitha you can either drive up the winding mountain road or take the funicular (€1) to the summit. The funicular runs every 15 minutes from 7am until about 4am all year round (except when very windy).

Ancient Eleusis

Once a glorious sanctuary devoted to Demeter, goddess of harvest and fertility, these days Eleusis is not so much a lush, hallowed ground as a marble scrapheap strewn with ancient rubble. Perched on the edge of the dusty, modern-day refinery town of Elefsina, 16 kilometres (ten miles) from Athens, Eleusis is the rough diamond of Attica's archaeological sites. Granted, it's not pretty to look at, but its

Roadside beaches

As well as the beaches (*paralias*) in the coastal towns, you can stop almost anywhere along Leof Posidonos and find yourself a spot for a swim and a sunbathe. From organised seafronts offering umbrellas and deckchairs to secluded coves that emerge suddenly from the jagged rocks, there's a beach at every turn (*see also pp123-6* **Beaches**). Just park on the hard shoulder or on the edge of the beach and cool off in the welcoming waters.

Five kilometres (three miles) out of Varkiza lies the secluded horseshoe bay of **Lombarda Beach**. With cheery chart pop drifting from the beach bars' speakers, this sandy strip, set away from the road, has a fun island feel. Even the sea is laid-back – shallow and calm, protected as it is by the rocky cliffs.

Further up the road is **Grand Resort Lagonissi** (Leof Posidonos, 229 107 6000, www.lagonissiresort.gr, closed mid Oct-Mar), a hotel whose plush pool and beach the public can use for a fee of 8 on weekdays and 12 at weekends. A deckchair and umbrella are included, though the fun things (watersports, massages, banana rides) are only available to hotel guests, so you might

prefer to head a kilometre (half a mile) further east to a very inviting strip of beach where you can sample the same sparkling Mediterranean sea for free.

Located between the towns of Saronida and Anavyssos, **Eden Beach** represents the middle ground between Lagonissi's luxury and the no-frills options. This pretty, rounded bay with crystal-clear waters in front of the Eden Hotel is served by a café-bar offering drinks and light snacks. Deckchairs and umbrellas are available for hire.

The long, flat bay of **Legrena**, around eight kilometres (five miles) from Cape Sounion, is dotted with gorgeous secluded beaches. The Capet Cove, on the edge of Legrena Bay between Harakas and Legrena, is one of the most scenic, but can get a little busy at weekends.

If bathing in the shadow of ancient monuments is a particular ambition, then head for the **Aegaio Hotel beach** on the western side of Cape Sounion or, for a more rugged (and private) dip, walk down the steep path that cuts down the left side of the Cape on the last stretch of road up towards the archaeological site.

Sounion. *See p243.*

vast mass of discarded marble blocks, crumbling walls and column stumps tells of a rich history.

First built in 2000 BC, the site is entrenched in the worship of Demeter and became home to the Eleusian mysteries – the name given to the cult's secret initiation process and ceremonial rites. As their name implies, little is known of what form the rituals took, but the Romans certainly took to them, spreading the cult throughout the pre-Christian world.

Because of its proximity to Athens, Eleusis was an important strategic stronghold and fought hard to retain its independence. However, despite its fortified walls, it was conquered many times – by the Athenians on a number of occasions, and later by the Romans. But all embraced the cult and added their architectural signatures to the sanctuary.

Eventually, though, after being conquered by Alaric's Visigoths in AD 395, Eleusis was abandoned and largely left to fend for itself until 1821, when it served as a military camp in the Greek War of Independence. Those intervening centuries go some way to explaining the chaos of the site today. Fortunately, a good (and air-conditioned) on-site museum filled with well-preserved relics is there to help you appreciate the sprawling remains.

Ancient Eleusis (site & museum)

Gioka 1, Platia Eleusis, Elefsina (210 554 6019). **Open** 8.30am-3pm Tue-Sun. **Admission** €4; €2 concessions; free under-18s. **No credit cards.**

Where to eat & drink

Unless refinery-spotting is a major passion, Eleusis is Elefsina's only draw. However, for a quick bite, **Café Tost** (Dimitrios 3, 210 556 1487, snacks from €2) is a well-priced café on the road directly opposite the site entrance. It serves soft drinks, coffee, beer and some fairly basic snacks. Those hankering for a bit of a sea view with their food should head south of the site to Elefsina's small port, which is dotted with cafés.

Getting there

By bus

Take either the A16 or B16 bus from Platia Koumoundourou near Omonia and get off at the Strofi bus stop. The site is a 5min walk. Buses depart frequently and take 1hr. Tickets cost €0.45 regular; €0.20 student.

By car

Take the Athens–Patras motorway towards Elefsina. Leave the motorway at Elefsina and follow signs to the archaeological site.

West Coast

Leof Posidonos – which runs from south Athens to the headland of Sounion with its quietly awe-inspiring temple – is a dusty old road that isn't quite as grand as its name suggests. But flanked to the north by lazy towns, rugged hills and (for some bizarre reason) a lot of fireplace-sellers, and to the south by countless secluded beaches, it's crammed with worthwhile coastal stopoffs offering a taste of Greek seaside life.

The road to Sounion

VARKIZA

Sleepy Varkiza is a peaceful alternative to its posher, more bustling neighbour, Vouliagmeni. Laid-back and off the tourist track, this child-friendly little harbour town is where many Athenian families make their summer homes. The narrow shingle beach – made up of a string of natural, shallow coves with calm waters – almost seems designed with kids in mind, while the local municipality has chipped in with some handy free canvas shelters to offer shade from the fierce summer sun. The leafy seaside promenade, along the main stretch of beach, is littered with cafés and restaurants offering the usual ice-creams, frappés, soft drinks and meals. For an inexpensive lunch option, visit **Artopolis** (Platia Varkiza & Leof Posidonos, no phone, snacks from €1.50). This bakery offers excellent-value, freshly made *tyropitas*, *spanakopitas*, ice-creams, traditional biscuits and baklava, which you can eat perched on one of the many seafront benches.

Further round the bay, beyond the fishermen mending their nets, the eastern side of the harbour is flanked by a strip of sandy beach.

SARONIDA

As the most cosmopolitan (and largest) of these coastal road stopoffs, Saronida attracts a trendier crowd than the rest and, come the weekend, the town's sandy seafront swells with well-heeled Greek families escaping the Athens heat. The town is equipped to handle the onslaught and its main strip – leading up from the beach – is filled with fashionable eateries, bars and ice-cream parlours. Among them is the swanky **Il Vento Art Caffè** (Leof Saronidas 4, 229 108 0080, main courses €10-€15), which, as its name suggests, takes pride in its smart decor and art-covered walls. Further up the road is the popular and industrial-themed **Reverso Café-Restaurant** (Leof Saronidas 20, 229 106 1331, main courses €5-€9), serving a wide range of food as well as an impressive choice of ice-creams and cocktails.

PALEA FOKEA

Perched on the eastern end of Anavyssos Bay, Palea Fokea is more a village than a town. But with its lively café-lined main square, quaint marinas and sandy beaches, it makes a great stop before the final assault on Cape Sounion.

The bustling no-frills souvlaki joint **Ta Thythima** (Platia Eleftherias 9, 229 103 8834, closed lunch daily, souvlaki sandwich €2) is well worth a visit for its succulent grilled chicken and lamb kebabs, as well as first-rate *gyros*. Of the fish restaurants that line the seafront at the top end of the town, **Remvi** (Leof Sounion 14, 229 103 6236, mezes €3-€6) and the **Four Brothers** (Leof Sounion 6, 229 104 0843, mezes €3-€6) are two of the best, offering excellent mezes, fresh calamari, grilled octopus and whitebait, as well as a wide range of fish by the kilo (€20-€40 per kilo) and meaty taverna staples. And if you want to avoid Sounion's sunset hordes, watch the sun slip behind Anavyssos Bay from the cool, grapevine-roofed **Café Fokea** (Leof Sounion 8, 229 103 6468, main courses about €10) on the seafront.

Sounion

With its stunningly well-preserved columns and unrivalled position on a dramatic cliff above the blue Aegean, the **Sanctuary of Poseidon** at Cape Sounion is one of the most impressive ancient ruins this side of Delphi (hence the steady stream of tourist coaches). Dedicated to the god of the sea, the temple dates back to the fifth century BC. If its proud Doric columns seem impressive from miles away, then up close they are simply breathtaking – particularly in the evening, when large crowds gather to watch the sun set over this most evocative of sites. Indeed, Lord Byron was so taken by this clifftop marvel that, when he visited in 1810, he etched his name into one of the temple's statuesque marble columns (a laurel wreath goes to anyone who can spot his legendary tag). Byron (who later referred to the temple in his *Don Juan*) wasn't the first or last to add his mark, but these days there are attendants on hand to stop any wannabe graffiti artists.

Set back behind the road that leads to the Sanctuary of Poseidon, 500 metres (1,600 feet) below, is the blink-and-you'll-miss-it **Sanctuary of Athena**. The scattered ancient rubble is not quite as incredible as the main attraction, but from this smaller sanctuary it is possible to get a great view of the towering big daddy of a ruin way up on the hill set back against the brilliant Attica sky. A well-stocked gift shop sells guidebooks and touristy knick-knacks.

Sanctuaries of Poseidon & Athena

Cape Sounion (229 203 9363). **Open** 9am-sunset daily. **Admission** €4; €2 concessions; free under-18s. Free to all Sun Nov-Mar. **No credit cards**.

Where to eat & drink

The site's cliffside café-restaurant (229 203 9190, main courses €7-€8) is surprisingly good value, especially considering the excellent view it offers, and pleasantly shaded.

Getting there

By bus

From Mavromataion, near the Pedion Areos park, board either of the two buses (210 823 0179) heading towards Sounion; both terminate at the Sanctuary of Poseidon. Buses leave every hour, 6.30am-5.30pm, and take 1hr 30mins. Check the timetable for the return journey – the last bus to Athens leaves Sounion only a short while after sunset. Tickets cost €4.30 regular; €3.20 student.

By car

If you are in too much of a hurry to enjoy the calming sea views from the coastal Leof Posidonos, take the Attiki Odos motorway in the direction of Lavrion and from there follow the signs for Sounion and the archaeological site.

Thorikos

Perched on top of Velatouri Hill, by a small bay just north of the Sounion headland, the **ancient theatre** at Thorikos is an archaeological mole hill compared to neighbouring clifftop Sounion. There are no attendants here – in fact, there isn't even a proper car park or an entrance fee, and information about the site is only available at the Lavrion Museum, two and a half kilometres (one and a half miles) away. But while Thorikos' scattered ruins, overrun by weeds, might not be as instantly impressive as Poseidon's towering marble columns, they are no less fascinating.

Dating back to the Mycenaean period in the sixth century BC, Thorikos became a miners' town processing metal from the nearby mines at Lavrion. These days the settlement is best known for its unusually oval-shaped theatre. Built into the hillside overlooking olive groves, the amphitheatre is charmingly rough and ready, but despite its age (and its obvious need for a gardener) the remains are incredibly well preserved.

Further back at the top of the hill there's also a sanctuary dedicated to Demeter and her daughter Kore, while scattered down the hill's west slope are the remains of a few houses.

Lavrion Museum

Platia Iroon Polytechniou, Lavrion (229 202 2817). **Open** 10am-3pm Tue-Sun. **Admission** €2; €1 concessions. **No credit cards**.

Getting there

By car

Turn right out of Sounion towards Lavrion. Once in Lavrion, follow the signs to the archaeological site.

East Attica

Destinations are covered in north-to-south order.

Rhamnous

With its serene hilltop setting overlooking the Euboian Gulf, the remote settlement of Rhamnous might look peaceful, but it's a site steeped in military history. Dating back to the sixth century BC, Rhamnous was home to the cult of Nemesis, goddess of retribution, and a grand temple dedicated to her once stood here. Appropriately, it's thought that the statue of the goddess within the temple was sculpted from the slab of marble that the Persians, confident of their victory at the Battle of Marathon in 490 BC, brought with them to build their triumphant memorial. Happily for the Greeks – though not for those cocky Persians – their assailants were vanquished and Nemesis received her well-won trophy.

Further down the hill is the fortress of Rhamnous – still under excavation and currently not open to the public. The fortress was permanently manned by an Athenian garrison and protected by a mighty 800-metre-long (half-mile) wall. Military buildings were enclosed on its upper level, with a gymnasium, unique natural theatre, burial grounds and private homes beneath. Sadly, little remains of either the sanctuary or the fortress after they were systematically destroyed by Christians at the turn of the fifth century AD.

Temple of Nemesis

Rhamnous (229 406 3477). **Open** *May-Oct* noon-5.30pm Mon; 8am-7pm Tue-Sun. *Nov-Apr* 8.30am-5pm daily. **Admission** €2; €1 concessions; free under-18s. Free to all Sun Nov-Mar. **No credit cards**.

Getting there

By car

Take the Athens–Lamia motorway in the direction of Agios Stephanos and Marathonas, then follow the signs to Grammatiko. When the road forks as you enter the village, follow it down the small hill to the

Byron in Greece

The admiration and love that Lord Byron felt for Greece, a 'beautiful country, with seasons all a-smile' and especially Athens ('Athens holds my heart and soul/Can I cease to love thee? No!') are well known. The feeling was reciprocated. When Byron died in 1824, weakened by an epileptic fit and thus unable to fight off a severe cold, the Greeks insisted on keeping his heart, and buried it beneath his statue in the Garden of Heroes in Mesolongi. Their affection for the English poet carries on to this day, with streets and children still being named after him.

Byron became fascinated by Greece at an early age. Born with a club-foot and becoming a sensitive and shy child, he spent most of his time reading. He was especially captivated by the glorious history and heroic myths of ancient Greece, and it is no surprise that later in his life he was so appalled by Lord Elgin's pillaging of the Parthenon (*see p80* **The making of a monument**).

He had a somewhat unstable childhood. His father, whom he scarcely knew, committed suicide and his mother treated him in an emotionally inconsistent manner. His nurse was rumoured to have made sexual advances to him, and he became infatuated with three of his cousins. The combination of this with his literary genius led him to become a self-willed young man, who vehemently resisted any attempts to control him. This is perhaps another reason why Byron admired Greece so much. Despite being under Turkish rule since the 14th century and despite attempts at oppressive assimilation, the Greeks managed to maintain their own cultural and national identity, traditions and religion virtually intact.

On coming of age and after leaving Cambridge University, Byron set off to travel around southern Europe with his friends. He first came to Greece in December 1809 (and visited it twice more over the next four months) and fell in love with not only the countryside, the sunshine, the architecture and the moral tolerance of the people, but also with a number of girls, about one of whom he wrote *Maid of Athens, Ere We Part*. He spent a lot of time on Platia Lysikratous, in central Athens, where he wrote some of *Childe Harold's Pilgrimage*. He also left his mark, quite literally, on the Sanctuary of Poseidon in Sounion, where he joined the vandalistic tradition of scrawling one's name into the columns. He even swam five kilometres (three miles) across Hellespont (the Dardanelles).

It was 12 years before Byron was to return to Greece. In 1823 the country was in upheaval and fighting for freedom from the Ottoman Empire. Byron had the honour of being appointed by the London Greek Committee as their agent in this cause. He threw himself into it with gusto, personally and financially, donating thousands of pounds to set up and arm the brig *Hercules*, although he himself never got to see any military action.

Lord Byron was an enigmatic and cynical man who effortlessly made women swoon, and perhaps there is more to his love of Greece than is known. Unfortunately, it's likely to stay that way – his memoirs, which were deemed too scandalous even by his closest liberal-minded friends, were thrown into the fire after his death at the tender age of just 37.

right. After about 1km (0.5 miles) the road bends to the right up a winding road. Stay on this road for just over 7km (4.5 miles) until you reach a T-junction. Turn left and follow the signs to Rhamnous.

Marathon

The site of Marathon is, of course, 42 kilometres (26 miles) from Athens, across the Attican peninsula on the Rafina Coast, and about three kilometres (two miles) from Marathonas town. It's more fascinating for the story it tells than for what ruins remain. It's basically a large mound, but a mound that evokes a sense of the ancient past, along with the serenity of a cemetery.

It was here that in 490 BC the Battle of Marathon was fought, in which an army of 10,000 Athenians and Plataeans defeated 25,000 Persian invaders by ambushing the foreign army from the sides. The Greeks' victory was conclusive: compared to 6,000 Persian dead, they lost just 192 men in the battle. The Tomb of the Fallen, a huge dome rising out of the ground in which the Greeks who died in the battle were buried, commemorates them.

Most famously, however, the Battle of Marathon gave rise to the modern race that still bears its name. After the battle, the messenger Pheidippides ran the 42 kilometres (26 miles) to Athens to relay news of the Greeks' tremendous

Rafina. See p247.

triumph. However, once there, having informed Athens of the victory, Pheidippides collapsed and died on the spot. The 2004 Olympic marathon started from here and retraced Pheidippides' steps.

The **Marathon Museum** lies two and a half kilometres (one and a half miles) to the west. It houses battle relics that tell the tale of the Greeks' amazing victory. There is no public transport between the site and the museum.

Archaeological site of Marathon

Spyrou Louis, Marathonas (229 405 5462).
Open 8am-3pm Tue-Sun. **Admission** (includes entry to museum) €3; €2 concessions; free under-18s, EU students. **No credit cards**.

Marathon Museum

Plataion 114, Vranas, Marathonas (229 405 5155).
Open 8am-3pm Tue-Sun. **Admission** (includes entry to archaeological site) €3; €2 concessions; free under-18s, EU students. **No credit cards**.

Where to eat & drink

There is nowhere worthy of recommendation to eat either at the ancient site or in Marathonas town. Your best bet is to head for Fragma at Marathon Lake (*see p247*).

Getting there

By bus

From the bus terminal at Mavromataion (210 821 0872), near the Pedion Areos park, take any bus to Marathonas, Grammatiko or Souli, and get off at the Tymvos bus stop. From there it is a short walk to the site. Buses depart every hour 5.30am-10.30pm and take 2hrs. Tickets cost €2.50 regular; €1.90 student.

By car

Take Mesogeion in the direction of Marathonas. Before you reach the town, follow the brown archaeological site signs for Tymvos.

Marathon Lake

Situated on the site of the ancient Marathon Lake, inland from Marathon, this massive reservoir was Athens' sole water supply right up until the 1950s. Although the dam (built in 1925) no longer shoulders such responsibility, it remains an impressive sight. Made out of marble, the structure, which measures 50 metres (160 feet) in height and 300 metres (a fifth of a mile) in length, rises imposingly out of the lake, surrounded by pine forests.

Although no one is allowed too close to the water, it is possible to walk on trails in the surrounding hills for beautiful views of the lake. The very smart Fragma restaurant on the east side of the dam offers a particularly stunning view of the serene lake from its spectacular terrace. Alternatively, there are observation platforms at either end of the dam and picnic areas on the west side from which to take in the sights.

Where to eat & drink

The fashionable and wonderfully situated café-restaurant **Fragma** (210 814 3415, main courses €20-€25) offers a selection of light snacks and traditional meze during the day and adventurous, well-presented modern European cuisine in the evenings (from lunchtimes at weekends). Dinner bookings are advisable.

Getting there

By car
Take Mesogeion in the direction of Marathonas. Once you reach the town, follow the well-marked signs to the lake ('*limni*').

Rafina

There's little reason to visit Athens' second port other than to catch a ferry, but there are certainly plenty of worse places to kill time in if you do happen to find yourself there. Rafina may be smaller and more out of the way than Piraeus, but ferry tickets from here to the Cyclades are generally cheaper, a taxi from the airport is just €20 and there are also plenty of buses, making the town a convenient alternative starting point for any island-hopping adventure.

And as ferry ports go, this one's not so bad. The catamaran and ferry ticket offices line the harbour front, but round to the right, on the south side of the town, lies a small but pleasant strip of beach. Rising above the harbour is Rafina's main square and, far from fulfilling any sailor clichés, it's a clean, wide, tree-lined space flanked by modern cafés and bars. Among the best are the bright and airy **Café Estoril** (Platia Rafina, 229 402 2490) and the elegant, brushed-wood and chrome-decorated **The Square** (Platia Rafina, 229 402 3400), both of which serve a selection of beers, cocktails, coffee and snacks. Head up the hill to the right of the square to find a very reasonably priced restaurant, **O Vraxos** (Platia Taxidromeiou, 229 402 2307, fish €37-€47 per kilo), which serves tasty fish mezes.

Any further information can be obtained from the offices of the **Rafina Port Authority** (229 402 2300), by the port.

Getting there

By bus
Buses (210 821 0872) for Rafina leave from Mavromataion, near Pedion Areos park, every 30mins and take 1hr 15mins.

By car
Take Mesogeion and head north towards Christopoulo and Pinkermi; from there follow the signs to Rafina. For the coastal route, take Mesogeion and head north in the direction of Loutsa. Once there, follow the signs to Rafina.

From the airport
An Airport Express bus connects Eleftherios Venizelos with Rafina. This route is run by coach company KTEL (229 402 3440). Single tickets cost €3; the journey takes about 20-30mins.

Sanctuary of Artemis Brauron (Vravrona)

This ancient site, 40 kilometres (25 miles) east of Athens, stands pretty much in the middle of nowhere. But its remoteness only adds to its romance. Surrounded by lush grasses and shady trees, this well-preserved temple is dedicated to Artemis, goddess of childbirth and hunting and protectress of animals. It dates back to the fifth century BC, when the worship of the goddess was the official cult of Attica. The site was particularly important during the Festival of Artemis, which took place every four years. For this occasion young girls aged between five and ten – priestesses in training – would wear bear skins and perform a ritual 'bear dance' where they'd imitate the movements of the goddess's favourite animal to celebrate her. You can still see the quarters where the young girls slept, as well as the preserved temple – and, thanks to its remote location, the chances are that you'll have the place to yourself.

The well-presented museum (which charges a separate entrance fee) is a kilometre (half a mile) further along the road and houses votive offerings found at the sanctuary.

Bear in mind that the site is miles from any town, and bars and restaurants are hard to come by. However, there are several fruit and veg vendors on the road to the sanctuary who would probably welcome a little custom.

Sanctuary of Artemis Brauron & Museum
Vravrona (229 902 7020). **Open** 8.30am-3pm Tue-Sun. **Admission** *Sanctuary* €3; €2 concessions; free under-18s. Free to all Sun Nov-Mar. *Museum* €3; €2 concessions; free under-18s. Free to all Sun Nov-Mar. **No credit cards.**

Trips Out of Town

Worship in peace at the remote **Sanctuary of Artemis Brauron**. *See p247.*

Getting there

By bus

Take the 304 bus from the Ethniki Amyna metro station until it terminates at Loutsa. The site is a 15min taxi journey from there. Buses depart frequently throughout the day. Tickets cost €0.45 regular; €0.20 students.

By car

Take Mesogeion and head north in the direction of Loutsa. Once there, follow signs for the Sanctuary of Artemis at Vravrona.

Porto Rafti

Once the exclusive summer playground of the wealthy, these days Porto Rafti welcomes a more varied crowd for the sunny season. Smart three-storey apartments stand tall over the grand old villas, while small boats mingle with flashy yachts in the peaceful bay.

Porto Rafti's family-friendly shingle beach is broken up into protected natural bays so it's perfect for paddling toddlers. Above, on the tree-lined promenade, young Greeks cool off in a string of fashionable shaded café-bars (open 10am-4am), whiling away the afternoons drinking frappés and playing *tavli* (backgammon) until the sun sets and beyond.

Where to eat & drink

The parasol-shaded **Café Status** (Leof Gregou 87, 229 907 2603, closed Mon-Thur from Oct to May) is among the busiest daytime cafés and at night it grooves to R&B and chart hits. The luxuriously whitewashed **Café del Mar** (Leof Gregou 41, 229 907 5698), on the southern tip of the town, exudes a chilled-out vibe during the day, while at night DJs pump chart pop from the nightspot's speakers. Further along the strip, the trendy **Smart Café** (Leof Gregou 67, 229 907 2270) has a funkier, more leftfield vibe.

Getting there

By bus

Buses depart about every hour 6am-9pm from Pedion Areos bus terminal (Mavromataion 29, 210 821 0872), next to the corner of Patision and Leof Alexandras.

By car

Take Mesogeion and head towards Markopoulo. Once there, follow signs for Porto Rafti.

Further Afield

Delphi

A majestic landscape at the foot of Mount Parnassus, the archaeological site of Delphi (226 508 2312) is on a plateau overlooking the silver-leaved olive groves of Amphissa and the Gulf of Galaxidi. According to ancient Greek legend, Zeus released two eagles at opposite ends of the world and Delphi is where they met.

At first a place where Mother Earth and Poseidon were worshipped, Delphi later became the Sanctuary of Pythian Apollo, before yet still more gods (including Dionysus and Athena Pronaia) became associated with the sacred

Trips Out of Town

location. Delphi was also the seat of the mystical oracle, the site of the first political allegiance among the city-states (the Amphictyonic League) and, along with Olympia and Delos, one of the most important sanctuaries in the ancient world.

Inside the **Sanctuary of Apollo** was the sanctum of the oracle where the Pythia (the priestess who delivered the oracle) would pronounce the dubious, and sometimes incomprehensible, prophecies in a state of holy intoxication. Following the victorious Battle of Marathon against the Persians, the Athenians asked the Pythia for an oracle in view of the next great expedition. The priestess pronounced that wooden walls would save the city. Interpreting this as a reference to their navy, the Athenians navigated their ships against the Persians and annihilated the Persian fleet in Salamis, ruling the seas for many years to come.

Follow the Sacred Way and gaze upon the offerings of the Athenians (Treasury of the Athenians) and other various treasuries, the Ancient Theatre in which theatrical and lyrical competitions were held, and the excellently preserved Stadium, where sports events took place as part of the Pythian Games, the second most important festival in the ancient world after the Olympic Games at Olympia.

Next to the Sanctuary of Apollo is the **museum**. On the other side are the **Sanctuary of Athena** and the Tholos, an impressive circular structure.

For hikers, the European path E4 offers a magical route (approximately seven hours) from the village of Agoriani (€20 taxi ride from Delphi) to the archaeological site of Delphi.

Museum
Delphi (226 508 2312). **Open** *June-Sept* 8.30am-6.45pm daily. *Oct-May* 8.30am-2.45pm daily. **Admission** €6 (€9 including Sanctuary of Apollo); concessions €3 (€5 including Sanctuary of Apollo).

Sanctuary of Apollo
Delphi (226 508 2312). **Open** 8.30am-2.45pm Mon; 7.30am-6.45pm Tue-Sun. **Admission** €6. **No credit cards**.

Sanctuary of Athena
Delphi (226 508 2312). **Open** *June-Sept* 7.30am-8pm daily. *Oct-May* 7.30am-sunset daily. **Admission** free.

Where to eat & stay

You'll find Greek specialities with a fabulous view at **Epicouros** (Vas Pavlou 33, 226 508 3250, closed dinner Nov-Mar, main courses €10), while **Vakhos Taverna** (Apollonos 31, no phone) has more of a family atmosphere, with traditional Greek cuisine, reasonable prices and a view over the valley below.

Delphi's most luxurious hotel is the A-class **Amalia** (Apollonos 1, 226 508 2101, €141-€190 double; €230 during Aug), where facilities include a restaurant, bar, pool and a majestic view over the olive groves towards the Gulf of Galaxidi. The **Acropole** (Philellinon 13, 226 508 2675, €45-€75 double) is ideal for those seeking peace and quiet, while the **Xenia Hotel** (Apollonos 69, 226 508 2151, €90-€120 double) has nice views and serves breakfast on the veranda.

Getting there

By bus
There are six buses daily from Liosion bus station. Information is available from KTEL Fokidos (210 831 7096). Tickets cost €11.

By car
Delphi is 178km (111 miles) from Athens on the Athens–Thessaloniki national road. Take the turning to Arachova-Delphi at the 84th km.

EXCURSIONS
The picturesque town of **Arachova** is 12 kilometres (eight miles) from Delphi on the main Athens–Delphi road. There are numerous rooms and hotels as well as some excellent tavernas – ask to try the local cheese (*formela*), honey and red wine – and a vast market of traditional products in the main street with wooden goods and rugs. A further 24km (16 miles) towards Athens, the 11th-century Byzantine monastery of **Osio Loukas** is beautiful both in its setting and its rich art and architecture, with notable mosaics.

Delphi. *See p248.*

Northern Peloponnese

Treasures of ancient Greece, feats of 19th-century engineering and the vigour of modern towns.

If it wasn't for a narrow strip of land (now cut across by the Corinth Canal), the Peloponnese – a wild, mountainous region, rich in historical significance and scenic grandeur – would be an island (its name means 'island of Pelops').

It is also an area steeped in classical history. The north-eastern Argolid and Corinthia regions contain some of the most celebrated remains of antiquity: **Mycenae**, centre of an influential early Greek culture and legendary home of Agamemnon; **Ancient Corinth**, destroyed and then rebuilt by the Romans, overseen by the eyrie-like fortress of Acrocorinth; and the magnificent theatre of **Epidaurus**, the largest and most complete Greek theatre in existence. And these are just the highlights.

To make the best of these sites, it's wise to find a local base, and they don't come any prettier and more relaxed than the town of **Nafplio** on the Gulf of Argolis. For something completely different, head west along the Gulf of Corinth to the lively, youthful port of **Patra**, gateway to the Ionian islands and Italy. Often overlooked by visitors, it's a messy but vibrant centre with a lively nightlife and the best carnival in Greece. South of here is ancient Olympia, venue of the original Olympic Games.

Ancient Corinth & Acrocorinth

One look at a map is enough to tell you why the city of Corinth played such a pivotal role in classical times. Commanding the narrow Isthmus of Corinth, it controlled both the lucrative sea route between the Adriatic (via the Gulf of Corinth) and the Aegean (via the Saronic Gulf), and the land route between the Peloponnese and the rest of the Greek mainland.

The city rose to prominence during the eighth century BC on the back of commerce. It founded the colonies of Corcyra on Corfu and Syracuse on Sicily, and was a major player in the various city-state power struggles that characterised the succeeding centuries (siding with Sparta against Athens in the ruinous Peloponnesian War at the end of the fifth century BC).

In 146 BC, following the Roman defeat of the Greek cities of the Achaian League, the vengeful Romans razed the city, which was then abandoned for a century. In 44 BC, however, Julius Caesar decided to rebuild Corinth on a grand scale as the provincial capital. The city prospered anew, and became famous for its wealth (and moral laxity, if St Paul is to be believed), until major earthquakes in the fourth and sixth centuries AD reduced it to rubble. It is the ruins of the Roman Corinth that can be seen today.

Modern Corinth is a hot, dusty, utilitarian sort of place, re-sited on the Gulf of Corinth in the mid 19th century. Give it a miss, and concentrate on the dual attractions of the remains of **Ancient Corinth**, and, looming above it, the spectacularly sited fortifications of Acrocorinth, just a few kilometres inland.

The excavated area of the ancient city, centred on a huge agora (market place), reveals only a fraction of what was once a vast settlement. The remains are fairly confusing, so it is wise to buy a guidebook. The one stand-out structure is a surprising survival from Greek Corinth, the seven remaining Doric columns of the fifth-century BC Temple of Apollo. Look out too for the Roman Fountain of Peirene, which stands beside a stretch of the marble-lined Lechaion Way. The site museum contains a fine selection of finds, all labelled in English, but, disappointingly, without any attempt to put them into their historical context.

While the excavations are certainly fascinating, most visitors will get more of a thrill out of ascending the rocky outcrop that supports the ruined citadel of **Acrocorinth**. Once home to Ancient Corinth's acropolis (and, on its highest peak, to a temple to Aphrodite tended by 1,000 sacred prostitutes), Acrocorinth became a formidable fortress in the Middle Ages, and was used until the end of Turkish rule in 1830.

The approach is via three gates that provide an architectural history lesson about the castle's various keepers. The first is Turkish, the second Frankish and Venetian, the third Byzantine. Beyond them lies a range of ruins scattered over a huge expanse of the rock-strewn hilltop, still largely encircled by its walls. A Frankish keep perches on the second

The Ancient Theatre at **Epidaurus**, renowned for its perfect acoustics. *See p252.*

highest peak, while for those seeking a bit of a physical challenge, take the paths from the car park leading to Acrocorinth's highest point. It's a tough half-hour hike, but the staggering 360-degree views from the summit are more than worth the gruelling effort.

Acrocorinth
No phone. **Open** 8am-7pm daily. **Admission** free.

Ancient Corinth Site & Museum
274 103 1207. **Open** *Apr-Oct* 8am-7pm daily.
Nov-Mar 8am-5pm daily. **Admission** €6.
No credit cards.

Where to eat & drink

In terms of views, **Acrocorinthos** (no phone), a café/restaurant by the entrance to Acrocorinth, certainly has the edge over the many touristy tavernas in the village that has grown up around the ruins of Ancient Corinth. However, for the ultimate atmospheric experience, take a picnic up to the peak of Acrocorinth.

Mycenae

In his epic poems, *The Iliad* and *The Odyssey*, written in the eighth century BC, Homer spoke of the 'well-built Mycenae, rich in gold'.

According to *The Iliad*, its king, Agamemnon – the richest and most powerful king of Greece – headed the Greek expedition to Troy after Paris, son of the king of Troy, abducted Helen, wife of Menelaus, king of Sparta and brother to Agamemnon, hence launching the Trojan War. The ten-year war (1193 BC-1184 BC) brought with it the heroic deeds of Achilles, the cunning of Odysseus and even divided the gods of Olympus.

Until the 19th century these poems were regarded as little more than enthralling legends. Then, in the 1870s, the amateur archaeologist Heinrich Schliemann (1822-90), ignoring the jeers of his professional counterparts, struck gold: first by excavating Troy in present-day Turkey, and then Mycenae. He uncovered the graves of more than a dozen people, all bedecked in gold and jewels, and was convinced he'd found the tomb of Agamemnon. Although these were later dated to at least 300 years earlier than the Trojan War, Schliemann had found evidence of Mycenae's wealth at its peak.

Neolithic settlements first appeared in Mycenae in the sixth millennium BC. In the late Bronze Age, the kingdom was the most powerful in Greece, holding control over the Aegean, and building a legacy of grand palaces

Relaxed little **Nafplio**. *See p253.*

and fortified constructions before beginning to wane around 1200 BC.

The citadel of Mycenae is surrounded by a gigantic wall so impressive that the Ancient Greeks believed it to have been built by a Cyclops, one of the fierce one-eyed giants described in Homer's *Odyssey*. It can be entered through the impressive Lion Gate, with the main path leading up to the ruins of Agamemnon's Palace, the Throne Room and the Great Court.

The best-preserved Mycenaean structure by far, however, lies outside the bounds of the citadel. The immense royal *tholos* tomb (built with blocks of stone, tapering to the top, and then covered with earth) is misleadingly known as the Treasury of Atreus or the Tomb of Agamemnon, but it was built several hundred years before Agamemnon's era.

The remains of the magnificent gold treasures of the Mycenaean civilisation are housed at the National Archaeological Museum in Athens (*see p106*).

It is worth buying a guidebook and perusing the excellent site museum before attempting to make sense of the ruins, which, tombs aside, are relatively scant and confusing.

Archaeological Site of Mycenae & Museum
275 107 6585. **Open** *Apr-Oct* 8am-7pm daily. *Nov-Mar* 8am-3pm daily. **Admission** €8; €4 concessions. **No credit cards.**

Where to eat & drink

The village of Mycenae offers plenty of touristy eating options. One of the best places lining the main road is **Mycinaiko** (275 107 6724, main courses around €7).

Epidaurus

Henry Miller dedicated over ten pages of his book *The Colossus of Maroussi* to the magical landscape of Epidaurus ('open, exposed… devoted to the spirit') and the surrounding area.

At the top of the archaeological site is the Ancient Theatre, which dates back to the fourth century BC. Unearthed by Greek archaeologists at the beginning of the 19th century, it is the largest and best preserved of its kind. The theatre seats up to 14,000 spectators and is renowned for its amazing acoustics – drop a coin in the centre of the amphitheatre and the sound will be heard as far as the highest seat. For a practical demonstration of this impressive venue, plan your visit in time for the annual Epidaurus Festival (*see p233* **Classics in situ**) when classical plays are performed just as they were more than 2,000 years ago.

At Epidaurus you'll also find the **Sanctuary of Asclepius** (dedicated to the Greek god of medicine), which includes the Katagogeion and the Temple of Asclepius, as well as the remains of a *tholos*, a gymnasium and a stadium.

Archaeological Site of Ancient Epidaurus
275 302 2009. **Open** 7.30am-5pm daily. **Admission** €6. **No credit cards.**

Where to eat

Having built up a healthy appetite exploring the sites, head to the **Leonidas** taverna (Epidavrou 103, 275 302 2115, closed *Oct-Mar* Mon-Fri, meal without drinks €10-€12) in the village of Lygourio, four kilometres (two miles) from the site. As well as serving top-class traditional Greek cuisine, Leonidas is also famous for its theatrical legacy. Decorated with photographs of performances at the Ancient Theatre, the taverna was reputedly Melina Mercouri and her husband Jules Dassin's favourite post-show hangout.

Getting there

By bus
From Kifissos station in Athens (100 Kifissou, 210 513 4110) to Nafplio there are 15 buses daily (fare €9); from Nafplio to Mycenae four local buses daily at 10am, noon, 2pm and 6pm (fare €2);

from Mycenae to Nafplio four local buses run daily at 11am, 1pm, 3pm and 7pm (€2).

From Kifissos station to Lygourio two buses run daily (€8.60); from Nafplio to Epidaurus four local buses daily at 10.15am, noon, 2pm and 2.30pm, which return at noon, 1pm, 4pm and 6pm (€2). There is also a local bus service between Nafplio and Lygourio (KTEL Argolidos, 210 513 4588).

Organised tours to Mycenae and Epidaurus are available from Chat Tours (210 323 0827, €69 incl admission and guide, €79 with lunch) and Key Tours (210 923 3166, €69 incl admission and guide, €79 with lunch).

By car

Take the Athens-Corinth-Tripolis national road to reach Ancient Corinth. Follow the signs to Argos-Nafplio and, after 9km (five miles), turn left for the archaeological site of Mycenae. For Epidaurus (27km/16.5 miles from Nafplio) follow the signs to Lygourio-Epidaurus.

Nafplio

This relaxed little town makes an excellent base from which to explore the north-eastern Peloponnese. Named after Nafplius, son of Poseidon, it wasn't until the Byzantines fortified the settlement at the end of the 12th century that it emerged as an important commercial and strategic regional centre. The following centuries saw it pass through many hands – Franks, Venetians, Turks – before it enjoyed a brief five-year glow of national importance as the capital of the newly independent Greek state, before Athens took over the role in 1834. In 1831, the town witnessed the assassination of Greece's first leader, Ioannis Kapodistrias, after he was shot dead in a vendetta outside the church of Agios Spyridon (the hole made by the fatal bullet is still visible behind a glass panel beside the door).

Modern Nafplio is split between a workaday new town and a lovely Old Town that sits snugly beneath the rocky outcrop of Akronafplia. But its eventful history is writ in stone. From the massive fortifications of the Palamidi castle on the hill to the multicoloured marble-paved and mansion-lined pedestrianised streets that lead down to the harbour, the town is alive with reminders of its varied past.

It's easy to do nothing in Nafplio, but the town has a handful of attractions worth seeking out. Its one-time military significance is obvious in the presence of not one, but three castles. The first of these is Bourtzi. Poised out on the harbour's edge, this picturesque little fortress was built by the Venetians in 1470, before being remodelled by them during their second period of occupation at the end of the 17th century.

The second, Akronafplia was once the site of a Byzantine town and a series of strongholds, but these days only remnants of their walls remain. The key destination for castle-lovers, however, is the mighty **Palamidi Fortress**, which can be reached either by car, or, for the fit, by an extraordinary 913-step staircase that leads out of the town and snakes up the almost-sheer slopes of a hill. The extensively fortified fortress was constructed by the Venetians in the early 18th century, and offers endless crenellated walls, dark passages and wide stairwells to explore, as well as look-out points from which to enjoy some glorious views.

Back in the Old Town there are a couple of museums worth a look. The award-winning **Peloponnesian Folklore Foundation** contains a beautiful selection of Greek folk costumes, though disappointingly little information about them. Same goes for the **Archaeological Museum**. Set in a prime location on the café-edged central square of Platia Syntagmatos, the museum houses a decent selection of local finds, including their prize exhibit, a very rare Mycenaean armour, but again offers precious little explanation. Also among its artefacts are some frescoes from Tiryns, a once-mighty Mycenaean city, the remains of which lie a couple of kilometres outside Nafplio.

Tiryns itself is well worth a visit, not least because it is mostly ignored by the tour bus convoys that hurtle round the better-known sites in the area, so chances are you'll be able to enjoy its ruins alone. While some parts of Tiryns have been dated to 2600 BC, the majority of what you see today dates from about a millennium later. The height and strength of its walls were famed in antiquity, and what is left still impresses, particularly when you hear they were originally twice their current height.

Once you've had your fill of ancient stones, head for the beach at **Karathonas**, a five-minute drive east of the town. This long, greyish, likeable strand is popular with Greek families and holds a scattering of beach bars and restaurants. Meanwhile the resort of Tolo, 15 minutes out of town, offers something a little more lively.

Archaeological Museum

Platia Syntagmatos (275 202 7502). **Open** 8.30am-3pm Tue-Sun. Closed for renovations until Oct 2005. **Admission** €2; €1 concessions. **No credit cards**.

Palamidi Fortress

275 202 8036. **Open** 8.30am-6.30pm daily. **Admission** €4; free-€2 concessions. **No credit cards**.

The archaeological site of **Olympia**, sanctuary of Zeus. *See p257.*

Peloponnesian Folklore Foundation

Ypsilantou 1 (275 202 8379/8947/5267/
www.pli.gr). **Open** 9am-3pm Mon, Wed-Sun.
Admission €4; €2-€3 concessions. **Credit**
DC, MC, V (gift shop).

Tiryns Archaeological Site

275 202 2657. **Open** *May-Oct* 7am-8pm daily.
Nov-Apr 8.30am-3pm daily. **Admission** €3; €2
concessions. **No credit cards.**

Where to eat & drink

Nafplio teems with tavernas. The main food
thoroughfare is pedestrianised Staikopolou,
which is filled with outdoor tables and waiters
exhorting you to choose their joint over their
neighbours'. Don't let this put you off, though.
To Fanaria (No.13, 275 202 7141, main courses
from €7) is excellent; try their lamb cooked with
tiny pasta in tomato sauce if it's available.

If you want to eat where the locals eat, and
don't mind sitting by a road opposite a car park
near the cargo port, then you can enjoy some
bargain-priced classic Greek cooking at
Nafplios (corner of Bouboulinas and Syngrou,
275 209 7999, main courses €5-€10), which
since 1966 has been knocking out the likes of
superb spit-roasted pork with crackling and the
most generous Greek salads you'll ever find.

For a more romantic setting, and some
seriously good fish, head round the end of the
peninsula, where a couple of restaurant-bars
enjoy an impossibly lovely setting right on the
water. The pick is **Agnanti** (Akti Miaouli, 275
202 9332, main courses €8-€30). It's great for a
sundowner, but if you want a livelier drinking
scene, the boisterous bars along Bouboulinas
will deliver. For dancing, head to one of the clubs
around the bay, or hop in a cab to the youthful
resort of Tolo, 15 minutes' drive away.

Where to stay

As a well-established resort, there's no shortage of places to stay in all categories in Nafplio. In summer 2003 it even got its own design hotel, the chic, sleek **Amphitryon Hotel** (Spiliadou 21, 275 207 0700, doubles €200-€320); each room has a terrace with wonderful sea views. Another luxury option, the **Nafplia Palace** (Acronafplia, 275 202 8981-5, doubles €200-€270), is perched just above it. You don't get the views at **Ilion** (Elthimiopolou 4 & Kapodistriou 6, 275 202 5114, www.ilionhotel.gr, doubles €95-€180), back in the Old Town, but you do get a lot more idiosyncratic character, with individually themed rooms flamboyantly decorated and decked out with antiques.

More affordable options include the six properties that make up the **Pension Acronafplia** (Papanikolaou 34, Vas Konstantinou 20 & Agios Spiridou 6, 275 202 4481/4076, www.pension-acronafplia.com, doubles €45-€70). A good mid-range choice is **Kapodistrias Traditional House** (Kokinou 20, 275 202 9366, www.hotelkapodistrias.gr, doubles €65-€120), while a popular budget spot is the **Dafni Pension** (Fotomara 10 & Iatrou 5, 275 202 9856, mobile 6972 708133, www.pensiondafni.gr, doubles €50-€80).

Tourist information

The information office is on 25 Martiou (275 202 4444, open 9am-1pm, 4-8pm daily).

Getting there

By bus

There are buses to Athens and to the nearby resort of Tolo every hour, and to Argos every half hour. Three buses a day go to Mycenae and four a day to the Theatre of Epidaurus. The bus station is on Syngrou (275 202 7323/7423). On weekends during July and August there are extra buses to Epidaurus from Nafplio at 7pm and from Athens at 5pm laid on for the drama performances at the Ancient Theatre. They return right after the performance.

By car

Nafplio is 146km (98 miles) from Athens.

Local treats

There's something about feasting on food in its natural habitat that seems to enhance its flavour. Just like fish eaten beside the sea, other food tastes best in context too. It's hard to imagine much cultivation of any sort when you're standing in Greece's traffic-clogged capital, but beyond the city is a country rich in natural produce – and you don't need to travel far from Athens to taste the fruits of this fertile soil.

Aegina (see p260) is just a short hop from Piraeus and while its surrounding sea teems with whitebait and sea bass, this charming island is best known for what grows on its trees rather than in its waters. Aegina has become synonymous with the pistachio, so much so that the delicate squat trees now almost threaten to overrun the island. So settle down in a seafront taverna and soak up the late afternoon sun with a glass of ouzo and a bowl of the island's world-famous pink and green nuts.

Across the Corinth Canal, the Peloponnese peninsula is rich in natural produce. The region's most famous exports are the succulent black olives and rich olive oils of Kalamata and the Mani, and these flat khaki-green groves carpet the surrounding hills, but the region produces excellent thyme honey too.

During the last 20 years, this verdant area has also been building an impressive reputation for its vineyards. The Greek wine-making tradition spans thousands of years but the Peloponnese's most famous tipple – a sweet dessert wine made from the indigenous Mavrodaphne grape – is only just over 100 years old. The top producer is the Achaia Clauss winery (261 032 5051/56, open daily 9am-5pm), situated eight kilometres (five miles) south east of Patras. Other local producers to look out for are Domaine Spiropoulos (279 606 1400, www.domainspiropoulos.com) in Nemea and the highly regarded Tselepos (271 054 4440, www.tsepelos.gr, open by appointment only) near Tripoli.

As well as olives and pistachios, Attica has its fair share of wine producers too. The Katogi-Strofilia winery and vineyards (229 104 1650, www.katogi-strofilia.gr) at Anavissos, just off the coastal road 55 kilometres (35 miles) east of Athens is a well-known example. Call ahead for directions and to arrange a tour before heading out to see the dazzling sunset from one of Greece's most beautiful ancient sites, Sounion.

For more about Greek wines and visiting vineyards, see p60.

The Corinth Canal

But for a mere six-kilometre (four-mile) strip of land, the Peloponnese peninsula would be an island. And if it were, how much quicker and safer navigation between the Adriatic and Aegean seas would be. Such was the problem that vexed minds as long ago as 602 BC, when Periander, tyrant of Corinth, considered, then rejected (following dire warnings from the Delphic Oracle), a plan to sink a canal across the isthmus.

The journey around the dangerous southern cape of the Peloponnese added 185 nautical miles to a ship's voyage between the two seas. Such was the risk and cost of the journey that, in the early sixth century BC, the Corinthians constructed a limestone-paved road called the *diolkos* between the Corinthian and Saronic Gulfs (traces of it are still visible today). Along this road ran the *olkos*, a cart that laboriously transported ships from one sea to the other. It proved a huge source of income and prestige for Corinth.

Yet the dreams of forging a nautical route across the isthmus persisted. In 307 BC another attempt was made. Demetrios Poliorcetes started a canal, before being scared off by Egyptian engineers, who persuaded him that differences in sea levels would result in the islands of the Saronic Gulf sinking under the waves.

The next serious attempt came in 67 AD, when Nero forced 6,000 Jewish slaves to start digging. They had created a trench 3,300 metres (10,830 feet) long and 40 metres (131 feet) wide before domestic troubles in Rome forced the Emperor back home and the project was abandoned.

The Byzantines tried, the Venetians tried. But time and again the enormity (and cost) of the task proved overwhelming. It wasn't until the technological advances of the Industrial Revolution that the canal project finally seemed feasible. A plan was considered, then put aside, by the new Greek government soon after independence from the Turks in 1830. It was the opening of the Suez Canal in 1869 that provided the spur – the Greeks assigned the mammoth task to a French company soon after. But yet again it stalled.

In 1881 Hungarian general Stefan Tyrr took over the project, and work commenced the following year. The canal took 11 years to complete, and followed almost exactly the route proposed by Nero 1,800 years earlier. It measured 6,346 metres (20,820 feet) in length, was 24.6 metres (81 feet) wide at sea level and around eight metres (26 feet) deep, and caused 12 million cubic metres (423,792,000 cubic feet) of earth to be displaced. On 25 July 1893 the Corinth Canal opened to traffic.

The greatest irony of this feat of engineering, two and a half thousand years in conception, is that within a century of its opening the development of super container ships, easily able to round the Peloponnese and too large for the canal, rendered it all but obsolete.

By train

Two trains a day run between Nafplio and Athens and Piraeus via Argos and Corinth. An additional train goes only as far as Argos. The rail station is by the port (for more information, call 275 202 9380).

Olympia

Ancient Olympia, the ancient Sanctuary of Zeus and home of the first Olympics, is deservedly the main tourist attraction of the western Peloponnese. Though packed during the summer months, it's well worth braving the crowds to explore the impressive site.

Olympia is about five hours from Athens, so we advise an overnight stay somewhere nearby or, better still, that you make it part of a longer trip exploring central or south-western parts of the Peloponnese.

Named after Mount Olympus which lies further north in Central Greece, Olympia was the most important sanctuary of the ancient world. The cult of Zeus started to develop around 1200 BC and, according to myth, Zeus's son Heracles appointed him patron of the Olympic Games. The Games took place every four years and were reorganised in 776 BC by Iphitus, King of Elis, who introduced the Sacred Truce (*ekecheiria*). Before and during the celebrations a ceasefire was declared among all Greek city-states for a month. Only free-born male Greeks were allowed to participate or spectate: neither slaves nor women could pass the gate of Altis, the sacred precinct – with just one single exception recorded throughout history. Kallipateira, a woman from Rhodes, disguised herself as a man and managed to enter the stadium, but her identity was revealed while celebrating her son's victory. Claiming her blood relationship with more than one Olympic champion, she was spared the death penalty, but thereafter it was decided that all participants and trainers should appear naked.

The most important monuments of the archaeological site include the Temple of Zeus (as large and impressive as its contemporary, the Athenian Parthenon), which once featured the now-lost gold-and-ivory statue of Zeus, one of the Seven Wonders of the Ancient World, created by Phidias; the Temple of Hera, where the famous statue of Hermes by Praxiteles was discovered in 1877; the Pelopeion, dedicated to the cult of ancient hero Pelops; the Treasuries, small edifices that operated as storage chambers of valuable offerings; and the Stadium, capable of holding up to 45,000 spectators.

The **Archaeological Museum of Olympia** holds some of the most magnificent examples of ancient Greek sculpture, including Praxiteles's Hermes and Paionios's Nike. Olympia is sited at the fertile confluence of the Alfeios and Kladeos rivers, and the surrounding rural areas have a lot of natural and historical interest, though Pyrgos, the regional capital, is somewhat less than scenic. The locals are looked down on as hicks by their compatriots, and though they do try to be helpful with foreigners they tend to come across as rather brusque and stand-offish. The modern town of Olympia, tediously overrun with souvenir shops, gives the impression that it was built just to serve the archaeological site. The **Museum of the Olympic Games** is its one and only draw.

After so many hours under the hot Olympian sun, you undoubtedly deserve a relaxing dip and you will get it if you head south to **Kaiafas** and its idyllic stretch of sand. To the west the beaches around **Katakolo** are a fairly good option as well. Another to try is **Skafidia**, just three kilometres (two miles) north, and the so-called **Aldemar** beach, named after the nearby five-star hotel (*see p258*). It will take you around 30 minutes to reach any of these beaches by car.

From mid July to mid August the **Floka Festival** at the recently built Olympia Theatre features drama, music, dance and other cultural happenings. For more information, contact the Municipality of Olympia (262 402 2549).

Archaeological Museum of Olympia

262 402 2529. **Open** 10.30am-5pm Mon; 8.30am-3pm Tue-Sun. **Admission** €6 (€9 incl site); €3 concessions (€5 incl site); free under-18s. **No credit cards**.

Archaeological Site of Olympia

262 402 2517. **Open** *May-Oct* 8am-7pm daily. *Nov-Apr* 8am-3pm daily. **Admission** €6 (€9 incl museum); €3 concessions (€5 incl museum); free under-18s. **No credit cards**.

Museum of the Olympic Games

Spiliopouliu (262 402 2544). **Open** 8.30am-3.30pm daily. **Admission** €2; free under-18s. **No credit cards**.

Where to eat & drink

Good value for money and a friendly atmosphere is what you will get at the traditional taverna of **Kladeos** (262 402 3322, main courses €7-€11), right behind the railway station in Olympia. Try **En Plo** (262 104 1300, main courses €8-€12) in Katakolo for home-made specialities by the sea. Popular with the locals, **Aigli** (4km off the Pyrgos-Patras road, 262 102 2502, main courses €8-€10) serves delicious home-cooked dishes.

Patra.

Where to stay

The **Aldemar Olympian Village** (Skafidia, Pyrgos, 262 105 4640, www.aldemarhotels.com, closed Oct-Apr, doubles €145-€200) is about a half-hour drive from Olympia, but the facilities and service are worth the extra drive. The **Amalia Hotel Olympia** (210 607 2000, www.amalia.gr, doubles €125-€150), two kilometres before Ancient Olympia, offers clean and comfortable rooms and well-kept patios. For an exceptional view of Olympia, try the recently refurbished **Antonios Hotel** (Krestena, 262 402 2348, www.olympiahotels.gr, doubles €56-€120). A good budget option is **Camping Diana** (262 402 2314, €5.50 per person, €3.50 tent, €3.50 car), a 15-minute walk from the archaeological site; facilities include a swimming pool and a mini-market for basic supplies. There is also a **Youth Hostel** (Praxiteli Kondyli 18, 262 402 2580, €8 per person plus €1 for extra sheets).

Getting there

By bus
KTEL buses to Olympia leave Kifissos station (Kifissou 100, 210 513 4110) twice daily (5.5hrs; €20). Call ahead to check the timetable.

By car
Olympia is 334km (208 miles) from Athens via Patras (coastal drive, national highway) or 323km (200 miles) via Tripolis (inland, windy drive). Both routes are well signposted.

By train
Trains to Olympia leave Athens' Larissa station (Karolou 1-3, 210 529 7777) twice daily (5hrs; €15). Call ahead to check the timetable.

Getting around

There is no direct bus service from Olympia to Katakolo, Kaiafas and the nearby villages. You'll need to get to Pyrgos first and then continue your trip. Buses leave Olympia for Pyrgos and from Pyrgos for the coastal and mainland villages every hour. For more information, contact the offices of KTEL Ileias in Athens (210 513 4110).

Patra

Patra doesn't get the best of press. For most visitors, the only reason to journey to this port 225 kilometres (141 miles) west of Athens, on the north-west edge of the Peloponnese, is to catch a ferry to Italy or the Ionian islands. Yet this irrepressibly lively little city (Greece's third largest, and its second port) is not without its charms, particularly when the sun goes down and the pavement cafés start to fill. In fact, it's Patra's zesty, youthful nightlife that is its primary draw – to enjoy the city at its buzzy best, visit during the Greek Carnival which runs for seven weeks leading up to Lent. The city is currently enjoying a spate of renovations and improvements to its infrastructure in anticipation of its upcoming stint as European Capital of Culture for 2006.

Patra is laid out on a grid plan, stretching uphill from the busy port, and becomes steadily more attractive the higher you climb. Its modern lower reaches are dominated by constant traffic and nondescript blocks, but the shopping here is good, particularly in the streets between and around Platia Olgas and Platia Georgiou.

A half day is plenty to take in the few sights. Overlooking the town is the ruined **Kastro** (Castle) (261 062 3390, closed Mon, Sun afternoon, admission free), built on the site of the ancient acropolis in the sixth century AD, and continually in use until World War II. There's not a lot to see, but the archaeologically inclined might enjoy untangling the architectural legacies of successive Frankish, Byzantine, Venetian and Turkish rulers.

Nearby stands the **Roman Odeon** (261 022 0829, open mornings Tue-Sun, admission free), described by Pausanias around 170 AD as the second-finest odeon in Greece (after the one in Athens). It was built some time before 160 BC and went out of use by the third century AD. Today, it's the venue for theatre and music events during Patra's enjoyable **Summer Arts Festival** (early June-late Sept, 261 062 0236).

Some of the local finds from classical times are laid out around the Odeon. Others are on display in the **Archaeological Museum of Patra** (Maizonos 42, 261 022 0829, open 8.30am-3pm Tue-Sun, admission free). The museum's pride and joy is a superb Roman mosaic pavement from a villa uncovered in the town.

You might also want to visit the vast bulk of the Byzantine-style church of **Agiou Andreou** (St Andrew), which was completed in 1974 and dominates the south-western corner of the city.

If you need a break from metropolitan life, a popular (though touristy) trip is to the **Achaïa Clauss** winery (Petroto Patron, 261 036 8100), just outside Patra, where the famed Mavrodaphne dessert wine is made.

If lying on a beach is more your thing, then the nearest is a ten-minute cab ride away at Plaz – just north of the city. Bikes are available free of charge from the extremely helpful Info Center on the waterfront, which also has an excellent English-language guide to the city.

Where to eat & drink

Though Patra is roaring with traffic noise from dawn until well after dusk, there are sanctuaries to be found on a number of pedestrianised, café-lined streets. The hippest alleyway in town is Radinou, one block south of Platia Olgas, which throbs with the chatter of Patra's sizeable student population and the clubby beats that waft from the street's strip of funky bars.

For a little more space and a little less volume, head a further block south to the cafés on Agiou Nikolaou, and those near the church of Agiou Andreou on tree-lined, traffic-free Trion Navarhon. The best eating in Patra is to be had at taverna-style places, and there's a great one here, on the corner with Riga Fereou, called **Mythos** (261 032 9984). Famed for its excellent meaty dishes, meze and salads, this cosy candlelit joint is a favourite among locals.

The other main pedestrianised nightlife area is at the top end of Gerokostopoulou and along the Ifestou, just below the Odeon.

For somewhere more chilled, keep heading upwards until you reach Papadiamandopoulou, immediately below the castle. Try meze and a carafe of the dark local wine at **Mourias**

(No.34, 261 027 6797, closed Oct-Mar and lunch Apr-Sept, main courses from €4.50) or **Kastro** (Panagouli 22, 261 062 2584).

The bars here stay open into the early hours, but if it's a heady club scene you're after, do as the city's dance kids do and head out to the summer resort of Rio, eight kilometres (five miles) north-east (a ten-minute No.6 bus ride away), where the waterfront is a continuous line of heaving bars and discos.

Where to stay

Until recently, accommodation options in Patra were hardly appetising. In its day, the big, blocky 120-room **Astir** (Agiou Andreou 16, 261 027 7502, doubles €115-€150) dominated both the waterfront and the classier end of the market. And while its rooftop bar and pool still appeal, these days two smaller hotels easily trump it for style. The 25-room **Byzantino Hotel** (Riga Fereou 106 & Asklipiou 26, 261 024 3000, www.byzantino-hotel.gr, doubles €150-€180) is cleanly designed in an updated trad style, while the **Primarolia Art Hotel** (Othonos Amalias 33, 261 062 4900, www.arthotel.gr, doubles €125-€185) is an incongruously gorgeous piece of contemporary design on Patra's grimy waterfront, with 14 rooms decked out with Jacobsen and Starck gems and hung with modern Greek artworks.

Further down the price scale, don't expect much character. The dull-but-reliable **Galaxy** (Agiou Nikolaou 9, 261 027 8815, doubles from €65) is well located, while those on a tight budget shouldn't have any complaints about **Pension Nicos** (Patreos 3 & Agiou Andreou 121, 261 062 3757, doubles €35-€40).

Tourist information

Othonos Amalias 6 (261 046 1740/1741). **Open** 8am-10pm daily.

Getting there

By bus

Buses to and from Athens leave every half hour (ten of these are express services). Journey time: 3hrs 30mins/2hrs 30mins express. The bus station is located on Othonos Amalias, the road that runs along the waterfront.

By car

It takes around 2hrs 30mins to reach Patra from Athens on the main E94 and E65 roads.

By train

There are eight daily trains to and from Athens. Journey time: 3hrs 30mins. All call at Corinth. The station is on the waterfront, close to the bus station.

Trips Out of Town

Island Escapes

If Athens gets too much, hop on a boat for an Aegean adventure.

It's well known that Piraeus is the ferry gateway to the Greek islands. But less known is the fact that you don't need to tempt seasickness with hours and hours aboard a ferry for the sake of an idyllic island escape. Some of the loveliest Greek islands are in fact within just a few hours of the mainland. Close enough, even, just to pop over for an island lunchdate – the enchanting **Aegina** is just 40 minutes away by fast boat.

The four islands listed below – pine-clad **Spetses** (two hours by fast boat), cosmopolitan **Hydra** (90 minutes), scenic, lively **Poros** (one hour) and the engagingly undeveloped Aegina – all make rewarding day trips or weekend destinations. If you do them as a quick side trip from Athens, it makes sense to take the fast boat rather than the regular ferry: journey times are halved. Two companies, Flying Dolphins (210 419 9200, www.dolphins.gr) and Saronic Dolphins (210 422 4777), run services to all four, leaving from the dockside at Piraeus about 200 metres south of the metro station, beside (Akti) Miaouli. Ticket booths (credit cards accepted at Flying Dolphins) are open from about an hour before each departure, but note that if you want to travel on a Friday afternoon or Saturday morning and return Sunday afternoon in high season (mid June to September), it is essential to buy tickets in advance. In high season there are several departures a day, but they are less frequent at other times, so make sure you've checked the timetable.

If you prefer to use the slower, cheaper, conventional ferries, we recommend that you book via a travel agent (*see p263*) as services can be confusing.

Aegina

Aegina, an island of 85 square kilometres (33 square miles) and a population of 10,000, is a mere 40-minute jaunt from Piraeus by hydrofoil. Yet it's a world away from the fumes and angst of Athens. Here you can visit one of the finest ancient monuments in the country, relax at a seaside taverna, or rent a bike and breeze through the endearing, pocket-sized port capital of Aegina Town. It's a pleasantly bustling town brimming with tavernas and cafés that overlook the fishing boats bobbing gently at the waterfront, and where horse-drawn carriages and pretty

neo-classical buildings hark back to the town's days as Greece's first capital after the War of Independence.

Twelve kilometres (about eight miles) east of Aegina Town is the intricate and immaculately preserved fifth-century BC **Temple of Aphaia** (229 703 2398, admission €4). Aphaia was a local goddess, later identified with Athena. It's a top-rank site and worth the journey, especially since en route are the **Monastery of St Nektarios** and the island's abandoned, atmospheric medieval capital, **Paleohora**.

Antiquary opportunities within walking distance of Aegina Town are at **Kolona**, home of the ruins of the **Temple of Apollo**, and the **Archaeological Museum** (229 702 2248, closed Mon, admission €3) located just north of the port.

The best spots for a swim are **Marathona** or **Aeginitsa** on the west coast, and **Kleidi** and **Keri** near the southern village of **Perdika** – an ideal place for a seaside lunch. The more commercialised eastern resort of **Agia Marina** also has some decent beaches. Shuttle boats leave from the main harbour.

Where to eat & drink

For great seafood in Aegina Town, try **Agora** (229 702 7308, closed Aug, main courses €5-€15) at the fish market, south of the port and a block inland, or **Lekkas** (229 702 2527, closed mid Dec-Feb, main courses €8-€15) on the seafront. The classic waterfront café **Aiakeion** (229 702 2249, closed Nov-Mar) serves cakes to die for. In Perdika, **To Proreon** (229 706 1827, main courses €8-€15) is a first-rate taverna on the seafront.

For nightlife in Aegina Town, **On the Beach**, **Belle Epoque**, **En Aigini** and **Ellinikon** are all lively hangouts. Clubs are clustered on the waterfront.

Where to stay

Most hotels quote a 'door price', but this can often be lowered with a spot of bargaining. In Aegina Town, the **Aegenitiko Archontiko** (Agiou Nikolaou & Thomaidou 1, 229 702 4968, doubles €50-€70) is traditional and friendly, while **Hotel Areti** (Kazantzakis 4, 229 702 3593, doubles €40-€50) offers sea

The cosmopolitan, car-free island of **Hydra** – the perfect place to unwind. *See p263.*

Pocket-sized **Aegina Town**. *See p260.*

views. In Perdika, **Hotel Hippocampus** (28 Oktovriou, 229 706 1363, doubles €35-€40) is traditional and cosy.

Tourist information

Aegina doesn't have an independent tourist information centre. However, **Aegina Island Holidays** (Dimokratias 47, 229 702 6430, closed Sun) is a helpful private travel bureau on the seafront.

Getting around

The bus station on Platia Ethneyersias runs an excellent service to most villages on the island. Regular services run to the Temple of Aphaia, and eight to ten per day run from Aegina Town along the west coast of the island, stopping at Marathona and Perdika. You could also rent a bike or scooter from one of several rental centres near the port, where you can also pick up horse-drawn carriages.

Spetses

The pine-clad island of Spetses is scenic, vibrant and cosmopolitan, steeped in history, and just two hours from Piraeus by hydrofoil. It covers 23 square kilometres (nine square miles) and has a population of about 4,000.

Rather quaintly, cars are pretty much banned on the island, so hire a bike or don comfortable shoes before setting out to explore the charming courtyards and grand neo-classical mansions of the port capital Spetses Town. Otherwise, horse-drawn carriages offer a romantic, if expensive, alternative.

The majestic Mexis Mansion in the town centre once belonged to the island's first governor, Hadziyiannis Mexis. But these days it's home to the **Museum of Spetses** (229 807 2994, closed afternoons & Mon, admission €3). As well as displaying relics from the 1821 Greek War of Independence, it houses the bones of Spetsiot heroine Laskarina Bouboulina, a leading figure in the fight against the Turks. The **House of Laskarina Bouboulina** (229 807 2416, closed Nov-Mar, tours every 45mins 9.45am-8.15pm, admission €4) can also be visited at the cannon-dotted modern port of **Dapia**. Once a rallying point during the revolution, Dapia is now the island's commercial centre and ferry port. The island's medieval district of **Kastelli**, the **Old Harbour** and the **Church of St Nicholas** (229 807 2423), with its giant pebble mosaics, are all nearby and worth a visit.

The **Anargyreios and Korgialenios School** (229 807 2206, call 8am-2pm to arrange a tour), about 15 minutes' walk west of Dapia, was an English public school where British writer John Fowles used to teach.

You can walk to some reasonable coves from Spetses Town, but the best beaches on the island are at **Agia Anarghiri** – a long, sheltered sandy bay in the south of Spetses – and **Agia Paraskevi**, a few kilometres further west (on the hill above it is the **Villa Yasemia** – used by Fowles as the setting for *The Magus*). Water taxis are an exhilarating way to get to secluded beaches, but they don't come cheap.

The little **Church of Panaghia Daskalaki**, on top of Spetses' mountain, also merits a visit. Though it's a bit of a hike from town it's not too strenuous and is a good way to build up an appetite.

Where to eat & drink

For fish and lobster spaghetti, try **Exedra** (229 807 3497, closed Nov-Feb, main courses €8-€10), on a jetty at the Old Harbour. **Lazaros** in Kastelli (229 807 2600, closed mid Oct-Mar, main courses €8-€12) serves good cooked dishes and home-made retsina, and the famed **Patralis** fish taverna (229 807 2134, closed Oct-7 Jan, main courses €8-€12) in the area of Kounoupitsa, west of the port, is also worth a visit. **Bracciera** and **Figaro**, near the port, are popular clubs.

Where to stay

A short walk from Spetses Town, in Kounoupitsa, the traditional **Economou Mansion** (229 807 3400, doubles €100-€205) is much loved for its huge balconies. Also in Kounoupitsa is the luxurious **Nissia** (229 807 5000/210 342 1279, doubles €135-€200). For more affordable comfort, a good bet is the **Yachting Club Inn** (229 807 3400, doubles €42-€70), near the beach half a mile from town.

Tourist information

The island's tourist police in the town centre (22980 73100, closed after 3pm and Oct-mid May) can provide you with information on accommodation, places to visit and where to eat and drink.

Getting around

You can reach most parts of the island by bicycle or motorbike – visit one of the various rental outlets in Spetses Town. Small boats ferry locals and visitors from Dapia to various beaches during the summer. Sea taxis are an expensive alternative but can take up to ten people for a set price. Horse-drawn carriages are also available.

Hydra

Arriving on this picturesque 50-square-kilometre (19-square-mile) island (population 3,000) after a 90-minute hydrofoil trip from Piraeus is like stepping into a painting. The distinctive neo-classical stone mansions of Hydra Town ascend amphitheatrically around the picture-pretty port where cafés teem with a cosmopolitan crowd and donkeys await their next expedition along cobbled lanes. (Like neighbouring Spetses cars are banned.)

For spectacular sea views, follow Boundouri, a pebbly path fringed with poppies that winds upwards from the port and towards the fishing village of Kamini; the route is particularly magical at night. Alternatively, climb the mountain from town to the **Monastery of Profitis Ilias** (229 805 2540, closed noon-4pm daily), the adjacent **Convent of St Efpraxia** (229 805 2484) and the nearby uninhabited **Monastery of St Triada** – the views from the top more than justify the one-hour trek.

Mandraki and **Vlichos** are the best beaches near the main harbour town, but for something a little more secluded head to **Bisti** and **Agios Nikolaos** in the west of the island and **Limioniza** in the south. Sea taxis take up to eight passengers at a time, to the above and other destinations, for a set price.

Drag yourself away from the island's natural beauty to visit the **Panaghia Mitropoleos** cathedral (229 805 2829, closed afternoons Sept-Apr), whose distinctive clock tower dominates the waterfront. It is here you'll find the ecclesiastical **Byzantine Museum** (229 805 4071, closed Mon, admission €1.50). Relics from the 1821 revolution are on display at the island's **Historical Archives & Museum** (229 805 2355, admission €3) at the port. Also worth a quick tour is the **Mansion of Lazaros Koundouriotis** (229 805 2421, admission €4) – once the home of the island's wealthy 18th-century merchant family – where the **Historical & Folk Museum** and **Public Art Gallery** are housed.

Many contemporary art collectors keep houses on Hydra, which each summer attracts a who's who of the international art scene. A must is the annual exhibition of works from the Ophiuchus Collection housed at **Hydra Workshops**, a gallery space located in the harbour area.

Where to eat & drink

Ydrargyros (229 805 4030, closed winter, main courses €8-€15) serves European cuisine in a sophisticated candlelit setting behind the port, while **Xeri Elia** (229 805 2886, closed three weeks Nov, main courses €8-€10) offers simple but quality fare in a square near the port. **Kondylenia** (229 805 3520, closed Nov-Feb) is situated in a charming location at Kamini. **Spilia Beach Club Café-Bar** (229 805 4166, closed Nov-Mar), built into the side of a cliff just before the cannons at Hydroneta, is a great spot for a coffee or a beer during the day. At night, visit the **Pirate Bar** (229 805 2711) for rock and 1980s nostalgia, **Nautilus** (229 805 3563) to sample some Greek music and **Heaven** (229 805 2716) for clubbing.

Where to stay

Bouayia (229 805 2869, doubles €70-€120) has a homely atmosphere; more stylish is **Bratsera** (229 805 3971, closed Oct-Mar, doubles €130-€150), set in a restored 19th-century sponge-processing factory. At the **Orloff** (229 805 2564, closed Nov-Apr, doubles €115-€130) guests can enjoy breakfast in a flower-filled courtyard. All are within walking distance of the port, which is rather handy as cars are banned on the island.

Tourist information

The tourist police (229 805 2205), in the town centre, can provide details on accommodation, eating and drinking out and places to visit.

Getting around

No motor vehicles are allowed on Hydra, so rent a bicycle or prepare yourself for plenty of walking (note that Hydra has a lot of steps). Donkey rides from the port are a quainter way of seeing some of the town. Sea taxis (229 805 3690) connect the port to all the island's beaches. Set prices: Kamini €7, Mandraki €10, Vlichos €10.

Poros

Covered in pine forests, Poros is a lively, scenic island just an hour from Piraeus and close to some of the most striking archaeological sites in the Peloponnese (*see p250* **Northern Peloponnese**). It has an area of 31 square kilometres (12 square miles) and a population of around 4,000. Poros (meaning 'ford' or 'crossing') is actually two islands – Sferia (the tiny volcanic peninsula that harbours Poros Town) and the more extensive Kalabria. They are separated from each other by a shallow artificial canal.

Poros Town's skyline is dominated by the characteristically island-esque **Clock Tower**, which looms over the animated, café-lined waterfront and rises distinctly from the hillside dotted with traditional and neo-classical houses. Among the characterful homes, on the west side of the island, lies the historic **Villa Galini**, famous among the literary set for having accommodated several writers in its time, including George Seferis and Henry Miller.

Points of interest in Poros Town include Constantinos Parthenis's magnificent wall paintings at the **Cathedral of St George** (229 802 3241, open Sat & Sun afternoons only), near the port, and the small **Archaeological Museum** (229 802 3276, closed Mon, admission free). The museum features finds from ancient **Troezen** (now Trizini), the legendary birthplace of Theseus and site of the ancient **Temple of Aesculapius**. Trizini is an eight-kilometre (five-mile) bus trip from Galatas, on the mainland. If you make the journey, the Gefira tou Diavolou, or **Devil's Bridge** – a natural rock formation spanning a gorge – en route makes for a pleasant walk, as do the nearby orange and lemon groves.

Elsewhere on the island, the sixth-century BC **Temple of Poseidon** (closed Mon, admission free), near the centre of Kalabria, has been reduced to a scant few pillars but remains an arresting sight. Legend has it that the exiled orator Demosthenes drank poison here after having been cornered by his enemies. For a serene excursion, visit the 18th-century **Monastery of Zoodochou Pigis** (229 802 2926), in an idyllic setting in southern Kalabria.

Poros isn't renowned for its beaches, but **Neorion Bay** and **Kanali** (north and south of Poros Town respectively) both make good swimming spots, as does the pretty sheltered cove of **Agapi**. More secluded beaches can be found near the ruins of the 19th-century Russian naval dockyard.

Where to eat & drink

For tasty home-cooked food, try **Mourtzoukos** (Neorion, 229 802 2438, closed Nov-Mar, main courses €5-€7) or **Panorama** (Askeli Bay, 229 802 4563, closed two weeks Nov, main courses €7-€9); for fresh fish, head to **Nikolas** taverna (Monastiri, 229 802 3426, closed Nov-Mar, main courses €7-€9), about four kilometres (two and a half miles) from the port.

The waterfront is swarming with vibrant bars, but for a catch-all experience, head to **Scirocco** (229 802 5790), south of the port. Warm up with a drink at its bustling café-bistro upstairs before heading downstairs to enjoy some music in the venue's popular club.

Where to stay

The **Sto Roloi** guesthouse (229 802 5808, www.storoloi-poros.gr, doubles €75-€250), housed in a restored neo-classical mansion just behind the port, is owned by the same people as **Anemoni** (229 802 5808, doubles €75-€250). The latter consists of two renovated farmhouses next to the Church of St Constantine; both are recommended. The newly refurbished **Poros Hotel** (229 802 2216, doubles €95-€150) has a prime location on the waterfront at Neorion Bay, while a cheaper option is the Hotel Saga (229 802 5400, www.sagahotelporos.com, doubles €65-€90), with its large balconies overlooking Kanali Bay.

Tourist information

If you have any queries regarding where to stay or eat and places to visit, call the tourist police (229 802 2256, closed end Sept-mid May). **Family Tours** (229 802 3743) is a helpful travel agent just behind the waterfront.

Getting around

To see the island, rent a scooter or bicycle from one of the rental outlets on the waterfront. Buses regularly leave Poros Town for the Monastery of Zoodochou Pigis. Frequent boats connect Poros Town with Galatas on the mainland from where there are regular buses to Trizini and the nearby Devil's Bridge. Travel agents on Poros can also organise day trips to Nafplio and to the Ancient Theatre of Epidaurus (for both, *see p250* **Northern Peloponnese**).

Directory

Features

Directory

Getting Around

Arriving & leaving

By air

Athens International Airport – Eleftherios Venizelos

210 353 0000/www.aia.gr.
The Greek capital is served by Eleftherios Venizelos Airport, about 27 kilometres (17 miles) north-east of Athens, linked by the six-lane Attiki Odos highway. There are now two new ways of getting to the city centre from the airport: the metro's Line 3, which will take you from the airport to Monastiraki station, and the new suburban railway (Proastiakos), which connects with Larissa station. Both of these link up to the broader public transport network.

The metro runs every half hour between around 6am and midnight and the journey time is 27 minutes. A single ticket costs €8, a return €12, a single for two people €12, for three €16, and for under-18s, over-65s, students and the disabled, €4.

After setting off from the airport, the suburban railway (Proastiakos) stops at Koropi, Pallini, Kantza, Doukissis Plakentias (where you can connect with metro Line 3), Kifisia, Nerantziotisa (connect with Line 1), Iraklion, and Aharnes Railway Junction, and terminates at Larissa, where you can transfer to metro Line 2. The entire journey takes 30 minutes and fares range from €0.70 to travel within Zone 1 to €8 for the trip from Larissa station to the airport. Services run every half an hour between approximately 5am and midnight.

Several public bus routes serve the airport exclusively, linking it with central Athens, Piraeus and the suburbs. All airport buses, known as Athens Airport Express, depart from outside the Arrivals Hall. Routes E92, E93, E96 and E97 run 24 hours a day. E95 goes right to the city centre (Syntagma) in roughly an hour; buses leave every eight to 30 minutes depending on the time of day. Route E96 will take you from the airport to the port of Piraeus. The journey time is a little over an hour and buses leave every 20 minutes to one hour, again, depending on the time of day. E92, E93 and E97 go to

Kifisia, Kifisou bus station and Dafni metro station respectively. The average journey time is 45 minutes. Route E94 takes you to Ethiniki Amyna, where you'll be able to connect to the city's metro network. The E94 runs from 5am to 11.30pm and leaves every 15-30 minutes, depending on the time of day. The journey time is around 30 minutes.

For more details on these routes, contact the Athens Urban Transport Organisation (OASA) on 185. The phones are manned by bilingual staff from 7am to 9pm daily.

Tickets for the Athens Airport Express cost €2.90 and can be purchased from all metro stations, blue-coloured public transport ticket booths or the bus driver – in this last case, make sure you have the right change. Your ticket is valid for one journey to or from the airport and you can use it within the city for 24 hours after the time you validate it (in the machine on board the bus) for an unlimited number of trips on all modes of public transport. If you are using one or more other forms of public transport prior to boarding the airport bus, validate your ticket once upon embarking on your journey and again on the airport bus.

Taxis will drop you off right outside the Departures entrance. There is a queue for taxis at the airport extending from doors 4-1 of the Arrivals entrance. An average taxi ride from Syntagma to the airport costs around €16 during the day and evening or €20 from midnight to 5am and takes 40 minutes (more in rush hour).

Be aware that frequent strikes and demonstrations can bring the city centre to a standstill so make sure that you allow plenty of time to get to the airport.

Airlines

Aegean Airlines *210 998 8339/ www.aegeanair.com*
British Airways *210 890 6666/ www.british-airways.com*
easyJet *210 353 0300/ www.easyjet.com*
Hellas Jet *210 353 0815/ www.hellas-jet.com*
Olympic Airlines *210 966 6666/ www.olympic-airways.com*
Virgin Express *210 353 0376/ www.virgin-express.com*

By rail

The national rail authority is called **OSE** (210 529 7777/www.ose.gr). Athens' main stations are Larissa (for trains from northern Greece and abroad) and Peloponnisou (for trains from the Peloponnese). The terminals are near each other in one of Athens' less savoury neighbourhoods. Keep an eye on your belongings and avoid accepting assistance from dodgy types outside the stations. Between 5am and 11.30pm the stations are linked to the city's transport system by buses, trams, metro and cabs, located right outside.

Larissa Station *Deliyianni 31 (210 529 7777). Metro Larissa Station.* **Open** 6.30am-midnight daily. **Map** p297 D1.
Peloponnisou Station *Sidirodromon (210 513 1601). Metro Larissa Station.* **Open** 6.30am-midnight daily. **Map** p297 C1.

By boat

From central Athens you can get to the port of Piraeus by metro (Line 1) or the 24-hour 040 bus from Syntagma (Filellinon). For more information, contact the Piraeus Port Authority (210 459 3000). An average taxi ride from Syntagma to the port costs €7-€11 during the day or €15 late at night (midnight-5am).

If you're planning to travel by boat in August, make sure you've reserved your tickets well in advance – it's the month when practically the whole of Athens escapes to the islands.

For information on routes and timetables, visit www.greekferries.gr, a comprehensive database detailing many of Greece's main ferry services. Piraeusferry.co.uk has timetables, information and booking facilities.

Ferry companies

ANEK Lines *Akti Posidonos 32 & Leocharous (210 419 7420/ www.anek.gr). Metro Piraeus.* **Open** 7.30am-8.30pm daily. **Credit** DC, V.
Hellas Flying Dolphins *Akti Kondyli & Aitolikou 2, Piraeus (Cyclades & Sporades 210 419 9000/ Saronic Gulf 210 419 9200/www. dolphins.gr). Metro Piraeus.* **Open** *Summer* 8.30am-8pm Mon-Sat. *Winter* 8.30am-4pm Mon-Fri; 8.30am-2.30pm Sat. **Credit** AmEx, MC, V.

Minoan Lines *Syngrou 98-100,*
Syngrou (210 920 0020/www.
minoan.gr). Metro Syngrou-Fix.
Open 8.20am-8pm Mon-Fri;
8.30am-4.30pm Sat; 3.30-4.30pm
Sun. **Credit** AmEx, DC, MC, V.
Map p301 D8.
Thermopylon 6-10, Piraeus (210
414 5700). Metro Piraeus. **Open**
7.30am-9pm daily. **Credit** AmEx,
DC, MC, V.

Yacht rental

Bear in mind that if you rent a motor
sailer without a crew, at least two
people on board need to be in
possession of a valid yacht licence.
Amphitrion Yachting *Defteras*
Merarchias 3, Piraeus (210 411
2045/www.amphitrion.gr). Metro
Piraeus. **Open** 9am-7pm Mon-Fri;
9.30am-1pm Sat. **Credit** AmEx,
DC, MC, V.
The average price for a ten- to 12-
person sailing boat, with crew, is
€20,000 a week in high season (June-
mid Sept). You can sail from one of
four different marinas: Alimos,
Glyfada, Vouliagmeni or Zea.

Nava Yachts *Sakkiotis*
Commercial Centre, Athinon 8,
Lavrion (22920 69018/www.
navayachts.gr). **Open** 10am-5.30pm
Mon-Fri. **No credit cards**.
Yachts for periods of seven days and
upwards (weekend rentals subject to
availability). The average price for a
ten-person sailing yacht is €4,500 a
week (skipper, crew and cabin crew
are available on request). You can
sail from Lavrion every Saturday or
other bases on the islands of Corfu,
Lefkas, Skiathos, Kos and Paros.
Triton Yachting *Eleftherias 5A,*
Alimos (210 981 1044/www.triton
yachting.com). **Open** 10am-6pm
Mon-Fri; 10am-3pm Sat. **Credit**
AmEx, MC, V.
Offers motor sailers, with crew, for
periods of two to 20 days. Prices for
a four-person boat start from €1,300
during high season. You can sail
from Alimos, Lavrion, Kalamaki and
various other harbours in Attica.
Vernicos Yachts *Leof Posidonos*
11, Alimos (210 989 6000/www.
vernicos.gr). **Open** 10am-7pm Mon-
Fri; 10am-2pm Sat. **Credit** MC, V.

Offers a wide selection of vessels,
from ultra-fast motor yachts
complete with swimming pools, to
traditional motor sailers. Bareboat
cruising and crewed yachts both
available. Charters begin and end
on a Saturday for multiples of seven
days, but in the low season flexible
arrangements can be made. Prices for
an eight-person boat start at €7,500.

Marinas

To book a berth:
Alimos Marina *210 982 1850.*
Glyfada Marina *210 891 2281.*
Vouliagmeni Marina *210 896*
0012.
Zea Marina *210 428 6100.*

By coach

The intercity coach service in Greece,
KTEL, serves destinations all over
the country. There are two coach
stations in Athens: Terminal A
(Kifisou 100), with buses to the
Peloponnese and western Greece,
and Terminal B (Liosion 260), with

Taxi revolution

In past years, the taxi experience was as
much a part of doing Athens as traipsing
around Plaka or gazing at fallen pillars. The
Athenian fleet was something of a freak
show, dominated by a tribe of Neanderthals
bursting at the seams with testosterone.
Back then, their untamed spirit obeyed no
speed limits, road regulations or personal
hygiene rules, and smoky interiors, noisy
confrontations with other road users and
'creative' charging were the norm. Drivers
and their vehicles were like miniature mobile
volcanoes, spewing fumes from cigarettes
and exhaust pipes, and creating enough
noise pollution to raise the dead, with
blaring radios, plenty of swearing and
heavy-handed horn use.

However, the Olympics provided authorities
with the golden carrot to persuade cabbies to
pull their socks up and start offering the kind
of services that their customers deserved.
Games organisers provided crash courses
in safe driving, protocol and languages, and
government investment provided drivers with
grants to improve their vehicles.

Taxi drivers are still not saints – be
prepared for a brief detour or two, a lecture
in world affairs or football, and don't be
surprised if you find yourself sharing a ride
with a complete stranger – but at least you

can be sure of finding an air-conditioned cab
and now drivers usually open the window or,
possibly, even ask before lighting up. Athens
is the only European city we know where
having one passenger on board is no bar
to picking up another. It's good for the
environment, good for your waiting time and
– since he gets two fares out of it – good for
the driver's pocket. Now *there's* a surprise.
Incidents of overcharging do still occasionally
occur, but they seem more rare, and in
Olympic Athens one cabbie famously retained
his dignity: when forgetful Dutch athlete
Diederik Simon left his silver medal in the
back of an Athens cab, the honourable driver
promptly returned it.

With a fleet of some 15,000 yellow cabs,
taxis greatly exacerbate the traffic problem in
this city of four million people, something
that becomes painfully and rather ironically
evident whenever the drivers try to persuade
the government to allow them to use bus
lanes by going on strike: on such days bus
travellers reach their destinations in record
times and the city's streets seem delightfully
calm. Last year, the Transport Ministry had
the novel idea of trying to lure some taxis off
the streets with the promise of bus driving
licences, though the subject seemed to sink
as quickly as it had appeared.

services connecting to central and northern Greece. For information on tickets and timetables, call 210 512 4910.

Travel agencies

Amphitrion Holidays

Syngrou 7, Makrygianni (210 900 6000/www.amphitrion.gr). Metro Akropoli. **Open** *Sept-May* 9am-5pm Mon-Fri. *June-Aug* 9am-6pm Mon-Fri; 9am-1pm Sat. **Credit** AmEx, DC, MC, V. **Map** p301 E7.

Argo

Xenofontos 10, Plaka (210 324 6000). Metro Syntagma. **Open** 9am-5pm Mon-Fri; 9am-3pm Sat. **Credit** AmEx, MC, V. **Map** p297 F5.

Aspida Travel

Filonos 46, Piraeus (210 413 2258). Metro Piraeus. **Open** 9am-5pm Mon-Fri; 9am-1pm Sat. **Credit** AmEx, MC, V.

Public transport

For information on public transport, visit www.oasa.gr and www.ametro.gr, or phone the Athens Transport Organisation (OASA) on 185.

FARES AND TICKETS

Metro tickets can be bought at ticket machines or ticket offices at all stations. Ticket machines do not give change for notes or take credit cards. The regular fare is €0.60 for Line 1 and €0.70 for Lines 2 and 3 (€0.70 for a journey involving a combination). A reduced fare of €0.40 is available for pensioners and students. Children up to six years old travel free.

You need to validate your ticket at the special machines before you board the train. Tickets are valid for 90 minutes from the time of validation and for interchanges on all three lines. However, they are not valid for return via the route already covered.

Fares for both **buses** and **trolleybuses** are €0.45. Drivers do not issue tickets, which must be bought prior to boarding from OASA ticket booths and kiosks. Tickets must be validated using the special machines on the bus itself.

A regular ticket for the **tram** is €0.60 (€0.30 for under-18s, over-65s, students and the disabled) and can be purchased from booths or special machines on the platforms. Tickets must be validated in special machines on the platform.

New €1 tickets are available that allow for travel on all types of public transport for a period of 90 minutes.

A day pass (€2.90) is valid for an unlimited number of trips on the metro, buses and trolleybuses and €10 tickets allow for a week's travel on all modes of public transport within the city.

Metro

The new underground train network is called the metro and the older line, which runs both underground and overground, is the ISAP (www.isap.gr). The stations are clearly marked with 'M' signs.

The network operates from 5.30am to midnight and has three different lines: Line 1 (ISAP) runs from the port of Piraeus to the northern suburb of Kifisia; Line 2 runs from Agios Dimitrios to Agios Antonios; and Line 3 from Monastiraki to Athens International Airport. Trains run around every five minutes at peak times (ten minutes off peak).

Suburban railway (Proastiakos)

The brand-new suburban railway, or Proastiakos, currently runs from Athens airport to the central Larissa station. A new link continuing down to the Peloponnesian city of Corinth is scheduled to open in May 2005. Services run every half hour between approximately 5am and midnight.

Buses & trolleybuses

Athens is well served by buses and trolleybuses. Their routes aren't particularly useful for visitors unless they need to get out to the suburbs and of course they can be delayed by traffic.

Blue buses and yellow trolleybuses run from around 5am until 11pm/midnight, depending on the route. For more information, contact OASA (185). You can pick up a bus map at metro stations.

Tram

The tram (www.tramsa.gr) went into service just before the 2004 Olympic Games and links central Athens (Syntagma) with the Peace and Friendship Stadium (SEF, which also links up with the ISAP line) in Faliro and the south-eastern suburb of Glyfada (Kolymvitirio). The service from the city centre to the southern coast has been criticised by commuters for its delays, but visitors with fewer time constraints will appreciate the Faliro-Glyfada route with its sea views and easy access to the beach. Trams run between 5am and 1am Sunday to Thursday and around the clock Friday to Saturday,

providing a much-needed night service for coastal clubbers in the summer. Between 5am and 10pm the average waiting time is 7.5 minutes, between 10pm and 1am 10 minutes, and from 1am to 5am 40 minutes.

Taxis

Taxis can get snarled up in traffic, especially during rush hour, but fares are reasonable and the service has greatly improved since the 2004 Olympics (*see p267* **Taxi revolution**). After midnight, when most public transport stops, taxis become a necessary form of transport.

Athenian taxis are yellow, with a 'TAXI' sign on the roof. They can be hailed in the street or booked by phoning a local cab company (€1 surcharge). One useful rank is on Syntagma between Ermou and Karagiorgi Servias.

Though it's pretty hard to find taxis during rush hour, most Athenian cabbies have no qualms about stopping to pick up extra fares. If a taxi slows down (or flashes his headlights) as he approaches you but has his light switched off, mouth your destination to him and he will stop to pick you up if he is going in the same direction.

Ask your driver for an estimate of how much your journey is going to cost before you set off. If you feel you're being ripped off, suggest that you find a police officer to get a second opinion; if your cabbie really is trying to take you for a ride, this kind of threat is usually enough to bring him back to his senses.

All taxis are obliged by law to use a running meter – if the driver doesn't switch it on when you get in, ask him to. There are two basic tariffs: No.1 and No.2. Depending on the time of day and the journey, the driver needs to select the correct rate. Tariff No.1 is the day rate, used from 5am to midnight, while tariff

No.2 is the night rate, valid from midnight to 5am. Also, tariff No.1 is used within the city limits and No.2 is used outside that zone. The number 1 or 2 should be clearly visible on the meter.

The meter starts at €0.73 and there is a minimum charge of €1.47. There is also a surcharge of €1.17 for taxi rides from and to the airport, and €0.50 for each item of luggage over 10 kilos.

Radio taxis

Europe 210 502 9764.
Express 210 994 3000.
Ikaros 210 515 2800/www.athens-taxi.gr.
Kosmos 18300/www.1300.gr.

Driving

You really don't need a car in Athens, but if you do have one, map your route before setting off and be prepared to keep your temper in check. Extensive roadworks and poor signposting make driving around the city extremely hard work. Athens' traffic jams (and its fender benders) are legendary. In the evening the police are on the lookout for drunk drivers, setting up checkpoints around the club districts. The summer months are especially messy, with accidents soaring around the coastal club strips.

Drivers should stick to the standard EU speed limits: 30km/h (18mph) in residential areas and around hospitals and schools, 60km/h (37mph) on central roads and 100km/h (62mph) on motorways. Seatbelts are compulsory.

Breakdown services

Check with the company you are registered with at home to find out about affiliated companies in Greece or register with a Greek breakdown company when you arrive.
ELPA Emergency Service 10400.
Express Service 1154.

Parking

Finding a parking place in Athens is notoriously hard. Most Greeks tend to park in the first available space, with no regard for pavements or blocking in other cars. There are no parking meters in Athens, but there are a few private car parks dotted around the city centre.

Lykavitou 3C, Kolonaki (210 361 5823). Open 24hrs daily. Rates €9.50 1st hr; €1/extra hr.

Zalokosta 8 & Kriezotou, Historic Centre (210 362 8863). Open 7am-1am Mon-Fri; 7am-3am Sat. Rates €9 1st hr; €1/extra hr.

Paparigopoulou 9 & Parnassou, Historic Centre (210 323 6606). Open 7am-10pm Mon-Sat. Rates €8/hr.

Platia Klafthmonos, Historic Centre (210 323 6698). Open 6.30am-11pm Mon-Fri; 6.30am-8pm Sat. Rates €6 1st hr; €1/extra hr.

PolisPark, Kanigos Square. Open 24hrs daily. Rates €4.50 1st hr; €1/extra hr.

PolisPark, Vas. Konstantinou & Rizari, Evangelismos. Open 24hrs daily. Rates €5 1st hr; €6.50 2-3hrs; €9 3-4hrs; €0.50/extra hr.

Petrol stations

Avin Oil *Solonos 56, Kolonaki (210 361 7767/210 362 8202). Open May-Sept 6am-9pm Mon-Sat. Oct-Apr 6am-8pm Mon-Sat. Open 24hrs every 1, 7, 17, 27 of each month. Credit DC, MC, V. Map p299 G4.*

Revoil *Mesogeion 17, Ampelokipi (210 770 5876). Open May-Sept 6am-9pm Mon-Sat. Oct-Apr 6am-8pm Mon-Sat. No credit cards.*

Vehicle hire

The minimum age for car rental in Greece is 21 and you must have held a licence for at least one year. EU citizens must hold an EU licence, while non-EU citizens must possess a valid national driving licence as well as an International Driving Permit.

Avis

Amalias 48, Historic Centre (210 322 4951). Metro Omonia. Open 7.30am-8.30pm daily. Rates from €45/day for a Hyundai Atos or Fiat Seicento. Credit AmEx, DC, MC, V. Map p297 F3.

Europcar

Syngrou 42, Makrygianni (210 924 8810). Metro Syngrou-Fix. Open 8am-8.30pm daily. Rates from €38/day for a Renault Twingo. Credit AmEx, DC, MC, V. Map p301 E8.

Hertz

Syngrou 12, Makrygianni (210 922 0102). Metro Akropoli. Open 7.30am-9.30pm Mon-Sat; 8am-9pm Sun. Rates from €60/day for a small car. Credit AmEx, DC, MC, V. Map p301 E7.

Reliable International Rent-a-Car

Syngrou 3, Makrygianni (210 924 9000). Metro Akropoli. Open 8am-9pm Mon-Fri. Rates from €35/day for a small car. Credit AmEx, DC, MC, V. Map p301 E7.

Sixt

Syngrou 23, Makrygianni (210 922 0171). Metro Akropoli. Open 7.30am-9pm daily. Rates from €30/day for a Daewoo Matiz. Credit AmEx, DC, MC, V. Map p301 E7.

Cycling

Although there are plans to introduce cycle lanes in the capital, there are no such facilities as yet and we wouldn't recommend risking it on two wheels.

Walking

The 2004 Olympics jolted the Athenian authorities out of their apathy towards the plight of the pedestrian. As a result they are now widening and improving existing pavements and have created a ten-mile pedestrian walkway to link the city centre's various archaeological sites.

Even so, pedestrians must be permanently alert, as red lights, stop signs, zebra crossings and one-way street signposts are often ignored by drivers. Even a green man doesn't give the pedestrian right of way. Always look both ways before crossing a street, even in pedestrian zones, which motorcyclists use as shortcuts.

Directory

Resources A-Z

Addresses

Most street signs in Athens are written in both Greek and Roman characters. Be warned, however, that spellings can often be quite imaginative due to the fact that there doesn't seem to be a standardised system of transliteration. For example, you could see Lykavitou, Licavittou (phonetic spelling) or even Lycabettus, all referring to the same street. In our listings we have used transliterations that sound recognisable, in case you need to ask for directions.

Age restrictions

The age limit for drinking, smoking and driving in Greece is 18. However, bars rarely ask for ID and most, especially small bars, will allow children in if they are accompanied by an adult. Driving below the age of 18 is strictly prohibited. The age of consent is 15.

Attitude & etiquette

Despite its laid-back attitude to most things, Greece is really a conservative society. Recent events involving skirmishes between tourists and locals in Athens and the islands have highlighted the need for mutual respect. While you may be on a carefree holiday, bear in mind that you are visiting a country with its own set of social rules and values. Drunk and disorderly conduct, overt displays of affection in public places and rude behaviour, especially towards the elderly, are not acceptable.

While Greeks are not famed for their gushing politeness, they will be helpful and friendly towards visitors. One real point of friction between visitors and locals, however, comes when paying a bill or taxi fare. Presenting a cab driver with a €20 note for a €2.50 fare or paying for a pack of cigarettes with €50 will trigger a long, heated argument. It is advisable to carry lots of loose change and, when changing money, to break €100 and €50 notes into smaller denominations.

Greeks are notoriously fond of arguing and shouting at each other in the street. Don't dwell on this too much – they never really act on these exaggerated displays. It's just their way of letting off steam.

Many locals still take a siesta at lunchtime in summer. Between 2pm and 5.30pm it's considered unacceptable to be noisy in residential areas or to disturb people at home.

If you plan to visit churches or monasteries during your stay, dress in a respectable manner (long trousers for men; sleeved dresses and no miniskirts for women).

Business

Meetings and conferences in Athens are generally held at the 'host' office or often in the lobbies of the better hotels, like the Divani Caravel, the Grande Bretagne, the InterContinental and the Hilton (*see pp52-72* **Where to Stay**). Lunch meetings are popular too.

Greeks may be somewhat lax in keeping time in their leisure hours, but not when it comes to business – be prompt. Also dress smartly if it is your first meeting.

Conventions & conferences

Conferences are generally held at the larger hotels. There are also a few official conference centres for fairs and exhibitions.

Helexpo *Leof Kifisias 22, Marousi (210 616 8888/www.helexpo). Bus A7, B7 from Kanigos.*

Piraeus Port Authority Centre (OLP) *Akti Miaouli 10, Piraeus (210 428 6842/www.olp.gr). Metro Piraeus.*

Zita Congress & Travel *1km Paianias-Markopoulou, Paiania (210 664 1190/www.zita-congress.gr). KTEL Koropi from Pedion Areos.*

Couriers & shippers

All courier companies will collect from hotels and offices for a fee. Unless otherwise stated, the companies listed offer both courier and shipping services.

DHL *Alimou 44 & Roma, Alimos (210 989 0000/www.dhl.gr).* **Open** 8am-7pm Mon-Fri; 8am-3pm Sat. **Credit** AmEx, DC, MC, V.

Travel advice

For up-to-date information on travelling to a specific country – including the latest news on safety and security, health issues, local laws and customs – contact your home country government's department of foreign affairs. Most have websites packed with useful advice for would-be travellers.

Australia
www.smartraveller.gov.au
Canada
www.voyage.gc.ca
New Zealand
www.mft.govt.nz/travel

Republic of Ireland
http://foreignaffairs.gov.ie
UK
www.fco.gov.uk/travel
USA
www.state.gov/travel

Greek etiquette

When it comes to cultural etiquette, it's usually best to take a monkey-see-monkey-do approach. In Athens, venture out of an evening before 10pm and, bar the odd über-eager maître d', you'll find the streets deserted. So instead, heartily embrace the daily diary of an Athenian: steal a kip after lunch, reserve your dinner table for late and, while you're at it, make time to greet even acquaintances with a kiss on both cheeks.

But blindly aping native habits is not always recommended. As in the case of the Trojan horse, there are times when there's more to Greek behaviour than first meets the eye. Like those rogue Greek letters that trick you with familiar shapes only to stump you with foreign sounds, some common gestures have altogether different meanings here.

Look out for the nod – or what to the untrained eye at least 'looks' like a nod. Far from indicating the affirmative, the casual dropping of one's chin followed by the tossing back of the head does in fact mean 'no'. For examples of practical usage, check out the city's cabbies who employ it with gusto when, as is invariably the case, they avoid being hailed.

The friendly wave is another innocent gesture lost in translation. Raise your hand – palm out, fingers splayed – and face the consequences. This is not the way to greet friends. It is an insult akin to lifting two fingers.

Having unwittingly committed such a social faux pas, you can soon re-ingratiate yourself with the locals with a spot of arguing. It's no surprise that 'drama' is a Greek word – nothing tickles an Athenian more than the chance to tell their side. The list of suitable topics is endless: pick anything from labour strikes to the cost of meat or tales of personal misfortune. Ears prick up, opinions are voiced vociferously and before you know it you're in the midst of a lively debate. To gauge the popularity of such a forum, just tune into the evening news where everything from a mild bus crash to a high church scandal is embellished with colourful eyewitness accounts.

However, there are times where the rules of conduct aren't nearly so clear cut: for instance, what to do when someone calls you *malaka* (roughly translated as 'wanker'). The word is the most common of insults, screamed at football referees and muttered at the mention of President Bush. So what do you do if it's directed at you? Well, it's a tricky call. You could nod with defiance or wave with anger. Or you could just smile, for among friends it is also a term of endearment. Go figure.

When in doubt remember the golden rule: never ask for milk in your *cafe elliniko* and when all else fails, grab some worry beads and fidget.

SpeedEx *(courier only) Spirou Patsi & Sidirokastrou 1-3, Votanikos, Western Athens (210 340 7190/ www.speedex.gr).* **Open** 8am-7pm Mon-Fri.

TNT *Zita 7, Elliniko, Southern Suburbs (210 894 0062/www.tnt.com).* **Open** 8am-7pm Mon-Fri. **No credit cards.**

UPS *Leof Kifisias 166, Marousi (210 614 6510/www.ups.com).* **Open** 9am-7pm Mon-Fri. **Credit** AmEx, DC, MC, V.

Office services

Fast Digital Copy Centre *Kolokotroni 11, Historic Centre (210 323 9865). Metro Syntagma.* **Open** 9am-5pm Mon-Fri. **No credit cards.** Map p297 F4.

Fototipies Strilinga *Aristidou 9, Historic Centre (210 321 2623). Metro Panepistimio.* **Open** 8am-7pm Mon-Fri; 9am-2pm Sat. **No credit cards.** Map p297 E4.

Secretarial services

IBS International Business Services *Michalakopoulou 29, Ilisia, Southern Suburbs (210 724 5541). Metro Evangelismos.* **Open** 9am-5pm Mon-Fri. **No credit cards.** Also offers translation services and conference organising.

Planitas *Spyridonos Trikoupi 20, Exarchia (210 330 6945-7/210 380 5663/www.planitas.gr). Metro Omonia.* **Open** 9am-7pm Mon-Fri. **No credit cards.**

Translation services

Executive Service *Athens Tower 2, Mesogeion 2-4, Ambelokipi (210 778 3698). Metro Ambelokipi.* **Open** 9am-5pm Mon-Fri. **No credit cards.** For legal and technical translations.

Com Translation & Interpretation *Xenagora 8-10, Platia Amerikis (210 862 3411/*

www.pra-zis.gr). Metro Victoria. **Open** 9am-5pm Mon-Fri. **No credit cards.**

Useful organisations

Athens Stock Exchange *Sofokleous 10 (210 321 1301).*

British-Hellenic Chamber of Commerce *Leof Vas Sofias 25 (210 721 0361/www.bhcc.gr).* **Open** Phone enquiries 9am-5pm Mon-Fri.

US-Hellenic Chamber of Commerce *Mesogeion 109-111 (210 699 3559/www.amcham.gr).* **Open** Phone enquiries 9am-4.30pm Mon-Fri.

Consumer

There is one main consumer protection service in Greece, INKA (Akadimias 7, 210 363 2443, www.inka.gr). However, although INKA can provide

Directory

advice, it doesn't have any legal power. In the case of an argument with a shop owner, hotelier, etc, it is better to seek advice from the tourist police (*see below* **Emergencies**).

Customs

When coming to Greece, you're allowed to bring in duty-free up to 200 cigarettes (or 100 cigarillos or 50 cigars or 250g of tobacco), one litre of spirits (or two litres of wine or liqueur), 50ml of perfume and 250ml of eau de cologne. EU nationals arriving from within Europe don't pass through customs. For further information about customs, contact Athens International Airport (210 353 0000).

Greece is naturally sensitive about its antiquities, which range from fragments of sculpture and architecture to a pebble picked up while touring the Acropolis, to coins and other relics. Taking antiquities out of the country without a permit is considered a serious offence, and the punishment ranges from a hefty fine to a jail term. To apply for a permit, you should contact the Central Archaeological Council (KAS) (210 820 1293) or consult the dealer you bought from.

Disabled

Compared to many other European cities, Athens is not very accommodating towards those with impaired mobility. The 2004 Paralympics highlighted what a nightmare the Greek capital was for the disabled to navigate and the authorities finally had to tackle the problems. In theory at least, all public transport (buses, trams, urban railway) and many cultural and archaeological sites – including the Acropolis – are now fully accessible for wheelchair-users. Many hotels,

shops and public buildings have also improved their ability to cater for disabled customers and efforts are being made to improve the city's pavements for both wheelchair-users and the blind. Transforming Athens into a truly disabled-friendly city, though, requires many more measures, the most important of which, perhaps, is raising public awareness, especially that of drivers as regards their parking habits.

National Committee for the Disabled

6th floor, Milerou 1 (210 523 8961/ www.disability.gr/esaea/).
Offers advice to disabled visitors.

Drugs

Do not get involved with any kind of drug in Greece, whether it be 'soft' drugs like marijuana or 'hard' drugs like cocaine, ecstasy or heroin. Penalties for possession of even small amounts are harsh and getting harsher. Depending on the amount you are caught with (and whether the crime is judged as a misdemeanour or a felony), you will get a suspended sentence, which you can pay off, or face a jail sentence (between five and 20 years).

Electricity

Greece uses 220-volt electric power (AC 50Hz). Appliances from North America require a transformer and British ones an adaptor. Bring one with you to save wasting valuable time searching for adaptors and transformers.

Embassies & consulates

American Embassy *Leof Vas Sofias 91, Ambelokipi (210 721 2951/fax 210 645 6282/www. usembassy.gr). Metro Megaro Mousikis.* **Open** 8.30am-5pm Mon-Fri.

Australian Embassy *Soutsou 37 & Tsocha 24, Ambelokipi (210 870 4000/fax 210 646 6595/www.ausemb. gr). Metro Ambelokipi.* **Open** 8.30am-12.30pm Mon-Fri.

British Embassy *Ploutarchou 1, Kolonaki (210 727 2600/fax 210 727 2876/www.british-embassy.gr). Metro Evangelismos.* **Open** 8.30am-3pm Mon-Fri. **Map** p299 H5.

Canadian Embassy *Ioannou Gennadiou 4, Kolonaki (210 727 3400/fax 210 727 3480/www.athens. gc.ca). Metro Evangelismos.* **Open** 8am-4pm Mon-Fri. **Map** p299 J4.

Irish Embassy *Leof Vas Konstantinou 5-7, Historic Centre (210 723 2771/fax 210 729 3383). Metro Syntagma.* **Open** 9am-3pm Mon-Fri. **Map** p299 E6.

Consulate of New Zealand *Leof Kifisias 268, Halandri (210 687 4700/fax 210 687 4444).* **Open** 10am-3.30pm Mon-Fri (by appointment only).

South African Embassy *Leof Kifisias 60, Marousi (210 610 6645/fax 210 610 6640/ www.southafrica.gr). Metro Marousi.* **Open** 8am-1pm Mon-Fri.

Emergencies

If you need immediate assistance, dial 100, free of charge, from any phone, or 112 from your GSM mobile.

If you've been robbed, attacked or involved in an infringement of the law, but don't require immediate attention, you can file a formal complaint at the Athens police headquarters (Leof Alexandras 173, Ambelokipi, 210 951 5111/210 647 6000) or at the Piraeus police headquarters (Iroon Polytechneiou 37, Piraeus, 210 411 1710).

For any problem, complaint or enquiry you may have, you can also contact the **Tourist Police**, where officers speak foreign languages. They can be contacted on 171 any time of the day or night, seven days a week, from all over Greece.

For hospital listings, *see p273* **Health**.

Useful numbers

Coastguard *108.*
Duty pharmacies *1434.*
Fire department *199.*

Poison Control Centre
210 779 3777.
Road assistance *10400.*
Tourist Police *171.*
Tourist Police Athens *Veikou 43, Koukaki (210 920 0724/210 920 0727). Metro Syngrou-Fix.*
Map p301 D8.
Tourist Police Piraeus *New Passenger Terminal, Xaveriou seafront (210 429 0664). Metro Piraeus.*

Gay & lesbian

Greeks are fairly tolerant of alternative lifestyles and, in Athens especially, there is a growing gay scene, mainly centred in the districts of Gazi and Psyrri, which have several lively gay clubs and bars. However, Greeks are also a bit conservative and gay/lesbian couples should exercise common sense about public displays of affection.

While Athens now has no exclusively gay hotels, the good news is that the majority of hotels in the city centre are perfectly willing to cater to gay couples, but you might want to check in advance.

Act Up Drase Hellas *Nikitara 8-10, Historic Centre (210 330 5500). Metro Omonia.* **Open** 9am-5pm Mon-Fri. **Map** p297 F3.

Gay Travel Greece *210 948 4182/www.gaytravelgreece.com.* Travel agency specialising in gay-friendly hotels and packages for Athens and the rest of Greece, including the Greek islands.

Health

Visitors do not need vaccinations prior to travelling to Greece. The sun can be punishing, and in summer it's a good idea to wear sunscreen, a hat and light clothing. Mosquitoes can be a nuisance: some insect repellent helps when going out in the evening, as does a plug-in zapper (available from supermarkets) for the bedroom.

Though in the capital and on the rest of the Greek mainland tap water quality is generally of a high standard,

remember that some of the islands do not have natural water resources and rely on desalination plants for their supply; the tap water in such places is briny and locals and visitors drink bottled water.

Accident & emergency

All visitors to Athens are entitled to free medical care in the event of an emergency. This may include helicopter transfer if necessary. Call 166 (free from any phone) to request an ambulance. All the hospitals listed below have 24-hour accident and emergency departments.

Agia Sophia General Children's Hospital *Thivon 3 & Mikrasias, Goudi (210 777 1811). Bus A5 or B5.*

Alexandra General Hospital *Leof Vas Sofias 80, Kolonaki (210 338 1100). Metro Megaro Mousikis.*

Errikos Dinan Hospital *Mesogeion 107, Ambelokipi (210 697 2000). Metro Katehaki or Panormou.*

Evangelismos General Hospital *Ypsilantou 45-47, Kolonaki (210 720 1000). Metro Evangelismos.* **Map** p299 J4.

Ippokratio General Hospital *Leof Vas Sofias 114, Ambelokipi (210 748 3770). Metro Megaro Mousikis.*

Contraception & abortion

Condoms are widely available at kiosks (some of which are open 24 hours a day in central Athens), newsagents, supermarkets and pharmacies. If you are on the Pill, however, we advise you to stock up for your holiday – Greek pharmacies require a doctor's prescription.

Though abortion is legal in Greece, there are no family planning clinics as such. Instead, contact one of the general hospitals or clinics, or one of the private gynaecological clinics below. Call to book an appointment or visit between 9am and noon daily.

Iaso *Leof Kifisias 37-39, Marousi (210 618 4000). Metro Marousi, then 010 bus.*

Mitera *Erithrou Stavrou 6, Marousi (210 686 9000). Metro Marousi, then 010 bus.*

Dentists

Some free dental treatments are available for EU citizens at Evangelismos Hospital (Ypsilantou

45-47, Kolonaki, 210 720 1000). Non-EU travellers are advised to contact their embassy (*see p272*).

In case of emergency, check the back page of *Kathimerini*'s English edition for duty hospitals, where you will be able to find a doctor to advise you, or call the SOS-Doctors on freephone 1016 (*see below*).

Doctors

You can also gain access to medical services by calling SOS-Doctors on 1016 (call is free of charge). This is an international organisation of 'house-call' doctors operating on a 24-hour basis. A doctor will be paged to come to wherever you are staying to assist with any medical need or emergency. For patients staying in hotel accommodation, SOS-Doctors fees are fixed at €80 (€100 between 11pm and 7am and public holidays).

If you wish to discuss your symptoms, but do not require immediate attention, the best option is to ask a pharmacist.

Opticians

See p182.

Private clinics

For those who feel uneasy about placing their health in the hands of a government-run hospital (though they really needn't – Greek medical services rank among the best in Europe, even if the hospitals might appear in need of a facelift), the following private clinics all have accident and emergency departments, and provide a range of thoroughly modern facilities.

If you have private health insurance in your own country, check if this brings any affiliations to private clinics in Greece.

Athens Euroclinic *Athanasiadou 9, Ambelokipi (210 641 6600/ emergency 1011/www.euroclinic.gr). Metro Ambelokipi.*

Athens General Clinic *M Geroulannou 15, Ambelokipi (210 692 2600/www.agclinic.gr). Metro Panormou.*

Central Clinic of Athens *Asklipiou 31, Kolonaki (210 367 4000/emergency 1169/www.centralclinic.gr). Metro Syntagma.* **Map** p299 E3.

Hygeia Clinic *Erythrou Stavrou 4 & Leof Kifisias, Marousi (210 686 7000/www.hygeia.gr). Metro Marousi.*

Metropolitan Hospital *Ethnarchou Makariou 9 & Leof Eleftheriou Venizelou 1, Neo Faliro (210 480 9000/www.metropolitan-hospital.gr). Metro Faliro.*

Pharmacies & prescriptions

Generally speaking, the opening hours for pharmacies in Athens are 8am-2.30pm on Mondays and Wednesdays and 8am-2pm and 5.30-8.30pm on Tuesdays, Thursdays and Fridays. Most are closed at weekends, except for emergency pharmacies – to find the nearest one, consult a newspaper, look on the door of a pharmacy, or call 1434.

EU citizens can exchange an E111 form (*see below*) for a health book (*vivliario ygeias*) at the Social Security Foundation (IKA), thereby entitling them to subsidised prescriptions; otherwise you pay the full whack (as do non-EU citizens).

The following pharmacies are centrally located:

Agamemnon Zisiadis *Pireos 1 (in the arcade), Omonia (210 524 8668). Metro Omonia.* **Map** p297 E3.

Bakakos *Aghiou Konstantinou 3, Omonia (210 523 2631). Metro Omonia.* **Map** p297 E3.

Litos *Stadiou 17, Historic Centre (210 322 8458). Metro Panepistimiou or Syntagma.* **Map** p297 F4.

Yiorgos Papaioannou *Asklipiou 144, Kolonaki (210 643 5586). Metro Panepistimio.* **Map** p299 G3.

STDs, HIV & AIDS

Visit the outpatient department of any of the main state hospitals (*see p273*) to arrange for free tests (a prescription issued by a state hospital doctor will speed the process up considerably).

AIDS hotline *210 722 2222.*

Kentro Zois *Diochorous 9, Ilisia, Southern Suburbs (210 729 9747).*

Helplines & support groups

For information on where to turn for help for various problems call a State Citizens' Information (KEP) centre. It will help you in cutting through red tape; call 1564 to access the multilingual 24-hour service to make an appointment at your nearest centre. All the centres listed can deal with English-speaking visitors.

Foundation for the Child & the Family *12A Herodou Attikou, Marousi (210 809 4419/ www.childfamily.gr). Metro Marousi.* **Open** 10am-6pm Mon-Fri.

HAPSA (Hellenic Association for the Prevention of Sexual Abuse) *Erifilis 12, Pangrati (210 729 0496/www.hapsa.netfirms.com). Metro Evangelismos.* **Open** hours vary; call ahead. **Map** p299 J6.

Hellenic Red Cross *Likavittou 1, Kolonaki (210 361 3563/www. redcross.gr). Metro Panepistimio.* **Open** 7.30am-2.30pm Mon-Fri. **Map** p299 E4.

OKANA (drug helpline) *Averoff 21, Omonia (210 889 8200-85/ 1031 hotline/www.okana.gr). Metro Omonia.* **Open** 9am-8pm Mon, Wed; 9am-4pm Tue, Thur, Fri. **Map** p297 E2.

The Parthenon Group of Alcoholics Anonymous *8th floor, Zinonos 4A, Omonia (210 522 0416). Metro Omonia.* **Open** hours vary; call ahead. **Map** p299 G3.

State Counselling Centre for Violence Against Women *Nikis 11, Plaka (210 331 7305/6). Metro Syntagma.* **Open** 8am-6pm Mon-Fri. **Map** p297 F5.

ID

By law Greeks must carry their identity cards at all times. Visitors are advised to carry a photocopy of their passports and visa (if travelling with one), especially in the capital, where it is not uncommon for police to carry out random spot checks in their efforts to clamp down on illegal immigrants. An EU driving licence with photo should also be acceptable.

You have to be at least 18 years old to legally buy or consume alcohol in Greece, but proof of ID is rarely requested.

Insurance

EU nationals should obtain an E111 form (available at post offices), which facilitates free medical care under the Greek national health service (IKA). E111s will cease to be valid after 1 January 2006, when they will be replaced by the European Health Insurance card. Visitors of other nationalities should arrange insurance prior to their trips.

Internet

Internet cafés are widespread in Athens. Most hotels also offer internet access, though at high rates.

Tellas is the only firm to offer free internet connection. Using the username 'tellas' and the password 'free', dial up an internet connection using the telephone number 801 500 5000 (or 211 180 5000 from mobile phones). CosmOTE and HOL are two other good and cheap providers. For useful Athens websites, *see p282* **Further Reference**.

Arcade *Stadiou 5, Historic Centre (210 321 0701). Metro Syntagma.* **Open** 9am-10pm Mon-Sat; midday-8pm Sun. **Rates** €3/hr. **No credit cards.** **Map** p297 F5.

Bits & Bytes *Akadimias 78, Omonia (210 330 6590/ www.bnb.gr). Metro Omonia.* **Open** 24hrs daily. **Rates** €2.50/hr 9am-midnight, €1.50/hr midnight-9am. **No credit cards.** **Map** p297 F3.

Quick Net Café *Gladstonos 4, Omonia (210 380 3771). Metro Omonia.* **Open** 24hrs daily. **Rates** €2.50/hr. **No credit cards.** **Map** p297 E3.

Language

The vast majority of Athenians have a basic grounding in English and many speak it well so you are unlikely to have problems communicating. However, you will be treated with more respect, especially in business liaisons, if you at least make an effort to learn the basics (*see p280* **Vocabulary**). Most Athenians will be flattered that you are trying and keen to help.

Left luggage

The left luggage facilities at Athens International Airport are situated on the ground floor of the International Arrivals terminal.

Travellers can also leave bags at either of the city's railway stations, Larissa and Peloponnisou, situated next door to each other between Deliyianni and Konstantinoupoleos (*see p266*). Both of central Athens' bus stations also have facilities

Dora's doggies

It wasn't just the city of Athens that got a makeover prior to the 2004 Olympic Games; its population of stray dogs did too. Dogged by criticism of the ill-treatment of animals and streets filled with packs of filthy, homeless hounds and felines, Mayor Dora Bakoyianni decided to finally get serious about the problem. Municipal teams were sent out to collect all the strays and take them to temporary kennels where they were bathed, neutered, treated for health problems, collared and electronically tagged before being adopted or returned to their original haunts once the Games had finished. Pet owners were also ordered to get their own animals tagged.

In spite of these positive measures, reports appeared in the UK press that exterminations were being carried out to reduce the stray population. Some welfare activists pinned the falling number of strays on to what they say was government-ordered poisoning of dogs and cats to 'clean up the streets' before the 2004 Olympic Games, allegations that the Greek authorities denied.

There are several reasons why Greece has such a large population of stray dogs and cats: the first is that sterilisation was – and still is in rural areas – taboo. Trying to convince a Greek man to have his dog neutered is like asking him to remove his own manhood, and many female cats and dogs are left unspayed by owners who consider the operation inhumane and unnatural. And although Greek law forbids the abandoning of animals, those who do so are rarely, if ever, found and punished.

In the cities, strays are, for the most part, fairly well cared for. Kind-hearted citizens often look after 'community' dogs or cats, providing them with food and water, and even taking them to the vet when necessary. Some shopkeepers 'adopt' a street dog or cat, and it's not uncommon to enter a chic boutique by stepping over a large, panting canine that has commandeered the doormat. Countryside strays tend to be worse off. Island tavernas may put out fish for families of stray cats or at least turn a blind eye when the tourists are there, but before the season starts the animals often fall prey to poisoners. Hunting dogs are abandoned in the fields if they perform poorly, and unwanted puppies of farm or guard dogs are also turned out to fend for themselves.

There is generally no need to be frightened by Greek strays. There is no rabies, and the city dogs especially tend to be friendly and harmless. The roaming packs of dogs that had been known to nip the heels – or more – of passing joggers, cyclists or walkers have also largely disappeared. The car-chasers, which continue to leap out joyfully attempting to bite the wheels of your car or moped, though somewhat distracting, are usually only interested in rubber tyres, not human flesh.

---

for left luggage, as do the Omonia and Monastiraki metro stations.

Legal help

Should you require any legal help during your stay in Greece, you should contact your embassy or consulate (*see p272*) and/or (where appropriate) your own insurance company.

Libraries

Visit the following libraries to browse through English-language books (note that the books can only be borrowed by members).

British Council Library *Platia Kolonaki 17, Kolonaki (210 369 2333). Metro Syntagma.* **Open** 8.30am-3pm Mon-Fri. **Map** p299 G5.
Hellenic-American Union *Massalias 22, Historic Centre (210 368 0044). Metro Panepistimio.* **Open** 10am-8pm Mon-Fri. **Map** p299 G4.

Lost property

The Greek transport police has a lost property office on the seventh floor at Leof Alexandras 173 (210 647 6000/ 210 642 1616). Bring your passport when making a claim.

Another lost property office is at Athens International Airport in Arrivals in the main terminal (210 353 0000).

Media

Newspapers & magazines

International magazines and newspapers are widely available at kiosks around the central Syntagma and Omonia squares, and on the main thoroughfares in Kolonaki.

Athens News is a local weekly English-language newspaper that comes out on Fridays, while *Kathimerini* is an English-language daily that comes out with the *International Herald Tribune*. Both newspapers feature news items as well as listings of things going on around the city, TV pages, emergency numbers, duty pharmacies and other useful information.

There is a weekly *Time Out* magazine for Athens. Its listings are in Greek and hard to figure out

Directory

unless you speak the language – in which case it's by far the best source of news, reviews, listings and opinion. Its summer *Visitors' Guide*, in English and widely available at newsstands, is an invaluable tourist and events guide.

Radio

Though there are no English-language radio stations in Greece, many play a wide range of British and American music, not to mention just about every other type, Greek and other – just zap through the stations until you find one you like.

For news bulletins in English, tune into the following: Antenna 97.2FM at 8.25am daily; Flash 96FM at 8.55am, 3pm and 8pm daily; ERA 91.6FM at 5am, 9am and 9.30pm daily.

No radio station offers English-language traffic news.

Television

There are three state-run TV channels in Greece (ET1, NET and ET3) as well as several private channels. While the former offer high-quality news and sports coverage and documentaries, the private TV stations tend to go for a tabloid style of news reporting. Their programming also includes soaps, quiz shows and late-night soft porn. Both state-run and private TV channels in Greece feature many familiar foreign programmes and films, and they're usually subtitled rather than dubbed. You'll find listings in papers mentioned above.

Money

The euro was introduced in January 2002. Notes in circulation are €5, €10, €20, €50, €100, €200 and €500 while coins come in denominations of €1, €2, 1 cent, 2 cents, 5 cents, 10 cents and 20 cents.

ATMs

ATMs are widely available in Athens. Most accept Visa and MasterCard (you'll pay interest on cash withdrawals) as well as debit cards of international networks such as Cirrus and Maestro. Syntagma and Omonia are focal points for ATMs.

Banks

Most banks are open 8am-2.30pm Mon-Thur and 8am-2pm Fri.
National Bank of Greece (NBG) *Karagiorgi Servias 6, Historic Centre (210 334 0500). Metro Syntagma.*

Open 8am-2.30pm Mon-Thur; 8am-2pm Fri. **Map** p297 F1.
As well as the usual banking services, this location offers a foreign exchange service on Saturdays and Sundays (9am-1pm).
Other locations: *Eolou 86 (210 334 1000/lost credit cards 210 483 4100).*
Eurobank's 'Open 24' *Leof Kifisias 44, Ambelokipi (210 955 5794). Metro Ambelokipi.* **Open** 10am-6pm Mon, Wed; 9am-8pm Tue, Thur, Fri; 9am-5pm Sat.
Not, as you'll notice, actually open 24 hours as the name might lead you to believe, but still good for an evening visit.
Other locations: *Sofokleous 7-9, Omonia (210 321 4811).*
Central Alpha Bank *(210 326 0000/lost credit cards 210 339 7250) Panepistimiou 3, Historic Centre (210 324 1023). Metro Syntagma.* **Open** 8am-2.30pm Mon-Thur; 8am-2pm Fri. **Map** p299 E5.
Filellinon 6, Plaka (210 323 8542). Metro Syntagma. **Open** 8am-2.30pm Mon-Thur; 8am-2pm Fri. **Map** p297/p301 F5.

Bureaux de change

Eurocambio *Apollon 5, Plaka (210 322 1527). Metro Syntagma.* **Open** 8.30am-4.30pm Mon-Fri; 9am-2pm Sat. **Map** p297 F5/p301 F5.
Stadiou 58, Omonia (210 331 4241-46). Metro Omonia. **Open** 8.30am-7pm Mon-Fri; 9am-2pm Sat, Sun. **Map** p297 E3.

Credit cards

Most major cards (AmEx, Diners Club, MasterCard, Visa) are accepted at hotels, department stores and some restaurants. Ask first if you're unsure.
If you lose your credit card or it is stolen, call:
American Express *210 324 4975-9 (8.30am-4pm Mon-Fri).*
Diners Club *210 924 5890/210 929 0200 (24hrs daily).*
MasterCard (City Bank) *210 929 0100 (24hrs daily).*
Visa *210 326 3000 (24hrs daily).*

Tax

Non-EU citizens travelling in Greece are entitled to a refund of the 18 per cent VAT (value-added tax) paid on certain goods bought during their stay here. Though this doesn't apply to hotel and food bills, it does cover items such as electronic goods, jewellery and furs, and could save you a fair amount of money. The store will

provide you with a form to fill in, which you should hand to a customs officer prior to your departure.

If you want to collect your refund before you leave, allow yourself plenty of time at the airport (or port, or border). Normally, you receive your refund by mail after you return home. Don't be surprised if it takes four to six weeks; this is normal (should you feel that you've been forgotten about, though, call the store where you made the purchase).

If your purchase is cumbersome or fragile, we recommend you have the store ship it home for you, in which case you only need to pay the shipping and import duties upon collection or receipt back home, if applicable.

Natural hazards

Greece lies in a seismic zone, so there are occasional earthquakes, but most are mild and result in no damage or injuries. If an earthquake occurs and you are indoors, get under a table or doorway away from windows. Do not use lifts. If you are outside, try to move to an open area to avoid any falling objects.

In extremely hot weather, avoid overexposure to the sun and drink plenty of water.

Over-the-counter remedies are available to treat jellyfish stings and mosquito bites.

Opening hours

Opening hours vary according to the business and to the season. Generally speaking, however, business hours are 9am-6pm Mon-Fri (8am-2pm for public services offices). Most banks are open 8am-2.30pm Mon-Thur and 8am-2pm Fri, while post offices open 8am-3pm Mon-Fri.

Shops generally open 9am-3pm Mon, Wed, Sat, and 8am-3pm and 5-8pm Tue, Thur, Fri. Large department stores generally open 8am-6pm Mon-Sat (or until 8pm in winter). When it comes to bars and clubs, even those with set hours tend to be flexible – usually closing when most customers have left.

Pets

If you're planning to bring a pet with you, bear in mind that Greeks aren't exactly animal lovers. You'd be hard pushed to find a hotel that accepts pets, and dogs are only allowed to travel on ISAP trains and the last carriage of the tram wearing a leash and a muzzle; otherwise forget about using public transport. The many stray dogs wandering the streets in the centre (*see p275* **Dora's doggies**) are eloquently indicative of the city's policy regarding animals.

Pets coming to Greece need to have an export health certificate, without which they will be refused entry; talk to your vet about this. If you acquire a pet during your stay and want to take it home with you, contact your embassy in Athens (*see p272*) to find out the correct procedure.

Postal services

You can buy stamps from all post offices and many kiosks. Post boxes around town are yellow and post offices are easily spotted by their blue and yellow signs.

Post office opening hours are 8am-3pm Mon-Fri. There are also four central post office (ELTA) branches (Syntagma, Tritis Septemvriou 28, Eolou 100, Koumoundourou 29) that stay open till 8pm. Local postage charges are approximately €0.50 for a regular letter and up to €4.50 for a letter weighing up to two kilos. Within the EU, prices range from €0.65 for a simple letter to €11.50 for a bulky letter. Prices are almost double for letters going outside the EU. The price for parcels going abroad ranges from €22 (in the EU) to €25 (outside EU) for small parcels, and from €95 (in the EU) to €120 (outside EU) for parcels of 20 kilos.

Tip: Parcels sent abroad are inspected, so don't wrap and seal them beforehand. You can buy brown paper, soft padded envelopes and cardboard boxes at most post offices.

See also p270 **Couriers & shippers**.

Poste restante/ general delivery

If you want to receive mail while you are staying in Greece but will have no fixed address, you can have it sent 'poste restante' to the main post office just off Omonia (Eolou 100) or the American Express location at 1st Floor, 2 Ermou Street, GR-102 25, near Syntagma. You must present your passport upon receipt.

Religion

Greece is a Greek Orthodox society with only a smattering of other religious groups: a sizeable Catholic community is mostly centred in Athens and on the island of Syros, and there is just a handful of Presbyterians. There are very few Jews and even fewer indigenous Muslims, and their communities are mostly found in the north. However, in recent years immigrants have brought Islam to Athens (migrants account for around a fifth of the city's population). For a long time, mosques were not licensed to operate in parts of the country and only recently has the government agreed to the construction of a large mosque outside Athens, in Spata, although this project was facing opposition at the time of writing. In the meantime, community centres run worship services in makeshift mosques (often set up in stores or basements) located mostly downtown around the Omonia area.

Anglican

St Paul's Anglican Church, Filellinon 29, Plaka (210 721 4906). Metro Syntagma. **Map** p297/p301 F5.

Armenian Apostolic

St Gregory, Kriezi 12, Psyrri (210 325 2149). Metro Thisio. **Map** p297 D4.

Catholic

St Denis, Omirou 9 & Panepistimiou 24, Historic Centre (210 362 3603). Metro Syntagma. **Map** p297 F4.

German Evangelical

Christuskirche, Sina 66, Kolonaki (210 361 2713). Metro Syntagma. **Map** p299 G3.

Jewish

Beth Shalom Synagogue, Melidoni 5, Keramikos (210 325 2823). Metro Thissio. **Map** p296 C4.

Protestant

St Andrew's Protestant Church, Paraschou 117, Pedion Areos (210 645 2583). Metro Victoria.

Safety & security

Though the crime rate has risen in recent years, Athens is still one of the safest cities in Europe. What crime there is tends to be of the organised variety between rival gangs. Also, the threat of terror attacks directed against foreign individuals has decreased since the arrests of suspected members of the notorious November 17 organisation in 2002.

Just to be on the safe side, however, here are a few tips:

Keep your money and other valuable items hidden away in a safe place while walking around the city, and especially on public transport.

Avoid poorly lit or dark deserted places at night.

Beware of bar hustlers. These characters target men out alone at night inviting them for a drink. The unsuspecting male is then taken to a bar where he is introduced to one or more girls whom he will be encouraged to buy drinks for before being presented with an enormous bill. If you try to dispute the price, the bar owner will probably bring in the heavies to help you recalculate. Don't get into this position.

Directory

Smoking

Despite the fact that Greeks are among the biggest tobacco consumers in the world, the recent European wave of campaigns against smoking seems to be making its presence felt. Smoking is now banned on all public transport and in public buildings (shops, banks, post offices, public offices, schools, hospitals, etc) and most indoor restaurants have no-smoking sections.

Cigarettes are cheap in Greece and the airport duty-free shops stock a wide range of brands.

Study

Language classes

There are several institutions that hold Greek language classes for foreigners in Athens. The centrally located Athens Centre (Archimidous 48, Pangrati, 210 701 2268) is one of the most popular.

Many teachers of Greek also advertise in the classified ads of the *Athens News*.

Useful organisations

For information on studying in Greece, from summer courses to language lessons, visit the Study Abroad website (www.study abroad.com/content/portals/ Greece_pt.html).

If you are interested in longer courses, the Greek Embassy in your own country will also be able to provide information on institutions, courses, prices and procedure.

Telephones

Dialling & codes

Several recent changes to telephone numbers in Greece mean that the numbers displayed in advertisements are not always valid. The area code must be included even if you are calling from the same area: for example, the area code for Athens is 210 and must be dialled whether you are calling from Athens or Thessaloniki. If you are unsure, check with directory enquiries (*see below*). The country code for Greece is 30.

Making a call

If you want to make an international call while in Greece, first dial 00, then the country code, before dialling the rest of the number, dropping any initial zeros as necessary (as it is for all British numbers). The country code for the UK is 44; for Australia it's 61; Canada 1; the Republic of Ireland 352; New Zealand 64; South Africa 27; and the USA 1.

Public phones

The cheapest way to make local or international calls is via the Hellenic Telecommunications Organisation (OTE) offices. Just walk into your nearest office – they're ubiquitous – and grab a booth. At the end of the call, the desk operator will present you with a bill.

Local and international calls can also be made from public cardphone booths and kiosks. Public payphones only take prepaid phonecards (*tilecartes*), which cost €3, €10 or €15 and are available from post offices and kiosks. You can also make calls from kiosk shops where the cost of your call is tallied up on a meter and you pay at the end.

A cheaper way to make calls, though, is to buy pre-paid cards that work like mobile phone top-up cards. They cost the same as payphone cards, but give you more call time for your money (approximately ten minutes for a €3 card). Smile and Talk Talk are two that give good value for money; look out for them at kiosks. As elsewhere in the world, hotels are notorious for charging ridiculously high rates for telephone bills. Avoid making calls from your hotel room, or use a pre-paid phone card.

Operator services

Directory enquiries *11888*.
International operator *139*.
International enquiries *139*.
International assistance *139*.

Mobile phones

Mobile phone connections in Greece operate on the GSM network, so you probably won't be able to use your phone here if you're visiting from the USA or Canada, unless it's a tri-band. In this case, your best option is to buy a 'pay-as-you-go' SIM card package to use while you're in Greece. B-Free Telestet, Cosmocarta, A la Carte and CU (€15 each, from Germanos) are four good ones; top-up cards cost from €9 upwards.

Visitors from the UK will be able to use their phones here if they have agreed roaming facilities with their service provider, or the terms of their pay-as-you-go deal allow it.

Germanos is a recommended mobile-phone service shop.

Germanos

Stadiou 10, Historic Centre (210 323 6000). Metro Syntagma. **Open** 9am-4pm Mon, Wed; 9am-8pm Tue, Thur, Fri; 9am-3pm Sat. **Credit** AmEx, DC, MC, V. **Map** p297/p301 F5.
Kanari 26, Kolonaki (210 361 5798). Metro Syntagma. **Open** 9am-4pm Mon, Wed; 9am-8pm Tue, Thur, Fri; 9am-3pm Sat. **Credit** AmEx, DC, MC, V. **Map** p299 G5.

Faxes & telegrams

There are many central print/copy shops from where you can send faxes, and every neighbourhood has at least one grocer or newsagent with access to a fax machine. Hotels also offer a (more expensive) fax service (and sometimes charge to receive too).

To send telegrams, call 136 or visit your nearest branch of OTE.

Time

Remember to adjust your watch to East European Time when you arrive in Athens. This is two hours ahead of Greenwich Mean Time, one hour ahead of Central European Time and seven hours ahead of Eastern Standard Time.

Daylight Saving Time starts at the end of March and ends in late September.

Tipping

You should tip in taxis, cafés, restaurants and some theatres. Ten per cent is normal, with some restaurants adding up to 15 per cent to your bill. Always check to see if service has been included in your bill.

Toilets

Public toilets in Athens are few and far between and generally little used. Your best bet is to pop into a fast-food outlet or department store. In bars and restaurants, it is best to ask.

Average climate

Month	Temp (°C/°F)		Hours of sun	Humidity (%)
Jan	10.3	50.5	4.12	68.9
Feb	10.7	51.2	4.48	68.3
Mar	12.4	54.3	5.54	66.3
Apr	16.0	60.0	7.42	62.8
May	20.7	69.2	9.24	59.5
June	25.1	77.1	11.12	53.4
July	27.9	82.2	11.42	47.6
Aug	27.7	81.8	11.00	47.3
Sept	24.2	75.5	9.12	53.7
Oct	19.4	66.9	6.42	61.9
Nov	15.5	59.9	5.06	68.9
Dec	12.2	53.9	3.54	70.1

Tourist information

The Greek National Tourist Organisation (GNTO) can provide details on places of interest, hotels and events, though not for many hours of the day or in a very convenient location (but there is a desk at the airport arrivals terminal). The GNTO office in your country can also supply information.

GNTO
Syngrou 98-100, Syngrou (210 928 7050/www.gnto.gr). Metro Syngrou-Fix. **Open** 8am-1.30pm Mon-Fri.

GNTO UK
4 Conduit Street, London W1S 2DJ (020 7495 9300/www. gnto.co.uk).

GNTO US
Olympic Tower, 645 Fifth Avenue, New York, NY 10022 (212 421 5777/www.greektourism.com).

Visas & immigration

EU nationals (exluding those from the 'new' eastern European EU countries, but including those from Cyprus and Malta) can travel without a visa and may remain indefinitely. Non-EU visitors can stay for up to three months without a visa. For longer periods, they should check with the Greek Embassy or Consulate in their home country. From 1 May 2006, citizens of the new EU countries will have the same rights as other EU nationals.

If you wish to extend your visa during your stay, go to the **Aliens Bureau** (Leof Alexandras 173, 210 510 2706). Be prepared to wade through a fair amount of red tape.

Weights & measures

Greece uses the metric system (kilometres, kilogrammes, litres, etc) rather than the imperial system (miles, pounds, pints, etc).
1 metre (m) = 3.28 feet (ft)
1 sq metre (sq m) = 1.196 sq yards
1 kilometre (km) = 0.62 miles
1 kilogramme (kg) = 2.2 pounds (lb)
1 litre (l) = 1.76 UK pints, 2.113 US pints

When to go

Climate

Summers in Athens are generally dry with next to no rainfall and plenty of sunshine. Between July and September the temperature hovers at around 35°C (95°F), and visitors should take precautions against the sun and heat (drink lots of water, wear a hat, etc).

Winter is wetter and cooler, with temperatures occasionally dropping to zero. However, mini-heatwaves with temperatures rising up into the mid 20s are not unheard of in winter.

Public holidays

Fixed
New Year's Day (1 Jan); Epiphany (6 Jan); Independence Day & Feast of the Annunciation (25 Mar); Labour Day (1 May); Dormition of the Virgin (15 Aug); 'Ochi' (No) Day (28 Oct); Christmas (25-26 Dec).

Changeable
Ash Monday (41 days before Easter); Easter weekend (Good Friday to Easter Monday); Whit Monday (50 days after Easter).

The Greek Orthodox calendar and its Western counterpart often diverge where Easter celebrations are concerned. Check ahead to avoid any unpleasant surprises.

Women

Athens is fairly safe, but it's best to avoid walking alone late at night in some of its dingier central districts (Omonia, Platia Vathis, Victoria, Pedion Areos).

See also p274 Helplines and *p273* Contraception & abortion.

Working in Athens

EU nationals (exluding those from the 'new' Eastern European EU countries, but including those from Cyprus and Malta) can work in Greece as long as they have a full passport. If you plan to be in Greece for over 90 days, apply in advance for a residence permit at the Aliens Bureau (*see above*). At the end of the financial year you will have to submit a tax form (available at a local tax office). You will also need to sign up with IKA, the Greek social security foundation, to which your employer has to make monthly contributions.

Non-EU citizens and those from the 'new' Eastern European EU countries should check requirements with their local embassy/consulate. After 1 May 2006 all EU citizens will have equal rights to work and stay in Greece.

Directory

Vocabulary

Pronunciation

a – 'a' as in cat
e – 'e' as in net
ee – 'ee' as in Greek
i – 'ee' as in feet
o – 'o' as in hot
oo – 'oo' as in fool
th – 'th' as in think
dh – 'th' as in that

Useful words & phrases

hello – yassoo; (plural/formal)
herete or yassas
goodbye – yassoo, ya;
(plural/formal) adeeo or yassas
good morning – kalee mera
good evening – kalee spera
good night – kalee nihta
How are you? – Tee kanees?;
(plural/formal) Tee kanete?
yes – ne
no – ohi
please – parakalo
thank you – efharisto
excuse me/sorry – seegnomi

open – anihto
closed – klisto
Do you speak English? – Milate
anglika?
I don't speak Greek (very well)
– Then milao ellinika (poli kala)
I don't understand – Dhen
katalaveno
Speak more slowly, please –
Boreete na milate pio seega,
parakalo?

Emergencies

Help! – Voeethia!
I'm sick – Eeme arosti
I want a doctor/policeman –
Thelo enas yiatros/astinomeekos
Hospital – nosokomeeo
There's a fire! – Ehi fotia!

Accommodation

hotel – xenodhoheeo
I have a reservation – Eho
kleesimo
double room – dhiklino
single room – mono
double bed – dhiplo krevatee

twin beds – dheeo mona krevateea
with a bath – me banyo
with a shower – me doosh
breakfast included – me proino
air-conditioned – kleematismos

Getting around

car – aftokeeneeto
bus – leoforeeo
bus stop – stathmos leoforeeo
coach – poolman
taxi – taxi
train – treno
trolley bus – trollei
aeroplane – aeeroplano
airport – aeerodhromeeo
station – stathmos
platform – apovathra
entrance – eesodhos
exit – exodhos
tickets – isiteeria
return ticket – isiteerio met
epeestrofis
(I'd like) a ticket to –
(Thaleethela) ena isiteerio ya
Where can I buy tickets? –
Pou boro n'agorazo isiteereea?
(Turn) left/right – (Strivete)
aristera/dhexeea

Greek letters and sounds

The alphabet

Αα alpha	'a' as in cat
Ββ vita	'v' as in vice
Γγ gama	'g' as in game
	'y' as in yes
Δδ thelta	'th' as in this
Εε epsilon	'e' as in net
Ζζ zeta	'z' as in zebra
Ηη ita	'ee' as in Greek
Θθ thita	'th' as in thing
Ιι yiota	'ee' as in Greek
Κκ kappa	'k' as in key
Λλ lamtha	'l' as in late
Μμ mi	'm' as in my
Νν ni	'n' as in night
Ξξ ksi	'ks' as in rocks
Οο omikron	'o' as in open
Ππ pi	'p' as in pet
Ρρ ro	'r' as in rope
Σσ (ς at the end of word) sigma	's' as in snake
Ττ taf	't' as in tea
Υυ ipsilon	'ee' as in Greek
Φφ fi	'f' as in food
Χχ hee	'h' as in heat
Ψψ psi	'ps' as in lapse
Ωω omega	'o' as in hot

Double-letter combinations

ει epsilon-yiota-	'ee' as in Greek
οι omikron-yiota-	'ee' as in Greek
αι alpha-yiota	'e' as in net
ου omikron-ipsilon-	'oo' as in food
μπ mi-pi	'b' as in bee
ντ ni-taf	'd' as in date
γκ gama-kappa	'g' as in get
γγ gama-gama	'ng' as in England
γχ gama-hee	'a' as in inherent
το taf-sigma	'ts' as in sets
τζ taf-zeta	'ds' as in friends
αυ alpha-ipsilon	'av' as in avenue
	'af' as in after
ευ epsilon-ipsilon	'ev' as in never
	'ef' as in left

Useful words

exit	εξοδος·
entrance	εισοδος
toilet	τουαλετα

Greek for cheats

Every Greek deeply appreciates any foreigner making the effort to butcher their beautiful and ancient language, so give it a go. And if you find Greek too hard, cheat.

For starters, speak slowly. Someone will finish the sentence for you. Speak quietly and your mistakes won't sound so bad. Speak quickly and blunders will be forgotten. This 'speak quickly' rule might appear to contradict the 'speak slowly' rule but Greek's like that.

Use your body (within limits). When you agree don't nod because, in Greece, a nod can mean 'no'. Instead, smile or just say 'Ne', the Greek for 'yes' (pronounced like the 'ne' in 'never'). To say 'no', remember 'hockey' and take off the 'h'. Strictly speaking, the 'ck' sound in 'ockey' should be more like the 'ch' in 'loch' but it's a quibble and cheats ignore quibbles. Hockey stays.

Let out a 'YA-sas' when saying hello to someone you don't know, or greeting more than one person. Why say hello to someone you don't know? It's a very friendly country. Speaking to a friend is YA-sue.

'How are you?' is 'tea-CAR-knees'. The polite and plural version can't be whittled down to a drink, an automobile or a part of the body, so forget it.

Asking the price of something depends on – dear, oh dear – whether it's singular or plural. You know what? Always say 'PO-sa', which rhymes with 'tosser'. Think pancakes and you'll be fine.

To introduce yourself: 'me-LE-ne Brian' (My name is Brian), the 'me' as in 'met', 'le-' in 'leg', 'ne' in 'net' and 'Brian' in 'Brian'. In this particular example, two Greek letters are needed to make the equivalent sound of the English letter 'B'. This happens quite a lot in Greek and you should either learn all the combinations or change your name to Petros.

What about 'thank you'? Many Greeks speak French, so 'merci' (if you know how to pronounce that) is one option. If you say this in a taverna, be prepared to have all the dishes explained in French.

The Greek for 'thank you' is pronounced 'ef-hari-STO'. Many books mention Mr F Harry Stowe as a way to remember this, cutting out the 'Mr' of course. A clipped version, 'sto', is like saying 'cue' at the end of a fast-spoken 'thank you' and probably works. One radical but fail-safe solution is never to say thank you.

● *Athens News* columnist Brian Church is the author of *Learn Greek in 25 Years*.

It's on the left/right – Eene ekee aristera/thexeea
straight on – eftheea
Could you show me the way to the Acropolis? – Boreete na moo dheexete to dhromoo ya to Acropoli?

Eating & drinking

I'd like to book a table for four at nine – Thaleethela na klino trapezi ya tessera stis enya
A table for two, please – Ena trapezi ya dheeo, parakalo
Can I see the menu? – Boro na dho to katalogho?
Some water – leegho nero
Waiter/waitress – servitoros/servitora
Is there a non-smoking section? – Eeparhee horo poo apaghorevete to kapneesma?
I am vegetarian – Eeme hortofaghos
Where's the toilet? – Poo eene ee twaleta?
That was (very) tasty – Eetane (polee) nosteemo.
That was not (very) good – Dhen eetane (polee) oreo.

bill – logariasmo
I think you've made a mistake on the bill – Nomizo ehete kani lathos sto logariasmo.

Shopping

How much does this cost? – Posso kanee afto?

Communications

phone – tilefono
stamp – gramatoseemo
letter – gramma
postcard – kartpostal
A stamp for England/the US – Ena gramatoseemo ya tin Angleea/Ameriki
Can I make a phone call? – Boro na kano ena tilefonima?

Days of the week

Monday – Dheftera
Tuesday – Treetee
Wednesday – Tetartee
Thursday – Pemptee
Friday – Paraskevee

Saturday – Savato
Sunday – Kireeakee
today – seemera
tomorrow – avreeo
morning – proee
afternoon – apoyevma
evening – vradhi
night – nihta

Numbers

1 – ena; 2 – dheeo; 3 – treea; 4 – tessera; 5 – pende; 6 – exi; 7 – efta; 8 – ohto; 9 – eneia; 10 – dhecca; 11 – endhecca; 12 – dhodhecca; 13 – dheccatreea; 14 – dheccatessera; 15 – dheccapende; 16 – dheccaexi; 17 – dheccaefta; 18 – dheccaohto; 19 – dheccaeneia; 20 – eekosi; 100 – ekato; 500 – penda-kosia; 1,000 – hilia

Times

Could you tell me the time? – Ehete tin ora?
It's... o'clock – Eene... ee ora.
quarter past... – ...ke tetarto
quarter to... – ...para tetarto
half past... – ...ke meessee

Further Reference

Websites

www.athensguide.com
A wide-ranging and knowledgeable home-made site from an American who clearly loves Athens with a passion.

www.athensnews.gr
The site for Athens' weekly English-language magazine. Good for features and news.

www.ekathimerini.com
The internet version of Athens' daily English-language paper. Good general information.

www.culture.gr
Created by the Culture Ministry, this portal highlights the artistic riches of Greece. It has a good list of museums, monuments and archaeological sites, and a regularly updated diary of cultural events.

www.gnto.gr
The site of the Greek National Tourist Organisation offers a wealth of information on where to stay, what to visit and how to get the most out of your stay.

www.gogreece.com
Loads of well-catalogued links provide information on myriad subjects, from arts to travel.

www.hri.org
Excellent information, media and links database for Greeks and Greek-Americans.

Films

The Attack of the Giant Moussaka
(Panos Koutras, 2000)
As silly as its name suggests.

Brides (Nyfes)
(Pantelis Voulgaris, 2004)
Set at the beginning of the 20th century when many Greek women were sent by boat to arranged marriages in the US, *Brides* tells the story of a Greek woman who falls in love with an American photographer during her voyage to the United States.

The Dawn (To Harama)
(Alexis Bistiskas, 1994)
A Star is Born set in Athens, complete with Greek ballads.

Edge of Night (Afti i Nighita Meni)
(Nikos Panagiotopoulos, 2000)
This film follows the ambitions of Stella, a young Athenian girl who dreams of becoming a famous singer.

End of an Era (Telos Epochis)
(Antonis Kokkinos, 1994)
An old man reminisces on his coming of age in Athens in the late 1960s, with the military dictatorship in the background.

From the Edge of the City (Apo tin Akri tis Polis)
(Konstantinos Giannaris, 1998)
A tale of sex and drugs set in the immigrant ghettos on the outskirts of Athens.

Hard Goodbyes: My Father (Dhiskoli Apoheretismi: O Babas Mou)
(Penny Panayotopoulou, 2002)
In the late 1960s a young Athenian boy struggles to come to terms with the death of his father.

Never on Sunday (Pote tin Kyriaki)
(Jules Dassin, 1960)
A US intellectual tries to reform a prostitute from Piraeus, believing her to be emblematic of the fall of the great Greek civilisation.

One Day in August (Dekapendavgoustus)
(Konstantinos Giannaris, 2001)
Follows a day in the life of three families in Athens at the height of the summer, when the rest of the city has left for the beaches.

Rembetiko
(Costas Ferris, 1984)
This film follows the fortunes of a female *rembetika* singer in Athens, from her childhood in the days of the Asia Minor population exchange (1922) to her rise to fame and eventual decline. Featuring original *rembetika* by Stavros Xarhakos.

A Touch of Spice (Politiki Kouzina)
(Tassos Boulmetis, 2003)
The story of a Greek boy who, with his parents, is forced to leave Istanbul during the deportations of 1964, with a focus on cooking and family.

When Mother Comes Home for Christmas (Otan Erthi Mama Gia ta Hristougenna)
(Nilita Vachani, 1995)
This documentary on the life of a Sri Lankan woman hired as a nanny in Athens reveals a dark truth behind some Athenian ladies who lunch.

Books

Classics

Aeschylus
Agamemnon, Persians, Prometheus Bound, The Suppliants

Aesop
Aesop's Fables

Aristophanes
The Acharnians, The Birds, The Clouds, The Frogs, Lysistrata

Euripides
Andromache, The Bacchae, The Cyclops, Electra, Hecuba

Homer
The Iliad, The Odyssey

Pausanias
Description of Greece

Plutarch
The Rise and Fall of Athens

Sophocles
Antigone, Electra, Oedipus the King

Thucydides
History of the Peloponnesian War

Fiction

Douka, Maro
Fool's Gold
The story of a young woman who becomes involved with the resistance movement, and her reaction to the events of 17 November 1973.

Fakinou, Eugenia
The Seventh Garment
The lives of three generations of Greek women reflect the history of the country, from the Asia Minor catastrophe, to the years of the Junta and on to modern Athens.

Finlay, David
The Nelson Touch
Nelson's Column is dismantled, taken from Trafalgar Square and held hostage for the return of the Elgin Marbles to Athens. Comedy and international intrigue.

Haris, Petros
Longest Night: Chronicle of a Dead City
Narratives detailing the brutal reality of the Nazi occupation of Athens during World War II.

Kazantzakis, Nikos
At the Palaces of Knossos
The author of *Zorba the Greek* mixes fact and fiction in this tale about the fall of Minoan Crete at the hands of the emerging city of Athens.

Kotzias, Alexandros
Jaguar
In 1964 the wife and the sister of a hero in the resistance who was killed 20 years earlier

meet in Athens. Their lives have taken a different path, but they share recollections of the main events in their lives, from the German occupation to the civil war.

Manning, Olivia
The Balkan Trilogy (Volume 3: Friends and Heroes)
A young married couple flees war-torn Romania for Athens, where they have to contend with more historical turmoil. Made into a TV series (*Fortunes of War*).

Mourselas, Kostas
Red Dyed Hair
This bestselling novel spawned a popular TV series in Greece. It focuses on the lives of a group of marginalised Piraeus dwellers.

Somoza, José Carlos
The Athenian Murders
When a student of Plato's Academy is found dead, foul play is suspected and Heracles sets about investigating the case. To make things murkier, a literary mystery unfolds within the murder mystery.

Non-fiction

Beard, Mary
The Parthenon
Beard demystifies the sacred temple on the hill.

Burn, AR
The Penguin History of Greece
A useful introduction to ancient Greece.

Church, Brian
Always on a Sunday
An irreverent, affectionate look at life in Greece from the shamelessly witty *Athens News* columnist.
Learn Greek in 25 Years
A tongue-in-cheek crash course for the linguistically challenged.

Davidson, James
Courtesans and Fishcakes: The Consuming Passions of Classical Athens
Sex, gluttony and booze.

Grant, Michael & Hazel, John
Who's Who in Classical Mythology
A thorough compendium of mythological personalities.

Henderson, John & Beard, Mary
Classics: A Very Short Introduction
How the classics have influenced our lives.

Holst, Gail
Road to Rembetika: Songs of Love, Sorrow and Hashish
For those who want to find out more about the blues of the Balkans and its singers.

Mackenzie, Molly
Turkish Athens
The history of Athens during its four centuries of Ottoman occupation.

Sacks, David, et al
A Dictionary of the Ancient Greek World
One-stop volume detailing the people, places and events that shaped the ancient Greek civilisation.

St Clair, William
Lord Elgin and the Marbles
The ultimate volume about the marbles that were taken from the Parthenon in 1801.

Storace, Patricia
Dinner with Persephone
A New Yorker living in Athens deconstructs the Greek sense of self, culture and attitudes with the clarity that only an outsider can have.

Theodorakis, Mikis
Journals of Resistance
The Greek composer and activist's journal during the years of the Junta.

Vlachos, Helen
House Arrest
Vlachos, editor of newspaper *Kathimerini* during the Junta years, was placed under house arrest when she refused to publish a censored paper.

Directory

Advertisers' Index

Please refer to the relevant pages for
contact details

Place of interest and/or entertainment	■
Railway & bus stations	■
Parks	■
Hospitals/universities	■
Olympic venues	■
Neighbourhood	PLAKA
Metro station	Ⓜ

Maps

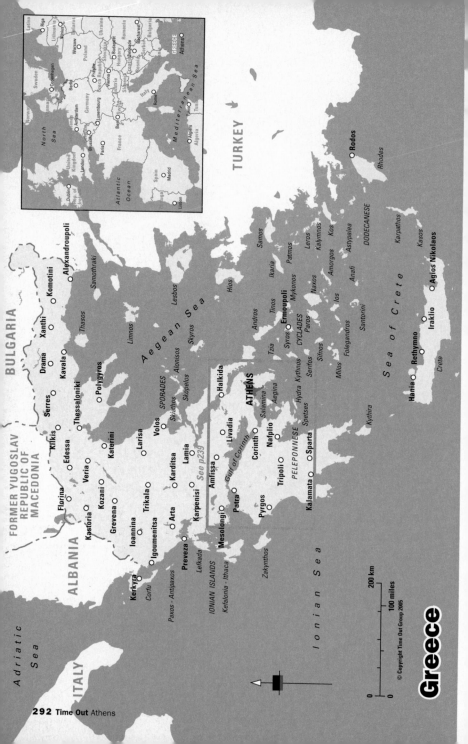

Greece

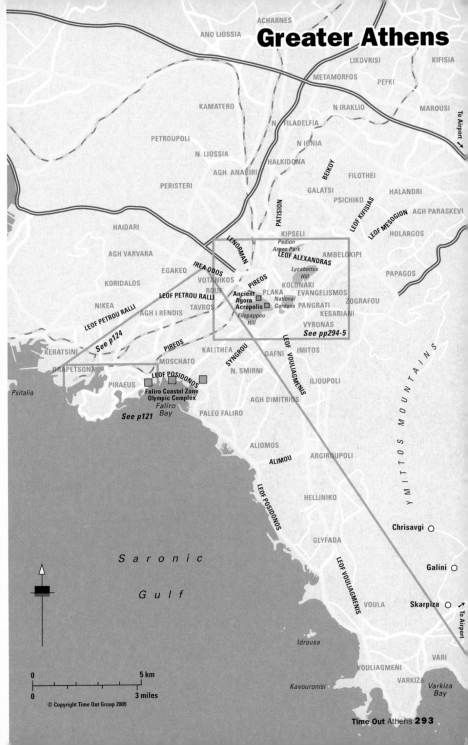

Greater Athens

ACHARNES

ANO LIOSSIA

LIKOVRISI

KIFISIA

METAMORFOS

PEFKI

N IRAKLIO

MAROUSI

To Airport

KAMATERO

N FILADELFIA

PETROUPOLI

N. LIOSSIA

N. IGNIA

BEIKOY

FILOTHEI

HALKIDONA

AGH. ANABIRI

PATISION

GALATSI

PSICHIKO

HALANDRI

PERISTERI

LEOF KIFISIAS

AGH PARASKEVI

KIPSELI

LEOF MESOGION

HAIDARI

HOLARGOS

Pedion
Areos Park

LENORMAN

LEOF ALEXANDRAS

AMBELOKIPI

AGH VARVARA

PAPAGOS

Lycabettus
Hill

EGAKEO

IREA ODOS

VOTANIKOS

PIREOS

KOLONAKI

KORIDALOS

ROUF

Ancient
Agora

PLAKA

EVANGELISMOS

LEOF PETROU RALLI

TAVROS

Acropolis

National
Gardens

PANGRATI

ZOGRAFOU

NIKEA

KESARIANI

AGH I RENDIS

Filopappou
Hill

VYRONAS

LEOF PETROU RALLI

PIREOS

See pp294-5

See p124

KALITHEA

SYNGROU

DAFNI

IMITOS

KERATSINI

MOSCHATO

LEOF VOULIAGMENIS

Psitalia

DRAPETSONA

LEOF POSIDONOS

ILIOUPOLI

PIRAEUS

N. SMIRNI

**Faliro Coastal Zone
Olympic Complex**

Faliro
Bay

AGH DIMITRIOS

See p121

PALEO FALIRO

ALIOMOS

ALIMOU

ARGIROUPOLI

HELLINIKO

Saronic

LEOF POSIDONOS

Chrisavgi ○

GLYFADA

Galini ○

Gulf

LEOF VOULIAGMENIS

Skarpiza ○

To Airport

VOULA

Idrousa

VARI

VOULIAGMENI

VARKIZA

0   5 km

Kavouronisi

*Varkiza
Bay*

0   3 miles

© Copyright Time Out Group 2005

Y M I T T O S   M O U N T A I N S

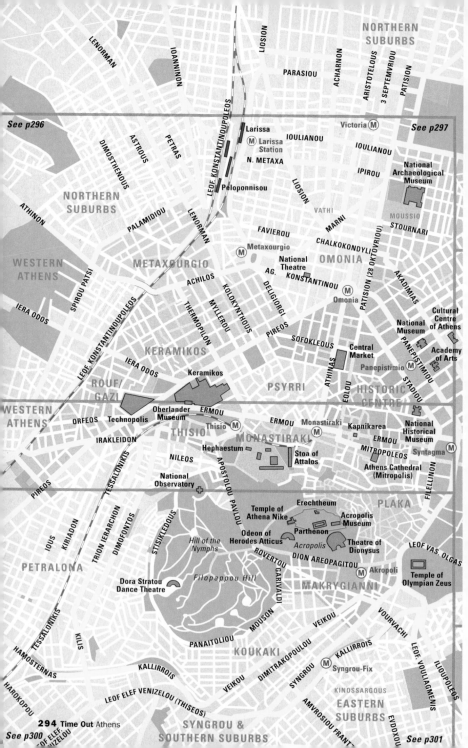

LENORMAN

IOANNINON

LIOSION

NORTHERN
SUBURBS

PARASIOU

ACHARNON

ARISTOTELOUS

3 SEPTEMVRIOU

PATISION

DIMOSTHENOUS

ASTROUS

PETRAS

LEOF. KONSTANTINOUPOLEOS

Larissa

Victoria Ⓜ

IOULIANOU

Ⓜ Larissa
Station

N. METAXA

IOULIANOU

National
Archaeological
Museum

ATHINON

NORTHERN
SUBURBS

PALAMIDIOU

LENORMAN

Peloponnisou

IPIROU

LIOSION

VATHI

MARNI

STOURNARI

MOUSSIO

WESTERN
ATHENS

SPIROU PATSI

IERA ODOS

METAXOURGIO

Ⓜ Metaxourgio

FAVIEROU

National
Theatre

AG.
KONSTANTINOU

CHALKOKONDYLI

OMONIA

PATISION (28 OKTOVRIOU)

AKADIMIAS

LEOF. KONSTANTINOUPOLEOS

ACHILOS

KOLOKYNTHOUS

THERMOPILON

MYLLEROU

DELIGIORGI

PIREOS

SOFOKLEOUS

Ⓜ
Omonia

National
Museum

Cultural
Centre
of Athens

PANEPISTIMIOU

Academy
of Arts

IERA ODOS

KERAMIKOS

Keramikos

Central
Market

ATHINAS

EOLOU

Panepistimio

Ⓜ
Panepistimio

STADIOU

ROUF/
GAZI

ORFEOS

Technopolis

Oberlander
Museum

ERMOU

Thisio Ⓜ

PSYRRI

HISTORIC
CENTRE

WESTERN
ATHENS

IRAKLEIDON

THISIO

NILEOS

Hephaestum

MONASTIRAKI

ERMOU

Monastiraki

Stoa of
Attalos

Kapnikarea

ERMOU

MITROPOLEOS

National
Historical
Museum

Syntagma Ⓜ

PIREOS

TESSALONIKIS

National
Observatory

APOSTOLOU PAVLOU

Athens Cathedral
(Mitropolis)

FILELLINON

IOUS

KIRIADON

TRION IERARCHON

DIMOFONTOS

STISIKLEOUS

Hill of the
Nymphs

Temple of
Athena Nike

Erechtheum

Odeon of
Herodes Atticus

Acropolis

Parthenon

PLAKA

Acropolis
Museum

Theatre of
Dionysus

LEOF VAS. OLGAS

PETRALONA

Dora Stratou
Dance Theatre

Filopappou Hill

ROVERTOU

DION AREOPAGITOU

GARIVALDI

MAKRYGIANNI

Akropoli Ⓜ

Temple of
Olympian Zeus

TESSALONIKIS

KILIS

PANAITOLIOU

MOUSON

VEIKOU

VOURVACHI

LEOF. VOULIAGMENIS

ILIOUPOLEOS

HAMOSTERNAS

HAROKOPOU

KALLIRROIS

VEIKOU

KOUKAKI

DIMITRAKOPOULOU

KALLIRROIS

SYNGROU

Syngrou-Fix Ⓜ

KINOSSARGOUS

EASTERN
SUBURBS

AMVROSIOU FRANT

EVDOXOU

LEOF ELEF VENIZELOU (THISEOS)

LEOF. ELEF. VENIZELOU

SYNGROU &
SOUTHERN SUBURBS

Athens Overview

SPETSON

EVELPIDON

PEDION AREOS PARK

Lofos Finopoulou

PEDION AREOS

NORTHERN SUBURBS

Panormou Ⓜ

PANORMOU

LEOF VAS KONSTANTINOU

LEOF ALEXANDRAS

Strefi Hill

EXARCHIA

Ambelokipi Ⓜ

LEOF ALEXANDRAS

AMBELOKIPI

HARILAOU TRIKOUPI

NEAPOLI

See p299

IPPOKRATOUS

Lycabettus Theatre

Lycabettus Hill

Megaron Mousikis

Eleftherias Park

LEOF VAS KONSTANTINOU

Megaro Mousikis Ⓜ

PAPADIAMANTOPOULOU

EASTERN SUBURBS

Gennadius Library

KOLONAKI

ILISIA

Benaki Museum

Goulandris Museum of Cycladic Art

Alsos Syngrou

LEOF VAS SOFIAS

LEOF VAS SOFIAS

Evangelismos Ⓜ

Parliament Building

Byzantine Museum

National War Museum

National Gallery

NATIONAL GARDENS

IRODOU ATTIKOU

RIZARI

EFTICHIDOU

Presidental Palace

LEOF VAS KONSTANTINOU

Zappeion

SPIROU MERKOURI

PANGRATI

YMITTOU

Panathenaic Stadium

ERATESTHENOU

Alsos Pagkratiou

Lofos Ardittou

ARCHIMIDOUS

EFTICHIDOU

N. THEOTOKI

STADIOU

EASTERN SUBURBS

LEOF. ETHNIKIS ANTISTASEOS

First National Cemetery

YMITTOU

FILOLAOU

FORMIONOS

ANALIPSIS

0   600 m

0   600 yds

© Copyright Time Out Group 2005

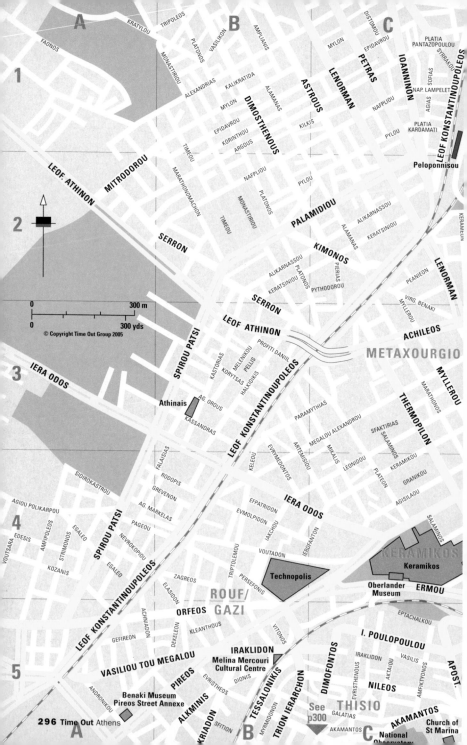

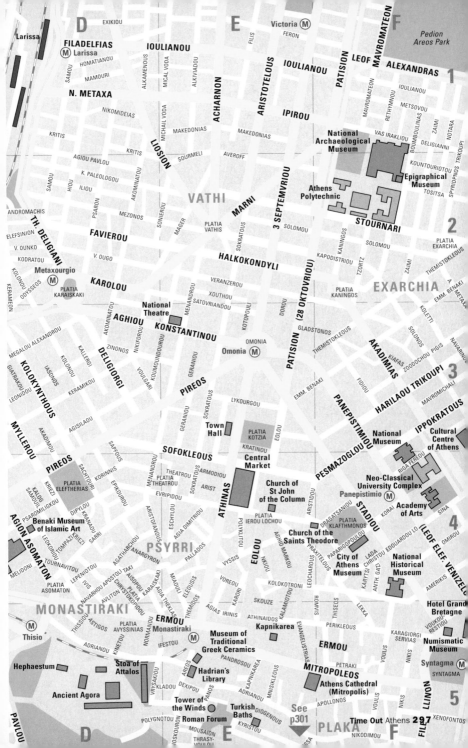

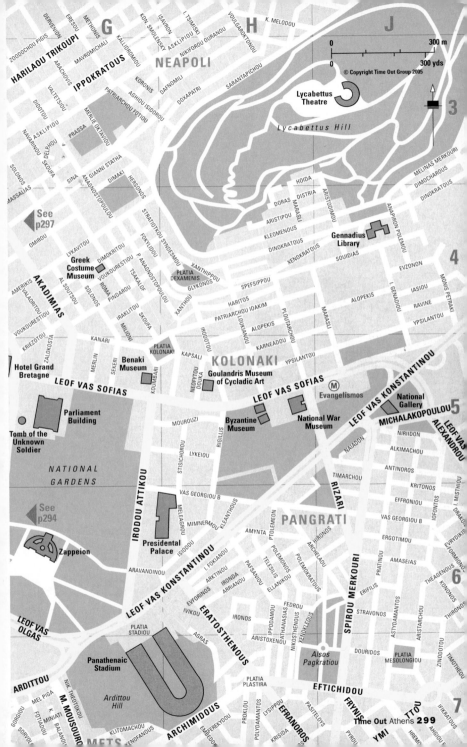

ZOODOCHOU PIGIS
DERVENION
ERESOU
METHONIS
KON SMOLENSKY
ISAVRON
I. TSIMISKI
ASKLIPIOU
NIKIFOROU OURANOU
VOULGAROKTONOU
K. MELODOU

300 m
0
300 yds
© Copyright Time Out Group 2005

HARILAOU TRIKOUPI
MAVROMICHALI
ARACHOVIS
KALLIDROMIOU
IPPOKRATOUS

NEAPOLI

Lycabettus
Theatre

3

VALTETSIOU
DIDOTOU
ASKLIPIOU
NAVARINOU
SKOUFA
DELFON
KORONIS
DAFNOMILI
DOXAPATRI
SARANTAPICHOU

Lycabettus Hill

SOLONOS
MASSALIAS

SINA
ANAGNOSTOPOULOU
GIANNI STATHA
DIMAKI
HERSONOS
STRATIOTIKOU SYNDESMOU

HOIDA

DORAS
DISTRIA
MARASLI
ARISTODIMOU

See
p297

OMIROU

LYKAVITOU
DIMOKRITOU
FOKYLIDOU
P. ANAGNOSTOPOULOU

ARISTIPOU
KLEOMENOUS
DINOKRATOUS

KENOKRATOUS

Gennadius
Library

ANAPIRON POLEMOU

MELINAS MERKOURI
DIMOCHAROUS
DINOKRATOUS

4

Greek
Costume
Museum

DIMOKRITOU
VOUKOURESTIOU
TSAKALOF
A. SOUTSOU
ROMA
PINDAROU

PLATIA
DEXAMENIS
XANTHIPPOU
GLYKONOS

SPEFSIPPOU

SOUIDIAS

EVZONON

AKADIMIAS

AMERIKIS
VALAADRITOU
SOLONOS
IRAKLITOU
SKOUFA

XANTHOU
HARITOS
PATRIARCHOU IOAKIM

ALOPEKIS

I. GENADIOU
IASIOU
RAVINE
YPSILANTOU

MONIS PETRAKI

KRIEZOTOU
ZALOKOSTA
KANARI
MILIONI

IRODOTOU
LOUKIANOU
ALOPEKIS
PLOUTARCHOU

KARNEADOU

VOUKOURESTIOU

MERLIN
SEKERI
KAPSALI
YPSILANTOU

Hotel Grand
Bretagne

Benaki
Museum
KOUMBARI
NEOFYTOU
DOUKA

PLATIA
KOLONAKI

KOLONAKI

Goulandris Museum
of Cycladic Art

LEOF VAS KONSTANTINOU

National
Gallery

LEOF VAS SOFIAS

LEOF VAS SOFIAS
Evangelismos
M

5

Parliament
Building

MOUROUZI

Byzantine
Museum

National War
Museum

MICHALAKOPOULOU
NIRIIDON

LEOF VAS ALEXANDROU

Tomb of the
Unknown
Soldier

STISICHOROU
LYKEIOU
RIGILLIS

ALKIMACHOU
ANTINOROS

NATIONAL
GARDENS

VAS GEORGIOU B

TIMARCHOU

KRITONOS
EFFRONIOU

IOFONTOS
DRAKON
MISTRIOTOU

See
p294

IRODOU ATTIKOU

MELEAGROU
MIMNERMOU
KLEANTHOUS

PANGRATI

VAS GEORGIOU B
ERGOTIMOU

EVRYDIKIS
FORMIONOS

Zappeion

Presidental
Palace

ISIODOU

AMYNTA
PTOLEMEON
HIRONOS
ARCHELAOU

AMASEIAS

THEAGENOUS
KONONOS
THIRONOS

ARAVANDINOU

LEOF VAS KONSTANTINOU

I. FOKIANOU
ARKTINOU
IRONDA
ARRIANOU

POLEMONOS
POLEMOKRATOUS

ERIFILIS
PRATINOU

ASTYDAMANTOS

LEOF VAS
OLGAS

EFVORINOS
IVIKOU

TELESILIS
PAFSANIOU
ELLANIKOU

SPIROU MERKOURI

PRATINOU

ARISTARCHOU
ZINDODOTOU
TIMOTHEOU

ERATOSTHENOUS

IRONOS
FEDROU
IPPODAMOU
ATHANASIAS
NIKOSTHENOU
XENOKLEOUS

STRAVONOS
DOURIDOS

PLATIA
MESOLONGIOU

ARDITTOU

PLATIA
STADIOU

AGRAS

ARISTOXENOU

Alsos
Pagkratiou

Panathenaic
Stadium

Arditou
Hill

PLATIA
PLASTIRA

EFTICHIDOU

M. MOUSOUROU
NIK. THEOTOKOU
K. MINIATI
FOTIADOU

KLITOMACHOU
XENOFANOUS

PROKLOU
LYSIPPOU
POLYDAMANTOS
PASITELOUS
KRISIDA

EFRANOROS
FRYNIS

YMI

IFIKRATOUS
AHGIOU
HREMO

ARCHIMIDOUS

Time Out Athens **299**

GORGIOU
SORVOLOU

MEL PIGA
BALANDIS

EKEEREKYOU
EMBEDOKLEOUS

PYROU

METS

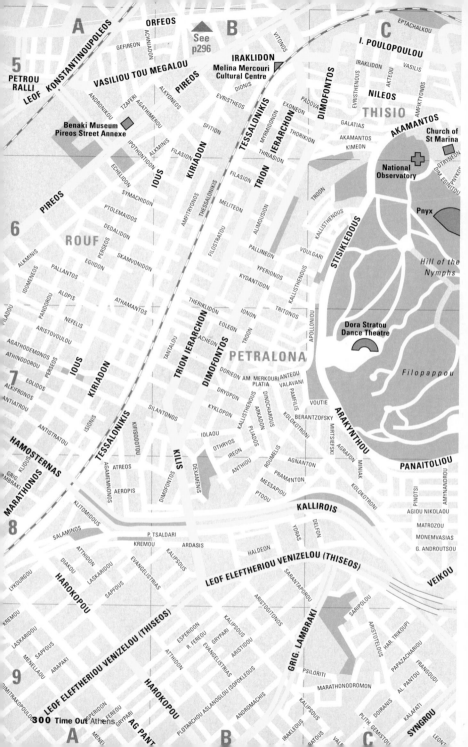

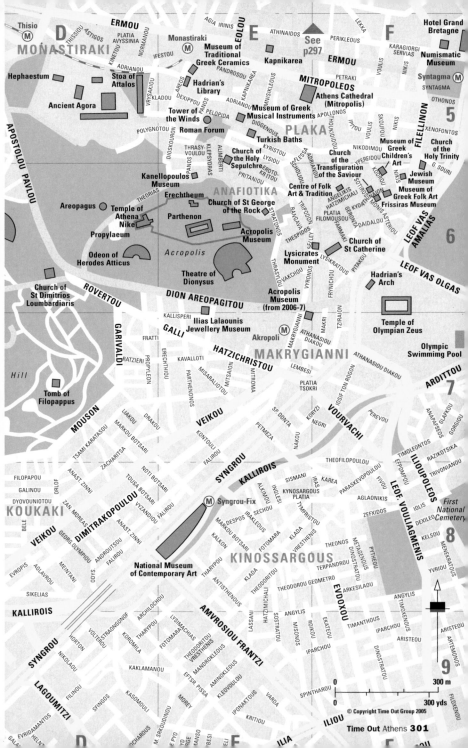

Street Index

Athens Metro

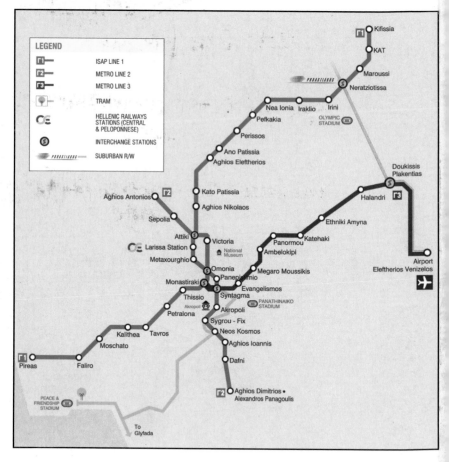

LEGEND

ISAP LINE 1	
METRO LINE 2	
METRO LINE 3	
TRAM	
HELLENIC RAILWAYS STATIONS (CENTRAL & PELOPONNESE)	
INTERCHANGE STATIONS	
SUBURBAN R/W	

Kifissia
KAT
Maroussi
Neratziotissa
Nea Ionia Iraklio Irini
Pefkakia
OLYMPIC STADIUM
Perissos
Ano Patissia
Aghios Eleftherios
Doukissis Plakentias
Aghios Antonios
Kato Patissia
Halandri
Aghios Nikolaos
Sepolia
Ethniki Amyna
Attiki
Victoria
Panormou Katehaki
Larissa Station
Ambelokipi
National Museum
Metaxourghio
Airport Eleftherios Venizelos
Omonia
Megaro Moussikis
Monastiraki Panepistimio
Thissio Evangelismos
Akropoli Syntagma
PANATHINAIKO STADIUM
Petralona Akropoli
Sygrou - Fix
Kalithea Tavros
Neos Kosmos
Moschato
Aghios Ioannis
Pireas Faliro
Dafni
PEACE & FRIENDSHIP STADIUM
Aghios Dimitrios • Alexandros Panagoulis
To Glyfada